IMPERIAL AIRWAYS

"HANNO" AT BAGHDAD AIRPORT

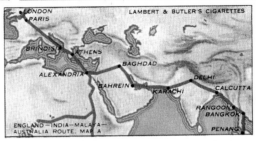

ENGLAND—INDIA—MALAYA—AUSTRALIA ROUTE. MAP A

IMPERIAL AIRWAYS

THE BIRTH OF THE BRITISH AIRLINE INDUSTRY
1914–1940

Robert Bluffield

CLASSIC
An imprint of
Ian Allan Publishing

Dedication

This book is dedicated to my dear wife, Frances

I also dedicate it to the crew, passengers and those on the ground who were the innocent victims of Pan Am Flight 103 that was blown from the sky over Lockerbie on Wednesday 21 December 1988

During the course of its short journey from London Heathrow on that fateful evening, the flight path of the Boeing 747 would have taken it over my home in Milton Keynes

I also dedicate this work to the innocent victims that lost their lives in the dreadful events of 11 September 2001

These events altered the whole ethos of flying for ever more

The Author

Robert 'Bob' Bluffield was born in London and has had a wide and varied career that includes advertising, cinema management, publishing and working as a private investigator. During the 1970s he started a successful photographic studio and wrote technical features for the photographic press which inspired three books; one on wedding photography, the others on the business aspects of running a photography business. More recently, he has been contributing editor to a Home Counties-based company that publishes business and lifestyle magazines, he has produced web copy for various clients and has completed a history for a Bedfordshire company. He also writes about political issues, travel, food and wine, cars, modern history and lifestyle subjects.

Bob has a lifelong interest in public transport but this is his first aviation book. He enjoys good food and wine, travel and reading non-fiction. He is married and lives in Milton Keynes.

His web site is at www.robertbluffield.co.uk

Imperial Airways
© 2009 Robert Bluffield

ISBN 978 1 906537 07 4

Produced by Chevron Publishing Limited
Project Editor: Robert Forsyth
Assistant Editor: Mark Nelson
(www.chevronpublishing.co.uk)

Cover and book design: Mark Nelson
© Text: 2009 Robert Bluffield
© Colour profiles: Tim Brown
Index: Alan Thatcher

Published by Ian Allan Publishing
Riverdene Business Park, Molesey Road,
Hersham, Surrey, KT12 4RG

North American trade distribution:
Specialty Press Publishers & Wholesalers Inc.
39966 Grand Avenue, North Branch, MN 55056, USA
Fax: 651 277 1203 Tel: 651 277 1400
Toll free telephone: 800 895 4585
www.specialtypress.com
Printed in England by Ian Allan Printing Ltd
Riverdene Business Park, Molesey Road,
Hersham, Surrey, KT12 4RG

Visit the Ian Allan Publishing website at:
www.ianallanpublishing.com

CLASSIC

CONTENTS

INTRODUCTION

MANY years ago by chance I picked up the Penguin paperback edition of Alexander Frater's wonderful book, *Beyond the Blue Horizon* (Penguin 1986). I was searching for some light reading to take on holiday and was browsing through the travel section in a local shop, when I was attracted by the cover. Until then I knew little about Imperial Airways; less still about the pioneering days of civil aviation and nothing at all about the people who surveyed the routes or founded and managed the first airlines. The inter-war period has often been referred to as the *Golden Years* of civil aviation but in reality flying during this period was anything but glamorous. Aircraft were extremely basic, unreliable, noisy, uncomfortable and frequently very unsafe and anyone who actually *wanted* to fly as a passenger in one of the early aircraft must have been either foolhardy or nurtured a death wish. Fortunately there were a number of innovative entrepreneurs, pioneering pilots and aircraft manufacturers who had the courage to follow their beliefs that commercial aviation had a future. A certain number of well-heeled members of the public were also brave enough to support the pioneers and were prepared to fly in the early machines. But, had it not been for the untiring efforts of individuals such as George Holt Thomas, Sir Sefton Brancker, the Short brothers, Frederick Handley Page, Geoffrey de Havilland, John Alcock and Arthur Brown, Alan Cobham, the Instones, Herbert Brackley and others, then civil aviation would not have progressed as rapidly as it did. Those prepared to take massive risks to follow their dreams pushed the boundaries and somehow, during the process, managed to create an amazing industry against overwhelming odds. Some lost everything, including their lives, but the tragedies and devastation that inflicted some merely strengthened the resolve of the remainder. The British Government was also extremely uncompromising and showed a remarkable lack of support, refusing to accept that the burgeoning industry would eventually replace merchant shipping as the most convenient way to reach the distant corners of Britain's once mighty Empire.

Frater's work is an intriguing account of a journey that he made to replicate, as closely as possible, the original path of the Empire Route to Australia that Imperial Airways had opened with Qantas Empire Airways in 1935. Flying on modern day aircraft between each stage, Frater used comparisons and contemporary reports to describe, in sharp detail, the conditions early passengers had to endure while travelling through Europe, the Middle East, India and South East Asia during the 1930s. The author searched for, and found, some of the remaining colourful characters who had been associated in some way with the route and Frater's lively prose managed to convey a colourful and interesting pot-pourri of a former age. The book paints a fascinating portrait of the formative years of civil aviation, but more importantly it compares airline travel then to now. The book is a thoroughly good read but it left me unfulfilled because it provoked a desire to learn more about the dreams and aspirations of the adventurous men (and a few women) who risked their lives to open a viable network of commercial routes. Being inquisitive by nature (my wife insists I am nosey) left me with a need to learn more about the lives of the individuals who surveyed inhospitable virgin territory to open mail and passenger services that would eventually span the world.

The book also left me curious about the role of the flying boats. These leviathans of the sky ceased operating long ago, leaving behind a legacy of intrigue that conjures up a very different way of travel since replaced by the cramped, sterile cabins of modern sub-sonic airliners. When I started my research, my experience of flying boats was restricted to the Short Sunderland exhibited at the Imperial War Museum's Duxford facility and to watching rare appearances of a couple of airworthy Consolidated Catalina amphibians performing magnificently at air shows. I also have a vague recollection when, as a ten year old, I went on a school trip to the Isle of Wight and my class was taken to see the huge Saunders Roe Princess flying boat that once sat neglected and forlorn on a ramp on the Medina River at Calshot. This vast, historic machine joined the great Shorts Empire boats and the Sikorsky, Martin and Boeing Clippers of Pan American Airways to the breaker's yards and I regret not being old enough to have ever seen any of these stately machines either statically or in flight.

My interest started to grow but it soon became apparent that there was relatively little in print about the formative years of British civil aviation. There are numerous excellent books dealing with aircraft types; especially those published by Putnam, but when I commenced this project there were few titles that told the stories of the early British airlines or anything about the people and the companies that operated the flimsy former war machines on the first London to Paris services. I was aware of Robin Higham's exceptional book *Britain's Imperial Air Routes 1918 to 1939*, first published in 1960, but my exhaustive efforts to locate a copy failed for some considerable time despite visiting second-hand shops and book fairs far and wide. My local library eventually located a copy and I also acquired a copy of *The Early Birds* that tells the story of the Instone Airline, one of the four independents that came together to form Imperial Airways.

As my quest for knowledge rapidly grew; I became conscious that my lust for information was developing into an obsession and I feared I was becoming a bore and turning into an 'anorak'. I attended a growing number of air shows, more to rummage through the shelves of old books and memorabilia than to watch the flying displays. It was at this point that I came into contact with a specialist book dealer that was at that time located in a run-down, dusty shop in Holloway Road, North London. There I met Simon Watson, who now owns The Aviation Book Shop, the business he formerly managed, but which he now runs from a new, brighter location in Tunbridge Wells. Using Simon's enthusiasm, knowledge and recommendations I bought every book I could find that contained the slightest reference to Imperial Airways (see the lengthy bibliography at the end of the book). This allowed me to form a picture in my mind of how the early airlines were conceived and operated. Simon then called me to say that he had located an almost mint condition copy of Higham's book. I was delighted. I wanted my own copy and to avoid the risk of entrusting the Post Office to deliver such a valuable title, I immediately set off to London keen to get my hands on the book. This became my bible. As I read and re-read the factual information held in its pages I was more convinced than ever that a modern version of the Imperial Airways story needed to be told, not least because Higham's book has become extremely rare. I owe much to Robin's authoritative work, and admire the way he examined the political intrigue behind the Government's first Chosen Instrument. However, I felt there was still plenty more to be told especially about the other independent companies that operated small aircraft on internal services, many of them between some surprising British locations. I also felt an urge to delve much deeper into the way commercial aviation was conceived in this country, domestically and internationally, during the unsettled period between two costly and devastating world wars. In order to do this I have drawn comparisons with developments in other countries that may have directly or indirectly influenced the industry's progression here. This has included an account of some of the earliest overseas passenger services and an examination of a short-lived obsession with lighter than air dirigibles that, for a period, captured the Government's imagination.

As tends to happen, during the lengthy process of bringing this project to fruition, I have witnessed a sudden growth in the number of parallel books that have appeared to satisfy a certain nostalgic interest in the old airlines. The most notable titles appeared not long after I had started my research but I remained undeterred. The first of these was *Imperial Airways and the First British Airlines 1919-40* by the late Archie Jackson; a title not dissimilar to my own. Next; a succession of books about flying boats; the late John Stroud's book on *The Imperial Airways Fleet* and a few other titles associated with the formative years of the British airline industry. I contacted the eminent historian, R E G Davies at his home in Virginia hoping his company, Paladwr, might be interested in my project. He replied pleasantly, taking the trouble to send me a lovely handwritten letter informing me that his book *British Airways: The Imperial Years* was already in production. He asked me to keep this a secret, but wished me well with my own project. I respected this and because I have many of Ron Davies' exceptional books in my aviation library I knew that anything with his name on the cover would be thoroughly researched, factual and concise in every aspect and it would certainly be a major challenge to my work. But, by then I was too far into my research to become dismayed and I remained resolute in my belief that no single title can ever hope to tell the complete story in a limited number of pages no matter how hard one tries. In spite of other books entering the market I hold the view that every writer brings their own element to a particular subject, often by adding previously undiscovered facts that can make a story slightly more unique from the next. Of course, it is also inevitable that there be some overlap. History is history after all, and the key facts of a non-fiction work should never be distorted to become fiction. As long as authors keep to this basic rule it is always possible to add a new dimension so that every book on a particular theme can compliment the next. This is the fun and challenge of writing. Every writer will describe events according to their individual slant, placing their own varied levels of emphasis according to the author's personal points of view. It is also human nature that different approaches to a comparable subject will inevitably give rise to a certain level of disagreement over key matters of fact but this is not necessarily a bad thing providing there is no straying from the truth.

I could not have anticipated, when I took the decision to write this book, that I was about to embark on a ten year journey that at times has become extremely involved. My quest was disadvantaged because I was hampered by the fact that almost everybody who had been involved with the airlines during the inter-war years were no longer living. This has meant having to rely on contemporary publications and archived records that are not always as accurate as they might be. Whenever possible I have gone to great lengths to double or triple check my facts. But, even by adopting a system of research that I consider to have been extremely vigilant, there have been occasions when officially recorded information has raised conflicts. When this has occurred I have done my utmost to arrive at what I believe has been a calculated conclusion after evaluating all of the material at my disposal. But on a few occasions I have been forced to take an 'educated guess' based on my judgement of which set of conflicting information appears to be the most reliable. Almost certainly this is bound to give rise to a few uncertainties which in turn might create disputes. If this subsequently leads to healthy dialogue then this is no bad thing and I will welcome your opinions if you care to contact me. If this can lead to me having the opportunity of rectifying any erroneous or uncertain material I will certainly be most grateful. In the meantime I offer my sincere apologies in advance for anything that might be construed as unintentionally inaccurate.

This book has really been a labour of love; my involvement has been mostly enjoyable, but like any love affair, at times it has led to certain frustrations. One of the major problems has been with trying to locate and obtain permission to use historic photographs and ephemera to illustrate the text. Few can ever earn a living by writing a work of this kind and the production costs are considerable if the book is to be as visually exciting as this one. Although I am extremely appreciative of the assistance I have been given by many people, especially by Jim Davies at the BA Museum, Peter Skinner of the Croydon Airport Society, Simon Watson and others named in the acknowledgements, I have been disillusioned by the high reproduction fees demanded by others.

Unfortunately this has meant that many photographs that I would have liked to have included have had to be omitted purely on economic grounds, but I hope those that have been obtained will more than compensate particularly as some of these images have never been published before.

My sincere hope is that the time I have spent on researching and writing this manuscript has not been wasted and that the end product will be considered as a valuable contribution by anyone who shares an interest in the history of British commercial aviation. My other hope is that the reader finds my text informative and interesting to absorb; nothing will displease me more than the thought that my prose might be considered laborious or boring.

Robert Bluffield
Milton Keynes
June 2009

ACKNOWLEDGEMENTS

THIS book would never have been possible without the help, encouragement and cooperation of a variety of individuals and organisations. Out of necessity I am eternally grateful to all of the authors and historians who have written on the subjects I have covered within my text. Regrettably many of these talented people were from a former generation and are now no longer with us, which reminds me in my own advancing years, of how so few aviation historians remain. Fortunately, when their souls departed, they left behind legacies in the form of their published works that can never be erased. I am extremely grateful to my predecessors for the amazing amount of tireless research most of them conducted to create books containing much priceless information. I am also conscious that almost all of the literature that precedes this book had been faultlessly researched without any aid from the internet, or even word processors. Both of these media have made my life far simpler and in this computer age, like others, I am guilty of taking them for granted.

All of the books that I have read and re-read as a major part of my research are included in the bibliography, but I owe particular thanks to the wordcraft of the late John Stroud; R E G 'Ron' Davies, Archie Jackson, George Holt Thomas, Robin Higham, John Pudney, Arthur W J G Ord-Hume, Alfred Instone, Herbert and Frida Brackley, Sir Alan Cobham and many others I never had the opportunity of meeting. Most of these prolific and proficient historians have long passed away, but their shapely prose remains as a testimony of their achievements. Although I have borrowed, and sometimes quoted, from their texts, I sincerely hope that I have given appropriate acknowledgement to their efforts where due and I trust that I will not be charged with plagiarism in any way because this has never been my intention.

I owe my first great debt to Simon Watson of The Aviation Book Shop (www.aviation-bookshop.com) who offered me early guidance on a subject I knew precious little about and I am thankful that he brought to my attention many of the books I refer to in the bibliography.

I am totally indebted to the help and facilities provided by Jim Davies during my frequent visits to the British Airways Museum at Heathrow Airport (www.bamuseum.com) and to his cups of coffee that kept me awake during lengthy reading sessions. It should be known that Jim, a modest man, is a volunteer but he goes about his work with great energy and enthusiasm and his wisdom should be regarded as a gem. I must also thank Jim's boss, Paul Jarvis, for allowing me access to the facility that he controls.

The Croydon Airport Society[1] (www.croydonairport.org.uk) keeps interest alive and maintains a vast archive of ephemera, books, magazines, artefacts and photographs related to the operation and preservation of Croydon Airport and the airlines that used it. I am proud to be a member of this worthy association but I regret it is now showing signs of decline because it is unable to attract sufficient young blood willing to carry its work into the future. Peter Skinner, the archives and artefacts coordinator of the CAS has given me much of his valuable time and a vast amount of assistance, allowing me to visit and scan many of the images and documents held in the Society's bulging filing cabinets. I urge you to take an active interest in this society and take the trouble to visit the beautifully restored airport terminal building and control tower to gain a first impression of the early years of airline operation in this country. Without Peter's kind assistance this work would have been struggling to find sufficient content to make it the visual feast it has become.

I have mentioned the value of the Internet as an aid to research, but it also provides access to organisations that hold historical artefacts, some of which have been reproduced in the pages of the book. One site contains an amazing collection of timetables and other travel literature that covers the entire worldwide history of airlines. After approaching Björn Larsson who operates The Airlines Timetable Images site (www.timetableimages.com) with David Zekra, he kindly sent me high resolution files of many early timetables for inclusion in this book and I cannot thank him enough for his consideration.

Mention must also be given to the US Library of Congress which maintains a website (www.loc.gov/rr/print/catalog.html) from which a number of fascinating photographs of Imperial Airways have been used for this book.

The process of bringing an initial idea for a book to eventual publication, as any writer will know, is frequently paved with trepidation and the success of any project depends on the efforts, enthusiasm and inspiration of those involved in the publishing industry. From an early stage in the process of writing I was greatly encouraged in my project by Robert Forsyth of Chevron Publishing (www.chevronpublishing.co.uk) who has been untiring and unselfish in his support. Robert is entirely responsible for the production you are now reading and he must be given full credit for introducing it to Ian Allan Publishing (www.ianallanpublishing.com) and making it a reality. Without his knowledge of the publishing industry this book simply would never have seen the light of day. I also wish to thank Mark Nelson, also of Chevron Publishing, who has been responsible for designing the book.

Jeremy Instone, the grandson of Theodore, one of the three founding brothers of the original Instone Air Line has also provided useful assistance by allowing me access to historic photographic images retained by his company, Instoneair (www.instoneair.com), that carries on the family tradition within commercial aviation. I would also like to thank Eddie Creek who helped with images of early German civil aviation from his collection.

Family and friends will always play a key role in the progress of any literary work, more especially as a work of this kind involves thousands of hours spent tucked away in libraries and archives while researching, usually alone in a quiet room with only the computer for company once writing commences. As any writer's spouse will know; they have to possess a single-minded resilience in order to accept their partner's obsession while they become totally absorbed with the project at hand, often to the detriment of all social activities including meal times. I thank my wife, Frances, for accepting the solitude that has become part and parcel of being an author's wife, and she has endured my single-mindedness, usually without complaint. It cannot be easy playing 'second fiddle' to my computer and a growing clutter of aviation books and documents that have threatened to engulf my tiny house. Hopefully our marriage of 20 years has become stronger as a result of her resilience and she knows that I could not have achieved the end result without her love and acceptance.

I am also extremely grateful to the comradeship of my closest friend, Christopher Kennedy, who has accompanied me to many distant air shows (including a mad weekend when we came close to freezing to death while attending the Confederate Air Force show at Midland, Texas). Chris has also been cajoled into providing his time as my research assistant during numerous visits to archives and has provided me with the encouragement to continue with the work in hand during periods when I may have considered giving up. Fortunately, although Chris is more an aficionado of military fast jets, he shares more than a passing interest in flying machines of every kind, so hopefully he has not regretted these forages.

When it comes to acknowledging those that have contributed their time and energy to bring any published work to fruition, it is always easy to forget an important role played by an individual. Hopefully I have mentioned all of those that have played a part but if I have omitted anyone unthinkingly; please accept my humble apologies because this has never been my intention. Finally, however, I must thank you, the reader, for taking the trouble to pick this book up and by reading this far you have expressed an interest, however slight, in what I have to say. Please enjoy.

[1.] Images provided by the Croydon Airport Society are referred to as CAS in the illustration captions.

CHAPTER ONE

LACK OF GOVERNMENT INTEREST
1914-1919

BEFORE the outbreak of the Great War in 1914 it was fortunate that a small hub of innovative individuals already fostered a belief that the future of flying could be viewed as a commercial proposition that could be developed to form a viable challenge to conventional travel by road and rail. The Government of the time however was not so convinced. Before the pioneers could put their ideas to the test, the needs of State dictated that every effort had to concentrate on training fighter pilots and building war machines instead of considering the feasibility of civilian flying. Thus, any development of commercial air transport as a worthwhile cause could not be considered until after the armistice had brought a halt to fighting. Even then, the Liberal Government of the day under David Lloyd George remained seriously reluctant to endorse the fledgling industry in a favourable way.

Despite the odds stacked against it, the British civil aviation story became embryonic as far back as 1910. Less than seven years before, Orville Wright had made history at Kill Devil Hill, Kitty Hawk, North Carolina when he briefly flew the first power-driven heavier-than-air machine on 17 December 1903. Between 18 May and 28 November 1910 The International Conference for Aerial Navigation (ICAN) had already debated issues relating to the use and sovereignty of the air. Germany registered a keenness to promote a freedom of the skies policy, but the British Foreign Office opposed this, preferring to protect the air space above the Kingdom as the sole reserve of British pilots. The Government construed that the air above *Her Majesties' Nations* must remain inviolable. This resulted in the Air Navigation Acts of 1911 and 1913 devised to protect the nation *against* aviation rather than to promote it. This, as was later discovered, proved to be a huge mistake that caused Germany, in an act of stubborn retaliation, to block Britain's attempts to establish early commercial routes to Prague, while France and Italy prevented the Imperial air service from being fully functional until as late as the mid-1930s. Britain's pompous stance also gave rise to lengthy delays in making progress on the India route because Persia (now Iran) forced flights to use the southern side of the Persian Gulf instead of allowing shorter, more direct access over its territory. By the late 1920s, the British Government had started to appreciate its own stupidity and backtracked, this time by arguing in favour of freedom of passage whereby before it had staunchly opposed it. It is no surprise that the nations the British Government had previously offended were now reluctant to support it.

A voluminous report

While the dark clouds of war were still hanging over vast tracts of Western Europe, the British Government was hardly in a mood to discuss peacetime aviation. Yet they were not able to ignore it either. The Civil Aerial Transport Committee formed on 26 April 1917, chaired by Lord Northcliffe, was empowered to consider and control the role of civil aviation. Forty members comprised the main committee that was appointed on 22 May 1917. This included interested parties from the Dominions, India and Newfoundland as well as members of governmental departments, the Services, aircraft designers, manufacturers and Members of Parliament. By February 1918 what was referred to as a *voluminous report* had been prepared and handed to the Air Council. This advocated '*State action for the development of aerial transport services*' and stressed a need to survey and open routes that would link the Empire to the motherland. After the initial meeting, Northcliffe, every bit an aviation protagonist, embarked on a fact finding mission to America leaving Major J L Baird (the Under Secretary of State for Air) to chair the Committee. Other notable members of the committee were, Brigadier-General W Sefton-Brancker who was later killed in the R101 airship disaster; Brigadier-General E M Maitland who, in 1919 flew both ways across the Atlantic in the R34 but later died in the R38 airship accident; Captain J C Porte, a Royal Navy flying-boat expert and H G Wells, the author.

The Foreign Office was consulted on the desirability of an international convention for aerial navigation and two principal issues emerged:

1. What should the Government's attitude be towards any future conference on the subject of international civil aviation?

Commander John Porte (left) glances at the camera from the hull of an America flying boat in late 1914/early 1915. In 1917 he served on the Civil Aerial Transport Committee.

A poster announcing the first UK Aerial Post flown between Hendon and Windsor by the Grahame White company.

Claude Grahame-White who, on 10 August 1910, made the first experimental air mail flight from Squires Gate, Blackpool to Southport, although he was forced down after just seven miles.

2. What terms would HM Government make with a foreign Government?

The future of Britain's air routes was largely dependant on the terms of the Committee's report, aided by the Committee of Imperial Defence who also opposed freedom of the skies on defence grounds. Mistrust and suspicions were rife. The International Convention for Aerial Navigation, led to the first Air Navigation Act in 1910, which formed the basis of the 1920 Act and any future amendments. The sub-committees appointed by the ICAN were given the task of investigating routes based on the limited aircraft types that were available in July 1917 and proposed:

• London–Edinburgh–Glasgow–Dublin–London
• London to the Riviera
• London–South Africa (suggesting East and West African routes)
• Atlantic Route (preferably via the Azores using aircraft carriers because of fog risks in Newfoundland)
• London–Norway–Sweden–Russia (this, and the Atlantic route was thought would best be served by existing airships)

The Committee also suggested that manufacturers should concentrate on designing aircraft with RAF usage in mind that could swiftly be re-deployed in the case of any renewed hostilities. This advice was later repeated in a Government Command Paper of 1920 suggested by Lord Trenchard who, it must be said, as RAF Chief of Staff, had a vested interest. The instability that remained in Europe gave some merit to the idea of developing aircraft with a dual role. Trenchard was far-sighted, astute enough to suggest the Government should consider putting money behind the development of civil air routes on a point of *national prestige*.

The Cabinet was asked to consider whether it felt civil aviation should be privately or state owned. It, in turn, advised that the Government should aid civil aviation while it weathered a development period and while advantage could be taken to utilise a glut of readily available surplus war stock.

Because so much of their communications networks had been destroyed by the hostilities, the French and Belgians had a greater need to re-establish a fluid and economic transport system than the British. Air transport began to be seen by these countries as a quick-fix solution that would help restore some of their mobility. In Britain, the rail and road infrastructure had not taken the same levels of battering as in mainland Western Europe, so there was little need to concentrate full scale efforts into peacetime aircraft manufacture. In any event, the British rail system at that time was the envy of the world. The Government viewed this as a good excuse *not* to invest money in a form of transportation that it neither considered necessary nor worthwhile.

Many trained pilots lucky enough to have returned unscathed from the skies above the battlefields of the Western Front were restless and had too much time on their hands. These were the fortunate ones. On average a front line wartime pilot was expected to live just fourteen days. Replacement pilots for those that had been killed in action or accidents had been no more than lambs to the slaughter. The carnage was horrific and many brave young men who arrived at an airfield in the morning were dead by afternoon. Still, those that did return needed work. Although some of these turned to stunt, exhibition and sports flying, others wanted a more steady form of income. A feeling of *air-mindedness* existed but there was no escaping the extreme dangers that confronted anyone reckless enough to take a flimsy wood and fabric machine into the sky and it was ironic that more pilots were killed in accidents than as a result of enemy action.

Pioneering mail flights

Developments in military aviation had come a long way in the four years since the outbreak of war. By 1918 twin-engined bombers had been built by Handley Page that could already reach Berlin carrying a considerable payload. These evolved too late to be of much use, and by the time they were ready, hostilities had already ceased. However these bombers could be converted without much difficulty from wartime duty to carry up to twelve passengers. Until then civilian flying had largely been restricted to experimental air-mail flights. The first of these took place on 10 August 1910 when Claude Grahame-White flying a Blériot from Squires Gate, Blackpool attempted to reach Southport but was forced down by bad weather after only seven miles. His exploit was followed on 18 February 1911 by Frenchman, M. Henri Pequet who carried 6500 letters and postcards six miles between the United Provinces Exhibition showground at Allahabad and Naini (Northern India) using a Humber biplane. This was an isolated journey but the flight is generally recognised by philatelists to be the world's first aerial

post and examples of covers carried on the flight still exist.

During the same year the Grahame-White Aviation Company established a postal service between Hendon and Windsor (Royal Farm) that continued for three weeks using three aircraft; a Farman biplane and two Blériot monoplanes. Between 9-26 September Gustav Hamel, Clement Greswell and E F Driver made a series of twenty flights to commemorate the Coronation of King George V (22 June 1911). A large crowd had gathered at Hendon to watch Hamel become formerly invested as a carrier of His Majesty's Mail. As the band struck up the final chords of the National Anthem his take-off was announced and his official departure time was noted as 1658 hrs. A few minutes later Charles Hubert flying the second mail plane, should have departed in a Farman, but after completing a trial spin his efforts to get airborne were thwarted by a strong breeze that forced him to abort his take-off. Hamel arrived at Windsor Castle at 1713 hrs, after a hazardous flight, to hand the despatch waybill and the mail to the Mayor of Windsor who informed the King by telegram that the mail had arrived. The Royal response was sent back by Lord Stamfordham from Balmoral with a reply thanking the Secretary of the Aerial Post, the Windsor postmaster Mr A A'Vard. Declining an offer of tea, Hamel departed from Windsor at 1832 hrs for Hendon with a return consignment of mail. A small crowd of well-wishers remained to carry him aloft to a rousing chorus of *See the Conquering Hero Comes*. A few days later during another attempt to carry mail from Windsor, Hubert crashed the Farman and broke both his legs. Hamel was joined by two other airmen, Greswell and Driver, for the remaining duration of the mail flights. In the three week period 26,288 letters and 97,017 postcards were carried bearing the inscription 'Coronation AD 1911, First UK Aerial Post by Sanction of HM Postmaster General'.

Although widely regarded as a stunt, the exercise achieved a healthy £1,438 profit to silence the critics. Hamel's departure from Hendon had also aroused considerable public interest when more than 3000 spectators had gathered. The mail flights had been arranged by Capt Walter Windham, who had previously organised the first official air mail in India. Air mails were also being carried with some considerable success in Italy and the USA around this time. Hamel unfortunately made headlines of a different kind when he knocked down and killed a five year old girl on 2 October 1911 who ran in front of his moving car near his home at Kingston-Upon-Thames.

Early passenger flights

Although many countries had started to make an effort, Germany was already leading the way towards establishing the first passenger-carrying company when Count Ferdinand von Zeppelin founded Die Deutsche Luftschiffahrt Aktien Gesellschaft (DELAG) on 16 November 1909 with his airships. The Hamburg-Amerika Shipping Line (HAPAG) invested in the company and took responsibility for booking seats on the six craft, of which three were later wrecked. Between March 1912 and November 1913 the company made 881 flights and carried 19,100 passengers over a distance of 65,000 miles. Despite claims to the contrary, it is generally understood that many of these flights were pleasure trips and short joy-rides putting the company's claim to be the world's first *scheduled* passenger air service title in considerable doubt.

The honour for this falls to the St Petersburg-Tampa Airboat Line which used a Roberts-powered Benoist flying-boat piloted by Tony Jannus, a pilot who had completed a ground breaking trip in 1912 that followed the Mississippi river for 1,700 miles, to ferry passengers between two cities across Tampa Bay, Florida. The service began on 1 January 1914 with the ex-mayor of St Petersburg, Abe Pheil, bidding $400 to be the first passenger. The service continued with two daily flights over a period of four months. Despite the small aircraft accommodating only one passenger on each twenty three mile trip, the service established a high level of regularity and managed to carry 1,200 passengers. As a tribute to this pioneering company the following poetic description of this epic flight is reproduced as it appeared in *The World's First Airline – The St Petersburg to Tampa Airboat Line* by Gay Blair White.

'The old Roberts wheezed, coughed, fired once and died. Tony Jannus inserted the crank again. It was a cold New Year's morning but he was warming up to the job.

'Once more he pulled down hard on the crank and this time the old two-cycle burst into life with a bellow of smoke from the stacks. Jay Dee leaned over the hull and adjusted the carb. The engine smoothed to a loud purr and Tony motioned to his passenger to climb in. Both waved to the excited crowd as the airboat slid into the water.

'Jannus headed for the west of the harbour. Then he turned the boat into the wind and opened the throttle. Slowly, coming up on the step, she picked up speed and skipped twice, floated into the air as she came to the mouth of the harbour. P E Fansler glanced at his watch as the Benoist came past the breakwater. It was exactly 10.00 am; the World's First Airline was on its way.'

Percival Fansler had instigated the Airboat Line after hearing the exploits of Tony Jannus. Fansler wrote to Tom Benoist to suggest establishing an air route across Tampa Bay. Benoist responded to his telegram and arrived in St Petersburg on 17 December 1913 and signed the first airline contract written anywhere in the world. Sadly Benoist and Jannus both died within a few years of creating the company. Benoist was victim of a most bizarre accident. While travelling on a St Petersburg (Florida) trolley-car on 14 June 1917, he collided with a telegraph pole while leaning from the side. His body fell to the ground and he died in hospital, aged 43. Jannus joined the Curtiss Aeroplane Company and went to Russia to train pilots. On 12 October 1916, while working at Sevastopol on the Black Sea, his aircraft suffered engine failure and dived into the ground and caught fire.

Ferdinand Graf von Zeppelin developed airships that pioneered passenger flights from 1909.

A poster advertising the very first passenger flights, inaugurated by the St. Petersburg-Tampa Airboat Line on 1 January 1914, across Tampa Bay, Florida.

Emblem of Deutsche Luftreederei.

Using converted First World War LVG (Luft-Verkehrs-Gesellschaft G.m.b.H.) C. VI aircraft, the Deutsche Luftreederei used the aircraft commencing in February 1919, to carry postal services on the routes between Berlin, Leipzig and Weimar.

Passenger flights by the RAF

By mid-April 1919 the British Government gave its approval for companies to provide civilian flying services. Before this, animosity between The Royal Flying Corps and the Royal Naval Air Service, mainly over procurement, had led to the creation of The Air Ministry (1917) and the formation of the Royal Air Force a year later. The RAF soon became instrumental in establishing a number of flights that carried passengers as well as mail. On 13 December 1918 the Number One Communications Squadron was formed at Hendon under the command of Major Cyril Patterson with a detachment based at Buc, close to Paris. At the same time the 86th Communications Wing under the command of Lt Colonel W H Primrose DFC was formed and flew officials and despatches to the Paris Peace Conference held at Versailles. DH4s capable of carrying two passengers were used initially that had been converted by Airco to include a hinged *coupé* cover, plywood sides and opening windows. Later, silver-painted twin-engine Handley Page 0/400s were put into service and given the designations HM Air Liners *Silver Queen, Silver Star* and *Great Britain*. These aircraft provided quick transport for Government officials attending the Paris conference from London and for mail to reach the Occupational Armies that remained as peacekeepers after the War. To provide some comfort, the cabins of these craft had been fitted with six to eight chairs but passengers were unable to escape the discomforts of engine noise or the vibrations caused by the aircraft's slipstream beating against the fabric lining above their heads.

It is claimed that *Silver Star* (D8326) became the first aircraft to carry non-military passengers across the Channel on 13 December 1918. It was also the first aircraft to make a passenger-carrying night flight between Britain and the Continent. Four days later the RAF and army postal authorities began airmail services between Marquise and Namur, Belgium (via Valenciennes) with DH9s. This route was later extended to Cologne and Spa (Belgium) via Hesdin, Valenciennes and Namur. A more regular service flew from Kenley to Buc using an assorted array of aircraft that ended in September after successfully making 749 flights and carrying 934 passengers and 1,008 sacks of mail.

From 3 March 18, 110 and 120 Squadrons operated an air mail service from Folkestone (Hawkinge) to Cologne to the Army of Occupational Forces. This carried 90 tons of mail on 1,842 flights but ceased on 31 August after maintaining a healthy 96% service reliability. Initially DH4, DH9, DH9a and DH10 aircraft were used, and a stop was made at Maisoncelle (and later at Marquise) but the service later operated non-stop. As these services were primarily organised to carry mail, single-engine fighters and some converted bombers were also used and carried two or three passengers in a covered, but unheated, cabin. On 15 August 1919 the service was taken over by Air Transport & Travel (AT&T) initially with a DH9 and, from 6 November with a pair of Napier Lion-powered DH9As (G-EAOF and G-EOAK). The service ceased completely in June 1920.

Britain was still bogged down by policies and negative discussions that held back any real commercial progress. Frank Pick, the driving force of the London Underground Group, argued that Britain did not have the same commercial and strategic strengths as it held as a maritime power. He stressed vehemently that France, Italy and Spain could block any progress Britain was considering to develop air routes to the Empire as well as to South America. Pick felt that civil aviation should have its own body instead of being controlled by the Air Ministry. He rightly argued that the Merchant Navy was controlled by the board of Trade, not the Admiralty, and civil aviation should be treated similarly. Nobody listened and it took until the end of the Second World War to create the Ministry of Civil Aviation.

Government indifference

The Air Ministry largely ignored civil aviation. When the Air Estimates were announced for 1919-20, it received none of the £54,282,064 that was allocated to commercial aviation. This situation did not change dramatically until the recommendations of the Cadman and Maybury Reports of the 1930s. Similarly the Air Council naively refused to appreciate that any value could be derived by developing civil air routes. They ignored the potential of civil air transport and refused to accept the role civilian aircraft had played in Iraq after the First World War in military control operations along the North West Frontier.

The issues regarding State enterprise versus State aid was taken up again in 1919 by a committee of ten; three of them veterans of previous committees. This was known as the Advisory Committee on Civil Aviation and the results of their findings were published in a document titled '*Report on Imperial Air Routes*'. This was the first study to be instigated by the Secretary of State for Air. A former Air Minister, Lord Weir of Eastwood chaired the debates and other influential members included Sir Hugh Trenchard, the Chief of Air Staff; Sir Frederick Sykes, the Director General of Civil Aviation; Lt. Colonel J T C Moore-Brabazon, Lord Incheape of Strathnaver and Sir James Stevenson of the Johnnie Walker Company.

The committee was unable to agree how civil air routes should be run. It was initially suggested that the RAF should operate some routes, but this was then dismissed. Instead it proposed that either chartered companies combining State and private interests, or State aided private enterprises should operate these services. It also recommended that the Government should be prepared to pay for the development of any routes, and to reimburse companies for any that were non-remunerative if private enterprises were chosen to run the airlines. But the Government generally shied away from the idea of funding a *national prestige* company despite Lord Trenchard's continuing view that it should.

Trenchard was keen to establish an efficient civil aviation industry because he believed private airlines could act as a reserve service should the RAF ever find itself again in need. Sykes, as Controller General and member of the Air Council, was responsible for implementing the Air Navigation Acts of 1911 and 1919 with direct access to the Secretary of State. The latter revision to the Act received Royal Assent on 27 February and provided '*conditions under which goods and mails are to be conveyed into and from the British Isles.*' Sykes, aided by department heads, became responsible for organising information, planning, communications, aerodromes and meteorology. The Treasury, in turn, approved the appointment of experienced RAF officers to implement Sykes' work by planning air routes at home and abroad, conducting communications, inspecting and organising aerodromes, aircraft and personnel and by investigating accidents (formerly carried out by the Royal Aero Club). Eventually responsibility for meteorology was passed from the RAF to the Air Ministry which issued weather forecasts; its first meteorological report for the next day being despatched on 31 January 1919. This stated that '*flying would be dangerous*' caused by low clouds, poor visibility and snow showers, over the British Isles. In May the Air Ministry took responsibility for licensing pilots, granting 'A' licences for private flyers and 'B' licenses for commercial pilots. A former naval officer, Flt Lt, Howard J Saint was the first recipient of a pilot's licence and H M Woodhams and Bill Kelly both of AT&T were the first ground engineers to be licensed.

Although the Committee felt that it had insufficient data or experience to recommend a rigid policy involving any immediate route planning, it did conclude that a route from the United Kingdom to India and onward to Australia would be of prime concern. It also considered that a UK-South Africa route should also be implemented. The Egypt and Karachi section of an India route was also considered as this had already been judged favourable in terms of aerial navigation.

The Committee decided who would best perform the role of information provider to include details of route navigation. It ruled out the RAF, instead suggesting a private company supported by State aid to provide wireless, telegraphy, weather and information on airfields. It concluded that the prime concern of any enterprise should be the carriage of mail; passengers and freight were, at that time, only given secondary status.

Civilian flying was allowed to begin from 1 May 1919 with the provisos that only service aircraft could be flown and by pilots having to remain within three miles of an airfield. By contrast, the forward thinking German Air Ministry had already approved civilian operations just two months after the signing of the armistice. This allowed the electrical combine, AEG, to form a co-operative with Zeppelin and the shipping company Hamburg-Amerika Line (responsible for bookings) which resulted in the airline Deutsche Luftreederei being formed. On 5 February 1919 it began flying between Berlin and Weimar, via Leipzig, using 5-seater AEG JII biplanes and 2-seater FFWs that completed the 120-mile route in 2hrs and 18mins.

A Hamburg-Berlin service was added on 1 March and later visitors to the Leipzig Fair were carried. On 5 July holiday passenger flights

One of the early pioneers of
aviation in the UK was A V Roe,
here shown with his brother (on
the right).

Advertisement for the first
domestic air service operated
by Avro in 1919 (CAS)

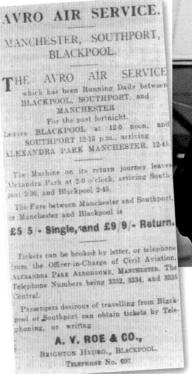

One of the early pioneers of aviation in the UK was A V Roe, here shown with his brother (on the right).

Advertisement for the first domestic air service operated by Avro in 1919 (CAS)

were introduced between Hamburg-Westerland and Berlin-Swinemünde. The early services may well have gathered more momentum had a severe petrol shortage in Germany not abruptly halted flying on 1 August and it took until late 1920 for DLR to resume fixed-wing flying. Nevertheless 1574 passengers had been carried.

Britain's pioneering companies

At the outset of 1919 50,000 men a day were being demobilised from the armed forces although a substantial Occupational Force was retained to keep order in Germany and Flanders. The arrival of peace meant that the frenzied production lines that had been supplying war machinery were grinding to a halt and companies were either closing or downsizing. Lord Weir, Secretary of State for Air, announced in the Commons on 2 January that legislation was being drafted to control civil aviation. Less than a week later, the prophecies of George Holt Thomas of AT&T were echoed in an address given at a meeting of the London Chamber of Commerce by former Chief of Air Staff, Major-General Sir Frederick Sykes entitled *Commercial Aviation in the Light of War Experience.* He stated: '*Ranging over every aspect affecting civilian use of aircraft, public confidence in the safety and security of flying must be engendered so that aviation could take its proper place in relation to older transport. Britain's immediate targets must be the routes to India, Cape to Cairo, European services, and short-haul runs at home.*'

On 11 January Lord Weir resigned and Sykes became Controller-General of Civil Aviation with Winston Churchill appointed Secretary of State for War and Air next day. Another key figure, later to play a vital role in the future of Imperial Airways, Sir Eric Geddes, took charge of improving the nation's social order with the task of providing better conditions of housing, employment and education all augmented under the guise of the Orwellian-sounding Ministry of Reconstruction.

Britain's civil aviation industry is indebted to a handful of early pioneers who fought relentlessly against overwhelming odds to keep their passions alive and their companies afloat. Despite their eagerness, regular commercial air transport had to wait until 10 May when A V Roe & Company began operating between Alexandra Park (Manchester), Southport and Blackpool using one of their own three-seater Avro aircraft. As many as 194 of 222 scheduled flights were completed between the start date and 30 September at a fare of £4 4s 0d (£4.20).

Air Transport and Travel (AT&T) had been registered by George Holt Thomas, the seventh son of newspaper proprietor George Luson Thomas, on 5 October 1916 with a capital of £50,000. Holt Thomas founded his original company, The Aeroplane Supply Company after meeting Henri Farman in Paris in 1909 and discovering that they shared common interests in aviation and motoring. The company became The Aircraft Manufacturing Company (AIRCO) in 1912 to build Farman aircraft and Gnome and Rhone radial aero engines under license. Holt Thomas was also the founder of The Society of Aircraft Constructors (SBAC). He had hired the highly talented aircraft designer, Geoffrey de Havilland, at the outbreak of war which led to Holt Thomas's company producing DH4, DH9 and DH10 warplanes. The DH4s and DH9s were later converted for commercial use and renamed the Airco 4 and Airco 9. Sir Sefton Brancker, one of the greatest ever protagonists for civil aviation, was appointed managing director. The company also operated a number of de Havilland DH42 light bombers that had also been converted from wartime use. These carried freight on relief flights between Folkestone and Ghent in Belgium. The same service was also operated by six DH9 machines that carried military markings but with *Aircraft Transport & Travel Limited. Belgian Service.* painted in white letters on the fuselages. These flights, made at the request of the Belgian Government, mainly carried woollen goods, food and other commodities that were badly needed to assist with shortages created by the War.

Holt Thomas was a highly intelligent man with concise ideas and a crystal clear vision of the future of commercial aviation. In 1918 he was ready to start a regular scheduled air service between London and Paris as soon as Government restrictions on commercial flying had been lifted. In an interview he gave to the *Observer* his views were painstakingly clear when he said *"I am just as enthusiastic over commercial transport as I was ten years ago over aircraft for military use; but the first point I have to recognise in linking the world by aerial routes is that unfortunately British celestial rights apparently end in mid-Channel. It is therefore unlikely that the French Government will allow an all-British enterprise to run Mail to Paris, or the Italians to Rome, nor the Norwegians from Aberdeen to Stavanger. An aerial service between London and Paris must include rights of Franco-British capital, Franco-British aircraft construction, Franco-British pilots and be an international combine in every detail. Facing these facts I have started a company of national importance at Christiana to link my company, Aircraft Transport and Travel Limited under the same direction as my aircraft company and other aviation enterprises. Similarly I have formed an allied company in France and another in Italy. I expect through Tata Ltd of India to link longer journeys from London, through France and Italy to India. Arrangements are also*

complete for a link to South Africa, from Cape to Cairo."

Holt Thomas was far thinking but the Government failed to subscribe to his views. History has a habit of repeating itself and the British Government was as apathetic then as it remains today and was remarkably slow to appreciate the necessities of a reliable transport system. Winston Churchill summed up the Government's attitude on 11 March 1920 when, as Secretary of State for Air, he uttered the immortal words in the Commons: *"Civil aviation must fly by itself; the Government cannot possibly hold it up in the air."* This confirmed the State's blind refusal to provide any subsidy for British companies intent on launching an airline. This was contrary to the facilities already put in place by foreign governments which were substantially supporting their fledgling air services. When the Advisory Committee on Civil Aviation delivered a second part to its report, the Under Secretary, Major Tryon attempted to play down Churchill's statement by saying that his superior really meant that commercial companies should "… *expect to fly by themselves right away!"* It is conjecture what Tryon intended by this, but he may have been trying to plant seeds by suggesting the Government might be open to reconsider funding airlines at a later date, assuming that they could survive the interim. The Advisory Committee disagreed with the Government and suggested it *should* provide funding of £250,000 for the financial years 1920-21 and 1921-22 but the Cabinet adamantly refused to comply.

Alcock and Brown cross the Atlantic

By May it was unclear where civil aviation was heading even though licences had been issued and RAF doctors had been assigned to pass civilian pilots who were considered medically fit to fly. Certificates of air worthiness were also being issued. Meanwhile, after a lengthy wait for temperate weather, Captain John Alcock DSC and Lieutenant Arthur Whitten Brown, his American-born engineer, left Harbour Grace, Newfoundland on 14 June for their epic non-stop flight across the Atlantic. The flight was marred by problems, not least the appalling weather that prevailed during a journey that almost caused their aircraft to spiral into the sea. With enough fuel remaining to take them on to London, the duo thought it unwise to add further stress to the airframe of their converted Vickers Vimy bomber. On sighting land, wisdom prevailed and they brought their aircraft down on what they thought was a green field. But the meadow was not all it seemed and the landing proved more haphazard. Instead of landing on flat grassland they had landed on a peat bog at Derrygimla near Clifden, County Galway with the nose of the Vimy nestling, undignified, in the mud with the tail pointing skywards. The journey had taken 16 hrs 12 mins but it left no

Alcock and Brown take off from St. John's, Newfoundland in 1919.

doubts that, with the right equipment, the potential existed for long-range commercial air transport to be developed.

Alcock and Brown were received as heroes and Winston Churchill announced at a celebratory luncheon held at the Savoy Hotel by the *Daily Mail "I am very happy to be able to tell you that I have received His Majesty's gracious consent to an immediate award of the Knight Commandership of the Order of the British Empire to both Captain Alcock and Lieutenant Brown."* This was met with rapturous applause from the gathered diners. Churchill presented the men with the £10,000 prize awarded by Lord Northcliffe to the first flyers to cross the Atlantic non-stop. Next day, although scheduled to appear at the Hendon Aerial Derby, Alcock and Brown had to disappoint the spectators and go instead to Windsor Castle where they were knighted by King George V. Although this was a momentous day for aviation, next day the front pages of the nation's press carried a very different story; the scuttling of the surrendered German fleet in Scapa Flow.

During the next few weeks Alcock and Brown remained in the public arena and performed their duties by making personal appearances and attending social events. By July their fame was almost forgotten. Brown by then had married his fiancée, Kathleen Kennedy and returned to his profession as an engineer. Alcock continued to fly as a staff pilot for Vickers at Brooklands but his life was cut short. On 18 December 1919, in his determination to deliver a new Vickers Viking Amphibian to the first post-war Aeronautical Exhibition in Paris, he shunned advice by departing in stormy conditions. Reaching northern France he found it enveloped in thick fog. Without a navigator, he descended in search of landmarks, hit a tree and crashed into a field at Côte d'Evrard about 25 miles from Rouen. He was found lying critically injured with severe head wounds by a local man who took him to a nearby farmhouse but he died of his injuries three hours later. Alcock was a month past his twenty-seventh birthday. The news of the tragedy hit Brown extremely hard and his grief was so pronounced that he immediately severed all connections with aviation and never flew again. The Vimy that made the Atlantic crossing, now repaired, was placed on display in the Science Museum in London. Former staff later described how Arthur Whitten Brown would quietly and anonymously pay homage by visiting the aircraft each year on the anniversary of the epic Atlantic crossing that he and Alcock had made. He continued this ritual until his own death in Swansea in 1948.

John Alcock's death stunned the British public and robbed aviation of one of its most distinguished flyers. It is likely that had he enjoyed a longer life Alcock may well have pioneered more long distance routes. His elder brother, E S J Alcock, who had been a Royal Flying Corps pilot during the First World War, became one of the best known captains to have served Imperial Airways. As holder of Master Pilot licence No. 4, he later flew on many of Imperial's commercial routes in Africa, Asia and Australasia. He flew land planes as well as flying boats, clocking up more than four-and-a-half million miles for the company. Although Allcock and Brown's journey did not lead to an immediate flood of people wishing to fly the Atlantic, their adventure proved that men and machines were quickly becoming capable of achieving what many had previously proclaimed to be impossible.

Brigadier-General W Sefton-Brancker (later Sir Sefton Brancker) was a well-known figure from the early days of aviation. He was later to die in the crash of the R101.

Civil flying begins

When an official map was published that showed air routes over Britain and to the Continent this could be taken as an indication that things had at last started to progress. The map showed the location of aerodromes that would be allocated Customs facilities and be designated entry/departure points to and from the British Isles. From 337 available fields at the signing of the Armistice, only a few received official sanction. These were the main airfield at Hounslow (west of London); Lympne (Kent) as the Channel entry field; Hadleigh (Suffolk) for the Netherlands and New Holland (Lincolnshire) for flights to Scandinavia.

On 30 April the *London Gazette* published the new Air Navigation Directions (AND) that gave schedules of aircraft and details of air worthiness certification; overhaul and examination; information about licensing pilots, navigators and engineers; log books; rules of the air; prohibited areas; arrival and departure procedures; signals; and control of import, export and unloading of goods. The 1919 version of the Air Navigation Act came into operation next day.

The public had become accustomed to expect a glut of flights from the first day and many aerodromes reported that they had been inundated with calls for seats on departing flights. But despite this interest, the industry had not responded in the way many might have expected and very few flights were made. This was not helped by appalling weather that may literally have dampened enthusiasm. Hounslow aerodrome readied a number of Avro five-seater aircraft a few days later and made them available to take passengers on fifteen-minute flights for one guinea a time. These were operated by a group of pilots; Lt Col G L P Henderson (formerly RAF), Capt Fagan, Lt Park, and Lt Hastings. Elsewhere it took until the following weekend for flights to begin from Manston, in Kent, to Margate in the same county and at Hamble where flights had been planned to Blackpool and Southport. The press reported an incident involving a '*large aircraft*' carrying a pilot and two passengers between Crayford, Kent and Norwich that had suffered engine failure and crash-landed in a field at Dunmow, Essex. The plane caught fire but this was extinguished by one of the passengers, saving the pilot in the process. The other passenger, Walter Jones, died in the accident. The dead man was unfortunate; he had survived the impact but was presumed to have died after being overcome by engine fumes.

AT&T were ready to start operating and by midnight had the engine running on a DH9 (G-EAAA) hired by the *Daily Mail* that Captains Howard J Saint and Greig would fly from Hendon to Portsmouth with a cargo of newspapers. The weather was bad on the night and the aircraft developed engine trouble causing it to crash at Portsdown Hill two miles from Portsmouth. Saint received a broken jaw in the accident but Greig, although badly shaken, was relatively unharmed.

On the same night, 1 May 1919, one of Handley Page's 0/400s flew from the company aerodrome at Cricklewood to Manchester with ten passengers in 3 hrs 30 mins. The company had also secured a contract to fly a special edition of the *Daily Mail* from Manchester to Edinburgh. The pilot was Lieutenant-Colonel William Sholto Douglas who, thirty years later, as Lord Douglas of Kirtleside, became chairman of British European Airways (BEA) from 1949 to 1964. Douglas battled against strong headwinds for three hours but managed to reach Manchester. Next day, when the bad weather continued, his flight to Scotland had to turn back and could not be completed until 5 May, when newspapers were successfully dropped by parachute at Carlisle, Dundee, Aberdeen, Montrose and Edinburgh. Major Orde-Lees, a passenger on the flight, decided to *drop in on a friend* literally by jumping by parachute as the aircraft flew over Aberdeen. During the first fortnight of May, Handley Page claimed to have carried 18,650 lbs of freight and 76 passengers on fourteen single flights between London and other UK destinations.

Bad weather continued to mar the entire first week of commercial flying and led to the death of a pilot, Capt E M Knott AFC, who crashed at Kenley while on a communications flight with Sir Frederick Sykes. The aircraft stalled at 50 ft and plummeted to the ground, but Sykes, although shaken by his experience was unhurt. But even his involvement in a fatal accident could not deter the Controller-General from giving a lecture on civil aviation at the Liverpool Chamber of Commerce three days later or from flying to an official engagement in Paris. It was not an auspicious start; the first Saturday of commercial flying had resulted in three separate fatal accidents.

First scheduled civil passenger flights

The Government's uncertainties about civil flying did not prevent AT&T from making a proving flight from Hendon to Le Bourget on 15 July 1919 carrying one passenger. This was Major Pilkington of the glass firm who paid £42 to charter the aircraft, a DH9 (K109 – later G-EAAC) flown by Lt H G 'Jerry' Shaw. Pilkington had read an announcement in the 14 July edition of the London *Evening News* about the Government's relaxation of the civil aviation rules. He contacted the flight manager of AT&T, the well known Davis Cup tennis-star Capt Donald Grieg, to explain his need to attend an urgent meeting in Paris next day. As the equivalent rail and sea journey would have taken a full day or night, air transport provided the solution to Pilkington's plight. The journey must have been quite an experience for the distinguished passenger who, after being kitted out in a heavy leather coat, goggles, helmet and gloves was subjected to torrential rain as the aircraft departed at 0730 hrs. Shaw, determined to make the first commercial passenger flight to Paris, ignored landing for Customs clearance at Hounslow after seeing a Handley Page 0/400 preparing to depart as he over-flew the airfield. He correctly reasoned that the aircraft was attempting to beat him to Paris. By not landing at Hounslow Shaw had put himself in deep water with the authorities. When he landed on the return he was confronted by angry customs officials who sternly reminded him of the regulations he had breached. This was in complete contrast to the relaxed arrival Shaw had received at Le Bourget, where there were no customs officials to meet them, and he and Pilkington merely left the airport and took a tram into the city despite Shaw having no passport. Pilkington's journey has been widely recognised as the first official international charter flight between Britain and the Continent although this has since been challenged. A record is believed to exist of a flight made on 1 March 1919 that carried Sir Woodman Burbridge, the managing director of Harrods, from Hendon to Brussels. This would have occurred before the Government had lifted the ban on civilian flights, therefore making it illegal; a probable reason why no published evidence of the flight appears to exist.

On 25 August, at 0910 hrs, a DH4a (G-EAJC) took-off from the grass strip at Hounslow Heath and headed for Le Bourget to claim the title of the world's first fixed-wing scheduled daily commercial service. There is also some debate over this claim because historians argue that the flight was made *before* the first official departure listed in a timetable to render it non-scheduled. Nevertheless this flight has since become extremely well-known. It was piloted by Lt E H Lawford and his passenger that morning was George Stevenson-Reece, a journalist, who accompanied a cargo of newspapers, leather, and fresh grouse to the French capital destined for Lord Derby, the British Ambassador, and a consignment of Devonshire cream for some gourmet restaurants. The flight lasted 2 hrs 30 mins and cost twenty guineas (£21). During the same day a second aircraft, a DH16 (K130) piloted by Major Cyril Patterson, flew four passengers on the route in 2hrs 15mins. One of the passengers was Bruce Ingham, editor of *The Illustrated London News*. This was a revenue earning flight that had departed in accordance with the published official timetable and many regard this to be the more worthy claimant to the accolade of first scheduled passenger service, discounting Lawford's earlier flight. The debate is really elementary because both aircraft were operated by AT&T.

Ingham was greatly impressed by his experience and was quick to praise the speed and convenience of air travel to his readers. '*What would have been thought some fifty years ago, if anyone had seriously made the announcement that our businessmen would in a few years be able to have lunch in London and tea in Paris, and return to London in time for dinner? And yet all this has now become possible. One cannot hope to describe adequately, the interest, the sense of security, and the comfort which such a journey gives, to say nothing of the time saved, the avoidance of inconvenience caused by change from train to boat, then from boat to train again, with the usual scramble for places, and the irritating delays at the Customs in the journey between London and Paris.*' Had he made that same journey today he would probably have been far more critical; for although jet travel may have shortened the flying time, the accumulated time it takes getting to and from airports, check-in procedures and waiting at the baggage carousel has made the equivalent journey in modern times far more arduous.

AT&T's claim to have operated the world's first scheduled fixed-wing passenger service has also been disputed, with some justification,

An Air Transport and Travel (AT&T) DH34 prepares to depart. (CAS)

by the Farman brothers. The French had laid claim to this honour after Lt Lucien Bossoutrot, flying one of Farman's F60 Goliaths, carried eleven military personnel from Paris (Toussus le Noble airfield) to Kenley on 8 February 1919. This flight was not recognised by the British authorities, nor could a *one-off* flight justifiably be regarded as *scheduled,* but the French may have a more reliable claim with the first service operated on the Paris-Brussels route. On 10 February a Cauldron C23 carried five journalists between the two cities on a trial flight. Bossoutrot followed this with a series of regular weekly flights for the Farman Company from 22 March. The journey took 2 hrs 50 mins and the fare was 365 Francs. It is recorded that Customs officials examined passengers upon arrival at Brussels after the third flight. As British Customs did not start operating at Hounslow until later the same year, the Belgians can also lay claim to the first airport customs inspection. The overseas editions of the *Daily Mail* carried advertisements in March 1919 placed by Farman to promote these flights with published fares, departure and arrival times for outbound and inbound journeys. By mid-August the French had already attempted a long distance Paris-Dakar flight of 2,800 miles. On the first day the Farman Goliath, referred to in *The Times* of 18 August 1919 as the *aerobus,* flown by Boussoutrot and Coupet with a crew of seven, had reached Cassablanca non-stop in 18 hrs 23 mins to set a record. After spending a day resting and a further day discussing the protocols of a Paris-Morocco service with General Lyautey at Rabat, the crew proceeded to Mogador before crossing 350 miles of desert between Tiznit and Port Etienne the next day. On 18 August Dakar lost contact with the aircraft. Little seems to be recorded about the fate of the Goliath, but it appears to have landed 90 miles short of its intended destination, probably after succumbing to a typhoon that had been reported at Dakar.

If anyone should doubt AT&T's claim to be the world's first *passenger* airline service, then there can be no disputing the regularity and reliability of its flights. The company maintained an impressive record despite the views of critics who believed it impossible to sustain reliability as well as safety. These opinions were based on the unreliability of aircraft in wartime which regularly suffered mechanical failures that led to crashes. But combat aircraft experienced more strenuous forms of flying and the machines, due to pressures to keep them operational, were sometimes less well maintained than their contemporary civil counterparts. During the first month of operation AT&T had successfully completed 54 of 56 scheduled services and during its first seven weeks made 99 completed flights from a schedule of 102. After fifteen weeks its reliability continued with 200 from 227 services completed. This is no mean feat considering that during that period only 90 days had been available for flying and 40

of these were considered climatically unfavourable, while 29 were deemed *unfit* due to severe adverse weather conditions. George Holt Thomas published the following chart in his book *Aerial Transport* (Hodder & Stoughton 1920) that shows the prevailing weather conditions encountered by his flights on the London-Paris route from 25 August to 18 September 1919. He also noted that between 25 August-11 October his aircraft had flown 24,750 miles. When placed in context against the primitive nature of the equipment available, it is proof that the company's service record was exemplary.

Rainy Days	6
Windy Days	6
Foggy Days	4
Misty Days	6
Cloudy Days	12

AT&T had been contracted by the British Post Office (GPO) to provide the world's first scheduled international airmail service, between London and Paris, on 10 November 1919 using an Airco DH4A (G-EAHF). The French Post Office awarded their contract to Compagnie Générale Transaraérienne used Breguet aircraft. Mail posted at several Central London post offices was collected by motor cycle and taken to Hounslow to meet the 1230 hrs flight. This reached Paris by 1445 hrs and mail was taken to the city centre for sorting, and delivered by 1600 hrs the same day. The air mail service considerably improved the delivery times of onward mail to other European capitals by almost 24 hours, and consignments bound for places such as Madrid and Rome continued on express trains leaving Paris during the evenings.

The first mail flight was piloted by Lt J McMullin in an aircraft that proudly sported an Air Mail logo attached to the rudder. Despite taking-off, low cloud and severe weather forced McMullin to return to Hounslow after reaching only as far as Epsom. This probably caused a number of red faces among the officials when the inaugural mail had to be returned to the Post Office for despatch by train and ferry. The French fared no better when even worse weather was encountered on the Continent. By next day, despite reported winds of up to 40 mph in the Channel, McMullin reached Paris five minutes early but the French service flown by Lt Lindley encountered strong head winds and was forced to alight at Kenley when Lindley ran out of petrol and a car had to transport the mail to London.

The company was paid 2s 0d (10p) from the charge of 2s 6d (12½p) per ounce that customers paid to send a letter by air, but loads were erratic and during the winter months the weather inevitably took its toll on schedules. Most of the aircraft were open to the elements. Pilots

would sit in exposed, unheated cockpits and be required to fly visually without any kind of sophisticated navigation equipment. The compasses were considerably unreliable and there were no radio aids. The conditions were appalling for much of the time, but the pilots were a hardy bunch that were willing to endure the hazards and extreme discomforts that their jobs entailed. Pilots would normally navigate by following railway lines and the names of stations at Redhill, Edenbridge, Tonbridge and Ashford were painted on the roofs to help them find their way. Enforced landings were common and emergency landing grounds were provided on both sides of the Channel every twenty miles or so (four in England; five in France) as a safety measure. The Department of Civil Aviation, founded 12 February 1919, published an official guide 'Aerial Route London (Hounslow) – France (St Inglevert)' that gave detailed directions along the entire route and provided pilots with a list of landmarks they should look for. The first passengers had to endure travelling in open compartments, always at the mercy of the weather and deafened by the noise of constantly droning engines that on occasions would also blow oil back into their faces. Low flying often meant enduring the considerable discomforts caused by any turbulence the aircraft encountered.

The difficulties of early flying can be found in a report of one particular flight. On 29 October 1919, Jerry Shaw left Le Bourget with one passenger in poor weather. His compass was not functioning so he flew in tandem with a second aircraft but the two became separated by poor visibility. Shaw got lost and was forced down in the English Channel but was fortunate to land close to a coaster. His passenger, bowler hat in hand, apparently made light of the experience, took everything in his stride and without complaint merely walked along the aircraft wing and stepped aboard the waiting vessel. After being landed at Weymouth, Shaw and his passenger continued their journey to London by train none the worse for wear.

In March 1920 the Air Manufacturing Company (AIRCO) that owned AT&T had been absorbed by the BSA (Birmingham Small Arms) and Daimler combines. BSA was well known for its wide number of interests that included producing explosives, arms, cars and bicycles. Despite the diversity of its business, the management failed to appreciate the future potential offered by air travel. It wound-up the Air Manufacturing Company and even though Holt Thomas's airline managed to survive for a short time after, without a Government subsidy its fate was sealed, it folded and BSA disposed of AT&T's assets. The situation after the War had become so bad that many aircraft manufacturers either closed down entirely or resorted to manufacturing other engineered products such as milk churns simply to remain in business. The finger was pointed at the Government for failing to acknowledge that aircraft production still had a future even though the requirement for war planes had ended. Without Government support, prospects for the industry were extremely grim and private backers were never likely to invest in a business that showed such little potential for making any money.

The viability of running an airline was extremely precarious. By the late summer of 1920 AT&T had just about broken even by charging £5 0s 0d to travel between London and Paris, but to remain viable the company had to sell every seat on its aircraft. If an aircraft departed with only 80 per cent capacity, to stay in profit the fare needed to be raised to £6 6s 0d (£6.30). Two years later an article in *The Aeroplane* on 1 February 1922 analysed the costs of making a London-Paris journey using a 450 hp aircraft:

Petrol	£ 9 0s 0d
Oil	£ 3 15s 0d
Pilot	£ 2 10s 0d
Repairs/maintenance	£ 3 0s 0d
TOTAL	£18 5s 0d

Against a revenue of £40 (8 seats sold at £5.00) the operating costs were £18 5s 0d (£18.25) that left a balance of £21 15s 0d (£21.75) to cover management, aircraft depreciation and other expenses. The difficulties faced by the company were obvious but the Government's

refusal to provide help forced the service to be discontinued in October. AT&T ceased operations altogether on 15 December 1922 despite Holt Thomas's relentless work and driving enthusiasm.

Before this, any honeymoon period there might have been for Holt Thomas's AIRCO Company following the absorption by BSA was extremely short lived. On 23 March 1920 *The Times* reported that Holt Thomas had resigned as chairman of AIRCO. In a lengthy and hard-hitting statement he gave to the newspaper he began by saying: '*By the amalgamation recently announced, the Birmingham Small Arms Company Limited, acquired control of my companies. Their interest naturally lies in the large factories, which although created for aircraft, are adapted for other productions such as motor bodies and engineering works; and equally naturally the first step is to foster these productions, and cut down all expense which is not likely to prove remunerative in the near future.*

'*Could I honestly advise my co-directors, in view of the present apathetic attitude of the Government to continue an expensive technical department devoted to the design of aircraft?*'

After emphasising how important the designs of Airco and de Havilland had been to the Government during the War, and how they had since been adopted by the United States Flying Corps for transporting 230,000 lbs of air mail that had been carried in the year up until June 1919, Holt Thomas continued: '*The form of design and factory equipment were described, and I feel rightly described, by Lord Cowdray in the capacity of our first Air Minister, as a 'national asset'. For 18 months no encouragement whatsoever has been given, and so far as I am aware there is no prospect or guarantee that the Airco will have orders for experimental machines, say for £100,000, a sum sufficient to keep the staff together for the next twelve months. Fundamentally the utter failure of the authorities to view in the proper proportion the importance of the air as compared with the Navy and Army is at the root of the matter. Minister after minister has publicly stated that we 'must retain our lead'. We are far from doing so.*'

He referred to the fact that any future attacks during a time of war would come from the air yet the British Government had done nothing to develop aviation and flight training in peacetime by encouraging civil aviation. He poignantly pointed out how the Air Service had been used to encourage civil aviation in every country but Great Britain. '*The French Government pays a subsidy almost amounting to the cost of a French machine flying to London and back. The American Government is establishing air mails everywhere. The British Government pays nothing, and the Air Ministry states that civil aviation must fly by itself. I cannot imagine the London-Paris air mail ceasing to exist. It is unthinkable that this and Airco design should disappear, but I resigned because I could not, as a businessman, see my way to advise my co-directors to continue under existing conditions.*' In this statement Holt Thomas had succinctly summed up the situation that prevailed during the period that led to the formation of Imperial Airways.

Handley Page enters the arena

The AT&T closure was not helped by the need to do battle with one of the greatest protagonists in aviation history. Handley Page had been one of the major manufacturers of heavy bombers during the Great War and it had been successful with its 0/400 aircraft in peacetime. A number of these aircraft were converted to civilian use for service anywhere the company thought there was a market. Frederick Handley Page was very adept at publicising and promoting his business and his prowess made him the main rival of AT&T in the race to launch a revenue earning air service. In March 1919 the company displayed the fuselage of a converted 0/400 in Selfridges, the prestigious London store, having added a plush interior that included upholstered lounge chairs for up to sixteen people. Handley Page had also been invited to tender for the supply of ten-seat, twin-engined aircraft for the Chinese Ministry of Communications. After winning the contract from Vickers, six commercial versions of the 0/400 were delivered. These were a more powerful derivation of the 0/400 known as the 0/700. By April, encouraged by the recently announced £10,000 prize offered by the *Daily Mail* for the first aircraft to fly the Atlantic Major Herbert Brackley DSO DSC was hired to fly the four-engined V/1500 loaned to the company by the Air Ministry. This was tested on 1 April using the 700 yard runway at Cricklewood. The flight had been a success but the Government, for reasons best known to itself, extended its ban on civil flying for a further two months. This outraged Holt Thomas and Handley Page prompting them to briefly support each other to formally

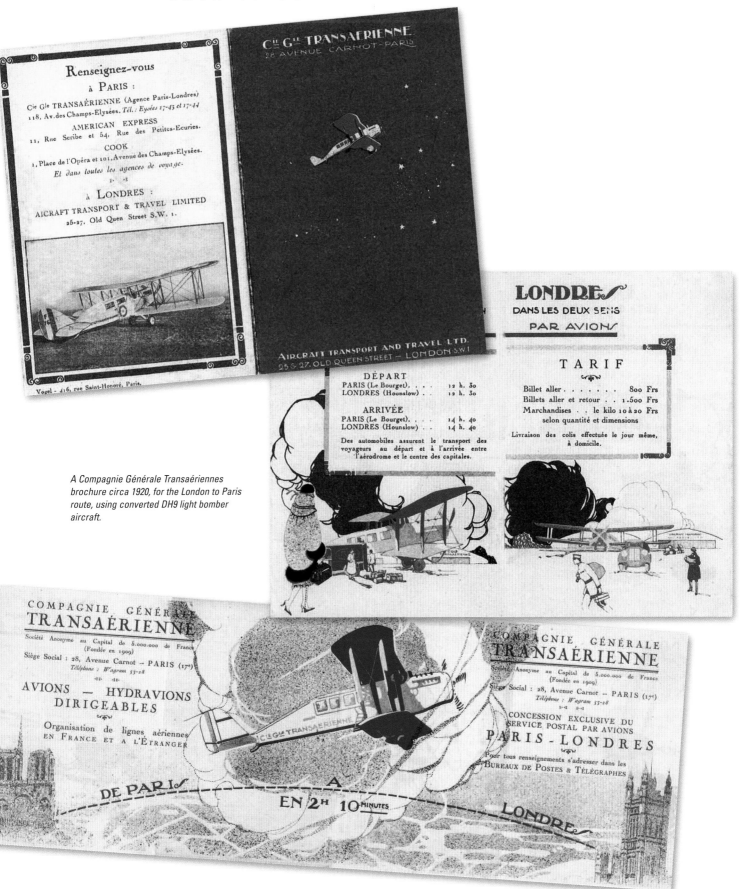

A Compagnie Générale Transaériennes brochure circa 1920, for the London to Paris route, using converted DH9 light bomber aircraft.

protest to the Air Ministry. This forced a stand-down by the Ministry that gave permission for local flying to begin from specified airfields which gave the public the opportunity to take joyrides offered over the Easter holiday. It came as a surprise when several thousand people flocked to one airfield and hundreds took to the skies despite appalling weather. Handley Page, as might be expected, seized every opportunity to gain publicity by using three 0/400 aircraft, one piloted by Maj Leslie Foot, that gave 800 fare-paying passengers the opportunity to take joy

flights from Cricklewood. To achieve this, these aircraft were converted to allow six passengers to be carried in the cabin with two more seated in the nose position formerly occupied by the gunner; a precarious location that could only be reached by step ladder. Aware of the risks of flying, the organisers were quick to print disclaimers in small type on their tickets informing passengers that any claims for death or injury were excluded and they were expected to fly entirely at their own risk.

Handley Page Air Services brochure circa 1919.

Tickets with such disclaimers were commonly issued by the early pioneering companies and became known as *blood-chits*.

The clamber for seats at air displays led Charles Grey, the highly outspoken editor of *The Aeroplane*, to write: '*Of the total population, two million will want the experience of having been up in an aeroplane, and some will go on joy-riding for as long as they can afford; so ultimately one might reckon there would be some five million joy-rides to be given before pleasure flying markets began to decline.*'

Handley Page Transport, formed as a separate new entity, from the aircraft manufacturing company, that became incorporated as a limited liability company on 14 June 1919 with a capital of £200,000 and appointed George Woods Humphery as manager. Within a few eventful years Woods Humphery progressed to play a key administrative role with Imperial Airways. On the day that AT&T had made its inaugural Paris flight (25 August 1919) Handley Page had flown a group of eleven journalists to the French capital who paid £15 15s 0d (£15.75) each for the privilege. He had intended to arrive before AT&T's DH42 but his aircraft had touched down ninety-five minutes later. Handley Page had already been making proving flights at weekends to Bournemouth and on the 19 July he flew to Brussels (Haren). On 2 September, Sholto Douglas inaugurated regular flights from Cricklewood to Paris and Capt Shakespeare made three flights a week to Brussels from 23 September (carrying seven passengers) using HP0/400s and an HP0/7. The French airline, Compagnie des Messageries Aériennes (CMA) had alternated with Handley Page on the Paris service using Breguet 14s. The first of these was operated by *Monsieur* Massot from London on 16 September. Ten days later *The Times* reported the excitement that had occurred when people rushed to a field at Dartford, Kent where Capt Shakespeare had made a brief landing to check his pressure pumps before continuing his journey from Brussels to London.

Business increased and during the week ending 15 October the companies jointly carried 60 passengers and 2,925 lbs of freight between London and Paris and 20 passengers and 60 lbs of baggage on the London-Brussels services. At that time regulations prevented the carriage of freight between London and the Belgian capital. As CMA was establishing relations with Handley Page, another French line, Compagnie Générale Transaériennes had been appointed Paris agents to AT&T but later introduced their own aircraft to compete on the route. In September Farman became the latest *personality* to join the already over-subscribed London-Paris route with the airline he had recently formed as Lignes Aériennes Farman.

Handley Page Transport had improved the London-Paris service pioneered by AT&T. The company was charging £15 15s 0d (£15.75)

for a one-way journey; £31 10s 0d return (£31.50) to either Paris or Brussels. By November the airline had carried 554 passengers and 9,600 lbs of freight. From 11 October a limousine car service provided transport to and from aerodromes and in an innovative move, passengers were offered lunch boxes for the first time containing six sandwiches, chocolate and fruit for 3s 0d (15p). Passengers ordered these in advance and the food was provided in wicker holders that were attached to the walls of the aircraft cabin. It is probable that few passengers consumed their in-flight luncheons because air sickness was a common occurrence that passengers had to endure and bumpy journeys were an everyday inconvenience that anyone wishing to partake in the flying experience had to get used to. The company also introduced a new, purpose-built, civilian aircraft, the W8 (G-EAPJ) which made its maiden flight to Paris on 4 December in 2 hrs 10 mins. The internal appearances of Handley Page aircraft were also enhanced to appear more luxurious than the machines operated by AT&T. Wicker armchair seating was introduced, there were brackets for holding fresh flowers, gilded mirrors and the windows, which could be opened, also had curtains. Despite these aesthetic modifications, seat belts and onboard toilets were still a thing of the future and flying continued to be a precarious and generally uncomfortable activity. In a move to imply that his aircraft were safer, Handley Page promoted the fact that his had two engines and that they were safer than the single-engine machines operated by AT&T. In reality the two-engines of the HP aircraft were no better; the aircraft were very heavy to fly, were extremely unstable and frequently were forced to make hurried emergency landings whenever one of these engines became unserviceable. Although Handley Page's propaganda would have passengers believe otherwise, in many respects the company's aircraft were lumbering giants with a light wing loading that caused them to rise and fall abruptly whenever they encountered turbulence.

In the formative years anything that involved civil aviation that appeared out of the ordinary was likely to appear in the newspapers. On 28 October 1919 *The Times* reported that three Paris, Amsterdam and Brussels flights to London had been caught in a gale. The story told of passengers and freight that had failed to reach London after being hit by 45-50 mph headwinds. The aircraft belonging to AT&T (named as Airco in the article) travelling from Brussels and the British Aerial Transport (see below) Amsterdam flight were both forced to land at Lympne and a Handley Page aircraft that had taken four and a half hours from Paris only reached Marden in Kent.

Handley Page flights were also hampered by having to land at Hounslow to undergo Customs clearance before passengers were allowed to re-board for the short flight to Cricklewood. The folly of this situation was addressed on 17 February 1920 when Customs facilities

were introduced at Cricklewood and flights no longer had to make the tedious stop at Hounslow.

In May 1920 Handley Page took over the mail contract between London and Paris that AT&T had lost when it had requested higher rates for the service. During the same month AT&T started a tri-weekly London-Amsterdam-The Hague-Rotterdam service in collaboration with the Dutch carrier, Koninklijke Luchtvaart Maatschappij voor Nederland an Kolonien (KLM) using a DH6 aircraft with a fare of £15 15s 0d (£15.75). The first of these flights was operated by Lt H Shaw carrying two passengers in a DH16 (G-EALU). The company gained a mail contract even though the GPO had reduced the rate from 2s 3½d to 2s 3d (11.25p) per ounce. In June a Brussels-London service was also launched by the Belgian company, Syndicat National pour l'etude des Transports Aériens (SNETA) using DH4 and DH9 aircraft. Handley Page had dropped this route in February in favour of Amsterdam although it was resumed on 19 July. The Amsterdam service began on 6 July in conjunction with KLM. This was followed on 26 July when Lt E Halliwell began flying an experimental service carrying British, Belgian and Dutch mails on the London-Brussels-Amsterdam-Rotterdam route that was discontinued on 30 October 1920 due to insufficient loads. Because of the rivalry between AT&T and Handley Page it was soon realised that the London-Paris route was failing to attract enough custom to support both companies and the latter ceased flying the route on 17 November.

A third airline had also been operating in the UK. Formed in 1917, British Aerial Transport Company (BAT) was started by Samuel Waring of the furniture company Waring and Gillow. Waring had encouraged the Dutch aviation engineer, Frederick Koolhoven to provide the expertise required for his venture and the company initially started services between Hendon and Birmingham (Castle Bromwich) on 30 September 1919. Koolhoven BAT FK26 aircraft were flown but on 7 October they were transferred to fly to Amsterdam (Soesterberg) carrying 600 lbs of cargo with Cyril Turner as pilot. The return on 10 October carried four passengers. This service continued in a fashion until January 1920 after which Koolhoven left and the company collapsed.

Instone starts an airline

A few days after BAT had inaugurated its Amsterdam route, S Instone & Company, a shipping line and coal exporter, began operating its own small airline, initially to carry staff and internal mail from Cardiff to Hounslow, then onward to Paris. Instone became the first trading company in the world to use aircraft for its everyday business. This came about after the Armistice when it took 7-10 days for mail to arrive on the Continent. This created problems by delaying Instone's ships from discharging its loads in Northern France because the bills of lading, sent in the post, had not arrived. The delays were creating extra expense for the company so it conceived the idea of buying an aircraft once Government approval had been given to transport their own mail. This decision proved to be prudent because Instone was able to gain an edge over its competitors who were forced to moor their ships while awaiting their paperwork. Frank Barnard was hired as chief pilot to fly the company DH4 aircraft (G-EAMU) that was equipped with a Rolls-Royce engine. This had been adapted from wartime to civilian use with the pilot up front in an open cockpit and enclosed accommodation behind for two passengers. The closed cabin gave passengers a modicum of comfort because they could fly in their own clothes and no longer needed to put on heavy flying gear. On 13 October 1919 Barnard took the aircraft to Cardiff on its initial flight, returning to Hounslow in just 56 minutes. Shortly after, it left for Paris carrying letters of greeting from Stanley Machin, chairman of the London Chamber of Commerce, to his counterpart at the British Chamber of Commerce in Paris. Barnard also released thousands of greetings cards while flying above the port of Boulogne. These showed an illustration depicting the Union flag and French tricolor with the following wording printed in French: *'son premier passage à Boulogne s/Mer l'aeroplane de la Societé Instone envoie à ses amis Boulonnais un salut fraternal'* and the cards were signed *'Barnard – Aviateur.'*

The Instone name was not new to aviation; it had previously been associated with flying as far back as August 1910 when it sponsored the Willows' gas-filled airship named *City of Cardiff* on a flight from the Welsh capital to London. During its early days as an airline Instone became involved in numerous other flying activities. According to

Alfred Instone, in his book *The Early Birds* the airline had undertaken the following:
- Carrying an edition of the *Daily Mail* to the Riviera during the French railway strike of 1920
- Flying a surgeon to perform an urgent operation
- Rain-producing experiments
- Printing and developing press photographs while airborne
- Announcing the result of the Dempsey-Carpentier boxing match with coloured signals
- Air ambulance flights
- Carrying jockeys between races in the UK and the Continent
- Special cargo flights and air excursions.

During the occupation of the Ruhr, Instone was chartered by the German Government to carry Marks to London and then back to Cologne. This became the country's only way of getting badly needed currency to its unemployed citizens who were under French occupational forces. Known as the *Marks Express*, the service, that had cost the Germans £120 per trip, came to an end on 7 October 1923 after the Allies had objected. The company also claimed a number of aviation 'firsts':
- Instone was the first to name an aircraft
- The first to provide uniforms for staff and pilots
- The first to provide aviation tuition for apprentices
- The first to operate wireless telephone conversations from office to aircraft.

On 15 May 1920 the company changed its title to The Instone Airline when it opened the Paris sector of its route to the public.

By May 1920 the single fare to the French capital had been cut to £12 and the company placed display advertisements in *The Times* of 19 and 26 May 1920 to promote its London-Paris service with a photograph of their Vickers Vimy Commercial *City of London* (G-EASI). The single fare was lowered again in June to £10 as an attempt to compete with the heavily subsidised French airlines operating on the same route. The British companies were finding it difficult to compete on an even keel against the heavily state-subsidised foreign airlines. But the British Government still refused to show any compassion. It was a bleak time. AT&T became the first to cease operations, but by 28 February Handley Page and Instone had followed suit. By the end of 1920 all British cross-channel operations had ceased and the money the taxpayer had contributed towards establishing aerodromes and navigation aids only benefited the foreign airlines that were flying into the United Kingdom unopposed. Ironically £514,900 for research and development and £805,700 towards civil aviation had been voted to go to the airlines from the Air Ministry but the funding had to be diverted by the Government to pay off war debts created by the Ministry of Munitions. Now that the war machine had been closed down, the economy had been briefly more stable but the Government refused to provide any help until it was forced to during the depressed year of 1921.

In the autumn of 1920 the Air Ministry had staged an air conference at London's Guildhall. Sefton Branker and George Holt Thomas had both suggested that all first class mail should be sent by air. Samuel Instone requested Government aid to rescue the companies from their inability to compete on equal terms with their European competitors. Instone had merely argued that the Air Ministry should offer the fledgling airlines the same assistance that had been given to merchant shipping through Admiralty money. He proposed that the Government should offer to pay part of a pilot's wages and, in so doing, make pilots employees of the RAF Reserve. He also asked for subsidies to be paid for aircraft manufacture, for the free use of airfields and hangars and for an insurance to build replacement aircraft to cover for the time when the supply of cheap wartime aircraft became exhausted. Instone and his brothers were successful colliery and shipping company operators with strong views that the airlines should be granted the same financial help that had previously benefited merchant shipping. They pointed out that private investment would not be forthcoming unless the companies could operate profitably, but this was impossible without subsidies.

Other pioneering operators
The previously mentioned companies had pioneered commercial air transport in British as best as they could but three other companies also

played a lesser role during the first year of scheduled service operations.

On 23 April 1919 the North Sea Aerial Navigation Company of Leeds was incorporated with the intention of providing an air link between various cities in the north of England. The name of the business was later changed to North Sea Aerial and General Transport. The company was a subsidiary of the Blackburn Aircraft Company of Hull and it used modified twin-engined, Blackburn Kangaroo ex-bomber aircraft to fly its routes. During the summer the airline operated a service between the Yorkshire towns of Scarborough, Hull and Harrogate with an Avro 504K (G-EAGV). On 30 September 1919 it began a regular service between Hull, Leeds and Hounslow using converted Kangaroos (G-EAIT and G-EAKQ) at a fare of fifteen guineas (£15.75) single; £30 return. The airline carried around 2,000 passengers before turning their interests to freight by introducing a service between Leeds and Amsterdam via London and Lympne. This was unsuccessful and the service launched on 5 March 1920 was suspended by October. Owner, Robert Blackburn, also issued publicity maps that outlined his proposals for future routes linking Hull with Copenhagen, Stockholm, Helsingfors (Helsinki) and Petrograd (Russia) but his ambitious plans never reached fruition.

An eccentric boat builder and aviator, Noel Pemberton Billing, dubbed by one newspaper as '*The Incredible*' because of his exploits, founded The Supermarine Aviation Company with a capital of £20,000. As far back as 1903, Billing had built a man-carrying glider and had almost killed himself when he launched himself from the roof of his house. In 1909 Billing had attempted to establish a large aircraft works at South Fambridge in Essex but the condition of the terrain made it difficult for machines to land and take-off causing the venture to fail within the first year. By 1913 he was attempting to develop a concept of boats that would fly and built the PB1, a flying-boat that was powered by a tractor engine mounted between the wings above a cigar shaped hull. During the previous year he had bought a factory unit next to Woolston Ferry on the River Itchen near Southampton. In the same year he challenged Frederick Handley Page to a £500 wager that he could learn to fly and gain a Royal Aero Club Aviator's Certificate within 24 hours. Pemberton Billing went to the Vickers school at Brooklands where, between 0545 hrs and breakfast, he amazingly gained Certification forcing Handley Page to hand over his money.

By 1914 Hubert Scott-Paine joined the company as works manager, becoming managing director two years later when the name of the company was changed to The Supermarine Aviation Works Ltd. A designer by the name of Reginald J. Mitchell joined the staff, who later gained fame for his Spitfire fighter and Schneider Trophy winning aircraft that bore the Supermarine name. The appointment of Scott-Paine allowed Billing the freedom to pursue his other activity as a political candidate. His election plan was to flatten the War Office aviation policy. He was aided in his views by his close, often outspoken friend, the editor of *The Aeroplane*, C G Grey, who in later years was openly accused of being a Nazi sympathiser. Billing's campaigning succeeded; he was elected Independent Member of Parliament for East Herts on 10 March 1916 at which point he relinquished his interests in the Supermarine Company.

Scott-Paine had worked closely with the Admiralty on flying-boat developments and the Channel Type aircraft evolved from his war-time design. This was an aircraft capable of carrying three passengers, seated in an outdoor cockpit in front of the pilot. These were originally built with the designation *A D Boats* (Air Department Boats) of which ten were bought back from the Admiralty with the intention of using five and keeping the remainder in reserve. They were later used for pleasure flights from the Royal Pier at Southampton to the Isle of Wight seaside resorts of Sandown, Shanklin, Ryde and Ventnor as well as for conveying passengers to and from the Cowes regatta. A Southampton-Bournemouth service was later inaugurated on 23 July 1919. One of these flights carried the oldest passengers to have taken to the air thus far; a man aged 75 years and a woman, three years his junior. Three aircraft were used on a daily basis; G-EAED. G-EAEE and G-EAEK.

In 1919 the company was able to take advantage of the rail strike that had prevented the ferries from sailing and it also provided flights for local mayors, chief constables and other dignitaries. During September, providing the weather remained favourable, it offered joy flights around the naval fleet that was anchored in Bournemouth Bay. Two passenger flights were made on 28 September to Le Havre and the next day it carried both mail and passengers. A month earlier one of the company's aircraft was used to make what is believed to be the very first fuel delivery by air. The Spencer motor launch that operated between the Isle of Wight and the mainland had run out fuel and was stranded at Ventnor. One of the Channel flying-boats was put to imaginative use and landed alongside to provide fuel for the stranded vessel.

An amusing episode occurred during September 1919 when an aircraft flown by its pilot Capt H C Biard was battling to reach Le Havre against massive headwinds. A somewhat irate Belgian millionaire was one of two passengers on board (the other was a naval officer) who had been annoyed at the inclement British weather. Scott-Paine was said to have given each passenger a lifebelt before escorting them to the waiting aircraft. During the flight the Belgian, seated in the outdoor cockpit took a drink from a flask of rum that Scott-Paine had offered before the flight to strengthen his morale. He tried to pass the flask to Biard who was seated in the pilot's cockpit in front of him but he only succeeded in causing the flask contents to blow back into the pilot's face. Biard was not only frozen, with ice hanging from his face and thick gloves but he now also had rum in his eyes and was having difficulty seeing. The Belgian then attempted to open an umbrella to shield his face from the weather. Biard, concerned that the wind would sweep this from the passenger's grasp and blow it into the engine had to take desperate action to gain some control over the boisterous Belgian. To quieten him down all he could do was to grab the flask and hit his passenger over the head with sufficient force to render the man unconscious. The rest of the flight, despite taking five hours, remained uneventful with no more disruptions from the Belgian passenger and, upon landing he expressed no malice by taking Biard into a local hotel where he bought him a stiff drink!

In May 1920 three of the Channel flying-boats were sold to the Norwegian airline Det Norske Luftfartrederi A/S of Christiania (Now Oslo). Bad weather had prevented the Supermarine from flying as frequently as the company would have liked and a lack of public support and too little mail led to the demise of the business at the end of 1920 although it was resurrected in 1923 as The British Marine Air Navigation Company (see next Chapter).

It is a little known fact that the news agency, Reuters had also expressed an interest in the possibility of operating its own airline, to speed up its communications between England and the Continent. During the First World War Roderick Jones, the agency managing director, had discussed the matter with Major Herbert Brackley. On 12 December 1918 Brackley, then still an operational officer of 214 Squadron of the RAF, wrote to Jones to offer his assistance in setting up a peacetime flying service. In his letter Brackley said '*Last year you expressed a desire to form an aviation service for the purpose of conveying dispatches to begin with from England to France and then, as the service develops, to other countries.*' However, Brackley's offer was never taken up by Reuters and Jones replied on 22 December: '*Since I last saw you our aviation ideas have undergone a change, and my intention now is to ally the Agency with one of the Air Transport Companies, rather than to conduct an air branch of our own.*' As Brackley joined Handley Page and later became an influential figure in the subsequent development of civil aviation, it is interesting to consider whether his involvement in this venture might have succeeded in creating a fully fledged airline operation able to compete with others on the European routes.

Finally, a company called Air Posts of Banks attempted to enter the London to Paris arena on 13 September 1920 using a pair of Westland Limousine aircraft (G-EAFO and G-EAJL). The enterprise was extremely brief, ending on 2 November when the company got into financial difficulties. The business had been set up to ferry documents and securities, out of office hours, for the banking houses, more specifically between London and the Continent. For the limited time it existed, the company also carried some freight and passengers between Croydon and Le Bourget and it set a record by completing one journey in1 hr 52 mins.

Despite their entrepreneurial spirit, it was obvious that the fledgling airlines could not possibly be expected to fly by themselves as Churchill had prescribed if they were to compete against the Continental airlines. It was obvious that the Government needed to radically change its policies towards civil aviation if Britain was to progress in line with other nations.

CHAPTER TWO

THE RISE AND FALL OF THE PIONEERS
1920-1923

A T the end of November 1919 a Government White Paper, *Imperial Air Routes,* was issued outlining the report of the newly formed Advisory Committee for Civil Aviation. The report stated that the Cairo-Karachi route that had been started for military purposes would be available for commercial flying in the future. A Cairo to the Cape route had also been surveyed with various landing stages established and full reconnaissance of the India-Australia route had also been completed. The Committee proposed that private enterprise, funded by State aid, should be developed to operate on these routes.

On 4 February 1920 two South African officers, Lt. Col. Pierre Van Rynevald DSO and Flt Lt C S Quinton Brand DSO MC DFC, financed by their Government, left the Vickers headquarters at Brooklands airfield at Weybridge in Surrey aboard the British registered Vimy IV *Silver Queen* (G-UABA) on the first successful attempt to reach Cape Town. After flying via Turin, Taranto, Sollum and Cairo they crashed at Korosko, 80 miles north of Wadi Halfa on 11 February. The flight continued using a surplus aircraft that they christened *Silver Queen II* that left Cairo eleven days later. This flew via Wadi Halfa, Khartoum, Mongalla, Kisumu, Shirati, Abercorn, Livingstone and Bulawayo where, on 6 March, the aircraft crashed on take-off. No doubt by now feeling extremely accident prone, the pilots took a third aircraft, a South African Government DH9 (H5648) *Voortrekker* and continued via Pretoria, Bloemfontein and Beaufort West eventually arriving in Cape Town on 20 March after what can only be described as a most eventful trip. A previous flight devised to test the practicality of the Cairo–Cape Town route that had previously departed from Brooklands on 24 January was unsuccessful. The Vickers Vimy Commercial (G-EAAV) piloted by Capt S Cockerell and Capt F C Broome DFC with mechanic Sgt-Major J Wyatt and rigger C Corby had reached Cairo by 3 February. Dr P E Mitchell of *The Times* who had chartered the aircraft joined the flight at the Egyptian capital but the Vimy later crashed on take-off while departing from Tabora, Tanganyika on 27 February and in so doing failed in its attempt to be the first aircraft to reach South Africa from the UK.

The desert furrow
Across a vast 500-mile expanse of the Middle East from Amman to Baghdad, a double-ploughed furrow had been created in the featureless desert. This was constructed by teams of men toiling in the searing heat, working tractors from either end under the leadership of Sir Hugh Trenchard, Chief of the Air Staff, to lay a long-distance marker that could be clearly seen from the air. DH9A aircraft of Number 30 Squadron (based at Ramadi) and Number 47 Squadron (from Amman) accompanied the ground workers. At suitable intervals, every twenty miles or so, landing areas were cleared and drums of fuel were placed as safety measures for any aircraft making a forced landing. At each of these landing grounds a circle was made that contained a letter or number to identify the site relevant to its location to the east or west of a place known as El Jid. The landing areas to the west had the letters A-R (omitting I and Q) and to the east, Roman numerals I-X (excepting 8

which was laid out in Arabic). The track was under the jurisdiction of the RAF Jordan Command to the west of El Jid and the Iraq Command to the east. As a further aid to pilots, arrows were placed in the sand that pointed towards the nearest landing ground. By necessity the track had to be maintained in good order and pilots using the route were required to report any areas that had been obscured by drifting sand. At the end of 1922 and again in 1923 the track was re-marked, generally tidied up and improved wherever possible. Today it seems preposterous that pilots had to rely on nothing more than a furrowed track to guide them safely across wastes of inhospitable desert, but in the 1920s there were no sophisticated aids and the idea worked extremely well.

From 12-30 March 1921 the Cairo Conference decided the future control of an area known as the Mandated Territory of Mesopotamia (later Iraq) that had been policed by troops. Trenchard proposed using aircraft and this suggestion led to the formation of the RAF Desert Air Mail that commenced in June 1923 between Cairo and Baghdad. During the next month the first air mails were carried from Baghdad to London and from 8 October between Cairo and London.

On 23 June 1921 the RAF commenced the Cairo (Heliopolis)-Baghdad (Baghdad West) mail service. This was operated by Number 47 Squadron based at Helwan, Egypt and Number 216 (Heliopolis) Squadron, both using DH9As. Vimys later replaced the squadron's DH9As and in 1922 45 and 70 Squadrons using Vickers Vernon aircraft worked the service while 216 Squadron continued to assist. By 28 July 1921 the first official Baghdad-London air mail service had started, arriving in London on 9 August. Mail from London left on 4 August to reach Baghdad on 17 August. The service was restricted at first to official mail but on 8 October it was opened to the public upon payment of a 1s 0d (5p) per ounce surcharge. This was later reduced to 6d (2½p) and then lowered again to 3d an ounce. Two extra services were operated on 13 and 20 October and from then on they ran fortnightly. RAF aircraft were only used on the Cairo-Baghdad sector, surface transport being used over the remainder of the route.

The ambitious Handley Page
While the RAF was establishing air mail routes in the Middle East, Frederick Handley Page had been looking elsewhere in his quest to broaden the horizons of his business. He was a far-thinking man who possessed a great deal of confidence and foresight about the future of commercial aviation. His vision certainly extended far beyond the proximities of domestic or European airline operations and he had plans for Handley Page aircraft to cover the world. After a successful deal to sell aircraft to the Chinese, he became embroiled in a series of negotiations that he hoped would launch his company onto a world wide stage. However these proved far less fruitful than he had anticipated. In September 1919 he won an important concession that gave him the monopoly to operate a passenger and mail service that stretched along a 2700-mile route in Brazil from Buenos Aires to Pernambuco. He intended to use twenty-four of his 0/400 aircraft that

Handley Page Transport HP W8b G-EBBI 'Prince Henry'. A commercial postcard from around 1922. (CAS)

would cover the route in eleven stages. These should have been shipped across the Atlantic in crates to be re-assembled once they had reached South America, but due to political wrangling the deal came to nothing.

This was shortly followed by a similar plan to run passenger and mail services in South Africa and India. In February 1920 Handley Page South African Transport Ltd of Cape Town was incorporated and in June the Handley Page Indo-Burmese Transport Company of Calcutta was launched. Both ventures failed to materialise although a private order was fulfilled for a luxury 0/7 aircraft fashioned with a fine pink silk interior that was bought by the Thakur Sahib of Morvi. The aircraft became known in the Handley Page works as *The Pink Elephant* because the fuselage was painted with high gloss pink paint with the engine nacelles picked out in blue.

Perhaps Handley Page's biggest mistake was to launch the American Handley Page Corporation that tendered, through an agent, William Workman, for a New York-Chicago mail contract that would also carry passengers and freight. On 10 July 1920 a perpetual injunction was issued in the New York Law Courts against Handley Page by the Wright Aeronautical Corporation. The injunction prevented the sale or use of foreign-built aircraft that embodied any features that infringed Wright patents. As this included warping or ailerons that would maintain lateral flight, the Handley Page aircraft were considered in breach of these patents and they were refused permission to operate. If this injunction had not already been enough, what really added insult to injury was that two aircraft that had already been shipped from England were impounded upon arrival in America by the US authorities.

A boost to the future potential of commercial flying, especially over long distances, was provided when a former bomber, a twin-engined Vickers Vimy, was entered into the England-Australia flying contest that offered a hefty £10,000 prize put up by Lord Northcliffe to the winner. This was flown by a former RAF pilot, Capt Ross Smith (who had previously surveyed the route) and his brother, Lt Keith Smith (navigator) with their mechanics, Sergeants J M Bennett and W H Shiers. The quartet departed from Hounslow at 0910 on 12 November and landed in Darwin on 10 December having flown an eventful 11,500 miles in stages totalling 124 flying hours. The flight was a mammoth achievement that stirred the imaginations of the residents of the many towns and cities that were encountered along the route. From Hounslow the flight continued via Lyons, Pisa, Rome, Taranto, Suda Bay, Cairo, Damascus, Ramadi, Basra, Bandar, Abbas, Karachi, Delhi, Allahabad, Calcutta, Akyab, Rangoon, Bangkok, Singora,

Singapore, Kalidjati, Sourabaya, Bima and Atamboea before eventually reaching Darwin.

On 15 December Alcock and Brown's Vimy that had completed the Atlantic crossing in June 1919 was presented to the Science Museum in South Kensington, where it remains in the museum's collection to this day. Not to be outdone by his rivals at Vickers, Handley Page also presented an aircraft to the museum; a W8 biplane, powered by 450hp Napier Lion engines that took centre stage among the other exhibits. This aircraft had been flown to Le Bourget by Robert Bager who had succeeded Sholto Douglas as the company's chief pilot. Essentially this was the world's first true airliner, a machine capable of carrying up to fourteen passengers in reasonable comfort that included the luxury of the first aircraft toilet. The same aircraft had taken second prize in an Air Ministry competition devised to promote safety, comfort and security on air transports. The entries had been limited and the Ministry felt unable to award a first prize. A Vickers Vimy Commercial took third prize and in the small aircraft category the main prize went to a Westland Limousine.

Despite the pioneers that were increasingly flying across vast and often inhospitable continental environments, flying was still an extremely hazardous and unreliable adventure. This was contrary to any public relations claims made by the early airlines. Navigational aids were still in their infancy and engine failures causing forced landings were only too common. Pilots had to fly by the seat of their pants using their local knowledge of the terrain, by following railway lines and by searching for familiar landmarks rather than to overly depend on compasses that tended to wildly oscillate if any sharp manoeuvres were made. Altimeters were notoriously unreliable and artificial horizons were still a thing of the future. During fine weather, flying could be an enjoyable experience. When pilots could find smooth air, travelling at 80 mph, 1500 ft above a passing vista of rolling countryside unfolding beneath them, could be delightful. If it was warm enough, cabin passengers could relax, remove their heavy outer layers of clothing and sit in their shirtsleeves and enjoy the view. In the winter it was a very different story and any romantic notions of flying were quickly dispelled. Dense clouds would frequently engulf the aircraft making locating any visual references impossible and controlling an aircraft against squalls and strong headwinds, rain and snow was anything but fun. Coal was still widely burnt by industry and used as domestic fuel and this created the dense, choking London smogs that would hang over the capital and Home Counties for days at a time causing the deaths of

thousands from severe respiratory diseases. Such smogs were just another safety hazard that pilots had to expect almost on a daily basis.

Before taking-off, procedure required pilots to telephone Lympne from Cricklewood or Hounslow to check the weather conditions close to the south coast. If the temperamental telephone system in France, still suffering from disruptions caused by wartime bombardments, was working, then a call to Paris might also provide an indication of the weather to expect at Le Bourget. But once in the air, conditions could change rapidly during a two hour flight, and pilots had to rely on their skills and judgement to reach their destinations. On return flights, soon after crossing the Kent coastline, a pilot might look for a flare fired from Lympne that would indicate whether he should end his journey and land instead of risking continuing to the capital where adverse conditions might prevent a safe landing. The big Handley Page aircraft were also physically exhausting to fly because they relied on a large control wheel that had to be manually turned to operate the ailerons. Pilots were also kitted out with heavy flight clothing to prevent them freezing to death in their open cockpits but this had the disadvantage of restricting their freedom of movement and made operating the controls still harder.

Passengers were also required to wear heavy flying jackets and helmets to keep out some of the cold when travelling in the open accommodation of AT&T's DH9s and DH16s. Capt Henry Spry Leverton, a former prisoner-of-war who worked as a manager with AT&T, was given the task of loaning garments to passengers when they flew from Hounslow. In Paris, Sydney St Barbe, the company's French representative, was responsible for retrieving the clothing from arriving passengers at Le Bourget as they disembarked but many attempted to keep this flying gear as souvenirs. The ground managers also had to greet passengers, check passports and luggage and generally act as liaisons that ensured that their charges were kept informed about the details of their flight.

Spry Leverton later became UK manager for KLM Royal Dutch Airlines after assisting a Dutch passenger by the name of Albert Plesman. When an AT&T aircraft bound for Paris became unserviceable, Leverton had helped Plesman by securing a seat on the rival Handley Page 0/400. When the Dutch airline was established on 7 October 1919 Plesman was appointed manager. He remembered the thoughtfulness shown to him by Leverton so contacted him and offered him a job at KLM which he accepted. The Dutch were not party to the Air Convention and the rules required pilots and aircraft to be from a signatory state so AT&T was hired to operate the cross-Channel service on their behalf. Some of the best known pilots of their day, including Hinchliffe, Olley and Shaw all worked for the Dutch carrier at some point in their careers.

The airfields at Cricklewood or Hounslow were not ideally suited for their purpose but the latter was selected to become England's main Customs aerodrome. Situated on what remained of Hounslow Heath, in earlier times a favourite haunt of highwaymen, the former RAF airfield had an area of only 800 square yards. Inbound aircraft would pick up the Thames around Tilbury and follow the course of the river through London to Richmond where the pilot would look for, and hopefully find the small landing field. At night landing would be aided by a gas lamp contained within a rotating beacon that would light automatically and be activated for three and a half hours after sunset. Flares were lit to form an 'L' shape on the landing area with the shorter part of the letter marking the end of the landing run. As a further aid to night landings, aircraft could be fitted with magnesium flares beneath a wing that were electrically triggered by the pilot immediately before touch down to illuminate the ground, but releasing these could often be a hazardous process.

Hounslow aerodrome was very spartan and lacked facilities. Fuel was available but there were no maintenance workshops and from a passenger point-of-view there was nowhere to obtain any kind of refreshments in the basic shed that served as a waiting room. There were however six Bessoneaux canvas hangars on the Bath Road side of the field and a large double-fronted hangar that was designated as the customs shed. To leave no doubt as to the purpose, this structure had 'CUSTOMS' painted beneath the left eve and 'DOUANE' on the right. To complete the rather limited equipment, a 15 ft map that displayed the weather forecast on both sides of the Channel hung on a door. As weather conditions were reported by telephone or by inbound

pilots, these would be chalked on to the board to keep the information as current as facilities would allow. An assortment of telegraph wires, trees, a disused wireless mast, railway signals and other such hazards were dotted about the landing field to complete an untidy panorama. Although the amenities were basic, pilots felt safe landing at Hounslow despite a tendency for it to become fogbound.

Cricklewood was altogether a different story. The Handley Page 0/400s that used it were heavy, cumbersome beasts that required a considerable amount of coaxing just to get them into the air. Take-offs required pilots to negotiate a ridge and then, if they succeeded at becoming airborne, aim for a narrow gap that would take the aircraft between the Handley Page factory and hangars. The large aircraft would gain speed very slowly over Cricklewood Broadway, barely 50 ft above the buildings and gradually gain altitude as they followed the Edgware Road towards Central London. This routine caused Robert McIntosh to comment in his autobiography, *All-Weather Mac* '*I followed the number ten buses. Usually I kept pace but the only time I could overtake them was when they stopped to pick up passengers.*' By the time a pilot reached Marble Arch, if the aircraft had reached an altitude of 500 ft, it was considered safe to continue providing an engine did not cut out. In many respects the scenario was an accident waiting to happen but this did not prevent Cricklewood from becoming an approved port of entry on 10 January 1920, with Customs facilities being added eight days later. Once the airfield was approved, Handley Page wasted no time inviting the press to a formal inauguration of his facilities and to witness Capt McIntosh take-off in G-EAMA bound for Paris. On the same day the company also introduced season tickets on the London to Paris route at a cost of £120 for twelve single flights. By the end of their first operational year (30 April 1920) Handley Page's performance had been impressive. The company claimed its aircraft had flown 4,460 passengers over a distance of 100,188 miles in the UK and across the world including France, Belgium, Holland, Poland, Scandinavia, Spain, Greece, India, China, South Africa and the USA. Additionally it had carried 35 tons of cargo mainly comprising of small parcels of valuable items such as silk, jewellery and pharmaceuticals.

Fatal accident at Cricklewood

It was only a matter of time before the inevitable happened. Just after noon on 14 December 1920 Handley Page's pilot, Robert Bager, crashed into a tree and the back wall of a house owned by a Miss Robinson at No 6, Basinghill, The Ridgeway, Childs Hill. The aircraft had taken-off in the limited easterly direction from Cricklewood in misty conditions bound for Paris. The area where the aircraft came down was reported as a '... *lonely district now being developed as a residential neighbourhood and the house which the aeroplane struck apparently with one of its wings, stands in an isolated position, on rising ground just above the aerodrome.*' The aircraft, (G-EAMA) had been in service only since November 1919 and was carrying Bager's mechanic, J H Williams and six passengers. The impact caused the aircraft to burst into flames and Bager, Williams and two passengers, Mr Van der Elst of Paris and Sam Sallinger of Boxmoor, survived the impact but perished in the blaze. Several local people attempted to rescue the injured occupants but the fire was too intense and they had to withdraw. Miraculously three passengers survived by climbing through the rear cabin windows while the fourth, Eric Studd, was flung from the nose cockpit apparently without much injury but oblivious to what had happened. A contemporary report suggests that it was initially feared that Studd had been burnt in the crash but he was found next day in Paris suffering from concussion and having no recollection of the incident or how he had managed to reach the city by surface transport after the accident. Apparently, after being knocked unconscious, he had woken up in the garden and remembered that he had to get to Paris. In a semi-conscious state he wandered off, took the Underground to Victoria where he boarded the overnight boat train for Dover and Calais. He must have presented quite a spectacle boarding public transport with his body and clothes showing visual signs of having been involved in an accident. The story now appears to be a little imaginative although one witness did report seeing a man in flying gear standing by the wreckage immediately after the crash who later disappeared. The witness believed this to be the pilot who he thought had returned to the wrecked aircraft and had died in the flames. The man the witness had seen was probably Studd. At the inquest held at Hendon Town Hall two days later, Studd's

recollections of the crash, provided in an affidavit, seemed perfectly clear and concise. He explained how he had tried, without success, to extricate two of the injured from the crash but was unable to make any headway and the aircraft then caught fire. He described how he felt that the pilot was *'cutting it fine'* when he saw the tree getting nearer. The statement appeared too concise to have been made by someone suffering memory loss. Major Herbert Brackley of Handley Page, when asked his opinion of what he felt Studd may have been meant by this statement, replied by saying that *'…he (Studd) may have believed that there had been something wrong with the machine and that the pilot had realised this and had tried to clear the tree.'* The Coroner concluded there was insufficient evidence to suggest either pilot error or machine failure had been responsible for the incident.

Robert Bager, the 34-year-old pilot, originated from Newcastle-Upon-Tyne and was formerly a member of the Naval Air Service, and he was wounded in the attack on Zeebrugge during the war. This was the first fatal accident involving a British scheduled airliner although it is a miracle that it had taken as long as it had to involve Cricklewood. The newspaper report published next day in *The Times* presented a graphic account of the incident. Handley Page was quoted to have carried 4,000 passengers over a flying distance of 320,000 miles since December 1919. This tends to exaggerate the operational statistics found elsewhere and the accuracy of the press report of the time has to be questioned more specifically as Herbert Brackley's name was referred to as *'Brockley'*.

Despite setbacks some progress had been made to improve the safety of airline operations. Handley Page had been instrumental in the use of wireless (W/T) and radio telephony (R/T). On 10 March 1920 R/T was used for the first time on a Handley Page aircraft when the pilot reported passing a homebound sister aircraft while crossing the Channel. By June Instone had also equipped their aircraft with R/T and by 1921 all British airliners were fitted with Marconi AD 2 sets.

Another new innovation was the directional finding (D/F) equipment that was installed on a Handley Page 0/400 aircraft piloted by Major Foot. Wireless stations had been established at Pevensey, Lowestoft and Chelmsford (where Marconi had its headquarters) to receive a signal from airliners. Each station could plot a bearing that would allow the operator to calculate the position of a transponding aircraft. Similar stations were established in France at Le Bourget, St Inlevert, Niems, Bordeaux and Maubeuge. The system, although fairly primitive, was a major aid to air navigation especially at times when aerodromes were shrouded in fog or thick cloud.

Across the English Channel the French airlines were forging ahead. By March 1920 they had already opened routes to Morocco (with a stop in Spain) carrying passengers and mail. A twice-weekly service was added to Turkey and an inaugural flight was made to Dacca (then French West Africa) with refuelling stops at Algiers and Timbuktu. By enlarging their route structure the French had already successfully opened aviation links with their colonies while in Britain there was little prospect of maintaining a cross-Channel service let alone establishing any Imperial routes to far flung corners of the Empire.

The General Post Office (GPO) followed the Government line by refusing to support the airlines when in contrast they too had actively encouraged the development of shipping since 1839. The GPO had also paid a subsidy to Cunard and had been very active in the development of faster and larger ships. In the USA the carriage of mail preceded passenger traffic and this had led to the rapid and healthy growth of their airlines since 1918, but in Britain the authorities were extremely slow to catch on to the benefits civil aviation had to offer. Dealing with an unsupportive Government was one thing, but the French were also acting competitively if not combatively. By cutting the London to Paris fare they had slowly but surely been hammering nails into the coffin of the entire British air transport industry. At one time during 1922 there were five airlines competing for the limited traffic on the London-Paris route. There were already 36 French aircraft operating the route compared to six of Handley Page. The coffin lid was closing tighter and the fledgling British airlines were being buried by a Government that did nothing to protect them. The lowest Handley Page fare was £10 10s 0d (£10.50) but they were unable to lower this any more if they were to remain in business. Without Government funding, the only thing Handley Page could do was to withdraw passenger services and concentrate on freight and mail. But the French had also cut their

freight charges. Handley Page was charging 2s 6d (12½p) per pound on packages up to ten pounds; the French had axed their rates to just 1s 0d (5p). The economics of the business was so precarious that Handley Page decided to quit passenger services altogether between London and Paris by 17 November.

Handley Page was in deep trouble. The debacle in America and other failed overseas deals, coupled with the end to wartime production, had created serious financial difficulties for the company. At the Annual General Meeting held on 25 June 1921 the company revealed a debt of £1,056,000. With interest accruing at a rate of £50,000 a year things were looking extremely bleak. The financial structure of the business had been entwined with that of The Aircraft Disposal Company (ADC), a once successful venture that Frederick Handley Page had set up to dispose of wartime aircraft and spares he had bought from the Government at knock-down prices. Much of the ADC's assets had latterly been used to prop up Handley Page Transport including the provision of £400,000 of the £500,000 it held in preference shares. Frederick Handley Page had also lost £176,000 of the personal money that had been due to be returned by the company. As a result of the management links with The Aircraft Disposal Company, it was formerly agreed not to liquidate Handley Page if ADC could nominate new management for the company. In June 1921 Lt Col W A Bristowe of Ogilvie and Partners (consulting engineers responsible for the mechanical side of Handley Page and the Instone Air Line) became chairman of the company but he was later replaced by Lt Col Barrett-Lennard of Marconi while Handley Page was away in America.

Daimler Hire

Despite the situation that had previously forced the other airlines to quit, a valiant newcomer, Daimler Hire Limited (incorporated 7 June 1919) began operating and became one of the companies that would later be a recipient of Government subsidies. The new company also introduced a new aircraft type to compete on the over-subscribed London-Paris airway.

The Daimler Hire airline arose in 1922 from the ashes of AT&T after the airline and its original company, AIRCO, had been absorbed by Birmingham Small Arms (BSA). Daimler and BSA had become partners in an engineering and motor business that had disposed of AT&T's aircraft along the way. But Daimler, inspired by Holt Thomas, had broken from the main concern to become Daimler Airways Ltd, the aircraft operating branch of Daimler Hire Ltd. Three *heavyweights*, later to be inspirational figures in British civil aviation, joined the management team: George Woods Humphery (engineer, ex-RFC pilot and formerly of Handley Page) as General Manager; Col Frank Searle (from the London General Omnibus Company) as Managing Director and the one-eyed airman, Walter George Raymond 'Bill' Hinchliffe (Chief Pilot).

Based at Croydon, the aircraft Daimler introduced was the prototype DH34 (G-EBBQ). This had been test-flown by Alan Cobham (later Sir Alan) at Stag Lane a week before Daimler started up on 2 April when Hinchliffe flew a consignment of newspapers to Paris. This was the first of a batch of ten aircraft built at Stag Lane of which seven had been delivered to the Air Council at Croydon on 31 March. Four of these were leased to Instone, the first, *City of Glasgow* (G-EBBR) was flown to Paris in 2 hrs 40 mins by Capt Barnard on the very day that Daimler made its own inaugural flight.

Daimler Hire had previously expressed considerable interest in the civilian version of the DH29 (G-EAYO) but the aircraft was found to have a number of control problems. This aeroplane was statically displayed at the Imperial Air Conference held at Croydon between 3-6 February but its sole public flying demonstration was held back until the final day of the event. Daimler opted instead for the DH34, an aircraft that incorporated many features of the previous DH29 but with significant improvements. The aircraft had a good reputation but it had inadequate heating. Daimler attempted to solve this by fitting a muff over the exhaust to provide heat to the cabin but this caused carbon-monoxide fumes to enter the enclosed space and the idea had to be dropped. The bright red aircraft could also carry a useful payload of nine passengers. Daimler soon added a second machine, G-EBBS, that went into service sooner than expected to maintain schedules single-handedly after their third machine, G-EBBU, had been damaged in a forced landing at Berck (France) on 3 November and turned over. The

The BAT EK26 of the Instone Air Line, G-EAPK 'City of Newcastle', circa 1920. (CAS/John Stroud)

aircraft had to be returned to Stag Lane where it was repaired before resuming service. On 23 May 1922 the same aircraft had been involved in a bizarre incident when another Daimler Hire aircraft (G-EBBQ) landed on top of it at Croydon. This left the stalwart G-EBBS to continue alone now that Daimler had two of the three aircraft out of action.

Having been compelled to work single-handedly, G-EBBS became the first aircraft to complete two round trips from Croydon to Le Bourget during the same day (1 May). Both were flown by Capt E D C Herne. This was increased to five single trips in a day on 2 June and by the end of the year the aircraft had established an amazing record by completing 122 daily services from a scheduled total of 165. Five further days were spent on Air Ministry tests and during the overall period, 45 same-day double return trips were made to Paris. G-EBBS achieved legendary status and gained a reputation as the company's most reliable aircraft. By 7 October 1922 this machine alone had made 332 flights on the London-Paris route (a distance of 240 miles) flying a total of 79,680 miles. This had increased to 100,393 miles by 5 December in 8,000 hours of flying without incident or overhaul. All good things eventually come to an end. At just after 1800 hrs on Friday, 14 September 1923 the outstanding success of the aircraft reached a dramatic conclusion when it crashed while attempting a forced landing at Ivinghoe Beacon in Buckinghamshire enroute from Croydon to Manchester. Eye witnesses reported the aircraft to be flying low and said the pilot had cut the engine, turned around and restarted the engine before the aircraft nose-dived into the ground at Ford End Farm, 600 yards from Ivinghoe Town Hall, close to The Raven public house. The engine was still turning as the aircraft hit and the propeller cut a hole in the ground. The conditions at the time were misty, and some eye witnesses claimed it was raining heavily when the accident occurred.

Capt Leslie George Scott Robinson and Capt George E Pratt together with three passengers – John Grimshaw originally of Manchester, Albert Hayward Turner of West Didsbury, Manchester and 21-year-old Mrs Ethel Russell Armitage, the English wife of an

American Naval officer of Boston, all died in the accident. The inquest took an intriguing turn when passenger Grimshaw's relationship with Mrs Armitage was discovered. Grimshaw was estranged from his wife and his employment with a hotel company required him to live wherever his job took him. During a point in the hearing, the Council for the Daimler Hire Company, Tristram Beresford, asked Harry Grimshaw, the brother of the deceased *'Did he ever tell you that on a number of occasions she had violently assaulted him?'* referring to

Daimler Airways timetable circa 1922.

Mrs Armitage. When the Coroner, Mr S E Wilkins, tried to divert this line of questioning by saying *'I don't know how that comes into the enquiry, unless you have something definite.'* Beresford responded: *'I have nothing definite but we have received information about this lady.'* At the time of the accident the body of Mrs Armitage had been identified by a friend, Mrs Jane Harriett Crook of Norton Terrace, Belgravia where the dead woman had been living, and she was presumed to be separated from her husband who did not attend the funeral at Ivinghoe Church.

The accident report stated that a sack of earth weighing 300 lbs and some stones of 20-30 lbs had been placed at the back of the cabin as ballast – a common procedure when loads were light and the passengers had not been carrying much baggage. Woods Humphery was questioned about this practice but assured the court that this was normal. There was some conjecture as to why an experienced pilot would land in a field when there were several airfields close by that could have been used. The discussion relating to Mrs Armitage that had

The Instone Air Line De Havilland DH34, G-EBBT, 'City of New York', circa 1922. (CAS)

INSTONE AIR LINER

occurred at the previous enquiry seemed to imply some kind of disturbance had taken place in the cabin, but the Coroner dismissed this to conclude that '...*whatever was taking place in the aeroplane, it was necessary to land.*' This by no means suggests that anything untoward may have taken place and certainly no evidence was put forward to support this. The Jury could reach only one verdict: '*accidental death*' as there was nothing to support any other reason for the crash. The Official Inspector's report concluded that the accident was caused by the pilot's error of judgement when he attempted to make a landing on account of the weather.

Frank Searle, the airline's General Manager, believed that aircraft costing £5,000 each should be utilised more fully to provide a faster return on investments. Based on an assumption that every motor car should cover 20,000 miles annually, this same principle was extended to aviation. While the other airlines only operated their aircraft for a few hours a day, Searle felt Daimler's aircraft could readily be flown for ten

An early gathering of Instone employees and the De Havilland DH34, 'City of Washington', in 1923. (CAS)

or more hours. This way they could achieve £160 gross daily on a double trip to Paris to return a net profit of around £100. Searle had a reputation for putting profits above all else and to achieve this he was an advocate of working people and equipment extremely hard. At that time the aircraft owned by rival companies were expected to be in the air for around 1000 hours annually; Daimler's method of intensive usage doubled this.

The intensive equipment usage policy allowed more flights to be achieved and more passengers to be carried, but it also created a stressful situation for Daimler's small fleet of aircraft. If an aircraft became unserviceable, or crashed, the company had none spare to bring into use and this created a situation where a flight would have to be cancelled. It also meant that maintenance staff and pilots needed to be more resourceful to ensure the greatest number of aircraft were kept flying at any one time. An occurrence happened in early 1923 when engine failure caused one of Daimler's aircraft to force-land at Rugby. Within 36 hours a new engine was located, put on a lorry from Croydon to Rugby and installed on the aircraft allowing it to return to routine service with a minimum of delay. Searle's operating theory, learnt from his time at London Transport, seemed to have credence that worked to Daimler's advantage but he had many critics who did not approve of his practices.

Croydon replaces Hounslow as London's Aerodrome

By early 1920 Hounslow was nearing the end of its useful life as London's international aerodrome and during March operations ceased. As the majority of air traffic headed to and from the South Coast, this necessitated a lengthy journey around the capital. There was a strong case to establish an aerodrome facility on the southern side of London. The RAF airfield near to Purley seemed the obvious answer. The site chosen was comprised of two adjoining fields; Beddington, the former RAF station and Waddon on the east side. A country lane called Plough Lane separated the two sites. This created a problem whenever an aircraft needed to manoeuvre from one side of the airfield to the other that required traffic or pedestrians to be stopped at a level crossing by a man waving a red flag. A decision was made to use the grass area of Waddon as the runway area with Beddington as the tarmac and terminal area. The site was far from ideal but it offered more potential for development than either Hounslow or Cricklewood. The operational field was rough, narrow and had a ridge which prevented aircraft from being seen from the apron. It was also subject to dangerous downdrafts whenever a south-westerly wind blew from the Purley Valley. This caused many pilots some nasty moments. There were also additional hazards around the perimeter of the former National Aircraft Factory (on the north-east corner of Waddon) and beyond that included the Wallington water tower. Nevertheless, despite the obstacles and the sheep that, on occasions, had to be cleared from the flying area, Croydon was destined to become London's Customs airport. It was officially opened by Lord Londonderry on 29 March 1920 and Hounslow

closed. A former RAF Major, S T L Greer was appointed manager.

At first there was no control tower and wartime huts along Plough Lane had to be converted to use as makeshift offices and for the Customs shed. The hotel owners, Trust House, spotted the potential of the old canteen on the site and quickly applied to convert this into a hotel. When applying for their liquors licence the smart chairman of the Bench remarked *'Do the passengers arrive in such a state that they require alcohol to revive them?'* There was no real answer to this but the licence was granted and the bar soon became a jovial and cosy meeting point for Europe's most flamboyant pilots. Local residents at nearby Wallington were less impressed by their new neighbour but the Borough of Croydon had no misgivings and adopted the aerodrome as its own. The new facility became known as Croydon Airport, and soon became synonymous as the first home of Imperial Airways.

AT&T wasted no time moving in to the new facility. It seems likely that they had already established a presence at Croydon in the week preceding the official opening. The company had been allocated two large, ex-RAF hangars to house its DH9s and DH16s. Robert Brenard, an employee of AT&T painted a colourful image of what he found when the company moved to Croydon. *'Actually the first little party of pioneer airwaymen to invade Croydon, driving in an old Ford car, lost themselves in a maze of roads between Sutton and Wallington, and it was some time before they located the aerodrome – then known as Waddon aerodrome – which had housed a wartime fighter squadron.*

'This military aerodrome they set to work to turn into a proper commercial airport. One of the most urgent needs was office accommodation. This was provided by purchasing old wooden army huts and erecting them on either side of what became a sort of 'main street' leading from Plough Lane to the aeroplane alighting-ground. Other people followed the first arrivals, erecting their particular kind of temporary wooden building. These were all of different shapes and sizes, until the final appearance of this 'main street' reminded one forcibly of a Wild West township. This resemblance was, in fact, so striking that some people visiting the aerodrome for the first time said they rather expected to see a group of cowboys come dashing round a corner to 'shoot the place up.'

Instone's brand new Vimy Commercial, *City of London* (G-EASI), looking splendid in its impressive silver and blue livery, did not arrive at the airport until 30 April 1920. The *City of London* held the distinction of carrying 472 passengers over a single weekend – 20-21 November 1920 – by providing joy rides at an air display.

Handley Page preferred to remain at its traditional home at Cricklewood for a further year because it had already established its own maintenance facilities at the site.

In May 1920, 27 countries signed the new ICAN Regulations. The neutral nations – Norway, Sweden, Denmark, Netherlands and Switzerland – refused to take part because Germany was still barred from membership and the northern European airlines needed to fly through German airspace to reach many of their destinations. The Dutch company, KLM, was especially concerned because as neighbours of Germany its Far Eastern services needed to cross the country. To solve the problem, a strange protocol was adopted that allowed foreign airlines to fly over German territory if they had *'reason of a good excuse.'* The neutral countries, now satisfied, quickly found their own good excuses and became party to the Regulations. On 17 May KLM started its weekly service to Croydon from Amsterdam (Schiphol) with AT&T. The French airline Cie des Grands Expresse Aériens also introduced a Goliath (F-GEAB) on the Croydon to Paris route but initially carried no passengers.

By the end of 1920 Handley Page was experiencing major operational problems. Its chief pilot, Herbert Brackley had tested the civilian variant of the 0/400, known as the A/10 (G-EATN) on Christmas Eve. The aircraft was unique because it had been fitted with the French designed Aveline Stabilizer, a kind of primitive auto-pilot. This allowed the aircraft, when flying in calm air, to maintain a steady course at altitude without the pilot needing to touch the controls. On 30 December Brackley reported in his log '*To Paris for French Govt. Competition with stabilizer. Flew for over an hour without touching controls.*' Brackley remained in Paris and on 4 January 1921 he again tested the Stabilizer '*Aileron and elevator controls splendid, could fly 'hands off' for any length of time.*' Colonel William Francis Forbes-Sempill, the Master of Sempill, one of Britain's leading aeronautical engineers was aboard the flight and was impressed sufficiently by the demonstration given by Brackley to invite him to join the British Aviation Mission to the Imperial Japanese Navy, which he was leading as a special instructor on large-type machines. With his work successfully completed at Handley Page, Brackley accepted the offer, went to the Far East and when the project there had been completed, he returned to England and became a prominent employee of Imperial Airways.

At the start of 1921 only a handful of revenue flights were completed and the six outbound and five inbound flights that were made produced only fifteen passengers in all. A temporary service of three flights a day was made for a time by Instone and one by Handley Page. Capt William McIntosh had succeeded Brackley as chief pilot at Handley Page and in realisation of the difficulties the company was facing, generously offered to fly without pay. Handley Page, although grateful, declined the gesture and by 28 February all British airline operations had ceased. During the same month the Belgians had lowered the Brussels-London fare to £5; about the same as the corresponding boat-rail ticket. Now too late, the British Government expressed an air of '*great concern*' over the demise of these services. The popular publication *The Aeroplane* was appropriately scathing and C G Grey's editorial read more like an obituary: '*British civil aviation died with the cessation of the Handley Page cross-Channel service, killed by the forward policy of the French government and the apathy of our own.*' Strong words indeed yet the statement was an illustration of just how apathetic the British Government had been.

Although British cross-Channel operations had ceased and all other regular commercial services had also ended, the Secretary of State's '*Memorandum to Accompany the Air Estimates*' finally made provision for £60,000 to be allocated to air transport. The Civil Aviation Vote had reached £458,000 but, as Sir Sefton Brancker noted, the decision to grant aid had '*arrived about a year too late.*' On 12 December 1920 Brancker's own company, AT&T was the first to cease trading and Instone and Handley Page had by then suspended their services.

The 'Temporary' and 'Permanent' Schemes

On 9 March 1921 Churchill announced the appointment of a special Air Ministry Cross-Channel Committee to discuss ways to revive British European air services. Churchill suddenly appeared to have reversed his views, and surprisingly said that it was '*short sighted*' to spend most of the Air Ministry's funding on military and naval air services. He continued, by saying that he felt it '*...right and necessary to spend money to build up the nation's commercial flying services.*' This was quite contrary to the official line given by Churchill almost a year previously

when he had made the infamous statement that the airlines must '*fly by themselves.*'

The newly formed Committee of three comprised of Lord Londonderry (Under-Secretary of State for Air) Sir James Stevenson and Major-Gen Sir F H Sykes (Controller General of Civil Aviation). Before the Committee had time to report, the coal workers had called a strike, the rail workers had threatened to join them and a national emergency had been declared. A new full-time Secretary of State for Air, Capt Frederick Guest, had also been appointed.

Lord Londonderry had asked Alfred Instone and his brothers, Samuel and Theodore, to devise a subsidy scheme that would aid the airlines. After the air industry meeting of 10 March, the brothers were sufficiently roused to debate the problem all night and presented Londonderry with their proposal the next afternoon. In simplistic terms they suggested that each airline should be given a minimum subsidy of £30,000.

Major George Woods Humphery (now unemployed) together with Colonel Frank Searle attempted to pull together a group of six that were prepared to fund a new airline to the tune of £5,000 each. Lord Weir, Sir Alfred Yarrow (the shipowner), Constantine and a textile producer were all in agreement but the project was short by two

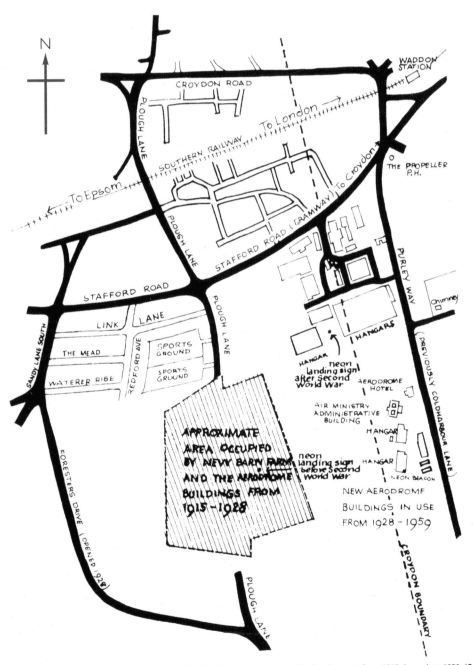

Croydon Aerodrome showing its development from 1915 through to 1959. (CAS)

The Handley Page Transport HP0/10 photographed in 1920. This aircraft crashed at Berck on 30 December 1921. (CAS)

backers. As they had failed to attract sufficient interest, Searle took the proposal to the BSA-Daimler group who offered to provide the full working capital of £30,000 and this was accepted by the Air Ministry on 9 September 1921.

By 19 March 1921 a makeshift subsidy scheme had taken affect that was based on proposals put forward by Alfred Instone and this became known simplistically as the *temporary scheme*. Under this proposal the Air Ministry would be expected to provide subsidies to Daimler and Instone up to a financial liability of £88,200 for the fiscal year ending 31 March 1922. The subsidy scheme was originally devised to run for just seven months until October, but it was continued for the remainder of the year. The funding was split, according to the contracts issued to the airlines; with £25,000 allocated for the first seven months ending 18 October, and £19,100 for the remaining months. The payments were intended to guarantee each airline a 10% profit on their gross

receipts and the Air Ministry also agreed to pay the companies an additional £75 every fortnight for each flight made. From 19 March 1921 to 31 March 1922, 1,072 single flights on the London-Paris route were maintained and a total of 5,804 passengers had been carried.

Business on the routes was not as good as the Government had predicted and Guest's optimism that the airlines would make a 10% profit on their first 24 flights turned out to be nothing more than a wildly inaccurate approximation. Government documents showed that two of the airlines operating under the scheme, Instone and Handley Page, had lost £5,398 between them even after the subsidies had been paid.

The operating loss between the two airlines was accounted for as follows, based upon figures derived from an analysis of operating costs that were drawn up in 1923: *(See table lower left)*.

The Cross Channel Committee continued to meet and was due to announce a *'permanent'* subsidy scheme on 21 October 1921. This was brought forward and by 15 June an announcement stated that no further funding would be introduced until the following April and then it would be shared by Daimler, Instone and Handley Page. The delays were caused firstly by Lord Londonderry's departure from his position as Under-Secretary of State for Air and later by the Geddes 'Axe' Committee that had been established to find ways to cut government spending. During 1920 the nation's financial position had been quite buoyant and exports had doubled those achieved in 1913. But the situation took a turn for the worse during 1921 when the financial costs of war had been tallied up and could no longer be ignored. In a very short space of time the economy of the country had slipped into a slump that was unfavourable to the struggling civil aviation industry.

In April 1922 Lord Gorell succeeded Londonderry as Under-Secretary for Air and the

INCOME:		EXPENDITURE:	
Passenger & Freight	£38,211	Operating costs (flying)	£23,039
Less agent's commission			
Car hire to aerodromes	£9,888	Operating costs (non-flying)	£59,882
	£28,323	Overheads	£36,732
Misc. receipts	£1,101	Total operating costs	£120,493
Total revenue	£29,424	Total revenue	£29,424
		Working loss	£91,969
		Subsidies paid	£85,671
		Loss to companies	**£5,398**

The overheads in the table includes a passenger operating cost of £20 15s 3d. (£20.76½) including the Government subsidy of £14 15s 0d (£14.75). British passengers had been expected to pay a £6 6s 0d (£6.30) fare between London-Paris; the French had lowered theirs to £5 5s 0d (£5.25).

The Instone Air Line Vickers Vimy Commercial, G-EASI, taking off in 1920. (CAS/Franklyn Barnard)

Vickers Vimy Commercial, G-EASI, *City of London*, of The Instone Air Line. This aircraft entered service in 1920 and was popular with passengers. It was transferred to Imperial Airways on 31 March 1924 and was withdrawn from service in August 1925.

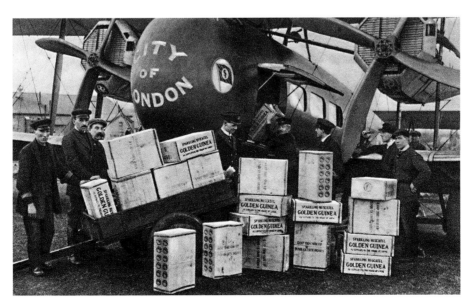

The famous dark blue Vickers Vimy Commercial of The Instone Air Line, G-EASI, 'City of London' being unloaded of a cargo of Golden Guinea sparkling wine in 1920. (CAS)

An Instone Air Line timetable from 1923. (CAS)

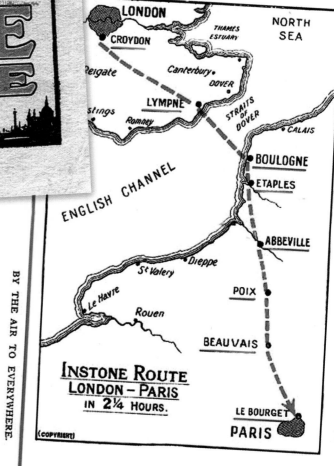

An Instone Air Line route map from circa 1922. (David Zekra)

Committee decided to set £200,000 a year aside under the 'permanent' subsidy scheme. This was an inappropriate amount by far in comparison to the £1,328,600 in direct subsidies paid by the French to their airlines. The French, still fearful of the Germans, were already creating a substantial airline industry that could be utilised alongside their efficient air force should hostilities begin again. Under the terms of the Armistice, Germany was prevented from developing an air force of its own, but this did not stop it concentrating on a massively enterprising scheme that encouraged major towns to support civil aviation in a cause that included paying airlines to land at their airports. The Germans were also operating a company for the Russians that flew between Königsberg and Moscow with a later extension to Tehran in Persia and Peking in China. To illustrate its level of commitment, one German company had single-handedly flown more services than all of the British companies combined. It was clear that most other European nations viewed civil aviation far more progressively than the British Government. The French and Germans were making good progress, so too were the airlines of Holland, Denmark, Sweden and Belgium but these were being soundly operated as state monopolies with funding provided by their respective governments.

Guest had announced that Sir Frederick Sykes would remain as Controller General of the Air Council for a further year after which the department would be downgraded to 'Directorate' level. When he heard of this Sykes resigned. Fortunately his place was taken by Sir Sefton Brancker who had become Head of the Air League of the British Empire after the liquidation of AT&T in May.

The Air Ministry had agreed to subsidise three companies on the London–Paris route – Daimler, Instone and Handley Page – and Instone on the Brussels route under the terms of the 'permanent' scheme that was introduced on 1 April 1922. This would pay the companies up to 25% of their gross profits on the carriage of passengers, freight, baggage and mail. Added to this would be a further subsidy of £3 for every passenger carried and 3d (1p) per pound for goods and mail. The Ministry also made it mandatory that all directors of the companies receiving subsidies had to be British. The Air Council agreed to finance half of each company's fleet on a hire basis at 2½% interest on the monthly cost, provided that it was British designed and built. Ownership of equipment financed this way would transfer to the companies once thirty payments had been made and the Air Council also agreed to cover half of the insurance premiums providing they did not amount to more than 10% of the equipment value. They also agreed to take back any equipment that was viewed to be in any way advantageous (presumably to the Air Council). A final clause in the contracts made the proviso that any excess profits above 15% of the total capital would be repayable to the Air Ministry up to the total amount of the subsidy paid. When everything in the small print had been analysed, the complicated terms attached to the subsidies appeared far less generous than any of the companies may have desired, but at least the Government was belatedly showing an element of willingness to provide a modicum of backing to the airlines.

The 'temporary and permanent schemes' failed to be the life savers the airlines desired. It soon became obvious that much more needed to be done to ensure that British operators would not only be permitted to survive, but would also be in a position to compete evenly with foreign competition.

Figures for the cross-Channel route between London and Paris for the week ending 19 August were published in The Times on 21 September. This demonstrated the load factor differences between all five companies that were competing on the route. In considering these figures the subsidies awarded by the French and British Governments should be taken into account. The French Government had paid CMA and GEA a subsidy of £1,655,290 for the year against the British provision of just £200,000 split between the three operators. (See table top right)

When Geddes wielded his mighty cost savings axe, he sliced £516,000 from the Civil Aviation Air Estimate and £500,000 from research and development. In all £5,500,000 had to be cut from the aviation budgets and the airlines lost out because the Air Ministry had

Company	Authorized Passenger Load	Passengers Carried	Percentage of Authorised Load
British Companies			
Handley Page	296	247	62.37
Instone	239	140	58.57
Daimler Airways	294	110	37.41
French Companies			
CMA	264	45	17.04
GEA	108	43	25.59

no wish to cut money destined for the RAF. It was a typical case of the State giving with one hand and taking back with the other. There was also a considerable level of public opinion against taxpayers' money being spent on airlines that many believed were only there to benefit the wealthy. There was some justification in this. Apart from the limited number that took joy flights at air displays, few from the working classes were ever likely to take a scheduled flight because the cost was prohibitive.

Handley Page became frustrated when his company was ordered to reduce the passenger capacity of his aircraft from ten to five on his 0/400s and to have the machine's main spars strengthened. This was the result of a number of incidents that had occurred at Croydon during take-offs. Capt Wilcockson, flying a heavily laden 0/400 bound for Paris, fell foul of the down-draught created by the south-easterly wind that blew across the Purley Valley. This caused him to struggle with the aircraft as it sank suddenly and he was extremely fortunate to touch-down safely in a field beyond the airfield boundary. The passengers were disembarked, returned to Croydon, and then, suitably shaken, were put back on the very same aircraft, now lightened, to re-commence their flight to the French capital. Only a week later a similar event occurred that forced down another aircraft close to nearby woodland.

Handley Page was not happy with the ruling but he had to comply by reducing the payload to prevent the Air Ministry from withdrawing the 0/400s' certificate of airworthiness. To deal with the problem the company appointed Walter Savage as engineering manager with a brief to check all aircraft. It was discovered that the weight of each aircraft varied by as much as 500 lbs. Riggings were checked and engine powers tested and when the work was completed and approved, certification was granted for the airliners to resume flying with their original compliment of up to eight passengers.

Because they were short of capacity, by April Handley Page adopted the Daimler Airways system of intensive usage by increasing the hours each machine spent in the air. Until then an aircraft would depart during the day from London, remain overnight in Paris and return to London next day. This could hardly be construed as making the best use of the company's limited resources. The company was also expecting delivery of two W8s fitted with powerful Napier engines but it had to wait until May 1922 for these to arrive. These were named Princess Mary (G-EBBG) and the Prince George (G-EBBH). Both had HP slats along the wing leading edges to reduce stall speed and could carry up to 25 passengers. Even with G-EAPJ and the two new aircraft operating four daily flights, an increase in passenger capacity meant that the company had to re-book any excess passengers onto French Air Union flights whenever its own aircraft were full. This was not helped when the Duchess of York (G-EAPJ) piloted by Wilcockson crashed at Poix en-route for Paris on 22 November 1923. Both engines had failed; one through lack of fuel, the other with a boiled-dry radiator. Skilfully Wilcockson managed to make a perfect forced-landing in a field and no injuries were sustained, but the field was hiding a sunken road that the aircraft fell into and the machine was wrecked beyond repair.

The Instone Air Line had operated Airco DH4 and 4a aircraft, a Vickers Vimy – City of London (G-EASI), a BAT FK26 and three Westland Limousines during 1920. By 1922 it had also started making full use of its DH34s. One of these, City of New York (G-EBBT) was delivered in April 1922 and made the inaugural flight from Croydon to Brussels on 2 May with Barnard in command. Traffic on the route was light and this forced the Director of Civil Aviation to re-allocate routes to prevent undesirable competition from causing a second failure in these services. As a result Instone was allocated the Croydon-Brussels-Cologne routes; Croydon-Paris was handed to Handley Page and a new

route to Berlin was assigned to Daimler Hire Ltd. On 19 September 1922 Hinchliffe piloted G-EBBS from Croydon to Germany accompanied by the directors of the company, Major Woods Humphery and Col Searle. Stopping en-route at Amsterdam, Bremen and Hamburg, the party reached Berlin (Staaken) at 1745 hrs where they met *Herr* Rusch of the Deutsche Luft Reederei Company. The two companies originally proposed starting joint scheduled operations on 10 October with intermediary stops at Amsterdam and Hamburg with a flying time of around seven hours. Searle told a correspondent from *The Times* that '… *the fare should be no more than the equivalent first class railway fare between London and Berlin.*' The intention was for the German airline to operate westbound flights from Berlin and Daimler the eastbound service from Croydon with each aircraft flying a return to their home base during the same day. The proposals failed to materialise because of regulations in place known as the '*Nine Rules*'. These related to the Inter-Allied Air Commission of Control disarmament procedures that had been drawn up after the War to prevent, theoretically, the Germans from constructing any new aircraft that could be used as a bomber. These rules governed the size, speed and horsepower of any aircraft they were allowed to build and the German Government decided to enforce a tit-for-tat manoeuvre that blocked any British-made aircraft of equivalent size capable of carrying nine passengers from entering its airspace. The power capacity of the DH34 effectively blocked it from any future flights until the rules could be relaxed. Daimler was also involved in discussions with other European operators and on 1 January 1923, a 180 hp German Dornier monoplane arrived at Croydon carrying the directors of Aero Union to meet with their counterparts at Daimler.

The Inter-Allied Air Commission had been formed in 1920 for a period of two years with the aim of disposing of the equipment of the former German war machine. The activity was led by General Masterman who was aided by 200 assistants from Britain, France, Belgium, Italy and Japan who were made responsible for destroying 14,800 German aircraft, 29,500 motors, 11 airships and 500 military and naval airship sheds. There was also a considerable amount of wireless equipment, armaments, ordnance and heavy hydrogen production plants to be destroyed. The hoard of equipment that was spread far and wide across German territory was comparable to everything the French and British jointly possessed and the task of ridding the defeated nation of its fighting prowess was a formidable one. The Commission's task was frequently obstructed by the Germans who, quite naturally, were unhappy with the situation. The Allies also had a vast amount of their own equipment to dispose of. In the end the task proved too large and the Germans had to be persuaded to cooperate by destroying their own ordnance. The Nine Rules had been established to consider the assumption that Germany, if it had been allowed to construct aircraft of a suitable size, might be tempted to present a renewed military threat. A sharp eye also had to be kept on Germany to ensure that it made no attempt to ignore the rules by entering the back door by building aircraft in a neutral country. The rules proved counter-productive towards civil aviation. Any aircraft built within the regulations would have been totally unsuitable for operating the distance between London and Berlin (650 miles). As a result the prospect of running regular services had to be put on hold until the dispute could be overcome. Without the assistance of a German airline, Daimler was forced to terminate its service at Amsterdam and a full Berlin service did not commence until 30 April 1923 when the destination airport had been changed to Tempelhof.

Daimler Airways took the initiative to become the first airline to employ a cabin steward, although the American airline, United, has also laid claim to this inspirational idea. Jack Sanderson, a man of very slight stature, attended passengers from his station provided at the rear of the cabin. There appears to be no record to confirm exactly what his duties entailed or whether he was employed to serve drinks and light refreshments during flights.

Negative views

When the time came for the 2nd Air Conference, London's Guildhall became a despondent place and the mood of the delegates was anything but convivial. Theodore Instone was confrontational when he argued a strong case against all three British airlines being subsidised to fly the same route (London-Paris) when there was already very strong French competition. He had a valid point. Guest explained that the Air Ministry was already converted to civil aviation and wanted to support it. The problem, he explained, was in trying to convince Parliament and the general public that the British tax payer should be forced to support it. Guest also made the mistake of expressing his opinion that the only worthwhile routes would be '*to connect Europe with the Imperial Services.*' He was extremely pessimistic towards commercial air transport and in today's parlance it is likely that he might have been regarded as 'unfit for purpose'. The conference delegates generally agreed that civil aviation and military flying should be kept completely separate. A member of the aeronautical press aptly summed up the attitude of the Conference: '*One fact was most startlingly brought out, and that is, the divergence of opinion that exists between the views of the Secretary of State for Air and those of more than ninety per cent of the speakers.*' Guest was also of the opinion that it would be many years before airlines operating in Europe would become profitable. With the Government's industry spokesman airing such negative opinions delegates might have been forgiven for wishing to separate the interests of the Air Ministry. Sir Sefton Brancker argued against Guest as well as against the ridiculous suggestion that the RAF should operate the air routes. '*The latter*' said Brancker: '*had a plentiful supply or aircraft but not of the type to carry passengers and freight.*' With this in mind he also put forward a proposition for a single state-run company to be established by saying: "*Competition might be good for trade, but not between British companies. We had plenty of competition from France. In 1920 we heard a lot about 'all red routes blazing the trail' and so on; the Controller General of Civil Aviation was then £300,000 in pocket, but no assistance was given to aviation.*' Brancker continued his paper by proposing a resolution on behalf of George Holt Thomas that the Government should establish an Empire Air Mail scheme.

The *Permanent* scheme of subsidies failed to work because the April weather of 1922 had been bad and traffic levels had dropped. Public confidence also took a nose dive when two aircraft crashed head-on in fog over Thieuloy Saint Antoine 4 km south of Grandvilliers, in northern France. As this involved a British aircraft, a DH18A (G-EAWO) operated by Daimler Hire Ltd, the affects of the accident were devastating. It was suggested that both pilots were leaning out of their cockpits so that they could see the Abbeville-Beauvais road instead of looking ahead. There was public outcry and the French pilot of the Farman Goliath F60 (F-GEAD) of Cie de Grands Express Aériens, M Mire, was largely blamed because of his country's lack of wireless telepathy and meteorological facilities. At the time of the accident on 7 April 1922, the British had three operational ground facilities but the French had only just commenced building two and the station at Le Bourget was said to be unreliable. As a result five died in the French aircraft and two in the British, Capt Robin E Duke and the boy steward, Hesterman who survived the terrible impact but died of his injuries in hospital. The British aircraft had lost a wing and the tail had hit the ground first. The French pilot was killed as were his mechanic and three passengers; an American honeymooning couple, Mr and Mrs Bruce Yule, and a French citizen, M Bouriez.

By May confidence had returned but in June passenger numbers fell once more. The airlines again called upon Brancker, a man with significant influence, to make changes in the subsidy structure. Brancker was also known to be sympathetic towards airline causes and frequently fought from their corner. His response was to work out what he called the Revised scheme. This was introduced on 1 October 1922 and was based upon the decision that the companies should no longer compete against each other on the same routes but look towards developing networks of their own. Brancker also scrapped the hire scheme that had previously been the method used by companies to acquire their aircraft and the equipment was given to them instead. This came with the proviso that allowed the Government to recover the aircraft of any company that went into liquidation. Subsidies were to be paid as a lump sum, but fines would be imposed if an airline failed to adhere to certain standards and conditions.

New routes were announced in September before the Revised scheme had come into operation. Daimler Airways were allocated to fly Manchester–London–Amsterdam with an extension to Berlin negotiated by Woods Humphery who had persuaded the German authorities to accept an informal agreement to relax their ban. Handley Page retained the London–Paris route as it had served it the longest, but Lausanne was added as an extension with lavish plans to later extend as

far as Malta, Egypt and the East. Instone was given London–Brussels–Cologne and onward to Prague with a proposal to continue east to Baghdad and India. The Czechs agreed to pay a subsidy on the Cologne-Prague extension and a further section was planned to Budapest using Czech-built DH34s. The Cologne sector opened on 3 October 1922 with *City of London* arriving in 3½ hrs. From May 1923 a non-stop service commenced using DH34s that departed from Croydon at 1030 and returned from Cologne at 1530. In the same year Instone negotiated with a Danish company for a through service to Copenhagen but the arrangement fell through.

Late in 1922, following a delivery of some underpowered Vickers Vulcans, Instone sued the makers for supplying aircraft that were not up to specification. Sir Sefton Brancker became involved in the dispute, favouring the airline which resulted in an agreement being reached with Vickers to re-equip the aircraft with more powerful Napier engines.

Significantly, by the end of the year the British had carried 65.6% of all passengers and 41.6% of freight on the London-Paris route. This was impressive considering the active competition that they faced from mainland European airlines. The Revised Scheme had given Handley Page a British monopoly on the route but the subsidy required the company to complete 300 flights although there was no stipulation to determine the percentage split between passenger and freight-carrying services. Much of the potential freight business was however lost to the French carriers who were licensed to carry newspapers. When the Conservatives came into power in October 1922 and Sir Samuel Hoare became the new Air Minister, he advised the House that extra funds should be provided to allow British airlines to carry English newspapers to France and Italy. He proposed that a further subsidy payment of £143 per round trip should be paid to match the subsidies the French were paying their operators. Passenger only flights earned just £21 without subsidies and it became important for the airlines to secure freight consignments in order to increase their profits.

Hoare also told Parliament that Daimler Hire owned two DH34s outright that could be utilised on routes other than those that qualified for subsidies. This resulted in G-EBBS flying a popular extension of the Amsterdam–Croydon route to Manchester from 23 October. From March-April, Daimler also included a service to Castle Bromwich that served the British Industries Fair. After G-EBSS crashed at Ivinghoe in September 1923, it was discovered that the DH34 had a high-speed stalling problem and, as a result of the accident, the sister aircraft, G-EBBX that was being rebuilt after a forced-landing on the beach at Coz-Sur-Mer near Ostend, had eighteen inches added to the wing tip overhang at a cost to the company of £171 17s 0d. (£171.85) The modifications led to the type being renamed the DH34B.

A view towards a single enterprise

By the end of 1922 the industry was starting to operate within a fairly stable environment, but the companies were still very small and all three operators combined accounted for the employment of only eighteen pilots and 117 other staff.

On 2 January 1923 The Hambling Committee was appointed under the official title of The Civil Air Transport Subsidies Committee and given until 1 March to report on Government financial assistance to the civil air transport companies. Sir Herbert Hambling (1857-1932) the deputy chairman of Barclays Bank and the Ocean Marine Insurance Company was appointed chairman. Assisting him were Joseph V. Broodbank (1857-1944) an associate of the London Dock Companies, The Port of London Authority and ex-president of the Institute of Transport; and Oliver V G Hoare, the younger brother of the Secretary of State for Air, Sir Samuel Hoare. The individual appointments gave considerable cause for concern because none of the selected members had any previous aviation experience. To the contrary, their interests were more readily associated with accountancy and the fiscal results than the vagaries of the airline industry. It is indicative that one of the conclusions reached by the committee was that the London–Paris and London–Brussels routes were too short to ever become serious revenue earners and that longer routes needed to be created. The controversial nature of the committee was further criticised when it was suggested that Sir Guy Hambling (son of Sir Herbert) had been approached by Prime Minister, Bonar Law, to pass the instruction to Sir Herbert: '*Can't you get them to amalgamate?*' This is precisely what George Holt Thomas

had said needed to be done three years earlier. Although it made good economic sense to merge, previously the idea had been completely ignored and had it been instigated when Holt Thomas made the suggestion, Britain's airlines might well have been in a more secure position.

Questions were raised in Parliament with Labour member Tom Johnston attacking Hoare over why the appointed committee had no aviation experience. The Minister responded by suggesting that this was irrelevant because the Committee had only been appointed to gauge the feasibility of the business operation of the companies. Johnston became more vehement and went for the jugular: '*Does not the right honourable Gentleman consider it inadvisable that of this committee of three persons, one should be his brother, another his brother's partner, and the third the late partner of the right honourable Gentleman himself?*'

This was a prudent point but Hoare remained unmoved. He continued by introducing the Air Estimates and by explaining that the contents were recommendations made by the Hambling Committee that the Government had already accepted. The Conservative Government's stand supported private funding and it was suspicious about the risks the Air Ministry were prepared to take with public money in return for having the profits. The Treasury was still not in favour of commercial aviation and it did not enjoy being involved in long term commitments. Johnston, of course, representing Labour's stand, was unrelenting and continued attacking Hoare. '*For my part, I trust that the Government will retain civil aviation in their own hands, that they will run air transport for the benefit and well-being of the British people, and that private finance, private plunder, and private capital will not be allowed to put its finger in this pie as it has put its finger in telegraphs and telephones.*' Certainly strong stuff, but the Government were unwilling to take ownership of the nation's air transport company.

The individual railway companies of Britain were grouped into four companies in 1923 and were nationalised in 1947 under the Transport Act as British Railways. The question of whether the airlines should be nationalised might have been on the mind of Johnston and the Labour Party at the time. Johnston's comments can be compared with what later transpired. British Railways strengths came from unification and it became a powerful and efficient force after nationalisation. Towards the end of the 20th century, when the railway system was broken up into various private entities, much of the unity was lost as the various private enterprises struggled to meet targets. As a result the debate will continue over whether the sum of a State controlled transport system funded by the tax payer is better placed to serve the needs of a nation than a number of individual privately owned corporations. If we examine the case of the railways in the UK today and compare them to the state-run systems in other countries, the argument in favour of State ownership might be considered very strong. The free enterprise approach in the UK caused major disruption, services to disintegrate and fares to increase out of hand. During the 1920s many believed that Imperial Airways should have been formed as a nationalised asset rather than as a subsidised privately owned monopoly, but whether this would have been of any real benefit to the nation is difficult to gauge more specifically as during that period the railways catered for the needs of the ordinary citizen when comparatively few could ever afford to fly.

Various proposals were suggested by the Committee. On the question of subsidies, it was agreed that £1m would be required over a period of ten years in addition to a capital requirement of the same amount. Some of this would be required to fund research, development and the building of new aircraft. An element of the national press was against any subsidy, but *Flight* magazine, which normally opposed public funding, agreed and the *Aeroplane* responded by saying that '*...it is not really a subsidy but a contribution towards national assets.*' In the five years preceding 1923 the individual companies had received a total of £313,824 in subsidies. This consisted of payments to Daimler Airways (£96,094), Handley Page (£94,472), Instone (£119,234), and The British Marine Navigation Company (£4,024) with a further payment made as gifted equipment totalling £65,027.

Hambling also agreed with previous proposals that all equipment and crews should be British with an additional requirement for crews to become members of the RAF Reserve. The committee ordered that in the event of a future war the Government would acquire the assets of the company for war service. As an extra safeguard the RAF was to be increased to 52 home defence squadrons so that their strength would

equal that of any potential enemy that was in range of our shores. Finally, it was proposed that the new company should have two Government appointed representatives as board members, presumably to protect the taxpayers interests.

As a result of the Hambling Committee's recommendations, discussions took place throughout the spring and summer to negotiate a suitable financial deal between any potential investors and the Air Ministry. Although the Committee had highlighted the need for a single, monopoly company, it nevertheless felt that the existing companies should be adequately rewarded rather than simply be allowed to go to the wall. After all, at the time of the amalgamation, domestic competition had become quite healthy. During 1923 the London–Paris services had carried 9,377 passengers; 7,179 of these by Handley Page. Instone operated a near monopoly, carrying 3,022 on the Brussels route and Daimler carried 1,736 from a total 2,712 passengers on the route serving London–Amsterdam and beyond.

Instone had prepared a 58-page proposal that suggested a Government funded company that would operate one internal and ten international routes from aerodromes in London and Glasgow. These would fly services to Vienna, Berlin and Marseilles but later extend as far as Cairo, Constantinople (Istanbul) Danzig, Dublin and Belfast. Their plan was to ask for a subsidy of £150,000 for the first year, based on a profit margin of 6% and a total expenditure of £250,000. This was £40,000 higher than a proposal made by the finance group favoured by the Hambling Committee.

Instone was out on its own. The other three companies, with George Holt Thomas as their spokesman, favoured a finance deal that was being brokered by Frederick Alexander Szarvasy, the chairman of the British Foreign and Colonial Corporation since 1919. Szarvasy was a millionaire, a naturalised Czech born in Hungary, who had arrived in Britain in 1901 when he was 26. His business acumen had come to the fore when, after the War, he had put together a rescue package for the ailing Dunlop Rubber Company. Szarvasy was also involved with the businessman Alfred Lowenstein who fell mysteriously from his own aircraft and was killed in 1928 and is the subject of a book by William Norris titled *The Man Who Fell From the Sky*.

Szarvasy's proposals called for a finance house to guarantee £500,000 in shares that would be used to buy the fifteen aircraft and assets from the four existing companies, including Instone. The British, Foreign and Colonial Group agreed to put up 50% of the capital. The proposal called for a continuation of existing routes but with an increase in mileage and a revenue of £285,000 (taking into account estimated receipts of £76,915 and subsidy of £137,000). During August an agreement between the companies was put on hold when Holt Thomas accused Instone of taking too many advanced bookings. In retaliation Instone accused Holt Thomas of trying to force the Government's hand over who should be appointed to the new company's board. Instone believed that his company was being forced out of a business even though he considered they were the most qualified to operate purely on financial grounds. *Flight* magazine supported Instone and added that whoever was appointed should be deemed to be in the public's interest.

In the spring of 1923 George Woods Humphery returned to Berlin to re-negotiate the Daimler service that would operate the Manchester–London–Bremen–Hamburg–Berlin route. The schedule was initially planned for one or two flights a week with passengers switching to the German company's aircraft at Amsterdam for the second sector of the journey. Although Daimler services began on 30 April using G-EBBS, problems over subsidies delayed the German Aero Lloyd inauguration until 21 May. It became apparent that to expect passengers to change aircraft part-way to their destinations was undesirable and it was not long before they were carried over the entire route on a company's own aircraft without the need to change planes. The service soon grew in popularity making it necessary for passengers to book more than two weeks in advance. Despite the growth in bookings on the route, the company soon dropped the Manchester connection to cope with the excess demands to fly from London to Germany and by September three flights a week were being operated. Daimler could have carried an extensive amount of freight over this route but it turned this away to concentrate its efforts on carrying fare-paying passengers.

Although there was a heavy demand for seats on the aircraft during the summer months, the cold winters and early sunsets across Northern Europe forced flights to terminate at Hamburg. When the service was later re-opened, the connection to Berlin was made via Hanover which cut the flying time from up to ten hours down to six. The passenger numbers that Daimler carried were at their highest from July to September when 206, 202 and 118 people were carried respectively but by January bad weather had cut passenger numbers to just 24.

The success of the service led to the North European Grand Trunk Airway being started that linked Daimler and Aero Lloyd with KLM and the Danish airline. From 30 April KLM operated two departures daily between Croydon and Amsterdam and Daimler one. The first of these services took-off on schedule using G-EBBS and reached Berlin in 6 hrs 45 mins. Single fares were set at £8 15s 0d (£8.75) for Manchester–Amsterdam and £6 10s 0d (£6.50) from London. Passengers wishing to fly to Copenhagen used Aero Lloyd with a night spent in Hamburg. Passengers for Moscow flew to Berlin where they would board the Berlin-Königsberg (formerly Prussia, now Kaliningrad, Russia) night train that would connect with the German run service that would fly them to the Russian capital. This service was very much a hybrid creation with a real international flavour. Although operated by a German company, it was registered in Russia and used Danish aircraft powered by British engines. The journey took two days from London but this was far quicker than making the same journey by surface transport.

Another company made a very brief yet mildly successful appearance during 1923. This was The British Marine Air Navigation Company (see previous Chapter) that was registered on 23 March with a capital of £15,000 in £1 shares. The Air Ministry also paid the company a subsidy of £10,000 a year and provided £21,000 towards aircraft and spares. Hubert Scott-Paine, who became a famous producer of motor boats, and James Bird were the company directors. The Supermarine Aircraft Company and the Asiatic Petroleum Company (the parent of Shell Mex) also held £5000 in share capital. The company aimed to operate three Supermarine Sea Eagle amphibian aircraft between Southampton, the Channel Islands and the French ports of Le Havre and Cherbourg. Delays prevented a spring launch because the company was unable to find a suitable airfield. Eventually it settled for a slipway at Woolston on Southampton Water where it launched its aircraft and built offices to satisfy the requirements of HM Customs and Excise.

It appears that a service of sorts was commenced from August but it was not properly allocated a schedule until 28 September when a pair of aircraft operated to and from the Channel Islands. The Sea Eagle usually took an hour and a half to reach St Peter Port (Alderney) from Southampton, departing daily at 1115 hrs (returning from Alderney at 1530 hrs), but on one occasion an aircraft bound for Southampton took more than 2½ hours to complete the short journey. The one-way ticket price was £3 18s 0d (£3.90). During October, Capt Bailey ditched G-EBGR into the sea off St Peter Port and seeing his plight, Capt Baird flying the sister aircraft (G-EBGS) landed alongside intending to tow the first aircraft to safety. However his attempt failed but a ship later rescued the stricken amphibian and towed it to Alderney.

Sir Sefton Brancker and Lord Apsley, a Member of Parliament who was a keen supporter of commercial air transport used the service on occasions to fly to and from the Isle of Wight. The company's third aircraft, G-EBFK, which gained a certificate of air worthiness in July entered the Kings Cup Air Race but blew a tyre on take-off from Newcastle and was forced to withdraw despite attempts to continue by landing on wheel rims.

Despite the differences between the parties concerned, by late October an agreement was finally reached in principle to pursue a single state-assisted airline and on 5 December 1923, *The Times* reported that the Air Ministry and British, Foreign and Colonial had put signatures to an agreement to form a new airline. Imperial Airways was about to become a reality.

CHAPTER THREE

THE BIRTH OF IMPERIAL AIRWAYS AND THE PILOTS' DISPUTE

1924

IF the Hambling Committee's original suggestion had been accepted Britain's new airline would have been known as The British Air Transport Service, or BATS for short. This really would have been most unfortunate considering that ironically the intended official opening day of operation had been set for 1 April 1924 – April Fools' Day! As it was, a pilot's strike prevented the launch and it is perhaps fortunate that George Holt Thomas was quick to spot the acronym before the company was formally registered. In view of the circumstances, it could have given rise to considerable ridicule more especially as there had been a previous company with a very similar name, British Aerial Transport Company (BAT) that existed only briefly during 1917

At the suggestion of Major Woods Humphery, the new company became the Imperial Air Transport Company Limited. This was a great deal more applicable especially if part of the Oxford Dictionary definition of 'Imperial' is taken into account which defines the word as '… of or relating to an Empire'.

Flight magazine had suggested that the company name might be shortened to use just the initials 'IAL' but noted that this might confuse it with the Instone Air Line, one of the founding companies. The respected journal also noted that the new company had been nicknamed 'The Million Pound Monopoly Company' on account of the subsidy that would be provided during the first ten operating years.

The two Government board members were named as Sir Herbert Hambling and Major Hill, who joined Sir Eric Campbell Geddes (of the Dunlop Rubber Company) as chairman, and his financial assistant Sir George Beharrell, along with the representatives of the four airlines that combined to form the new company. These were Lord Invernairn of Beardmores (Instone), Lt-Col. Barrett-Lennard (Handley Page Transport), Sir Samuel Instone (Instone), Col. Frank Searle (Daimler Airways), and Hubert Scott-Paine (The British Marine Air Navigation Company). Searle was appointed managing director and Woods Humphery as general manager. By 28 December 1923 the activities of the company were formerly announced.

As well as the proposals of the Hambling Committee mentioned previously, the document set down the operational duties of the company. It provided for the formation of the Imperial Air Transport Company to operate heavier than air services in Europe, the Mediterranean and the Black Sea. Imperial Airways was to be regarded as the Government's Chosen Instrument in the same way that Pan American Airways was unofficially recognised as such by the US Government.

Politically, a national air carrier should have been considered a necessity that would link the mother country with her Empire.

A 1930s cigarette card caricature of Sir Eric Geddes – Chairman of Imperial Airways, 1924-1937.

Now that it had been made possible, it had become imperative to work towards linking the far-flung British territories with a reliable air service as quickly as possible. There was, as Trenchard had implied, a certain amount of national pride at stake but evidence suggested that Britain was already falling behind the more progressive European nations in the aviation hierarchy. Considering that Britain had for centuries dominated the high seas, it would be slipping in its duties if air transport was not permitted the same prominence. The country badly needed an efficient airline in order to transport mail and other cargo, officers of the HM Government, ambassadors, emissaries and governors who would ultimately all benefit. Manufacturers also needed the impetus to develop and sell new aircraft now that the priority to produce military machines had diminished and a single national carrier would be the ideal enterprise to determine what should be built. The public still showed very little interest in a national airline and most people believed that they would never have the opportunity to fly. Tickets were far too expensive and flying was still the sole domain of Government officials and the wealthy.

Although the company had been formerly registered, there was still a great deal to be done before any services could begin. During the early part of the year Lt Col Mervyn O'Gorman and Brig Gen R K Bagnall-Wilde were engaged to place a value on the old companies. It was agreed that each of the four airlines would receive one third of their values in cash with the remainder in £1 shares in the new company. After valuations had been completed Handley Page was set to receive £51,500; Instone £46,000; Daimler Airways £30,000 and The Marine Navigation Company £21,500. Shares worth £99,168 were included in these figures.

Despite initial optimism the sale of shares was not going as well as expected. The directors intended to raise £1m in £1 shares with a further working capital of £250,000 in 10s 0d (50p) shares. Under the Labour Government there was a general reluctance by the public to invest in a commercial enterprise that was also a monopoly. There was talk of the State imposing a levy on shares and the future of the company under the new Government was anything but certain. There had also been early rumours of floatation; even nationalisation and these were probably instrumental in causing the directors to delay registering the company until they knew which way the Government was likely to react. Labour was also considering a subsidy proposal to build two huge airships; one to be privately owned, the other Government sponsored. Many critics believed airships were the safest and most feasible way to reach far flung corners of the Commonwealth. The Government reserved its right to subsidise a lighter-than-air programme but it was not prepared to subsidise any other heavier-than-air operators.

Imperial Airways De Havilland DH50, G-EBFO.
(CAS/Robert Pearson Brown)

Originally Commander C D Burney had initiated a scheme in April 1922 to build six airships that he intended to operate between Britain, India and Australia. The Government, in its usual way dithered, taking until 14 May 1924 for the new Prime Minister, Ramsay Macdonald, to announce that only two giant airships, the R100 and R101, were to be built, abandoning the original plan for six.

On stock sales, Imperial Airways proposed to pay a 10% dividend to paid-up shareholders on profits and a further bonus once development costs and subsidy repayments had been taken into account. Despite this, 70% of the stock remained unsold until the company started to pay dividends and stockholders were expected to pay sixpence (2½p) to anyone who bought shares. The subscription lists closed by 6 June 1924 still under-subscribed, but by then the company had already been funded through the deal brokered by the millionaire, Frederick Alexander Szarvasy (see Chapter Two) that dispelled any need for concern.

Szarvasy was involved with the new issue and company promotion business. He bought the Cornhill Contract Corporation and then joined the board of the British Foreign and Colonial Corporation (BFCC) becoming chairman in 1923. BFCC was a major issuing house during the mid-1920s and Szarvasy quickly became known as one of the City's leading financiers, gaining the respect of H C Clifford-Turner, a London solicitor well known for his involvement with many company flotations. Like Holt Thomas, four years earlier Szarvasy, through BFCC, had proposed the establishment of a monopoly airline that would combine the interests of a number of small carriers. Despite initial opposition to his proposal, the Air Ministry began to appreciate the wisdom of his thinking in 1923 and reached an agreement with BFCC to combine the existing airlines for a public flotation. Szarvasy was made responsible for brokering a deal with the individual companies and he managed to persuade Geddes to become chairman of the new enterprise. Because of the national importance attached to the venture, BFCC generously offered their services without charge and conducted the flotation for just their out-of-pocket expenses.

Geddes had got to know Szarvasy through the Dunlop Rubber Company where they had worked together. The former chairman of Dunlop, Sir Arthur Du Cross, had brought the company to the brink of collapse owing to bad speculative activities and during 1920 Szarvasy had been engaged as a trouble-shooting chairman to repair the damage Du Cross had created. Szarvasy introduced proper accounting systems where there had been none, organised new finance that eased the company out of its problems and rid the boardroom of several directors

who were non-productive. In 1922 he handed the chair of the now sound and financially viable company to Geddes. During the course of the 1920s Szarvasy's reputation was enhanced after he had intervened in the rescue of several other leading companies, including the Marconi Wireless and Telegraph Company and William Beardmore.

The first board meeting of Imperial Airways was held at BFCC's offices at 81 Gresham Street, London EC2 on Monday, 31 March 1924. This was attended by Geddes, who took the chair; Col Searle (managing director); Sir George Beharrel; Samuel Instone; Scott Paine and Clifford Turner of the solicitors Clifford Turner and Hopton. The solicitors confirmed the incorporation of the company and announced that the Certificate of Registration would be issued on 2 April. The directors were appointed and Ian Dismore was appointed secretary; Messrs Whinney Smith and Whinney were appointed auditors and Clifford Turner and Hopton were officially appointed as solicitors. Each director was issued one share each that were registered numerically as shares 1-7 on the Memorandum of Association.

The company immediately found itself embroiled in a dispute with the pilots that had been retained from the original companies who refused to accept the employment terms they were offered. Searle had attempted to negotiate with the pilots and prepared the following statement that he read to the board: '*Early last week at the request of Sir Eric Geddes I interviewed three of the four Daimler pilots. I discussed with them various points, and mentioned, among other things, that there was a possibility that Major Woods Humphery would be appointed as manager, to which there was no word of dissent. It was voluntarily stated by one of the pilots, and agreed to by the others that they would sooner fly Daimler machines, so far as safety was concerned than any other machines on the aerodrome.*

'*I indicated to them the proposed budget, so far as pilots pay was concerned was then £100 a year retaining fee and 2d a mile flying bonus. In this I had calculated on each pilot flying 810 hours, making total pay of £782 per annum. The only comment on this rate of pay was a question as to whether they would be allowed to fly more miles, and on being assured that they would do this, they went away apparently satisfied..*

'*On Wednesday last, Capt Barnard of the Instone Airline rang me up at Knightsbridge and asked if he might bring three pilots with him for an interview. On arrival, after going into the importance of the pilots calling generally, Capt Barnard said he thought the retaining fee was much too low. I at once agreed that this should be increased to anything within reason, but I would write him on Friday morning making him an offer embodying a higher retaining fee.*

'*On Thursday last I had an appointment with Capt Alfred Instone at Croydon, when I heard from Major Greer that the pilots would most likely refuse to fly on Tuesday morning. I asked if I could see some of their pilots, and four were brought in, including Capt Barnard and we went into the question at some length and they indicated that such was the case and that they would not fly on Tuesday morning unless they were satisfied with their pay. I immediately made them a proposal of £400 a year, which with flying pay would at least equal what I had put in the budget. I asked them if, under such circumstances, they would carry on for the new company. Capt Barnard indicated that although he thought there was no question that they would carry on under such circumstances he could not speak for the others.*

'On Friday morning I received an ultimatum from the Pilots Federation of which the original is attached. On Friday night I sent each pilot a letter notifying them of an offer of £400 a year retaining fee and 1 3/8 ths pence per mile flying pay. This they received on Saturday morning by hand.

'On Sunday I was at Croydon Aerodrome when Capt Baker informed me that he had done everything possible to get the Federation to withdraw their letter as he thought it was an impossible situation for the Directors to accept. Whilst I was in the office I was handed another letter from the Federation which was a further confirmation of their ultimatum. Capt. Baker asked whether I would meet the pilots and I said I was at their disposal any time they chose to appoint. I met them at 6 o'clock and found Mr Bob Williams of the Transport Workers Union was in the room. I explained to him that I was meeting the pilots of the three companies for the first time, and I failed to see the reason for his presence, and that if he remained in the room I could not go on with my proposals. After some discussion, whilst I was out of the room, Mr Bob Williams retired. We discussed pay at length. The question of Major Woods Humphery was also brought up, on which subject they were most dictatorial, bringing up all those accidents which have already been investigated by Sir Eric Geddes. I finally left them, and stated that I would do the very best I could for them with the Directors, but I was quite certain that the Directors had made up their minds definitely that the pilots should not dictate to them as to who should be employed in the management of the new company. The pilots finally asked what was the position with regards to the Mechanics, because they had told the Mechanics that they would stand or fall by them. I informed them that this was a very serious attitude for them to adopt, and in any circumstances the pay of the Mechanics would be equal to, if not slightly in excess, of the Standard Union rates.'

As the meeting continued the board proposed to devise a scheme consisting of a pilot's council that was to be comprised of the chief pilot and others. This would duly act for the pilots in their interests and be reportable to the management.

The board proposed a suspension of all services operated by the founding airlines pending a complete overhaul of all equipment that would be carried out by Brigadier General R K Bagnall-Wild OBE and Col O'Gorman who would be asked to make a joint report as to the value of the aeroplanes, engines, stores and plant. This was done by referring to the mandatory aeroplane and engine logbooks that were kept and signed by the aircraft inspection department of the Air Ministry.

As can be judged from Col Searle's report, the pilots who had flown for the four airlines were unhappy with the terms offered by Imperial Airways. Technically they became unemployed on 31 March, the day before Imperial Airways was due to begin operations, and the intention was for the new airline to smoothly re-employ the majority of them. Despite being formed during 1923, Imperial Airways was only registered as a company the day before flying was due to start; such delay may have been caused by the board's uncertainty over the pilots' grievances. Although jobs were waiting for them, the pilots considered that the board of Imperial Airways had been underhanded and secretive by assuming that the pilots, now officially out of work, could be expected to be employed for considerably less than they had been paid by their old companies. The pilots were further angered because they claimed that the Imperial Airways board had failed to discuss pay and flying hours with them nor had the directors allowed them any say in the appointment of their general manager, Woods Humphery, who was not popular. He had an autocratic manner that would never endear him to the Croydon pilots and he certainly would never have been their ideal choice. The pilots claimed that he had made it public knowledge that he regarded their status on equal terms to engine drivers on the North East Railway; a company where Woods Humphery had previously reigned. The pilots felt that the board lacked the skills necessary to deal with them and this was hindered from the beginning by management's failure to seek the pilots' cooperation. Naturally the pilots were furious but because many had come from military

backgrounds they lacked the necessary commercial experience required to deal with disputes. After consulting with the TUC they had formed The Federation of Civil Airline Pilots while the mechanics and ground crews started their own union, The Federation of British Aircraft Workers. Having done this, the pilot's union met with the Secretary of State for Air, Lord Thomson, on the very day the new airline was due to have started flying. The proclaimed Socialist, Ben Tillett, of the Dock Workers Union, and Bob Williams of the Transport Workers gave their support and led a group of disgruntled pilots intent on putting their case to Thomson, who had been in office only since Labour came into power on 23 January. Tillett was widely regarded as an agitator who, in 1921, had tried to encourage the entire TUC to strike in support of the miners. There was some suggestion, not without foundation, that the pilots' grievances were being used to foster left wing activists. The delegation explained to Thomson that the old companies had paid their pilots a retainer of between £450 and £550 a year with an additional 10s 0d (50p) paid for every hour flown. In consequence the annual salaries of Handley Page pilots could reach £915, Instone £827 and Daimler £1000. They felt that the deal they had been offered by Imperial Airways fell substantially short of what they had earned before. Even with a retainer of £100-£200 and a mileage payment of 2d, their basic salaries, (later changed to £400 and 1d) were still less than they expected. The pilots were also concerned about their lack of security after learning that the board was intent on entering a clause in their contracts that would allow the company to terminate their employment on just one-days notice although this was later amended to a more reasonable three months.

The negotiations between the board of directors and the pilots were destined to become complex and various allegations and counter allegations were exchanged. At the initial board meeting on 31 March the board had proposed to pay pilots an average of £750-£850 a year depending on seniority. This was based on an average wage of £680 that the company claimed was the same as the old airlines had paid.

An Imperial Airways flyer from 1924. (CAS)

Cabin of the De Havilland DH34 showing leather-covered seats – 1924. (CAS)

The prototype De Havilland DH34, G-EBBQ, *City of Glasgow*, originally flown by Alan Cobham. This aircraft served with Daimler Airways and was transferred to Imperial Airways in 1924.

Next day, following the pilots' visit, Searle and Geddes were summoned to Lord Thomson's office to explain why there was a delay in starting operations. They unwisely covered up the truth and put the reason for the delay down to the need for the aircraft to undergo certificates of air worthiness inspections. They explained that once these had been completed they would employ the pilots to fly them. They also told the Minister of State that the pilots would be offered a retainer of £400-£500 with a further mileage payment of 1 pence which they claimed would provide them with an additional annual income of £355 based on a daily two hour flight at 85 mph. Searle claimed that offers of employment had already been sent out during March but no replies had been received until 31st when the pilots had collectively responded by 'making certain demands'. C J Grey, of *The Aeroplane* (9 April 1924) made a scathing attack calling the pilots '… *silly, inexperienced, un-businesslike, temperamental, young pilots'* over the demands they were making upon the Imperial Airways management. He may well have had a point. They were really in a no-win situation. Had their refusal to accept the contracts they were offered continued, they would have been left unemployed because there was nowhere else for them to go. There was no longer a need for military pilots and there were no other British airlines. Despite being criticised, Searle genuinely cared about the welfare of his pilots. Many of them had been loyal to him during the

period when he headed Daimler, but he was no longer his own man and had become answerable to a board of directors who were less than sympathetic to his views. A year later, when he was forced out of the company, it was claimed in *The Aeroplane* of 1 April 1925 that he had never been given the full support of the board during the strike, an accusation that the Imperial Airways minutes appear to confirm.

At the second board meeting held on Friday, 11 April Mr Quin-Harkin was appointed company accountant at a salary of £400 per year and Samuel Instone asked BFCC to underwrite an issue of 500,000 shares. This was passed and was followed by Instone calling attention to an allegation that accused him of being party to the agitators amongst the pilots and mechanics. This he denied and Geddes assured him that the board did not believe these rumours and that some of the directors had not heard them. The remark specifically referred to an incident when filings had been placed in a fuel tank on an Instone airliner that Scotland Yard were investigating as an act of sabotage. Geddes read a report concerning the pilot negotiations and informed the meeting that specific charges against Woods Humphery had been made that were being investigated by the board. Woods Humphery produced documentary evidence to defend himself that he claimed proved that the allegations were incorrect. Despite these allegations (see below) Woods Humphery's appointment was confirmed.

A vote of no confidence

Further anger arose over the appointment of Woods Humphery at a conference between the directors and pilots. This time it was over a claim that he was a qualified pilot with nearly 500 hours flying experience. This was untrue and a pilot, Colonel Henderson, advised that no Air Ministry record could be found to support any such claim. Capt Barnard said that Woods Humphery was an equipment or technical officer, not an experienced pilot as Geddes had previously claimed. Geddes responded by saying he had not meant to say '*experienced*' pilot and explained that the board's opinion of Woods Humphery's reputation had been confirmed by a cablegram received from an independent pilot named as Capt Herne, and by a letter from underwriters. Two of the pilots, Henderson and Robertson, agreed that Woods Humphery was '*…an excellent maintenance engineer but that maintenance was the only phase of his position.*' Geddes added that the underwriter could think of no man more suitable than Woods Humphery for the position but the pilots remained unconvinced and continued to create problems over his appointment. Their attention turned to issues mainly relating to maintenance, safety and reliability. One grievance concerned a replacement engine fitted to a Berlin flight made by Robertson that was said to be new when it was not. He was required to fly a circuit of the airfield to check the engine after it had been run on a test bed. These ground tests had been vital as the water pipes, controls and other equipment needed to be adjusted before the aircraft could be made serviceable. Despite this, Robertson had been expected to fly it in service with a troublesome carburettor and an oil fault. Henderson said that this was unavoidable but the company had telegraphed for a new engine to be sent but it had not arrived.

Another complaint raised the problem of carburettors that choked in the snow. Henderson had been told that nothing had been done to solve this problem but he had letters proving that Woods Humphery had written to the manufacturers about the situation. A number of pilots claimed to have been reprimanded by Woods Humphery for refusing to fly due to weather or technical problems. The board asked Henderson if this had ever happened to him and although he admitted he had refused to fly, no action had ever been taken against him by Woods Humphery.

Geddes proposed that Searle and Woods Humphery should be asked to discuss allegations that had been made against them, but the pilots refused to do this and called for a public enquiry. Geddes asked the pilots to consider the company's point of view. Geddes confirmed his view that Woods Humphery was the best manager they could have appointed, but the pilots refused to concur with this opinion. The situation had become heated and Geddes tried to calm things by agreeing, when special circumstances occurred that put pilots at risk, provision would be made for the chief pilot acting with a committee to look after their interests. He also said that the pilots, if applicable, would also be allowed to attend every board meeting. Geddes also told the conference that the pilots had been given a very generous allowance that insured that their welfare would be personally collectively looked after by the board in future. But the pilots remained confrontational.

On the point where Capt Herne had supported Woods Humphery's appointment with a letter to the board, Henderson asked Dismore, the company secretary, for the reason why Herne had left Handley Page Transport. He replied saying that Herne had been discharged by Woods Humphery owing to financial difficulties after trying to gain an exchange using the company's money. It seemed strange that he should follow his dismissal by backing Woods Humphery's appointment, but it appeared the board never questioned this.

Sir Samuel Instone had initially opposed the appointment of Woods Humphery owing to the evidence that was given to him. But, when the facts had been investigated and it was proved to him that the rumours were incorrect, and that satisfactory explanations had been given, he withdrew and supported the appointment. He asked the pilots to accept the company's offer and to give the proposals a trial.

Major Hills, as a board appointee of the Air Ministry, said that he was particularly anxious to see the trouble settled, and that he too considered Woods Humphery to be most fitted for the position. He went on to say that he was against the pilot's expectation to appoint the manager, and in urging them to accept the company's conditions said that a great concession had been made to them.

The chairman informed the pilots that there was to be no compulsion to fly under unfavourable conditions, no question of unsafe acts, and no victimisation and he urged them not to decide too quickly. Capt Barnard felt that negotiations were impossible with such a lack of confidence in Woods Humphery. Meanwhile Henderson said that he would demand a public enquiry into past fatal accidents, and referred specifically to the Ivinghoe crash that had killed Pratt. He explained that there was a letter from a Dutch company before the accident that stated Pratt should be dismissed as an incompetent pilot. Olley added that the pilots had not had any confidence in Woods Humphery in the past and would have none in the future. He agreed that his maintenance qualifications were excellent but it was his recklessness in management which was at fault. Barnard added that if the company's account of Woods Humphery was correct why should the pilots collectively lack confidence in him? Henderson wanted to vote on the issues with the mechanics but the chairman strongly advised against this and told them it was also wrong to expect that they could fix the mechanics' wages.

The dispute had gained heated momentum and the meeting hardly created the right kind of environment for launching a new company. Geddes requested that a written statement about each complaint be sent to him giving the name of the pilot, the incident date and the reference to the aircraft (where possible). A list of sixteen separate accusations had been levied at Woods Humphery and these were presented at the next conference held at 55 Pall Mall on 14 April 1924. Geddes (chairman), Beharrel, Major John Hills, Samuel Instone and Szarvasy represented Imperial Airways; the pilots that attended were Henderson, Barnard, Olley, Wilcockson, Robertson, Walters, Jones, Robins, Wolley-Dod, Rogers, Robinson, Dismore, Hinchliffe and McIntosh. S A Dismore (not the pilot) was secretary. The chairman told the pilots that there would be no question of safety ever being compromised and he would make it his business to be available for them and he would always insist on every precaution being taken to make the service safe. He asked the pilots to forget any suggestion that Woods Humphery had any flying experience and to work on the understanding that all flying matters would be decided by a flying man. This personal guarantee from the chairman, and with the chief pilot being permitted to attend board meetings, gave the pilots an increased level of security. Despite this, they continued to press for an enquiry but the chairman expressed this could only happen with Woods Humphery's agreement.

It is important to include here the extensive list of grievances that was presented by the pilots at the conference as an indication of their reasons for doubting Woods Humphery's credibility. These have been taken from the Imperial Airways minutes and should be considered in context because they were made by pilots who were highly regarded for their experience and professionalism. Their statements present an extremely damning testimony against the company and the man Imperial Airways had employed to manage its pilots' interests. Some of the wording has been abbreviated without removing any of the key information:

1. *Bager's accident on 14/12/20 – Engine revs were not correct but the engine was not touched since the previous flight from Paris. Major Woods Humphery personally arranged departure and compositions of load. Visibility 500-700 yards.*
2. *At Handley Page in 1920 Woods Humphery told mechanics that it was "a damned waste of time to clean spark plugs." A petrol system designed by Caddick and approved by Woods Humphery was bad and the pump was tied together with string.*
3. *September 1919 Olley was sent to Paris by Woods Humphery carrying one passenger. He had never flown an 0/400 before or flown to Paris.*
4. *1920 accident of G-EALX. Engine cut out on take-off and pilot was discharged. Insurance Company refused to pay because of an unfavourable report although another pilot who was a witness said it was not the pilot's fault.*
5. *Six Handley Page crashes within a few weeks; underwriters refused to insure.*
6. *Pilot Rogers sent to Norway to fly flying-boats. He was told by Woods Humphery to say that he had been on a course at Felixstowe even though he had not.*
7. *April 1922; Handley Page: Duke's accident. Pilot had never flown a DH18 before and was given a test of only 20 minutes. He did not know the route; he was not insured and collided with a French machine. No passengers or goods aboard but pilots say he should never have made this flight.*

8. *Collision between Robinson and Dickinson. Pilots told not to make a circuit by Woods Humphery and a collision resulted. Dickinson dismissed. Union Canton Insurance Company refused to pay. McIntosh was asked to give evidence but was told what to say by Woods Humphery.*

9. *Ivinghoe crash; Pratt had no proper practice and had crashed at Rotterdam. Dutch Company wrote asking for his dismissal. Insurance Company passed Pratt out of pity after only two weeks of flying. He had made only one previous flight in a DH34 and again on the day of the accident then flew with Chief Pilot as passenger. Woods Humphery, giving evidence at inquest, said "Chief Pilot going as passenger was an Insurance Company regulation." Ballast not weighed and no method of arranging – afterwards it was weighed and sand issued instead of stone.*

10. *April 1922; Gebbs first flight to Paris. Pilot Hinchliffe overloaded – pilots want log book.*

11. *Safety precautions neglected. Labourers used at Amsterdam instead of skilled mechanic. One man with one month experience sent to inspect engine. Form giving mechanical details not filled in.*

12. *New engine required at Berlin. Considered too costly.*

13. *Hinchliffe asked for new engine because he had a leaky block. He was told this was unnecessary as they knew the block was leaking when he left.*

14. *No magnetos or spare parts kept in Berlin. Henderson had to take chance because of this. Woods Humphery left everything to chance.*

15. *Robertson left Berlin with a broken tail skid because there were no spares.*

16. *Generally Woods Humphery highly vindictive, Daimler sacked Robinson and Woods Humphery saw Greer to stop Instone from employing him. Breakell, when applying for a job, was told that there were no vacancies until some of the present pilots were sacked. Robertson crashed into the sea: flying mechanic Wilmott injured. The mechanic had lost all his tools and had to have two weeks off work. Woods Humphery gave him only £3 compensation and told him that mechanics should not carry tools. Money was not provided to pilots for petrol etc. In forced landings they were told they must supply themselves. Handley Page and Instone did provide. Woods Humphery tried to stop dismissed mechanics from obtaining jobs elsewhere.*

Although it would have appeared obvious, Henderson had emphasised to the board that the pilots had no confidence in Woods Humphery. He also added that comments that had been made by the pilots had been brushed aside by the board. Geddes said he had asked the pilots to verify the report of these complaints but they had refused to do so. Henderson apologised but said that the board could not know all about Woods Humphery and suggested a private enquiry by a court of five should be convened. This, he suggested should include two members appointed by the company; two by the pilots and a chairman to be chosen by the other four. He told the meeting that the pilots and mechanics were prepared to abide by any decision made by a court of enquiry. Geddes had suggested each side putting forward a short list of eight names with two members chosen as representatives by the other side and said that if the court's suggestion was agreed by the board then the company would adopt the decision. After Henderson had read the list of grievances (above) he asked the board for a comparison of insurance quotes bases on: a) Woods Humphery and new pilots and b) Other manager and old pilots. He said that the pilots thought the board would be surprised at the difference.

The chairman informed the meeting that if a Court of Enquiry would be held it would have to take samples of the complaints and investigate them. He added that he doubted whether a court would be empowered to take evidence on oath and there were also other issues involving the pilots that needed to be settled. As well as the issues relating to Woods Humphery's appointment, they needed to reach an agreement over the mechanics wages and the pilot's pay and terms of employment.

A board meeting followed next day. Briefly, the discussion moved away from the pilots' dispute while the issue of 500 ordinary £1 shares were allotted to each of the following directors (with a sum of two shillings (10p) payable upon allotment): Lt Col J Barrett-Leonard CBE (share numbers 8-507), Sir George Beharrell DSO (508-1007), Sir Eric Geddes GCB GBE (1008-1507), Sir Samuel Instone (1508-2007),

H Scott-Paine (2008-2507) and Lt Col Frank Searle (2508-3007).

When the board next met on 23 April there was still no settlement in sight with the pilots. A letter was read from Woods Humphery denying the charges against him and he produced documentary evidence against the pilots' allegations. The Secretary of State had asked the company to agree to an enquiry and the board agreed, but they responded by adding that a full investigation had been made. It was confirmed that evidence would be taken on oath with each side being represented by counsel. The board offered a 'little latitude' to enable the pilots until the following Monday to decide whether to work for the company. The company was still being pressed to provide the Secretary of State with a reason why flying had still not started and why other pilots had not been engaged to replace those that were refusing to work.

Herbert Brackley – the Imperial Airways Air Superintendent

The appointment of Brackley

Such was the ferocity of the dispute that Woods Humphery saw fit to take drastic action by filing a libel suit against the leaders of the pilots union. Some pilots had claimed that he would push them to the limits, often forcing them to fly in appalling weather against their professional judgement and then blaming them if they had to make a forced-landing or their aircraft became damaged. Woods Humphery had also been ready to hire RAF pilots with no commercial flying experience if the existing pilots continued to refuse to work. Fortunately, the Air Ministry intervened and by 30 April the dispute had been settled, Imperial Airways formerly announcing two days later that the strike was over. In a move that could be construed as a face-saving exercise, Sir Samuel Instone suggested that an air superintendent be appointed to represent the pilots' interests. It was no surprise when the name of Major Herbert George Brackley was put forward, ironically by Woods Humphery. Brackley's appointment apparently upset Geddes because he viewed it as a costly and unwarranted expense that would eat into the dividend payments that he, and the other directors, could expect to receive from the company. However it appears evident from letters published in Frida Brackley's biography of her late husband that Brackley's popularity at that time was instrumental in achieving the settlement between the pilots and the company. The levels of animosity between the pilots and Woods Humphery had become intense. It was a situation that would have become far dirtier had positive action not been taken. If RAF pilots with no commercial experience had been hired to fly Imperial Airways aircraft passenger safety might have been impaired, especially so had they been pushed into immediate service without adequate training. Certainly this would have created a certain lack of public confidence in the company. In any event, the protracted accusations that had been exchanged did not create a satisfactory working environment and Woods Humphery could not have drawn comfort from knowing that his pilots despised him. After all that had transpired, Woods Humphery demonstrated that his skin must have been incredibly thick to continue in his appointed role; many lesser men would have walked from the job long before the atmosphere had deteriorated as far as it had. His attitude in this respect was admirable.

While the accusations and denials were being exchanged, the board had met during the interim and agreed the insurance values of the aircraft that they had acquired from the former companies.

- The three DH34s from Daimler Hire (G-EBBX, G-EBBY and G-EBCX) were valued at £5000 each
- The four DH34s of Instone (G-EBBW, G-EBBT, G-EBBV and G-EBBR) at £5000 each
- The Vickers Vimy Commercial (G-EASI) from Instone with two Rolls-Royce engines at £4000
- The Vickers Vulcan (G-EBBL) from Instone with one Rolls-Royce engine at £3800
- The three former Handley Page W8bs (G-EBBG, G-EBBH and G-EBBI) at £7000 each
- The 0/400 from Handley Page (G-EATH) at £2000.
- The two Sea Eagle flying-boats (G-EBGR and G-EBGS) of British Marine Air Navigation at £5600 each

When the board next convened on 6 May, talk surrounded the four vendor companies that had been absorbed to form Imperial Airways that were still waiting to be paid for their assets. Mr Szarvasy agreed to set aside £30,000 to pay for any disbursements as well as the current expenditure of the vendor airlines. The purchase prices agreed with each them was – Daimler Hire £10,000; Handley Page £17,166; Instone £15,333 and British Marine Air Navigation £7,083; a total of £49,582. However the board proposed to hold back the money owed to the four companies until Imperial Airways shares issue had been completed. This prompted the secretary of Daimler Hire Limited to send a letter chasing for payment for the sale and he also reminded Imperial Airways that Daimler were still waiting for the agreement for the purchase of the airline that the board had neglected to send. Imperial Airways had hardly got off to a favourable start.

With the pilot issues nearing settlement, the board set to work to build the infrastructure of the business. Thomas Cook was appointed as official agents for passengers and freight and a discussion turned to finding a headquarters for the airline. A suite of offices at Wolsely House, Piccadilly was considered for an annual rent of £700 consisting of four small first floor offices and one large room. An advertising budget was allocated of £5,000 and Sir Charles Higham and Mr Sidney Walton were hired as Imperial Airways' advertising agency. In line with traditional advertising protocol, the agency was allowed to retain the commission they earned from buying space in publications and they were also paid an annual retainer of £1,000. The board considered these payments to be 'overgenerous' and the chairman was asked to approach the agency with a view to reducing the agency's charges.

Although a settlement had been finally made with the pilots, they still refused to write a letter of apology to Woods Humphery who, in turn, had been asked by the board to withdraw his writ against the pilots. This had been on the understanding that they would agree never to repeat their allegations. The disgruntled mechanics had also settled in spite of Imperial Airways' refusal to employ all of their colleagues from the former airlines and with no guarantee that they would do so in the future.

Brackley was appointed as the air superintendent at an annual salary of £1,000. He was an excellent choice; highly respected throughout aviation, military and political circles. He was fair, meticulous and cared greatly about his fellow men. As time went on he personally tested every aircraft that Imperial Airways flew and he was only prepared to release a new machine to his pilots for passenger service once he was completely satisfied that it was totally safe. He was also highly influential in the design of many of Imperial Airways' successful later aircraft, notably the HP42, Short Empire flying boats and the Armstrong-Whitworth Atalanta. Brackley was also firmly behind buying British, a policy that the company relentlessly stuck to – at times unwisely.

On the same day of his official appointment, Brackley met with Geddes and the board of Imperial Airways and then went immediately to Croydon to introduce himself to the pilots. He was well received and was ready to discuss their concerns. Brackley wrote a letter to his wife at midnight the next day while she was convalescing after a minor operation: '*Yesterday afternoon I spent three hours with Sir Eric Geddes and met the board of Directors. I was duly appointed and left Pall Mall immediately for Croydon to try and get the flying personnel together… At Croydon I found more difficulties than expected. Questions of insurance; withdrawal of writs; making up and signing of agreements; inspection of machines; insurance of machines, and the hundred and one questions connected with the taking over of a new job and meeting new staff. After doing as much as possible, I left Croydon at 7.45, it being essential to return this morning to continue. Instones and Handley Page had not handed over their machines and we could not touch them.*

'This morning I had to get out temporary agreements for all the pilots, sixteen in number, to cover the period during which the proper agreements are being drawn up. Timetables for all routes, terminal aerodromes and accommodation – all these things have to be thought out and action taken. All the old offices at Croydon are to be pulled down and one central office will take their place. Meantime I will makeshift for an office. Difficulties arose between pilots' solicitors and Humphery's solicitors over the writ question, the pilots naturally demanding that Humphery should withdraw the writs. After a great deal of discussion, I have got this settled, and the papers will be signed tomorrow morning.

Then I had to interview disgruntled men who had been thrown out of employment and demanded work with the new Company. After a great deal of talk with the managing director, I got him to send letters to them stating that they will be taken on as soon as there is work for them to do. One of the best foremen died very suddenly today. He had been working very hard and this morning, after cycling to work, fell unconscious and died within an hour. The net result of all this is that so far only three machines are definitely ready with insurance covered and inspection finished, so I shall start with these machines. There are tons and tons of freight waiting to go.'

Frank L Barnard was confirmed as chief pilot and with the title came the responsibility for vigorously insuring that the employed airmen carried out their duties as expected. His chairman, Sir Eric Geddes, was known as a hard task-master, lacking in patience but with a reputation for problem solving and an ability of getting things done. He was bombastic in a bullying way that caused Oswald Short, the aircraft manufacturer, to order him from his Rochester factory at one time. Geddes, one of two Scottish brothers, was said to have a penchant for cutting everything, financial and personnel, to the bone and he believed that he could control Imperial Airways by spending just a day a month, in a role he shared with his leadership at Dunlop. Delegation was his tool and he left others to do the work and to solve the many problems that he left them in his wake.

Barnard was immediately expected to obtain written reports from any pilot who refused, for any reason, to fly on any given day or in a particular aircraft. Sixteen pilots of the twenty-one available signed for the airline at a revised pay scale of £780 to £880 per annum and with £1,000 life insurance. The contracts ran for a year after which termination could be made by either party giving three months notice. The board had intended the notice period to be three weeks, but this was amended probably on the insistence of the pilots. The remaining five pilots were sent letters promising employment as soon as the airline had work for them. Initially, a shortage of aircraft made it impossible for the company to employ the extra pilots. While they waited for the Instone and Handley Page fleet to be handed over, Imperial Airways had only a depleted fleet comprising two Supermarine Sea Eagles (formerly of British Marine Air Navigation Co) and three DH34s (from Daimler). The three HPW8bs of Handley Page and the Vickers Vimy Commercial and DH34s of Instone were handed over later together with a selection of unserviceable aircraft that was scrapped. The company had inherited a strange assortment of machines, all of them still painted in the liveries of their previous owners. The fuselages of the former Instone aircraft were painted in the familiar deep blue; those from Daimler were pillar box red and the Handley Page machines had silver painted fuselages picked out with blue silhouette lines. The wings of the small fleet were all painted with silver dope that was retained as part of the Imperial livery when the aircraft were eventually re-branded.

A Handley Page timetable from 1924. (CAS)

Although the pilots strike did not reach a formal end until May, the airline commenced operations on 26 April when Capt H S Robertson flew a DH34 (G-EBCX) on the first Imperial Airways service from Croydon to Paris (Le Bourget). On 1 May, a Sea Eagle operated the Southampton-Guernsey flying boat service and two days later regular services commenced between London-Brussels-Cologne (Capt A L Robinson in the DH34: G-EBBY) and on the London –Ostend–Cologne daily services. The new airline had belatedly become operational after a teething period of concerned uncertainty.

Records show a discrepancy over the number of pilots originally hired. According to Capt Robert McIntosh in his autobiography, *All-Weather Mac*, nineteen had formally signed contracts. These, with their commercial flying licence numbers in brackets, were listed as W Armstrong (289); F J Bailey (2250); F L Barnard ((305); F Dismore (632); C F Wolley Dodd (?); W G R Hinchliffe (235); H J Horsey (99); O P Jones (449); R H McIntosh (314); F F Minchin (371); G P Olley (307); G Powell (300); P D Robins (407); A L Robinson (264); H S Robertson (675); W Rogers (475); L A Waters (740); A S Wilcockson (425) and A C H Youell (694). Brackley's diaries record that, initially, there were three less.

It seems that the directors of Imperial Airways were highly embarrassed and very sensitive about the strike. In the first part of a short history of the airline that was published in the company's official magazine, *Imperial Airways Gazette*, of April 1934 there is no mention of the dispute. Under a section entitled *'First Services'* the start up delay is explained: '*During the immediate three weeks following the formation of the Company no services were run, as there was* a period of reconstruction (author's emphasis) *which had to be undergone.'* Whilst this is certainly true, the *Gazette's* editor makes no reference to the pilots being the cause of the delay. The *Imperial Airways Gazette* was a very informative public relations tool that the company sent to travel agents, members of the public and other interested parties. It was also given away as a free insert in *The Aeroplane* magazine. The omission of the strike from the pages of the *Gazette* could be taken as an indication that even ten years on, the company still considered the strike to be a detrimental part of its history.

Despite all that had gone before, Woods Humphery continued to demand the highest levels of discipline from his pilots. They were issued with a copy of a blue book entitled 'Pilots Handbook and General Instructions'. This contained the rules and conditions of service, the international agreement, aerodrome rules, forced landing procedures, customs requirements, AD6 wireless operation, cargo regulations, routes and an explanation of the duties of the air superintendent. It also included fares and timetables, freight charges and *'Points for the Passenger'*. The little blue book was a mine of information and it was deemed of sufficient historic interest for British Airways to issue a reprint when the 50th anniversary of the founding of Imperial Airways was celebrated in 1974.

Pilots were also expected to learn the fundamentals of every aircraft in the fleet and be able to fly all types on every route. Barnard, Robinson and Powell had to convert from the single-engine DH34 to the larger Handley Page W8 despite having no previous experience of flying twin-engined machines. After making a brief fly-around over Croydon they were required to take a machine straight into service on the cross-Channel route. It was no surprise that mishaps occurred on a regular basis and it is doubtful whether members of the public were ever aware of this dubious and potentially dangerous practice. It is unlikely whether they would ever have stepped on to an Imperial Airways aircraft had they known the truth. Fortunately most of these minor accidents occurred on the ground while taxiing, but a DH34 was written off when one pilot crashed into the memorial at Ostend during a poorly executed take-off. These were exactly the sort of issues that had fired the pilots complaints about Woods Humphery's appointment, but the board chose to ignore these hazardous practices. The pilots were no longer really in a position to bargain; had they attempted to make any determined complaints the alternative was unemployment.

The airline was keen to establish a corporate identity that would give it a more professional image even if its operational methods were in doubt. Aircraft fuselages were painted blue and the pilots were fitted with blue naval-style uniforms and peaked caps and were no longer permitted to wear civilian clothes while on duty. A fleet of Daimler limousines was introduced to ferry passengers from the comfortable lounge at the company's Central London terminal to Croydon Airport,

a journey that took around 40 minutes. Passengers could also be collected from several out of town pick-up points. The weight carried on flights was crucial and passengers with their bags could not exceed 170 lbs. Passengers were weighed with their luggage before boarding an aircraft. A simple method was adopted to avoid any passengers feeling embarrassed by others seeing their weight. The face of the scales was discreetly turned towards the check-in clerk so that he was the only person who could see it. The weight issue was sometimes open to abuse because smaller passengers sometimes felt they should be allowed extra luggage to compensate for their slight stature.

Croydon airport was also undergoing some important changes. Plough Lane disappeared and the old flight sheds were demolished and replaced by new structures. The rural atmosphere, that had included a horse-drawn mower for cutting the grass, gradually dissipated as the aerodrome started to take on a more functional appearance. This included the construction of a new central office building on the eastern boundary near the main road where the terminal was located. The local residents had started to complain about the noise caused by aircraft movements, especially during times when pilots flew too close to houses as they struggled to gain height after take-off. The situation was made worse at the end of the year when a new pilot, 34-year-old David Arthur Stewart, who had previously flown large RAF bombers, took off towards Purley in a DH34 (G-EBBX). It was Christmas Eve and the wind was quite gusty. Stewart appeared to have experienced engine trouble as he fought to gain height over the ridge along the Purley Valley. By attempting to turn back towards the airfield to avoid houses he stalled, sending the aircraft into a steep dive from 200 feet. The aircraft came down on a plot of open land between Kingsdown Avenue and Mount Park Avenue close to the Brighton Road and fortunately nobody on the ground was injured. However, as frequently happened in accidents of this kind, the aircraft caught fire and all eight aboard died. At a subsequent inquest held at the Law Courts, Brackley revealed that Croydon Airport was unsafe for flying in bad weather.

There was a great deal of consternation over the crash. Hinchliffe had reported the engine of the DH34 as faulty after a previous flight but apart from a brief ground run-up before the ill-fated departure, the engine had been signed off by a ground engineer as serviceable. Hinchliffe had found it necessary to lighten the load by 300 pounds before leaving on a previous flight from Amsterdam for Croydon but he had not suggested that Stewart do the same prior to his final departure. Nevertheless, the aircraft had safely flown in from Brussels on the day of the accident, landing at Croydon at 12.24 hrs and the pilot on that occasion had reported nothing untoward. At the subsequent board of enquiry comprising of Woods Humphery, Dismore, Brackley (who, owing to his wife's illness, was later replaced by Barnard) and Major Beaumont (a member of Beaumont and Sons, Solicitors, retained for the purpose) it was concluded that no blame could be attached. The cause of the accident was determined to have been a stall following a turn. On 14 November 1924, the Air Ministry reported the following relevant factors associated with the incident:

- That a contributing factor was a partial engine failure immediately after the aircraft had taken-off which precluded a successful forced landing.
- The cause of the engine failure could not be determined after the accident.
- That the trees in the south west corner of the aerodrome constituted a dangerous obstacle to aircraft taking off in that direction more especially as the prevailing wind was in that direction.

G-EBBX was first commissioned on the Channel Service in January 1923 and it had completed 1,780 hours of flying, but it had been 507½ hours since a major overhaul by the manufacturers and 152 hours since its last complete overhaul. Stewart had completed 81½ hours in the type.

Residents near to where the aircraft had come down reported seeing a woman who, for many years, would visit the crash site on Christmas Eve and lay flowers by a pillar that had a white cross painted on it marking the location. Although nobody could ever confirm the identity of the woman, it was assumed to be Mrs Stewart, the dead pilot's widow, who lived at nearby Wallington. During the course of time the woman's visits ceased and the pillar with the painted cross became covered in weeds and undergrowth. In recent years, as a mark of respect, members of the Croydon Airport Society cleaned up the area and re-painted the cross. On Christmas Eve 2005 local residents joined Society members for a plaque laying ceremony in memory of the eight people who had perished in the crash.

Another tragic incident occurred on 26 July as R H McIntosh was running up his engines in preparation for a departure to Zurich. The Imperial Airways mechanical superintendent, Albert Percy Sergeant, walked into the turning propeller of the HP W8b which fractured his skull. He was rushed to Purley Hospital but later died from his injuries. The mechanic had been more familiar with Daimler aircraft that had greater ground clearance and it was concluded that the mechanic had misjudged the proximity of the airscrews on the W8b, but it was another tragedy that should never have happened.

Croydon Airport was quickly becoming the focal point of British commercial aviation but the success of the airport was causing local residents to strongly voice their opposition to developments. The Aircraft Disposal Company, based at Croydon had its own small airfield next to the main airport where it regularly tested engines, often during early morning. This came in for special criticism when residents demanded that an underground testing facility be built. The local Member of Parliament, Mr R J Meller put this proposal to the House. A resident of South Beddington, Mr Francis Barry, reported Imperial Airways to the police because of aircraft noise and then appealed to other residents to form an action committee. R.M.Chant, chairman of the Magistrates, informed the complainant that it was a civil matter and therefore not within the jurisdiction of the police. As a result the local press became a focal point for debate and regularly carried letters from protestors who were openly opposed to the existence of the airport.

Despite improvements that had been made during the previous years, flying was still generally considered to be a hazardous, if not a downright terrifying experience. Arrangements had been made on both sides of the Channel for the railways to carry airline passengers who had become stranded whenever an aircraft was forced to make an emergency landing. In a public relations exercise devised during October 1924 to build confidence, Imperial Airways invited members of the press to join it on a flight from Croydon to Brussels to report on the safety aspects of flying. It was fortunate that the flight had operated smoothly without anything going wrong. From the stories that later appeared, it seems that most of the reporters found the experience enjoyable. The airlines needed all the positive publicity they could get and the Imperial Airways management could breathe a sigh of relief when the press reported favourably.

While on the subject of safety, it is appropriate to reflect on the impressive records enjoyed by AT&T and the four airlines that merged to form Imperial Airways. Considering the flimsy construction of the aircraft, particularly those used in the beginning that were converted military machines, the lack of navigational aids and the appalling weather that was frequently encountered, the record was exceptionally impressive. In the period from August 1919 to the end of March 1924 34,605 passengers had been carried on British civil aircraft. Instone enjoyed an accident free record without any casualties at all; Handley Page lost Capt Bager in December 1920; AT&T lost Bradley in 1919 and Daimler had lost Duke (early 1922); Robinson and Pratt in 1923. During the formative period it is astonishing, yet nevertheless extremely commendable, that only five pilots lost their lives in operational accidents together with the steward, Hesterman who flew with Daimler Airways and was killed in the head-on collision over France. In the very few serious accidents that did occur, five passengers also lost their lives. Although accident-related deaths are never acceptable, when all things are considered, the numbers were considerably low. When the combination of fragile airframes, a lack of safety features and inclement

A pair of Imperial Airways flight tickets from the early 1920s. (CAS)

flying conditions were combined this was a cocktail for disaster, but good fortune probably played a major part in keeping the accident rate down.

Political upheaval

At the time of Imperial Airways formation, Britain was going through a period of political instability. The coalition Government that had been led by David Lloyd George since the end of the War had reached the end of the road. In 1922 there was a Conservative revolt when the Liberal, Lloyd George, called for a continuation of the coalition. Bonar Law, terminally ill with throat cancer, called for a party vote and the idea of another coalition was beaten two to one. On 20 October Lloyd George resigned and the general election that followed in November gave the Conservatives a victory. Bonar Law became Prime Minister with Stanley Baldwin his Chancellor, but the partnership was uneasy from the outset. Law resigned, handed the reigns to Baldwin and died six months later. Baldwin had been an MP for 15 years but little was known about his strengths and weaknesses. The country was witnessing a post-war rise in unemployment and the economy was stagnant. This was not the ideal time to be starting Britain's national air carrier.

Baldwin aimed to re-instate import duties, thus abandoning the free trade policies that had been introduced by his predecessor. This proved to be his downfall and a second general election was called within a year. This time the Conservatives lost. On 24 January 1924 Herbert Asquith led his Liberal party in support of Labour and together they won 92 more seats than the Tories and Ramsay MacDonald was voted in as the first Labour Party Prime Minister. The newly elected Government was uninformed about air travel and the appointed Minister for Air, Brigadier General C B Thomson was no exception, although he worked hard to become familiar with his brief. The Prime Minister's term of tenure at Downing Street was short-lived after various scandals had been revealed and by 4 November, Baldwin was once again in power with Winston Churchill as Chancellor and Sir Samuel Hoare as the Secretary of State for Air, a position he held in four different administrations. Ramsay McDonald's tenure as Prime Minister had ended with his resignation following the defeat of his Government over a motion to prosecute the acting editor of the *Workers' Weekly* for attempting to incite soldiers to mutiny instead of being used to break strikes. Under Baldwin's Government, civil aviation was granted £355,000 in state subsidies, a pittance considering that £14,728,000 had been set aside in the Air Estimates announced the previous March. As Britain's flag carrier, Imperial Airways needed all the help it could get but in the topsy-turvy political situation that prevailed this was hardly likely to be forthcoming.

During 1924 a new domestic airline owned by a pair of tennis players, Donald M Greig (Davis Cup player and former manager of AT&T) and E Higgs made a brief appearance. Greig was also a brother-in-law to Spry Leverton of KLM. Northern Air Lines officially opened on 30 April with a service from Belfast (Malone) to Liverpool (Aintree) at a fare of £3. The inauguration, of the intended daily service, was flown by Alan Cobham with the Lord Mayor of Belfast and High Sheriff aboard his DH50 (G-EBFP). At the same time V N Dickinson departed from Aintree in the opposite direction but was forced to land at Southport due to bad weather. The service was short-lived, lasting only until 2 June. Undeterred, the little airline battled on and even tempted Robert McIntosh away from Imperial Airways to become chief pilot on a temporary basis. McIntosh was taking unpaid leave from Imperial Airways and had agreed to spend the last four months working for Northern. At the end of June a number of experimental flights were operated between Glasgow and Belfast, and on 2 September a series of mail and newspaper flights were flown from Carlisle to Belfast. The company was also hired by London's *Daily Chronicle* to carry newspapers to Belfast for onward distribution next morning by rail

throughout Ireland. The newspapers were printed in Leeds, sent to Stranraer by train where they were loaded on to the aircraft. The system permitted the last newspapers to leave the presses at 21.00 hrs and be delivered next morning in Ireland before their rivals appeared on the street. According to McIntosh's account, he carried copies of the *Belfast Telegraph* on the return flight for distribution in England along with the occasional passenger. These flights ceased around 3 November but on the 22nd of the month the airline was incorporated as a private limited company with a capital of £50,000. Two further aircraft, both DH9s, were bought from the Aircraft Disposal Company and a third was ordered. The company intended to operate a Belfast-England mail service throughout the year to various airports but carried only one consignment to Malone Aerodrome when the pilot, unable to land, had tossed the sack out of the aircraft window but it was never recovered. Needless to say, Northern Air Lines were never awarded a contract. It planned to use Carlisle for eight months and transfer operations to Stranraer during the four months of winter. During March 1925 Northern Air Lines was based at Stranraer and opened a brief service to Belfast but by June 1925 the company abandoned its efforts to operate a long-term regular service and went into liquidation. It has been the only domestic airline to operate in the UK since the inception of Imperial Airways.

Alan Cobham, after his brief flirtation with Northern, was ready for something more adventurous. He was already regarded as a highly innovative and enthusiastic pioneering pilot. On 19 September he flew from Croydon in a DH50 (G-EBFP) owned by the de Havilland Aircraft Company hire service to reach Tangier the same day. Returning next day, his marathon flight notched up 3,000 miles in just 28 hours.

On 2 June, Imperial Airways commenced a weekday London-Amsterdam service that extended to Berlin via Hanover in association with Deutsche Aero-Lloyd AG. The German operator ceased trading six months later forcing Imperial Airways to drop the Amsterdam-Berlin sector from its schedules. Fifteen days later (17 June) another route was introduced for the summer that linked London, Paris, Basle and Zurich three times a week.

During 1924 it became obvious that Imperial Airways needed larger, more powerful aircraft to fulfil the future development of the company. It was looking to acquire equipment with two engines and company policy was starting to edge away from single-engine machines. It was felt that two engines were needed to improve the safety margins that the company required. As time progressed, three and four-engined aircraft would take preference in the airline's plans. In line with this, the method of allocating Government subsidies was changed from a system based on a ratio of aircraft/miles to horsepower/miles. Britain was already starting to lag behind in the design race and Germany was already developing monoplanes. By 1926 Luft Hansa was operating the Junkers F13, a single-engine monoplane capable of carrying four passengers in a heated cabin. The need for purpose-built passenger machines led to Imperial Airways commissioning its first three-engined airliner. This was the Handley Page W8F Hamilton (G-EBIX) that it named *City of Washington*. This aircraft had originally been designed to operate with a single Napier Lion engine in the nose and two Armstrong Siddeley Pumas on the wings, but to save money the Air Ministry decided to replace the Lion with a less expensive Rolls-Royce Eagle powerplant. The aircraft cost £8,000 with the engines and instrumentation provided free on an embodiment loan. The provision of three engines was based on the assumption that if one engine failed the aircraft could maintain height and continue flying safely on the remaining two. The Belgian airline, SABENA, had also confidently ordered the W8b and W8e variants for operation on its long-distance Belgian Congo routes. The aircraft was considered the best option for safe flying on hitherto undeveloped routes over territory that could be extremely inhospitable. Arthur Wilcockson conducted the first test flight of the new machine at Cricklewood on 20 June but although the aircraft was already painted in the livery of Imperial Airways it was not handed over until 3 November. The proving flights successfully illustrated the value of three engines against two and despite reports of vibrations the airliner was adopted as the standard machine for operation on the Cairo–Baghdad–Karachi route that was about to be relinquished to Imperial Airways by the RAF.

While the introduction of the Karachi service was progressing, further consideration was being given to the carriage of mail.

The company planned to carry this on part of the route that crossed the Transjordan Desert and Iraq that was controlled under a British mandate. This sector linked Ramleh, Rutbah, Ramadi and Baghdad. A ground-based mail service had been operated by an Anglo-French business called The Eastern Transport Company that provided an overland service between Caiffa, Bayreuth, Damascus and Baghdad across territory that was partly French-controlled and partly British. A second motor transport company, Nairn Brothers, also operated and during 1924 it was anticipated that the two ground services might merge to form a single company.

On 10 November Alan Cobham set off in foul weather on a lengthy survey flight of India and Burma that covered 18,000 miles in 210 hours. He was accompanied aboard the Puma-powered DH50 (G-EBFO) by Sir Sefton Brancker (now Air Vice-Marshal) and A B Elliott his engineer. The Croydon runway was so sticky with mud that Brancker had expressed doubts about whether the aircraft would become airborne even with such a highly experienced pilot at the controls. The aircraft struggled but managed to un-stick, although the flight was curtailed by appalling visibility across the Channel that forced them to land at Poix. As conditions improved they continued to Berlin's Tempelhoferfeld (Tempelhof), a facility that Brancker proclaimed as the world's best.

During the trip Brancker became ill and contracted a terrible cold while travelling through Romania by train while the aircraft was being serviced. This turned to pneumonia and pleurisy that hospitalised him for two weeks in India. He was also suffering from exhaustion, but his determination and enthusiasm for the project never dampened and he regarded the three-day sea voyage from India to Rangoon as the therapy needed to regain his strength. While in India sites were investigated for airship bases and Brancker discussed internal airline proposals with the Indian Air Board. The Government had intended Brancker to travel the entire route by sea but, as Director of Civil Aviation, he typically viewed this as '… a preposterous idea.' Cobham had called on Sir Samuel Hoare to discuss ways to fund the survey and he agreed to provide the money set aside for Brancker's sea voyage. Cobham was not easily discouraged from getting his way, and by using his powers of persuasion he cajoled industry leaders and other patrons to come up with the necessary funding whenever he needed it. The venture was eventually financed jointly by Imperial Airways, the Air Ministry, the Aircraft Disposal Company, Anglo-Persian Oil and the Society of British Aircraft Manufacturers.

On 30 November the first operating figures were announced at the Imperial Airways board meeting that covered the period 1 April-30 November 1924 but they were far from convincing and demonstrated that 52% of all departures left, on average, 49 minutes late. The causes were attributed to:
- weather: 36% (average 48½ mins late)
- operating/mechanical: 9% (79½ mins)
- traffic: 6% (6 mins)
- miscellaneous causes: 1% (42 mins)

Arrivals fared only slightly better. 43% services were on time but the remainder were late by an average of 52 minutes. The causes were:
- weather: 36% (47 mins)
- operating/mechanical: 5% (98 mins)
- traffic: 1% (7 mins)
- miscellaneous: 1% (33 mins)

During the same period Imperial Airways cancelled as many as 783 services (157 of them during November alone) and only 80.1% of all departing flights were completed; (only 59.95% during November).
These were caused by:
- bad weather: 125 during November (455 over the whole period)
- mechanical: 25 (264)
- no machine being available: 7 (29)
- miscellaneous: none in November (28)
- no loads: none during November and 7 for the entire period.

In most respects, Imperial Airways had experienced a considerably shaky year.

CHAPTER FOUR

THE MIDDLE EAST AND SURVEYING
THE CAPE ROUTE
1925

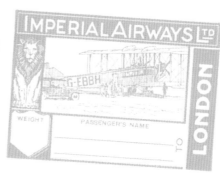

I N February 1925 new European routes were considered to fulfil the one-million-mile requirement set by the Government to comply with the terms of the subsidy agreement. Imperial Airways needed to fly an additional 300,000 miles and a circular route was proposed serving Paris-Amsterdam-Cologne-Paris. This would be used as a stop-gap operation that would fulfil the company's obligation to the Government without the need to incur any additional employment costs because staff were already located at these destinations. In consideration of the viability of this route, the journey times were compared with rail. Amsterdam-Cologne took nine hours, but only 90 minutes by air and Paris-Cologne was 13 hours by train, and three hours by air, proving beyond a shadow of doubt how valuable the airlines could be when saving time was a consideration.

The company felt the DH50 was no longer a suitable platform for passenger operations and there was a proposal to close the Berlin service because the Germans maintained that this was the only machine that would be permitted on the route under the nine rules treaty. The Germans were only allowing three flights a week and because of this there was a proposal to operate a Hanover-Berlin service using a German company that would connect with a daily Imperial Airways London-Amsterdam service at Schiphol. The directors had also considered a proposal for a London-Marseilles route that would continue onward to Madrid. This would either have used Toulon or Lyon as an intermediary stop but the International Air Convention ruled that only through traffic could be carried if the route became operational. A Paris-Zurich service was also considered after the Swiss Government offered to provide a subsidy of 310 Francs per flight if 200 flights could be completed during 1925. This subsidy had however been cut from the 560 Francs the Swiss had offered the previous year. Nevertheless, the viability of the route was investigated more specifically because the German issue was also preventing the company from securing rights on a proposed London-Prague link via Frankfurt. At this time the Channel Islands service was not proving to be worthwhile and the board concluded that £720 in staff wages would be saved over a three-month period if it closed it down.

During March discussions continued over the Prague routing and the chairman was asked to write to the Air Minister about the continuing difficulties being caused by Germany which was denying Imperial Airways the use of its airspace. Geddes informed the board that he would approach Mr Sachsenberg of the Junkers group in an attempt to gain his support for a relaxation of air rights. This prompted Samuel Instone to comment to Geddes about the Germans: '*Dealing with the first proposal (the route to Prague) the difficulties are enormous. In their present mood the Germans are determined to agree to nothing which does not include removal of the nine-point disability and their attitude is a "brick wall" one.*'

He hinted that England ought to use its occupation of Cologne '… *and its "possibilities" to bring pressure upon the German mind, and it must not be forgotten that apart from the question of flying our big machines over*

Germany, flying permission must be obtained for a machine of any kind, however small, to be flown over the territory.'

The Czech Government were keen to make the Cologne-Prague route feasible and agreed to operate the service on a 45/55 subsidy split with the British Government. Imperial Airways estimated that, after subsidies, it could show a £4,700 profit that would be shared with the Czech Government. With view to this it was decided to ask the British Government to negotiate with the Czechs to secure a ten-year contract. The practicalities of commencing the Prague service also meant that the company could withdraw the equivalent mileage from the circular route as this would be replaced by the mileage gained by linking the Czech capital. By April there were further provisos to the negotiations. The Czechs wanted to operate the service using Czech and British aircraft equally. This was generally agreed but Imperial Airways would lose its subsidy on any miles that were not flown by its own aircraft. Proposals were also discussed relating to the subsidy levels the Czechs expected to pay once any service got under way. If they were prepared to pay a mileage subsidy over the entire route, this would be based on 1s 8d (about 9p) for each mile flown that would increase to 3s 0d (15p) per mile over the Cologne-Prague sector. The service looked favourable but if the restrictions associated with the nine rules could not be overcome the route could not operate.

On 17 March Brancker and Cobham returned from their survey with the conclusion that an air route linking England with India and Burma was feasible. A great deal was gained from the trip and Brancker was able to judge the way air transport would be perceived from the people he met in the countries along the route. He appreciated that most European nations now accepted that civil aviation could be used to further their political influences as well as a means to boost their military reserves. The War had done nothing to foster harmony between nations and there was still little friendly cooperation between neighbouring states. Brancker viewed this as the major stumbling block that would hinder any progress towards the expansion of international routes.

In Iraq he found that the authorities were favourable to air services providing that their government would not be involved in too much expense. At Rutbah Wells, half-way across the desert, where a police post was being established, he noted the potential of the site as an ideal refuelling point for aircraft travelling between the Mediterranean and Baghdad.

To his dismay he found that the German Junkers firm had already established a strong presence in Persia (now Iran). He believed this to be detrimental to the future of British aviation unless swift action could be taken to establish a route between Iraq and India that included the Persian Gulf. Brancker noticed that in India there was a general reluctance to take the initiative although the nation was keen to play its part in establishing links with the United Kingdom. Brancker offered his help in setting up a civil aviation department and sent a member of the Air Ministry staff on temporary secondment to organise an establishment. He discovered that the Indian, Burmese and Chinese commercial communities were all keenly in favour of developing commercial aviation but warned that a lack of knowledge and experience in Government and business circles could slow the progress of establishing an air route in the subcontinent. Despite this Brancker felt that an air operation in the east would be much simpler to run – specifically between London and Rangoon – than it would be to increase routes in Western Europe in view of the political turmoil that existed.

Brancker's vision

After his arrival back in England Brancker wrote favourably: '*I believe therefore that an aeroplane service along this route will fly with extraordinary regularity. I had anticipated that the journey might be a difficult one in places. The nearer we came to our anticipated difficulties, the less serious they appeared. I have always maintained that travelling by air was the most comfortable form of progression, and I have returned from this journey more convinced of this than ever. I was never actually too hot or too cold while in the air, and whether starting from the slush and snow of Europe or the intense heat of Rangoon I was comfortable from the moment we took off and began to fly.*' Brancker went on to recommend using a three-engined aircraft on the route.

Nobody realised more than Sir Sefton Brancker just how the British Government's lethargy had lost the nation the opportunity to lead European civil aviation. Convinced of the value to be gained by linking the British Empire to the motherland, he threw his energy behind creating a network of international commercial routes. As director-general of civil aviation he produced a thesis upon his return from India that clearly outlined his opinions. '*Our particular national conditions present somewhat of a paradox... It seems obvious that the nations which must naturally become the great air powers of the world both in war and commerce will be the great continental nations. It is a great continent such as the United States that gives the population a national incentive to fly and to create national air commerce.*

'*At home we started into the development of this new enterprise under most crippling conditions. We have a bad climate, short distances and excellent*

A Junkers G 24 airliner of Luft Hansa photographed in 1925. (CAS)

railways, with the result that the time which can be saved by flying within the United Kingdom is comparatively small, while the risk of being held up by weather during the winter, at all events is considerable. In addition to these disadvantages, we have no through traffic as exists in the central European countries; we are on the edge of Europe, and aircraft have not yet reached the stage of development at which they require ports of arrival and departure for crossing the Atlantic. Thus the British public have no real incentive to fly and no opportunity of learning the value of air transport, and in consequence few people care whether the new industry flourishes or not.

'But, while we labour under disadvantages at home, when the Empire comes into consideration we have more incentive to become a nation of airmen than any other people in the world

'The continents of Australia, Canada and British Africa offer everything that air transport can ask for in a way of opportunity – good climate, long distances and undeveloped communications. Australia has already started off with commendable vigour and enterprise and has proved to her people the great benefits to be realised from air communications; Canada is just beginning; South

Africa and the East African Colonies realise what air transport can do for them but have not yet been able to find the money necessary for serious development. But, beyond all this, we have the unrivalled incentive of Imperial Communication between Great Britain and the rest of the Empire. Though we may have been slow in starting, the demands of air communications of the Empire must eventually force us into a leading position in air commerce. It is unthinkable that we can let other nations become responsible for our Imperial Communications.

'At present the British Government has certain first objectives:

1. A service of aeroplanes via Iraq and India to Australia
2. A service of aeroplanes via Egypt, the Sudan and the East African Colonies to South Africa
3. An airship service to some part of the Empire, probably Canada.

The first two of these objectives will not only save time but will provide frequency. Once established, these routes should provide sufficient traffic to justify a daily service along their whole length. Think what it would mean to the British settlers in Central Africa to receive the London newspapers every morning only

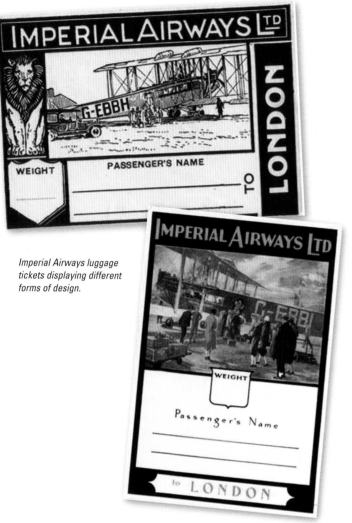

Imperial Airways luggage tickets displaying different forms of design.

a few days after publication. Up to date, our efforts towards the accomplishment of the first two objectives have been delayed by lack of money and by international difficulties.

'Broadly speaking, the policy of the Government regarding the provision of subsidies is that the Imperial Government is responsible for Imperial air connections between the various Colonies and Dominions outside their territories. Thus, the Imperial Government has committed itself to the establishment of the lines from London to Karachi and London to Egypt; Karachi to Rangoon has been accepted by India; and the other links will be judged on the merits within the basic policy as they arise.'

As a part of Brancker's vision for the future he encouraged the founding of light aeroplane clubs as a means of training a national reserve of civil pilots. However, Government funding for civil aviation continued to remain minimal and when the Air Estimates were announced on 12 March only £357,010 from £15,370,010 was allocated to the industry.

Outdated equipment

Although three-engined airliners were being developed by de Havilland, with the Hercules, and Armstrong Whitworth with the Argosy; progress was slow. These were considered to be advanced passenger aircraft that coupled good performance with economic passenger costs per mile but these aircraft were not available for immediate delivery. The air superintendent, Herbert Brackley was also considering the twin-engined Napier-powered Supermarine Swan to replace the Sea Eagle flying boats that had operated the Southampton-Channel Islands route during the summer. The Supermarine Sea Eagle used a single pusher Rolls-Royce engine and carried six passengers in an enclosed cabin. In contrast, the amphibian Swan had twin-engines and carried a compliment of pilot, flight engineer and ten passengers. Amphibians were being considered for the Australian route chiefly because they were considered to be more cost effective over long distances. The route between Madras and Penang, for example, was 1,250 miles which would be uneconomical to operate using a flying

boat because they were not fuel efficient. It was also felt that an amphibian would better suit the company's requirements because it would be able to make use of any existing land based aerodromes and not be restricted to landing on water. Geddes, recently back from the USA, told the board how American long-distance flyers, such as MacLaren, had favoured amphibians. Barnard had suggested converting the existing flying boats into amphibians by adding landing gear to make them more versatile and able to operate from Croydon. But, his proposal was set aside in favour of an alternative site that had been found at Southampton to accommodate the flying boats at an annual rent of £250 with an annual costs estimate of £1,000. The Air Ministry agreed to provide a hangar without charge on the site and to pay £500 towards the cost of a slipway to enable the aircraft to leave the water.

The stark differences between the aircraft being developed for Imperial Airways and those that were already in use on the continent were obvious to passengers who had travelled on the through service to Scandinavia introduced on 15 May. The Imperial Airways DH34 (G-EBBV) that operated the London-Amsterdam sector was grossly inferior to the Junkers G23 operated by AB Aerotransport (Swedish Air Lines) on the Amsterdam-Copenhagen-Malmo sector. Although this was the earlier version of the airliner that visited Croydon a few months later, it was still much more advanced than the dated DH34. The Junkers was the first low-wing monoplane of its kind to enter airline service and it was viewed as a major advancement in aircraft design. This was in spite of the fact that the version operated by Swedish Airlines was underpowered owing to the restrictions on performance enforced by the Allies in the aftermath of the War.

There were at least a few positive aspects about Imperial Airways. Passengers did have the advantage of being able to book direct flights that would connect them with up to 30 major European cities. The Air Express Company Ltd was formed at Croydon as an air transport agency that linked the various airlines of Europe together to simplify passenger bookings and the carriage of freight. The work done by this agency allowed Imperial Airways to connect with the Europe-Union system in Amsterdam and similar services that made travelling to Austria, Switzerland, Hungary, Germany, Sweden, Denmark, Poland, Estonia, Latvia, Lithuania and Finland more feasible. Bookings to all of these destinations could be made directly through Imperial Airways, Air Express or Thomas Cook offices. Geddes had visited America intending to establish an agency that would enable passengers travelling to Europe to book their flights before leaving. His trip took in New York, Washington and Chicago but he had been disappointed to find that there was very little interest in passenger flights. The existing agencies largely ignored the needs of passengers once they had left America, and if they wanted to go to Continental Europe after arriving in England by ship, individuals had to organise their own bookings. Geddes offered agents a fixed commission of 10% for all bookings made in the USA for travellers who wished to continue their journeys using air, rail or ship between London and Paris. He offered a net commission of about 2s 6d (12½p) that increased to 12s 7d (approx 63p) if an agent booked his clients on an Imperial Airways flight. Geddes had met a man named Trowle, who as a vice president of American Express, had agreed to instruct his managers to encourage air travel. The Americans had thought it desirable to have a source where they could obtain information about the pros and cons of flying that could then be passed on to their customers and Mr S E Piza, the manager of Daimler Hire's New York office, was approached to provide this function. He was appointed as Imperial Airways temporary agent at a salary of £250 a year plus £50 to operate an office in the USA. Although Piza's appointment had its unsatisfactory features, Geddes felt it would be a far cheaper alternative to appoint him as agent than to open a self-contained American office.

Routing problems

At the start of April, Imperial Airways had ended its first trading year. It had not kicked off on the right foot with the pilots' strike and there had been a variety of operational and management problems that needed to be overcome. But, in the end. the company could take some credit for what had been achieved. The mileage figures were reasonably impressive considering that they were still operating within an environment that, by modern standards, can only be called primitive. The following table show the mileages flown from 1 April 1924-31 March 1925.

1924	
April	1,350
May	46,590
June	99,710
July	146,820
August	139,315
September	110,354
October	72,140
November	47,280
December	36,420
1925	
January	27,105
February	43,810
March	54,839
Total	**825,733**

On 21 April a proposal was made for an extension of the Ismailia service to Karachi on a weekly basis. This would accumulate 255,000 miles a year that would make any shortfall to meet the Government's one million-mile target. If the Cologne–Prague route was to reach practicality this would also add a further 104,000 miles a year towards the target and allow the equivalent distance to be dropped from other, less profitable, routes. These included the Cologne-Paris and Paris-Cologne-Amsterdam sectors of the circular route for part of the year that would achieve an annual saving of 208,000 miles. This was considered worthwhile even if the Cologne-Prague service had never been inaugurated.

Any transfer of mileage between routes was dependant on the acquisition of new, smaller aircraft to replace the obsolete types that were still being flown. On the 23rd the board met and formerly approved the Karachi extension although the chairman reported that the current equipment situation was making it impossible to make a profit. The previous decision to buy only multi-engine aircraft was revised because there was a realisation that additional single-engine aircraft would be more suitable on shorter routes. With the liability of having to fly a million miles a year the company felt it was impossible to operate with any degree of profitability.

At the start of April 1925 the press reported that Colonel Frank Searle had resigned his position on the board of Imperial Airways and Woods Humphery was promoted to managing director. It was well known that Searle had always placed safety before profits and it is likely that there had been major differences of opinion between him and Geddes who was firmly in favour of minimising expenses to maximise profits. Searle had fallen out with Geddes earlier during their time together at AT&T where the latter was very much regarded as a single-minded martinet determined to get his own way. Imperial Airways had flown more than 800,000 miles during the first year in spite of the limited equipment at its disposal, but this had been achieved at a considerable financial loss. Geddes appeared to have cast the blame for the losses on Searle and had pushed him to resign. The two accidents that had befallen the company's aircraft during the year had created disharmony in the boardroom and the heated exchanges that would have permeated the air can only be imagined. Unfortunately it is not possible to gauge the verbal tension from the company minutes because they record only the facts of a debate and little of the emotion. But Searle did comment quite vehemently afterwards: '*The Board consists of very successful men who know the danger of trusting the unknown, but none of them had successfully operated any new form of transport. My experience has in fact been unique, but such men want a lot of convincing, and in such company my rhetoric may have left a lot to be desired, but at least I have the satisfaction of knowing that what has been accomplished has placed the company in a very strong position for its second year of operations.*'

Brancker's suspicions gained from his trip to Asia were realised when the Germans secured a monopoly for all internal flying rights over Persia. With a view to this Brancker returned to the Middle East, this time on a lengthy covert mission that extended from 21 August to 12 October 1925 with the aim of negotiating Britain's rights to fly along the Persian Gulf. The British Government had also decided to commercialise the RAF's Cairo-Basra route and to extend it onwards to India. This could not be achieved with any level of success without

flying along the Persian Gulf and Brancker visited Tehran to conduct negotiations.

The Government wanted Imperial Airways to consider operating the Kantara-Basra mail route that had been established by the RAF. The Air Ministry proposed subsidising a service for a year with a grant of £50,000 and a free supply of aircraft and engine spares. The board estimated it would cost at least £51,631 to operate between Basra and Karachi prompting the Air Ministry to throw in free use of wireless facilities, ground stations, aerodromes and weather reports. The board responded, by informing the government that the grant was insufficient to cover all of the running costs and raised a number of objections to the service. The board considered the service would run at a loss even with the grant and it felt that the Air Ministry would be unable to maintain aerodromes beyond Basra. There were also no spares or fuel available between Basra and Karachi and no wireless facilities beyond Basra except at Karachi. Apart from the Basra-Karachi sector, it was not possible to fly the remainder of the route at night. In short the service was fraught with problems, many of them potentially dangerous.

The debate continued over the alternatives of operating this service in view of the restrictions being imposed by Persia. An air route between Port Said and Bombay was considered but this would have offered little benefit because it would have been hampered by having to make a five-day boat journey between Basra and Karachi along the Persian Gulf. The fastest boat, operated by the British India Steam Navigation Company, left Basra at noon on Saturday and did not arrive in Karachi until noon the following Thursday. The Board concluded that if an aircraft left Kantara on Friday morning it would take 6½ days to arrive in Karachi. Mail sent by boat between Port Said and Bombay took 9 days. A Baghdad to Basra air service would take around three hours; a huge time saving on the comparable 21 hour train journey. The RAF had produced a set of figures that showed the load factors of mail that they had carried:

Period:	Cairo-Baghdad	Baghdad-Cairo
August-December 1921	1210 pounds	939 pounds
January-December 1922	6027 pounds	7016 pounds
January-June 1923	5488 pounds	5746 pounds
July-December 1923	6264 pounds	5043 pounds
January-June 1924	4433 pounds	3965 pounds
July–December 1924	4347 pounds	3930 pounds

Average mail carried per year in fortnightly service 17,082 pounds.
Estimated load for weekly Imperial Airways service 42,328 pounds.

Earlier in the year Brancker had chaired the eighth session of the ICAO held on 3 April when further modifications were made to the traffic regulations. The conference agreed on further minimum requirements for air worthiness certification and passed rules on the composition of aircrews. This was still an age of male chauvinism. This was highlighted when the convention ruled that women would be excluded from all aircrews engaged on public transport. It was widely considered that flying was a job for men and that any appointment of women as aircrew would create public outrage. Political correctness was non-existent, and the members could never have foreseen just how important women would become during the Second World War as fighter delivery pilots, let alone as captains and first officers on modern day jet airliners.

Sir Samuel Hoare, the Secretary of State for Air, had also been on his travels to the Near East. Upon his return he addressed a banquet at the Royal Academy on 2 May by loudly singing the praises of British commercial aviation: '*That the air will become the great Imperial highway was shown by the fact that in a few weeks we have made a journey which would otherwise have taken twelve months. Traversing Iraq from end to end and visiting the mountains of Kurdistan and the Persian plains through which the British pipe line brings oil for the use of the Fleet. We stayed in Transjordania, Palestine and Egypt, and inspected every British activity, military and civil, in those distant and largely inaccessible countries. It was a long and varied journey, but British pilots, British machines and British organisation enabled it to be performed without risk, delay or incident. This spirit of enterprise will drive through the air a new highway for the British Empire and enable ministers and traders and travellers to pass swiftly and easily as a matter of*

ordinary routine from one end of it to another united by an aerial line of closer and quicker intercourse.'

Despite his comments, the Imperial Airways route network was still limited to a few destinations within Europe and after more than a year there were few signs of the Empire being linked by air even though this was the prime purpose of the company. It was also causing concern that Imperial Airways was flying fewer miles in 1925 than the four founding companies had operated independently in 1923. The Germans, in spite of losing the war, were already expanding their route networks in leaps and bounds. The British position was blamed largely on the Government's apathy about commercial flying and its lack of initiative to get things done. This attitude was well illustrated when, during August, the all-steel Junkers G24 tri-motor airliner flew into Croydon. Although the monoplane caused considerable interest from those who saw it, the obvious advances in the aircraft's design still failed to impress the Imperial Airways directors or the British Government who were still firmly committed to buying outdated British made biplanes that relied on doped canvas stretched across steel framed wings.

On 15 May Sir Samuel Instone chaired a committee that presented unfavourable news relating to the Germans. Woods Humphery reported that the existing London–Paris–Cologne service could be maintained for five more years using existing aircraft but the London–Berlin service would only be permitted using smaller aircraft that conformed to the nine rules. However, having previously agreed verbally to a five-year tenure, the Germans refused permission to fly to Prague and Paris from Cologne. Woods Humphery was furious: '*The Committee regarded these refusals as very grave and felt that the Company were not receiving that official support which was afforded to foreign companies by their Governments. It was therefore decided that with a view to meet the Air Minister a letter be first sent to him explaining the seriousness of the situation and appealing for the support of the Foreign Office to overcome the political restrictions which were preventing extensions in Europe.'*

Developing the image

Imperial Airways was frequently subjected to considerable criticism. Racing driver, S.F. Edge, returning on a flight from Paris was quick to complain about the way the airline was being operated. He was the only passenger on the outbound flight and one of just three on the return. He put this down to inadequate publicity and suggested that the names of prominent flyers should be listed in the press together with safety statistics as a means of encouraging others to fly. Edge was not impressed by the level of smartness at Croydon nor enamoured of the facilities on board the aircraft. The seat legs were restrained only by a strap with the feet of the chair fitting into thimble-like slots, and when Edge leaned back he was concerned when the seat disengaged from its moorings. He suggested that Imperial Airways should issue a pamphlet telling passengers that the steep climb out on take-off was normal and that it was necessary for the aircraft to lean while making a turn. An explanation of bumps caused by turbulence would also provide passengers with some relief from the feeling that the aircraft was out of control. He further advised that aircraft should have two pilots and while one was flying the other should be employed in the cabin explaining routines to passengers. Finally, Edge's diatribe added that all passengers should be issued with ear plugs to counter the terrible noise from the engines.

Edge's suggestions seemed fair enough especially when the out-of-date fleet the company had at its disposal was considered. This still only consisted of three W8bs, three ex-Instone DH34s and a further three from Daimler Hire; a Vickers Vimy and a Vickers Vulcan (both used solely for freight). To counter the problem the Air Ministry had commissioned the three-engined version of the W8 that was named the Hamilton W8f. To promote the aircraft Imperial Airways issued a handbook called '*Points for Passengers'*. This informed that: '*The passenger cabin is entirely enclosed. The windows on either side can be opened and closed at will. There is no more need for special clothing than there is on a railway journey.'* But there was no mention of the vibration caused by the nose-mounted engine that could be felt clearly in the passenger cabin.

The letter that Edge had written may have had some influence on the board who were evaluating the advertising proposals put forward by their advertising agency, Charles F. Higham. The directors voted to spend £8,500 on advertisements placed in London daily and weekly newspapers (£2,500), a few selected American journals (£1,500), an English language Parisian newspaper and some European publications (£1,000) distributed in Amsterdam, Brussels, Switzerland. Other advertising and promotional costs included £1,000 spent on timetables, brochures and posters and an additional £100 on salaries paid to publicity agents. £1,500 was also made available to Imperial Airways managers in Paris and Brussels to launch a campaign that was specifically aimed against Air Union and to promote the airline's Brussels and summer Ostend services. The money earmarked to launch the advertising campaign was quite considerable. Behind the scenes the board was also working with the General Post Office to improve the air mail services. This resulted in a new poster that was displayed in every post office throughout the UK, produced at a cost of £146 that was split with the GPO. This intended to draw attention to a new pamphlet that was available from any Post Office counter. The GPO had also supported the campaign by placing suitable references in the newspapers to further promote the air mail services.

Imperial Airways, assisted by the Air Ministry, took a large stand in the Palace of Housing and Transport at the Wembley Exhibition. The Vickers Vulcan freight aircraft and a ten-seat Bristol biplane were exhibited alongside a model of a lighthouse and a replica of the Croydon Airport control tower. As messages from aircraft were received at Croydon these were relayed to the exhibition stand to provide visitors with an element of realism. Aircraft models were displayed and pamphlets were handed to visitors extolling the wonders of air travel. The exhibition, visited by 300,000, was deemed a great success and bookings were taken worth £851. It had cost the company very little to exhibit and once all expenses had been accounted for, a £104 profit had been made.

As a further example of Imperial Airways willingness to promote the company, Highams had entered an agreement on the company's behalf with someone called Newton who launched a magazine at the board's request called '*Airways'*. Imperial Airways agreed to pay £100 per month for a period of six months to help the publication survive its formative period. In return the company was given two pages of advertising and 4,000 copies of the magazine for distribution. These were mailed to customers and others selected from specific mailing lists and free copies were also handed out at the London terminal, at Croydon Airport and at other outlets connected with the airline. Highams had negotiated an exceptional deal with the publisher that was extremely beneficial to the airline. As well as free advertising and a substantial number of complimentary magazines, Imperial Airways had the right to object to any competing or damaging advertising intended for publication. It was also given the right to cancel the agreement with three months notice and as an added benefit it negotiated a deal that paid Imperial Airways 15% of any profits the magazine managed to make.

The promotional literature produced by the company has a distinct historic value and most things associated with Imperial Airways remain highly collectable throughout the world. Much of the literature was tastefully designed, with excellent graphics in the Art Deco style of the period. The artist Theyre Lee-Elliott, who had also designed posters for London Transport, created many original designs for Imperial Airways including the famous '*Speedbird'* logo in 1931 that appeared initially on luggage labels and from 1939 on aircraft, starting with the DH91 Albatross. There were no computers or instant lettering transfer sheets and the original artwork would have been hand-drawn by skilled commercial artists. The period is widely regarded as the 'golden days' of advertising, a term similarly applied to flying during the period, and the posters, brochures and other publicity items of Imperial Airways reflect this.

At home Imperial Airways latest aircraft, the HP W9, designated the Hampstead (G-EBLE) was unveiled and test flown at Cricklewood on 1 October by Bill Hinchliffe. This was the modified version of the Hamilton, *City of Washington* (G-EBIX) that had been flying since November 1924 but had given concern because of the severe vibration caused by the original engine configuration. The latest aircraft, although still a biplane, was impressive and had cost Imperial Airways £9,200. The price had escalated to £18,398 once a 'package' had been added that included six Jaguar engines costing £1,533 each with starting gear and auxiliary drives. This version of the aircraft had accommodation for up to fourteen passengers, with a toilet at the rear of the cabin and a large baggage hold. For the first time in the 'W' series of Handley Page

aircraft, the pilot was given the port-side seat in the cockpit to comply with a six-year-old ICAN ruling that had so far been ignored. After solving some problems with the exhaust system, Hinchliffe took delivery of the aircraft and flew it to Croydon on 19 October with Frederick Handley Page, Col Outram and Maj Turner as passengers. Geddes met the flight at Croydon and was taken aloft to experience the aircraft first-hand. However the Hampstead still required certification before entering service, a procedure normally carried out at Martlesham. Before this could be awarded the rudder configuration had to be re-designed. Once this had been successfully completed, Flt Lt Oddie of the RAE certified the aircraft at Croydon. The aircraft was named *City of New York* and entered service on 3 November. On 10 March 1926 it completed the London–Paris route in 86 mins setting a new record. In April the Jaguar engines were replaced by Bristol Jupiters and completed 250 hours of endurance flying under normal airline conditions. Impressively, after completing the test, the only replacement parts required during the engine service that followed cost just £1 15s 0d (£1.75).

The company had by now outgrown its offices at Wolseley House and by the summer the board was actively looking to move. There were certain criteria that needed to be met that were quite stringent. The rent on any new premises could not exceed £3,000 a year and the building needed to have a shop window frontage of no less than 25 feet that faced, or was close to, a main thoroughfare. The building that the company sought had to be located in an area where there would be no objections from local residents or from the police over traffic converging on the street to pick up and drop-off passengers, baggage and freight. A side entrance was also needed for vehicles to depart for Croydon. The selected building had to have a minimum ground floor area of 100 square feet to provide sufficient space to accommodate a passenger waiting room, shop counter and space for porters and clerical staff to handle baggage. The ground floor or basement of 800 square feet was required for freight. A tall order it might seem, but offices were found just off the Haymarket at Charles Street at a location opposite the stage door to His Majesty's Theatre. The premises were considered ideal although another site next door to the Criterion Restaurant in nearby Lower Regent Street was also viewed as an alternative possibility.

A Little Light Music

There was the occasional strange interlude that served to keep Imperial Airways in the public eye. On 14 October 1925 Hinchliffe was asked to take a group of six BBC musicians (one of them ironically named 'Hinchliff': without the 'e') and a sound engineer for a 45-minute flight aboard the DH34 (G-EBBV). The purpose was to determine whether musical instruments could be successfully played in the air for broadcasting purposes. Hinchliffe obliged his passengers by climbing to 7,000 feet and then, after cutting his engine to quarter power, glided down while the musicians played several selections of music. The BBC sound engineer had been suitably impressed with the results to request a second trip, although this time a piano was somehow squeezed into the aircraft. After further tests, a live broadcast was scheduled for 6 November when the Savoy Band was carried along with West (the sound engineer) and Messrs Sayers and Yearsley of the BBC. On this occasion Hinchliffe flew the HP W8b (G-EBBH) on a 25-minute trip over Keston, close to the BBC's experimental station at Hayes. Later that day another flight departed carrying a group of well-known singers who performed while aloft, but the sound quality was marred by the engine noise that could be heard through the microphone. Undeterred, another attempt was made on 9 November aboard the newly delivered Vickers Vanguard (G-EBCP) that Hinchliffe had only flown for the first time for licensing purposes during the morning. After reaching 8,000 feet, the engines were cut as before and the aircraft was put into a long glide, but this time there were a few technical problems. This did not deter the musicians from playing a lively jazz piece as the aircraft descended. The live radio performance was scheduled to be broadcast next day but had to be postponed because of fog. Although the Vickers Vanguard managed to get airborne to conduct further tests, technical problems were again encountered forcing the flight to be aborted after only fifteen minutes.

In view of the weather and the problems with the aircraft, the live broadcast had to be re-scheduled rather ominously for Friday, 13 November. Aboard were the Savoy Orpheans Orchestra, singers Robert

Hale, Dion Titheridge, Arthur Chesney, Marion Brown and others named as Gawthorne, Sayers, Cock, West and Oldfield. Hinchliffe again commanded the aircraft and later reported 'BBC concert from the air. Foggy and had difficulty finding Keston receiving station. Took off in the dark at 17.15. Music results good in spite of a slight background of engine noise.'

The party was airborne for an hour but a fractured oil pipe delayed the second half of the broadcast. Hinchliffe again reported: 'Second half of the BBC programme. Weather much better now and fog dispersed. Concert received very well. This is incidentally the first concert ever broadcast from the air and was a great success in spite of the date being Friday the 13th.'

The next day coincided with the third anniversary of the start of official broadcasting in the British Isles; the first broadcast having been made from Marconi House in the Strand when BBC station 2LO had gone on the air by announcing the results of the 1922 general election.

The success of the aerial concert created so much excitement for the pianist and two other orchestra members that they privately hired a DH50 (G-EBKX) for a further flight to celebrate their success. In a trip that lasted three hours, Hinchliffe took the party on a route that over-flew Littlestone, Folkestone, Dover, Calais, Gravelines, Dover, Lympne, Redhill, and Central London. It was quite a high-spirited flight, leaving Hinchliffe to later comment: 'They had not been to bed and had consumed Champagne in large quantities.'

As strange as a live aerial BBC concert might have been, this was surpassed with an in-flight dancing lesson being given aboard an Imperial Airways Argosy 'Silver Wing' service. This took place during 1926 when leading dance exponent, Richard Granville, gave a demonstration of his own particular form of Charleston. He was accompanied by Babette, his partner, as they danced aboard the aircraft. This was followed by a lesson given to a passenger in a space that had been cleared in the cabin. The first in-flight entertainment on an Imperial Airways flight, other than the BBC concert or a dance lesson, was provided for twelve passengers aboard the HP W8b (G-EBBI) on 7 April 1925. A silent film adaptation of Sir Arthur Conan Doyle's book *The Lost World* starring Wallace Beery and Lewis Stone was projected onto a screen as a demonstration aboard the flight from Croydon. Newsreel film of the event still exists and can be viewed on the internet. The American company, Aeromarine Airways, can legitimately claim to have beaten Imperial Airways by screening the first in-flight movie almost four years earlier. The company projected a short film called 'Howdy Chicago' to eleven passengers aboard the amphibian aircraft *Santa Maria* while flying over the city during the Chicago Pageant of Progress in August 1921. There is also a further claim that a single-reel 'short' was projected on a Deutsche Luft Hansa flight on 6 April 1925.

Further survey flights

On a more serious commercial level, Lt Col H Burchall was appointed manager of the Egypt-India route on 10 August at an annual salary of £1,500. The appointment was for a three-year period to coincide with the progression being made to open the corresponding air route. Plans had started to be formalised on the development of the Cairo-Basra service. During November Imperial Airways had placed an order for five Hampsteads costing £10,500 each that were required to enter service as soon as the route opened. Handley Page had been expected to supply the aircraft with an all-metal fuselage but was unable to guarantee the delivery date. In view of this, the order was cancelled and de Havilland was awarded the contract to produce DH26 Hercules in its place.

While the Imperial Airways directors deliberated over which aircraft to buy, Alan Cobham was en-route to Cape Town to survey the Africa route. He departed from Stag Lane on 16 November 1925 in an Armstrong Siddeley Jaguar-powered DH50J (G-EBFO) accompanied by his faithful engineer, Arthur Elliott and a cameraman, B W G Emmott. They arrived in Cape Town on 17 February 1926 after an 8,000-mile flight from Croydon that landed at Paris, Marseilles, Pisa, Taranto, Athens, Sollum, Cairo, Luxor, Assuan, Wadi Halfa, Atbara, Khartoum, Malakal, Mongalla, Jinja, Kisumu, Tabora, Abercorn, Ndola, Broken Hill, Livingstone, Bulawayo, Pretoria, Johannesburg, Kimberley, Bloemfontein and finally Cape Town. The return retraced the same route with fewer stops. Cobham had set a challenge for the captain of the Union Castle liner, SS *Windsor Castle*, that was leaving the same day. Cobham had wagered that he would beat the ship to England and succeeded by two days, arriving at Croydon on 13 March 1926, despite

delays caused by headwinds. Cobham was mobbed by the public as he stepped from the aircraft and was later summoned to Buckingham Palace to meet the King who awarded him the Air Force Cross for his services to aviation. Selfridges grabbed the chance to associate with Cobham by acquiring the aircraft on loan, appropriately painted in the livery of Imperial Airways, to display in their Oxford Street store.

While Cobham was in Africa, Wolley Dod and Col Shelmerdine were conducting a ground survey between Kantara and Karachi. Colonels Minchin and Burchall meanwhile had been gaining experience by flying the proposed India route on behalf of Imperial Airways and were judging the condition of every potential landing ground. This went well, but operational incidents at home were still occurring with astonishing regularity. During March alone eight flights had to be curtailed or cancelled altogether owing to bad weather and a further six experienced mechanical failures. At the end of his qualifying flight for the type, Armstrong had made a good landing in the Vulcan but the undercarriage collapsed. Rogers was forced to land at Lympne after strong winds across the Channel that almost rendered G-EBBI out of control and Olley, on a gold-carrying mission from Basle to London in the Vickers Vimy Commercial (G-EASI), was forced down by snow. His engines had cut out at only 500 feet over what was described as *'bad country'* near Belfort and the aircraft hit a hidden tree stump on landing. This required the aircraft to be dismantled and taken to Luxevil for repairs. Snow had also caused the forced-landing or cancellations of several other flights which gave rise to some comments that the airline was unable to operate its aircraft whenever snow fell. After Dod's DH34 (G-EBBW) toppled over and was damaged during yet another bad weather forced-landing, Brackley

recommended to the board that all cross-Channel passenger flights should cease until Napier Lion engines could be thoroughly tested as replacements for the existing powerplants. Although Dod's aircraft had not been badly damaged, this too required dismantling for transportation to Cologne for repairs and spent five days out of service.

The board meeting minutes provide an interesting portrayal of some of the non-operational aspects of the company and the costs related to them. In March 1925 it was resolved that Imperial Airways would join the International Chamber of Commerce at the princely sum of six Guineas (£6.30). At the same meeting, the board agreed to buy a motor car, costing £300, '...*to be used by the commercial manager while going about his business'* and £200 was also paid to the general manager for using his own car on official company business. Woods Humphery was less fortunate when he was required to sell his company Daimler because the running costs were considered to be too high!

A more disturbing issue concerned an incident involving Capt Rogers who had been temporarily thrown from his seat while encountering climatic forces during a flight. In 1925 there was still no legal requirement for pilots or their passengers to wear lap belts and it was considered that those on board the ill-fated Daimler Hire DH34 that crashed at Ivinghoe in 1923 may have survived if seat belts had been worn. The board collectively agreed to approach the Air Ministry to suggest making seat belts mandatory for pilots. No action was taken and they did not become for pilots and passengers in open cockpits until 1928, but they did not become commonplace until the 1930s, although the first reported use of a belt was credited to Adolphe Pegoud, a Frenchman, when he became the first person to fly upside down in 1913.

Capt Barnard had successfully competed in the 1925 Kings Cup Air Race in an aircraft sporting Imperial Airways decals, although he had not been flying in an official capacity for the company. Even this caused a disagreement after some board members felt Barnard should be financially rewarded for winning the race, if only to offset some of his costs. A heated debate ensued before an agreement was reached to pay Barnard a hundred guineas (£101). Instone vehemently opposed this payment, claiming that had Barnard crashed he would have brought adverse publicity to the company. Apart from this, Barnard had entirely financed his own entry although it later transpired that the aircraft had in fact been entered in the name of Eric Geddes.

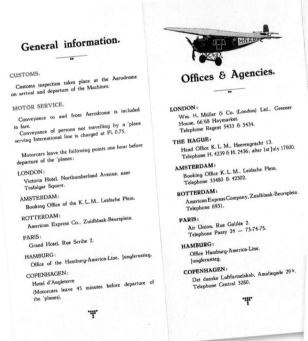

Another European operator running alongside Imperial Airways was the Dutch airline, KLM. This KLM timetable dates from 1924. (CAS)

CHAPTER FIVE

COBHAM SURVEYS THE LINK
TO AUSTRALIA

1926

THE British Public welcomed in the New Year of 1926 full of hope and there appeared to be a greater feeling of confidence among the population. Cars were selling well and there was a boom in entertainment as wireless and gramophones became more widespread in people's homes. The weather, always a British preoccupation, was dreadful as gales and floods swept across the country early in the year forcing many commercial flights to be cancelled. There was also a feeling of increased buoyancy in the economy, but this was short-lived, lasting only until 3 May when the coal-miners went on strike. The miners had gained support from three quarters of the TUC membership and more than three million backed what became dubbed 'The General Strike'. Baldwin was belligerent, refused to hear the miners' grievances and unwisely added fire to the strikers' anger by telling them they were 'breaking the law.' Perhaps, had he been prepared to listen and been less bullying, the strike might have been prevented. The miners remained resilient and stayed out for six months, but the industrial action taken by others failed to last long, ending just nine days after it began. But the strike did prove how an action of this magnitude could rapidly snowball to bring the entire country to its knees. The airlines continued to fly and were inundated for requests for seats because the cross-Channel ferries were not operating. The Paris service was tripled to cope with demand but there were scuffles at Le Bourget as passengers without tickets tried to board aircraft that were already full. Imperial Airways was still hampered by having too few aircraft, allowing foreign competitors to gain an advantage. Newspaper and mail deliveries were maintained during the strike by the RAF which had been joined by flying club aircraft organised by the Royal Aero Club. In February the Air Estimates announced that from £15,755,000 civil aviation would get £462,000 – not a vast amount but more than it received in the previous year although still insufficient to be of much benefit to the burgeoning industry.

Early in the year Col Shelmerdine and Wolley Dod were still away undertaking the ground survey between Kantara and Karachi, and Cols Burchall and Minchin were also still in India assessing appropriate landing grounds.

The Handley Page W10; the commercial version of the military W8d *Hyderabad*, made its maiden flight in February. This was followed by a fortnight of air trials before the type quickly gained its certificate of air worthiness. Within a short time three more were completed and certificated for delivery to Imperial Airways by 30 March. In a ceremony held at Croydon next day, Lady Maud Hoare christened the new equipment *City of Melbourne* (G-EBMM), *City of Pretoria* (G-EBMR), *City of London* (G-EBMS) and *City of Ottawa* (G-EBMT). The prototype W9a Hampstead had previously been named *City of New York* (G-EBLE). At the celebration dinner that followed, Frederick Handley Page took the opportunity to prompt Geddes into saying that Imperial Airways, having started with a nondescript fleet of mixed aircraft, had consolidated by operating 75 per cent of one type, '*The good old Handley Page aircraft.*' The reality of the situation was that the W10

was a 1926 aircraft built to a 1919 design. It was still a bi-plane, it still had wires and struts and un-cowled engines, and it was still far from being passenger friendly. In spite of this it was probably the best British-built passenger aircraft available at that time. The cabin was noisy, draughty and had only low-backed wicker seats that provided little if any comfort, but the Imperial Airways management seemed proud of its new acquisitions. By 13 April the W10s had replaced the DH34s on the Paris route at a fare of 6 guineas (£6.30) for a single ticket, 11 guineas (£11.55) for a return. These had been increased in April but passengers could also use their tickets on the French airline, Air Union.

Armstrong Whitworth was competing with Handley Page with its comparable Argosy, an aircraft of similar size and power to the W10 but with a capacity to carry 20 passengers at 95 mph for up to 520 miles. The first Argosy was flown in mid-March by Frank Barnard who was on leave from Imperial Airways. Barnard was however not a test pilot; nevertheless he enthused over the aircraft's handling despite the failure of one of the Jaguar engines shortly after take-off. Frank Radcliffe BSc, a young engineer employed at the Gloster Aircraft factory was prompted to comment: '*I recently flew in both the Hampstead and the Argosy and can say neither offers the comfort of an old Ford car. As for noise, even the cotton wool did little good. The side bracing wires come through the woodwork in the Argosy with a good big clearance for the draughts to come through. In my opinion the engines should not be attached to the body, but placed on the wings; the noise is far too great with them as they are, and it would appear that a better position would be nearer the trailing edges because the noise would be behind the passengers. Further, the nose engine makes you aware of its presence by the vibration it transmits to the passenger cabin, especially if there is irregularity in cylinder firing. The 'Ripping Panels' on top of the cabin ought to be water-proof, so that when there is rain they do not become 'dripping panels' to the discomfort of the passengers. Then there is the design of the Hampstead's chairs that cause cramped knees, and the Argosy a stiff neck as one's head cannot rest against the chair back. With the present wide wings of a biplane all that some of the passengers see is an expanse of fabric, which is a dull sight. A cantilever monoplane wing seems an absolute necessity; if we place it above the cabin the passengers have a clear view and flying becomes a little more interesting, but when the novelty goes, flying in a commercial airliner is dull.*'

When compared to the smooth lines of the new high-winged, three-engined Fokker aircraft being built by the Dutch, both the Hampstead and the Argosy looked positively dated and Radcliffe's educated opinions were completely justified. He knew what he was talking about, so why did British designers not heed his advice?

The spring of 1926 brought a number of incidents. At the end of March Dismore was flying thirteen passengers from Paris to Croydon in the Handley Page W9 Hampstead *City of New York* when the starboard engine ceased and the propeller sheared off and damaged a wing. Fortunately he was flying high enough to glide the aircraft to land at Littlestone without causing any injuries. Three weeks later the same aircraft suffered another engine failure shortly after leaving Croydon but it was again landed safely. Barnard may, quite literally, have had the

A line-up of Imperial Airlines Handley Page W10 variants at Croydon during their naming ceremony held on 31 March 1926. (CAS/John Stroud)

IMPERIAL AIRWAYS PASSENGER AEROPLANE, CITY CLASS.

Handley Page W10 'City of Melbourne' G-EBMM, which was sold to National Aviation Day Displays in 1926. (CAS)

A cheery group of European pilots celebrate at Croydon in front of the Handley Page W9 Hampstead G-EBLE, City of New York, circa 1926. This aircraft was sold subsequently to New Guinea in January 1929 and became VH-ULK. The pilots are from left to right, C F Wolley Dod (Imperial Airways), A B H Youell (Imperial Airways), Charles Corsin (Air Union - France), Emile Bouderie (Air Union General Manager), Robert McIntosh (Imperial Airways), H G Brackley (Imperial Airways - Air Superintendent), Robert Bajac (Air Union Chief Pilot) and Walter Rogers (Imperial Airways). The last man on the right is unknown, but believed to be a KLM pilot. (CAS)

biggest shock of his flying career when the *City of London* was struck by lightening near Beauvais. This was still a phenomenon most pilots were still yet to encounter. The lower wing had been hit by what he described as '…*like a loud explosion.*' It burnt a hole through the fabric and scorched the main spar causing damage to the aileron. With a misfiring engine and a compass that had gone haywire, Barnard landed safely at Lympne to the relief of his fourteen passengers.

When Horsey also experienced engine problems at 1,000 feet over the Channel en-route to Amsterdam he badly damaged the wings and collapsed the undercarriage when he force-landed in a rough field after barely clearing the cliff tops. It was a close shave and he had luck on his side when he brought his machine to a halt without any injuries. A KLM Fokker nearly came to grief two days later as it approached the English coast in fog so low that the pilot was suddenly confronted with a cliff wall directly in front of him. He was fortunate; by climbing quickly he managed to climb clear of the obstacle to land on the beach at Hythe but the experience had left the pilot badly shaken.

As a safety issue, the board for a second time decided it should scrap all single-engined aircraft. This also helped to satisfy the Government million-mile subsidy stipulation that was later amended to a more complicated ratio requiring the company to fly 425 million horsepower miles. Because of cruise speed differences, it was deemed that every mile flown by a slower marine aircraft would equate to 1½ miles against the total requirement. This led the *Aeroplane* to comment that '*The essence of success is the frequency of service.*' It also meant that the airline had to concentrate on buying aircraft that produced greater engine power.

The progression of the Continental airlines

On 6 January 1926 Deutsche Luft Hansa AG (DLH) was formed although operations did not begin until 6 April. The airline was founded by the amalgamation of Deutsche Aero Lloyd and Junkers Luftverkehr who had both hitherto, operated under subsidies provided jointly by their parent companies, local municipalities and the German State. Aero Lloyd mainly operated services to parts of North Western Europe while Junkers concentrated throughout Central and Northern Europe on routes that were operated by their affiliates Nord-Europa-Union and Trans-Europa-Union. Although Aero Lloyd and Junkers may have cooperated on occasions, more frequently they fought a fierce rivalry to compete for the limited business available on the same routes. The situation was much as it had been in Britain prior to 1924 when the Minister of State for Air aptly referred to things as 'cut-throat.' It clearly made better sense for the two airlines to pool resources as the British airlines had done to form Imperial Airways.

Kurt Weigelt, a key figure at Deutsche Bank and Deutsche Petroleum had written a pamphlet that he titled '*Fusion In the Field of Air Traffic*' that he presented to interested parties. This recommended merging the two German airlines into a single company and this suggestion was accepted by Ernst Brandenburg, the head of aviation at the German Air Ministry. Junkers operated only aircraft of its own manufacture while Deutsche Aero Lloyd had an assortment of equipment that also included a few Junkers that it based at Danzig. By combining these assets the newly formed Deutsche Luft Hansa inherited 126 aircraft consisting of 19 different types that formed a very

The Supermarine Sea Eagle G-EBGS of Imperial Airways that was rammed by a ship and sank at St Peter Port, Guernsey on 10 January 1927. (CAS)

formidable fleet. The company had an initial capital of 50,000 marks with stock split between the German Government (26%), German regional cities and provinces (19%), regional companies (27.5%) and private organisations (27.5%). The assets were later increased by a group of individual investors to a share capital of 25m marks.

The treaties enforced by the Allies after the War had, at least in theory, considerably restricted German aviation practices. But, with typical German aplomb, the country's aviation industry had overcome most of the obstacles imposed upon them by the Allies. In order to operate a large fleet of aircraft the Germans flew many under the trading names of different companies that, for appearances at least, had enlisted foreign involvement. It was estimated that by 1925 the ancestors of Luft Hansa already accounted for 2/5ths of the world's entire commercial aircraft services. One such company was Deutsch-Russiche Luftverkehrs GmbH (Derulft) that was operated by Aero-Union in association with the Russians. The progress the Germans had made to overcome adversity was admirable more especially considering that their entire aviation industry had to be rebuilt from scratch after the War.

The air transport industry throughout Continental Europe was growing at a steady rate and an impressive route structure was developing. During the week ending 1 May, the Belgian operator, SABENA (Société Anonyme Belge d'Exploitation de la Navigation Aérienne) began operating a Brussels-London service using Handley Page W8b and W8e aircraft. Although the Germans had the largest and most efficient of all the airline networks, the French were also making a major impact. The Farman Company Société Générale de Transport Aérien (SEFTA) continued to operate in Northern Europe and on 26 May they commenced a Paris–Berlin service in eight hours using a high-wing Farman F170 monoplane capable of carrying eight passengers.

The Italians had been slow starters but during 1926 there was a flurry of activity with the emergence of several new companies. Although the Italians were progressing they were less advanced than the Germans, French or British. Some of their airlines had been founded for more than a year but none began operating routes until the spring. On 1 April Società Italiana Servizi Aerei (SISA) launched a Turin–Venice–Trieste service, followed by S A Navigazione Aerea (SANA) who opened a domestic service between Genoa-Rome–Naples that began on 7 April. By 1 August Aero Expresso Italiana (AEI), founded in 1923, began flying a long-distance route between Brindisi and Contantinople (now Istanbul) and Transadriatica, S A Italiana di Navigazione Aerea (Transadriatica) opened two routes; Rome-Venice (from 1 February) and Venice-Vienna (from 18 August). A fifth airline, S A Avio-Linee Italiane (ALI) was also formed on 13 November.

On 4 May Capt O P Jones piloted the Handley Page W10 *City of Pretoria* (G-EBMR) that carried the heir to the British throne, HRH Prince of Wales (later King Edward VIII), from Paris to London. This was a landmark in the history of Imperial Airways because it was the first time that an heir to the throne had crossed the English Channel by air or had been flown by Imperial Airways.

The death of Elliott

On 30 June Alan Cobham returned to long distance travels and left the UK to survey the route to Australia. He took off from the River Medway at Rochester to fly to Melbourne in a DH50J seaplane (G-EBFO). On the final sector of the route, Darwin to Melbourne, a wheeled undercarriage was fitted in place of the floats to enable the plane to alight on land. According to his account in *Australia and Back*, it would appear that the pioneering flyer was not in the best of health to make this arduous journey. Sandstorms and monsoon rains battered the aircraft while flying through the Middle East causing Cobham to fly low for extended periods in order to keep the terrain in visual contact.

SIR ALAN COBHAM'S AIR DISPLAY

SIR ALAN J. COBHAM, K.B.E., A.F.C.

This caused Cobham considerable exhaustion but it was a minor inconvenience considering what happened next. A most bizarre incident occurred as he and his engineer, Arthur B Elliott, were cruising at low altitude close to Basra. Cobham suddenly heard what he thought was an explosion coming from the cabin behind. As he turned to discuss the problem with Elliott, he realised that his colleague was quite badly injured, caused by what Elliott believed was a ruptured fuel line. Upon landing at Basra he arranged a hurried transfer of his engineer to hospital and Cobham was told by an RAF engineer that it would have been impossible for a fuel line to have failed in this way. When examined, Elliott was found to have a gaping hole in his side and air was escaping from his lungs. He was obviously in a far worse condition than was first thought and it took a little time to discover that the cause of his severe injury was a bullet that was found lodged in Elliott's body. Examination of the aircraft revealed a distinct hole through the cabin floor and the fuel line that marked the path of the bullet.

Local officials insisted that Cobham should re-trace his route in an attempt to locate the place where the shot had been fired at his aircraft. Eventually, convinced he had found the exact location, local tribesmen in the area were interviewed about the shooting. By chance a wandering nomad admitted firing at the aircraft and was subsequently charged. Meanwhile, despite believing Elliott would pull through, his condition weakened during the night and he died from his wound. Cobham was naturally distraught and it required much encouragement from others for him to regain sufficient willpower to continue with the journey.

The flight was remarkable and it is not only surprising but is a demonstration of the enormous courage Cobham possessed to push himself to continue the survey after the tragic and violent loss of Elliott. Lesser men would have given up there and then, and nobody could have questioned their action. But, through persistence, Cobham fought against his own doubts to reach Melbourne by 15 August, where he rested until he regained his confidence to make the return flight a fortnight later. He covered a total of 28,000 miles in 78 days and spent 320 hours at the aircraft's controls before making a spectacular touch-down on the Thames alongside the Houses of Parliament on 1 October to be greeted by Sir Samuel Hoare, before being subsequently knighted by King George V.

During July the annual report on the progress of civil aviation for the year ending 31 March 1926 was released. This showed that Imperial Airways had carried 14,675 passengers (an increase on the 1,197 for the corresponding period of 1925) although the miles flown had decreased from 890,000 to 865,000.

Route	May to September	October to April
London to Paris	Twice Daily	Daily
London-Paris-Basle–Zurich	Daily	No Service
London-Ostend	Twice Daily	No Service
London-Brussels-Cologne	Twice Daily	Daily
London-Amsterdam (Hanover-Berlin)	Daily	Daily
Southampton-Channel Isles	No Service	Weekly

The first Armstrong Whitworth Argosy began operating on the Imperial Airways London-Paris route on 16 July. This was the first three-engined aircraft to be commissioned and was named *City of Birmingham* (G-EBLO). Barnard, with eighteen passengers, completed the first flight in 1 hr 15 mins with the benefit of a tail wind, but the return flight was considerably longer and took 2 hrs 33 mins.

Brackley dismissed

Politics was never far away from the everyday operations of the company. A strange upheaval took place during 1926 when Herbert Brackley was dismissed by Woods Humphery from his position as air

superintendent; the very man who had recommended him for the job. Surprisingly Frida Brackley makes little comment over the sacking of her husband in *Brackles – Memoirs of a Pioneer of Civil Aviation*, the biography she wrote based on his diaries, although Woods Humphery had been quite scathing in a letter confirming his action. It appears there had been some kind of misunderstanding between the two men that prompted Woods Humphery to write:

Dear Brackley

With regards to our conversation regarding your position in this Company, I have given very careful thought to this matter, and whilst I do not doubt that you have done your best to carry out your duties satisfactorily and much as I regret being obliged to say so, you have not rendered the standard of service which the Company expects from a highly salaried official in your position.

You pressed me to say where you have failed – it is in the case of a post such as yours almost impossible to do so without inviting controversy but, amongst other things your failings have included a lack of foresight, tact and leadership; also a failure to take advantage of the talent which undoubtedly exists among our pilots to provide the Company with information, well considered and balanced views, on matters of importance to the technical development of the Company, or to assist me in the question of policy which should arise in your mind from time to time in your daily work. I have therefore with regret had to tell you and the board that it is not in the best interests of the Company for you to continue in your post.

You asked to be given a further opportunity to show whether you can give the service for which the board look and they have, on my recommendation, consented to give you a further period in which to demonstrate this; I think I need not assure you that I shall only be too pleased to give you all the assistance and advice that I can. I am instructed to say, however, that this letter must be taken as six months' notice to terminate your engagement with this Company, which notice will therefore expire on 1st May, next. If, as you assure me you can render a higher standard of service during this period, the question can be reconsidered by the board, and I would suggest that you come and see me on this subject in say three months time to see how things are progressing.

If you wish to adopt my suggestion I shall be glad to have your acceptance of it.

Yours very truly,
G E Woods Humphery
General Manager

In today's parlance this might be regarded as an official written warning over matters relating to Brackley's work standards although Woods Humphery initially appeared to be dismissing Brackley but then retracted his action by giving him a second chance. This letter can only be viewed as quite a bizarre episode in the relationship between the two men prompting Brackley to respond on 21 November.

Dear Major Woods Humphery

With reference to your letter dated 25th ult., I will do as you suggest and come to see you about the end of January regarding my position in the Company. Before you leave England (author's note: Woods Humphery was preparing to leave for Cairo on 24 November to finalise arrangements for the start of the Cairo to Karachi service) *I want to assure you and I shall be glad if you will convey to the chairman that I will do my utmost during your absence to prove my value to the Company. Our recent talks have, I trust, cleared away any misunderstandings and I must thank you for your kind offer of assistance and advice…*

There was a suggestion that some of the pilots may have felt that Brackley had become too intent on personally conducting the testing of all new aircraft instead of delegating the task to them. But this was because he had always felt it was his responsibility especially if there was any element of risk being involved. Brackley and Woods Humphery were both strong-willed individuals and it was unavoidable that a collision course between two headstrong, ambitious men could have occurred quite regularly. Mrs Brackley summed up the relationship perfectly in her book:

'*Both were young, enthusiastic, ambitious, self-made and single-minded in their devotion to their ideal of work; temperamentally poles apart with a new science and unexplored business to pursue. I can only wonder more and more, despite all the difficulties, disillusionments and misunderstandings of others, mostly, and at times between themselves, what an amazing record they both achieved.*'

Needless to say, Brackley must have satisfied the doubts expressed by his general manager because the sacking seems to have been cast aside and he continued in the position of air superintendent for the duration of Imperial Airways. The debacle appeared to have cleared the air and the two men seemed to have cemented a stronger relationship based on the mutual respect they shared for each other.

The rift between Brackley and Woods Humphery may have reached a satisfactory conclusion, but the airline continued to be plagued with technical problems. On 8 December Jones was flying an Argosy with 12 passengers to Croydon when a tappet rod broke causing an engine to lose power. If that had not been suitably problematic, another of the Jupiter engines simultaneously started to lose oil pressure. Despite the engine power rapidly fading, Jones skilfully performed a safe landing at Pluckley and the passengers were transferred to a train to continue their journey to London. After repairs had been carried out, Jones returned the aircraft to Croydon next day, touching down just as the first of the new DH66 Hercules airliners arrived. With no time for fuss or ceremony, and no route proving trials, the Hercules was immediately put to work next morning, flown by Barnard on a flight to Paris with nine passengers. Unfortunately the weather was bad enough to force an unscheduled landing at Beauvais where pilot and aircraft spent the night before returning to Croydon next morning.

De Havilland had performed a remarkable job with the Hercules. They had designed, built, tested and had three aircraft delivered to Imperial Airways all within a year. The first (G-EBMW) was impressively flown by the de Havilland test pilot, Hubert Broad, in front of an audience of staff at Stag Lane, the manufacturer's Edgware headquarters. Broad performed a number of passes, firstly with one engine shut down and then followed by two of the three closed down. The aircraft had performed admirably.

On 24 November, Woods Humphery and Burchall left England for Karachi to finalise the arrangements for the start of the India service and by 18 December, Wolley Dod had been appointed chief pilot of the new Eastern Route. He flew from Croydon with Brancker to position the Hercules (G-EBMY) at Heliopolis (Cairo) in time for the inauguration of the Egypt–India sector that was due to commence on 12 January 1927. Other passengers aboard the aircraft included Warner (2nd pilot), Air Commodore James G Weir of the RAF Reserve, Mrs Weir and Capt T A Gladstone (who later operated the Cairo–Kisumu sector of the Africa route). Leaving at daybreak, the flight soon encountered heavy snow storms that gave the passengers an extremely bumpy ride which caused Brancker to be violently sick. Despite being commercial aviation's greatest advocate, Brancker had the misfortune of frequently being airsick yet he refused to allow any discomfort to mar his professionalism or to dampen his lively enthusiasm.

The party landed at Lyon for the first night; spent the second at Marignane near Marseilles and refuelled at Pisa to arrive at Naples during the third evening where two more passengers joined the flight. By next day the bad weather had returned causing the passengers further discomfort as they crossed the Gulf of Salerno en-route for Malta. At one point the rain was so heavy that it caused the fabric to strip from a propeller with such a loud report that those on board feared they had encountered serious engine trouble. The weather settled for at time until the Straits of Messina where the Hercules encountered a severe down-draught that caused it to drop 400 feet sending passengers and baggage into free-flight within the cabin. Miraculously nobody was injured and the flight resumed to land at Catania four hours later.

A second Hercules had also left Croydon the same day. This was piloted by Hinchliffe, and bound for Baghdad with Warner and Dudley Travers as co-pilots. The third DH66 Hercules (G-EBMX) left for India on 27 December with the Secretary of State for Air and his wife, Lady Maud Hoare, Air Vice Marshall Sir Geoffrey Salmond (AOC for India) and Lt Bullock (Hoare's private secretary) as passengers. This was a survey flight flown by Barnard as far as Aboukir where Wolley Dod took command for the remainder of the route. Brancker had flown out earlier to join the flight at Baghdad with Woods Humphery. Lady Irwin, wife of the Indian Viceroy, later christened this aircraft *City of Delhi* in a ceremony held on 10 January 1927.

The epic India flight is recorded in a book published in 1927 by Sir Samuel Hoare, *India By Air*, which contains the text of an interesting letter carried by the party, written in five languages, for use in emergencies:

'The bearer of this letter is Lieutenant-Colonel the Rt Hon SIR SAMUEL JOHN GURNEY HOARE, Baronet, Companion of the most distinguished Order of St Michael and St George, Member of Parliament, a Principal Secretary of State and one of the chief ministers of His Most Excellent Majesty George the Fifth, by the Grace of God King of the United Kingdom of Great Britain and Ireland and of the British Dominions beyond the Seas, Emperor of India. He, with his wife, staff and servants, is proceeding by air on an urgent and important British mission. The safety of this exalted personage and his companions is a matter of closest concern to the King of England, who will amply reward persons who may give them any assistance they may need on their historic journey.'

The Seal of the Air Council has been affixed in the presence of SIR WALTER FREDERIC NICHOLSON, KCB, Secretary of the Air Council.

This document aptly sums up the attitude of self-importance that was adopted by British officialdom. Had the aircraft come down killing or injuring the occupants, it would have been interesting to have known what reaction this letter would have received, if any, particularly if it was picked up by an illiterate resident in some remote location. Fortunately, it was never put to the test.

Imperial Airways produced photographs of its pilots that could be bought or given to passengers. Seen here is George Powell (left) and Lionel L. Leleu (above). (CAS)

CHAPTER SIX

MOVING FORWARD

1927-1928

DURING the first week of January, the RAF's 216 Squadron operated its final mail flights on the Cairo to Basra route. From the 7th of the month the first sector of the British Overseas Trunk Route was opened and Imperial Airways DH66 Hercules biplanes began flying from Heliopolis to Basra via Baghdad. The service operated fortnightly carrying passengers and mail with the return flights from Basra timed to meet the P&O mail ships that linked Cairo with Port Said and Marseilles. The initial flight reached Heliopolis on 9 January 1927 having flown from Basra with stops at Baghdad and Gaza. Three days later, the first eastbound service departed from Heliopolis with Dudley Travers in command of G-EBMW that arrived at Basra on 14 January. The aircraft was named *City of Cairo* by King Faud of Egypt. A second Hercules (G-EBMY) left Croydon on 18 December to be positioned for the commencement of the service and was named *City of Baghdad* by King Feisel of Iraq.

In England the winter weather had closed in and during a heavy snow fall at the start of January a canvas hangar collapsed at Croydon Airport damaging an operational Handley Page W10 and several other aircraft that had been withdrawn from service and were being stored.

Behind the scenes the hard working Sefton Brancker had interrupted his Indian visit to hold discussions with the Persian authorities who had revoked a 1925 agreement that allowed Imperial aircraft to over-fly their territory. The Persian Government had become heavily influenced by the Russians and were blocking progress on the next sector of the Trunk Route that would link Basra to Karachi. In freezing weather, Brancker braved treacherous roads to drive to Teheran. Unscathed by the experience, he returned to Baghdad on 14 January where he boarded the scheduled Imperial Airways flight back to Basra.

Two further aircraft were despatched to compliment the three already in position and these were delivered to Cairo between 23-27 January. The fourth was G-EBMZ that was later named *City of Jerusalem* by the High Commissioner to Palestine, Lord Plummer; and the fifth named *City of Teheran* (G-EBNA).

At the start of January, the North Sea Aerial and General Transport company attempted to make its first mail flight from Khartoum to Kisumu in a DH50J Pelican seaplane (G-EBOP) flown by T A Gladstone. The Kenya and Uganda Governments had agreed to pay £2,500 each and Sudan £2,000 to help fund the service but the venture was very short-lived after the aircraft hit a piece of jetsam and crashed on take-off.

On 1 February the DH66, *City of Delhi* (G-EBMX), departed Delhi to head back for England after completing the India survey that had left Croydon on 27 December 1926. It landed at Heliopolis on 7 February after making the flight from Delhi in 32 hrs and 50 mins.

The Air Estimates announced during March suppressed any hopes that civil aviation would receive an appropriate sum; only £464,000 from £15,360,000 was allocated to the industry. Of this £111,000 had been assigned to the Cairo-Karachi service, £137,000 to Imperial Airways European routes, £8,000 for meteorological services and £10,000 for wireless/telegraphy. The start of April marked the third anniversary of the formation of Imperial Airways but the closure of routes indicated that the subsidies awarded by the Government were still insufficient. Of the original services that were operated, only Paris, Zurich, Ostend, Brussels and Cologne remained. Amsterdam and Berlin had been abandoned although Karachi had been introduced. Encouragement was gained when the Cairo to Baghdad and Basra service was increased to a weekly service on 13 April.

The Silver Wing service

Although *The Times* reported on Saturday, 30 April 1927 that the new *Silver Wing* service between Croydon and Paris was due to start that day, services did not officially begin until next day. There was great excitement as the silver-painted Armstrong Whitworth Argosy *City of Glasgow* (G-EBLF) flown by Gordon Olley prepared to depart at noon for Le Bourget. Special pre-inaugural local flights had been made from Croydon two days prior to the service proper being introduced. The *Silver Wing* offered a luxury lunchtime service in the most comfortable aircraft that Imperial Airways could offer at that time. This had an improved interior with eighteen cushioned seats with armrests, curtains and a toilet located at the rear of the cabin. During the 2 hrs 30 mins flight, passengers were treated to a full cabin service that included bar and a light lunch served by a steward from the buffet located at the rear starboard side of the aircraft. This first class service was available for a single fare of 6 guineas (£6.30), or £1 more than the normal fare. The standard version of the Argosy could carry two more passengers that still sat in wicker chairs, but the accommodation was less comfortable than on the luxury service. The *Silver Wing* schedule was also faster and reached Paris in 2 hrs 30 mins and, compared to the DH34, the operating cost per ton mile was considerably improved. By October HP W10 had been introduced as a second class alternative to the *Silver Wing* but there was no steward or bar service provided and it took twenty minutes longer to reach Paris.

Three months later, the French company Air Union responded by announcing its competing *Rayon d'Or* (Golden Ray) service that operated three Loirée et Olivier Le 0 21 twin-engined biplanes. The main cabin of this aircraft was lavishly fitted with restaurant style tables and white linen table cloths along one side of the cabin, with an aisle on the opposite side that allowed the steward to serve passengers. The restaurant aircraft, operated in conjunction with Cie des Wagons-Lits, could accommodate twelve passengers for dining based on a four-per-table configuration. In addition a nose cabin could accommodate six additional passengers when required. Although the aircraft fuselage contained the wording *Avion restaurant Londres-Paris-Marseilles-Tunis* there is doubt whether this service ever flew beyond London and Paris. But the French service was no match for the Argosy which proved so popular that by the following year Imperial Airways was carrying almost 70 per cent of all traffic on the London-Paris route.

Armstrong Whitworth Argosy, G-EBLF 'City of Glasgow', in a publicity photograph to promote the Silver Wing Service in 1928. (CAS)

Armstrong Whitworth Argosy, G-EBLF, *City of Glasgow*. The aircraft was certificated on 29 September 1926, and operated the first Imperial Airways Silver Wing luxury service between London and Paris on 1 May 1927. The aircraft was withdrawn from use in September 1934.

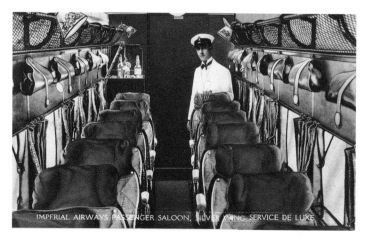

The interior of an Armstrong Whitworth Argosy on the Silver Wing Service. (CAS)

To court some much needed publicity, Imperial Airways began introducing joy-riding flights over London using a W8. The fare of two guineas (£2.10) included transfers from London and provided passengers with a reasonably priced introduction to air travel. The airlines were searching for innovative ways to attract customers to the concept of flying. An interesting experiment was made by Air Union during May when it installed four sleeping berths in a Farman Goliath for passengers travelling overnight between London and Marseilles.

At Croydon there was immense excitement when the lone flyer, Charles Lindbergh, arrived at the aerodrome from France after completing his 3,610-mile solo Atlantic crossing that reached Le Bourget on 21 May. Lindbergh had battled against exhaustion and came close to falling asleep several times during the 33-hour flight The crowds that gathered at Croydon a week after his record-breaking journey were so vast and so enthusiastic that Lindbergh was unable to land his 230hp Ryan monoplane on the first attempt. An estimated 120,000 people had crowded onto the airfield, mobbing the aviator as soon as his aircraft reached the apron. C G Grey in his inimitable way remarked: *'They behaved like a lot of foreigners.'* There had never been scenes approaching the hysteria at Croydon that day. Historians have compared it with the scenes at Heathrow when the Beatles returned from New York in 1963 and to the crowds that gathered at Hong Kong's Kai Tak airport during the final hours before operations were transferred to the new airport at Chek Lap Kok in 1998. Robert McIntosh, *'All-Weather Mac'*, had been commissioned by a national newspaper to fly close to Lindbergh to obtain photographs, but his airspace became overcrowded by amateur flyers when he reached Dartford. McIntosh later remarked how the crowd came so close to his propellers that it was a miracle nobody was decapitated as he taxied after

landing. Dan Minchin, who was also following Lindbergh in the Handley Page Hampstead, was unable to shift the crowd despite flying low enough over Croydon Aerodrome to create a dust storm in an attempt to clear some space. Minchin, seriously low on fuel, was forced to land on a recreation ground in Chipstead. Yet, miraculously, despite much pushing and shoving, the crowd remained amicable and the American pioneer was carried aloft to the control tower by his admirers while the *Spirit of St Louis* was safely hangared for the night.

On 15 July Imperial Airways introduced a weekday summer service between Croydon and Le Touquet to capture the day-tripper and holiday market. On 11 August, Wolley Dod, with the RAF navigator C H Keith, made the first flight to Bahrain in a DH 66 chartered by a pearl merchant. A night stop was made at Basra before completing the journey next day. A Southampton-Guernsey service commenced on 6 October 1927 using the Supermarine Swan flying boat, G-EBJY, that operated until February 1929.

Minchin was in trouble again when he crashed the Handley Page W9A Hampstead (G-EBLE) into a field at Cudham near Westerham on 27 June after again running out of fuel, just 11 miles short of Croydon. The tri-motor aircraft had been returning from Paris with a compliment of nine passengers which all escaped injury. The aircraft narrowly averted complete disaster by narrowly missing a house, but it hit some trees that damaged the starboard wings and undercarriage. In an official enquiry held on 17 August the Accident Investigation Branch concluded that Minchin was an experienced pilot who had served with distinction in the RAF and had flown for Imperial Airways for three years. In the ten days prior to the incident, Minchin had flown the Paris-London route on five occasions and on three of these he had used special 0.708 gravity petrol that contained a small amount of Ethyl fluid. The report failed to mention whether this fuel type may have been significant to the cause of the accident but it seems unlikely. The fuel tanks of the aircraft were empty but no leaks were found in the fuel pipes and there appeared to be no engine problems. Consequently the accident investigation concluded that '... *the accident was due to errors of judgement, amounting to carelessness, on the part of the pilot in that he (1) flew the aircraft at a speed considerably above the normal cruising speed (2) failed to make use of a fuel economiser, and (3) failed to keep watch on the amount of fuel in the tanks.*' The report added that the aircraft would have reached Croydon if it had been flown at a normal cruising speed, but it criticised the fact that an insufficient amount of fuel had been carried to permit the aircraft to remain in the air for three hours. It was known that a friendly rivalry existed between Minchin and Hinchliffe. They were friends who, on occasions, would be known to race to be the first to reach their destination. On the day of the crash there had been a report that suggested Minchin had overtaken an unidentified Argosy of the company. Hinchliffe's logbook revealed that he had also been flying from Paris to Croydon in Argosy G-EBOZ which was suffering some kind of engine trouble. It is likely that Minchin recognised the Argosy, concluded his friend was flying it and decided to increase speed to beat him home. The investigation sealed Minchin's fate and he was dismissed by Imperial Airways although his name would re-appear later, but not in a context associated with the airline.

A major tragedy struck on 28 July when one of the most acclaimed pilots of the day, Frank Barnard, was killed while testing his Jupiter-powered Badminton bi-plane that he had intended to fly in the Kings Cup Air Race during the August Bank Holiday. Barnard had stalled while trying to turn into the wind and the aircraft swiftly plummeted into the ground. This prompted a tribute by the often vehement founder/editor of *The Aeroplane* C G Grey: '*He was one of the best fellows we have ever had in British aviation. He had an unusual gift for imparting information. Few have done more to establish the practical side of commercial aviation.*' Barnard was a well respected and much loved character who had piloted royalty and his funeral on 3 August at Deauville, France was well attended by airmen from both sides of the Channel.

In order to improve communications all Imperial Airways aircraft were fitted with fixed aerials to replace the trailing wires that had been

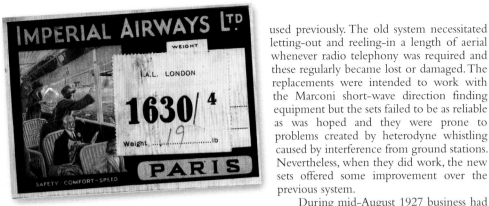

A 1927 Imperial Airways Baggage Label. (author's collection)

used previously. The old system necessitated letting-out and reeling-in a length of aerial whenever radio telephony was required and these regularly became lost or damaged. The replacements were intended to work with the Marconi short-wave direction finding equipment but the sets failed to be as reliable as was hoped and they were prone to problems created by heterodyne whistling caused by interference from ground stations. Nevertheless, when they did work, the new sets offered some improvement over the previous system.

During mid-August 1927 business had been booming for Imperial Airways. The *Silver Wing* service was proving extremely popular and during the course of a single week, the airline carried 565 passengers on 87 flights. The winter months were foggy, causing delays and cancellations which gave pilots ample opportunity to indulge in banter and practical joking with the ground crews. There was an element of stiff competition between the pilots and as soon as the meteorological officers announced a break in the weather there was a scrimmage to be the first in the air. The winter also brought complaints from passengers flying in the W10s and Argosys because the cabins were exceptionally cold. Muffs had been installed around the engine exhausts to enable heat to be transferred to the cabin, but these were ineffective and the engineers had to invent a different way to keep passengers warm. They devised a system that relied on physics to use the low pressure from the cockpit to draw warm air forward

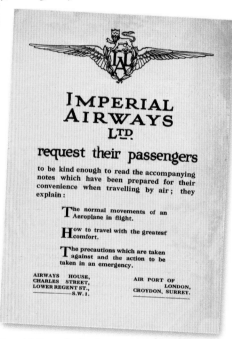

Imperial Airways' notice to passengers from 1927. (author's collection)

from the rear of the aircraft to the front of the cabin to provide heat for the passengers. The Argosy was also susceptible to turbulence caused by its low wing loading. On occasions this caused the aircraft to drop like a stone without warning, often during meal service, giving rise to a great deal of concern among the passengers. Although pilots liked the long-travel undercarriage that allowed them to manoeuvre more easily over the undulating grass runways, the heavy controls made them very tiring to fly.

By the end of the third financial year, Imperial Airways had made a small profit of £11,000 that was achieved by maintaining operations on 92 per cent of all European flights and on all of the Middle Eastern schedules. The latter could be maintained more readily because the good weather of the region made it unnecessary to cancel flights. The extension to Karachi was still being blocked by the Persians but the British Government, as usual, procrastinated by providing little in the way of diplomacy to rectify the problem. There was the usual call by Imperial Airways for the Government to increase the subsidy it needed to maintain efficient and profitable services. Geddes was quick to remind politicians that the success of foreign competition was owed much to the support their airlines were receiving from their governments, but the British Government refused to address the status quo.

Cobham Surveys Africa

On 17 November Sir Alan Cobham returned to his long-distance travels and departed on a long survey of Africa. This was the Charles Wakefield Africa Survey, a round trip of 20,000 miles in a Rolls-Royce

Condor-powered Short Singapore flying boat (G-EBUP). He left Rochester, re-positioned at Hamble then flew via Malta, the Nile, Great Lakes and around the coast of Durban to finish at Cape Town. After 82 take-offs and landings, Cobham returned to the UK via the west coast of Africa and reached Plymouth on 31 May 1928 after completing 330 flying hours. Lady Cobham accompanied him on the venture along with H.V. Worrall (pilot), crew members F Green and C E Conway, as well as the Gaumont film cameraman, C R Bonnett who made a full-length film of the journey. The progression of the survey was far from smooth. When reaching Malta, Cobham had to divert to St Paul's Bay because of high seas at Valetta. Later, while under tow to the Grand Harbour at Valetta, the starboard wing float was torn off in stormy seas. The port float then became waterlogged as the aircraft was being dragged up a slipway by a team of 200 men and a part of a wing had to be cut off because a wall prevented the aircraft from being removed safely from the water. The Shorts works had to be called into action to build an entirely new wing complete with floats and elevators that was shipped to Malta before the flight could resume. It miraculously finished the job within a fortnight, but Cobham's aircraft was further damaged by the violence of the storm that continued unabated for ten days. When the weather eventually eased the flight resumed via Benghazi, Tobruk and Mongalla, then on to Entebbe and Mwanza on Lake Victoria. More delays followed when the Colonial Office required Cobham to side-step to Khartoum before re-tracing his route to Lakes Tanganyika and Nyasa before turning inland to Beira. Once there Cobham turned his aircraft to follow the coastline via Lourenço Marques to Durban where the Singapore underwent a three-week inspection. This was the first flying boat to be seen in Cape Town and when the aircraft eventually landed at the city it was greeted by a rapturous welcome.

The return flight was also plagued with delays. After leaving Cape Town Cobham flew to Banana Creek at the mouth of the Congo, where crew member Green was taken ill and had to be off-loaded and transferred to hospital by boat. A hailstorm forced the aircraft to take refuge at Libreville before continuing via Lagos where an engine vibration caused by a fractured crankcase had to be repaired at Fresco Bay. More time was lost when barnacles encrusting the hull outer skin had to be removed at Freetown, but things improved and the Singapore returned to England via Bathurst, Port Etienne, La Luz (Grand Canary), Casablanca, Gibraltar, Barcelona and Bordeaux.

Cobham's latest epic flight created a renewed interest in the flying boat and Imperial Airways was not slow to realise the potential of these machines as future airliners. Short Brothers had almost completed a sister design to the Singapore that Cobham had flown called the Calcutta. The aircraft was a three-engine bi-plane with open cockpit and comfortable accommodation for 15 passengers in a cabin configuration that comprised of four rows of three, one row of two and a single seat at the rear. The aircraft had a toilet and separate washroom on the starboard side at the rear of the cabin and there was a steward's buffet cabinet and a twin oil cooker. The seats had pneumatic cushions covered in royal blue leather that could quickly be detached to use as buoyancy aids. The Calcutta was an impressive machine with a higher level of comfort and finish that air passengers had so far been denied.

As 1927 progressed towards another year, Britain was gripped by one of its severest winters. Villages were cut off by deep snow drifts and Air Taxis, the Imperial Airways charter division managed by Gordon Olley, was fully occupied in delivering food parcels that were dropped to isolated communities. In marked contrast to the conditions at home, Dudley Travers piloting the DH66 Hercules, *City of Cairo* (G-EBMW), above the Iraqi desert experienced a period of concern when strong headwinds exhausted his fuel, forcing him down between landing grounds numbers 5 and 6, two hundred miles west of Baghdad. Ground vehicles were sent out with fuel for the stricken aircraft and an air search was instigated but Travers could not be located for two days. By chance, Capt Warner, flying another Hercules along the desert track, spotted the grounded aircraft and was able to land nearby. There was no need for concern while they waited to be rescued. Travis, his crew and four

Imperial Airways timetable cover circa 1928.
(CAS)

passengers were entertained by a friendly crowd of Arabs. The passengers and mail were transferred to Warner's aircraft while Travers had to sit and wait for the petrol to arrive before he could fly his aircraft back to Baghdad.

The new airport

In February 1923 Sir Sefton Brancker, in a lengthy speech given at the Third Air Conference, made mention of a scheme that was being considered to build an aerodrome on top of one of the London railway terminals. This would certainly have been an interesting concept, but it was dismissed on financial grounds when it was realised that the estimated cost of the project would have been in the region of £4m. Something built on terra firma was selected as a more practical option and a major event occurred in British civil aviation history when the new Croydon Airport opened for business. The Croydon Aerodrome Act had been passed in 1925 allowing the Waddon and Wallington airfields to be combined and Plough Lane to be extensively developed. Work had started during 1926 on a design drawn up by staff at the Building and Works Department of the Air Ministry. Wilson Lovatt and Son Ltd were contracted to undertake the work and by January 1928 the airport was ready to open having cost the Government £267,000. The redevelopment of the original aerodrome enlarged the facility so that for the first time part of it fell within the boundary of the Borough of Croydon from where the airport took its name.

The main buildings were situated on the east side of the aerodrome close to the former Coldharbour Lane. The road had been developed as a major artery, a part of the A23, named the Purley Way that linked London with Brighton. The fifty-room Aerodrome Hotel, half with private bathrooms, was built at the entrance to replace the former Trust House establishment. This became a popular meeting place and was the focus for celebratory dinners including the official airport opening luncheon held on 20 September 1928 attended by Sir Samuel Hoare. The former huts and sheds in Plough Lane that had served as offices to the fledgling airlines since 30 March 1920 were abandoned and staff moved into the impressive steel and concrete terminal building. This was constructed using a steel frame and around 50,000 concrete blocks that were faced on the exterior using a ¾ inch aggregate of china clay, sand and rapid hardening Portland cement. The building was 250 feet in length, 180 feet deep and stood 30 feet high with the addition of a 50 feet high control tower built on the rear. This overlooked a concrete apron and to the side aircraft hangars and workshops were built. The terminal contained a central booking hall with individual airline desks, check-in facilities, cafe and a shop. In the centre there was a clock displaying the current time at world airports and a map, regularly amended by staff that displayed the prevailing weather across Europe. Although the new booking hall facilities were opened, the old control tower in Plough Lane remained in use until the new one became fully operational on 25 April.

Although the official opening of the new passenger terminal by Lady Maud Hoare had to wait until 2 May, flights began operating from 30 January 1928 with the departure of the 0800 hrs Imperial Airways service to Paris.

During the winter discussions were held between Imperial Airways and Government members of the Irish Free State over proposals to operate a London to Dublin service using Handley Page aircraft, and between Liverpool and Dublin using the Calcutta flying boat. Imperial Airways also made an attempt to enter the holiday market. Advertisements were placed from the end of January 1928 that promoted an aerial pleasure cruise around Europe and North Africa using the Argosy with an on-board steward. For a cost of 435 guineas (£456.75) (more than £20,061 at today's values) including hotel accommodation, the tour was planned to depart from London and visit 23 destinations: Paris (twice), Bordeaux, Biarritz, Barcelona, Alicante, Malaga, Seville, Tangier, Cassablanca, Marakesh, Fez, Oran, Algiers, Biskra, Tunis, Catania, Naples, Rome, Venice, Pisa, Marseilles and Lyon before returning to Croydon via Paris. Evidence to confirm whether this ambitious excursion ever took place has been impossible to find,

An Imperial Airways Short S8 Calcutta flying boat on the Sea of Galilee. (CAS)

but because of the prevailing economic situation in Britain at that time it seems unlikely. Similarly the proposed routes to Dublin never got beyond the discussion stage.

The Calcutta's debut

On 13 February 1928 the first Short S8 Calcutta flying boat was launched on the River Medway at Rochester carrying the registration G-EBVG. After a very brief two-minute jaunt the following day, the first proving flight was not made by John Lankester Parker until the 20 February. Brackley had made a strong impression on Imperial Airways to adopt the flying boat

The Air Union Golden Ray that competed with Imperial Airways on the London-Paris route 1927. (CAS)

after the work he had done in Japan with the Imperial Japanese Navy who had effectively used Short FS flying-boats. Oswald Short had first shown plans of the Calcutta to Air Commodore J G Weir at the Air Ministry. Some weeks elapsed before Short and Parker were summoned to meet Sir Sefton Brancker, the Director of Civil Aviation. Brancker offered to order three aircraft at a cost of £42,000 and although Short accepted, he explained that he would lose £6,000 per aircraft on the deal. The order was revised a few days later and one Calcutta was axed allowing Short to increase the unit price to £18,000.

After some modifications had been made following the first flight, Brackley took the Calcutta to 12,000 feet with a full load on 27 February. Sir Samuel Hoare was given a six-minute demonstration flight on 10 March and five days later the aircraft was flown from Rochester to Felixstowe to undergo sea trials. Brackley had intended to make his own proving flight on 26 July on the Southampton-Guernsey route but fog forced it to be abandoned. The next day G-EBVG (later named *City of Alexandria*) was granted a certificate of air worthiness and was returned to Rochester the same day. What followed was probably a well-devised publicity stunt by Short and Parker flying the Calcutta from Rochester to Westminster where they landed on the Thames between Lambeth Bridge (then a suspension footbridge) and Vauxhall Bridge. A Port of London Authority launch towed the aircraft to the Albert Embankment where it remained moored until 5 August allowing Members of both Houses to visit including Winston Churchill. Oswald Short was supported in his guided tours by Colonel, the Master of Sempill who had moored his Blackburn Bluebird nearby. At the end of the period, Parker took-off from a stretch of river near Vauxhall narrowly missing Lambeth Bridge as he gained height. He followed this with a low pass in front of the Palace of Westminster. On 9 August Brackley took delivery of the Calcutta for Imperial Airways and flew it

Nearest to the camera, the Air Union Rayon D'or (Golden Ray) circa 1927. (CAS)

from Rochester to Southampton prior to making the return proving flight to Guernsey next day.

After making an initial trial flight two days before with Brancker on board, Imperial Airways provided the Short Calcutta (G-EBVH) with F J Bailey and Donald Drew who flew a special service to support the celebrations for Liverpool Civil Week that were held from 24 September to 4 October. This carried passengers and mail between the River Mersey to the Musgrave Channel in Belfast for a single fare of £3 10s 0d (£3.50) and £6 10s 0d (£5.50) return.

On 12 March the Air Estimates for 1928 clearly proved there had been no change to the policy of allocating as little as possible to civil aviation. From £16,042,000 only £415,000 was destined towards the development of the industry. The lack of resources provided by the

A very evocative Imperial Airways fold-out timetable/brochure
for services between London and Le Touquet from 1927.
The aircraft depicted is the Armstrong Whitworth Argosy
G-EBLF 'City of Glasgow'. (author's collection)

Government was no doubt bothering Brancker when he gave a lecture at the Institute of Transport during the previous week. The subject was *Progress in Air Transport* and Brancker, speaking as vice-president of the Institute, compared what was being achieved in mainland Europe, the British Empire and America with the situation in Great Britain. In a speech that was both profound and somewhat futuristic he criticised the lack of progress caused by successive British Governments that had continued to show a remarkable lack of insight and remained unwilling to support issues that should be addressed as priorities. This was particularly poignant considering this remains the case today. Brancker's speech was, as to be expected from a man of his stature, straight to the point: '*It must be asked why Great Britain is so far behind in the volume of operations as compared to the rest of the world? The answer is simple. This country has been spending much less money than any other, and for various reasons: as a nation, it is naturally opposed to the granting of subsidies for commercial enterprises; it is by nature conservative, and it does not adopt new ideas with rapidity; and it is endeavouring to pay its debts: as a result it is ruled by a ruthless Treasury in regard to expenditure on commercial flying. Last year British civil aviation received only £230,000 in subsidy. For 1928 France has allocated approximately one million pounds sterling, Germany has voted nearly one million pounds sterling and, in addition, the local States and Municipalities contribute the equivalent of about £300,000 in direct subsidies. Britain is spending less than a quarter of the same that these two nations are each applying to this particular industry.*

'*Germany is in an exceptionally advantageous position respecting air transport. By the Treaty of Versailles, Germany is forbidden to maintain any military air organisation or to own any military aircraft. The result is that all her brains, energy and money are being devoted to the development of commercial aviation.*'

'*America also has great advantages over us in this new form of transport. It is a huge country, with a wonderful climate and a big, intelligent and wealthy population separated by long distances; it is also free of all international complications. The result is today air transport is really booming.*'

'*One thing Britain can claim unhesitatingly: its quantity may not be great but its quality is good. Its administration and aircraft provide a model of safety and reliability which is the admiration of the whole world. Having established its high standard of safety and reliability, Britain's main problem now is to reduce the cost of operation and so eliminate the necessity of artificial assistance.*'

'*A flourishing aircraft industry is of vital importance to Great Britain. At present the chief markets of the world require military aircraft and the demands for commercial aircraft are comparatively small. When air transport can pay its way without Government assistance this position will be completely reversed. There will be numerous demands for commercial aircraft in every part of the world and the market for military aircraft will become comparatively unimportant. Thus, I hope that, in the not very distant future, the aircraft industry of this country will be chiefly concerned in the production of commercial aircraft for every nation in the world.*'

The Atlantic was a major challenge to all air-minded nations but some progress was being made to bridge this vast expanse from east to west. Capt Hermann Köhl (1888–1938) and Commander James Fitzmaurice (1898-1965), with their passenger, Baron Günter von Hünefeld (1892-1929), known in some quarters as 'The Crazy Baron', crossed from Baldonnel, near Dublin to Greenly Island off Labrador. The journey was made in the all-metal Junkers W33 *Bremen*. (D1167) and took 37 hours. It had been nine years since Alcock and Brown had made their epic west-east crossing. On 12 April 1928 the trio; two Germans and one Irishman, left Ireland and headed for New York. They carried no radio and the small aircraft had no heating. The Junkers controls were heavy and the two pilots each took half hour spells flying while the other tried to rest. Strong headwinds made the flight difficult, restricting forward movement to a maximum of 100 mph. Next morning, as dawn broke, with their fuel supply starting to run perilously low, they were anxious to spot land. Eventually, through the mist, they spotted what they first thought was the smoke plume from the funnels of a liner. As they got nearer they realised this was not a ship but the profile of a stone lighthouse. They decided to land but the rocky terrain ripped off the landing gear and broke the propeller causing the aircraft to skid to a halt on its belly. Fortunately the occupants were uninjured

An IA London to Paris passenger ticket dated 2 August 1927. (author's collection)

but they were dismayed to find they had been blown badly off course. Instead of arriving near New York they were on a tiny island to the far north-west tip of Newfoundland. An astonished lighthouse keeper informed the Point Armour radio station of their arrival and news was passed to the Canadian authorities. A pair of Fairchild aircraft were sent from Lake Saint Agnes, Quebec Province 700 miles away to rescue the *Bremen's* crew. These left on 14 April but took till the next day, flying through snow storms and with an overnight stop, to reach the stranded aircraft. Although the *Bremen* was repaired there was insufficient room to take-off and it was damaged again on the rough terrain in an aborted attempt to get airborne. The aircraft was later dismantled and sent to the USA by sea where it was vandalised by souvenir hunters while being displayed at a New York railway station. It was finally acquired by the late Henry Ford and placed in the Ford Museum at Greenfield Village at Dearborn near Detroit and at the time of writing is believed to be on loan to Bremen Airport after being renovated by Lufthansa.

All three of the Junkers crew had made unsuccessful attempts previously but this time their single-mindedness was being rewarded. Hünefeld and Köhl had attempted their earlier crossing from Dessau, Germany in the same aircraft, the *Bremen*, on 14 August 1927 but were defeated by bad weather. They had intended to make the first double crossing and were accompanied by an identical Junkers, the *Europa*, piloted by Edzard and Ristiez that had taken-off at the same time but was forced back by engine trouble. Fitzmaurice had also made a previous attempt on 16 September 1927 with Imperial Airways pilot Robert McIntosh in the Fokker monoplane (G-EBTS) but they too were defeated by the elements. Strong headwinds had cut the aircraft's forward motion by half and after three hours the attempt was aborted. McIntosh, the one known as *All Weather Mac*, had failed to live up to his name. He had taken unpaid leave from the airline to attempt the crossing, but delays quickly ate up his allocated leave time. McIntosh wrote to Woods Humphery requesting further unpaid leave but this was denied in a stark reply: '*Unless you return by the date specified we must ask you to resign from Imperial Airways.*' McIntosh, forced to make a quick choice, stuck with his attempt to be first to make the first east-west Atlantic crossing. The choice had been a bitter one to make and McIntosh felt it was totally uncompromising and remained convinced that, had his attempt succeeded, Imperial Airways would have benefited.

On 25 July a stone cairn and a plaque was erected at Greenly Island to commemorate the *Bremen's* epic flight. This served as a poignant reminder of the 20 who had already died attempting to make the perilous crossing. One of these was Capt Walter R (Ray) Hinchliffe, the one-eyed Imperial Airways pilot and his passenger, the Hon. Elsie Mackay, daughter of Lord Inchcape, who had left Cranwell, Lincolnshire on 13 March 1928 and were never seen again. Hinchliffe had bought a single-engine Stinson Detroiter monoplane that he had shipped from America. This was prepared in readiness for the crossing and was named *The Endeavour*. It had been known that Hinchliffe would be accompanied, but the identity of his passenger remained secret until after the aircraft was reported missing. Rumours abounded but nobody guessed the mystery passenger to be a woman, especially someone as prominent as Ms Mackay, an accomplished pilot in her own right.

Another former Imperial Airways pilot who lost his life attempting to cross the Atlantic was the accomplished flyer, Lt Col Frank '*Freddy*' Minchin CBE DSO DFC, who had previously been dismissed by Imperial Airways (mentioned earlier) in June 1927. He had been financed for the venture by Princess Lowenstein-Wertheim, a married daughter of the Earl of Mexborough who was a passenger on the flight. The test pilot and flying instructor, Leslie Hamilton had accompanied Minchin and the Princess when the flight departed on 31 August 1927. A Fokker monoplane with a 450 hp Jupiter engine was bought and specially strengthened for the attempt and before leaving this had been christened *St Raphael* and blessed by the Bishop of Cardiff, but no Godly intervention could prevent tragedy from occurring. The aircraft was extremely heavy and had difficulty getting airborne. Around 2200

This page and opposite: Although there is some damage to these photographs, they nevertheless show some interesting detail in a ceremony photographed at Kalendia Aerodrome near Ramallah, north of Jerusalem. The British High Commissioner, Lord Plumer, is seen (below) pulling off the cover of a nameplate to christen a de Havilland DH66 Hercules airliner of Imperial Airways as the 'City of Jerusalem'. The ceremony is believed to have taken place on or around 18 March 1927.
(US Library of Congress)

hrs the aircraft was spotted flying high over the mid-Atlantic by the crew of the oil tanker *Josiah Macy* but this is believed to have been the final sighting. Nothing more was heard and the aircraft and the occupants disappeared without trace.

24 April 1928 saw the incorporation of Alan Cobham's Aviation Company with North Sea Aerial and General Transport Limited, the two companies involved in the Khartoum-Kisumu African venture mentioned earlier. The new company became known as Cobham-Blackburn Airlines Limited with the intention of operating the Blackburn Nile flying boat over parts of Africa. The project became thwarted by the Government when, two years later, it directed that all Empire routes must be operated by Imperial Airways.

A further long-distance breakthrough occurred when Charles Kingsford Smith and his crew departed from Oakland, California on 31 May to make the first crossing of the Pacific. On board the Fokker F VIIb-3m *Southern Cross* was co-pilot C T P Ulm, Harry Lyon (navigator) and James Warner (radio operator). The flight touched down at Eagle Farm, Brisbane on 9 June after a flight time of 83 hrs 11 mins. Stops had been made at Honolulu, Suva and Fiji. The *Southern Cross* was preserved and was exhibited at Eagle Farm Airport until the closure of the facility when it was moved to a special glass hangar at Airport Drive close to the International Terminal at Brisbane Airport.

An interesting experiment was conducted on 15 June 1928 when the Argosy aircraft, *City of Glasgow* (G-EBLF) flown by Gordon Olley competed against the London North Eastern Railway's famous *Flying Scotsman* to be first to reach Edinburgh from London. The Argosy took off from Croydon with eighteen passengers en-route to Edinburgh Turnhouse Airport as the train left Kings Cross for Waverley station. After making two refuelling stops and brief diversions to view picturesque scenery, the Argosy reached Edinburgh with fifteen minutes to spare. The margin should have been wider but Olley and his passengers had to make their way from Turnhouse to the railway platform to await the train's arrival. As Olley pointed out in his book, *A Million Miles in the Air*, the contest was not a genuine race; had it been, the airliner with its superior speed would have won hands down. It was more a publicity stunt organised to compare the two forms of travel for comfort and convenience. An assortment of journalists were aboard both modes of transport and a train driver accompanied Olley in the Argosy cockpit and an Imperial Airways pilot rode the locomotive footplate. The two were connected by radio that gave rise to some good humoured banter during the journey. The train driver aboard Olley's aircraft was amused when they were due to rendezvous with the train and fly above as it crossed the River Tweed at Berwick for the benefit of press photographers. As he reached the Royal Border Bridge Olley could see the train about to cross and positioned the Argosy overhead. But Olley had arrived late and was unaware that the *Flying Scotsman* had already crossed and the train he had located was the local stopping train! The plane was obviously faster between the two cities but economically it was the loser because it could only carry 18 passengers against several hundred on the train. Taking the payload and convenience issues into consideration, it is difficult to appreciate what the exercise was meant to prove apart from achieving a certain level of free publicity. A contemporary report published in the *The Bystander* of 27 June 1928, reached its own conclusion: '*The passengers were agreed that from the point of view of comfort the airway quite held its own.*'

In the summer of 1928, a new ten-year agreement was signed between the Air Ministry and Imperial Airways that came into effect from 1 April 1929. This outlined the subsidy levels the airline would receive on a decreasing scale for the European and India routes. For 1929-30 and 1930-31 this was set at £335,000; thereafter the amount reduced to £310,000 for the next four years; for the seventh and eighth years to £170,000; £120,000 for the ninth and £70,000 for the final year of the agreement.

There was still a strong reluctance, even a fear of flying. In a book written in 1928 entitled *European Skyways* by Lowell Thomas the author of *With Lawrence in Arabia,* Thomas's wife vividly describes her first, horrific, flying experience. This paints a vivid description by an early airline passenger that might have deterred many from stepping aboard an aircraft. It aptly emphasises the fear factor and the unpleasantness associated with cruising at low altitudes. In the following excerpt, Mrs Thomas describes her flight on the Imperial Airways *Hampstead* from Croydon to Amsterdam:

'*We swoop up and down and lurch from side to side. Every time we plunge into the cloud or emerge on the other side of one, we get a bump. The sky bristles with invisible bumps. We have been in the air nearly half an hour, and at last I am plucking up courage to look at the world below. I feel like a giantess flying over pygmy villages. Even the horses in the fields run when they hear the mighty hum of our three Jaguars.*

'*But by the time we have passed over Ashford and start over Romney Marsh, where the smugglers used to hide, I no longer have an interest in scenery. I feel my first suggestion of airsickness. When I have the ambition to look around me, I discover that there is a special basin under each chair. Most of the passengers are holding them in their laps now. They are ghastly green and apparently feel far worse than I do. If this merciless dipping doesn't let up, I don't care whether I land in Holland or drop into the Channel.*

'*I forget my air misery for a moment, as we soar over the famous chalk cliffs. Down where the boys are gathered with their butterfly nets is the very spot on which Julius Caesar and his legions camped when they crossed the narrow seas from Gaul. That town built of red bricks is Folkestone, where we have come ashore so many times on our way from Boulogne. The big cliff covered in shrubs is the Leas. I climbed it once and found a memorial to William Harvey, discoverer of the circulation of blood. If he could take a sample of mine now, he would need a powerful microscope to find any red corpuscles. The heavy rain clouds through which we have been flying and which have caused all the bumps are called 'Folkestone Girls'. Just leave it to the men. They know where to put the blame even for fickle weather.*

'*A few small steamers are darting across from Folkestone and the water looks smooth as a billiard table from the edge of the Folkestone Girls. I feel safer flying over the sea, although I realise this is a land plane. Our landing gear, or undercarriage, as airmen call it, consists of huge shock absorbers and two big wheels with pneumatic tyres to soften the jolts when we come down into a field. All the same, I think it would be less disagreeable to fall into the English Channel than into Romney Marsh or into one of those chalk quarries back in Kent.*

'*There are lifebelts in the narrow rack that runs along each side of the cabin above the windows. They are not inflated and a notice requests passengers not to blow them up except in an emergency. But I calmly disobey, because I am curious to see how long it will take to inflate one. And, after all we might take a flop into the Channel! I find it takes me fifteen minutes! Anything and everything can happen in an aeroplane in fifteen minutes. For instance, by the time my lifebelt is of any use as a life-saver, we have crossed the Channel, turned north at Cape Gris Nez, and are skirting the French coast, with the harbour and buildings of Calais behind us, and the sandy beach leading north to Dunkirk and Ostend just ahead…*'

Her husband then took up the story: '*When I saw my wife and the other passengers reaching for the basins under their chairs I began to feel pea-green myself; in all my experiences in aeroplanes, never before had I flown in an enclosed cabin instead of the open air. The difference is preponderantly in favour of flying outside. The other passengers insisted on keeping the windows closed and the atmosphere rapidly grew unbearably stuffy. Some of the passengers were whiffing aromatic salts. One young man was sadly biting into a sandwich and another desperately sucking lemon. The lady in front of me clutched to her heaving bosom a bottle labelled 'Mother Sills' Remedy for Sea Sickness'. As the trip grew bumpier and bumpier and my neighbours sicker and sicker, I unbuttoned my shirt collar and I would have given one hundred pounds for one pint of fresh air.*' Enough said!

In an attempt to establish more airports throughout Great Britain the Air Ministry circulated letters to the town clerks of communities with a population of more than 20,000 hoping to encourage councils to become more 'air-minded'. This had little effect and there was not the expected mass clamour by local authorities to construct new airfields.

When the Air Estimates board had met the future equipment requirements of Imperial Airways was debated. The Hon F G Guest put forward a strong argument to further the development of flying boats. He felt that the geography of many of the Dominion countries favoured landings on water and suggested that Southampton should be adopted as the main base for these aircraft. Guest prompted a programme of '*bold expenditure*' to ensure that a permanent, assured and prosperous aircraft industry could be established.

A Parliamentary debate ensued that decided to set aside £450,000 to defray civil aviation expenses. This was to be paid to the industry by 31 March 1929. Sir Robert Lynn advocated that subsidies should be paid towards operating an internal service between Southampton,

A selection of pages from a 1928 KLM brochure outlining routes and fares. (David Zekra)

Liverpool and Manchester as well as between Liverpool and Belfast and Glasgow. Sir Harry Britain felt that funding should go towards flying boats that would operate to the West Indies, Bahamas and Florida. These might be viewed as rather obscure destinations in the priority of things, but in 1924 Imperial Airways had considered proposals to fly from Georgetown (British Guiana) to Key West (Florida) via Trinidad, Puerto Rico, Santa Domingo, Porto Prince, Kingston, Santiago (Cuba) and Havana. It also discussed a route in Chile from Valparaiso northward to Coquimbo and southward to Coronel.

Sir Samuel Hoare explained that Imperial Airways '… is the envy of every country and has a remarkable record for reliability. We are now at the stage where with possibly two or three more changes from present types to more up-to-date, our aeroplanes will cover the expenses and our airline will be self supporting.'

During the spring, Brancker had been inviting tenders from Britain's leading manufacturers to build aircraft based on separate provisos. He emphasised the need for aircraft capable of carrying 40 passengers, powered by three and also four engines with different types being courted to serve Europe and the Middle East. Because of the high temperatures encountered in the Middle East there was an extra stipulation that aircraft should not have stalling speeds below 52 mph. It was already known that stalling speeds noticeably increased with a rise in temperature. Designers were given a fairly free hand to express their own ideas and inspirations as long as safety, the cost per aircraft, payload capacities and operating costs were their fundamental considerations. The manufacturers were also tempted by bonuses to be paid for any aircraft that was built ahead of schedule but there were also penalties for any that fell short of the expected requirements. Handley Page was selected as the winner of the tender from the five that entered.

At a shareholders meeting of Imperial Airways on 7 September, Sir Eric Geddes announced a substantial increase in profits from £11,000 to £72,000 and the company was able to pay a 5 per cent dividend to shareholders for the first time. Passenger figures had increased from 11,395 during the airline's first year to 26,479 in the fourth and the company reached a milestone by carrying 1,000 passengers in a single week. Traffic revenue had also increased by 60 per cent from two years before. Geddes explained that the company had been given greater security of tenure through the support of the Government and he welcomed the extensions of the grants by five years for the European routes and seven years for the Middle East. Geddes later departed on the Calcutta he had chartered for an air cruise of Britain. The weather must have been more favourable than it had been for Mrs Lowell Thomas, mentioned earlier, for the chairman's comments were reported at some length in the Liverpool Echo of 17 September: 'We have done 1,000 miles and had no discomforts at all. It is not merely transportation that people pay for in these days, it the saving of time that matters … there is no flurry, no rush, no scrambling for seats and no indiscriminate tipping.'

Lagging behind Europe

Hoare had indicated that the role of Imperial Airways was to be, as the name implied, Imperial, and it should not be regarded solely as a European carrier. In 1928 European routes were taking less prominence and Imperial Airways was looking towards the Empire to broaden its horizons. Many considered it to be short-sighted to neglect the development of a European network during the formative years. However, it was easier to negotiate rights on distant routes than it was nearer to home because of the sensitive diplomatic situation the War had created for Britain with many European nations. The company was criticised for embarking on costly, time-consuming surveys of Africa and Asia before aircraft had been developed that could reach them. This left Imperial Airways in an untenable situation. It is certainly true that the right aircraft did not exist with the capabilities to cross vast continents, but had the company sat back and made no attempts to link the Empire, albeit it with primitive equipment, there would have been no incentive for designers to have developed advanced aircraft and the industry would have been left in the dark ages. The other European nations, most specifically the Germans, had overtaken Britain and had established an enviable concentration of routes, but they had the full support of their government. Perhaps Imperial Airways had been unwise to give away the Berlin route to the German flag carrier, Luft Hansa, but this was in part due to political incompatibility. The French and Italians were also giving Imperial Airways an impressive run for its money in Europe but were less influential elsewhere in the world. Much of Imperial Airways' lack of progress was created by the short-

sightedness of the Government for failing to support commercial aviation fully from the outset. It had been a continuing uphill struggle for a management trying to compete on even terms against foreign competition that was heavily subsidised. The airline had, at one point, attempted to abandon all European operations to concentrate on the Empire routes but the Government would neither allow it to do so nor provide the funding to make the routes a viable proposition. The company was split between a rock and a hard place by being expected to deliver on all fronts without the equipment or financial means to comply.

During the period 1925-1930 the Germans had taken economic control of the airspace across much of Europe, often by operating joint services with various companies from other countries. As a nation that was meant to be flat on its back after losing the War, Germany had exercised enormous commercial prowess despite being hampered by restrictions imposed by the Allies that prevented it from building warplanes. The following routes indicate how far Deutsche Luft Hansa (founded 6 January 1926) had progressed in so little time:

- 21 March 1927: Berlin-Vienna via Dresden in collaboration with Austrian and Czech airlines
- 13 April 1927: Munich-Milan with ALT (Italian Airlines); Berlin-Oslo via Stettin; Copenhagen and Gothenburg; Stuttgart-Barcelona via Basle
- 5 January 1928: Geneva-Marseilles with through connections with Iberia to Madrid
- 23 April 1929: Geneva-Malmo via Basle, Frankfurt, Hamburg & Copenhagen
- 14 May 1928: Berlin-Zurich Express
- 6 June 1928: Berlin-Leningrad via Königsberg, Tilsit, Riga and Reval in 14 hours. Lufthansa had 50 per cent stock in Deutsche-Russische Luftverkehrs (Deruluft) and continued operations to Moscow

These routes had previously been under the control of German cities but were transferred in 1926 to a new organisation controlled by the Messerschmitt company. This had been granted a small number of routes by Nordbayerischen Verkehrsflug, a company that had taken over Luftverkehr Thüringen in February. These routes were mostly diverse and offered no competition to Lufthansa and were served entirely by Messerschmitt and Focke-Wulf aircraft.

The French had also been overshadowed by the Germans. Nevertheless, Air Union had taken over Aéronavale in 1926 and had extended their interests beyond the Paris–Marseilles route to North Africa. This was followed by services to Ajaccio and later, Tunis and Bone using CAMS 53 flying boats. Farman's Société Générale de Transport Aérien (SGTA) operated routes to Northern Europe, including an eight-hour Paris-Berlin service started on 26 May 1926. In 1927 Farman entered a pool arrangement with DLH for various routes that terminated in Berlin. Further routes were added to the Low Countries and Copenhagen-Malmo via Cologne and Hamburg.

By 1930 Italy had increased to six operational airlines that used German Dornier and Junkers aircraft, Dutch Fokkers as well as some Italian-built machines. It was poignant that throughout the whole of Europe only the Belgians considered buying British aircraft.

On 8 October 1928 Brancker gave the Presidential Address at the Institute of Transport with a speech titled 'Cooperation in Transport' that gave an insight of the official line of thinking at the end of 1928: 'I am convinced that aircraft have not necessarily come as rivals to ships, trains and motor vehicles – but as an antidote to relieve the increasing complications of modern civilisation, and particularly to relieve existing forms of transport from the constant and growing demand for quicker communication. … in a few years the passenger traffic carried by air across the Channel will represent a very appreciable percentage of the total first class travellers to the Continent.

'Motor road transport is the most modern form of travel. Aviation as we know it owes its existence to motor transport, for without the internal combustion engine we should not be flying today. Cooperation between motor transport and air transport is to some extent automatic. The latest aeroplane carries at the most 2 tons of paying load; obviously the best means of collecting and distributing such a cargo is by road vehicle. On the other hand, the light aeroplane bids fair to be a serious rival to the motor car in the future as a means of luxury travel both for business and pleasure.

"Air transport has a good deal to learn from the railways with regard to overhaul of equipment, engines etc., and the handling of peak traffic, which I think affects railways and air transport more than it does shipping. Through booking of passengers and goods involving the cooperation of various foreign lines is a problem common to railways and air transport – and a problem in which the latter can reap the fruits of experience from the railways. Railways so far have made no real use of air transport, but there are great possibilities in this direction.[1] The great railway companies will do well to watch the development of air transport very carefully and seize every opportunity of making use of this new auxiliary in meeting their many and complicated local requirements. The long Imperial and international air services do not call for their attention, but the local and feeder lines which will undoubtedly be established in the future are surely very much their concern.

'It is generally admitted that, with the technical developments at our disposal, ships have reached the limit of their economic speed. The remedy seems simple. Let the big shipping lines, in their future programmes, arrange to carry first-class mail matter, and speed passengers by air. They will then be in a position to build slower, more comfortable, and more profitable ships for the ordinary passengers and for the rest of their freight. It is generally believed that the railways in the British Isles would have benefited considerably if, at an early stage in the development of road transport, they had stepped in and pushed on the new activity for their own purposes; to those who believe in aviation, the shipping companies today appear to be in almost exactly the same position with regard to air transport.

'We are on the threshold of vast and far reaching development in air commerce; that air commerce will benefit every activity in the civilised world, and among them, the older forms of transport which can so adjust their spheres of activity as to avoid clashing and so make full use of the facilities offered by the air. I can visualise both the railways and shipping companies adapting aviation to their own particular needs, while above and beyond fly the great aircraft operating companies to every quarter of the globe – all working in genuine cooperation.'

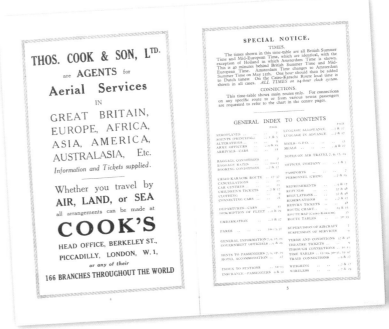

---

[1]. The Imperial Airways board had considered forming a joint rail and air company for the distribution of freight but it failed to obtain Government approval. There was also a rumour that the railway companies were getting together to apply to Parliament to form an airline in an attempt to put Imperial Airways out of business. In 1934 Railway Air Services Limited was formed jointly by the Great Western Railway (GWR), the London Midland Scottish (LMS), the London North Eastern Railway (LNER) and the Southern Railway (SR) together with Imperial Airways as equal shareholders. By then any idea to form an airline that could endanger the future of Imperial Airways had been dismissed.

DUNLOP
Wired-Type TYRES

—so completely victorious in the world of motoring—are now being used in connection with aeroplanes.

Dunlop wired-type equipment is renowned for safety and efficiency wherever the car and motorcycle are used, and will earn the same high reputation in the world of aircraft.

DUNLOP RUBBER CO., LTD., FORT DUNLOP, BIRMINGHAM.

Branches throughout the World.

C.F.H. 491

6

INFORMATION FOR PASSENGERS ON "IMPERIAL" EUROPEAN AIR ROUTES.

BRITISH AIR SERVICES.—Imperial Airways Limited is the only British Company operating aeroplane services between Great Britain and the Continent.

AEROPLANES.—Only British-built aeroplanes, seating 12 to 20 passengers (driven by two or three British engines), are used on the regular services. They all have lavatory accommodation.

PILOTS.—All the pilots have brilliant records and long flying experience. They are licensed only after passing rigid medical, flying and technical tests, conducted by the British Air Ministry, and they are regularly re-examined at least once in every six months.

MECHANICS.—Each aeroplane carries a highly trained and certified mechanic licensed by the British Air Ministry.

THROUGH ROUTES AND FARES FROM LONDON—continued

THROUGH ROUTES AND FARES FROM LONDON—continued

13

ARMSTRONG SIDDELEY
LONG EIGHTEEN 6 CYLINDER

MADE BY THE MEN WHO MADE SIR ALAN COBHAM'S AERO ENGINE

ARMSTRONG Siddeley aero engines are in regular use on the London-Paris Airway, where reliability, economy and speed are so essential.

These aero engines are made side by side with the six cylinder Armstrong Siddeley car engines which give the same kind of service on the highway that the aero engines give you in the sky.

The Armstrong Siddeley Long Eighteen Six Cylinder maintains its wonderful performance for thousands of miles on a petrol consumption of 21 m.p.g. and an oil consumption of 1,500 m.p.g. Water consumption is nil, and over 10,000 miles are covered on a set of tyres.

There is plenty of room for the family and friends in the completely-equipped range of open and closed coachwork.

Closed Carriages from
Open cars from (500) **£795** *Ex Works* Dunlop Tyres

ALL-BRITISH

Write for your copy of the Armstrong Siddeley Mileage Chart and Calendar for 1927.

ARMSTRONG SIDDELEY MOTORS LIMITED, COVENTRY.
London: 10 Old Bond Street, W.1. Manchester: 35 King Street West.
The Largest Manufacturers of Six Cylinder Cars in Europe.

18

LONDON—ROTTERDAM—AMSTERDAM
(A) KONINKLIJKE LUCHTVAART MAATSCHAPPIJ
(B) DEUTSCHE LUFT HANSA A.G.

(A) From April 19 daily, excluding Sundays
(B) From April 18 daily, excluding Sundays
(C) From June 15 daily, excluding Sundays

LONDON—OSTEND
(IMPERIAL AIRWAYS AND SABENA JOINT SERVICE)

IMPERIAL AIRWAYS
CHART OF EUROPEAN AIR ROUTES

THE NUMBERS ON THE ROUTES INDICATE THE PAGES ON WHICH THE TIMETABLE WILL BE FOUND. THE CHART IS NOT GEOGRAPHICALLY CORRECT.

24   25

Opposite page left and this page: A selection of pages from an early Imperial Airways brochure, indicating routes, timetables and fares. (David Zekra)

*A selection of pages from an early Imperial Airways
brochure, indicating routes, timetables and fares.
(David Zekra)*

CHAPTER SEVEN

THE START OF THE INDIA SERVICE
1929

O CTOBER 24 1929 became known as 'Black Thursday', a day of mass panic that culminated in the New York Stock Exchange on Wall Street 'crashing'. Shares fell sharply and many investors lost everything. In the United Kingdom Baldwin, unable to gain a clear majority, resigned as Prime Minister and on 4 June, Ramsay MacDonald was invited to form a Labour Government. Four days later, Lord Thompson was appointed as Secretary of State for Air to replace Sir Samuel Hoare.

There was a sad start to the year for civil aviation when, George Holt Thomas, aircraft constructor and founder of Air Transport and Travel (AT&T) died on New Years' Day at his home at Cimiez, Southern France, aged 59. In every respect Holt Thomas had been a visionary with sound opinions and able to predict with great accuracy how the future of commercial air travel would pan out. He was far ahead of his times, yet few believed him when he said that aircraft would circle the world. Holt Thomas had the courage of his convictions, and proved this by registering the first British airline in October 1916 '...to enter into contract for the carriage of mail, passengers, goods and cattle'. A great deal of Holt Thomas's thinking is revealed in his fascinating book of 1920, *Aerial Transport*, that many at the time considered was more science fiction than probability. When he lectured at the Aeronautical Society and promised a *'two day journey to Baghdad'* this prompted Sir John Rees MP to declare mockingly that Holt Thomas's prediction *'...seems like the magic carpet of the Arabian Nights.'* Holt Thomas was a very private man, little known beyond immediate aviation circles despite his knowledge and the pioneering work that he did during the formative years of commercial flight.

On 1 February the Guild of Air Pilots and Navigators (GAPAN) was inaugurated at a meeting held at Rules Hostelry in London's Maiden Lane with Squadron Leader E L Johnston appointed chairman. The Guild's purpose was to boost the professional integrity and standing of its members. Fifty pilots joined, 26 of them from Imperial Airways who formed the largest single group. Most of these were senior pilots with over 1,000 flying hours under their belts, 900 in command of a multi-engine aircraft that included some night-flying. As existing B Licence holders, this entitled them to be granted Master Pilot's Licences by default.

On the 28 February, Imperial Airways withdrew from the Southampton-Guernsey route. The airline, still desperately short of aircraft, required the Calcutta flying boats that had operated the route in the Mediterranean in readiness for the start of the London–India service. The curtailment was not seen as a great loss to the company because the Channel Islands had never been viable and only 43 passengers had been carried during 1927 and 160 in 1928.

In March the Air Estimates voted a meagre £450,000 from £15,983,000 to civil aviation. In the debate that always followed the Estimates, there was concern that Britain possessed only nineteen

A commercial postcard of an AW Argosy arriving over the airport hotel at Croydon. (CAS)

commercial aircraft in regular service while the USA, which had been late industry entrants, already had 250 and Germany, 240. It was seen as encouraging that 75 local authorities had been persuaded to consider establishing airports. Their ultimate decisions rested on the subsequent development of air taxis and internal charter services. Lt Cdr Kenworthy considered that, in his opinion, the routes for expansion should be New York-Galway, across Ireland to Wales and from the Humber to Hamburg, where links should be established via the European and Asiatic routes to Peking. He expressed scorn that the Egypt-Karachi route was still not yet open despite the Air Ministry's assurance in 1926 that operations with three-engine aircraft would commence in January 1927. The start of the service was nevertheless on the horizon.

March was a very special time for Imperial Airways because it formerly marked the start of the aforementioned overdue weekly service to India. However, the belligerent attitude of the British Government had created disagreements that prevented aircraft from over-flying or entering the airspace of countries it had fallen out with. By blocking Mussolini's plans for Mediterranean supremacy and by refusing Italian aircraft landing rights at British bases including Gibraltar, they could hardly expect to be awarded reciprocal favours. This irritated the Italians causing them to retaliate by banning British aircraft from entering Italy from France. This denied Imperial Airways access to a lucrative link on its eastern air route that might have added Rome as a profitable intermediary destination. Not only were over-flying rights refused, but Imperial Airways was also barred from using Tobruk as a refuelling stop because Libya was under the control of the Italians. Like so many of its actions over the years, this was another historical example of Government short-sightedness. This is especially true if the potential traffic between Italy and Gibraltar is to be considered. The route would have been less rewarding for the Italians, but Imperial Airways stood to gain much had they been permitted access to Italian cities. But, typically, Britain failed to learn from its mistakes and instead of opting for any give-and-take they remained at odds with the Italians.

A celebration for Alexandra Day –
Sir Sefton Brancker with a group of
dignitaries and guests at Croydon
during the late 1920s. (CAS)

During the autumn the British government had also blocked Italian plans for a suggested pooled Genoa-Alexandria service. To bypass Italy a route was suggested via Vienna, Budapest, Skopje, Salonika and Athens but during the winter months the danger of icing made this impractical. At that time no effective way of dealing with the icing problem had been devised. With the equipment Imperial Airways had available it was not considered safe to fly over the Alps and the alternative was to transfer passengers to a steam train for a lengthy trek across Europe. This was inconvenient and time consuming because the 600-mile rail journey through Switzerland to Genoa required a night spent on the train. The journey could be extremely tedious and uncomfortable, and it created a somewhat ridiculous and embarrassing situation for the airline through its inability to fly its passengers over the entire route to Karachi. However, because of a lack of détente, it was a situation that was to continue for quite some time.

The three Armstrong Whitworth Argosies that had originally been ordered for the Middle East that had gone into service from July 1926 on the London-Paris *Silver Wing* service had proved to be so successful that four more were ordered. These were designated as Mark IIs and they arrived between May and July 1929 and carried the registrations G-AACH (*City of Edinburgh*); G-AACI (*City of Liverpool*); G-AACJ (*City of Manchester*) and G-AAEJ (*City of Coventry*). These aircraft were fitted with servo-assisted ailerons that the manufacturers claimed required less effort to operate than the earlier equipment that had to be manually adjusted. The aircraft type could carry 19 passengers and came equipped with a buffet and a cabin designed by the acclaimed interior designer and decorator, Ionides. This included scientifically efficient cabin ventilation that kept passengers warm without needing extra

Handley Page W9 Hampstead, G-EBLE 'City of New York', circa 1926. This aircraft was
subsequently sold to New Guinea in January 1929 as VH-ULK – the pilot went with it.
(CAS)

layers of clothing. The armchair seats were designed for comfort and relaxation and the windows gave a sweeping view of the panorama beneath the aircraft. The walls and upholstery were fashioned in a '…cheerful shade of silver-blue' and the overall interior décor was designed to be airy, spacious and restful on the eye. The Argosies were destined for the England-India route as well as on the *Silver Wing* service as soon as they became available.

In 1929 Imperial Airways acquired a second depot ship that was purchased by Societa Anonima Navigazionne Aerea of Genoa which also operated a weekly service between Italy, Greece and Egypt. The new vessel was called *Alice* and was stationed at Tobruk to compliment the other Imperial yacht, *Imperia*, that was based at Suda Bay in Crete.

The India Route opens

On 30 March the Argosy, *City of Glasgow* (G-EBLF), left Croydon on the first through service to India. The aircraft carrying 364 lbs of mail departed on time at 10.00 hrs with Capt Wilcockson in command for the first stage of the scheduled flight that in future would carry passengers to Karachi in seven days at a fare of £130. The same aircraft had established a record by completing the London-Paris journey on 20 January in just 105 minutes at an average speed of 128 mph. Sir Samuel Hoare and his private secretary, Christopher Lloyd Bullock, Air Vice-Marshall Sir Vyell Vyvyan, and the Air Ministry board member of Imperial Airways flew on the inaugural service. Brackley accompanied Wilcockson in the cockpit as far as Basle, returning to Croydon at 07.30 hrs next day. The inaugural flight carried no fare-paying passengers but 12,000 items of mail were on board. The flight was fortunately blessed with good weather and reached Paris (Le Bourget) by noon (departing 13.30 hrs) and Basle ahead of schedule at 16.30 hrs. From there, the small party of VIPs boarded the train to Genoa and joined the Calcutta flying boat *City of Alexandria* (G-EBVG). This departed for Rome (Ostia), Naples and Corfu, then on to Athens where the party alighted in choppy seas off Phaleron Bay onto the waiting Imperial Airways motor launch that took them to shore. After an overnight stay, the group continued to Alexandria via Suda Bay and Tobruk. Hoare then left the party to make a 4,000-mile tour of the proposed Cairo-Cape Town route. Vyvyan joined the DH66 Hercules, *City of Jerusalem* (G-EBMZ), and accompanied the mail consignment on the final sector to Karachi

via Gaza, Rutbah Wells, Baghdad, Basra, Bushire, Lingeh, Jask and Gwadar. The political wrangling with the Persians was continuing and British aircraft were unable to follow a more favourable coastline route along the north side of the Gulf. Instead pilots were forced to route along the Trucial Coast of Arabia before crossing the sea at Gwadar to make the final leg to Karachi. This added much extra time and stretched the flying distance to 4,966 miles.

Sir Vyell Vyvyan arrived in India on 6 April after being delayed by a sandstorm. Next day, the reciprocal return service left Karachi with the airline's Vice Chairman, Lord Chetwynd, and his daughter, Vyvyan and Sir Geoffrey Salmond aboard the DH66 Hercules, *City of Baghdad* (G-EBMY), with the London-bound mail. Hoare later joined the flight after completing his trip through Africa.

Following Hoare's return to England there were positive signs that things were coming together on the proposed Cape route. Hoare had flown up to 750 miles a day, and was exuberant when he announced: *'We certainly hope that the service from Egypt to Cape Town may be started on April 1st next year.'* The Union of South Africa government was equally bullish when it agreed to operate the air mail service between Cape Town and Port Elizabeth that would extend to East London, Durban, Bloemfontein and Johannesburg with the intention of linking with the Imperial Airways service. On 6 June, Imperial Airways (Africa) Limited was registered with 100 per cent ownership vested in Imperial Airways Ltd.

On 1 April the subsidies agreed between the Air Ministry and Imperial Airways referred to previously became a reality to provide badly needed funding for the UK-India service.

There was excitement in Hong Kong during September when the local Post Office took in over 374 items of mail destined for Britain. These were taken by sea on the steamer *Kakusan Maru* to Singapore and on to India where they were loaded onto the Imperial Airways India air mail flight bound for Croydon. The letters took 24 days to reach their destinations, longer than it took on the Trans-Siberian Railway that normally carried the Hong Kong mail. Despite the jubilation created by the mail service, Crown Colony residents were dismayed that a direct air link had not already been established with Britain although a local commentator had remarked that the territory was *'… not in the slightest degree air-minded.'* This may have been one man's view, but this idea was later dispelled by a display of joyful celebration when the first Imperial Airways aircraft eventually landed at Kai Tak in 1936.

While Imperial Airways was unable to operate an all-air England-India service, the RAF did what the airline could not do and completed its first non-stop flight from England to Karachi. From 24-26 April, Squadron Ldr A G Jones-Williams MC and Flt Lt N H Jenkins OBE DFC DSM flew a Fairey Long-Range Monoplane, *J9479*, equipped with a single 530 hp Napier Lion XI engine, 4,130 miles from Cranwell, Lincolnshire to land at Karachi 50 hrs 37 mins later. They originally intended to reach Bangalore to establish a world distance record, but strong headwinds cut short their remarkable attempt.

Promoting 'air-mindedness' was also high on the agenda for Imperial Airways and during the summer, the airline attended major air shows where it offered short pleasure flights. In June the company continued promoting civil aviation by launching sightseeing 'Tea Flights' over London that gave passengers the opportunity to enjoy a traditional tea served by a uniformed steward for just two guineas (£2.10p). These flights using the slogan *'Tea in the Air over London'* commenced on 8 June and operated every Friday and Saturday afternoon throughout the summer.

On 16 July the Prince of Wales opened the Seventh International Aero Exhibition at London's Olympia (the first since 1919) and although Imperial Airways took part, the press were less than enthusiastic over the quality of its display. The company had shown a mock-up of one side of an Argosy cabin that was intended to demonstrate the comforts of air travel. Unfortunately this was considered to be unprofessional and visitors complained that the seats were uncomfortable and the under-seat tin cuspidors (receptacles for passengers suffering from air-sickness) and the opening windows were dirty. A rolling painted panorama located behind the windows was intended to simulate actual flight and showed a painted backdrop of the England–Egypt–India route that was reported to be extremely amateurish and unconvincing. The company also displayed an illuminated glass map of Europe that they called *'The Automatic Guide to*

Air Travel.' This showed the airline's key destinations that lit up when the appropriate button was pressed to display departure/arrival times and ticket costs. This provided, if nothing else, novelty value that amused any children that were taken to the exhibition, who spent hours of fun pushing the various buttons.

Handley Page also supported the exhibition and used its space to promote its association with Imperial Airways by displaying an impressively long, white-painted mock up of its new four-engine HP42 airliner that had recently been ordered by the airline. This aircraft had an enclosed cockpit with Triplex glass windows, never used before on an Imperial Airways aircraft, and a cabin that demonstrated impressive levels of style and comfort previously unknown. The aircraft was impressive although before delivery the cockpit layout needed to be extensively changed to meet the demands of Wolley Dod before it could enter service on the Eastern route. One of the highlights of the exhibition should have been the appearance of a complete Imperial Airways Armstrong Whitworth Argosy (instead of a cabin mock-up), but visitors were denied the opportunity to see the aircraft at close quarters because an increased popularity in flying had forced every available aircraft into service.

Riots in the Near East

Dod took a break from running the Near East Division at Heliopolis (Cairo) and Brackley was sent in his place on a temporary assignment that extended to almost four months. From the outset it appeared that Woods Humphery, the Imperial Airways general manager, had plans to make life difficult for Brackley that would keep him out of the way for as long as possible. It is clear from Brackley's diaries that relationships with Woods Humphery had again become strained and the tone of a memorandum he sent to Brackley is blunt and seriously lacked humanity: *'I am informing Cairo that you will be leaving London on 13 July to relieve the Manager, Near East Division, while he comes home on leave. His leave is for three months in England and you will be away from home for a period approaching 3½ to 4 months in order that you may overlap in Cairo at beginning and end of period.*

'… You will act on exactly the same powers as the Divisional Manager … you can get replies to queries by cable within 48hrs. and of course consult departmental chiefs of your own division … I do not anticipate this will be necessary and my belief is that your trip will be as valuable to you as giving you an insight into the operation of our work outside Europe as it will be to the Company to have you there carrying on in Mr Dod's absence.'

Brackley departed on a difficult journey, spending 26 hours in the air and further period on the train. His outbound journey spanned five days. After taking the Argosy from Croydon to Paris, he boarded an ageing HP W10 for Basle and took the train to Genoa. From Italy he boarded the scheduled Calcutta flying boat to Alexandria where the final sector of his journey was made by Hercules to Cairo. Long distances were slowly being conquered but progress was hampered by the time it took to get anywhere. Flying beyond the closest European cities required passengers to call upon vast amounts of stamina. This was a far cry from the image that the airlines wanted to project.

No sooner had Brackley arrived in Cairo on 17 July than troubles began to arise in Palestine. This reached a head on 24 August when Arabs massacred 47 Jews. British troops were called in to restore order, but 86 more Jews and over 100 Arabs were slaughtered, most of the latter shot by the British peace-keepers. According to Brackley, the bloodshed had begun after an Arab had urinated against Jerusalem's Wailing Wall. As might be expected, the Jews viewed this as a serious act of blasphemy and they reacted by causing mass riots that the small local police force were powerless to control. The Acting High Commissioner sent for British forces and Brackley witnessed an RAF Vickers troop aircraft carrying re-enforcements crash on take-off killing four of the six occupants. A further fifteen troops were reported missing when the aircraft transporting them came down in hostile territory.

Brackley wrote to his wife, Frida, expressing concern over the problems he was enduring in order to protect the Imperial Airways staff, passengers, aircraft and mail. His entire staff at the Gaza office had been commandeered by the police and military and ordered to quell the riots that had erupted around Gaza, Jaffa and Hebron. With his workforce depleted, Brackley had a difficult task protecting the passengers on the company's east and westbound flights. On 25 August he again wrote to Frida: *'Personally, I feel a good deal of responsibility at the moment. The Air*

Main photograph: Armstrong Whitworth Argosy, G-EBLF, 'City of Glasgow' in front of a Handley Page W8f of SABENA. (CAS/John Stroud)

Armstrong Whitworth Argosy, G-EBOZ, 'City of Wellington' in 1929 (this aircraft was renamed 'City of Arundel' before being written off in October 1934). (CAS)

Officer Commanding and the RAF have been very kind and helpful, but they have been quite frank about the great risk I am running. I'm not going to leave a stone unturned to maintain our services to schedule. It's an excellent chance to show what we can do, not by mere bravado, but by carefully laid plans…'

Throughout August the Jews continued to be driven from their homes and many were systematically and horrendously murdered while their houses were burned. The British were also under threat from the Arabs who considered that the troops were supporting and protecting the Jews against them. On 30

August, Brackley reported that '… *the Navy, Army and Air Force turned up, of course very late.'* In spite of the troubles, Imperial Airways flights departed without problems and on the 29th, a record was created when the westbound service covered over 1,000 miles from Basra to Alexandria in a single day. This was maintained for a second week during a period when the situation had become too dangerous for flights to stop at Gaza. At the same time, the Jerusalem authorities had forced the eastbound flight to re-route via Kantara and Amman to avoid danger. The eventual arrival of extra British troops had quelled the violence allowing the Gaza station staff to return to airline duties and the routeing of flights was restored to operate Basra-Alexandria via Gaza. When all this was over, the Director General of Posts and Telegraphs in India openly praised Brackley's efforts in maintaining the punctuality of the air mail service in spite of the troubles. However, further evidence of the rift between the air superintendent and Woods Humphery came with the only communication Brackley ever received from London throughout his spell at Heliopolis. This was blunt and contained no mention of the welfare of Brackley or his staff in a note that referred only to the company's wish not to endanger passengers by night-flying to

Alexandria. This arrived *after* protective action had already been taken by Brackley and caused him to comment in a letter to his wife: '…*Woods Humphery hasn't written me a word since I've been here.*'

Herbert Brackley certainly had his hands full. If the slaughtering of Jews and Arabs had not been sufficient to cause him more than a little concern there was usually a myriad of staff problems to contend with. He reported that certain members of his station staff had become more than a little eccentric in the desert heat. One of the managers had to be sent home for three weeks because he had 'gone native' and had taken to wearing Arab dress, had hennaed his feet and was being worshipped by a native girl and had moved in with her family. The local English doctor had become a religious maniac who did '…*strange things*' although there is no hint of what he meant by this. At the same time the wives of a pilot and a member of the engineering staff were expecting babies that required them to be assigned a period of home leave.

Accident at Jask

On Friday, 6 September disaster struck when the DH66, *City of Jerusalem* (G-EBMZ), crashed and caught fire at Jask while attempting a night landing. One passenger was killed outright, two were injured and a record amount of 25,000 items of mail from London were destroyed.

Capt Woodbridge, a popular member of staff, who was piloting the aircraft, was thrown clear and was uninjured. He scrambled back into the cabin, attempting to rescue a trapped passenger unaware that the injured passenger, Mr V G Bell of Watlington, Oxford, had already died in the resulting fire. Woodbridge's clothing caught fire and although his burns were not considered to have been fatal, he died shortly after of heart failure. Another Imperial Airways employee, John Court, aged 25, was also killed but flight engineer, H C Amor, and wireless operator H Bourne, survived the ordeal. The cause of the accident was believed to have been attributed to the pilot's tiredness caused by heat exhaustion and the last words Woodbridge was said to have uttered moments before dying were '*Tell them I am sorry.*' Night-flying was still a dangerous occupation and at

A commercial postcard of Croydon Aerodrome. (CAS)

Jask there was no aerodrome lighting. Pilots had to rely on wing flares to illuminate their path as they came into land; a system that always had a degree of risk. When the DH66 crashed, one theory suggested that a wing tip struck the ground causing the entire wing to tear and be forced back in towards the fuselage causing the flare to set the cabin alight. This turned what was believed to have been a survivable accident into an inferno offering little chance of escape.

In September news had reached Brackley that Dod would not be returning to Cairo as planned. Instead he was sent to Africa to carry out further detailed work in conjunction with the South African Government on the route to Cape Town. Brackley, in turn, was ordered to review the future of flying boat operations and to research developments in Karachi for an extension that would stretch the route across India to Australia.

Woods Humphery did not break the news to Brackley himself; Colonel Burchall, his assistant was left with the responsibility of contacting him by memo that he received on 16 October:

'You will doubtless be anxious to know something regarding the movements of Wolley Dod and the arrival of the next '66'.

'After a great deal of negotiation, it has been found necessary to send Wolley Dod to conduct a survey of the Africa route, commencing at Cape Town. He is accordingly leaving here on the 25th instant and probably not be back in Cairo for three months after that.

'The General Manager is accordingly anxious that you shall remain in Cairo to look after the Near East Route, and I hope this will not be inconvenient to your private arrangements. It is, however, exceedingly difficult to see any other solution to the matter, and I trust therefore that having stood the heat of summer, you will rather look forward to remaining in Cairo for part of the Season,'

Frida Brackley had been due to fly out to spend time with her husband. The long-planned trip was unreasonably delayed when the head of the Imperial Airways Passenger Department, a man appropriately named Handover, informed Frida as she was about to board the eastbound flight that an important company member needed her seat. She was expected to stand-down and wait a considerable time for another flight. In today's terminology this is known as being 'bumped' from a flight and it is not hard to imagine Frida's despondency at being removed minutes from departure in such a blatant way. Handover spitefully added that there was no need for Frida to hurry to Egypt to meet her husband '...*because he was going to be away in that country for a considerable period.'* At that time Brackley had not been informed that his time in Heliopolis had been extended and Handover's comment had come as a shock. The conspiracy continued when Frida discovered that Handover had been lying and the aircraft was not full. She eventually persuaded him to allow her to board, but this was only on the understanding that the majority of her luggage would have to be left behind even though it had been weighed and cleared for the flight

the previous day. It appeared that management was doing everything it could to prevent Frida from flying to Egypt. When this became obvious, it gave her the resolve to reach her husband as quickly as possible and to determine a reason for the company's behaviour. The woman suffered further indignation when a company trainee took the passports from her and an Imperial Airways employee travelling aboard the flight '...*to speed their progress through Customs'* at Basle. Having boarded the train, the trainee apparently had '*dined too well'* and retired to bed taking the passports with him. Fortunately Mrs Brackley was able to retrieve her documents by the time the train reached the Italian frontier. The indignation continued and when Frida arrived at Genoa she was told that the Calcutta flying boat was overweight and she would have to wait five days for another flight. But Frida, now more determined than ever to reach her husband, enlisted some sympathetic members of the Imperial Airways staff who booked her a passage on a Lloyd Triestino ship that was about to set sail for Alexandria from Naples. This involved her making an overnight train journey from Genoa to Naples to reach the ship and she eventually arrived in Alexandria on 5 October. Her husband meanwhile had not been informed of the circumstances and had been left waiting to meet his wife when the flying boat arrived. He was not surprised to find that the aircraft was *underweight.* By the time Frida arrived, Brackley had still not received notification of his prolonged stay in Egypt and he later concluded that this had been a deliberate attempt by Woods Humphery to minimise his involvement as the pilots' representative on the board. Brackley had made many personal sacrifices for the company and he was justifiably appalled at the way he and his wife had been treated.

It appears that Brackley's concerns were not restricted to the bad personal treatment he was receiving from Woods Humphery. For the only time in his career he was also starting to doubt the safety of flying on Imperial Airways aircraft operating in the Near East. This was a dreadful indictment from a man that was as regarded as safety-minded as Brackley.

Herbert and Frida Brackley had passages booked on the Calcutta, *City of Rome* (G-AADN), that subsequently crashed off Spezia but the continuing antics of head office had ironically spared the couple from boarding the flight. Frida returned to Britain by sea and rail and by the time she arrived home on 2 November, all flying boats had been grounded. Before leaving for home, Brackley had promised his wife that he would speak to Geddes upon his return to London once he had considered it safe again to use the company's aircraft. It took him until 4 December to make the meeting but it gave Brackley the opportunity to clear the air and to re-establish his role within Imperial Airways. However, according to Frida's book, as he was leaving the room Geddes curtly remarked: *'I understand your wife was with you in Heliopolis.'* One can make what one might of this comment but it appeared indicative of the political rivalry that was developing at Imperial Airways during that time. It had been a very difficult time for Herbert Brackley and he returned to Cairo on the understanding that his real role within the company was in London representing the interests of the company's flying personnel.

On 26 September Imperial Airways held its AGM and announced a 7½ per cent dividend to shareholders. Geddes, who had originally tendered his resignation from the board the previous year, explained that he was still very much at the helm of the company after being pressured into staying by his colleagues. There were several positive aspects to the chairman's report. He announced that the airline had flown in excess of one million miles and had safely carried almost 35,000 fare-paying passengers and 870 tons of mail and freight. The airline had achieved 75 per cent capacity on the European routes and 61 per cent in the Near East. Geddes commented on the excellent staff and management relationships that existed within the company, but presumably failed to consider the difficulties Brackley had experienced with Woods Humphery who, incidentally, was given a vote of thanks.

The Post Master General openly praised the way that the Eastern Route was being operated. Mail was leaving Croydon for Karachi every Saturday morning with the westbound returning each Sunday. During the first six months of operations 14,656 lbs of mail had been carried to various destinations from London and 17,529 lbs had been delivered to Croydon on the westbound flights. The Post Master General commented that there was no other long distance service that could compare with this success. The mail had been late on only two occasions eastbound, caused by floods and sandstorms, and the accident at Jask had resulted in a load being lost. On the return to London another sandstorm had dusted an aircraft's occupants with a light coating of sand and had delayed one consignment. Two more had been late by missing the train connection at Genoa, but overall the service was considered to be extremely successful.

As we have seen, Brackley and his wife were fortunate to have been excluded from the passenger list of the Calcutta, *City of Rome* (G-AADN), on 26 October that was lost causing a major setback in Imperial Airways' operations. All seven on board the aircraft were drowned and in retrospect it seemed that the aircraft should never have departed from the Neopolitan flying boat port at Molo Beverello. The weather in the area at the time was extremely bad, the journey was predicted to be dangerous and no other flights on similar routes even attempted to take off. The *City of Rome* alighted safely at Ostia before continuing to Genoa where it was forced down off the Tuscan coast between Bocca d'Arno and Vigreggio, probably due to an engine that was either shut down or had become faulty. SOS signals were sent by the pilot, Capt L S Birt, when he realised his aircraft was in danger of being swamped in the high seas whipped up by the prevailing south-westerly gale that was reported to be gusting at 70 mph. Even a destroyer sent from Spezia was forced to return due to the violent weather, but the steamer *Famiglia* eventually found the aircraft and managed to get a tow line connected. As the tug slowly towed the Calcutta, the aircraft had its engines running to assist progress, but the cable snapped and the aircraft disappeared from view and sank quickly taking all on board with it. As well as Birt, flight engineer, F T Pembroke, wireless operator, S J Stone and passengers Mr H Turney, Mr H K Robinson, Mr Ritchie and Miss M Bromford were all lost. Turney was a customs officer at Croydon who was on holiday.

Despite the loss and the obvious warning of the dangers of landing on high seas, the Court of Inquiry failed to connect any blame to the prevailing conditions. The Calcuttas continued to fly and only four days later, the remaining pair was also damaged in heavy seas and had to be repaired. *City of Alexandria* (G-EBVG), flown by Stocks, was badly damaged at Mersa following a forced-landing at Suda and *City of Athens* (G-EBVH), flown by Bailey, suffered from severe hull damage after hitting a rock.

Following the fatal loss of the *City of Rome* the Italians wasted no time withdrawing the rights that had allowed the Imperial Airways flying boats the use of Italian ports. This decision was also symptomatic of the company's refusal to pool receipts from the Genoa-Alexandria route with the Italian company S.A.Navigazione Aerea which began operating smaller Dornier Do J *Wal* (Whale) flying boats on 11 April. As a result re-routing became necessary. From Croydon, flights flew via Cologne and Nuremberg then on to Vienna, Budapest, Belgrade, Skopje, Salonika and Athens. The Argosy was used for the first part of the route, thereafter passengers were transferred to flying boats at Athens. The route across the Balkans was extremely short-lived, lasting for only two services, and from 2 November it was abandoned. Flying the route in winter was still considered unsafe and passengers and mail were assigned to the train between Paris and Athens.

While the Calcuttas were grounded, an Air Ministry Supermarine Southampton (G-AASH) was hired for a brief period between 15 November 1929-19 February 1930 to provide cover on the route. This was the only Southampton flying boat ever to be used by a British airline. While Imperial Airways was sorting out its routing problems, developments of a different kind were taking place in England. The HM Airship, R101 (G-FAAW), was completed and moored at Cardington, Bedfordshire on 8 October in preparation for its maiden flight on the 14th. The sister ship, R100 (G-FAAV), made her first flight of 140 miles in two hours from Howden, Yorkshire to Cardington on 16 December. (see Chapter 8)

On 21 December, Imperial Airways extended the India service from Karachi to Jodhpur. The route was placed under charter to the Indian Government which wanted to take control over all commercial flights that transversed India. The route was further extended nine days later to Delhi and the first service was flown by the DH86 Hercules, *City of Delhi* (G-EBMX).

By the end of 1929 the relationship between Brackley and Woods Humphery had improved. The general manager, no doubt mellowed by his recent marriage, arrived in Cairo with his wife and took Brackley to dinner. Following this a dinner-dance was held for the staff that Brackley records was a '*great success*' and he and Woods Humphery took the opportunity to make speeches. Mr and Mrs Woods Humphery and Brackley also spent a considerable time together dining and visiting the Pyramids and it appears that the year ended more positively for the air superintendent. As 1930 began, Brackley flew with Woods Humphery to visit the stations along the India route. According to Robin Higham's excellent work *Britain's Imperial Air Routes 1918 to 1939*, there is some doubt over the *persecution* (author's word) that Frida Brackley suggested her husband had been subjected to by Woods Humphery. There are of course two sides to every story and Higham points out that the company may have considered Brackley had reached the end of the road as far as his abilities were concerned. After interviewing Woods Humphery, there was a denial that a private meeting between Brackley and Geddes ever took place because he claimed that Geddes never discussed the duties of subordinates behind his manager's back. Higham also gained the impression from Frida's memoirs of her late husband that Brackley was perhaps '...*overly concerned with private affairs while apt to be annoyed by small detail.*' This may be so but the situation is not a subject ever likely to be verified by first-hand accounts now that almost everybody concerned with the Imperial Airways story are long departed. In order to attempt to obtain a balanced perspective it has been necessary to rely on accounts written previously by those involved with the company, or by third parties fortunate enough to have conducted personal interviews with those that had known Brackley, Woods Humphery or the other key individuals. However, as this book neared completion, the writer raised the issue with Major David Brackley, Herbert's son, when he visited him at the old family home at Blakeney, Norfolk. Although he was only a young boy at the time, David implied that there was a strong indication that although his father and Woods Humphery *became* friends during the latter stages of their

The ill-fated Vickers 170 Vanguard that was loaned from the Air Ministry and which crashed at Shepperton on 16 May 1929. (author's collection)

relationship, he believed that an element of friction between the two men existed particularly during the early part of their working time together.

Nevertheless, according to Higham's research, Imperial Airways had made a concerted effort to replace Brackley as its air superintendent. General van Ryneld was approached to join the company although in a higher grade than air superintendent and following his rejection of the offer, Maj R H Mayo, became General Manager (Technical) and Col Burchall took over as General Manager (Commercial) leaving Brackley in his post with direct access to the board. C G Grey reported in *The Aeroplane* that the senior pilot, Armstrong, '… *had sternly occupied his* (Brackley's) *official chair. Then one morning Mr Wilcockson was there looking like Mussolini with a liver. A few days later the air superintendent was positively portentous.'* This may be taken as an indication that at least some of the pilots did not regard Brackley as highly as he regarded himself. Brackley had reason to be concerned and he may have been right to conclude

that during this tricky period there was a management move, behind his back, to replace him. As will be revealed, further evidence of this evolved in 1939 prior to the amalgamation with British Airways.

During the year there was a further incident that reflected a lack of political correctness. Lord Chetwynd, a new director of Imperial Airways, appointed with a view to being groomed to take over from Geddes when he retired, dropped more than a major 'clanger' during his visit to India. He was there to participate in negotiations to set up a subsidiary company that would take Indians on to the board. During the course of these discussions he came up with the classic faux pas: *'Who would ever fly with Indians?'* It is fortuitous that this did not give rise to a riot, but it did cause immense anger and embarrassment to those present. But Chetwynd continued by erring further when, on the flight home, he refused to allow the pilot to wait for the returning mail at Baghdad. This could have cost the company dearly, but fortunately the RAF intervened by sending two pilots in pursuit of the Imperial

Airlines flight to repatriate the missing mail. Questions were later raised in Parliament and an announcement was made that Chetwynd had strangely '… *resigned from the company because of ill health.*'

There were a number of other interesting matters involving the company that occurred during 1929. Among the snippets that appeared in the *Imperial Airways Gazette* during the period was an article concerning the carriage of what were referred to as *'strange cargos.'* In the modern age of jet transport none of the articles carried at that time would be anything other than ordinary, but in 1929 when a consignment of albino rats, or a number of valuable birds were carried by air, this became newsworthy. The rats were used for scientific research for a substance known as Ostelin that occurred in vitamin D. Ground-breaking experiments were being carried out on the rats in London and a number of the rodents were flown on an Imperial Airways cross-Channel flight on their way to the University of Barcelona. The birds were more fortunate and were carried from Germany, France, Switzerland and Holland to participate in a show at the Crystal Palace. There was no limit to the numbers of species that the airline carried. One hundred and fifty guinea pigs were flown on the Paris-Croydon freight service; a lion cub and tropical fish destined for London Zoo and an equestrian horse, transported in a specially built crate, were all included among the livestock flown by Imperial Airways. When the DH86 Hercules, *City of Baghdad*, was under routine inspection at Karachi, it was found to have attracted livestock of the wrong kind. It was noticed that portions of the wall fabric were showing signs of having been chewed. Traps were set overnight and the following morning a medium-sized rat was discovered in the freight compartment.

The *Gazette* also reported that Chritsmas mail on the India route had reached record proportions with 35,000-40,000 items carried on 7 December alone and 50,000 (weighing half a ton) a week later. Record shipments of gold – about two tons per aircraft – were regularly flown

The Armstrong Whitworth Argosy Mk II, G-AACJ 'City of Manchester', circa 1929. (CAS)

A commercial postcard of Croydon Aerodrome.

as cargo on the London, Paris and Switzerland routes. In all, the airline was responsible for carrying 40 tons without loss or incident during a nine-day period. Pilots on gold-carrying flights were issued with revolvers to protect their cargo from robbers, but exactly what the company expected them to do if a robbery had been attempted is difficult to imagine.

Imperial Airways sets new records

People, naturally, are key in some of the major stories surrounding the airline. While no passengers could be carried by air on the London-Alexandria sector of the India route during November owing to a temporary diversion, elsewhere passenger figures had looked promising. The *Imperial Airways Gazette* reported that during the year a London businessman completed his 200th Imperial Airways flight. His normal routine consisted of leaving London in the morning, doing business on the Continent during the day and returning home in time for dinner. At one stage the gentleman (who was not named) chartered an Imperial Airways aircraft for a week to visit many major European cities. Had he travelled overland the same journey would have taken him several months and he covered the costs of this aerial assault on his clients with a worthwhile increase in business. On 7 September, Prime Minister Ramsay MacDonald accompanied by his daughter, Miss Ishbel MacDonald, took the morning flight from Paris (Le Bourget) on their way back from Geneva. Afterwards Miss MacDonald expressed her enthusiasm for flying and declared her intention to repeat the experience. In November the movie stars Mary Pickford and Douglas Fairbanks were accompanied by Lady Louis Mountbatten to Croydon where they joined the *Silver Wing* service to Paris. Meanwhile a pair of women Members of Parliament, Miss Ellen Wilkinson and Miss Jenny Lee, chartered an aircraft so they could have lunch in London, fly to inspect a Yorkshire colliery during the afternoon and return to the capital in time for dinner. On 22 June a child made a flight that the company claimed to be record-breaking. Master Denis Lithgow, aged 3½, was accompanied by his parents on the 2,350 mile journey from London to Alexandria that was considered to be the longest distance a child had flown. By 7 February the 100,000th passenger had been carried by Imperial Airways between Croydon and Paris and three days before, the airline had announced it had completed 400,000 flying miles between the UK and the Continent. Some of the longer serving pilots were also breaking records. A L Robinson notched up 6,000 flying hours during October; the equivalent to 250 days or eight months in the air. After beginning his career at Brooklands, Robinson had served with the RAF in France but since 1919 had spent most of his time flying passengers across the English Channel. In all, he had safely carried 15,000 passengers on 1,500 flights. There was also the strange occurrence of Capt G I Thompson being 'sold' with his aircraft. When

the HPW9 Hampstead *City of New York* (G-EBLE) was sold to a new owner in New Guinea (and re-registered VH-ULK) the pilot went with it although the terms of the deal are not known.

Despite the records that the airline was creating, the final days of November and much of December were interrupted by the worst weather in the history of aviation. The conditions prevailed throughout Britain and Western Europe and on 9 November all flying services were suspended. Ten days later, when dense fog prevented a pilot from seeing the ground, he flew entirely blind using only directional finding wireless to guide him throughout the entire journey from Paris to Croydon.

During September an experimental service organised by a tour company proved quite revolutionary for its day. Advertised at an inclusive price of fifteen guineas (£15.75), passengers could book a flight from Le Bourget to Croydon where they would be met by a car that would take them to a London hotel for dinner. This was followed by the theatre, supper and a cabaret before being flown back to Paris in time for breakfast next morning. From 14 September, a similar programme was organised in reverse allowing British passengers to enjoy a similar programme of events in Paris. The success of the venture is unknown but an edition of *Imperial Airways Gazette* from October 1929 reported the intention to operate these flights twice-weekly subject to demand.

The Air Taxi service was also growing in popularity and a Westland IV (G-AAGW) long-distance aircraft was acquired by Imperial Airways for charter work. The aircraft was a three-engine monoplane powered by 105 hp Cirrus Hermes 1 engines. It was the second of the type to be built by the Yeovil-based manufacturer and it was initially on display at the Olympia exhibition earlier in the year. Imperial Airways promoted a service whereby a customer could telephone the airline offices day or night to charter an aircraft that would be available within an hour. In addition to the Westland IV, any of the other aircraft in the Imperial Airways fleet, subject to availability, could be made available for private charter work at the following rates:

No. of seats	Maximum weight:	Cost per mile:	
1	200 lbs	1s 9d	(8p approx)
3	600 lbs	2s 0d	(10p)
4	1000 lbs	3s 0d	(15p)
6	1200 lbs	3s 6d	(17½p)
12	2500 lbs	5s 0d	(25p)
20	4000 lbs	10s 0d	(50p)

There was no charge made for waiting time providing the aircraft returned to Croydon no later than the next day and the rates charged were applied from the time that the aircraft departed from Croydon until its return.

Additionally the Airline had started to operate short flights for parties visiting Croydon Airport at the following rates:

No. of seats	10 minutes:	30 minutes:
4	£2 2s 0d (£2.10)	£ 5 5s 0d (£5.25)
13	£6 6s 0d (£6.30)	£15 15s 0d (£15.75)
20	£9 9s 0d (£9.45)	£21 10s 0d (£21)

In comparison to the average working man's weekly wage, flying was still the very much the province of the wealthy, but the carriage costs for baggage could still be favourable. The free personal baggage allowance for passengers in 1929 was 30 lbs, but the company would carry trunks by air for less than the equivalent cost by surface transport. It would cost £4 for two trunks to be carried by rail and steamer from London to Brussels and the transit time was ten days. Imperial Airways boasted that it would carry the same two trunks with a maximum weight of 250 lbs by air for the same price in a much shorter time.

CHAPTER EIGHT

THE R101 DISASTER AND THE ARRIVAL OF THE HP42

1930

THE New Year had commenced with Brackley, still entrenched in Cairo, playing host to Woods Humphery who was combining his honeymoon with a working trip. On 2 January both men departed before dawn for Baghdad in a DH66, arriving 9 hrs 40 mins later after a stop at Gaza. Next day they flew on to Basra, a destination that was causing some consternation among passengers due to the conditions of the overnight accommodation. On the 4th they called in at Bushire and Lingeh and continued on to Jask where they visited the grave of the pilot Woodbridge. For the next few days they continued their journey to India stopping at Gwadar, Karachi and Hyderabad. From here Woods Humphery went to Delhi while Brackley returned to Cairo via Karachi. En route Brackley had given assistance to Francis Chichester at Gaza who was on his way to Australia single-handedly in his Moth. In more recent times the New Zealand-born pioneer was knighted by HM Queen Elizabeth II following his epic round-the-world sailing exploits in his tiny yacht *Gipsy Moth*. Brackley reached his Cairo office on 12 January only to encounter two weeks of gales and torrential rain that made aircraft operations difficult. He was thankful when the former AT&T pilot, Bill Armstrong, newly appointed as manager of the Near East Division, arrived in Egypt to replace him.

At home a new service was announced. Imperial Airways had linked up with the railway companies to enable a joint rail and air freight service. This was due to take effect from 1 April 1931 and, in theory, meant that a parcel handed in at any one of 140 prime British railway stations could be forwarded on an Imperial Airways aircraft for delivery to addresses in Egypt, Iraq, and India, Central and South Africa. A similar agreement had also been made with the trans-Atlantic shipping operator, Cunard, to carry freight between the USA and Greece, Egypt, Palestine, Iraq and India. This would provide huge time savings; nine days on items sent this way to the USA and Alexandria; eighteen days on goods sent to Baghdad. Packages sent by surface transport would otherwise have spent many weeks in transit.

The Air Estimates announced in March voted £500,000 of the £17,850,000 to civil aviation. The Under Secretary of State for Air, Mr Montague, pointed out in the Commons that developments in India were moving forward with the Indian Government extending the Karachi service to Delhi using aircraft chartered from Imperial Airways. He announced that operations were reaching an advanced state for further extensions to Calcutta and Rangoon, Burma with Air Ministry proposals being put forward for the remaining Rangoon-Australia sector. On 5 May Montague moved a Commons resolution that proposed a new Air Transport (Subsidy Agreements) Bill that would

A picture postcard of the main booking hall at Croydon Aerodrome. (CAS)

empower the Secretary of State to provide up to £1m in a Government subsidy that theoretically would be granted to anyone with the necessary organisation to operate a commercial airline. This withdrew the Imperial Airways monopoly and allowed others to compete with it and to draw state funding.

Organising the Cape route

On 11 April Capt Frederick Tymms, who had been leading the joint Air Ministry/Imperial Airways survey, completed the operational work of the Cairo-Cape Town route bringing a second major scheduled Empire link closer to realisation. The British Government, when negotiating the route, had also represented the interests of the Dominion of South Africa and the various colonial territories involved. The agreement was to run for five years from the date of the first through service. Each of the other countries that the route passed through agreed to share a proportion of the operating costs. This was offset by the maximum subsidy of £940,000 that was to be paid over a five-year period. This was split between the British Government (£270,000), the South African Government (£400,000) and the remainder by the colonial territories. The route from Cairo to Cape Town was 5,625 miles long and the first sector to open, Cairo-Tanganyika covered 2,670 miles. Although the entire route did not open until the spring of 1931, a great deal of preparation was required to establish airports, navigational aids and emergency runways across vast stretches of virgin territory that

The seven-passenger DH66 Hercules helped to open up the great air routes of the Empire. This example has an enclosed cockpit, tail wheel and note that the port engine is not running.

This De Havilland DH66 Hercules, G-EBMX, '*City of Delhi*', entered service with Imperial Airways in 1926 and was used on the India route. The aircraft was sold to the South African Air Force in November 1934.

A picture postcard of DH66 Hercules, G-EBNA, 'City of Teheran' that crash-landed at Gaza on 14 February 1930. (CAS)

contained inhospitable swamp, bush, rivers and jungle. No fewer than 27 main air stations were established between Cairo and the Cape with around 30 intermediate points that would be available as extra landing and boarding destinations that would be made available to passengers on demand. Staff quarters, hotels, hangars, workshops, wireless and meteorological facilities had to be built at every main stop. Once the route had been completed, the travelling time between London and Cape Town was cut from 17 days overland to 11 by air. Three days were still consumed by the European rail connection and on the flight across the Mediterranean; the remaining eight by flying down the eastern side of the African continent. It was viewed as a positive development that aircraft flying the Africa route were able to keep in touch with a ground station at all times using wireless, telegraphy or telephony. Each aircraft was fitted with long and short wave radios that enabled contact to be maintained with any of 17 wireless stations that were located within a flight range of 300 miles.

Imperial Airways decided to use flying boats on the Khartoum-Mwanza sector. The soil of the Southern Sudan was liable to flooding during the rainy season, where it quickly turned to dark black mud and the airfields did not provide all-weather capabilities especially at Malakal and Juba. Over the remainder of the route conditions were more favourable enabling land aircraft to be used.

Much of the proposed route had never been thoroughly surveyed and there were no accurate maps. According to *The Time Shrinkers* by David Jones, Captains Egglesfield and Prendergast had been engaged by Imperial Airways and posted to Egypt in November to operate the flying boats. They lacked information and found themselves having to make their own sketch maps and organise schedules as part of their everyday duties. Egglesfield recalled in the book that the maps were extremely sketchy: '*...sometimes because there was nothing to put on them, as between Wadi Halfa and Kareima which was completely barren and uninhabitable desert, except one hill seventy miles out from Halfa.*' It was not uncommon for pilots to write remarks on their basic hand-drawn maps to remind them of any minor features that would help them to navigate the harsh terrain when they flew it next time. Comments such as '*...line of trees on the horizon*' and other such remarks could provide vital aids for retracing a route across an otherwise featureless land mass.

The Air Ministry had also been discussing the possibility of operating along the eastern seaboard of the North American continent in cooperation with the Canadian Government. A debate was held in the House of Lords to discuss relating issues, but it seemed Secretary of State, Lord Thomson, was keen to omit Imperial Airways from his plans and the consultative committee that was set up had noticeably excluded representation from the company. Exactly who they had in mind to operate the service remains a mystery, but as it stood, Britain had no commercial aircraft capable of flying the Atlantic so it seems more likely that aircraft would have been shipped across, and be based in Newfoundland or Montreal to operate a coastal route.

On 12 April the arrival of spring meant the re-introduction, albeit briefly, of flights across central Europe and the Balkans to replace the much despised train journey. Apart from the sector between Skopje and Salonika the route was still by train, passengers could cross the majority of Europe by air, cutting two days from the journey time to Karachi. Ten days later, the entire European route opened to air traffic providing a massive improvement to the service. However arguments continued over rights, especially with the Italians, and further operational difficulties in Central Europe caused by adverse weather meant that it was not long before the arduous train journey from Paris to Brindisi was reinstated and the number of days taken to reach India reverted to eight and a half.

Imperial Airways' main European competitors had been introducing new services. On 14 April the Belgian airline SABENA began a Brussels-Croydon night mail service five times a week using the popular Fokker FVIIb-3m three-engine monoplanes. The service was subsidised by the Belgian Government and the airline claimed 100 per cent

reliability during the first four months of operation. Imperial Airways also entered an arrangement with the Belgian company to share the London-Brussels-Cologne service. Imperial Airways operated this on Tuesdays, Thursdays and Saturdays, Sabena on the remaining days. The arrangement enabled Imperial Airways to maintain a route presence despite having insufficient aircraft of its own. The German company, Deutsche Lufthansa, also opened a Croydon-Hanover-Berlin night mail service the following month. Imperial Airways were unable to reciprocate, although a domestic service was added on 16 June that operated an Argosy three times a week between Croydon, Birmingham, Manchester and Liverpool to link with their European services at Croydon. Having carried around 600 passengers, the company withdrew the domestic services on 20 September.

Women had begun to make a mark on civil aviation albeit as pioneering pilots. While the South Africa survey was underway, the 64-year-old Duchess of Bedford, Mary Du Caurroy, known as 'The Flying Duchess', left England with the former de Havilland instructor, Capt Charles Barnard, and relief pilot, engineer and navigator, Bob Little. They too were Cape Town-bound in the latest of the

Imperial Airways' Captain O. P. Jones, who flew during the 1920s and 1930s and then with BOAC. (CAS)

Duchess's aerial exploits. Mary had learned to fly a Moth during her more mature years and she was partial to making long-distance flights with Barnard in a series of aircraft that she had owned including the Jupiter powered Fokker F VII *Spider* (G-EBTS). They had previously flown through Europe and North Africa in 1927, India the following year and had returned to the Sub-Continent in 1929 in a record of 7½ days. Her ventures to India were made when Imperial Airways could still only contemplate flying the route themselves. On the Cape trip the party left Lympne just after dawn on 10 April and in a little over 12 hours they had covered 1,000 miles to reach Oran in North Africa. They continued, flying in stages through heavy rain to reach Tunis, Benghazi, Assuit, Khartoum, Dodoma, Broken Hill and Bulawayo, reaching Cape Town nine days after leaving England. With a break of only two days they left for home, retracing their route to Egypt and then to Aleppo and Sofia to land at Croydon on 30 April. The editor of *The Aeroplane*, C G Grey, unable to resist the opportunity, quipped at Imperial Airways: '*Though Her Grace is not competing with Imperial Airways, she will have done that organisation a great service if those responsible will profit by it, for she has shown the kind of competition it will have to compete with.*' He continued: '*...that without the slightest trouble mail can be flown from London to India in less than three days, and allowing twenty-four hours for reply, the answer could be back in England the same week. Likewise she now shows that letters can be sent to the Cape and the answer back in England in less than a fortnight – which is the same time letters take for the single journey from England to the Cape by steamer.*' Grey suggested that if an aircraft that Vickers were building (the Viastra) were to be used then the mail could be speeded up considerably. However, he neglected to mention the vast logistical differences that separated operating a commercial airline on a scheduled footing from a few adventurers setting out independently. A pioneering pilot was able to fly more or less where and when they pleased without having to consider shareholders, Government interference and dealing with the Postmaster General over contracts. Another intrepid lady flyer who courted the public imagination was Amy Johnson who, on 5 May, departed from Croydon for Port Darwin, Australia in her second-hand DH Gipsy Moth (G-AAAH).

The airships

Progress east of Karachi was still slow and the British Government were favouring the use of two lighter-than-air dirigibles that were under construction. These were the mighty rigid airships R100 and R101 that the Government viewed as the great hopes to link the most distant parts of the Commonwealth. In view of the work done by the Germans with their huge *Graf Zeppelin* and the progress being made by the Americans, many in British aviation circles remained convinced that lighter-than-air dirigibles were the only appropriate solution for long distance operations. The future use of rigid airships on transcontinental routes

The Zeppelin airship – built for war and peace: completed at Friedrichshafen and commissioned in July 1915, the L13 was commanded by Kapitänleutnant Heinrich Mathy the following September when it bombed central London. Mathy flew 14 airship bombing missions over England, more than any other German Naval airman.

was highly favoured by Lord Thomson and supported by Sir Sefton Brancker, not least because of the problems caused by unreliable engines on fixed-wing machines. The use of engines in airships had less critical considerations. A failure would hardly mean that an airship would fall from the sky, while with a heavier than air, fixed-wing machine an engine loss could be critical. If an airship engine failed it was possible to carry out repairs while in the air although the exercise might have been precarious. As airships did not require engines for speed; they could be used sparingly and more economically for forward motion. A dirigible could also remain airborne for thousands of miles, but a conventional fixed-wing aircraft had to refuel at regular intervals and at most could only travel a few hundred miles without having to land. The airship also had the advantage of being able to fly above great tracks of barren land without the need to establish fuel dumps and landing grounds at close intervals.

In order to draw some perspective about the use of dirigibles for civilian flying, it is worth outlining how successfully the Germans had employed their Zeppelin built lighter-than-air craft. The Zeppelin LZ7 *Deutschland* had been the first powered aircraft to carry passengers. The maiden flight was made on 19 June 1910 and a group of journalists was carried on the first passenger flight on 28 June. This press outing came to grief when the flight commander, Capt Kahlenberg of the Prussian Airship Battalion, was blamed for making a series of miscalculations in bad weather that caused the *Deutschland* to crash into the trees in the Teutoburger Wald in Westphalia. Fortunately the cabin was barely damaged, the craft did not catch fire and the passengers were able to escape the wreckage virtually uninjured apart from one individual who broke an ankle.

The dirigible project had commenced long before when *Graf* Ferdinand von Zeppelin's first LZ7 made its maiden flight at Manzell on Bodensee (Lake Constance) on 2 July 1900. A lack of funding caused the craft to be abandoned after making only three flights and five years lapsed before the *Graf* had sufficient money to build another airship. On 16 November 1909, Deutsche Luftschiffahrts AG (Delag) was formed with the task of training Zeppelin flight crews. Once suitable crews had been found it took only a short while for a series of routes to be established that carried revenue paying passengers with great success. Huge sheds to house the Zeppelins were built at the main base at Friedrichshafen, at Baden-Baden and Düsseldorf. Other sites were added and by the latter part of 1911 Johannisthal, near Berlin, and

Ferdinand Adolf Heinrich August Graf von Zeppelin (centre) on board the airship 'Viktoria Luise'. To the left is Alfred Colsmann, general director of the Zeppelin company.
(US Library of Congress)

Gotha were opened. During the next few years the system was expanded to include sheds at Frankfurt-am-Main, Potsdam, Dresden, Hamburg and Leipzig. By 1913 a circular route from Friedrichshafen was being advertised that linked these stations. No scheduled flights were operated during the 1914-18 War years but in the period immediately following, the company claimed to have operated a route network of 107,205 miles and carried 33,722 passengers and crew without a single passenger being injured despite some Zeppelins being written-off in accidents.

When the *Deutschland* was lost the LZ6 (built 1909) was adapted for passenger service with Delag but after flying only 1,946 miles and carrying 726 paying passengers, the airship was destroyed by fire in its hangar. A replacement *Deutschland,* the LZ8 *Ersatz* (substitute) was built in 1911, funded from the insurance claim paid on the original craft. This too had only a short life, making just 33 flights before its back was broken at a point between the two suspended gondolas while being manoeuvred from its hangar in strong winds. Passengers were on board at the time and photographs of the incident portray them being coaxed by rescuers to climb from the gondolas onto long flimsy ladders in an extremely hazardous and terrifying operation.

Next in line was the Baden-Baden based LZ10 *Schwaben* that made its first flight on 26 June 1911 and subsequently went into service with Delag. This airship was 459 feet long, 46 feet in diameter with power supplied by a pair of Maybach A-Z 150 hp engines. The craft could reach 44 mph and it had a range of 900 statute miles. After only 218 flights this Zeppelin also met a tragic end when it was destroyed during a storm at Düsseldorf on 28 June 1912 and static electricity caused the hydrogen within the rubberised fabric gas cells to ignite. During the same year Delag took delivery of the LZ11 *Viktoria Luise* and for a brief time the company had two airships in service at the same time. The *Schwaben* and *Viktoria Luise* must have presented an impressive sight when they flew in tandem from Mannheim to Heidelberg on 4 April. After a distinguished career, the *Viktoria Luise* was dismantled during 1915. It flew mainly on the Heligoland, Norderney and Sylt route and ended its civilian career on 21 July 1914 after making 489 flights in 981 hours and had carried 2995 revenue passengers. During the early part of the war *Viktoria Luise* had served with the XVIII Corps of the German Army before being transferred to the Navy as a training vessel. By the time she was retired, this airship had carried more than 22,039 people in complete safety.

Two more Zeppelins went into service with Delag prior to the First World War. The LZ13 *Hansa* was the same size as the *Viktoria Luise* – 486 ft long x 46 ft diameter – the *LZ17 Sachsen* was slightly larger at 519 ft long x 49 ft diameter, and both craft were powered by Maybach engines. The engines on *Viktoria Luise* and *Hansa* were 170 hp each while those on the *Sachsen* were 180 hp giving the latter a range of 1,400 miles, but the two smaller craft could travel only half this distance. The *Hansa* operated initially from Hamburg but was later transferred to Potsdam prior to being moved again to serve the VII Army Corps at Johannisthal as a trainer. The *Sachsen* was originally based at Leipzig and on 9 June 1913 she made the first Zeppelin flight between Baden-Baden and Vienna. On 25 October she was transferred to the German Navy at Dresden for crew training after most of the previously trained personnel had been killed when the LZ14 was lost at sea and the LZ18 exploded in the air. During 1914 *Sachsen* briefly returned to Delag enabling the company to increase its compliment to three serving passenger Zeppelins that operated until services were suspended at the outbreak of War. This Zeppelin carried 24 passengers at any one time and it is reported that *Sachsen* carried 2,465 fare-paying passengers in all. During the War this Zeppelin was transferred to the German XIX Army and served at Cologne. On 2 September 1914 it was flown to bomb Antwerp and later served on the Russian front before being used as a trainer by the Navy. After an interesting and distinguished career *Sachsen* was dismantled.

During the War years 95 rigid Zeppelin airships were built that left the production line at the rate of roughly one a fortnight. During 1917, one such ship, the L59 serving the Navy was used to fly urgently needed supplies to the German Army in East Africa. During a five day period it left its base in Jamboli (Bulgaria) and reached Khartoum before being recalled. During this time it flew more than 4,200 miles in less than 100 hours and carried a payload of 15 tons.

Graf Zeppelin had made a definitive mark. His company had employed 23,000 workers during the War years, 13,600 of them at Friedrichshafen. He survived to witness the L59 flight to Khartoum notch up a world distance record for that time, but died soon after on 8 March 1917 leaving behind a company that would add much to the annals of early aviation history. By 1918 there was no decline in the potential use of the dirigible and production of civilian versions re-commenced with the building of the LZ120 *Bodensee*, first flown on 20 August 1919 and the *Nordstern* (North Star) that was delivered later the same year. *Bodensee* was used on the Friedrichshafen-Berlin (Staaken Zeppelin Station) service that commenced on 24 August. Northbound flights were flown on odd dates; southbound on even dates and it took four to five hours to fly the 372 mile route non-stop. Originally a stop was made at Munich until 4 October when the service became direct. Delag's original plan was to operate an international service that would link Berlin and Friedrichshafen with Switzerland, Spain, Italy and Sweden but the service never commenced.

The *Bodensee* differed in design from the pre-war Zeppelins. It was shorter, more streamlined and the four 245hp Maybach Mb IVa engines improved the airship's performance, providing a cruising speed of 82 mph. The crew and passengers were accommodated in a single cabin structure that fitted flush to the underside of the hull that enabled passengers to view the passing countryside through large panoramic windows. Twenty seats were lined along these windows with an additional single seat placed behind the rear of the crew control room. When atmospheric conditions provided sufficient lift, up to six extra wicker chairs could be added in the aisle to increase the number of fare paying passengers to 27. Before being retired, *Bodensee* completed 103 flights in 104 days, including a return trip between Berlin and Stockholm, and carried 4,050 people (2,253 of them revenue paying passengers).

At the end of the First World War there was still a great deal of bitterness between the opposing nations, and as part of the peacetime requirements Delag was forced to retire *Bodensee* and *Nordstern* and to hand them to the Allies as war repatriations. The former was flown to Ciampino, Rome and passed to the Italian Navy who renamed it *Esperia*. It was later flown to St Cyr near Paris and handed to the French Navy who renamed it again; calling her the *Mediterranée*. The craft was

The Graf Zeppelin over the Mount of Olives in east Jerusalem. (US Library of Congress)

dismantled in 1927; *Nordstern* was broken up a year earlier. A pair of military airships, known as the V Class Super Zeppelins L64 and LZ109, found their way to England as part of the repatriation demands. These formed part of a fleet that had bombed Leeds, Grimsby and Hull. The first of these was flown to Pulham, Norfolk by its German crew on 22 June 1920 and handed over, but neither Zeppelin ever flew again. Although the airships were only a few years old, British design and construction had already progressed beyond the limitations of the German craft and the Zeppelins were no longer considered to be of any real value. Subsequently both were eventually broken up.

Despite the repatriation of her airships, Germany remained undeterred in her effort to gain civilian air supremacy. After the death of *Graf* Zeppelin, the prominent wartime commander, Hugo Eckener, held considerable influence within the Zeppelin company. The great works at Friedrichshafen were reprieved from the threat of post-war destruction by cunningly offering to build airships for America and eventually the company formed an alliance with the Goodyear Corporation in 1923. The Americans controlled the production of Helium, a rare non-flammable gas that was obtained from a small source in Texas previously unavailable to the Germans. However, the helium-filled airships were of less sturdy construction than the more vulnerable hydrogen craft and subsequent efforts to build reliable American airships were marred by mishaps. In 1925, the *Shenandoah,* an American replica of a Zeppelin came to grief when it was ripped in half by strong winds over Ohio. Later, the first joint Goodyear-Zeppelin venture, the *Akron* crashed into the sea off New Jersey. By then Luftschiffbau Zeppelin was already involved in building its LZ127 *Graf Zeppelin* (D-ENNE), a mighty dirigible that stretched to over 774 feet in length with a diameter of 100 feet. On 8 July 1928 Count Zeppelin's daughter, Countess von Brandenstein-Zeppelin, christened it and by 18 September it had made its maiden flight. This was an endurance test that lasted 36 hours. On 11 October, less than a month later, the *Graf Zeppelin* left Friedrichshafen to cross the Atlantic heading for Lakehurst, New Jersey with a

Stereograph of the Graf Zeppelin overflying the 4,000-year-old pyramids of Gizeh, Egypt in 1929. (US Library of Congress)

compliment of ten revenue-paying passengers and ten guests. The airship became a familiar sight over much of Europe and during March 1929 it cruised to Egypt from Friedrichshafen and flew below sea level over the Dead Sea. On 8 August the airship was positioned at Lakehurst where it commenced a round-the-world flight that would moor at Friedrichshafen, Tokyo and Los Angeles carrying 41 crew and 20 passengers and a load of mail and freight. The round trip of 21,251 miles was accomplished in just 12 days 14 hrs and 20 mins at an average speed of 70 mph thus proving that the mode of transport had huge potential for covering vast distances.

The success of the world orbital flight spurred the Germans into making further long-distance journeys with the *Graf Zeppelin*. On 18 May 1930 it embarked on its first flight to South America from Friedrichshafen. The routing was made via Seville in southern Spain to Pernambuco (Recife) in north-eastern Brazil, then to Rio de Janeiro returning via Recife, Lakehurst, and Seville and finally back to Friedrichshafen. From August-October 1931 further trial flights were made to South America before a regular Friedrichshafen-Recife service carrying fare-paying passengers began on 20 March 1932. Between making the South American proving flights, the Zeppelin was taken on an Arctic cruise and reached Franz Josef Land, an archipelago of 191 islands, in the far north of Russia.

The British had studied the early progress that the Germans had made and in July 1908 the Admiralty proposed that the Royal Navy should build a large airship because of the usefulness as a bomb platform that could attack an enemy's resources. Prime Minister Asquith, aware that the German Government had allocated funding to its project, agreed with the Admiralty that Britain should do the same. Proposals were put through the appropriate Government departments and because of their previous naval connections, Vickers, Sons and Maxim (later Vickers Ltd) was offered a £30,000 contract to build an airship. The first design was known as the HMA No1 (His Majesty's Airship, nicknamed *Mayfly*) that was built at the Barrow naval construction yard. The designers followed Zeppelin's example by building the 512 ft long airship afloat, using Cavendish Dock. Vickers obtained the rights to a new alloy called duralumin, ironically a German invention, and fabricated the skeletal structure from this. Vickers had secured the proprietary rights to the metal and, as a result, it was four years before the Germans were able to use the alloy they had invented to construct a craft or their own. On 22 September, after various modifications had been made to the original construction, the revised airship was inflated and readied for tests due to take place two days later. The project was very short-lived; the airship broke in two after being hit by a squall causing great embarrassment to all involved. It is perhaps significant that Churchill, sitting at the subsequent Court of Inquiry, refused to allow publication of the outcome of the incident and the official report mysteriously became lost. Typically of so many Government contracts, it is believed that the cost of developing the *Mayfly* had escalated to more than double the £30,000 originally allocated to the project. After this catastrophe, the Vickers airship department was disbanded but resurrected in 1913 when it was again called upon to develop dirigibles

for the Admiralty. The designer appointed at that time was H B Pratt from S F Saunders of Cowes who took on a young man by the name of Neville Barnes Wallis as his apprentice. As we know, many years later, the same Barnes Wallis would become synonymous with the infamous 'bouncing bomb' and was knighted for his work.

The continuing military projects became embroiled in the normal Government departmental squabbling and work was cancelled, then re-scheduled causing delays and an excess in public spending. The eventual outcome was an airship with insufficient power that became known simply as No 9. On 16 November 1916 this became the first British rigid to fly. After engine changes and other modifications, the airship was damaged in a storm during 1918 and was broken up. The estimated cost was reported to have reached £120,000-£150,000 – a vast sum of money for the time, that was wasted in mismanagement and failure. Projects came and went to build dirigibles for naval anti-submarine patrols but in September 1916 significantly, the L33 Zeppelin was captured over Essex after being damaged by British air-to-air fire. The crew, realising that the escaping gas would prevent their escape to Germany, put the airship down near Mersea and attempted to destroy the craft by setting fire to it. However, insufficient gas remained, preventing the structure from burning. It was soon realised that the German design and performance was far ahead of any British development. Prior to this £11,500 had been spent on the girder design and construction to build the R30. A detailed analysis of the captured Zeppelin caused drastic alterations to the British way of thinking and the existing projects were scrapped and the German design formed the blueprint for a new classification of airship named the 33-class after the design of the captured German ship. The first of these was the R33, an airship that was very similar to the captured Zeppelin. Nevertheless, Barnes Wallis continued with his design work at Vickers and from his drawing board evolved the R80 ('R' for rigid) a streamlined airship version with a range of 4,000 miles. This stylish-looking dirigible flew for just 75 hours before it too was scrapped by the Labour Government in a move that was doubly foolish and narrow minded. The criticism aimed at the Government pointed to the fact that the Vickers R80 was costing considerably less to maintain than the equivalent airships, R33 and R34 that Armstrong Whitworth and Beardmore were developing on behalf of the Navy. When Vickers suggested that the R80 could be used as civilian transport it is not surprising that the Government refused to listen. Meanwhile the R33 built at Barlow first flew on 6 March 1919 and eight days later, the Beardmore-built R34 was launched at Inchinnan. The two airships were considered to be the most successful of the British craft and the R33 flew more than any other, spending over 735 hours airborne before being dismantled in 1928. The R34 gained acclaim when it departed from East Fortune, Edinburgh on 2 July 1919 to make the first east-west crossing of the Atlantic reaching Minneola, New York 108 hours later despite prevailing headwinds. Six days later it returned in just 75 hours to achieve the first double crossing. In September 1919 the R33 made a 20-hour flight to demonstrate the feasibility and comforts of the airship as a means of commercial transport. A group of invited businessmen was

treated to a trip along the Belgian and Dutch coasts and given an aerial view of the Flanders battlefields before returning to England. An on-board chef cooked a five-course meal and beds were provided in an attempt to win favourable reports from the passengers. In May 1920 the R33 was involved in a strange experiment to test a fire-proof fuel tank fitted to a pilotless Sopwith Camel with its engine running that was launched from the airship. Exactly how the success of the experiment could be judged is a mystery because the aircraft was deliberately crashed into the ground, although the Sopwith fuel tank did remain intact and failed to ignite when the aircraft impacted. Shortly after, on 14 January 1921, the R33 was re-registered as the civilian airship G-FAAG. During the same year disaster struck the entire airship programme when the R38 broke in two over Hull causing the gas tanks in both halves to explode killing 44 crew members.

It became clear that potential disaster was never far away. The bow and stern of the R33 was fitted with a ballast tank containing a ton of water that could be released from the control gondola. These tanks saved the aircraft from probable destruction when, during a local flight, a rigger fell through a gas bag causing the airship to tilt dangerously towards the stern. The crew transferred their weight to the bow and then released the stern ballast to re-trim the airship to avert disaster. The rigger, despite his fall and any discomforts caused by filling his lungs with gas, survived the ordeal. The R33 was then used for a lengthy tethering exercise that involved mooring her to the mast at Pulham for 96 days during which she was subjected to severe weather with snow squalls and winds of up to 55 mph. Emerging unscathed, the airship was later used to evaluate the recently-installed lighting system along the Continental air route and to assist in traffic control operations via a wireless communication with the police during the Epsom Derby race meeting.

By 28 June 1921 the Government, with their usual wisdom, decided that the airships were no longer economical and all of the remaining British-built craft (R33, R36, R37 and R80 and the surrendered German Zeppelins L64 and L70) were disposed of. They were initially offered free to any would-be operator who applied for them by 1 August but nobody expressed an interest in using them commercially or otherwise. However, they escaped from being scrapped for a time and were put in storage. In May 1924 the Government, inspired by the Empire scheme proposed by Commander Burney, revised their thinking and the R33 emerged from her vast shed at Cardington once more to be flown to Pulham where she was used in air pressure and hull stress experiments. On 16 April, after being moored at the Pulham mast for ten days, the R33 was struck by severe winds that damaged the nose and deflated the front gas bag. The airship broke away from the mast with Flt Lt R E Booth, a flight sergeant and 18 civilians aboard. Booth took command of the airship, ordering the release of two tons of ballast that enabled the airship to climb rapidly and avoid a potentially devastating collision with the station gas tank. Under engine power, the airship continued to ride the storm but was moving backwards at a rate of 20 knots. Despite the inherent danger, crew members climbed to the top of the structure to secure the flapping fabric to make safe the deflated gas bag to regain stability and to repair a protective bulkhead. The R33 continued to be blown backwards in the storm, crossed the coast at Lowestoft and reached the Dutch coast near Ijmuiden by 18.30. The Dutch authorities gathered 300 men in readiness for a landing and a gunboat shadowed the R33 to render assistance in case a tow was required. But the winds abated and 29½ hours after the adventure began the R33 returned safely to Pulham. The nose was subsequently re-designed and rebuilt and the airship continued with experimental work

until early 1926 when the Treasury once more decided to place the R33 and the Pulham station on a 'care and maintenance basis'. The remarkable exploits of the R33 continued when she was revitalised again in October 1926 to test the new mooring mast that had been erected at Cardington for the R100 and R101. In a further experiment, heavy Gloster Glebe fighters were attached beneath the hull to test the stability and trim of the airship. These were launched in flight without any noticeable difference to the airship's handling ability. The R33 made her last flight to Cardington on 21 November 1926 before being dismantled to make room for the R101.

Armstrong Whitworth closed its works at Barlow in October 1919 ending its association with lighter-than-air machines although briefly, there was some consideration given to forming a joint commercial scheme with Beardmore and Cunard presumably to commercially employ airships to cross the Atlantic. It is reported that the company wanted to be guaranteed against loss and, as a result, the idea never progressed.

Vickers continued its work on non-rigid airships but these were generally smaller, slower craft, known as blimps, that were used for coastal patrols and defence work around the East Coast and over the North Sea.

The Burney Scheme

By the end of the First World War, the idea of using airships for trans-Atlantic work was being discussed seriously by Cmdr C D Burney who proposed a scheme for operating private airships to India and Australia with funding provided by Vickers, the Shell Petroleum Group and the Government by way of a £2m subsidy. Burney formed the Airship Guarantee Company in 1924 with Vickers and with Barnes Wallis as designer, Major P L Tweed as metallurgist and Nevil Shute Norway, the famous novelist, as engineer. In response, the Government set up the Empire Communications Scheme with Brig Gen Lord Thomson of Cardington at the

The R101 was built by the Royal Airships Works and made its first flight on 14 October 1929.

helm. A contract was issued for £350,000 and two rigid airships were commissioned. The R101 was to be built by the Royal Airship Works at Cardington near Bedford; the R100 to be built by Vickers at the hitherto disused Howden (Yorkshire) works that it purchased for £61,000. There was a considerable amount of rivalry between the two organisations and the Government had set down its usual provisos that included a requirement for the airships to be capable of reaching a maximum speed of 70 mph. Failure to reach this speed would have rendered a £1,000 penalty payable for every half mph below the target. The airship also had to be capable of flying the North Atlantic from the UK to Canada and back. Vickers had no worries; its R100, built as cheaply as possible with a three-deck configuration, surpassed the demanded speed and achieved 81 mph on its first test flight after being delivered to Cardington from Howden on 16 December 1929.

On 29 July 1930, HM Airship R100, commanded by Sqn Ldr Booth, left Cardington with 43 crew members and an invited list of passengers to cross the Atlantic bound for Canada. She successfully reached St Hubert Airport, Montreal in 78 hrs 49 mins on 1 August against headwinds. The return flight, made between 13-16 August was accomplished in under 58 hours. The R100 completed this test relatively unscathed although two stabiliser fins were damaged during a violent electrical storm over the St Lawrence Seaway. The crew managed to repair these in-flight with no disruption being caused to the schedule and it was reported that the R100 handled extremely well.

The British airship programme, initially heralded as a success, was suddenly plunged into deep despair so soon after the return of the R100. At 02.02 hrs on the morning of the 5 October the R101, commanded by Flt Lt H C Irwin, was heading for Egypt and India

The R33 attached to her mooring mast wearing the code G-FAAG, after she was 'demilitarised'" and given over to civilian work.

The wreckage of R101 in France, 4 October 1930.

when it crashed into a hillside at Allone near Beauvais in northern France. Forty-eight of the fifty-four on board died. Among the dead were Lord Thomson, the Air Minister, and Sir Sefton Brancker, the highly respected Director of Civil Aviation. It was a time for deep contemplation and, as an outcome, the British Government decided to end its brief flirtation with the airship. Criticism has long been directed at the design of the R101 and the airship had been described as '*leaky, overweight and short of lift.*' It was not built to the same standard as the R100 and had been constructed on a low budget with a sense of 'make-do'. Notwithstanding, Lord Thomson, in his hurry to make the India flight declared the airship to be as '*safe as a house*' although many who had worked on it strongly disagreed with his pronouncement.

Despite the use of hydrogen, a highly volatile gas, the R101 was considered to be so well insulated against stray sparks that any risk of accidental fires was believed to be beyond the realms of probability. Because of the low flashpoint of petrol, the airship carried heavy oil to power its engines as this was considered to be safer. Cooking was done by electricity and all electrical components had been insulated against stray sparks. The level of confidence was so high that people were allowed to smoke for the first time during flight in a fireproof compartment installed within the passenger quarters. Nevertheless contemporary writings reveal that Sir Sefton Brancker appeared unchacteristically tense, unsettled and more than a little agitated about making the epic flight. A colleague who knew Brancker well, Lt Cmdr S Deacon RN, who served as the aerodrome officer in charge of Lympne, stated that he had never before seen Brancker in such a nervous state. In his 1935 book, *Sir Sefton Brancker*, Norman MacMillan tells of a meeting between Brancker and Deacon that took place during the morning of 4 October, the day before the fateful flight: '*...that morning he was fidgety; he fingered the ornaments on the mantelpiece. His manner was noticeably different. One saw the same thing so often in the War that one knows the signs. What rhyme or reason is there in such feelings? One does not know. They are super organic; but sometimes terribly real. They must have been real to Brancker that day.*'

If what has been written is true, it suggests that Brancker was nursing his own personal doubts about the R101 and his own safety. His view of the future for long distance air travel was made clear by a remark he made after visiting the Dornier works at Friedrichshafen where he had been taken up in the huge Dornier-X flying boat: '*That machine is the father of long-distance airliners.*' There is also documented evidence of self-doubt over his forthcoming flight on the R101. Brancker had written expressing his concerns that things were not right with the airship and a key worker at Cardington had also spoken of his feelings that the flight should have been delayed but these views were ignored. Maybe Brancker had experienced a premonition of his destiny; we will never know. In any event it is known that the gas bags had been chafing against the girders prior to the final flight and wrappings had been put round the stainless steel framework to provide added protection. This make-do remedy had failed to solve the problem by the time the flight to India was due to depart. The pressures had been against the doubters and it seemed Lord Thomson was pushing for a successful trip to be made to India and back in time for the Economic Conference that was being held in London on 28 October. With the

world watching, the flight had to go ahead without question. The possibility of failure could not be contemplated because this would have caused Thomson to lose face and the Government would never have been permitted to live it down. During a meeting between Thomson and Brancker that took place a short while before departure, Brancker is believed to have expressed his doubts about the safety of the R101. His concerns about flying in the airship were only met with a stern rebuff from Thomson who is said to have accused him of being a coward. Thomson was quick to add pressure by informing Brancker that there were plenty of men who would gladly take his place.

Other members of the works crew at Cardington were also opposed to the flight because they believed that the airship was far from ready. The *Bedfordshire Times* reported in October 2008 that a diary had been found written by one of the Cardington ground engineers that recorded his safety fears for the airship. If any of these views were ever passed to a higher level then it is certain they were never heeded. Indeed, it had been evident during the R101's appearance at the Hendon air display in June that the level of control left much to be desired and during the short return flight to its mooring at Cardington the airship had almost come to grief when it went into a steep dive. Any difficulties the crew had experienced controlling her were played down by those who did not have to fly in her, but for the operating crew the dangers were only too real. Apart from her appearance at Hendon the airship had made only limited test flights, the longest lasting just 24 hours. The Cardington workforce had also put in hundreds of hours splitting the airship in half, inserting a new bay, modifying the engines and replacing damaged cables with stronger chains. Yet, many believed that the R101 still had not received anywhere near the amount of time in the air necessary before embarking on a flight of several thousand miles. Nevertheless, when the due day arrived, doubts were firmly cast aside as the time came for the great airship to lumber from her mast at Cardington on a wet and gusty night. As the winds increased so too did the handling difficulties. The lashing rain brought with it a big depression that reduced lift. When she did separate from the mast the rain that fell had created so much extra weight that the crew needed to battle with the controls to overcome the elements in order to gain just a modicum of height. The airship had only managed to reach 1,500 feet as she approached the high ground around Beauvais. The gas bags, despite the added wrappings, continued to chafe and were leaking inside and outside the skin and the R101 was flying perilously far beneath the recommended minimum height set at two-and-a-half times the airship's overall length. The R101 measured 769 feet from nose to tail but the combination of wind and heaviness caused by the rain had brought her altitude down to barely 1,000 feet; too low to recover from the sudden down-draught that forced her nose to drop in the airship's penultimate manoeuvre. Although the airframe had initially reacted to the elevator controls made by the coxswain, control was brief. The engines were shut down to tempt more lift but this failed to prevent the nose from going down again in one final gesture. Inevitably, against a strong headwind, the nose struck the ground, the leaking hydrogen exploded and the mighty airship almost instantaneously became a massive fireball. Eight men were thrown clear, saved either by the escaping water from the ballast tanks or tossed through the ripping fabric. One of these later died in hospital. Thomson's verbal assault would probably have been playing on Brancker's mind when the reality of the huge airship's final plummet signalled its fate. Ignorance, foolishness and downright stupidity had all combined to snuff out the lives of so many prominent members of the British flying community, but above all the nation had lost aviation's greatest protagonist and a most likeable character; Sir William Sefton Brancker KCB, AFC, the Director of Civil Aviation.

In the aftermath of the R101 disaster some major developments took place during the autumn of 1930 that would shape the future of British commercial aviation. The first occurred on 22 October with the signing of an agreement between the Air Ministry and Imperial Airways for the operation of a weekly service between Egypt and the Cape, and an additional £60,000 was allocated from the Air Estimates to assist with the funding. The other important event was the maiden flight of the Handley Page HP42E, *Hannibal* (G-AAGX) at Radlett, an aircraft that was to epitomise the new comfort levels and safety standards that were to become synonymous with Imperial Airways during the next decade.

During six weeks of the summer, Imperial Airways operated a service with Short Calcutta flying boats between Alexandria, the Palestinian oil port of Haifa and Famagusta. This service was provided at the joint request of the Air Ministry and the Government of Cyprus.

From 20 September the European sector of the India route was modified and the mail was flown between Croydon, Cologne and Nuremberg; then by train from Nuremberg to Vienna and by air through Central Europe on the Vienna-Budapest-Belgrade-Nish sector, with rail used between Nish and Athens. Because of the vagaries associated with flying the Central European route, passengers were advised to travel on the Simplon Orient Express between Paris and Athens,

The Air Superintendent and his role

Although Wolley Dod, Tony Gladstone and Frederick Tymms had by March finally completed the survey of the northern section of the Cairo to Cape route, much still needed to be done before the entire route could become fully operational. One problem was in finding suitably experienced staff to run the numerous landing stations en-route. A training scheme was set up at Airways House to entice new recruits to join a two-year programme that would provide the fundamentals of international commercial aviation management. The programme included three months spent overseas and six months at one of the company's divisional headquarters. Within a short time a number of good candidates had enrolled and some of these progressed through the company hierarchy. During the same period the association formed by the pilots regularly met at Croydon's Aerodrome Hotel to socialise but they also became influential in improving the education and training standards that the company was implementing.

The dust had not settled in the aftermath of the R101 disaster when public opinion of commercial flying was dampened further by the crash of the Imperial Airways Handley Page W8f Hamilton on 30 October. One passenger and two Imperial Airways staff died when the aircraft hit a hillside at Neufchâtel, Northern France in fog. A second passenger died in hospital a few days later. The *City of Washington* (G-EBIX) had been converted from three to twin-engine operation, had left Le Bourget at 10.43 hrs bound for Croydon. The accident happened around 12.30 hrs but the scene was not discovered for two hours when farm labourers found an injured passenger who had crawled more than a mile from the wreckage. The injured passenger and the pilot, J J 'Paddy' Flynn (ranked only as a flight officer) both had leg amputations at Boulogne hospital. The Hamilton was nearly seven years old and was being used on the route as a relief aircraft. The cause of the crash was attributed to poor visibility and the failure of both engines after Flynn had reported that the right-hand engine had been giving trouble prior to the crash. The accident was another stark reminder of the inherent dangers that still awaited anyone who contemplated flying, especially in adverse weather. It had been suggested that the Imperial Airways management had reverted to giving pilots a directive that impressed the importance of departing and keeping to schedules irrespective of the prevailing conditions. This was something that had always concerned Brackley who, during mid-1930 was again at loggerheads with Woods Humphery and had been trying to determine exactly what his role as air superintendent meant within the company. On 6 May Brackley felt obligated to write to Woods Humphery outlining what he believed his role should be. The letter, reproduced in full, provides a clear insight into the way that Imperial Airways had been operating at that time.

FROM: Air Superintendent
TO: General Manager
'I submit herewith for your consideration a draft of what I consider should be the main duties of the Air Superintendent of the Company, together with an outline of the scheme for the selection and training of Pilots.*

In the main of course, the duties are similar to those previously carried out by the Air Superintendent, but in the past too much time has been taken up with details of the operation of the European Division only, leaving insufficient time for the development of work in both day and night flying which obviously should advance with the general progress of aviation.

With the expansion of the Company's operations it is considered reasonable that the scope of the Air Superintendent's duties should be extended. To carry out the duties at all satisfactorily it would be necessary, I submit, to appoint one of the senior pilots to supervise the duties of the European Division pilots only, and

to be responsible for the smooth working of the Pilot's Roster. The details of these duties, I feel, cannot be carried out satisfactorily by the Stand-by Pilot only, owing to liability of being sent away on duty at a moment's notice.

It is most desirable for the Air Superintendent to keep in very close touch with the Management, and this can best be done if the Air Superintendent is based at Airways House, where all the Pilot's records and correspondence affecting the Air Department should normally be kept.

The Air Superintendent's normal day could be spent partly at Airways House and partly at Croydon.

I feel too, that the Air Superintendent should be taken into the Management's confidence and be allowed the same privileges as the Chief and Consulting Engineers and Traffic Manager by taking part in the Management and other meetings at which the Company's operations and subjects affecting the Air Department are discussed.

In regard to the development of night flying on the European Routes, as well as the Near East, I would suggest that a meeting be held to discuss certain basic principles which have retarded night flying progress in Europe and to formulate plans for future development.

In conclusion I submit that with your backing and confidence, I can carry out the duties to your and the board's entire satisfaction.

The attached figures taken from the Company's Record, giving total numbers of flights per year from 1925 to date with the percentage of services interrupted or cancelled for weather causes or what might be termed 'Pilotage causes' show, I submit that there has been no falling off in pilotage efficiency. In fact the figures show an improvement'.

Brackley attached the following document.

'AIR SUPERINTENDENT'S DUTIES
The main duty of the Air Superintendent is to be responsible to the Management for the organisation and supervision of all subjects affecting the Pilots and their work for the Company.
This embodies:-
1. *Selection and training of Pilots for all Routes – Land and Sea*
2. *Supervision of the duties attached to Pilots and selection of Pilots in co-operation with the Divisional Managers and with the approval of the Management, for the various routes operated by the Company.*
3. *To collect the Pilot's Reports and Flying Returns from the Divisional Managers and to consolidate these into the monthly Air Department Report for the board.*
4. *To represent the collective views of Pilots at meetings held to discuss and decide on new types of aircraft★*
5. *To be responsible to the Management for the flying acceptance tests of all new aircraft and to work in closest co-operation with the Management, Chief and Consulting Engineers, in all matters affecting test, development and service flying, navigating instruments and other aids to flying.*
6. *To assist the Management in the development of night flying, ground organisation for night flying, the training and keeping in practice of Pilots and ground personnel for night flying. To keep in touch with the development of night flying in other countries. To watch closely the developments in Direction-finding wireless, wireless telephone and telegraphy apparatus in this and other countries, and to co-operate with the Management in the endeavour to obtain the most efficient types of D/F and other wireless equipment for aircraft, suitable for both day and night flying.*
7. *To attend Management and other meetings at which the Company's operations or any other subjects affecting the Air Department and Pilot's work are discussed.★*
8. *In order to investigate the conditions under which the Pilots are working on the various routes, it is desirable that the Air Superintendent should be allowed to fly on the routes at irregular intervals and work in closest co-operation with Divisional Managers in matters affecting pilotage, wireless, 'dromes and performance of aircraft.★*

SELECTION AND TRAINING OF PILOTS
1. *All applications from Pilots wishing to join Imperial Airways should be carefully considered and their records kept on an efficient card-index with the interviewer's recommendations placed on record for reference. Divisional Managers should send to Airways House, London, full details of an applicant's qualifications, together with copies of testimonials and their recommendations.*
2. *Briefly the applicants should possess*
   a) At least 1000 hours Piloting experience as Captain of aircraft.

LONDON

TO EGYPT & INDIA

PARIS

The presentation of this folder issued by your agent

will ensure special attention at any IMPERIAL AIRWAYS OFFICE

IN EUROPE THIS SUMMER

BRUSSELS

COLOGNE

travel by AIR

BASLE

ZURICH

IMPERIAL AIRWAYS

FOREMOST IN SIZE AND SAFETY

ALWAYS FLY ACROSS THE ENGLISH CHANNEL

LONDON
AIRWAYS HOUSE
CHARLES STREET
LOWER REGENT STREET, S.W.1
Telephone : Regent 7861 (Night & Day)
& Croydon Aerodrome

PARIS
AIRWAYS HOUSE
38 AVENUE DE L'OPERA
Telephone : Opera 09.16 (Night & Day)
& Le Bourget Aerodrome

BASLE
BIRSFELDEN AERODROME
Telephone : Safran 5966

BRUSSELS
68 BOULEVARD ADOLPHE MAX
Telephone : Brussels 164-61
& Haren Aerodrome

COLOGNE
DOM HOTEL
Telephone : Rheinland 222774
& Bickendorf Aerodrome

ZURICH
DUBENDORF AERODROME
Telephone : Dubendorf 126

The giant three and four engined air liners of Imperial Airways—the Big Ships of the Air—will bear you safely across the Channel in cushioned comfort on your trip to Europe this year. Whether your hunting ground be France, Belgium, Switzerland or Germany, you can travel there in the shortest time by Imperial Airways.

The 'planes are all of British construction and the British standards of safety are higher than any in the world. Every passenger 'plane on these services has three or four engines and can carry from 18–40 passengers. On all flights food and drinks may be purchased during the trip.

The journey will be one of uncrowded calm from hotel to hotel. There is no crush at Customs, no hectic change from train to boat and back again to train; just an effortless speeding through the air at twice the speed of an express train, sunk in the embrace of an easy chair, while all the panorama of Europe's countries slides gently away below.

Your comfort is studied to the smallest detail and every fleeting minute helps to build an experience that you cannot afford to miss.

Every detail of Imperial Airways is British.

BE SURE YOUR TICKET IS MARKED "IMPERIAL"

Any accredited Travel Agent will make reservations for you, before you leave the States if you wish, or the Company's city offices in New York, London, Paris and other Continental Cities, will reserve for you if desired.

Imperial Airways European timetable c 1930. (David Zekra)

b) *Experience on various types of aircraft but mostly on multi-engined types.*

c) *Flying-boat applicants should have had experience on float and boat aircraft and should be accustomed to flying out of sight of land.*

d) *Cross-country and night flying experience as Captain of aircraft in the British Isles and Near East.*

e) *A Second Class Navigator's Licence.*

f) *Must be of steady and sober habits and possess the right mentality and character for a commercial Pilot. He should not have any heavy responsibility such as a large family etc.*

3. *Special consideration should be given to applicants who have had most of their experience as Captain of aircraft on multi-engined craft and have to their credit a considerable amount of cross-country flying and night-flying, but not have completed the full 1000 hours.*

4. *Close touch should be kept with the Air Ministry and a record kept of Pilots whose qualifications are likely to be of use to the Company at the termination of their service with the Royal Air Force.★*

5. *Applicants selected by the Air Superintendent should be interviewed by the General Manager or by the Assistant General Manager, before the offer of employment is made.★*

6. *Successful applicants will be placed on two periods of probation of three months each.*

7. *As the most important part of a Pilot's work is the actual pilotage, the candidate's ability as a Pilot must be tested before a course of lectures is given on the various subjects affecting his future work. To put this into effect, the Air Superintendent or Chief Pilot should first test the candidate. Then he should be sent on service flights as Second Pilot on aircraft fitted with dual control. A careful record should be made of all flights so undertaken and a report attached by the Captain of Aircraft who should be one of the Company's most experienced Pilots.★*

8. *If after one month the reports are considered satisfactory, by the Air Superintendent, the candidate should be given a course of lectures on all subjects affecting the Pilot's responsibilities, on the Traffic and Engineering Department, and lectures should also be given on the Company's policy, International Legislation, Rules and Regulations at foreign aerodromes, Pilot's direct responsibilities etc.*

9. *At the end of the second month an examination should be held. Successful candidates should then be given as much flying as possible as Second Pilot until the end of the third month.*

10. *The Pilots should be allowed to qualify as Captain of Aircraft and should be sent on the short sectors of the European Routes such as the London-Paris, or Paris-Zurich, and London-Brussels-Cologne routes. If there is a freight service operating on any of these routes, then the probationary Pilot should operate it.*

11. *If at the end of the second three months the Pilot has carried out his duties satisfactorily, a report should be rendered to the General Manager recommending that he be taken on the permanent staff on the usual terms of the Pilot's Contract.'*

The items marked ★ represent the views that Brackley was most passionate about.

Following this lengthy prose, Brackley received confirmation of his duties and his simple diary entry on 26 May 1930 recorded: '*Return to duty as Air Superintendent.*' Brackley had requested a pay rise in a subsequent letter but this was turned down and during the six years he had been with the company he had never had an increase.

On 16 November, Woods Humphery took a passage on the *MS Mauretania* bound for New York where he met Juan Trippe, the 31-year-old president of Pan American Airways. The purpose of the trip was to discuss the potential for a New York-Bermuda service that Imperial Airways proposed to operate with an onward connection to London via the Azores. Trippe was also negotiating with André Boilloux-Lafont of Aéropostale and at the Frenchman's insistence the discussions were mostly conducted in French. This suited Trippe, who had a basic understanding of the language, but Woods Humphery had no grasp of it at all and was out of his depth. The discussions, spanning three weeks, were laborious and progressed slowly due to the language difficulties and were usually held at Trippe's fashionable Manhattan apartment at 1111 Park Avenue. At the end, a tripartite agreement was made to collaborate across the Atlantic and not to operate singularly, with New York, Paris, Lisbon and London suggested as the destinations. Trippe conducted his own negotiations for Pan Am but Woods Humphery and Boilloux-Lafont were acting as representatives of their respective Governments. The business to be derived from the discussions was not equally divided and by the end of the sessions the British took responsibility for control and landings in the United Kingdom and

Handley Page HP42W, G-AAXE, 'Hengist'. (CAS)

Handley Page HP42E, G-AAGX, *Hannibal*. This machine was one of only eight HP42 aircraft ever built. This aircraft went into service in 1931 and had its tail torn off during an emergency landing in Kent (August 1931) and later the wings were torn off in November 1932 at Tiberias. The airliner continued to serve Imperial Airways faithfully, but sadly was lost at sea between Jask and Sharjah on 1 March 1940.

Ireland and the French would control the Azores in an exclusive agreement with the Portuguese. Trippe's negotiating skills were such that although he did not have the right to control New York, he still managed to secure half of the traffic rights for himself, while Aéropostale and Imperial Airways had a quarter each. Trippe was a master at getting what he wanted. This was achieved by wearing down his opposition by embroiling them in long, hard discussions. He had a reputation for appearing genteel, even at times to act naïve, innocent and even bumbling, but he was renowned as a formidable negotiator. One of his contemporaries, an investment banker named Frank Russell, summed him up: '*He'll talk to you in his suavest, most deferential manner. You'll think there is no one like him and believe every word he says, and all of a sudden he's stolen your pants.*'

New comfort levels

The long awaited Handley Page HP42 bi-plane, G-AAGX (later named *Hannibal*), took to the skies for its maiden flight on 14 November 1930 seven months overdue. The airliner was very different from anything Imperial Airways had ever operated in the past and it had been designed

specifically to fulfil the company's requirements in two versions: one for the European routes (the Western version that became known as the HP42W), the other for the Cairo-Karachi route (the Eastern version HP42E). Passengers were accommodated in two luxurious saloons that were bright, airy and not dissimilar to railway Pullman cars in terms of comfort and interior finish. The passenger compartments were heated, well ventilated and soundproofed against the considerable engine noise from the four slightly-supercharged Bristol Jupiter X1F air-cooled radial engines. Passengers sat, four to a table, facing each other and were able to enjoy a full, in-flight meal service that was prepared on board by a uniformed steward. Unobstructed views of the ground were provided through the large windows. The galley, toilets and baggage compartments were located between the two passenger cabins in a vestibule set on the same geometric plane as the airscrews. This was determined by the noise factor; the drone from the engines in this part of the aircraft was considered too noisy for passenger comfort. The pilots occupied a forward enclosed cockpit in the extreme nose of the aircraft where they had an uninterrupted forward view making flying the aircraft more comfortable than in any of the company's earlier

airliners. They were no longer exposed to the elements but an enclosed cockpit was not altogether welcomed. Such were the peculiarities of the day that many pilots preferred to be in the open air where they could feel the wind in their faces. Old habits died hard and one of the reasons given for a pilot's preference for the open cockpit was that they felt they were easier to escape from if there was an emergency.

The first HP42 was constructed at Cricklewood before being transferred for final assembly by road to the new Handley Page works a few miles away at Radlett. Sqdn Ldr Thomas Harold England, the company's 37-year-old chief test pilot and commercial manager, flew the aircraft with his assistant, the elegantly named Major James Broome Lucas Hope Cordes. Initial problems were encountered because the long aircraft nose made it difficult for pilots to accurately judge attitude, and the high cockpit position made the judgement of level flight tricky. An external device was fitted as a temporary measure that acted as a very primitive form of artificial horizon that aided level flight at low altitudes. The unequal span upper and lower wings had no bracing wires. They were joined instead by a series of diagonal struts that were made of a light duralumin that had been used in the last airships. A major problem on the maiden flight was caused by flutter of the upper wing and aileron

'The New Road to the East' advertising brochure for Imperial Airways showing DH66, G-EBMW. (CAS)

when the aircraft built up speed. During the initial flight Cordes had applied full aileron causing a strut to buckle. To counteract this, George Rupert Volkert, the designer, added a pair of bracing wires to the outer wing sections on all production models to strengthen the struts and this solved the problem. On 2 December Brackley took the right hand seat and flew the aircraft for a brief period at Radlett for his first taste of the HP42. In view of the small, yet nagging teething problems discovered during the test flights, the aircraft was further delayed coming into service and had to wait until May 1931 to be granted a certificate of airworthiness at Martlesham Heath.

In 1930 Imperial Airways became involved in a number of non-scheduled special flights. The air tour that had been advertised in 1929 was re-launched and a short feature in *Imperial Airways Gazette* reported that the idea was *'becoming more popular but still sufficiently novel.'* Flights were offered on a 21-day air tour that departed from Croydon and visited the South of France, Madrid, Lisbon and Seville before crossing to North Africa with time spent in Tangier and Fez. Returning to Spain travellers were rewarded with the delights of Granada, Alicante and Barcelona before heading back to London by way of the Rhone Valley to Lyon, and Paris. The tour was advertised at £140 per person excluding accommodation and incidentals, but the *Gazette* emphasised it was not a conducted tour but a trip that would allow several days to be spent at each port of call.

In another promotion, Imperial Airways offered seats on a 20-seat *Silver Wing* airliner for an aerial weekend in Scotland. This flight left Croydon on 23 May and flew to Glasgow. For a one-way fare of £5 5s 0d (£5.25); £10 return, passengers would be driven to Croydon from Airways House, be offered in-flight refreshments and taken by car from Renfrew Airport to the centre of Glasgow. The entire round trip was accomplished in under ten hours and in certain respects was the equivalent to the modern *'Away Day.'*

Imperial Airways was making full use of every aircraft it had at its disposal. For eight guineas (£8 8s 0d/£8.40) passengers could fly to the Grand National at Aintree with entry to the prestigious reserved

Carriage Enclosure. Trips were also offered to watch the University boat race between Oxford and Cambridge from the air at two guineas (£2 2s 0d/£2.05p) including car transportation between London and Croydon. Larger aircraft were used for Easter trips to Paris, Brussels and other European cities as well as to the France-Wales rugby international in Paris. Another airliner was specifically chartered to fly delegates to a convention of sales managers in Scarborough and 300 livery company employees took flights aboard the Argosy *City of Coventry* after being given a conducted tour of Croydon Aerodrome. This venture gave Imperial Airways the ideal opportunity to promote their *Silver Wing* service to large groups of influential people. On Derby Day 17 passengers aboard an Imperial Airways airliner flying north of Paris were able to tune in to a live broadcast of the famous horse race being run at Epsom using individual headphones installed on the aircraft. The Prime Minister, Ramsay MacDonald and his daughter took *City of Glasgow* on 23 May for a flight to the Scottish city of the same name to attend an air pageant. The Argosy was being used to provide short flights for pageant visitors to promote the airline's regular services. This encouraged a record number of people to fly that weekend; most of them for the first time. In all 1,071 people took flights on Saturday 24 April and 1,280 the next day. In another promotion a company called Aviation Tours Limited hired a Handley Page airliner from Imperial Airways for a 5,000-mile tour of Britain and gave short demonstration flights to residents of several provincial towns and cities. The company expected to fly 10,000 people during the tour but no record could be located to clarify whether this was achieved. The popular tea flights over London were again provided from 14 June until the end of September on Friday, Saturday and Sunday afternoons.

The number of days it took to reach far-off destinations had already shown some improvements. On 2 June a flight between Egypt and England was completed in less than 60 hours to set a new record, and the extension of the air mail route from Karachi to Delhi using rail cut a further 24 hours from the journey time between the two cities. Passengers could now travel the entire India route in 8½ days.

During the year Imperial Airways used the extensive six-window frontage to its Charles Street headquarters to imaginatively promote its freight services. Central to this was a display of flowers picked in Egypt on Saturday morning that were on display by Tuesday. The company had made a series of experimental flights to import foreign fruits and vegetables into the UK that were displayed to promote the fresh, out of season produce the airline was carrying. All kind of produce was displayed including cabbages and green tomatoes grown in Egypt that were ripened in the UK, as well as foreign produce including bananas, apricots and fresh strawberries. Imperial Airways was also hired to fly fresh fruit into Croydon from overseas that was offloaded and driven to a London jam factory. As well as fresh produce, the office window displays also contained a range of scientific, medical and commercial items that had all been air freighted into Croydon. On 25 September, as a further example of how air freight was being considered for all kinds of commodities, a consignment of live canaries had been flown from Croydon to India.

By the close of 1930, Imperial Airways had flown 6,441,998 miles on domestic, European and Empire routes and had carried 159,026 passengers and 4,823 tons of freight, figures boosted with the help of the various tours and promotional flights that the company had commenced operating.

CHAPTER NINE

THE HP42 ENTERS SERVICE, THE AFRICA ROUTE AND AIR MAILS TO AUSTRALIA

1931

BRITAIN under the Labour Government was suffering from mass unemployment that, by spring, accounted for 25 per cent of the entire working population, double the number of 1928. The situation was much the same in other parts of Europe. In Germany the banks were failing and as many as five million people were unemployed. By August, the MacDonald Government had fallen and a coalition was formed with the Liberals and Conservatives that became known as the 'National Government'. Then a strange state of affairs occurred with a call for a general election that was held on 27 October. No fewer than 473 Conservatives were returned while Labour held just 52 seats, but MacDonald remained as Labour Prime Minister with 13 National Labour colleagues forming the Cabinet. Colonel Francis Shelmerdine was appointed Director of Civil Aviation after the death of Sir Sefton Brancker had left the position vacant. India was also experiencing economic problems as well as civil unrest. Her Government had remained adamant that only Indian nationals should operate flights across the Sub-Continent but this was hardly feasible considering that all State expenditure on civil aviation had been suspended. Nevertheless, Frederick Tymms, a civil servant, was given the difficult job of negotiating with a belligerent Indian Government.

Despite the difficult economic climate, Imperial Airways continued to progress and it was always an exciting moment when an important new aircraft was introduced to the fleet. The Handley Page HP42 airliner very quickly became a popular attribute for its comfort, safety and reliability. In contemporary times it was this airliner more than any other that unofficially became the trade mark of the company. It has been said that anyone fortunate enough to have witnessed the great aircraft in flight would have been enthused by the special rich sound, referred to by many as the 'symphony' that the airliner's four Jupiter engines made. Today it seems inconceivable that only eight of these magnificent aircraft were produced; four of each of the two variants, and it is sad that none survive. The aircraft was fondly referred to as the 'Flying Banana', so named on account of its curved-shaped fuselage. During October 2005, Capt Eric J Flanagan, the last surviving pilot of the HP42, died at the grand age of 97, severing the last living connection with the aircraft.

In February 1931 the manufacturer's test pilots, Sqn Leader Tom Harry England and Capt James Cordes, made their 22nd test flight together in the HP42 and took Frederick Handley Page's wife and three daughters for a brief flight. After landing, Cordes noticed that both ailerons were drooping abnormally. Handley Page's attention was discreetly drawn to the problem while his family were cautiously led away to prevent them from being alarmed by the damage. The cause was attributed to the aileron outrigger hinge brackets that had buckled during the tight turns and bumps the crew had exerted on the aircraft during the short flight. Strengthening brackets were fabricated and once fitted, the problem was promptly rectified and never reoccurred. As an amusing anecdote it is claimed that the original brackets were taken away and used to reinforce the bottom of a pond Handley Page was having built in the grounds of his home at Limes House, Stanmore. He later hinted jokingly that if archaeologists at some future point dug these up they might be mistaken for believing they had come from the chariot of Queen Boadicea who was believed to have been buried nearby!

Imperial Airways, keen to promote its magnificent new airliner to the public, announced the imminent arrival and named all eight production aircraft in accordance with its new policy of using mythological titles. Its faith in the HP42 was such that firm orders were placed for the entire fleet to be built before the first aircraft had even made its maiden flight. Imperial Airways' confidence was rewarded by the special price that the company was able to negotiate at around £21,000 for each aircraft. The first HP42, G-AAGX, was named *Hannibal* and the other three eastern variants followed; *Hadrian*

Imperial Airways Air Liner in the Clouds

1068

A contemporary postcard of G-AAGX, 'Hannibal' in flight.

AM701 IMPERIAL AIRWAYS "HERACLES" AT CROYDON 1939   Pamlin Prints, Croydon

The Handley Page HP42W G-AAXC 'Heracles' at Croydon – as seen on a commercial postcard. (CAS)

(G-AAUE), *Hanno* (G-AAUD), and *Hecate* (G-AAUC). The four western versions were *Heracles* (G-AAXC), *Horatius* (G-AAXD), *Hesperides* (G-AAXE), and *Helena* (G-AAXF), although because of objections from Handley Page over the Hell-Fire associations with the names of *Hecate* and *Hesperides* these were swiftly changed to *Horsa* and *Hengist*. Although Imperial Airways always referred to all eight aircraft collectively as HP42s (adding an 'E' at the end to identify the eastern variant and a 'W' for the western variant) Handley Page referred to the western variant as the HP45.

Imperial Airways promoted its new fleet auspiciously and, without doubt, the new aircraft offered passengers unprecedented levels of comfort. Its looks were considered to be fussy, consisting of two upper-wing engines, two lower and a box-like tail arrangement that made use of triple fins that were still very reminiscent of the past. The design also indicated that the Imperial Airways management remained set in its ways by continuing to favour biplanes. In many respects the airline was

regarded as a dinosaur, living in a time warp, afraid to investigate the potential offered by a more contemporarily designed aircraft. Instead it believed that the biplane would continue to serve as the vehicle that would carry the airline into the future. This was hardly enterprising for a company that was aspiring to become the world leader in air transport while elsewhere others were already turning to more streamlined designs in the form of the emerging cantilever-wing monoplanes. In Germany, Dornier and Junkers were paving the way in monoplane design, while Fokker was also successfully pushing the single-wing concept. The HP42 was nevertheless considered to be a safe concept. Additionally, it provided low operational and maintenance costs, but the original design dated back to 1921 when Hugh Oswald Short designed an easy access, low-fuselage aircraft with the same four-engine wing configuration and undercarriage layout but never used the patent. Subsequently, when the patent expired and was never renewed, Handley Page's designer, George Volkert, took advantage of Short's lack of foresight. Armstrong Whitworth also entered the frame by accusing Handley page of infringing its rights by employing continuously-rolled, drawn high-tensile steel strip in the fabrication of wing spars. Handley Page argued that the material it had used was duralumin that had flat surfaces that permitted the attachment of ribs. Its argument was not accepted and a High Court action ensued that Handley Page lost although it later won an appeal when the case went to the House of Lords. It is a matter of pure conjecture whether Frederick Handley Page's two brothers, Arthur (a judge), or Theodore (a barrister), had exerted any influence on the appeal hearing.

The HP42 had an upper wingspan of 130 feet that was fitted with Handley Page automatic slots and ailerons. The lower wing had a much shorter span. Both wings were built of duralumin around two metal box spars and the two fabric covered wings were braced together by rigid Warren-girder struts. The fuel tanks had a capacity of 500 gallons and were incorporated into the upper wing in typical Handley Page fashion. Initially there were two engine choices; the Armstrong Siddeley Jaguar and the Bristol Jupiter, but the latter was selected with the 490 hp Jupiter X1F being fitted to the HP42E and the more powerful 555 hp Jupiter XFBM on the HP42W. A Bristol gas starter was built into the

An Imperial Airways 'limousine' unloading at Croydon Airport during the 1930s. (CAS)

port side of the fuselage to provide external as well as internal access. This proved effective when no ground engineer was available to fire up the engines.

The HP42 consisted of a two-section fuselage made from metal monocoque (to the front) and of welded steel fabric covered structure to the rear. The forward section was covered in an outer skin of corrugated duralumin lined with plywood and the mid-section, where the galley and toilet were located, was lined with soundproofing materials to deaden some of the considerable noise from the engines. This area was closest to the propeller discs, hence, for safety reasons it was kept free of passenger seating as a precaution in case a blade failed and broke through the fuselage skin. The rear end of the fuselage was fitted with a shock-absorbing tail wheel.

The HP42Ws were based at Croydon and served the European sector of the India and South Africa routes. These were configured to carry 18 passengers in the forward cabin, and 20 in the rear with the freight and mail being transported in a 250-cubic foot central section located between the cabins. The cabin configuration on the Cairo-based Eastern variant accommodated only six passengers in the forward cabin and twelve in the rear. This was later changed to seat 12 passengers in each. Initially the central mail and baggage section was doubled to 500 cubic feet, but when extra passenger seats were added this was reduced accordingly.

The aircraft had some in-built design features that were incorporated to enhance safety. The four moderately supercharged Bristol Jupiter air-cooled engines had initially given some concern because the two upper units were fitted 27 feet above the ground and added considerable weight to the upper wing. Because of an incident involving a British manufacturer, W G Tarrant Ltd, which had built an aircraft known as the Tabor which had six engines, a throttle box was installed on the HP42 to force a delay between the power being applied to the uppermost pair of engines before those on the lower wing. In the Tabor incident, the uppermost engines had been started prior to the lower causing the aircraft to nose over. This resulted in both pilots being killed. The throttle box was an innovative piece of equipment that prevented the top engines reaching full power ahead of those on the lower wing, and it also prevented the lower engines from being throttled back before the upper units. The safety aspects imposed by this power control to the engines at take-off was the reason for the HP42's unique sound. The lower engines would reach take-off power first, followed, after a slight delay, by power being applied to the upper engines to produce a sound that was described as being like a chorus. The upper engines could never run at full-thrust ahead of the lower to prevent a recurrence of the Tarrant accident, and when taxiing the upper engines were allowed to idle, while the lower set provided the power to manoeuvre the aircraft along the ground.

Another design feature had also caused some concern when the aircraft underwent certification tests at Martlesham. The throttle levers, when pushed from idle to close had an automatic system that shut down the fuel supply to the engines. This prevented a well-tried method from being used that relied on opening the throttles before cutting off the fuel supply should a fire break out in flight. However the system was not considered to be a dangerous feature and certification was awarded without any modification.

On 6 June 1931, *Hannibal* appeared before the public for the first time when it was flown to the Royal Aeronautical Society garden party at Hanworth where it was demonstrated to members of both Parliamentary Houses. Five days later it operated on the London–Paris route with fare-paying passengers on a series of proving flights. On 8 August the aircraft became involved in a unique accident. A cowling fastener broke away and hit the port lower propeller causing it to disintegrate. This in turn set up a serious vibration. Fred Dismore was flying the aircraft and he took the prudent decision to land as soon as possible rather than to head for Croydon. The size and weight of the aircraft caused him some control problems as he headed for a field at Tudeley, near Tonbridge. As he made his approach he was conscious of nearby houses and telegraph wires, but in his efforts to land he clipped

An Imperial Airways DH66, with the later style enclosed cockpit.

a telegraph pole with the lower starboard wing but managed to land safely. However, the field was small and he also caught a tree stump that snagged the tail bracing wires and ripped off the rear section of the fuselage. Thankfully, nobody was injured in the incident but the aircraft had to be dismantled and taken back to Croydon by road for repair.

On 8 July, the second aircraft, *Hadrian* was delivered to Croydon after a few hiccups during its final certification tests. On 19 June it had been weighed at Radlett but was found to be 215 lbs lighter than *Hannibal*. During the first test flight on 23 June, the engines leaked oil and were misfiring, but the resident Bristol engineer had worked all night enabling Capt England to take the aircraft up next morning. Everything went well until the seventh test flight on 29 June when both England and Walters were on the flight deck. Walters complained of aileron snatch when banking to port. Two days later, Cordes took the aircraft up with Walters but was unable to find any problems and a series of tight turns were made. On this occasion the outer diagonal wing strut on the starboard side buckled and collapsed. Cordes blamed Walters, claiming he had placed undue stresses on the aircraft. As a consequence the struts were changed to crossed streamline tie-rods and the aircraft experienced no further problems.

The African adventure

1931 was a landmark year for it heralded the start of the weekly Central African service. The route aimed to cover the 5,124 miles between Croydon and Mwanza on Lake Victoria over a scheduled period of ten days. The inaugural flight left Croydon on 28 February, but carried only mail. After leaving Croydon, the service, flown by an Argosy, continued via Cologne-Nuremberg-Vienna and Budapest to Athens, a route that was still only considered safe and practical during the summer. During winter, the Simplon Orient Express continued to be used. From Athens the Short Calcutta flying boat operated via Mirabella, in Crete, to Alexandria but for the sector between Alexandria and Cairo the train was used. At the Egyptian capital another Argosy, *City of Arundel* (G-EBOZ), commanded by Capt Shepherd operated the first Cairo-Assuit-Luxor-Assuan-Wadi Halfa-Kareima sector to Khartoum, and a second Calcutta crossed the swamps of Southern Sudan and Uganda, stopping at Kosti-Malakal-Shambe-Juba-Port Bell-Kisumu and finally Mwanza. On the inaugural service this was operated by *City of Khartoum* (G-AASJ) flown by Capt Prendergast. Imperial Airways had established its Central African base at Kisumu where a connecting flight was operated by Wilson Airways in both directions that connected the town with Nairobi. Mail bound for the Belgian Congo was transferred at Juba and a special connecting flight was operated between Masindi-Kampala (Port Bell) because the inaugural service from Croydon did not serve Butiaba.

When the Air Estimates allocation was announced in March, only £651,000 from £18,100,000 was destined for civil aviation. Despite a contribution of £155,000 from the Dominion and Colonial Governments towards the costs for operating the Africa service, this

figure was low and continued to reflect how the Government was refusing to attach much significance to the industry.

Despite the long distances involved there was no provision for additional pilots to be carried on flights although according to Capt Egglesfield in *The Time Shrinkers* by David Rendel, '...*there was no time (nor inclination) for proving flights but, as a concession, two pilots were carried on the first two flights in each direction.*' Although the Imperial Airways rule book specifically forbade anybody who did not hold a pilot's licence from handling the controls of an aircraft, in practice it appears likely that at times during the cruise, the pilot would hand control to the flight engineer or wireless operator while he took a break. For obvious reasons, this was a dubious practice that Imperial Airways would not have wanted publicised but it seems it turned a blind eye.

On 10 March the return flight departed from Mwanza and followed the same northerly track to Cairo but with an additional stop at Butiaba. From Vienna, the European routing called for stops at Basle and Paris before reaching Croydon on 19 March. This was amended from 16 May when passengers were flown from Croydon to Basle where they joined the train to Genoa. But the European sector changed again from 11 June and reverted to Croydon-Paris by air using the HP42 *Hannibal* (G-AAGX), then by rail to Brindisi to rendezvous with either a Short S8 Calcutta or Short S17 Kent flying boat.

At the end of the year Capt Egglesfield made an unofficial night landing on the Nile at Kosti in the Sudan. Engine trouble on the Calcutta had delayed the progress of the northbound flight at Juba and he realised that he would not make the connecting flight at Khartoum. Arrangements were made for the Argosy to fly down to Kosti so that the Cairo-bound passengers could transfer there. Although there was very little light by the time Egglesfield made his approach he was able to identify the outline of the Kosti railway bridge that spanned the river and approached low over this, switched off any lights to reduce glare, and alighted safely on the water.

In the 1930s to fly any part of the Africa route must have been an extremely arduous experience; to travel the entire distance as a passenger for ten days, especially in the earliest period must have been an experience of extreme trepidation and discomfort. Yet, even the discomforts of flying at low altitude in unpredictable weather over territory that could be extremely hostile was preferable and offered greater security than the equivalent overland journey. Operating fairly basic aircraft over the African continent was never an easy exercise. The temperatures and cruise altitudes of the aircraft restricted the load capacity of the Argosy and the passenger compliment had to be reduced to ten or twelve. Cabins were not pressurised, forcing pilots to fly quite low over extremely hot terrain that would have frequently made the air unstable. Passengers would have had to endure severe discomfort from 'bumps' that would have caused all but the hardiest to experience airsickness. Frequent landings were required, not just to refuel but also to give passengers some respite from the hardships of the journey. Although overnight accommodation was provided at the many stops en route, in the early days these were scantily staffed hotels where the food served was often little more than watery soup with some rice and vegetables. At Aswan, for example, there was a stop for lunch but passengers complained about the pre-prepared sandwiches they were offered that had curled and almost toasted in the African heat. At most, passengers could not be expected to fly more than 1,000 miles a day, with a limit of around 700 miles being more realistic. After a hot, sticky night spent in very basic accommodation, passengers usually had to rise before dawn and be ready to depart at first light. There was no time for breakfast and refreshments would be provided later by the cabin steward during the flight. In addition, the health of passengers and crew could be a major consideration. Herbert Brackley on one of his enforced Africa jaunts had made reference to the conditions in his diary entry of 24 July 1931: '*Only this morning, when we thought everything was going well again, there comes a signal stating that Lumsden, the pilot of the southbound service, has gone sick at Malakal and the service is held up; Egglesfield, on the northbound service has an engine seized at Khartoum. Another pilot went sick at Kampala last week – the usual trouble out here, malaria. ... these fever stricken countries are most trying and in spite of all the medical care and precaution there seems to be no way out once a wretched mosquito has bitten one, or an animal for that matter. The tribes from Malakal southwards are chock-full of malaria and disease and the abortion and infant mortality*

is high. If only they could exterminate the mosquito – but that seems impossible where stagnant water lies in such huge areas such as the Sud.'

William Armstrong, a long-serving captain with Imperial Airways, was transferred to run the Near East Division from the Cairo station. He managed the commercial and technical operations from his base at Heliopolis almost independently and had to ensure that the aircraft maintained the schedules stipulated by head office. The RAF provided most of the radio and navigational support necessary to cover 3,000 miles of air routes. Imperial Airways did have a small maintenance team at the RAF station at Heliopolis and from there carried out repairs and servicing on engines and aircraft. They were also required to perform the annual inspections to conform to the requirements for the renewal of an aircraft's certificate of air worthiness. Armstrong by necessity had to be a 'Jack of all trades' responsible for selling tickets, catering and providing overnight accommodation for passengers. At times, he and his staff had to go out and search for a missing aircraft. He also had to keep records, accounts and statistics up to date. The small deployment of staff was all housed in a spare RAF hangar and they were required to work long and unsocial hours, rising in time to attend the departure of eastbound flights on the India route that took advantage of the cooler air to leave at 04.30 hrs.

Once the Africa route was opened Cairo became the home to three Imperial Airways divisions. Armstrong took responsibility for the Near East and was joined by Wolley Dod (in charge of North Africa) and Cross (the Mediterranean).

The typical schedule maintained on the first section of the Africa route to Mwanza (Lake Victoria) as advertised on 16 May 1931:

London Croydon	Dept	Saturday	08.30
Paris Le Bourget	Arr		10.45
		Dept	11.00
Basle (Birsfelden)	Arr		13.45
Central Station	Dept		16.04)Train
Genoa Station	Arr	Sunday	03.31)Train
Genoa Airport	Dep		06.44
Naples	Arr		11.30
	Dept		12.30
Corfu	Arr		17.45
	Dept	Monday 06.00	
Athens	Arr		09.00
	Dept		09.45
Alexandria	Arr		16.30
	Dept		19.00)Train
Cairo (station)	Arr		22.15)Train
Cairo Heliopolis	Dept	Tuesday	05.30
Assuit	Arr		08.00
	Dept		08.45
Luxor	Calling by arrangement		
Aswan	Arr		12.20
	Dept		13.05
Wadi Halfa	Arr		15.25
	Dept	Wednesday	06.00
Atbara	Arr		11.15
	Dept		12.00
Khartoum	Arr		14.00
	Dept	Thursday	03.00
Kosti	Arr		05.20
	Dept		06.05
Malakal	Arr		09.35
	Dept		10.20
Juba	Arr		15.45
	Dept	Friday	04.00
Butiaba	Arr		07.00
	Dept		07.30
Port Bell	Arr		09.20
	Dept		10.05
Kisumu★	Arr		12.05
	Dept	Saturday	06.00
Mwanza	Arr		08.50

★ At Kisumu the mail for Kenya would be flown by Wilson Airways to Nairobi in a D H Puss Moth.

Silent Travel

Travelling in the luxurious air liners of Imperial Airways is as quiet as in a Pullman car and conversation is carried on without raising the voice

4 Bristol 'JUPITER' 9-cylinder air-cooled Radial Engines developing 550 h.p. each in the 'HERACLES' and 490 h.p. in the 'HANNIBAL' class

Forward Luggage and Freight Hold

Handley-Page Automatic Safety Slot

First Officer

Captain

Wireless Operator

Steward

Trailing Wireless Aerial in Tube

Wind-driven Generator for supplying current for lighting and wireless apparatus

Two fully-equipped Lavatories

Connecting passage between forward and aft cabins

Steward's Pantry

Forward Cabin holding up to 18 passengers in the 'HERACLES' and 10 in the 'HANNIBAL' class

A contemporary piece of artwork, showing details of the then new HP42W Heracles class of airliners, then entering Imperial Airways service. This particular aircraft is 'Horatius', which crashed on Tiverton golf course, Devon, 7 November 1939.

Navigation Light

pan of top plane—130'·0"

Aileron

Length of Aeroplane - - 86'-6"
Height of Aeroplane - - 27'-3"
Maximum speed - - 130 m.p.h.
Cruising speed - - 100 m.p.h.
Approximate 'all-up' weight - 13 tons

Fixed Wireless Aerial

g cut
cabin

G · AAXD

ROYAL MAIL
GR

Aft Freight Hold

Royal Mail Insignia

International Registration Number

g up to 20 passengers in the
4 in the 'HANNIBAL' class

The 'HERACLES' type of Imperial Airways liners carries 38 passengers. There is a crew of four: Captain, First Officer and two stewards. There is also ample luggage accommodation and two lavatories

A Short Brothers S17 Kent flying boat introduced into Imperial Airways service in 1931. Three of the type served with the company and G-ABFC 'Satyrus' is seen here.

The mail service to Africa was not always smooth sailing. The southbound service that had departed from Croydon on 2 April ran into trouble and failed to arrive in Nairobi until the 17th owing to engine trouble. This snowballed, causing the northbound service to be delayed by three days. Equipment failures could readily upset services which led to the Nairobi Chamber of Commerce making a complaint and suggesting that all experimental work on the route should be completed before subjecting the public to such a poor service. The complaint escalated and it was requested that the Kenyan Government suspend subsidies until a reliable service could be guaranteed. Imperial Airways did not help its own cause when it published a cartoon showing an elephant holding a letter in its raised trunk, saying *'Where's my mail?'* The Chamber of Commerce responded to this self-ridicule by asking the very same question!

This was not the only problem to befall the Africa route. On 5 May, Tony Gladstone, the director of Imperial Airways (South Africa) Ltd was killed when the overloaded DH Puss Moth he was travelling in with Glen Kidston crashed into the Drakensburg Mountains in Natal. The two executives had been involved in negotiations for the sale of Union Airways to Imperial Airways when the accident happened. Union Airways was operating the Cape Town, Durban and Johannesburg via Port Elizabeth air mail link. The airline, started in 1929 by Major A M Miller, was a private company that operated a fleet of five DH Gipsy Moths that later expanded to include Junkers F13s, W34s and a Fokker Universal. The purchase failed to materialise and Union Airways was eventually taken over by South African Airways on 1 February 1934.

The Kent flying boat

Another new addition to the Imperial Airways fleet arrived in 1931. This was the Shorts S17 Kent four-engined flying boat that made her debut flight under the control of John Lankester Parker on the River Medway on 24 February. The new aircraft was essentially a larger, upgraded version of the Calcutta with an extra engine. The first of three aircraft was registered G-ABFA and named *Scipio*. The type was intended as a replacement for the Calcuttas on the Mediterranean routes that were proving vulnerable to rough seas. The flying ban in Italy, relinquished later in the year, also prevented Imperial Airways from making a refuelling stop at Tobruk, the Italian controlled Libyan port.

PASSENGERS BOARDING "SCIPIO" AT BRINDISI

LAMBERT & BUTLER'S CIGARETTES

REFUELLING "SCIPIO" IN ALEXANDRIA HARBOUR

This resulted in the company making the decision to fly Mirabella-Alexandria without a technical stop and the Kents were designed to fulfil this role. On 27 April *Scipio* left the UK bound for the Mediterranean.

The Kent flying boat was a great improvement over its predecessor. It had a fully enclosed cockpit, four moderately supercharged Bristol Jupiter XFBM engines and a stressed-skin metal hull, a design feature that had first been used on a flying boat by the Calcutta. Jupiter engines had become standard where possible throughout the Imperial Airways fleet giving the company an engineering advantage due to parts being interchangeable between the Kent and other aircraft in the fleet. The Kent was fitted out luxuriously in a way similar to the HP42 that mimicked the style of Pullman railway carriages and those on the French 'Blue Train'. The cabin had 15 comfortable, high-backed lounge seats arranged in facing pairs with tables between. The passenger accommodation, located below the wings, was spacious at 14 feet long and 6ft 6ins high with large curtained windows and a central gangway. Aft of the cabin, the steward's galley was located on the port side with a toilet and washroom opposite. A mail section was placed in front of the passenger cabin on the port side opposite the entry hatch, with a larger freight and mail compartment with two-ton capacity behind the cabin. The cockpit contained side-by-side pilot seats with dual controls with a radio station on the starboard side.

Much of the test flying and pilot certification was conducted by Brackley, but he was keen to include other Imperial Airways captains such as Walters and Wilcockson as co-pilots on alternate flights as well as flying with Major Mayo and Capt Bailey. On 2 May, Sir Samuel Instone was taken aboard for the second flight of *Satyrus* (G-ABFC) and it is believed that the aircraft sustained some damage during this flight. Col Shelmerdine, the Director of Civil Aviation, had been due to fly in the first Kent on 26 February but he arrived too late and darkness prevented the flight from taking place. During the same period, night-flying was being tested and Brackley flew an Argosy from Croydon with

Olley on 6 March without experiencing any difficulties. During the same month Brackley, at the suggestion of Shelmerdine, was offered the appointment as Deputy Director of Civil Aviation to the Government of India. This was a post he respectfully declined after discussing his future with Woods Humphery, again suggesting they were once more on amicable terms. Despite the politics, it was perhaps fortuitous that Brackley remained with Imperial Airways because his experience contributed much to the everyday operations of the company.

Syvanus had been prepared at Rochester for a demonstration flight staged for the directors of Imperial Airways and members of the press. Oswald Short made his dislike of Geddes obvious when he reluctantly escorted him to the moored flying boat. He was still harbouring an issue involving the chairman of Imperial Airways that had occurred in 1919 that had caused Short extreme embarrassment. As a result of the previous contretemps, Short had refused to show Geddes round his aircraft works. The original dispute had occurred in January 1919 while the Shorts airship works at Cardington was working on the R38. The contract was cancelled without warning and Short was summoned to a meeting at the Admiralty where Sir Vincent Raven bluntly informed him that his factory had been nationalised under the Defence of the Realm Act. Although Short received compensation, the Government changed the name to the Royal Airship Works and reinstated the contract for the R38. The decision to remove Short from the programme had been made by Raven's superior at the Admiralty. This was Geddes. Short refused to forgive Geddes and for axing another project he was involved with during 1922. From then on Geddes was never made welcome at Rochester and in snubbing Geddes, Short had gained an element of revenge that he was quick to reinforce when he wrote to Brackley to thank him personally for the work that he had done during the testing of the Kents. He made no reference to Geddes: '*The whole firm feels indebted to you for the prompt and safe manner in which you put the three Kents through their final tests.*'

The Australian Mail

As the year got under way battles between the international airlines increased as they fought to compete for long distance routes across the globe. The British retained India but wanted to establish a regular route to Australia and the French and Dutch had colonies in South East Asia that they needed to serve. On the African continent, the British, French, Belgian and Italians were all committed to expanding their networks to link with their respective colonies. The French Air Orient Company was a competitor Imperial Airways viewed as a potential threat because it intended to open a route to Saigon via Beirut, Baghdad, Karachi, Calcutta and Rangoon. This pointed to increased competition on the Iraq-India route that the British did not relish. The Germans were also concerned about the threat being posed by the French, but responded well by introducing night-flying on their Baghdad-Basra service. Imperial Airways did likewise by starting night-flying from 11 April; it cut the overall journey time between England and India to 5½ days. Imperial Airways also reacted by extending the London–Delhi mail service on an experimental basis to Australia that commenced at Croydon on 4 April although things failed to work out as planned. Using a DH66 Hercules, *City of Cairo* (G-EBMW), flown by Mollard and Alger, the route operated via Jodhpur, Delhi, Allahabad, Calcutta, Akyab, Rangoon, Victoria Point (Burma), Penang, Muntock, Singapore, Batavia, Semarang, Sourabaya, Rambang and Koepang (Timor Island) where the aircraft ran out of petrol and crashed on 19 April. At a point only six miles short of an airfield the crew realised they had insufficient fuel left to make a landing. With little option, they chose to bring the aircraft down in what they thought was a flat field of smooth grass. As they touched down they realised that the ground was strewn with rocks which caused the Hercules undercarriage to collapse on impact. Charles Kingsford Smith, the great Australian aviator and George 'Scotty' Allan of Australian National Airways (ANA) were hired to retrieve the mail in their Fokker F VIIb-3m, *Southern Cross*, (VH-USU). The Australians delivered the mail to Darwin on 25 April and from there a well organised relay operation was set up:

Captain Percy delivers the mail at Croydon after the first experimental Australia/UK mail flight in 1931.

- Darwin-Brisbane by Capt Russell B Tapp in DH61 *Apollo* (VH-UJB)
- Brisbane-Sydney by Capt P Lynch Blosse of ANA in an Avro Ten, *Southern Sun* (VH-UNA) that arrived on 29 April
- Sydney-Melbourne by Capt J A Mollison in a second Avro Ten, *Southern Star* (VH-UMG).

Embarrassingly for Imperial Airways, the delivery had taken 24 days to arrive from London. The return relay was operated again to carry the returning mail. This left Melbourne for Sydney on 23 April on *Southern Star*, continued next day on *Southern Sun* to Brisbane; to Darwin aboard the DH61 *Apollo* and by Kingsford Smith aboard *Southern Cross* to Akyab. The final haul to London was made by the Imperial Airways DH66, *City of Karachi* (G-AARY), that arrived on 14 May. The return flights had shaved five days from the time taken to carry the outbound Croydon-Brisbane mail but the success of the exercise was badly marred.

On 25 April a second attempt was made to fly a consignment of 5,000 letters to Australia aboard the regular Croydon-Karachi service. This was more successful and the mail arrived in Sydney and Melbourne without any major mishaps. On 5 May, the *City of Karachi* commanded by Capt Alcock had carried it from Karachi to Akyab where Kingsford Smith and Allan took over for the stage to Darwin on *Southern Cross*, where it arrived on 11 May. Tapp flew the next part of the relay from Darwin to Brisbane aboard the DH50, *Hippomenes* (VH-ULG), arriving two days later and a pair of ANA Avro 10s flew the last sectors: Capt Taylor with *Southern Moon* (VH-UMI) on the Brisbane–Sydney sector, and Capt Chaseling aboard *Southern Sky* (VH-UMH) the sector to Melbourne. The mail arrived on 14 May, ironically the same day that the first return mail had reached London. Two days later the westbound mail for Croydon left Australia.

Although Australian pilots and aircraft began the return mail flight with Capt Mollison in command of *Southern Sun* that left Melbourne for Brisbane, and with W Hudson Fysh flying the DH50 *Hippomenes* from Brisbane to Darwin, an Imperial Airways aircraft operated the next stage to Karachi. For the purpose, the company had bought a DH66 from West Australian Airways, (VH-UJO), that was flown from Perth to Darwin to arrive on 18 May. The registration was later changed to G-ABMT and the aircraft was named *City of Cape Town*. Capt Mollard flew this machine on the Darwin-Karachi sector, arriving in India on 21 May and transferred the mail to the scheduled service that reached Croydon six days later. Progress was being made, albeit slow. The mail had taken 16 days, but this was half the time it would have taken by sea. The success of the venture prompted Kingsford Smith and Charles Ulm to apply to the Australian authorities for a permanent mail contract that they proposed would link with Imperial Airways at Karachi.

While the Australian–Imperial Airways efforts were gaining some credence out of the confusion, the Dutch company, Koninklijke Luchtvaart Maatschappij (KLM), under the direction of the irrepressible Dr Albert Plesman, decided to stage a show of its own. It had already commenced operating a scheduled service linking Amsterdam with Batavia (now Jakarta) to establish the longest regular air route in the

The closed cockpit of an HP42W Heracles class, which must have made for a much better environment for the crews to conduct their long flights.

world (8,540 miles), but it wanted more. Plesman's next vision was to operate a mail service from Holland that crossed the Australian coast at Wyndham, to arrive at Sydney on 18 May, eighteen days from Amsterdam. KLM was extremely well organised and keen to take advantage of the lucrative Australian mail contracts. Having already established its presence in Batavia it was only a comparatively short 'hop' across the Timor Sea to either Port Darwin or Wyndham on the Australian coast. The stakes had risen. Now KLM, ANA, and West Australian Airways were all competing with Imperial Airways for the Australian mail contracts. The British were angered and considered that the Empire route between London and Darwin was their birthright. The competing companies disputed any divine rights that the British made claim to. Fortunately for Imperial Airways, KLM's plans did not always run as smoothly as expected either, and it was also being challenged strongly by the Australians. A suggestion was made by ANA to operate a high-volume Christmas mail service to London that H P Brown, the Head of Australia's Post Office, approved. Kingsford Smith and Ulm were never slow to react to an opportunity and, on 20 November, they despatched 'Scotty' Allan in the Avro X *Southern Sun* from Melbourne. 1,500 lbs of mail and a single passenger were aboard

the heavily laden aircraft as it struggled to gain height. The passenger was Colonel Horace Clowes Brinsmead, the Australian Controller of Civil Aviation who ironically was London-bound to discuss the air mail and passenger links between England and Australia. Brinsmead has been described as a tireless worker with a gift for cutting diplomatic red tape and had been responsible for framing the Australian air navigation regulations. He had worked, much as Brackley had for Imperial Airways, investigating commercial routes and landing grounds over thousands of miles of harsh territory. After stopping in Malaya at Alor Star, the *Southern Star* bogged down on a waterlogged airfield and crashed after the centre engine failed. Nobody was hurt but the aircraft was unable to continue. Kingsford Smith again responded to the call by flying *Southern Cross* to collect Allan and the mail but Brinsmead chose to continue his journey by taking the KLM-scheduled Fokker FVIIb service. The man's luck ran out because this aircraft also crashed at Bangkok's Don Muang airport killing five people. Although Brinsmead narrowly escaped death, he suffered dreadful head injuries. He was flown home from Siam (Thailand) in February 1932 but remained an invalid until his death in 1934 and he never worked again.

Hudson Fysh, founder of Queensland and Northern Territory Aerial Services and known universally as 'The Flying Fysh' heard of the mishap that had befallen *Southern Star* but as his airline still had only single-engine aircraft that were not suitable for crossing large expanses of water, Qantas could not respond leaving Kingsford Smith unopposed to deliver the mail to Croydon. He arrived on 16 December but more bad luck followed. The day before the *Southern Star* was due to depart for the return to Australia, she too crashed in fog at Croydon and repairs to the aircraft delayed her departure until 7 January 1932. Although time was subsequently made up, the belated return mail did not reach Sydney until 21 January.

Fysh used the opportunity to send air mails to various people highlighting the Australian spirit behind the mail flights and was gracious enough to praise the efforts of his rivals, Kingsford Smith and 'Scotty' Allan. One cover was destined for Woods Humphery, no doubt in good faith, but the Imperial Airways manager's response was uncalled for and characteristically pompous: '*We are fully alive to the intentions at the backs of the minds of the promoters of the air mail flight to London and back as we have, unfortunately, other experiences of people with little behind them creating nuisances; as we call them.*'

Details of the HP42 passenger aircraft – showing the large biplane tail unit with triple rudders and the large size of the main undercarriage - in comparison with a cotemporary motor vehicle. The aircraft shown here is G-AAXE, 'Hengist'; she was the only HP42W not to survive until the Second World War, having been destroyed in a hangar fire at Karachi on 31 May 1937.

Fortunately for Imperial Airways, despite this rebuff, Fysh and McMaster were not prepared to give up the idea of establishing a link with the company. In the interim, Fysh sent a telegram to McMaster concerning the ANA bid for the mail contracts: '*Application made by ANA to operate permanent route Brisbane-Darwin and to India receiving considerable support. Position fairly critical to our own interest.*' West Australian Airways had also made waves for an immediate mail connection with KLM through Wyndham. Until then, Qantas had never been considered a serious contender beyond its own backyard in the sheep-rearing outback of Queensland and Northern Territory. Since the company's formation in 1919 this was the first major challenge it had encountered, but Fysh viewed the situation as something he had to face up to or in his words be '...*forced to close its doors.*' As often happened, fate played a hand and Kingsford Smith's efforts were seriously hampered. On the morning of 21 March, one of ANA's most experienced bad-weather pilots, T W Shortridge, disappeared on a flight from Sydney to Melbourne in the three-engined Avro X *Southern Cloud* with six passengers. Shortridge had more than 4,000 flying hours to his credit and he knew the route he was covering like the back of his hand. Ahead of him on this fateful morning lay a cyclone with winds raging to over 60 mph. The aircraft never reached Melbourne and speculation at the time suggested that the Avro had either been blown out to sea or crashed in dense forest. No trace was found of the aircraft until twenty-seven years later when the wreckage was discovered during 1958 in the Snowy Mountains of New South Wales.

The disappearance of *Southern Cloud* naturally caused the public to lose confidence in ANA. The economic depression that Australia was suffering had already had a marked effect on the company's balance sheet caused by a downturn in passenger traffic forcing the board to suspend services on 26 June. This was initially decided on a temporary basis while negotiations were held with the Australian Government, but any financial assistance that might have been expected from the State never came and the airline ceased operations. On 15 May Fergus McMaster set out his plans to establish a formal link between Qantas and Imperial Airways in a letter that he sent to Hudson Fysh: '*You might be able to suggest in some way that if Qantas was the operating company from Darwin, Imperial Airways might have representation on the Qantas Board and that a subsidiary company of Qantas would operate the service, keeping all operations of that service separate from its other activities. If there were any future interruption such as that caused by the City of Cairo (a crash), the organisation at Darwin would have suitable machines and staff to do the work done by Kingsford Smith this time.*

'*If a subsidiary company consisting of Qantas and Imperial Airways interests were formed, it would mean that the Darwin-Brisbane-Sydney-Melbourne service would not only have the advantage of direct Australian management, but would also be in the closest touch and of assistance to the overseas section from Darwin. Suggestion could also be made that this organisation could make contact with a branch service of West Australian Airways at some suitable point, thus allowing the mails to get to Perth and Adelaide by the quickest route.*'

McMaster also instructed Fysh to hasten contact with British and American aircraft manufacturers with view to buying three-engined machines for his company. On 16 June Fysh contacted Woods Humphery again in what he termed the '*first definite approach*'.

While developments were accelerating in the race for the mail contract between England and Australia, back home, Imperial Airways proudly carried TRH Prince of Wales and Prince George from Bordeaux and Paris and landed them on Smith's Lawn in Windsor Great Park on 29 April 1931 to end the Royals' tour of South America. Originally Their Majesties were to be flown from Lisbon but the political situation in Spain had caused their ship to be diverted to Bordeaux. Gordon Olley had the honour of flying the Royals on this occasion, accompanied by Brackley, in the Argosy *City of Glasgow* (G-EBLF). Olley later wrote in his 1934 book *A Million Miles in the Air* how the Prince of Wales was a staunch advocate of flying: '*The Prince not only loves flying as a swift method of travel, but he himself can pilot an aeroplane with judgement and skill. When he makes one of his journeys by air, he is not content*

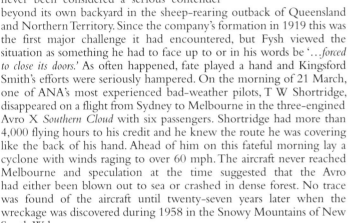

ELEPHANTS IN THE SUDD

to remain seated in his arm-chair in the saloon. When His Royal Highness charters an airliner in that way, he has not been long in the air, as a rule before he jumps up and makes his way to the cockpit, taking his seat beside the pilot, and interesting himself keenly in every aspect of modern aerial navigation. The Prince is, as I have said, an expert pilot, while what interests him particularly is the system of wireless communication between an aeroplane in flight and ground stations, which has been brought to such a state of perfection in modern airway working. On the flight to which I referred just now, when I piloted the Prince on his return from South America, we had a capital example of the value of wireless. Bad visibility – the airman's bugbear unless he has a wireless to help him – dogged our aerial path. But, being as I was in constant touch by wireless with the control tower at Croydon, I came through accurately to schedule, and without a moment's doubt as to my position above the obscured face of the earth below. The Prince, sitting out with me for long spells in the cockpit, followed attentively each phase of this application of modern science to aerial navigation: and after I had landed him in his own private aerodrome at Windsor Great Park, he spent some time in discussing the technical development of commercial aviation. His Royal Highness has a clear grasp of the one essential fact, and this is that speed is the vital asset of the aeroplane. It is speed which brings us our loads in commercial flying; and what the Prince advocates keenly – always bearing in mind the need for safety and reliability – is a steady increase in the speed in which our civil 'planes fly. He wants to see Britain lead the world in this new industry which may, ere long, prove to be as important as, and perhaps even more important than, our great shipbuilding industry.'

Although Brackley recalled the flight in his diary, Olley fails to mention in his account that the air superintendent was on board. If anything can be read into this omission is a matter of conjecture, but it may indicate a further suggestion that Brackley's popularity among his charges was less than desired.

The Prince of Wales satisfied his interest when he took the controls of the Kent flying boat *Sylvanus* (G-ABFB) at Hythe on 27 May, the day after Brackley had flown it on the final acceptance flight at Rochester. The Prince had gone to inspect the new Canadian Pacific ocean liner, *Empress of Britain*, before she set sail on her maiden voyage from Southampton and he later accompanied Brackley at the controls of *Sylvanus* during the flypast as the ship sailed into the Solent.

The political wrangling that had taken place with the Italian Government finally reached an amicable agreement that, for the time being, changed the structure of the European sector of the India route. The ban on Imperial Airways was lifted, allowing aircraft to operate to Genoa, Rome and Naples. From 18 May the route was changed to Croydon–Basle by air, Basle–Genoa by train and onward by air using the new Kent flying boats. The first southbound flight was operated by *Satyrus* (G-ABFC) on 16 May while *Scipio* flew the homebound sector with the mail from India. But *Scipio* was damaged when Capt Horsey landed on heavy seas at Candia and ripped a wing-tip float from the aircraft. Sensing the danger, Horsey immediately commenced a take-off run and flew the damaged aircraft to Mirabella where he landed safely in more sheltered waters. The damage put the aircraft out of commission for a month and it had only just gone back into service when a second aircraft, *Sylvanus*, collided with a Dornier *Wal* in Genoa harbour causing damage to two of her engines. The Calcuttas had to be recalled to service but their range made it difficult coping with the distance between Mirabella and Alexandria. By August all three Kents were back in operation and by October they were using Brindisi in compliance with the recent agreement with the Italians.

Sir Alan Cobham set off for a second time to survey 12,300 miles of the African route on 22 July 1931 in a Short Valetta S11 float plane (G-AAJY). The new survey was conducted at the joint request of Imperial Airways and the Air Ministry to look at landing places along the Nile and to evaluate a new Central African route from Entebbe to the West Coast. By 5 August the team of six had reached Entebbe. The next stage required surveying the Ruwenzori Range, the high country that stretches between Lake Albert and Lake Edward. Severe turbulence and continuous bad weather forced the team back and after a week battling against the elements Cobham gave up, returned to

Entebbe and then back to England, landing on Southampton Water on 31 August.

During July Brackley was also in Africa on an inspection tour of the central states. Flying on one of the Calcuttas his diary reveals some of the discomforts that had to be endured in Africa. At the start of the month he was in Khartoum, having flown there on the Argosy from Heliopolis. He complained of the sand flies that had pestered him for several hours en-route at Wadi Haifa. On 7 July he had a forced-landing at Kampala after encountering '*large size thunderstorms*' between Kisumu and Mwanza. When one of the engines completely failed Brackley tried to return to Port Bell, but was forced down in what he termed as '*...sleeping sickness country*' at a place called Kubanga. He reported that '*... the place was lousy with crocodiles...*' and the '*...wireless operator had accidentally dropped the generator pulley into the water and we couldn't communicate with anyone!*' Brackley's journey continued after a kindly native took him eight miles on his motorbike to the nearest 'Englishman' who then drove him in his car to the telegraph station, six miles away. By chance another British national was testing the equipment and Brackley was able to use the engineer's small telephone to communicate with the Imperial Airways office at Kampala. A spare engine was located at Kisumu, 220 miles away, and Brackley was driven there with the freight and mail from the Calcutta '*...over the worst roads I have ever met*' to collect the engine and continue to Nairobi. Meanwhile a tug had been organised to tow the crippled flying boat to Port Bell.

With the engine replaced, Brackley reached Entebbe before returning to Khartoum and being thrown about in severe storms: '*...a series of violent rain-squalls and thunderstorms, in one of which we continued to be sucked up to 5000 feet in spite of all engines being throttled right down and our air-speed over 115 mph. Gliding wasn't in it!*' The Africa route was perilous and it is surprising that anyone wanted to fly there, let alone pay for the privilege. Diseases and misery were widespread throughout the continent and Brackley wrote of this to his wife: '*... the mosquito boots are a blessing, as these pests are terrible in this part of the world. The hospitals are chock-full of malaria, enteric and typhoid patients. One cannot be too careful. I am feeling very fit and hope to remain so.*'

At the 7th AGM of Imperial Airways, Geddes announced that the company profits had fallen by £60,000 to £27,140. When he informed shareholders that the company possessed 41 aircraft this was an exaggeration because he had included the Atalantas that were still under construction, three charter aircraft and three obsolete W8s. At least he was able announce some good news; that five HP42s and three Shorts Kent flying boats had all been put into service during a difficult trading year. During November three of the HP42s, *Horsa*, *Hadrian* and *Hanno* were flown to Cairo in readiness to operate on the Eastern Route.

Changes were made from 21 October when Imperial Airways announced the independent departures from Croydon of the India and Africa services that had previously operated as a single departure as far as Athens. At the same time, the trans-Mediterranean section frequencies were doubled. The India service departed from Croydon at midday on Saturdays; the African at the same time on Wednesdays. The agreement reached with the Italians earlier in the year had been short-lived and the political differences returned forcing passengers back on the train across 975 miles between Paris and Brindisi, where they boarded the flight for Athens. India service passengers flew from Athens via Castelrosso (eastern-most of the Dodecanese Islands) to Haifa where they transferred to cars from Haifa to Tiberias, where they rejoined a flight to Karachi via Baghdad. The first re-routed Africa service departed from London on 21 October and from Athens passengers flew to Alexandria via Mirabella (Crete) on to Haifa. By 29 December the Karachi-Delhi sector that had been operated by the Indian State Air Service ended and was taken over by the Delhi Flying Club using a Gipsy Moth.

At the end of the year Brackley and Alger returned to Africa to make the final survey of the Cairo-Cape Town route. They delivered the DH66 Hercules *City of Karachi* (G-AARY) with the Christmas mail on 21 December in readiness for the opening of the experimental service in January 1932. The aircraft name was also painted on the fuselage in Afrikaans that read '*Stad van Karachi*'. Brackley and Alger were accompanied by Air Commodore Fletcher, Capt Durrant of the Air Ministry and Mr Vleery, a Dunlop Estate Manager from the East Indies (described as '*an expert on malaria*'). After leaving Croydon they flew via Marseilles to Pisa in good weather, but after spending a night in Rome appalling weather was encountered en route to Naples that forced them to fly at 500 feet. From Messina and Etna to Catania they found clear air and after a smooth flight spent the night at Malta but were delayed by a failed elevator rod. Over the next two days the flight continued to Tripoli, Syrte and Benghazi; then Tobruk, Matruh and Cairo, but after leaving at dawn on 23 November they were forced to land at Luxor to make adjustments to one of the engines. By the 25th they had reached Khartoum via Wadi Halfa but the engines were performing badly and further adjustments had to be made.

Writing in his diary for 1 December at Kisumu, Brackley records

LAMBERT & BUTLER'S CIGARETTES

"SCIPIO" OVER ATHENS

that: '*Although we did not intend to stay here more than two days to give the City of Karachi a good look-over before proceeding to the South African Division, so much work was found necessary that we shall not get away until Thursday the 3rd, and then we fly only to Nairobi, spend the rest of the day there seeing the Governor of Kenya and heads of departments, Posts, Wireless and Meteorological before going on to Moshi, Dodoma and Mpika...*' Heavy rain and electrical storms further delayed their progress at Entebbe.

Brackley also commented about the importance of the mail in his diary entry for 16 December: '*... It is difficult to realise the havoc distance plays with letters in the great continent of Africa, and the public are only too anxious to have the air mail to speed up things a bit. When one realises that from Central Africa it takes two months to get a reply from England, poor homesick husbands are almost in despair...*' The flight had reached Johannesburg via Nairobi before flying on to Moshi across the mountain ranges of Kilimanjaro and Meru. After landing at Mpika, the route continued towards Broken Hill where the worst weather of the entire trip was experienced forcing Brackley to fly low over forests and mountainous country. He had attempted to turn back but the storms had also closed in behind him and the party had to shelter at one of the emergency landing grounds at Kanona. This was located at an altitude of more than 5,000 feet and the small airstrip meant that Brackley had to send Fletcher and Durrant, the party's rigger as well as luggage and spares by lorry to Broken Hill to reduce the take-off weight in order to get the Hercules airborne. Next day, 10 December, they left for Salisbury and crossed the Zambezi River. Crowds gathered to greet them and to see them off at dawn, bound for Bulawayo where they rested a couple of days. On 12 December they set off on the final sector of this difficult journey via Pretoria to Johannesburg where Brackley had a series of meetings to discuss wireless communication, meteorology and the many other essential requirements for the opening of the Cape route. On 19 December the tireless Brackley was present for the official opening of Germiston Aerodrome, in the Witwatersrand to the south-east of Johannesburg where he took the Governor General for a flight in the Hercules.

During 1931 there had been little progress in establishing an independent air service in the British Isles. Only one operated and this, by its nature, flew a rather strange route. The operational details are obscure, but a pilot named Michael Scott ran a twice-daily summer service across the Wash from Skegness (Lincolnshire) to Hunstanton (Norfolk) for the company he later called Eastern Air Services. A DH Puss Moth (G-AAXL) was flown at a return fare of £1.00 for the 17-mile journey. It was hardly a route that was destined to make a profit, yet the tiny airline survived.

Towards the end of 1931 another historic flight had been made and on 7 December, Herbert 'Bert' Hinkler (1892-1933) flew into Hanworth Air Park from Paris in his Puss Moth after becoming the first person to fly single-handed across the South Atlantic. His record flight had began in Canada and continued to New York, Jamaica, Venezuela and Guyana before embarking on the 22-hour crossing in terrible visibility from Natal (Brazil) to the Gambia. The journey was completed in stages along the West African coast to Europe.

CHAPTER TEN

THE ATALANTA AND THE OPENING OF THE CAPE ROUTE

1932

THE start of the regular mail-only service to Cape Town, a journey covering approximately 8,000 miles, was heralded by the 12.30 hrs departure of the HP42W, *Helena* (G-AAXF), from Croydon to Paris on Wednesday, 20 January with Capt Youell in command. The aircraft continued to Cairo where it was positioned for later flights and on the first stages of the flight *Helena* was accompanied by her sister, *Hengist* (G-AXEE). Afterwards the company celebrated with a South African themed lunch at Croydon for several hundred invited guests and presented each of them with a folder, *The Dream of Flying to Africa*, which contained cartoons and quotations. Lt Col Sir George Beharrel, a director of Imperial Airways, greeted the guests and another board member, Lt Col Barrett-Leonard, proposed a toast to which Mr George W Klerk, the Secretary to the South African High Commissioner responded. A special guest, Major Ewart Grogen, an adventurer who had walked from the Cape to Cairo in 1900, gave a speech and toasted Imperial Airways by saying: '*To fly across Africa and back is no longer an adventure but an entrancing experience in which 8,000 miles of Empire unrolls beneath your armchair.*' An evocative description, except for the moment, Imperial Airways was only carrying mail on the Africa service although Francis Bertram of the Air Ministry and Sir Vyell Vyvyan were on board the inaugural flight. The main purpose was to ensure His Majesty's Mail was carried safely, and a hefty consignment of 20,000 letters and 150 parcels were heading for the Cape. This was achieved using a variety of aircraft but it took 10 days for the mail to reach its destination. *Helena* ended her involvement at Cairo where the consignment was transferred to the Argosy, *City of Birmingham* (G-EBOZ). This flew the Cairo-Khartoum sector where a Calcutta flying boat waited to carry the cargo to Kisumu. A DH66 Hercules, believed to have been *City of Baghdad* (G-EBMY) flew the final Kisumu-Cape Town stage, arriving on 1 February. Fare-paying passengers had to wait until 27 April to use the service.

Typically, the official launch of the service failed to go to plan. The *City of Baghdad* arrived eighteen hours late at Nairobi after being forced to make an un-scheduled landing due to tropical storms. By the time the aircraft reached Johannesburg it was already late enough, but by Cape Town it had fallen a full two days behind schedule. Things were no better for the return operated by *City of Basra* (G-AAJH) that left The Cape on 27 January. If the delays on the outbound flight from Croydon had caused the critics some consternation, this could hardly be compared with what happened next. Upon reaching Salisbury, the aircraft wheels sank in a boggy hole on the airfield causing damage to the tail and fuselage. A relief aircraft was sent but this was forced down after only 40 miles by bad weather and tipped onto its nose on a waterlogged landing ground. The mail eventually reached England but

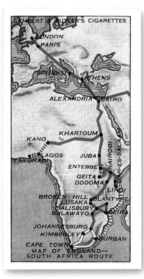

it was nine days late. The airline's critics were far from amused. This included Capt Harold Harrington Balfour, a Member of Parliament, who raised embarrassing questions in the Commons about the fallibility of Imperial Airways. Balfour had personal interests at stake. As a director of Whitehall Securities he had joined the board of Saunders-Roe, the aircraft manufacturer. Later still he became involved in Spartan Airlines (a company set up by Whitehall Securities) and he had also piloted a Spartan Arrow aircraft in the 1930 Kings Cup Air Race. On 10 February he raised the issue of low passenger yields on the Imperial Airways India service by rightly pointing out that only 75 passengers had flown the route during the whole of the previous year. These were mostly oil and other workers and it appeared there was little public interest in flying to India. Two days later he was on his feet again, to point the finger at Sir Philip Sassoon, the Secretary of State for Air, enquiring whether he was aware that the Government subsidy for the Cairo-Karachi service amounted to £1,800 per ton of payload which, when converted into passenger yield, equated to £180 for every passenger carried. Because passengers were only paying £58 for the privilege of flying the route he considered, with due cause, that the Government subsidy was being squandered. He had a point, but surely was this not the price that had to be paid in the name of progress? Sassoon, in his reply, was forced to concede that the figures Balfour had quoted were correct although he said he failed to appreciate the relevance of the debate. Balfour continued, questioning why Imperial Airways had been granted a £20,000 subsidy towards the cost of flying boats. This was a pointed question that suggested Balfour harboured a hidden agenda and was bitter because Imperial Airways had not awarded Saunders-Roe a contract. Balfour's involvement with civil aviation continued and he was later appointed Under Secretary of State for Air (1938-1944) and was bestowed the title, Rt Hon Lord Balfour of Inchyre PC MC.

Balfour refused to be silenced and continued his attack during the usual debate that followed the announcement of the Air Estimates. This time his comments were aimed at Imperial Airways' state monopoly that he claimed '*retarded civil aviation*'. He criticised the route to Egypt because it required passengers to travel 970 miles by rail and only 1,200 miles by air. He also mocked the Australia route by reminding the House that it had only been flown once and that resulted in a crash and then remarked that the trans-India route had become impractical because of political bungling; the same kind of thing that was causing problems on the Persia sector. Turning his attention to South Africa, he proclaimed the route was not credible and reminded members that the Hambling Report had recommended a 50/50 split in subsidies between public and private enterprise, but Imperial Airways had been paid £2m

HP42W, G-AAXC 'Heracles', in a publicity photograph with a Marconi van at Croydon c1930. (Author's collection)

while the shareholders had only contributed £500,000 of their own money. In conclusion Balfour proposed that there should be no further agreements in favour of Imperial Airways. On this occasion, the Air Estimates had provided £473,000 to civil aviation from a total of £17,400,000.

Balfour's criticism in Parliament about the Persia route had some justification. The political debates continued but the Persian Government refused permission for British aircraft to use their landing grounds. In consequence the route flown by Imperial Airways had to be changed (see later) to fly along the southern coast of the Gulf by way of the British Protectorate of Bahrein (Bahrain). This necessitated the need to fit extra fuel tanks to the HP42s. What concerned Imperial Airways more was that no similar ban had been enforced on KLM who was enjoying free rights over Persia on its Amsterdam-Batavia (Jakarta) service. There was further concern for Imperial Airways because it feared the Dutch airline might be awarded the Batavia-Sydney route that it was attempting to negotiate with the Australian Government that could have been devastating for the start of the Empire service.

With Cape Town now becoming the final destination in Africa, the stage from Kisumu to Mwanza was withdrawn. With the exception of the inaugural flight, the journey across Europe was still relying on the train between Paris and Brindisi as Balfour had correctly pointed out to Parliament. Future services were due to be operated by the Hercules from Croydon but only as far as Paris and passengers did not reconnect with an aircraft until boarding the Scipio flying boat at Brindisi. This flew them to Alexandria but rail was also being used from there to Cairo. To fly the entire Africa route was extremely involved and required a bizarre mixture of trains and aircraft. As they had on the inaugural flight, the Argosy operated Cairo-Khartoum, the Calcutta between Khartoum and Kisumu and the DH86 Hercules on the final stage to Cape Town. With this number of changes the journey was made incredibly arduous and it could never justify being called 'direct'.

The African route from Kisumu operated via Nairobi, Moshi, Dodoma, Mbeya, Mpika, Broken Hill, Salisbury (now Harare), Bulawayo, Pietersburg, Johannesburg, Kimberley and Victoria West. As strange looking machines descended from the skies at these townships local people could be excused for musing over the alien experience that confronted them. Their reactions can only be imagined when they saw an aeroplane descend from the sky for the first time. This would have encouraged a feeling of trepidation, excitement, perhaps even fear and hostility. Aircraft were things that tribal people simply

were unable to comprehend. A wonderful story tells of an elderly African tribal chief, who witnessed the landing of an early flight. He slowly approached the Imperial Airways crew to enquire whether he might acquire one of the eggs of the great bird to propagate on his land. The captain politely refused his request but some years later the chief was rewarded with the opportunity to fly to London to participate in an African conference.

Passenger traffic opens to the Cape

On 27 April the route to the Cape was opened to passengers with a one-way fare of £130. This may have further incurred the wrath of Harold Balfour once he became aware that the price included all meals and hotel accommodation. Despite the progress being made on the route structure, something needed to be done to eradicate the lengthy train journey. This situation was not exactly satisfactory and it must have added considerably to the stress passengers had to face. Flying in Africa was still preferable to going overland but there were disadvantages. There was a lack of restaurants between Cairo and Mwanza and passengers frequently had to be content with the unappetising dry sandwiches they were offered. Flying was still falling far short of the glamour that the airline advocated.

The first northbound flight from the Cape was also scheduled to depart on 27 April and although 25 passengers had been carried over short sectors of the route, only one person completed the entire journey to arrive at Croydon on 8 May. The next day, *Horatius,* (G-AAXD) operating the outbound flight was struck by lightning while flying over Tonbridge causing the wireless and trailing aerial to be burnt out. Capt O P Jones was quick to respond and turned the aircraft about and returned to Croydon. *Helena* (G-AAXF) was assigned as the replacement but only thirteen of the original passengers were prepared to board the aircraft. The other five were sufficiently shaken by the experience and refused to continue their journey. There was still a lack of public confidence in air travel and, because a lightning strike was a rare occurrence, it is understandable that some of the passengers had been terrified by the ordeal.

In spite of the mounting criticism levelled at Imperial Airways over its inability to attract sufficient numbers of fare-paying passengers, this failed to deter the company from advertising low cost air cruises in a concerted effort to conjure up a different kind of business. This was an early attempt to enter the package holiday market by advertising a 16-day trip costing £80. The price included all flights, first class sleeper

accommodation on the train, hotels and motor tours. The tour took the scheduled flight to Paris, rail connection to Brindisi, flying boat flights on the Kent class to Athens, Castelrosso and Galilee where passengers were offered a three-day car tour of Damascus, Jerusalem and other parts of the Holy Land. This ended on the 8th day with a trip from Tiberias to Cairo where four further days were spent visiting Egyptian tourist sites. On the twelfth day passengers would join the Cairo-Alexandria train then fly to Crete and Athens next day, spending the final three days travelling back to England. Passengers also had the option to extend their holiday by adding a week at any of the locations before joining the scheduled flight that was returning to London.

On 16 April the India service incorporated an extra stop with aircraft scheduled to call at Limassol, Cyprus and three days later the Short Scipio *Sylvanus* (G-ABFB) opened the service that flew Alexandria-Haifa-Limassol. The service received little support and by 12 October it was withdrawn. There was also a welcome change on the Africa route when the HP42s were brought into extended use between Cairo and Kisumu from November to replace the Calcutta flying boats and Argosy biplanes.

The independents
During 1932, although the nation was in the grip of a severe recession that had seen the unemployment figures reach 2.8 million, a number of home-based airlines opened. The bank base rate stood incredibly low at just 2% which offered some encouragement to the fledgling companies, but not to the majority of people who were hardly able to afford a seat on an aeroplane. The domestic airlines addressed this and many of their fares were extremely low. The economic situation failed to deter those with an entrepreneurial spirit and the low bank rate encouraged some to use this to their advantage when they felt a niche market for an air service existed. A number of small airlines were started in association with regional bus services to connect with their regular routes. Today some of the air routes that evolved would seem rather diverse and almost all of the routes operated involved crossing expanses of water.

Even one regional daily newspaper got into the act during January when the *Bristol Evening Times* ran a twice-daily experimental service between Bristol and Cardiff. This lasted only a week and used an Avro 10 chartered from Imperial Airways. The British Air Navigation Company Ltd (BANCO) was launched on 10 February to fly experimentally between Cardiff (Splott) and Bristol (Whitchurch) using an impressive looking silver and blue Fokker FVIIA (G-EBTS) named *The Spider,* the aircraft used by Barnard and the Duchess of Bedford on some of her pioneering flights. Barnard was also a pilot for BANCO and four flights a day were made at a fare of 15s 0d (75p) single; 27s 6d (£1.37½p) return. During the first year BANCO claimed to have flown 48,542 hours on contract and hire work. It added services to France with a route to Pourville and, from 12 July, added Heston-Deauville and Heston-Le Touquet services in mid-1934. BANCO also flew a pair of Ford Tri-Motor aircraft and employed T W Morten as a pilot, but despite carrying 585 fare-paying passengers the company was wound up in March 1935.

British Amphibious Air Lines was registered on 22 February to operate between various UK seaports. The company was founded by Messrs Kirston and Mace with a small group of other directors and had a capital of £3,500. One of these was Howe Monk who, during the summers of 1932-33, operated an irregular service between Blackpool and the Isle of Man using the Saro Cutty Sark amphibians, G-AAIP and G-ABBC *Progress.* Around 5,000 passengers used the service that had been organised to link with Progress Buses which provided through bookings on their coaches that ran between Blackpool-Leeds, Bradford, Dewsbury, Huddersfield, Halifax, Burnley and Barnsley. Between June and the end of September, the company flew 8,920 miles and carried 348 passengers. Monk departed in 1935 and joined Portsmouth, Southsea and Isle of Wight Aviation Ltd, (PS & IOWA) founded in 1932 when Wight Aviation Ltd re-organised.

A second amphibian operator, a company called British Flying Boats Ltd ran a regular, but short-lived, experimental service between

HP42W, G-AAXE 'Hengist' in north Africa c1932.

Greenock and Belfast (Musgrave Channel) using the Saro Cloud, *Cloud of Iona* (G-ABXW). The company also operated between Stranraer, the Isle of Man and Belfast but this lasted for only one week.

PS & IOWA was a well-financed private organisation with a capital of £100,000. The company operated a Portsmouth-Ryde ferry service using a Westland Wessex (G-ABVD). From 1 July it began operating in conjunction with Solent Coaches to provide connecting road-air services. By 1934 the company was still operating quite successfully and had opened air routes between London (Heston)-Ryde-Shanklin, Portsmouth-Ryde-Shanklin and Portsmouth-Shanklin that ran four times a day. The summer services were extremely popular and during a single week in 1934 the company carried 2,338 passengers between Portsmouth and the Isle of Wight and 181 on the Heston-Isle of Wight service. Amy Johnson worked for the company at one stage and Sir Alan Cobham became chairman in 1935 and forged an association with North Eastern Airways at Heston to fly routes linking the south of England with Leeds, Doncaster, and Newcastle and later, Edinburgh.

Another route operated in association with Hillman's Airways between Southampton, Portsmouth and Paris using a five-passenger Airspeed Envoy.

During October, National Flying Services (registered in 1929) briefly operated flights between Hull and Grimsby with a Desoutter monoplane at a fare of 14s 0d (70p) return. The company was initially set up to establish a nationwide chain of flying schools, but moved into air charter and taxi operations. Cobham was also a director of this company along with the Colonel the Master of Sempill, but the business was not a success and it was advertised for sale as a going concern in June 1933, failing to attract a buyer and it subsequently went into receivership.

Another small airline, Eastern Air Transport Ltd, was formed during 1932 (see previous chapter) by Michael Scott who had previously started Eastern Air Services a year earlier which operated across The Wash. Scott's new company ran a seasonal service every day between Skegness and Nottingham and later added Skegness-Leicester, Nottingham-Skegness and Leicester-Nottingham, all at rock bottom fares. The first flight was made on 22 May between Nottingham and Skegness and was flown by Scott with Alderman W Green, the Lord Mayor of Nottingham, as his first passenger. The history of the company is vague but it is thought to have gone into liquidation during 1935 when its base aerodrome at Skegness was sold.

Hillman's Airways opened a service on 1 April between Romford (Maylands) and Clacton using a DH Puss Moth and a Fox Moth. Such was the popularity of the service that by June the company was operating every three hours from 09.00 hrs at a fare of £1 return. The airline was the brainchild of Edward Henry Hillman of Gidea Park, Essex who operated a very successful coach company before launching

LAMBERT & BUTLER'S CIGARETTES

TEMPLE OF QUEEN HATSHEPSUT

'The British Air Line': a period brochure cover for promotional purposes.

Hillman's Saloon Coaches & Airways Ltd in November 1931. Hillman was every bit the entrepreneur despite being illiterate. He began as a bicycle repairer and later had a car hire business before evolving as one of the most successful independent transport operators in the country. Prior to turning his attention to aircraft, Hillman had built his coach business to more than 200 vehicles. He learnt to fly and operated Puss Moths *Gilford* (G-ABVX), *Babs* (G-ABSO) and *Sonny* (G-ABSB) before adding three Fox Moth biplanes to his fleet (G-ABVI, G-ABVJ and G-ABVK). A De Havilland Dragon (G-ACAN) was also bought and this was christened *Maylands* by Amy Johnson at Romford prior to the aircraft being put to work on the Romford-Paris (Le Bourget) route. Hillman's offered daily air trips from Maylands (originally known as Hillman's Aerodrome) and published a tariff of long distance domestic flights at 3d (less than 1½p) a mile.

A further successful operator was Norman Edgar who started a charter service known as Bristol Air Taxis. Later, using a DH83 Fox Moth (G-ABYO) flown by W N L Cope, between Somerdale (Somerset) and Heston, he carried chocolate under contract to J S Fry & Son. In September a twice-daily service was flown across the Bristol Channel linking Bristol (Whitchurch) with Cardiff (Splott) using the Fox Moth that Cope also flew on the route until it was abandoned as uneconomical by the British Air Navigation Company (see above). The airline changed its name to Norman Edgar (Western Airways) Ltd in September 1933. Dragons and Dragon Rapides were added to the fleet to operate between Weston-Super-Mare, Bristol and Cardiff; Bristol-Bournemouth and on a limited basis, Cardiff-Bristol-Le Touquet-Paris.

On 20 May the race between the famed *Flying Scotsman* train and an aircraft was repeated. Capt Jones commanded the Handley Page HP42W, (G-AAXC) *Heracles*, although on this occasion the flight was to test radio communication between the aircraft and the train.

Mishaps were never far away and it is indicative of the times and the fairly primitive equipment available that accidents and mechanical failures were inevitable. An embarrassing moment occurred at a garden party on 19 June being staged by Dick Fairey, the President of the Royal Aircraft Establishment at Hanworth. *Heracles* had been the star of the show and tea flights were made by the airliner at five shillings (25p) to promote the Imperial Airways flying experience. A scrimmage for seats occurred that kept the airliner busy. With 32 passengers aboard, the aircraft suddenly went through the ground when a conduit beneath the surface ruptured. The port wheel of the HP42 sank causing damage to a wing, propeller and undercarriage. *Heracles* remained stranded for several days and a cordon of Boy Scouts was assigned to surround the aircraft to prevent onlookers and souvenir hunters from getting too close. Frederick Handley Page was one of the more prominent people blocked from reaching the aircraft. Baden Powell's boys were not to know who he was, and as far as they were concerned he was to be barred with the same indifference as any other spectators who got too near the stricken aircraft.

The first monoplane
1932 also heralded the introduction of the new four-engine cantilever monoplane, the Armstrong Whitworth AW XV Atalanta Class that commenced engine runs during May. This aircraft was a major break from the Imperial Airways tradition of commissioning and operating only biplanes on its scheduled services and a monoplane was still a very new concept especially with British designers. The biplane remained the popular choice because the double-wing arrangement created a sufficiently large wing area to enable landing speeds to be kept low enough to cope with extremely short runways. When John Lloyd was designing the AW XV he felt that the extra power created by four engines would make the aircraft safer and more reliable even if this caused landing speeds to rise. Lloyd envisaged an aircraft with a lighter, single wing that would produce greater aerodynamic efficiency. The design that emerged was considered to be a breakthrough that was well ahead of its time and the Atalanta was a great improvement on its predecessor, the Argosy.

The Atalanta was designed with sleek, smooth lines that were more streamlined than any previous Imperial Airways aircraft. The wing-mounted engines were fitted to and recessed into the leading edges and were faired in a tidy fashion. The undercarriage was streamlined and although not retractable, it did fit partially within the lines of the fuselage. The aircraft had been developed using a wind tunnel and this

Armstrong Whitworth AW XV Atalanta Class G-ABTH, 'Andromeda' in Africa, note G-AAXE 'Hengist' in background. (CAS)

Armstrong Whitworth XV Atalanta Class G-ABPI, 'Atalanta' in Africa. (CAS)

work had contributed much towards the reduction of drag that was a feature of the design and was half that of the Argosy. Had the designers gone the whole hog and incorporated a retractable undercarriage, the aerodynamics would have been even more efficient. As much as 25 per cent of the fuselage drag was caused by the exposed landing gear yet, for no apparent reason, retractable undercarriages were still viewed with some suspicion in Britain.

The aircraft was made of wood and mixed metal and the overall design allowed for a generous amount of cabin space for the passengers.

Originally only nine passengers were carried on the Africa route and these were accommodated in a well-ventilated cabin fitted with adjustable-back wicker chairs that were arranged either singularly or in pairs facing a table. The flight deck was also spacious − built to accommodate two pilots and a wireless operator. Behind the cockpit there was a large mail compartment with room for one ton of cargo and beyond this a luggage compartment and the steward's galley. When the aircraft was subsequently used on other routes the passenger seating was increased to seventeen.

Commercial postcard of G-AACJ 'City of Manchester', Armstrong Whitworth Argosy MkII in 1932. (CAS)

AM745 IMPERIAL AIRWAYS Armstrong Whitworth "City of Manchester" Pamlin Prints
at Croydon Aerodrome c1932 Croydon
(By Courtesy of Morgans (Purley) Ltd.)

Commercial postcard of Short L17 G-ACJJ 'Scylla' at Croydon in the early 1930s. (CAS)

"SCYLLA"
IMPERIAL AIRWAYS AIR LINER
K 1594

The Atalanta was powered by a pair of 5-cylinder Mongoose moderately supercharged radial engines on each wing that were linked together to provide a pair of 10-cylinder two-row engines. These were capable of producing up to 375 hp at 4,500 feet. The power units were initially known as 'Double Mongoose' engines but the name was later changed to Serval. In service the aircraft recorded a true cruise speed of 118 mph at 9,000 feet and it had a rate of climb from the ground of 550 ft/min. If an engine failed, the designers claimed the Atalanta could remain aloft at 9,000 feet at a speed of 51 mph with the engines throttled back and a fully laden aircraft needed just 375 yards in which to take off.

The Atalanta made her maiden flight on 6 June 1932 after going straight into production from the drawing board, which for the time was considered to be an unprecedented move. On 27 June the Atalanta made her first public appearance at the SBAC Display at Hendon. The first aircraft was flown on tests at Martlesham Heath on 11 July and was certificated in August. By September two more of the type had been delivered, *Amalthea* (G-ABTG) and *Andromeda* (G-ABTH). The remaining five were completed and delivered to Imperial Airways in April 1933. From the outset pilots reported the Atalantas to be easy and enjoyable to fly and no major problems were encountered, either during testing or in commercial use. The only minor downside was that pilots had to exercise care to lift the tail at the right time to get airborne and at certain speeds the aircraft had a tendency to sink rather suddenly. There was also moderate vibration caused by the engines that resulted in some damage to the bracing wire, engine mounts and oil tanks which

Passengers disembarking from Short L17, G-ACJJ 'Scylla' at Croydon aerodrome during the mid-1930s. (CAS)

had to be rectified by fitting stronger wires, steel tubes and rubber mounts for the oil tanks.

On 26 September *Atalanta* made her Imperial Airways debut on the service to Brussels and Cologne on the same day that the third aircraft, *Andromeda* was delivered. For the remainder of the year the aircraft were operated irregularly on the scheduled services between Croydon, Brussels and Cologne and on the Croydon-Brussels-Basle-Zurich route before being introduced to the Empire routes.

Some minor modifications were required to *Atalanta* and she was flown to Coventry for the work to be carried out. However, while she was being test-flown on 20 October a more serious problem occurred and the aircraft suffered a sudden loss of all four engines. This was found to be caused by fuel starvation created by the use of a new type of fuel tank vent and was soon rectified. The aircraft was being flown by Alan Campbell-Orde who had just been given clearance to take off when the incident occurred. Fortunately he was able to land just beyond the airfield boundary on a hillock. The landing was heavy, causing substantial damage to the fuselage and undercarriage and Donald Salisbury Green, the test pilot operating the aircraft with Campbell-Orde was injured seriously enough to end his career, but Campbell-Orde was unhurt. The incident was embarrassing for the manufacturer, Armstrong Whitworth, and it did its best to keep the accident concealed. A few reports appeared in the press but it only revealed that the aircraft had received *'minor damage'*. While *Atalanta* was undergoing repairs, the aircraft's name was secretly transferred to G-ABTI, the fourth production aircraft. This was probably carried out as an attempt to further cover up the incident even though the new *Atalanta* now had a different registration. After extensive repairs, the original *Atalanta* reappeared carrying the fleet name *Arethusa*.

G-ABTI, the newly named *Atalanta,* was delivered to Imperial Airways on Christmas Eve and entered service on 5 January 1933 on a proving flight to Cape Town where it arrived on 14 February.

On 13 July, Imperial Airways took part in an operation devised to speed air mail between Britain and Canada during the period when the Imperial Economic Conference[1] was being held in Ottawa. This exercise clearly illustrates the complex organisation that was sometimes

devised to ensure that mail reached a destination. In this particular case a Westland Wessex was used on 13 July, 30 July and 13 August to fly mail between Croydon and Cherbourg. This connected with the SS *Empress of Britain* that carried the consignment on the five-day Atlantic crossing to Red Bay (Strait of Belle Isle) where it was transferred to a Bellanca seaplane bound for Havre St Pierre. From there it was loaded on a Vickers Vancouver flying boat, for the journey to Rimouski before completing the final part of a relay to Ottawa aboard a Fairchild FC 2.

Continuing problems with Persia

During the autumn of 1932 the political situation with Persia was increasingly fragile and permission was withdrawn for the previously approved limited passage of British aircraft over Persian territory on the north side of the Gulf. The India service had, until 1 October, used the direct routing Basra-Bushire-Lingeh-Jask-Gwadar. This sector had been agreed under a three-year term by the Persian Government in 1929. Persia had insisted that aircraft should take the inland route that would require departing from Baghdad (missing out Basra) and flying the route via Shustar-Isfahan-Yezd-Kirman-Bam and then Gwadar. This was a lengthy diversion over difficult terrain that the company considered too dangerous. Instead, aircraft were forced to fly the longer southerly tract that would route the aircraft from Basra to Kuwait and then onwards via Bahrain, Yas and Sharjah on the Arabian side of the Gulf. At that time Sharjah was little more than a patch of desert and the landing ground consisted of a row of tents surrounded by barbed wire that was guarded by local tribesmen. Brackley aptly conjured up a vivid description of the journey from Baghdad on *Hanno* in a letter sent to his wife on 22 November 1932. *'Up again at two o'clock local time (we had one hour's sleep) and flew on to Basra, 280 miles before daylight. Breakfast at Basra then off again in less than one hour for Kowsit, where we landed to pick up more passengers. Only ten minutes here and on to Bahrein, where we refuelled… It was very hot at Bahrein and sun helmet was essential. Off again for a long sea crossing of over 300 miles to our next and final stop for the day. It was dark before we got to land again, and we alighted at Sharjah by the usual flare path… This station at the moment consists of tents surrounded by barbed wire and guards armed to the teeth. Near by the "Works and Bricks" are building our fort.*

---

[1] This was a conference organised by the Canadian Government and had no connection to Imperial Airways as the title might suggest.

We had to taxi the aircraft inside a barbed wire enclosure and this is rigorously guarded all night by a gang of real toughs, under order of the Sheik, who came over to greet us and was quite genial, but looks an old brigand...

'A pleasant dinner in the tent with our 9 passengers and a sit-put in the cool air of the desert, and we were already for our 4 hours' sleep. Up again at two o'clock, and off we set over the mountains of the Oman Peninsula to Gwada in Baluchistan, keeping 3 miles off the Persian coast. This hop of 440 miles is quite a long one and nearly all over water. Refuelling at Gwada, up again for the final hop to Karachi, where we arrived at 4.30 on Sunday afternoon.'

After Sharjah the aircraft would cross the Gulf to reach Gwadar en-route to Karachi. The first service to use the Arabian route was operated by the HP42E *Hanno* (G-AAUD). During mid-November strong gales swept across the area around Galilee causing damage to *Hannibal* that temporarily put her out of action

Imperial Airways 'cabin boy' 1930s. (CAS)

The previous account in Brackley's words summed up brilliantly what passengers could expect during their brief desert stops in the Persian Gulf. Another account, this time by William Armstrong, a former pilot who managed the Near East division at Heliopolis for four years, described a journey between Cairo and India during the 1930s. Armstrong's delightful passages, taken from his 1952 book, *Pioneer Pilot* painted a lively picture of an arrival at a primitive airport and a typical early morning departure:

'The robust three-engined de Havilland Hercules was used between Cairo and India until replaced by the much larger Hannibal.

'With both planes our flight-stages were short, the first from Heliopolis to Gaza, 212 miles, then to Rutbah Wells, 365 miles, to Baghdad, Basra. Lingeh, Jask, Gwadar, Karachi. We used to take three days for the journey with night stops, sometimes at one place and sometimes at another. We had scheduled every place at one time or another as a night stop, except Lingeh and Gwadar.

'Come with me in the imagination. After arriving at Cairo railway station in the heat of a hot, dry Egyptian summer day, from Alexandria where you had arrived three and a half hours before by flying boat, you are housed in a hotel for the night.

'If you have spent the early part of the night sightseeing, you will probably be too fatigued next morning to do much more than doze in the plane because you have had to rise long before dawn for the four-thirty departure from Heliopolis.

'To drive out to the aerodrome in the very early hours of the morning is dull and irritating, and however early you went to bed the night before, you feel only half awake now; you take no notice of your fellow passengers, nor they of you. You feel a vague emptiness inside which does not come from hunger; it is because your routine has been disturbed.

'After only a few minutes you are bundled out at the aerodrome hangar which serves as office and passenger reception building. You notice that you are walking on sand, but in the darkness you can scarcely see the building itself. The reception area is crude, although attempts have been made to make it attractive. There are not-unattractive Egyptian carpets on the concrete floor, with their blacks, browns and fawns, and made of camel hair; and there are comfortable wicker chairs, tables and magazines – and the place is clean.

'You are met by a bright young fellow in uniform, an Imperial Airways commercial trainee who is destined to become a station superintendent in a year or two, or more, depending on how he conducts himself. He is at least alert and wide awake. He collects passports, examines tickets, conducts you and your fellow passengers to the waiting room, sees you are well provided for, then arranges for customs and police to see you, takes your weight and completes the 'ships' papers.

'Meanwhile you have a cup of tea brought to you, while behind the scenes the mail is checked and loaded into the plane under the supervision of the station superintendent. The pilot finally examines his load sheet, checks that it is within the authorised weight limits, and having worked out his flight ahead announces that he is satisfied. You are then conducted aboard the waiting plane, until a moment before an object of great activity. Now it is quiet; all the dead load of mail and freight are aboard and the plane awaits you and the other passengers.

'You are led over the few yards of soft sand, and step aboard; the door is closed and the atmosphere is funereal. But now the silence is shattered by a sudden, rattling clangour which tells you that the first engine has been started; then follows the other two engines and you feel the plane begin to move. You look at your watch, and unless you have passed through Cairo before you feel a little surprised to find that the time is precisely that advertised. If you had been able to see out and ahead you would have discovered a young traffic assistant with a torch showing a red light, holding the plane back until the exact time of departure, when he would change the colour to green.

'The plane bumps across the sand in the darkness. You cannot see anything, until away to one side you see first one, then another, paraffin flare; then a long line of flares, flickering golden and ruddy in the darkness. You feel the plane turning; you catch another glimpse of the line of flares, through the struts between the wings, you lose them again and then, all of a sudden the engines open up to full power. You bump along the rough sand and see the flares go by one by one; then suddenly the bumping ceases – you are off.

'There has been so much activity within the last hour that you imagine that all the world must be awake. But looking down on to the lighted streets of Cairo and Heliopolis, you see that there is not a soul about. Quickly the lights of the town are behind and you head out into the darkness of the desert; but we are not yet separated from civilisation; the delta keeps bearing along with us to our left and from time to time we see the lights of villages, Bilneis and Tel el Kebir and we almost skirt the RAF aerodrome at Abu Suir.'

In his book Armstrong continued with the narrative to describe the places that the passengers would be able to see from the air. If they were able to endure the discomforts, during the early years, passengers were at least compensated by the outstanding vista they could watch pass by their cabin window.

The mother of the editor of this book, Muriel Forsyth, poses elegantly for a photograph at the fuselage door of HP42E, G-AAXE 'Hengist', at Heliopolis, Egypt in the late 1930s. Note the crude access ladders to the wings, weighted down by sandbags and the very rudimentary door locks. (Robert Forsyth)

CHAPTER ELEVEN

THE ENGLAND-AUSTRALIA ROUTE
NEARS FRUITION
1933

ALTHOUGH the Armstrong Whitworth AW XV was an impressive new machine, in certain respects it failed to entirely live up to expectations. On 5 January Herbert Brackley was aboard *Atalanta* (G-ABTI) that departed from Croydon at 10.20 hrs for the proving flight to Cape Town where he was scheduled to meet Woods Humphery. The crew consisted of Campbell-Orde and Capt Egglesfield who flew the aircraft to Cairo. For the journey beyond, *Atalanta* was under the command of Capt H W C Alger. The aircraft had been fitted with new wireless equipment enabling the crew to maintain contact with Croydon all the way to the Egyptian capital. This was an incredible advancement in aircraft communications for the time, but it made little difference having good radio contact if the aircraft was not in the air. After leaving Malta on 9 January one of the engines had started giving trouble forcing a return to the airfield. The weather en route had been bad, particularly across the Mediterranean forcing Brackley to opt for a shorter crossing to Sirte instead of flying direct to Benghazi. When the party arrived at Cairo next day mechanics and engineering staff spent the entire night looking for the fault. This was eventually located to the oil system that required modification, but it had delayed the flight by several days and a replacement engine had to be sent out from England. In the end, all four engines had to be taken out to be overhauled before *Atalanta* could continue. Thirteen days had been spent holed up in Cairo, but the crew could at least gain some comfort by being stranded at the best-equipped of all the Imperial Airways bases along the Cape route. Further delays were endured when the crew reached Johannesburg. While they waited the arrival of special gauges needed for monitoring the engines. Woods Humphery, angry and tired of waiting for the flight to arrive, gave up on his rendezvous with Brackley and impatiently returned home by ship.

The bad weather that had befallen the *Atalanta* had also caused havoc with the India service. Storms in the Eastern Mediterranean made it necessary to change the routing. Instead of flying Athens-Castelrosso-Cyprus-Galilee, they were forced to revert to the Brindisi-Athens-Alexandria-Gaza tract. At least, by 11 February there was a positive outcome when the Alexandria-Cairo section could be operated by air for the first time casting the tedious Egyptian train journey into history.

The good news continued. By 18 February Imperial Airways announced that the airline had completed ten million miles in the air. This was achieved by operating a route network of 12,000 miles that served 19 countries. Imperial Airways also acted as booking agents for other airlines serving six countries. The growing route structure was considered a massive achievement especially considering that during the airline's first year only 1,000 miles were in operation. In tandem with this came news that passenger insurance premiums had been greatly cut in line with the company's safety record. The insurers had effectively reduced the premium for £1,000 of cover from 12s 0d (60p) to just 1s 0d (5p). This was positive for those that could afford the cost of a ticket to India because the premium to fly the entire route had also been reduced to just 14s 0d (70p). This was a great saving considering it had once cost as much as £7 4s 0d (£7.20) for cover amounting to £2,000. The underwriters had started to take air travel seriously and in 1933 it cost only 2s 0d (10p) more to buy cover for an entire trip to India by air than to travel there by surface transport. It was also generally cheaper to buy insurance for less arduous air journeys than for the equivalent rail or boat journey. In some respects Imperial Airways' reputation had escalated and it was widely regarded to be the best-organised passenger airline in the world. This did not stop the company having to fend off heavy criticism for the frequent delays that affected flying mail to its destinations. In the early 1930s delays to passengers did not appear to matter greatly; but when the mail was put at risk it was viewed as an entirely different matter.

"HANNO" AND "ATHENA" AT KARACHI AIRPORT

By 28 March any thoughts of the company's impressive safety record took a severe hammering when Lionel Lelew, an Imperial Airways pilot since 1926, crashed the *Argosy City of Liverpool* (G-AACI) near Dixmude, Belgium. The aircraft caught fire in the air and went into a vertical dive. The probable cause was thought to be a cigarette discarded by a passenger smoking in the toilet that ignited acetate contained in some baggage. There was no steward on board to ensure that passengers obeyed the no smoking rule. Although never proved, it seems likely that the fire went undiscovered and the pilot had no knowledge that anything was wrong until the fabric burnt off the tail causing the aircraft to immediately plunge out of control. All twelve passengers and three crew members were killed. When Brackley, Mayo and representatives of the Ministry arrived at the scene next day many of the bodies were still buried in the ground where they had fallen and debris spread for miles around. Fortunately the renewed public confidence in flying failed to be dampened too much and next day the early morning flight to Paris was full to capacity and had a waiting list.

Part of the problem facing the company was the unreliability of its aircraft. Matters had improved enormously but there was still a shortage of equipment and the equipment that it did have regularly developed faults. Imperial Airways urgently needed two more HP42s, aircraft that it insisted should be fitted with more powerful Armstrong Tiger engines, but the cost of these was considered too prohibitive. Major Mayo, an expert on these matters, put forward a solution that suggested building an aircraft with an under-slung fuselage attached to a set of Shorts Kent flying boat wings and engines. Oswald Short agreed with

this, more especially as it gave him an edge over his main rival, Handley Page. This resulted in the evolution of a pair of hybrid land planes capable of carrying 38 passengers that became known as the Short L17 and named *Scylla* (G-ACJJ) and *Syrinx* (G-ACJK) that were developed to come into service during 1934.

The domestic airlines expand

Some of the smaller airlines had started to flourish. On 1 April, Hillman's Airways commenced a twice-daily service to Paris from Romford (Maylands) using de Havilland Dragons at a fare of £3 10s 0d (£3.50) single; £5 10s 0d (£5.50) return with a weekend return offered for just £4 15s 0d (£4.75). By 8 April Hillman's had added a twice-daily summer service between Romford and Manston (Ramsgate) to encourage Essex holidaymakers bound for Margate and the Kent coast.

The spring of 1933 marked an active period of development for the smaller companies. On 2 February, Spartan Air Lines was registered as a limited company. This was a subsidiary of Spartan Aircraft Ltd that built the popular three-engined Spartan Cruiser. The company began flying a summer weekend service between Cowes on the Isle of Wight and Heston with its Cruisers. This service operated twice-daily from 12 May until it ceased on 2 October for the winter, but it maintained an impressive record by carrying 1,459 passengers and having flown 50,000 miles.

On 10 March Midland and Scottish Air Ferries Ltd was registered. This had been founded by John Sword, the owner of the Scottish Bus Group, with a capital of £20,000. By 3 April two more companies, Blackpool and West Coast Air Services Ltd and Highland Airways Ltd of Edinburgh evolved. The latter linked the Orkneys with Inverness and carried two tons of newspapers and 2,000 passengers and two tons of newspapers in an eleven month period. The company also operated

IN THE CABIN OF "ATHENA"

Britain's first scheduled domestic air mail service (see next chapter). The Great Western Railway inaugurated a passenger-carrying air service between Cardiff and Plymouth (Roborough) on 12 April following a proving flight made the day before by Gordon Olley. This operated a Westland Wessex (G-AAGW) chartered from Imperial Airways that flew twice each way during the week via Haldon, an airport that provided bus connections with Torquay, Newton Abbot and Teignmouth. The aircraft was re-painted in the smart chocolate and cream livery of the railway company in time for the first service. A second Wessex (G-EBXK) was also used to carry dignitaries and their guests. The popularity of the service was such that the company expanded it to Birmingham (Castle Bromwich) on 22 May, but this was short-lived and was suspended on 30 September. The company had been granted permission to carry letters by the General Post Office (GPO) at a surcharge of 3d (1¼p). This was the first sustained air service operated by a railway company under rights they had been granted in 1929. Because the company was able to fly directly across the Bristol Channel, the flying time cut more than three hours from the equivalent railway journey. Despite the short duration of this first operation, the company flew 62,400 miles and carried 714 passengers, 454 lbs of mail and 104 lbs of freight.

A lack of surface transport and the need to link many of the outlying Scottish island communities provided the right conditions that aircraft owners attempted to exploit. One such was Capt Ernest Edmund Fresson who began an Inverness (Longman Aerodrome)-Wick-Kirkwall (Wideford) service for Highland Airways on 8 May using the four-seat Monospar ST4, *Inverness* (G-ACEW). The service was scheduled to provide a link with trains that arrived at Inverness from the south. Another service operated between Kirkwall, Wick and Aberdeen. During gaps in the return service, a route extension was added between Kirkwall and Thurso (West Murkle) but this was ceased

Armstrong Whitworth Atalanta
G-ABTL 'Astrea'. (CAS)

on 6 September when Thurso was considered to be unsafe as a landing ground. On 19 April, Capt W B Caldwell became the first pilot to land an aircraft in the Shetland Isles at Sumburgh. This was the Fox Moth (G-ACEB) owned by Scottish Motor Traction (SMT) that carried officials of the Commercial Bank of Scotland. Another 'first' occurred when Scottish Air Ferries operated the first recorded air ambulance flight with the DH84 Dragon (G-ACZ) between Islay and Renfrew. There is a discrepancy over the date and it is shown in different sources as either 8 or 14 May.

Politically there was still much that the Government needed to do for the airlines. In July a committee was formed by Lord Londonderry to determine the current requirements relating to the Air Navigation Regulations. The independent committee chaired by Lord Gorell and with Capt Balfour as one of the six members, set out to challenge the controls being forced on international air travel by Geneva. The Germans operated the largest route system in Europe but had adopted a policy that was heading towards totalitarianism. The British were not without faults and demanded freedom of the air wherever it suited them, but they were still reluctant to allow reciprocal rights to foreign airlines in the airspace over the United Kingdom. America, despite being late starters to the airline industry, was already streaking ahead of Europe in aircraft design and production, and it was also quick to appreciate how speed should be paramount in the quest to fly. United Airlines already operated 60 twin-engine Boeing 247 low-wing aircraft that could cruise above 170 mph with a flight deck crew of two, a steward and ten passengers. The aircraft had also seriously reduced in-flight drag by incorporating a fully retractable under carriage; a feature the British were yet to come to grips with. The most modern British aircraft was the *Atalanta* class, but only eight were built, and compared to the latest aircraft leaving the Boeing production line it was a cumbersome machine.

Nevertheless, the Atalanta was the most up to date aircraft that Imperial Airways had in its fleet. In February *Atalanta* (G-ABTI) left Croydon bound for the Cape. It was joined by three other aircraft of the type that were destined to replace the ageing DH66 Hercules. These

were *Amalthea* (G-ABTG), *Andromeda* (G-ABTH) and *Artemis* (G-ABTJ). The journey took around 71 hours but it provided time that was usefully used for in-flight crew training. Although the Atalantas were welcomed on the service, there were occasions during periods of heavy traffic when they proved to be inadequate due to their size and the DH66s were frequently recalled to provide a relief service.

Atalanta heads 'Down Under'

During May the relationship between Brackley and Woods Humphery had experienced a period of harmony. The latter decided that Brackley should team up with Capt J V Prendergast to take *Astraea* (G-ABTL) on a 13,000 mile proving flight to Australia where they would have the opportunity to meet Hudson Fysh of Qantas to discuss the potential UK-Australia route. *Astraea* left Croydon on 29 May and had a trouble-free journey to Rome in 8 hrs via Paris and Lyon. The flight continued with stops at Brindisi, Athens, Alexandria, Cairo, Gaza, Baghdad, Basra, Bahrein (Bahrain), Sharjah and Gwadar before crossing into India and landing at Karachi on 4 June. In addition to Brackley and Prendergast, the flight crew comprised C Griffiths and W Hickman (engineers) and E Brown, the wireless operator loaned by Marconi. On 6 June the crew continued via Jodhpur and Delhi where Brackley took a night train to Simla for meetings with the '...*Viceroy and Government people*' returning next evening in time to continue flying *Astraea* to Calcutta and onwards via Akyab, Rangoon and Bangkok in what he called '*dirty*' weather. Bangkok airport was under floods when they arrived and the heavy storms continued via Prachaub to Alor Star, Malaya where the party was delayed an hour before continuing to Singapore where an oil leak caused a day to be lost. But all was well to continue via Palembang, Batavia and Sourabaya (Java) where an engine was giving vibration problems. This caused no further delays and the flight proceeded as planned to Bima and Koepang. Strong 30 mph head winds were encountered across the Timor Sea forcing an un-scheduled refuelling stop at Bathurst Island after 6½ hours in the air. Brackley recalls in his diary that they were '...*well looked after by Father Gsell and the Aborigines*'. The intention had been to reach Darwin but the winds had created a low-fuel situation that might have been catastrophic had they not reached Bathurst Island by the skin of their teeth. At the time, none on board *Astraea* knew whether the island was inhabited or not; neither did they know whether there was a suitable area large enough for the aircraft to land. The alternative to a forced-landing was to ditch in a shark-infested sea, an option the crew were not keen to face. They were lucky. With Brackley at the controls they sighted a clearing in the jungle and landed. This passage from Brackley's diaries provides a wonderful insight into the inherent adventures that still faced aviators even as late on as 1933. '*Almost as in a dream, because so great was the surprise, there appeared Father Gsell, that amazing Alsatian Franciscan and great missionary (later Roman Catholic Bishop of Darwin), whose brilliant imagination had foreseen the day when European airmen would need the sanctuary of his island home where his life-work of Christian civilisation would be a bulwark against the forces of unbridled nature. He had so won the devotion of the Aborigines to his ways of life that he had been able to get them to make with crude implements this elementary landing ground for the great winged invention they had never seen and now crowded around in spellbound wonderment.*' Thereafter, the crew revelled in the hospitality and dined on Australian delicacies such as kangaroo tails and turtle soup for two days, while the missionary motor launch braved the rough seas to fetch fuel from Darwin.

After the forced landing at Bathurst Island, the remaining journey to Port Darwin was routine despite flying across territory that had only been roughly charted and required the crew to navigate using tracks and telegraph wires. They landed at Camooweal, Cloncurry and Longreach where they dined with the directors of Qantas. After being grounded by torrential rain that swept across 500 miles of outback, they landed at Roma, and the quaint sounding towns of Chinchilla and Toowoomba, before reaching Brisbane. Brackley met Hudson Fysh and despite the Australian's cynicism about the Atalanta, the meeting with the Qantas managing director set the foundation for a long-lasting friendship. Fysh felt the aircraft was too slow, too expensive and too comfortable. He was strongly committed to a single-engine four-seater aircraft and he had already placed an order for the DH86 to operate the Darwin-Brisbane route. Wherever the Atalanta went in Australia the crew attracted a hero's welcome. *Astraea* was the first large aircraft ever to be seen in the country. At Archer Field, Brisbane on 23 June the aircraft was mobbed

Two De Havilland DH50s as used by QANTAS from the 1920s through to the early 1930s.

and a young boy was run over by the aircraft's tail wheel. Fortunately he was uninjured. From Brisbane the party continued to Sydney where local dignitaries were given the opportunity to fly on the aircraft before it continued to Canberra and Melbourne.

While in Australia Brackley was invited to speak as a guest on several radio broadcasts that gave him a platform to promote Imperial Airways and the Empire route to the people of Australia.

At Brisbane he had the following to say:

'We had a splendid reception this afternoon on landing at Brisbane after our 13,000 mile flight from London at an average speed of well over 100 mph. We are here with a message of goodwill from the Old Country to Australia and to show the British Flag on the latest addition to our Empire fleet of aeroplanes – the four-engined monoplanes of the Atalanta type, of which we have the Astraea, one of eight comprising the class.

'My visit to Australia is purely technical and the objects are to make a final survey from the flying point of view of the route from Karachi to Singapore and between Singapore to Australia so that Imperial Airways will have full knowledge of this route, and if they are able to tender for the Contract, they will make an earnest bid for the operation of the extension from Singapore to the Australian terminal through their Australian company, the Australian Empire Airways, in cooperation with Qantas – your great Queensland organisation with whom a happy alliance has been formed. Their record for safety and reliability cannot be beaten and has done so much to create air mindedness in Australia.

'Now Imperial Airways is anxious that a comprehensive service shall be established comparable with and in every respect a complement of the other Great Empire lines. As you no doubt know, we run a weekly service – London, India and South Africa. Bookings are heavy, three months ahead, and the extension will operate shortly to Singapore. Astraea has an all up load of 20,000 pounds – and top speed of 150 mph.'

Following the exploits at the Corpus Christi Bathurst Island Mission, the 13 July issue of the Australian magazine *Table Talk* carried a story about the incident and, more fittingly, included a portrait of Brackley's career.

'He has attained the summit of a pilot's ambition and he is well under 30! But that was ten years ago. In the decade that has elapsed, he has seen Imperial Airways grow from a baby into a giant, spreading its limbs down through Africa to Cape Town, across Europe in every direction, across Iraq and Arabia to India, and now across India and the East to Australia, to Melbourne. It has all been carried out under his direction. He is in control of all pilots, machines, wireless, and the organisation of new routes. He is the Big Noise in Civil Aviation today. After a long yarn with this quiet-spoken, diffident young man in Melbourne one understands why.

'It is a pity that he was not commandeered while in Melbourne by some enterprising person to give some talks to the boys. What tales he would have had to tell them! He is the sort of man who makes First Grade, Super He-Man boy's hero, but the trouble is that he doesn't look the part, nor play it. Dapper, short, softly spoken, a clerical collar is all that is needed to turn him into a curate... on the outside. But inside there must be nerves of steel under a calm and placid disposition.'

This was a very befitting tribute to the air superintendent o Imperial Airways. Brackley was later joined by the Australiar representative of the company, Albert E Rudder, who flew on the promotional tour when *Astraea* visited the major cities. Rudder, as a trusted advocate of Hudson Fysh, became a major prime-mover in the successful negotiations between Imperial Airways and Qantas tc establish the Empire Mail service that followed.

While Brackley and Prendergast and the crew were enjoying the hospitality of their Australian sabbatical, the political situation within Australian aviation circles was fai from certain and a level of animosity was starting to erupt between the various parties. Australian National Airways (ANA) under the leadership of Charles Ulm was being reconstructed after being on the brink of going bust, and there was no love lost between Hudson Fysh of Qantas and Sir Norman Brearley of West Australian Airways (WAA) when it concerned negotiating for the first overseas rights to be granted to an Australian airline Brearley was in favour of linking up with KLM, but Hudson Fysh favoured an all-red route that would associate Qantas with Imperial Airways. In June 1932 the three main players in the debate, ANA, WAA and Qantas had composed their

Wilmot Hudson Fysh in 1935.

proposals and listed the routes they hoped to operate under their own identities. These were: WAA to be granted the rights to Perth-Wyndham and Wyndham-Adelaide; ANA, Calcutta-Wyndham and Qantas, Brisbane-Newcastle Waters. Additionally Qantas and ANA would share the traffic on the prime Brisbane-Sydney route. According to its proposal, ANA intended to operate the only overseas route using Avro X aircraft. However any agreement that might have coordinated the route proposals of the companies soon broke down when Brearley decided to drop Perth from his plans to concentrate on Wyndham. He had proposed operating a Batavia-Wyndham service in collaboration with KLM. Had he intended to make an agreement with Imperial Airways, Brearley would initially have needed to suspend any connection with KLM. Ultimately his plans to work with the Dutch company came to nothing and by the end of 1932, ANA's poor financial position made it inevitable that no agreement could ever be forged between the three Australian companies. Fysh was also suspicious of Brearley's motives and on 2 February he wired his chairman, Fergus McMaster, to warn him that: 'Brearley is undoubtedly out to trick us,' later adding: 'Qantas, WAA and ANA can never be happy bedfellows.' and after a considerable time spent in private meetings with the various parties, concluded that Qantas had three options:

1. To form some sort of joint operation with Imperial Airways
2. To form an amalgamation with ANA and WAA in a wholly Australian company; best avoided because he felt that any link with the other companies would mean Qantas and its way of life would be altered beyond recognition
3. To go it alone, even though he felt this was beyond the financial resources and experience of Qantas if overseas operations were involved.

From the choices Fysh believed that some form of alliance with Imperial Airways would provide the best solution. Brearley and Ulm had always been against an arrangement that involved Imperial Airways and even though a full agreement could not be reached the three nevertheless decided to operate what they loosely referred to as a working agreement. Rudder, the Australian representative of Imperial Airways, was pushing Qantas hard to establish the British link but Fysh wanted to be certain that Qantas, the Australian Government and the citizens of Australia would all benefit from any arrangement. The people wanted any link forged between Brisbane and Singapore to be all-Australian and the debate in Government went along similar lines. In due course Rudder was invited to Brisbane where he attended the Qantas board meeting of 22 February. Once the board's main business had been discussed, he was ushered into the room. By then Fysh's earlier options had already been narrowed to just two; 1) the agreement with ANA and WAA or 2) the formation of a company with Imperial Airways. In Fysh's mind there was no doubt that a deal with Imperial Airways was the preferred course to follow.

An arrangement was offered based on what those present termed a 'Gentleman's Agreement'. The company was to be operated with an 'Australian Atmosphere' and it would tender for the new Australian services on a 50/50 basis. The meeting historically laid the foundations for the Empire Mail Scheme to become a reality. Those present were: Hudson Fysh, Fergus McMaster (chairman). F E Loxton and Alan Campbell (standing in for A N Templeman who was unable to attend). Rudder was given the opportunity to present a proposal to the Qantas board that Woods Humphery had drawn up that the Australian directors accepted as follows:

'It was moved by Mr Campbell, seconded by Mr Loxton and carried unanimously, that Qantas should associate itself with Imperial Airways in connection with the proposed new service to England as the basis of the terms and conditions submitted by them, but subject to certain modifications to be arranged with Imperial Airways.'

The seeds of an agreement had already been sown prior to this when Sir Walter Nicholson, an Imperial Airways director, had visited Australia early in 1932 to examine the potential of a joint venture between the two airlines. Correspondence had been exchanged between Imperial Airways and Fysh as far back as October 1929, but nothing substantial had been discussed until Fysh wrote positively to Woods Humphery on 16 June 1931. While Nicholson had been in Australia Fysh had handed him a proposal that would ultimately form the basis for a joint venture that would lead to the formation of Qantas Empire Airways. The document drawn up by Fysh at that time was fairly simple:

'Formula proposed by Qantas for Scheme of Co-Operation between Qantas and Imperial Airways.

A definite understanding with Imperial Airways to form a company which would be called 'The Commonwealth and Imperial Airways Ltd' to operate the England-Australia service from say Singapore-Darwin-Brisbane etc. or Calcutta-Darwin-Brisbane etc. The necessary capital to be raised by Imperial Airways and Qantas and representation on the board to be proportional to Share interests.

'In calling Australian Capital, option would be given to 'ANA', 'West Australian Airways', 'Larkin' and other Australian operators to subscribe and these groups would have representation on the board proportional to their Shares but Imperial Airways and Qantas to hold controlling representation.

Imperial Airways to operate to Darwin and Qantas organisation to operate from Darwin to Brisbane etc.'

While steady progress was beginning to be made in Australia, on the Sub-Continent Indian Trans-Continental Airways (ITCA) had applied to share the trans-India route with Imperial Airways. India was still strongly committed to using Indian-registered aircraft on flights across the country. Thus, on 1 July Arethusa (G-ABPI) was flown to Karachi where it was given the Indian registration VT-AEF. Before continuing to Calcutta on 7 July, Arethusa opened the mail route between England and the Indian city by carrying 500 lbs of mail and five passengers. In April Aurora (G-ABTM), the last of the Atalantas, emerged from the

production line. This aircraft was flown to Belgium in June at the request of the King of the Belgians who flew in her for an hour. The aircraft was then flown to Karachi where it too was given an Indian registration (VY-AEG) and was the second Atalanta leased to ITCA.

ITCA was formed on 21 June 1933 with Imperial Airways retaining a controlling 51 per cent stake in the company. The remaining shares were owned by the Government of India (24 per cent) and Indian National Airways (25 per cent). In the equivalent to what is now referred to as 'wet-leasing', the Indian company had hired the Atalanta aircraft from Imperial Airways with crews, technical support and management. These alternated on the trans-Indian routes from Karachi via Jodhpur, Delhi, Cawnpore and Allahabad to Calcutta with Indian-operated aircraft. This route was extended to Rangoon on 23 September via Akyab with Aurora making the inaugural flight that returned on 2 October. By 9 December the route had progressed as far as Singapore. Astraea (G-ABTL) inaugurated the sector with return flights that commenced on New Year's Eve, but KLM was quicker off the mark by seven months and had already established its Singapore link with Batavia (Jakarta) on 3 May.

Indian National Airways (INA) Ltd had been formed during May to become shareholders in ITCA and to develop feeder services for the company in North India. INA was registered in Delhi with a capital of 3m Rupees, but the largest shareholders were the non-Indian Govan brothers who owned a 60 per cent stake. INA was also appointed as the principal ticket agents of the Imperial Airways/ITCA joint services and made bookings from their eleven offices.

Australian hostility

In Australia Hudson Fysh was content in the knowledge that the Qantas proposal to form an alliance with Imperial Airways was going ahead. On 19 July he took his seat aboard Astraea at Darwin for the long trip to London. Although he had previously claimed that the speed of the British aircraft was unimportant, his opinion probably changed when he was swiftly flown to Koepang courtesy of 140 mph tail winds. Fysh flew on to Singapore without problems but by the time he boarded the aircraft for the next sector to Calcutta a monsoon had developed that delayed his progress by 24 hours at Karachi. Since leaving Croydon Astraea had completed 23,430 miles on the Australia trip and had spent 210 hrs and 37 mins in the air. Astraea was now based at Karachi so Brackley and Fysh continued to London on the regular service aboard the trusty HP42E Hannibal as far as Cairo, where the usual mix of aircraft and train were used to complete the journey. Brackley's epic two-month venture ended as Heracles touched down at Croydon at 11.15 hrs on 24 July where he was met by Woods Humphery. Fysh was in London to negotiate the agreement with Imperial Airways that would form the contract for the Singapore-Darwin-Brisbane sector of the England-Australia Empire Mail service.

Astraea's visit to Australia had caused shockwaves in the country that continued to reverberate. As the aircraft toured Sydney, Canberra and Melbourne large crowds, some estimated as large as 10,000, gathered to see it. With a wingspan of 90 feet it was far larger than any aircraft seen in Australia previously, but the aircraft was too large to fit into any existing hangar. Yet, while public acclaim for the aircraft was generally good, many members of the aviation hierarchy scorned the aircraft's intrusion on their domestic scene. One such was Jimmy Larkin, who, as owner of Larkin's Australian Aerial Services (later changed to Larkin Aerial Supply Company – Lasco), had crossed swords with Qantas and the other operators. During 1932 Larkin and others had attempted to dominate Australian air transport by organising the First Annual Air Convention. The main airlines, including Qantas, ANA and WAA were all deliberately excluded from the first meeting on 25 May 1932 when Larkin planned to set his own policy for civil aviation in Australia. In modern times this would be tantamount to an association of scheduled British carriers being formed that excluded British Airways, Virgin and BMI. The main companies responded by forming the rival Association of Australian Aviation Industries that thoroughly discredited Larkin's organisation. Subsequently Larkin's Air Convention was sued for

Captain Travers leaves AW XV Atalanta Class, G-ABTH, 'Andromeda' at Nairobi in 1933. (T Samson)

defamation after it had sent a derogatory letter to Sir George Pearce; the Minister for Defence. Larkin conducted his own defence but lost, but he refused to be silenced. He again became instrumental in trying to condemn *Astraea* on behalf of his Air Convention by sending telegrams containing the following text to the proprietors of every major Australian newspaper urging them to refrain from giving Imperial Airways any publicity:

'*By clever propaganda and methods beyond reach of Australian aircraft operators, Imperial Airways' monopoly is endeavouring to stampede government, press and public into pre-supposing that company will secure subsidy contract for Singapore-Australia air link. As tenders not yet called, and as several Australian companies propose tendering, appeal to you to place fair limit on space devoted to Imperial Airways, and make it clear to public that tenders have yet to be called, and the Government has started its intention (of) giving preference (to) Australian companies.*'

Brearley of Western Australian Airways was similarly vindictive and attacked Imperial Airways in his WAA *Bulletin*. This caused Rudder of Imperial Airways to suggest to Fergus McMaster that '*It seems to me that a little more Australian character might be added if the tenders are submitted in the name of Qantas.*' Brearley also attacked the efficiency and safety record of Imperial Airways, causing Fysh to be uncharacteristically bitter about his rival, when he penned a response to McMaster after reaching London. In retaliation he referred to WAA's own fatal crash by responding: '*He has forgotten the opening of his own north-west route and the fact that surplus revenue has not gone into his service but to enrich himself and his shareholders.*'

While Fysh remained in London embroiled in negotiations with Imperial Airways, heated debates were ensuing within the Australian Parliament. The Labour member for New South Wales, Senator Dunn took up the attack on any Qantas-Imperial Airways alliance by praising the efforts of Ulm, Kingsford Smith and other Australian aviators by saying: '*Apparently these men are to be left on the beach, while this profitable contract goes to Imperial Airways to be run on British capital, manned by British airmen, and paid for with good Australian cash. What chance has Smith or Ulm, or any other Australian without money, to compete with this wealthy monopoly in open tenders? They will be frozen out and the Government by its encouragement of the propaganda stunt of the Astraea is already preparing the public mind to see them frozen out.*'

Dunn continued by quoting a 1931 report by the Auditor-General that condemned any proposal of an English-Australian air mail service because of the financial recession that the country was still suffering.

'*Although it is perfectly clear that the Australian financial position is such that it cannot afford the huge subsidy which would be necessary to maintain such*

a service, endeavours are being made by certain commonwealth interests to influence the Commonwealth Government with a view to establishing the service. No real justification for an English-Australian air mail service has been established.'

Dunn vehemently suggested that Imperial Airways was the '*Nigger in the woodpile*' and that '*...Australia is not the first to feel the imperial tentacles of this octopus.*' Harsh words indeed although his remarks were not so much aimed directly at Imperial Airways but at the tendency for Australian concern to become linked to British interests. He did however make specific mention of the Imperial Airways connection by attacking '*...the mammoth Dunlop interest*' and the '*...powerful British-Australian financial Baillieu group*' that controlled the *Melbourne Herald* and many other newspapers within the Commonwealth that had so warmly acclaimed the arrival of the *Astraea*.

As the differences of opinion permeated the Australian political debates Fysh wrote to McMaster on 17 September from his room at the Grosvenor Hotel in London to inform his colleague that '*...there is not the slightest doubt but that control would remain in Australia*' and added that he was '*... only more settled in my opinion that Woods Humphery is a great leader and that his executives are excellent. Their policy is our policy to an extraordinary extent. Their principles of operation are right, and they are not out to make points.*' Fysh concurred with the observation that obtaining the Brisbane-Singapore route would not create a monopoly because they still had to contend with whatever Brearley had planned in his proposal to link up with KLM.

Fysh returned to Australia via the USA where he inspected some of their airline operations, reviewed the Douglas DC2 and DC3 and flew at night with United Airlines between Chicago and San Francisco on a route lit by night beacons. This form of flying had made use of landing grounds every 20 miles that were illuminated, and revolving beacons had been established every 10 miles that enabled pilots to follow the route. This worked well when visibility was clear but in bad weather flight crews had to rely on their two-way radios. Fysh described this as '*... a remarkable experience in 1933.*' Before leaving London some of Fysh's friends had expressed concerns about him flying at night on the Boeing 247 all-metal monoplane. This aircraft, and the Douglas that he had seen, created a positive impression and he wrote to Woods Humphery on 17 October: '*...All these high speed machines here make everything look out of date in England except the Handley Page 42, which is supreme in its class. The new DH86 will also be supreme in its class but it should be built of metal and have a retractable undercarriage – still it will be a job without peer in America, but I do hope some of your manufacturers will go to it on this high speed stuff, because I feel you must be interested for the Empire Route.*'

Fysh's letter continued by describing the way that United Airlines operated: '*United Airlines booking staff, aerodrome staff and operating staff work in shifts day and night – intensive activity all the time. They have 42 services in and out of Chicago every 24 hours. American aviation as you suspected has impressed me enormously, but I have not lost my sense of proportion by any means. The Handleys and the new Short for the London-Paris route stand alone in the world. The Atalantas are still good to me, but it seems, somehow or other, the long Empire routes have got to be speeded up without too much loss of time – and I realise your difficulty in this. Whether the new KLM machine will solve the problem I do not know. I would I think put up the night air mail here because of the intensely organised route but what of the flying at night – all night – between say Cairo and Karachi! Those beacons were what comforted me. By the way, an extraordinary thing – there is not one airport here to anywhere touch Tempelhof or Croydon – I thought this strange, as I expected something grand ...*' After seeing the Douglas DC3 being developed for TWA Fysh wrote again to Woods Humphery extolling its virtues, saying: '*... Impressive in every way and evidently superior to the Boeing ...*'

In the Australian Parliament the battle had commenced as the vehement members turned their attack towards the proposed route the

Empire service would take. The Australian Government was firm in its view that this should be from Darwin to Charleville (Queensland) and onward to Cootamundra where it would terminate at the mid-point of the Sydney-Melbourne railroad. Brisbane would be connected only by a local route from Charleville. It seems inconceivable that the Australian Government did not consider it favourable to operate an air service between Sydney and Melbourne, preferring to terminate an international route at a nondescript, sheep-rearing town with a name that translated literally from the Aboriginal as 'swamp with turtles.' Cootamundra is 300 miles north-east of Sydney and even as recently as 2006 claimed a population of 7,695.

McMaster's proposal was for the route from England to continue via Brisbane to Sydney which made far more sense. The press naturally had a great deal to say about the Government's proposal. The Brisbane *Courier Mail* expressed '*European airmen ridicule the idea of terminating the world's longest air service at Cootamundra, instead of Sydney via Brisbane; nowhere in Europe is the influence of railways allowed to retard air development.*' Fysh had rightly argued that to operate a route that terminated in the back country instead of at a major centre was contrary to the development of an airways system. The Australian Government failed to agree and instead issued tender forms on 22 September that confirmed Cootamundra as the termination point of the England-Australia service. Three different tenders were issued; the overseas division (Singapore-Darwin); the eastern division (Darwin-Brisbane-Cootamundra) that had subsections Darwin-Mount Isa-Longreach; Longreach-Brisbane and Charleville-Cootamundra and the western division between Katherine and Perth with sub-divisions Katherine-Broome, Broome-Carnarvon and Carnarvon-Perth. The tenders also had conditions attached that required applicants to provide aircraft capable of cruising at 110 mph with a range of 600 miles against 30 mph headwinds for the overseas division; and a range of 300 miles for the other divisions. Because there were still few aircraft capable of the prescribed cruising speeds in Australia, a sub-condition was added permitting a company to operate aircraft with a minimum cruising speed of 95 mph for the first five years of an awarded contract. This drew a considerable amount of flak from the aviation press who concluded that the 110 mph ruling was ridiculous because within five years developments in aircraft design were expected to push the cruising speeds up to 250 mph.

Prior to agreeing to the Qantas association, Imperial Airways registered a new company that it called Australian Empire Airways with the purpose of tendering for the Australian overseas contract. The intention was to merge this with Qantas once it had secured the operating contract. The newly registered company never traded and it seems it was only formed for negotiation purposes and was liquidated almost as soon as it was announced.

Fysh had concluded that an aircraft as large as the *Astraea* would be too big and uneconomic to operate on the Qantas sector of the England-Australia route. He had also decided that the cost of such an aircraft would be too prohibitive more especially as the Australian Government was not in a position to provide subsidies. Fysh had been negotiating for a considerable time with de Havilland for the production of a much smaller airliner that would be capable of cruising at a speed of 135 mph with a payload of 1,800 lbs that would be powered by four DH Gipsy engines. In April 1933 Fysh had written to Woods Humphery outlining his belief that the acquisition of such an aircraft would be a positive move in their strategy to secure the contracts.

When the time eventually came to tender, Imperial Airways sent out its capable company secretary, S A Dismore, to prepare the documentation. This resulted in Qantas Empire Airways becoming a reality, formerly registered on 18 January 1934. Things were starting to fall into place on a service that would benefit the future development of both Qantas and Imperial Airways.

On the UK domestic front, several of the smaller, privately owned airlines were continuing to open new routes. Many services were short-lived or were operated either on an ad-hoc basis or during specific times of the year. Blackpool and West Coast Air Services operated a pair of

Fox Moths (G-ACFC *Progress* and G-ACFF *Progress* II) and a Dragon (G-ACGU) on a regular Blackpool-Liverpool-Isle of Man service. This began on 22 June and during the summer a daily Liverpool-Blackpool service was added.

For a brief time Hillman's Airways extended its Romford-Paris service to Vichy on summer weekends from 30 June, but this ceased on 4 September because of a shortage of passengers. Between June and September, Eastern Air Transport ran a daily service from Nottingham to Skegness using a Fox Moth (G-ABVJ) and from June to October, British Amphibian Airlines re-opened its Blackpool-Isle of Man service with the Saro Cutty Sark amphibian (G-ABBC).

North Sea Aerial and General Transport Limited operated their aerial services to link with the bus company, East Yorkshire Motor Services, to run an air ferry service across the River Humber between Hull and Grimsby (Waltham) that commenced on 1 July. This was maintained three times daily and increased to nine per day on 4 September using a Blackburn Seagrave (G-ABFR) and a Fox Moth that incorporated an air link from Hedon to Waltham.

During August a company known as International Airline Ltd made a mail-carrying flight from Croydon to Plymouth via Portsmouth and Southampton that it called 'The Western Air Express'. Two Monospar ST 4s aircraft (G-ACJE and G-ACJF) were operated on the route that opened on 24 August. This company became Provincial Airways Ltd on 12 October that began a 'West Country Air Service' on 25 November linking London, Southampton and Plymouth.

On 1 September Midland and Scottish Air Ferries began flying a thrice-weekly summer service with an Avro 10 (G-ACGF) between Hooton, Liverpool (Speke) and Dublin (Baldonnel). The company was founded by John Sword (1892-1960) who had also been a bus operator, but sold Midland Bus Services, which owned 509 buses, to SMT. At one time Sword's airline operated 17 aircraft and the company also employed Scotland's first woman pilot (20-year-old Winifred Drinkwater). At the end of September, London Midland and Scottish Railway was in negotiations with the Scottish Motor Traction Company (SMT) to operate a joint Scotland-Western Isles-Ireland service.

On 7 September another independent airline that made a major impact was formed as Norman Edgar (Western Airways) Limited with a capital of £7,500. The company operated initially Bristol-Cardiff, Bristol-Bournemouth and a weekend charter between Cardiff, Bristol, Le Touquet and Paris.

In France there was a significant development on 17 May when the four main airlines, Air Orient, Air Union, SGTA (Farman) and CIDNA, combined to form Société Centrale pour l'Exploitation de Lignes Aériennes (SCELA) with the purpose of negotiating with the French Government to form a national airline. On 30 August, Air France was inaugurated at Le Bourget following a buy-out of Cie Générale Aéropostale which had gone bankrupt following a scandal. This airline had previously made its name by pioneering routes across the South Atlantic. The Government held 25 per cent of the resulting company's stock while the former individual companies held the remainder in differing proportions. The new airline had 259 aircraft at its disposal (172 were single-engine machines) that consisted of 35 different types. During the autumn Air France introduced at least two three-engined Wibault Penhoët 282 T12 '*Golden Clipper*' low-wing monoplanes (F-AMNH and F-AMHO) on the Paris-London service to compete with the Imperial Airways HP42s. They were also operated on the company's Paris-Cologne-Berlin service. The Wibault carried ten passengers at 150 mph — 50 mph faster than the cruising speed of the lumbering HP42s. The British airliner was more comfortable, but the French now posed a serious threat with their faster machines on what had been dubbed 'The Golden Airway.'

Jersey Airways Limited was formed on 9 December with a capital of £120,000. Six days later the company took delivery of its first aircraft, the DH Dragon (G-ACMJ) that it named *The St Aubin's Bay* that operated proving flights between Stag Lane and Jersey with Bill Caldwell as pilot. By 18 December the company started operating daily from Portsmouth to Jersey with a hired Dragon (G-ACCE). The company's own Dragon also flew a second service to Jersey the

Winter Timetable

**Brisbane—
Singapore
Air Service**

Linking with the
associated company
IMPERIAL
AIRWAYS
LIMITED

Singapore--London

**QANTAS EMPIRE AIRWAYS
LTD.**

43 Creek Street, Brisbane
Queensland, Australia

Air Union, F-AIXY, Breguet 08T was a visitor to Croydon during the 1930s. (CAS)

same day and in the absence of an airfield, the public beach at St Aubin Bay served as the landing ground for the island.

Croydon Airport witnessed several changes during 1933. H L Hall, the chief engineer of Imperial Airways, who had a reputation for being a strict disciplinarian, devised a system that would ensure that the company's aircraft were kept in the air for as long as possible. He believed that a swift efficient turn-around was essential for the airline to remain profitable. The arrival of an HP42 on the apron at Croydon signalled a period of rapid activity. Passengers were quickly disembarked, the mail and baggage taken off, and the aircraft towed to the hangar. Within fifteen minutes of landing, two-storey rostrums had been placed around the aircraft allowing a team of fitters to work simultaneously on all four engines. While this was being done the aircraft interior was cleaned, the galley restocked and fuel was pumped into the tanks. Inspectors finally checked the external structure and working parts and the outgoing mail was loaded. Hall's system aimed to return each aircraft to the apron, ready for boarding prior for the next flight within 30 minutes. Apart from the times aircraft were grounded for intermediate inspections every thirty hours, or for an annual 1,500-hour check, its time in the air was greatly improved.

During November, the Croydon control zone, known as QBI, was introduced in a *'Notice to Airmen'*. This comprised an area covering ten miles in each direction from the airport, bounded to the north by the Thames from Kingston and Tilbury; and from the west, south and east by a line that ran from Kingston through Dorking, Horley, Penshurst and West Malling to Tilbury. During times when the visibility was less than 3,000 feet or the cloud base was below 1,000 feet, entry to the zone was only permitted to aircraft fitted with radio equipment. When restrictions applied, any aircraft without permission to fly inside the control zone were forced to land elsewhere. During the winter of 1933 the weather was so bad at times that all aircraft that were unable to fly blind were required to divert to other landing grounds. But even when adverse weather forced the cross-Channel ferries to be cancelled, aircraft fitted with the system could operate safely and efficiently. Very few flights failed to land at Croydon and flying had to be cancelled entirely on only one day.

At the Imperial Airways AGM on 30 October, Geddes boasted that the company profits had increased by £42,707 to £52,894. This was largely attributed to a 75 per cent increase in traffic on a scheduled route network of more than two million miles.

Discussions regarding a service to link America to Europe was again on the agenda. On 11 May the Secretary of State for Air asked Imperial Airways for its proposals for crossing the Atlantic, fearing that Britain would be caught out by Juan Trippe of Pan American Airways. The British Government had so far failed to develop a long-range flying boat capable of reaching America. Imperial Airways could still only fly a maximum of 500 miles with the aircraft at its disposal and this was one reason why the Indian and African services could only be flown in short hops. This was hardly very progressive and it pointed to the urgent need to develop long-range aircraft that could remain in the air for considerably longer than those the airline possessed. It was revealed that Imperial Airways had criticised the Government in a secret report.

The board was angered over the Government's refusal to provide the necessary funding to allow the company to develop the Atlantic route. This was certainly a justified criticism. On one hand the Air Ministry was pushing for the airline's urgent proposals while, with the other, it was refusing to financially back anything that Imperial Airways put forward. It was a clear-cut case that was made even more damning by the US Government's pledge to subsidise Pan American's involvement with an investment equivalent to almost £1.5m. With so little Government funding it was really quite an achievement that Imperial Airways had progressed as far as it had. Despite the inherent rivalry, it was also encouraging that the airline had already established a good understanding with Juan Trippe of Pan Am and it seemed only a matter of time before something positive would materialise from the association.

Debate arose over the carriage of air mails; a subject that was always seen as a priority. Kodak had been called in to discuss cheaper and more efficient ways to transport mail. Microfilm and a development by the name of Airgraphs were among the topics put forward, but the GPO objected to these methods on the grounds of confidentiality. Nevertheless, in 1933 Britain (including the Empire) was carrying more mail by air than any other nation with the exceptions of the United States and Germany.

Air Mail tonnage carried by other nations

United States of America	3489 tonnes
Germany	460
British Empire (all parts)	455
France (including South American Service)	219
Switzerland	181
Holland (including North-east Indies)	178
Japan	96
Spain	70
Italy	62
Belgium (including Belgian Congo)	56

Tragically, 1933 ended with another bad accident. Just after midday on 30 December the Avro Ten *Apollo* (G-ABLU) piloted by Capt Gittens from Brussels to Croydon entered thick fog at Ruysselade, near Bruge and struck a stay on a 900 feet-high radio mast. This became entangled with the aircraft and the Avro fell into a steep dive, killing all ten on board when it hit the ground. Two minutes after impact the ruptured fuel tanks caught fire and two Belgians who had rushed to the scene of the crash also sustained major burns.

Left and below: Imperial Airways Avro 618 Ten, G-ABLU, 'Apollo' (a British licence-built version of the Fokker F.VIIB/3m) is seen here at Gaza in 1931, with HP42E, G-AAUD, 'Hanno' in the background. The pilot is unidentified. The Avro had, at the time of the photograph, been chartered to the Iraq Petroleum Transport Company and was used by that company until returning to Imperial Airways in 1933, whereupon it was lost in a crash near Bruges in Belgium on 30 December 1933. (US Library of Congress)

THE PRINCIPAL EUROPEAN OFFICES OF IMPERIAL AIRWAYS

LONDON

CENTRAL ADMINISTRATIVE OFFICES, PASSENGER DEPARTURE STATION AND FREIGHT RECEPTION OFFICE

Airway Terminus, Victoria Station, S.W.1

Telephone : Victoria 2211 (Day and Night)
Telegrams : *Impairlim, London*

WEST END BOOKING OFFICE

Airways House, Charles St., Lower Regent Street

Telephone : Victoria 2211
Telegrams : *Impairlim, London*

PARIS

CENTRAL ADMINISTRATIVE AND BOOKING OFFICE

Airways House, 38 Avenue de l'Opéra

Telephone : Opéra 0916
Telegrams : *Flying, Paris*

PASSENGER DEPARTURE STATION AND FREIGHT RECEPTION OFFICE

Hotel Bohy-Lafayette, Square Montholon, Rue Lafayette

Telephone : Opéra 0916 (Day and Night)
Telegrams : *Flying, Paris*

THE AIR PORT OF LONDON, CROYDON

Telephone : Croydon 2046   Telegrams : *Flying, Croydon*

ANTWERP

The Air Port, Deurne

Telephone : 93513

Telegrams :
Airsabena, Antwerp

AMSTERDAM

K.L.M. Leidsche Plein

Telephone : 25039

Telegrams :
Transaera, Amsterdam

COLOGNE

Dom Hotel

Telephone : Rhineland 222774

Telegrams : *Flying, Cologne*

BASLE

The Air Port
(Birsfelden)

Telephone : 25966

Telegrams : *Flying, Basle*

BERLIN

Lindenstrasse 35 S.W. 68

Telephone : A7 Dönhoff 8360

Telegrams : *Luft Hansa, Berlin*

BRUSSELS

19 Rue St. Michel

Telephone : Brussels 17.64.62
Telegrams : *Flying, Brussels*

32-34 Boulevard Adolphe Max

Telephone : 17.10.06
Telegrams : *Airsabena*

OSTEND

The Air Port, Steene

Telephone : Ostend 513

Telegrams : *Airsabena Ostend*

ZÜRICH

The Air Port
(Dübendorf)

Telephone :
Dübendorf 126

Telegrams : *Flying, Zürich*

UNITED STATES OF AMERICA

NEW YORK—The Plaza, Fifth Avenue, and 59th Street

Telephone : PL 3.0794 & PL 3.1740   Telegrams : *Flying, New York*

★ *In addition to these offices, any air line operating company or any travel agent in Europe can supply information relating to the various air services operating in Europe*

LOCAL AGENT

[1A/ABC/38.100M. 2/33]

*Printed in Great Britain by Spottiswoode, Ballantyne & Co. Ltd., 1 New Street Square, E.C. 4.
Published by Imperial Airways, Ltd., from Airway Terminus, London*

12

IMPERIAL AIRWAYS

TO AND FROM LONDON

PARIS
FRANCE—SWITZERLAND
BELGIUM—GERMANY
BELGIAN COAST
HOLLAND—GERMANY
GERMANY—DENMARK—SWEDEN

EUROPEAN TIME TABLE

1933

SUMMER SERVICES

10

FARES

The Fares (which are liable to alteration without notice) must be paid in the currency of the country from which the service is scheduled to leave

● All return tickets are available for use on the return journey any day within the period of their validity

★ The ordinary return ticket is normally valid for 30 (thirty) days from the date of issue, but those to and from the places marked * on the list given below are valid for 2 months

From LONDON to		Single	Return	15-day Return	Rate per Kg for Excess Baggage
AMSTERDAM*	.. .. ..	£5 0 0	£8 10 0	—	9d
ANTWERP	.. .. ..	£4 0 0	£7 4 0	£6 8 0	9d
BERLIN*	.. .. ..	£10 0 0	£17 0 0	—	1/8
BREMEN*	.. .. ..	£8 5 0	£14 0 6	—	1/5
BRUSSELS	.. .. ..	£4 0 0	£7 4 0	£6 8 0	9d
COLOGNE	.. .. ..	£5 10 0	£9 18 0	£8 16 0	1/1
COPENHAGEN*	.. .. ..	£12 0 0	£20 8 0	—	1/6
DORTMUND	.. .. ..	£5 16 0	£10 9 0	£9 5 6	1/2
DÜSSELDORF ..	.. .. ..	£5 10 0	£9 18 0	£8 16 0	1/1
ESSEN/MÜLHEIM	.. .. ..	£5 15 0	£10 7 0	£9 4 0	1/1
HAMBURG*	.. .. ..	£8 5 0	£14 0 6	—	1/1
HANOVER*	.. .. ..	£7 7 6	£13 7 9	—	1/4
LE ZOUTE	.. .. ..	£3 5 0	£5 17 0	£5 4 0	9d
MALMÖ*	.. .. ..	£12 10 0	£21 5 0	—	1/6
OSTEND	.. .. ..	£3 5 0	£5 17 0	£5 4 0	9d

To LONDON from		Single	Return	15-day Return	Rate per Kg for Excess Baggage
AMSTERDAM*	.. .. ..	48 Guilders	81.60 Guilders	—	0.50 Guilders
ANTWERP	.. .. ..	550 Belgian Francs	990 Belgian Francs	880 Belgian Francs	5.50 Belgian Francs
BERLIN*	.. .. ..	150 Reichs Mark	285 Reichs Mark	—	1.50 Reichs Mark
BREMEN*	.. .. ..	120 Reichs Mark	204 Reichs Mark	—	1.40 Reichs Mark
BRUSSELS	.. .. ..	550 Belgian Francs	990 Belgian Francs	880 Belgian Francs	5.50 Belgian Francs
COLOGNE	.. .. ..	90 Reichs Mark	162 Reichs Mark	144 Reichs Mark	0.90 Reichs Mark
COPENHAGEN*	.. .. ..	215 Kroner	365.50 Kroner	—	1.00 Kroner
DORTMUND	.. .. ..	105 Reichs Mark	199.50 Reichs Mark	168.50 Reichs Mark	1.05 Reichs Mark
DÜSSELDORF ..	.. .. ..	90 Reichs Mark	162 Reichs Mark	144 Reichs Mark	0.90 Reichs Mark
ESSEN/MÜLHEIM	.. .. ..	95 Reichs Mark	167.40 Reichs Mark	148.80 Reichs Mark	0.95 Reichs Mark
HAMBURG*	.. .. ..	120 Reichs Mark	204 Reichs Mark	—	1.00 Reichs Mark
HANOVER*	.. .. ..	120 Reichs Mark	204 Reichs Mark	—	1.20 Reichs Mark
LE ZOUTE	.. .. ..	475 Belgian Francs	855 Belgian Francs	760 Belgian Francs	6.00 Belgian Francs
MALMÖ*	.. .. ..	225 Kronor	382.50 Kronor	—	1.00 Kronor
OSTEND	.. .. ..	475 Belgian Francs	855 Belgian Francs	760 Belgian Francs	6.00 Belgian Francs

● A French edition of this timetable is published and may be obtained on request from Imperial Airways, Airway Terminus, Victoria Station, S.W.1, or from Airways House, 38 Avenue de l'Opéra, Paris

Passengers are advised to ask for the booklet *Notes for your Comfort and Convenience when travelling by Air in Europe* in which much useful information will be found

---

11

DO YOU KNOW

this about air travel ?

THAT, as well as its European services, Imperial Airways operates a regular weekly service from London to Greece, Egypt, Palestine, 'Iraq, the Persian Gulf and India, and from London to Greece, Egypt, the Anglo-Egyptian Sudan, Uganda, Kenya Colony, Tanganyika Territory, Northern and Southern Rhodesia, Transvaal and Cape Province ?

THAT, by means of these services, you can fly to India in 6½ days and to South Africa in 11 days, sleeping comfortably on land each night ?

THAT on these Empire services all meals and hotel accommodation, and even tips, are included in the fares, which are very reasonable ?

THAT the latest Imperial Airways liners are as comfortable and as quiet as Pullmans, carry stewards and are equipped with a buffet, ample luggage accommodation and lavatories ?

THAT you can post letters for Air Mail as easily as for ordinary mail and that by air your letters arrive much sooner ?

THAT freight sent by air to anywhere in the world is generally insurable at about half the rate charged for surface transport ?

IMPERIAL AIRWAYS

THE BRITISH AIR LINE

CHAPTER TWELVE

QANTAS EMPIRE AIRWAYS AND
RAILWAY AIR SERVICES
1934

THE year began in a solemn mood as Imperial Airways had to deal with the repercussions of the accident to the Avro 10 *Apollo* (G-ABLU) that had crashed in Belgium on the penultimate day of 1933. The parents of one of the victims, a Polish passenger by the name of Samuel Halperine, were pressing to claim damages of £40,000 from the company. At the time there was a Warsaw Pact agreement in force that limited accident damage liability claims to just £1,560 but this was on the proviso that the party responsible for the accident could prove they had taken all precautions to avoid the incident. This could hardly be said of Imperial Airways because Gittens, the pilot who had commanded the aircraft, was 12 miles off course and flying far too low when he hit the wireless mast in his path. It appears that he may have been hopelessly lost and it is understood that he was radioing to ascertain his position at the moment his aircraft collided with the stay of the mast.

The year also commenced with an agreement between the French and British governments that permitted passengers travelling on flights between Paris and London to dispense with the need to take their passports. Strangely the concession only applied to journeys made between Fridays and Tuesdays in either direction. Why travellers on the other days of the week still needed their passports is a mystery.

January was a busy month for Imperial Airways. The new DH86 was ready and was undergoing tests at Stag Lane prior to being flown to Martlesham where it was granted a certificate of airworthiness just one day prior to the deadline for inclusion to operate the Australian route. At a meeting in Brisbane on the 18 January, Qantas Empire Airways (QEA) was formed to operate the Australia-Singapore sector of the Empire route. During the evening of the 22nd, the board was elected at a meeting held at the Wool Exchange Building in Eagle Street. This was attended by four men; two from Imperial Airways; the others from Qantas. Albert E Rudder and S A Dismore from the British side met with their Australian counterparts, Fergus McMaster and Hudson Fysh, to elect the officers of the new company. McMaster was appointed chairman; Rudder vice-chairman; Fysh managing director; Harman secretary and W A Watt and F E Loxton as directors. The elected board approved tenders for the air mail contract and the proposed prices for carrying the mail. The new company was launched with a capital of £A200,000 with Qantas and Imperial Airways owning

Control Tower, Croydon Aerodrome

49 per cent each of the stock. Sir George Julius took up the remaining 2 per cent and was fondly referred to as 'the umpire' in the negotiations. Because of the good understanding that Imperial Airways and Qantas enjoyed, Hudson Fysh later remarked that Julius was '...the umpire who never had to blow his whistle.' Clause 26 in the association proposed by Imperial Airways formed the basis of the agreement and summed up the remarkable spirit that was behind its foundation: 'It is the intention of both parties that each shall have a "square deal" in the sense that that expression is understood by fair and reasonably minded men.' A commonly held view by many who had not been privileged to become a part of the joint venture still was that the arrangement should have been kept entirely Australian.

On 24 January Fysh travelled with Dismore by train to Melbourne taking with them a black tin box that contained their twenty-two submissions for the various routes and route variations they were seeking to win. Spaces were left on the documents for the tender prices of their bids to be added at the very last minute. The two men shared a sleeping compartment and the box containing the valuable documents was kept within their sight throughout the entire journey. After all, the future of QEA depended on the vital documents inside the box. Some light-hearted relief was enjoyed when their rivals, Charles Ulm of Australian National Airways, and Norman Brearley of West Australian Airways, also en-route to Melbourne with their tenders, looked into the compartment. While some friendly banter was exchanged, the two competitors casually glanced at the box, then decided to rest their feet on it as they chatted. They were completely unaware that their footrest contained their rival's tenders. No doubt they would have been keen to have known the details written on the documents inside their temporary footrest. Fysh and Dismore found the episode highly amusing which sufficiently inspired the Imperial Airways man to write some lines of poetry, reproduced from *Qantas Rising – The Autobiography of the Flying Fysh* by Hudson Fysh (published by Angus & Robertson Ltd 1965):

DEDICATED TO SOMETHING VERY 'TENDER'
Said Charley Ulm to Norman Brearley
They'll have to tender very queerly
To beat our combination

With an abomination
Like Qantas Impairlim
Said Uncle Norman to Charlie Boy
Very true but still t'would be a joy
And it is my fervent wish
To know what's in the mind
Of that stiff, Hudson Fysh

The QEA tenders, four alternatives in all for the Singapore–Darwin service, and those for other routes was lodged just 51 minutes before the expiration of the official application deadline at the obscure time of 5.06 pm on 31 January. Brearley and Ulm tendered six for the same route. The lowest tender came from Qantas at £A207,248, but this was rejected because the aircraft contained in the proposal was considered to be too slow. Using faster aircraft (the DH86), Qantas had tendered at £A228,478. Ulm and Brearley tendered £A44,483 more than Qantas forcing them out of the running. What followed was a long period of waiting as the proposals were examined, scrutinised and considered. More than 70 years later the tension can only be imagined, especially as the entire future of the companies concerned, not least the success of the Empire route, had rested on these contracts being granted or refused. The waiting period finally came to an end on 19 April 1934 with the announcement by the Australian Prime Minister, the Hon J A Lyons, that Qantas Empire Airways had been awarded the Singapore-Brisbane service. The only other tender for the Overseas route came from the Ulm–Brearley combination. Qantas had also tendered for the eastern route between Darwin, Brisbane and Cootamundra at £A180,764 for five years, as well as the Cloncurry-Normanton branch.

The former went to QEA with a total tender across the Singapore–Darwin–Brisbane–Cootamundra route of £A339,486 over five years. Ulm and Brearley had priced their tenders too high and although they also offered to operate the DH86, their efforts went without reward and QEA won the contract at a price of 2As 11d (approx 14.9p) per mile for the first four years, reducing to 2As 5d (approx 10.6p) in the fifth. However, when the proposals reached Cabinet, the southern portion of the route, Charleville-Cootamundra, was handed to C A Butler of New England Airways and Aircraft Pty (Butler Air Transport) who tendered using DH34 Dragon aircraft. Butler was already well known for his record solo flight from Australia to England in 1932. His airline was founded on 1 March 1931 on the back of the New England Motor Company that operated buses and operated a Brisbane-Lismore service that was extended to Sydney in July 1931 and operated daily during 1934.

The DH86 is unveiled

The DH86 that Qantas proposed operating was the fastest British aircraft of the time and was the first four-engined aircraft to be used in Australia. The airline had contracted for five but Fysh was concerned that the price he had quoted in the tenders was too low to be profitable. He need not have worried; once the route became operational his doubts were proved unfounded and the company recorded continuous yearly profits thereafter. On 23 May, Lester Brain, the Qantas senior pilot, departed Australia bound for the de Havilland works in England where he tested the DH86 before flying it back to his homeland. On 14 June, Fysh also left Australia to check the route to Singapore to ensure that the landing grounds were in order. Albert Plesman also

Railway Air Services' DH86, G-AEFH Neptune, photographed in the mid-1930s. (CAS)

announced KLM's intention to compete to Australia, even suggesting seeking '… *an equitable division of traffic with Imperial Airways.*' Parkhill, the Australian Postmaster General retaliated, stating that any extension of the Royal Dutch Air Mail Batavia-Darwin service would be '…*a matter of arrangements between governments.*'

The de Havilland DH86 was designed and produced in just four months to the specifications of the Australian Government. It was the first four-engine aircraft to be built by the company. It had to be fast, efficient and capable of flying safely across the Timor and Java Seas. This was achieved by using the reliable Gipsy VI engines designed by Major F B Halford and was a six-cylinder version of the Gipsy Major. The first of these power plants was hastily tested in time to be added to the prototype DH86 that first flew at Stag Lane on 14 January 1934. This was successfully piloted by Hubert Broad before the aircraft was certificated at Martlesham on 30 January. The resulting aircraft was flown by a single pilot sitting in the nose, aided by a wireless operator/navigator who sat behind the pilot on the starboard side. Ten passengers and mail could be accommodated within the plywood box-style cabin. The outside was covered in fabric and the aircraft had an attractive rounded appearance. But, despite appearing more modern, the DH86 was nevertheless still a bi-plane with all four engines mounted on the lower wing. There was still no break from the tradition of a fixed undercarriage either, although on the DH86 the wheels were at least partially hooded by fairings to provide a smoother air flow.

LAMBERT & BUTLER'S CIGARETTES

COMMONWEALTH CLASS. QANTAS EMPIRE AIRWAYS LINER

The DH86 variants that were introduced to the Australian route had significant design modifications to those flown in Europe. The longer Australian routes required the fuel capacity to be increased from the two 57 gallon tanks on the domestic aircraft, to 183 gallons. The Australians did not approve the original idea of seating the first officer behind the pilot, and the cockpit was changed so that they sat side-by-side. In the end, from a total of 62 that were manufactured, until production ceased in 1937, only four retained the single pilot configuration of the original design. The re-fitted prototype was painted in the colours of Imperial Airways and entered service as *Delphinus* (G-ACPL) during August.

The weekly mail service between England and Australia officially opened in bad weather on 8 December 1934. Imperial Airways operated the London-Karachi sector; the Karachi-Singapore sector was operated by Imperial Airways in association with Indian Trans-Continental Airways and Qantas Empire Airways flew the final stage to Brisbane. By the time the service started, Qantas was still awaiting the arrival of its own compliment of DH86s and flights between Singapore and Darwin were initially operated using Imperial Airways aircraft.

There was increasing consternation over the fact that Hong Kong still had no international air link despite the improvements that had been made at Kowloon's Kai Tak airport. In July 1932 a rumour had circulated that the French Compagnie Français Air Orient was about to

operate a series of test flights between Hong Kong and Vietnam to link with its Saigon-Marseilles air mail service. The managing director of the company proudly announced *'Hong Kong will shortly be within ten days journey of France by regular airmail and passenger service.'* Much speculation followed and on 16 June 1933, following a visit by Francis Love of the American Aircraft Export Corporation, a claim was made that *'Hong Kong and Shanghai* (were) *to be linked.'* There was a sudden flurry of interest when Pan American Airways as well as the French and Thai airlines were said to be preparing to serve the vast Chinese market. The best option open at that time was for passengers to take the five-day sea voyage to Singapore where they could link up with the KLM flight to Amsterdam.

Prior to the first scheduled Australian departure from Croydon on 8 December, the Secretary of State for Air, the Marquis of Londonderry KG, MVO conducted a brief ceremony with Sir Eric Geddes, who was handed the mail by the Postmaster General, Sir Kingsley Wood. Letters from the HM King George V, Queen Mary and HRH Prince of Wales were given to a postman by Wood who ceremonially placed them in his mail bag that he handed to Geddes for loading onto the aeroplane. 100,000 letters and 500 lbs of parcels comprised the initial load. The route was operated in a relay:

- Capt Walters flew HP42W *Hengist* (G-AAXE), on a positioning flight, and carried the mail to Karachi.
- The Imperial Airways AW Atalanta *Astraea* (G-ABTL) and AW XV *Arethusa* (VT-AEF) jointly operated the Karachi-Darwin sector, arriving 18 December.
- On 19 December the Qantas DH61 *Diana* (VH-UJC) (Capt Allan) and DH50J *Hippomenes* (VH-ULG) (Capt Lester Brain) collected the mail at Darwin. *Diana* was damaged at Camooweal and its mail was taken aboard *Hippomenes* to Mt Isa.
- Finally, a DH50A (VH-UJS) (Capt E Donaldson) flew the final leg, Mount Isa-Brisbane arriving on 21 December.

The returning westbound mail had already left for England on a service inaugurated by HRH the Duke of Gloucester at a ceremony held at Brisbane's Archerfield Aerodrome on 10 December.

- Lester Brain commanded the repaired Qantas DH61 *Diana* and carried the mail to Darwin.
- Capt Tapp took it as far as Roma on *Hippomenes*
- Capt Allan flew Roma-Darwin.
- From Darwin the Imperial Airways, Australian registered *Arethusa* flown by Capt R O Taylor carried it to Paris.
- At Paris the mail was split and loaded onto the Armstrong Whitworth Argosy, *City of Coventry* (G-AAEJ), flown by Capt Percy and the Short L17 *Syrinx* (G-ACJK), which arrived at Croydon on 24 December.

The domestic airlines became increasingly active during '1934; further new enterprises evolved, while inevitably others failed. Whitehall Securities, a wealthy company owned by the powerful Pearson family, were beginning to wield great influence in the civil aviation industry. A senior family member, Weetman Pearson (1856-1927) became Lord Cowdray and served as the Liberal MP for Colchester until his death, when his eldest son Harold inherited the title. The family owned other prominent businesses including Formed Metal Propellers Ltd and Anglo-Mexican Petroleum Products. The Pearsons also controlled Simmonds Aircraft that became Simmonds Spartan Aircraft (later Spartan Aircraft Ltd), the parent company of Spartan Air Lines.

On 28 January Jersey Airways inaugurated their daily London (Heston)-Jersey service with a 10.55 hrs departure that carried five passengers. A DH84 Dragon operated the service that used the public beach at St Helier in the absence of an airport. On 18 March the company extended its Jersey-Portsmouth service to include Southampton (Eastleigh), and by 28 February 1935, Portsmouth was dropped in favour of a non-stop service between Eastleigh and Jersey. On 4 June 1934 operations were further extended to include a twice-weekly St Helier-Paris service. The States, Jersey's legislative body, was concerned about an infestation of Colorado beetles that could destroy the Island's potato crops, and this caused the service to be suspended on 27 September fearing that the bug might be transported by air. It was

later resumed and the route became so popular that on one day all eight of the company's Dragons flew an impressive formation to land one after the other on the beach. Timings had to fit within a tight time-slot to coincide with the tides and it was normal for scheduled flights to arrive and depart at very close intervals.

From 19 February-2 March, Midland and Scottish Air Ferries operated flights in conjunction with Redditch Garages Ltd between Liverpool (Hooton)-Birmingham (Castle Bromwich) and Heston-Birmingham in connection with the British Industries Fair. The company became the first airline to use the rather ungainly looking three-engined Airspeed Ferry biplanes on these services. On 6 April, the company staged a ceremony at Liverpool to inaugurate its London–Liverpool–Belfast and London–Liverpool–Glasgow services that used an Avro 642, *Marchioness of Londonderry* (G-ACFV). Afterwards the Prime Minister, Ramsay MacDonald, and his party returned to London on board the aircraft. Further route expansions followed three days later when the company launched London (Romford)–Birmingham–Liverpool–Glasgow and Liverpool-Isle of Man–Belfast that flew twice-weekly. The airline later adopted Abridge on the outskirts of east London as its base until operations ceased during July.

As flying started to grow in popularity several small companies struggled to establish routes. On 19 March London Scottish and Provincial Airways began experimental flights with an Airspeed Courier between London, Nottingham, Manchester and Renfrew. On the same day a different airline with a similar name, Provincial Airways Ltd, began flying from Croydon to Southampton, Haldon and Plymouth with Fox Moths. During May the company used a DH Dragon on the service, but following the fate of many, its future was shaky and it went into liquidation on 10 December 1935.

The progressive Dutch company KLM was continuing to be a major threat and was attempting to dig a thorn deep into the side of Imperial Airways. After attempting to grab the lucrative air mail contracts to Australia, the company's leader, Albert Plesman, attempted to court the Lord Mayor of Manchester at a conference by offering to place the city more prominently on the aviation map, more especially as it had largely been ignored. In a proposal put to the Mayor, Plesman announced that KLM was ready to establish a direct air link between Manchester and the Continent; a service he planned to start from Amsterdam via Hull. Imperial Airways, for its part, remained unconcerned and its attention was on the more pressing issues associated with the Empire air mail services. As it turned out, KLM launched its northern England service on 1 June, but instead of Manchester, the airline announced it would fly instead to the rival city of Liverpool from Amsterdam via Hull. The airline was given rights to carry passengers on the Hull-Liverpool sector and GPO mail was carried to Holland, Northern Germany and Scandinavia. During 1934 the service carried 969 passengers, 398 kgs of cargo and 564 kgs of mail to and from Liverpool. The service continued until the outbreak of the Second World War, normally using Fokker F XII monoplanes. From 1936 Doncaster replaced Hull as the intermediary destination and the proposed Manchester service was eventually introduced but not until 27 June 1938.

KLM and the DC2

During October the Dutch company was able to score a valuable success over Imperial Airways when the low-wing, all-steel, American-built monoplane, the Douglas DC2 was successfully entered in the MacRobertson air race. This was won by the bright red purpose-built DH88 Comet racing machine, *Grosvenor House* (G-ACSS), flown by C W A Scott and Tom Campbell-Black within three days flying time. Many were surprised when the Douglas put in a highly polished performance to finish second in the 12,300 mile race from Mildenhall (Suffolk) to Melbourne. KLM's entry in the race had made a positive statement about the speed and reliability of the DC2 and it emphasised how the Imperial Airways fleet looked slow and dated in comparison. Captained by K D Parmentier with J J Moll, the Douglas completed the race in 3 days, 18 hrs and 17 mins with three passengers and 191 kg of mail on board. In comparison, even the faithful Fokkers that KLM had relied on since the 1920s, were looking tired and the company's race success encouraged the company to order a further 14 DC2s from Douglas. This heralded the start of the future dominance that American aircraft would have in Europe.

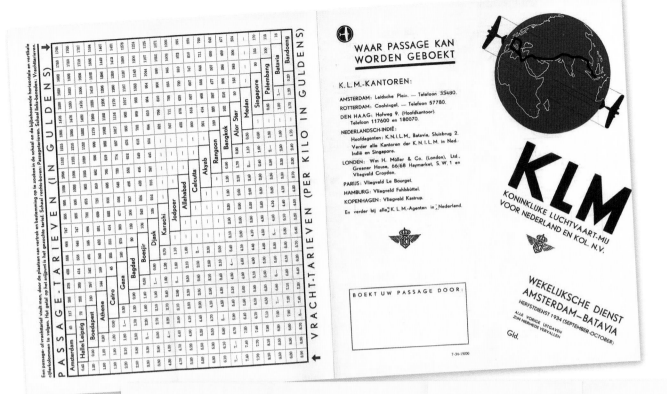

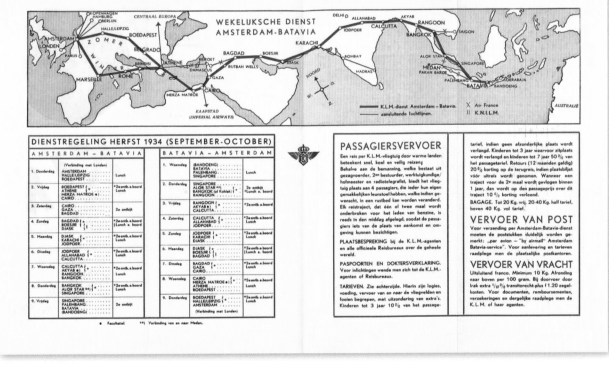

A KLM brochure, including a timetable for flights from Europe to Indonesia.

Railway Air Services

By far one of the major developments to occur in the domestic airline agenda came with the registration of Railway Air Services (RAS) on 21 March. This was formed by the four mainline members of the Railway Companies Association; the London Midland and Scottish, London and North Eastern, Great Western and the Southern Railway who were attempting to compete with an expanding number of bus operators. Many bus companies had already established successful associations with airlines and in Scotland, SMT operated its own aircraft. Imperial Airways also ventured to become a founder member of the new company. RAS had a nominal capital of £50,000 and the board consisted of Sir Harold Hartley of LMS Scientific Research (chairman) and one director from each of the other companies including Imperial Airways. These were S B Collett (GWR); O H Corble (LNER); G S Szlumper (SR) and Lt Col H Burchall of Imperial Airways. Wing Commander Harold 'Daddy' Measures of Imperial Airways was

appointed air superintendent. Measures had joined Imperial Airways in 1930 and became Divisional Engineer (East Africa) a year later and Operations Manager (India) in 1933. Brackley was given the task of training the new RAS pilots. The headquarters of the new concern was housed in a single office on the top floor of the Imperial Airways headquarters at Airway Terminus in Hudson's Place adjacent to Victoria Station.

Gordon Olley, who had been successful as GWR's chief pilot was surprisingly overlooked for a managerial appointment. Angered by the decision, he left the company to set up Olley Air Services with a capital of £6,015. Olley was given a retirement luncheon by his former Imperial Airways colleagues at the Croydon Aerodrome Hotel with a menu specially devised with courses named to represent the pilots who had been his colleagues. The *Au Revoir* menu, as it was called, is shown on the following page with the pilot's names in italics where the references may be less than obvious:

A policeman stands guard in front of a pair of Olley Air Services Dragons outside an Imperial Airways hangar at Croydon (CAS)

Thick *Horsey's* Tail
Fried Fillet of Sole taken from deep *Walters* by a *Dizzy* pilot
(Dismore)
Sauce from *Rog* who said she was a Tartar

Veal Cutlets Milanaise
Youell eat these if your *Arm is Strong (Armstrong)*
Petits Pois *Perry*
Who is not the *Pater's Son (Peterson)*
Pommes from the
Chateau *Wilky* (Wilcockson) is searching for
(Sent by Special *Messinger*)

Cup a l'Aerodrome
The Winner Must Make *Hay*
Whilst the sun shines

Cheese it *Jonah*

The Café in the Rue Blondell

Good-bye d'*Olley* we must leave you.

One of the summer services Gordon Olley performed with his airline was to launch sightseeing flights along the Kent coast that returned over the county's hop fields.

Railway Air Services was formed to forge internal links within the United Kingdom in conjunction with Imperial Airways. The railway companies had considered that they had an expanded role to play in aviation, but this proved to be a fairly rash opinion. The company launched a more brutal objective by attempting to absorb any smaller airlines it considered were operating on a sound basis that were likely to pose it a threat. This idea was to snuff out or restrict the activities of these companies and it attempted to do this by ordering all railway travel agents to cease handling bookings for all other British domestic airlines. All routes operated by RAS fell within the financial responsibilities of the particular railway company within the region a route was being flown. The revenue from the airline was paid to the railway companies and then reimbursed by way of the airline's full operating costs, overheads, interest and depreciation. This led to some losses as Southern Railway later discovered from its joint operations with Spartan Airlines.

Despite LNER requesting that a route be opened by RAS to operate between London–Norwich–Hull–Newcastle–Edinburgh and Aberdeen that loosely followed its east coast railway line, the service never materialised and the LNER never operated any air routes. The other three railway companies had intended to bring Irish Railways into

their network to provide a valuable link to Northern Ireland and the Irish Free State (Eire), but this never happened. The GWR's attempts to establish a service to the Republic was also prevented because the Irish Government had already provided monopoly rights to fly in and out of its country to an independent company.

On 5 November Sir Eric Geddes addressed the shareholders at the 10th AGM of Imperial Airways by announcing a net profit of £78,571 from a gross surplus of £314,661. He also used the occasion to clarify the company's stance in relation to Railway Air Services:

'As you doubtless know, the railway companies, who suffered severely from road competition in years gone by before they acquired the powers to operate road motor services, took precautions to avoid being caught in the same way by air transport and acquired Parliamentary powers to operate air services. Their powers permit them to operate not only within the United Kingdom, but also on the Continent of Europe, therefore, we faced the possibility of competition by the railway companies in our services to the Continent, but we were faced with the possibility of our establishing air services within the territories served by their railways. Under the circumstances, the main line railway companies and our company have jointly, by agreement, founded Railway Air Services Ltd – a company intended mainly to operate internal air lines in the British Isles…"

The decision that had faced Imperial Airways was a case of 'if you can't beat them, join them,' but Imperial Airways also stood to gain by providing RAS with aircraft, crews, training and maintenance.

In time for the launch of the new airline, Croydon Airport had made some further significant improvements. A new direction finding mast had been installed as well as a microwave system (known as HF) that coordinated with a system the French had installed across the Channel at St Inglevert. This enabled telephone and teleprinter exchanges to be improved so that departures and arrivals could immediately be signalled. The microwave system was a major breakthrough that was capable of producing cloud and darkness penetrating rays that gave aircraft the ability to remain in touch with the ground in all prevailing conditions.

The internal air mail

The first of a new fleet of aircraft needed for the launch of RAS was delivered on 3 May. This was the DH84 Dragon II (G-ACPX) that arrived at Croydon and was destined for the routes operated by GWR and SR. LMS selected the four-engined DH86 Express Airliner that could accommodate ten passengers, for the route between London and Glasgow. Two of these aircraft were ordered, together with a number of DH89 Dragon Rapides. Brackley had test flown the DH86 *Delphinus* (G-ACPL), and had demonstrated the aircraft to Col Shelmerdine (the Director of Civil Aviation) during July. Later that month he flew the Dragon (G-ACVB) over a period of three days to Manchester, Liverpool, Glasgow and Blackpool on routes operated by RAS. Brackley was also involved with Britain's first internal air mail service

between London and Glasgow via Birmingham, Manchester and Belfast that officially opened on 20 August. As dignitaries gathered at Croydon to greet the arrival of the first mail consignment from Glasgow, the celebrations were almost abandoned when terrible weather prevented the flight reaching London. In order to prevent the gathered throng from being disappointed, Brackley astutely instructed William Armstrong to load a *Wessex* with mail and take-off for the return trip to give the VIPs something to see. On the same day mail had also been scheduled for flights between Belfast, the Isle of Man and Manchester on a shuttle basis, and between Liverpool-Plymouth and Birmingham-Cowes (Isle of Wight), but these operations were also marred by the weather. The southbound Glasgow–Belfast–Manchester flights flown by Capt J H Lock aboard DH86 (G-ACVY) *Mercury* and by Capt E Poole on (G-ACPL) *Delphinus,* the London–Birmingham by Westland Wessex (G-AAGW) (Capt W Armstrong), the Belfast–Isle of Man–Manchester (southbound) by Dragon (G-ACXI flown by Capt Gordon Store), the Liverpool–Birmingham–Cardiff–Haldon–Plymouth in both directions by Dragon (G-ACPX) and the Birmingham–Bristol sector of the Birmingham–Cowes route in both directions by Dragon (G-ACPY) did get through. The following day conditions improved and normal services were resumed.

Spartan Air Lines Ltd, (see previous chapter) had been operating a successful service from London (Heston) to Cowes (Isle of Wight) during the summer of 1933. When the service re-commenced on 1 May for the summer season of 1934, Spartan operated the route under the new title Southern Air Services. This name was adopted when the company became newly associated with the Southern Railway. At the same time the airline's London terminus was moved from Heston to Croydon where RAS had its operational base. The Isle of Wight towns of Ryde and Bembridge (where aircraft stopped by request) were included in the thrice-daily schedules operated each way by Spartan Cruiser aircraft. A fourth service was added on 15 May 1934. Capt P W Lynch-Blosse flew the inaugural service in the Spartan Cruiser II *Faithful City* (G-ACDW). A flight between Croydon and Cowes took 50 minutes and cost £1 10s 0d (£1.50) single and £2 10s 0d (£2.50) return. An arrangement was also put in place permitting passengers holding return tickets to travel first class on Southern Railway trains if they preferred. On the day that Spartan re-opened its Isle of Wight service, Portsmouth, Southsea and Isle of Wight Aviation (PSIWA) also began flying between Heston, Ryde and Shanklin using a Wessex (G-ABVB) and a Dragon (G-ACRF). The company later added routes connecting Shoreham, Portsmouth and Bournemouth and Ryde, Shanklin and Bournemouth using the Wessex, a pair of Fox Moths (G-ACCA and G-ACIG) and the Dragon (G-ACRF).

The first RAS service operated on the Plymouth (Roborough) –Haldon–Cardiff–Birmingham (Castle Bromwich) route previously flown by GWR that opened on 7 May was then extended to Liverpool (Speke). A once-weekly service was made in each direction by the Dragon (G-ACPX) that was flown by Imperial Airways pilots and this aircraft was the first to be painted in the red, green and silver livery of RAS.

During May, Capt Oscar Philip Jones of Imperial Airways, affectionately known as 'O.P' among his contemporaries but 'Mister' by junior aircrew behind his back, celebrated flying his one millionth mile. This accomplished feat was duly mentioned in the press together with the fact that he had safely carried 65,000 passengers during his long career. Two months earlier Capt L A Walters

Raymond Hinchliffe, the one-eyed pilot of Imperial Airways. (CAS)

had celebrated becoming the first pilot to receive a Master Pilot's Certificate.

Imperial Airways remained drastically short of aircraft. The L17 *Scylla*, the rather ungainly hybrid land version of the S17 Kent flying-boat was being built in the open air by Shorts, but it was viewed very much as a stop-gap aircraft that lacked any kind of refinement. G-ACJJ made its first flight on 26 March at Rochester when Lankester Parker took it aloft for fifteen minutes accompanied by the aircraft's designer. Brackley flew it on a second flight and tested the dual controls and reported that the handling was '...*very good.*' Next day he flew the aircraft to Martlesham for further trials that continued into mid-May when the aircraft was certificated before entering service. On 16 May Capt Youell carried mail and passengers between London and Paris on the first sector of the Africa service. In June *Scylla* was joined by her sister aircraft, *Syrinx* (G-ACJK), to provide support to the HP42s that were assigned to the London to Paris, Brussels, Basle and Zurich services. Brackley's confidence in the aircraft's handling abilities was not shared by all Imperial Airways pilots who had to fly the type. The aircraft were said to *wallow* in gusty weather and they were heavy and uncomfortable to control even in favourable conditions. On 3 August a wheel brake jammed on *Scylla* at Le Bourget causing it to tip forward onto its nose and the aircraft's centre of gravity was moved aft to put extra weight on the tail. The aircraft was not liked and thankfully for the pilots, only two were ever built.

In June a mail version of the Heinkel He 70A (V2) was flown into Croydon by the German carrier Lufthansa. The aircraft was sleek and described as having a torpedo-like futuristic appearance that prompted a comment from an eyewitness to say *'It would make a good bomber.'* But the appearance of the German aircraft served only to emphasise how dated *Scylla* and *Syrinx* were in contrast with the designs evolving from other nations. Britain seemed caught in a time warp and was still lagging stubbornly behind the USA and the progressive aircraft manufacturing countries.

The 1934 Air Estimates allocated £513,000 towards civil aviation; the highest contribution for ten years. Funding was provided for an extension to the India service to Singapore and the New Zealand Government offered an annual subsidy of £5,000 towards the Antipodean service. Unreasonably £50,000 was cut from the subsidy of the Egypt-South Africa service although provision was made towards

The sleek, 'torpedo-like' shape of Lufthansa's Heinkel He 70 caused a stir when it arrived at Croydon in June 1934. The appearance of the aircraft served only to emphasise how dated Imperial Airways' Scylla and Syrinx were in contrast with the designs evolving from other nations. Seen here is He 70, W.Nr. 403, taxying during a press demonstration in Germany in the mid-1930s.

better meteorological services, establishing new radio stations and air route lighting for night operations. A night beacon in Transjordania on the Cairo-Karachi service was also funded. Sir Philip Sassoon had also hinted to Parliament that a £10,000 subsidy would be granted for a weekly service being proposed between New York and Bermuda that Imperial Airways intended to operate in conjunction with an American airline as an integral part of a future Atlantic service.

Expansion in Africa

There had been a setback for Imperial Airways when, on 1 February, South African Airways (SAA) bought Union Airways. SAA was a subsidiary of South African Railways that in turn was owned by the Ministry of Railways and Harbours. Union Airways had been started in 1929 by the former wartime flying ace, Alister Miller, to carry mail. The airline was funded by the Atlantic Refining Company and had commenced operations with a fleet of five DH Gipsy Moths. By 1930 passengers were being carried using a pair of DH Puss Moths and a Fokker Super Universal, but the safety record had not been good and all three aircraft crashed the following year, with two of the accidents resulting in fatalities. The company replaced the lost aircraft with the Junkers machines of South West African Airways, a business owned by Junkers. Union and SWAA amalgamated, but continued operating under their own identities until the SAA takeover. In so doing, SAA inherited the Junkers machines bought by Union and improved the fleet by adding more up-to-date Ju 52/3ms that served the Johannesburg–Bulawayo route from 1 November. During the same month Woods Humphery announced that Imperial Airways intended to operate a new route to West Africa, either to be linked with Khartoum or by a new flying boat service via Portugal, the Cape Verde Islands and Bathurst (Gambia). Apart from at Bathurst, Accra and Lagos, there were no other suitable landing grounds in West Africa and this stalled any decision. There was a further proposal to land at Tamala in the Gold Coast (later Ghana) but this was considered unsuitable. Nigeria was rapidly developing aerodromes and in addition to Lagos those at Maiduguri, Yolam, Bauchi, Jos, Kano, Kaduna, Katsina, Mina and Ilorin were all considered destinations. Nigeria was also suited to seaplane operations with potential landing sites available at Lagos, Forcados, Port Harcourt, Calabar, Onitsha, Makurdi, Lokoja and Jebba. Despite this, little aviation activity took place in the country until Elder Dempster began a mail service between the Gold Coast and Nigeria. On 27 October, in a letter sent to the Nigerian Governor, Sir Arnold Hodson KCMG, proposed a route between Takoradi, Accra and Lagos using multi-engined aircraft that could fly over water in order to avoid sensitive French-controlled territories. Elder Dempster, who operated a shipping company, decided to form the service in conjunction with Imperial Airways under the name Elder Colonial Airways Limited.

1934 marked the tenth anniversary of Imperial Airways and the BBC celebrated the occasion on 3 May with a special hour-long broadcast written and produced by Lance Sieveking (Lancelot De Giberne Sieveking DFC) a popular radio personality of the day. In the two days prior to the broadcast, several hours were spent rehearsing. Although many characters associated with the company were heard on the programme, only Wolley Dod, who flew the first regular flight to

LAMBERT & BUTLER'S CIGARETTES

MOUNT KENYA, KENYA COLONY

IMPERIAL AIRWAYS TO-DAY AND TO-MORROW

Below are extracts from the speech of the Chairman (Rt. Hon. Sir Eric Geddes), at the Annual General Meeting of Imperial Airways Ltd., on Monday, 5 November 1934

The Chairman said:

¶ During the year under review, the traffic carried on the European services has not only been maintained but improved

¶ The traffic on the Indian and Malayan route shows a gratifying and steady growth

¶ The traffic on the whole of the Africa route increased by more than 40 per cent over the previous year

¶ We are quite convinced that our services are by far the quietest and most comfortable in the world. . . . Our standard of efficiency, service, and discipline are also, we believe, second to none in the world

¶ The line from England to South Africa, at least as far as Johannesburg, is to be doubled in frequency almost immediately, so that there will be two services each way a week between London and Johannesburg

¶ We also have under immediate consideration the question of increasing the frequency of our Eastern service to twice weekly

¶ The extension from Singapore to Australia will commence just before Christmas

¶ We decided some months ago to order two flying-boats and two land-planes as prototypes on which experimental work could be conducted. . . . These aircraft will be much larger than anything at present in our Company's service . . . and they will, of course, be faster than the existing fleet

¶ When our present fleet is replaced, the public may expect a substantial increase in speed as well as frequency

¶ No amount of written matter can ever equal the visit of a director, a salesman or an inspector. I hold the view that 'Trade follows the passenger' far more than that 'Trade follows the mail'. . . . To separate the mail and passenger services would merely mean that instead of both classes of traffic getting the benefit of increased frequency, neither of them would, and we believe that the passenger services are as important as mail services

¶ The Directors recommend the payment of a dividend on the Ordinary shares of the Company of 6%, less tax, as compared with 5% for the previous year. The net profit for the year was £78,571.15.0 as compared with £52,894.1.10 for the previous year

Full report on application to the Company

IMPERIAL AIRWAYS LTD

Airway Terminus, Victoria Station, S.W.1

Basra in 1927, Major Richard (who discussed air traffic control) and Brackley were named for their contributions. According to reports that were written after the broadcast, it is apparent that this was a rather contrived affair. Voices were used to introduce a build-up of speakers from various parts of the world that culminated at Croydon. Brackley was critical about having to work from a rather pedestrian script and the following commentary from the broadcast is taken from *Brackles – Memoirs of a Pioneer of Civil Aviation;* it provides a unique insight into the way Imperial Airways operated:

'It falls on my lot to describe briefly the type of work necessary to establish an Empire Route. Having studied all available traffic and mail statistics of the territories over which we are to fly, the Management decides the type of aircraft to be used and the route to be flown. The Chief Engineer then prepares the specification of the required aircraft and invites the aircraft builders to tender for their construction and supply. Then comes my part of the business as air superintendent to test for acceptance by the Company new types of aircraft, both landplanes and flying boats. I select and am responsible for the training of those who are to pilot the aircraft and operate the wireless.

'Whilst all this is going on our Ground Services, Engineering and Traffic Departments deal with the problems connected with the preparation of landing grounds, alighting areas and their equipment, wireless and meteorological services, as well as the accommodation for passengers who will set out on a flight varying from 200 to 10,000 miles, through rapidly changing climate conditions.

'The pilots and the operation of the aircraft are my special responsibility, so I must ensure that they are provided with the best possible aids to navigation and the most up-to-date wireless equipment. Then, when all is ready, I test again the aircraft and its capabilities over the actual route, usually in company with one of the Captains who will later operate the services. Together we test the suitability of the aerodromes and alighting areas, wireless and meteorological organisations, and the accommodation for passengers.

'Last year was my privilege to make two journeys to South Africa, and on the first of these journeys to test on the actual route the new four-engined Atalanta Class of aircraft specially designed for the service, and also to make the flight over the Australian route to Melbourne with one of the four-engined Atalanta Class. Before the year is ended it is hoped that the long awaited air service from London to Brisbane will be completed by the inauguration of a service from Singapore to Brisbane by our associated Australian Company, Qantas Empire Airways Ltd.'

On 20 July political changes were recommended in a report issued by the Gorell Committee. This contained several proposals, the most important being the recommendation to set up a Civil Department of State, known as the Air Registration Board, to deal with certification, air worthiness, supervision of competency, mandatory third party insurance and registrations.

Hillman's Airways

Parliament was not without its usual inter-party wrangling. Sir Kingsley Wood, the Postmaster General, made a proposal that all airmail charges should be fixed at a single flat rate to anywhere in the Empire. This was frowned upon by many who thought it impractical. To the surprise of many, Hillman's Airways was granted an air mail contract (from 1 December) that would operate daily between London, Liverpool, Belfast and Glasgow. This was a service previously operated by Railway Air Services. Capt W Anderson operated the first Hillman's northbound

An Imperial Airways publicity photograph showing a Short L17 Scylla-class flying over an AW XV Atalanta-class and its crew. (CAS)

flight in the Dragon (G-ACPN), Capt C E N Pelly the first southbound in the Dragon *Brentwood* (G-ACEU). On being awarded the contract, Hillman formed a new company to celebrate his success. This was known as Edward Henry Hillman Limited, a company with £150,000 share value (£120,000 fully paid up). Sir Charles Harris of Cotton Plantations Ltd was appointed chairman, Hillman managing director, and his son as works manager. The airline also attempted a European challenge against Imperial Airways by expanding its existing services to include regular flights from its Essex base to Ostend, Brussels, Dieppe, Cherbourg and Paris at cut-price fares. On 1 June the airline's operations were transferred from Romford (Maylands) to Stapleford Airport also in Essex, and on 16 July, Hillman's took over the route London (Stapleford)–Liverpool–Isle of Man–Belfast (Aldergrove) vacated by Midland and Scottish Air Ferries two days before.

Hillman however was in poor health. He was overweight, suffered from hyper-tension, worked too many hours and this combined to cause a massive coronary that killed him on New Year's Eve 1934 aged just 44. Hillman was a genuine entrepreneur. Born in 1890 at Laindon, Essex, he started work as a farm boy earning a pittance. Before the Great War to '...*secure three good meals a day*' he joined the cavalry and reached the rank of sergeant major. From the army he went into the diplomatic corps and became a driver in charge of a Rolls-Royce. After the war, like the Wright Brothers, he started a bicycle-making business. He then became a taxi driver, but turned taxi owner in 1928 when he realised that a cab's owner made more money than the driver. This evolved into a car hire company, but in 1928 Hillman bought his first motor coach and launched Hillman's Saloon Coaches. By the year end he had rapidly established regular services between Stratford (East London) and Chelmsford, Essex via Romford and Brentwood. When he entered aviation, Hillman was operating a fleet of 300 coaches that criss-crossed East Anglia. He kept his costs low, charged below average fares, but also refused to pay his staff much money. Hillman was criticised for regarding all airmen as no more than '...*bus drivers of the sky.*' When the Government decided to bring in regulations that prevented the uncontrolled expansion of bus routes, Hillman was forced to sell the coach business to London Transport but he received £145,000 compensation. He used this to start Hillman's Airways in November 1931 and his first charter took place with a de Havilland Puss Moth on

Christmas Day. By the following April, he was operating his first scheduled service between Maylands and Clacton-on-Sea; hardly an inspiring destination but a stepping stone towards greater success. The low fares he charged made the service popular among holidaymakers. On 11 March 1932 he expanded, adding a pair of de Havilland Fox Moths that he paid for on-the-spot during a visit to the manufacturer. Hillman was the first to acknowledge that he was poorly educated and when he was required to sign a contract to buy his aircraft, he demonstrated his illiteracy by asking someone to read the clauses to him before he wrote an 'X' for his signature. Despite this he had an amazing penchant for business. When the company expanded he remained loyal to de Havilland and bought the DH84 Dragon for £2,899 plus £105 for a job-lot of six seats. He also demonstrated a natural edge for publicity. When the time came to christen his new aircraft, he invited the famous female pilot, Amy Johnson, to break the Champagne bottle over the Dragon's nose to name it *Maylands*. He quickly put the aircraft to work on a twice-daily service to Paris. Although his flights offered no frills or meals, his prices considerably undercut Imperial Airways HP42 services by offering a round-trip fare equivalent to Imperial Airways single fare. In many respects he was the first cut-price airline. When RAS was launched and put their DH Dragon into service, Hillman went one better, by introducing the Dragon Rapide to his fleet to become the first commercial operator of the type. He lived modestly in a small semi-detached house in Essex but through his thriftiness he managed to build an enviable business, allowing himself one indulgence; a rather unique Rolls-Royce with a special body, one of only four of its kind ever built.

When one of his aircraft, the DH89 Dragon Rapide (G-ACPM) became involved in a fatal accident near Folkestone on 2 October killing all seven aboard, the incident was probably instrumental in bringing Hillman's life to an end. Despite being something of a 'rough diamond', Hillman was also an inspired pioneer who, during his short life, contributed much to British commercial aviation heritage. The airline he founded did not immediately die with him. Shortly before he passed away, Hillman's Airways became a public company with all 400,000 five-shilling (.25p) shares being sold within the space of an hour but less than a year later, following a takeover by British Airways, the Hillman name disappeared from the aircraft.

A view inside the control tower at Croydon Aerodrome during the 1930s. (CAS)

Scottish Developments

On 27 September, a few days prior to the Hillman's Airways crash, an Airspeed Courier (G-ACSY) owned by London Scottish and Provincial Airways went down at Sevenoaks killing four people. For Imperial Airways, the year had ended without any major incidents.

1934 marked another year of pioneering activity by entrepreneurs willing to try their luck in the precarious airline business. On 7 May, Highland Airways started a service from Aberdeen (Seaton) to Wick and Kirkwall every weekday using a Dragon *Aberdeen* (G-ACIT) flown by Capt E E Fresson. On 29 May the airline had carried the first regular British internal air mail when it flew 2,000 letters from Inverness (Longman Aerodrome) to Kirkwall (Wideford) in the Dragon *Caithness* (G-ACCE). Fresson, again the inaugural pilot, was proudly handed the Royal Air Mail Pennant by Sir Frederick Williamson, the Director of Postal Services. Three days earlier, the Postmaster General had handed Sir Eric Geddes of Imperial Airways his airline's first official Royal Air Mail Pennant for the India mail that was flown on *Hengist* (G-AAXE) from Croydon for Paris. By 6 August Highland Airways had expanded its routes to include a weekday inter-islands service linking Longhope, Stronsay, Sanday, North Ronaldsway and Westray with Kirkwall. By 1 December an additional contract was awarded to the company to fly mail between Inverness and Wick, with mail for Thurso being included from 10 December that was carried by overland transport on the final stage. Meanwhile, a new airport at Dyce, Aberdeen opened on 28 July and by 11 September, Aberdeen Airways had commenced a twice-daily service from the 'granite city' to Glasgow using a Dragon and a Short Scion (G-ACUV). This was cut to twice a week during the winter. New services were quickly springing up in other parts of Scotland. George Nicholson formed Northern and Scottish Airways Ltd on 21 November with a capital of £7,000 that operated from Glasgow (Renfrew) to western Scotland. Services started on 1 December using a Dragon (G-ACFG) to operate a twice-weekly Renfrew–Campbeltown–Islay service. These were later split to operate Renfrew–Campbeltown and Campbeltown–Islay.

Dragons combined low costs with reliability and were becoming the popular choice with many smaller airlines. Wrightson and Pearce used the type for early morning newspaper deliveries from London to Paris and at weekends passenger services were offered between Heston and Le Tourquet. It is understood that operations only lasted until 24 October and by 17 December the company re-appeared with a new name, Wrightways Ltd, with a capital of £6,000. Another newspaper service was launched by a company called Commercial Air Hire Ltd on 7 August that registered with a capital of £500 and operated a Dragon (G-ACCR) between Croydon and Paris.

A short-lived international service was also operated by a company called The British Air Navigation Company (BANCO) between 18 May-18 September using Dragons and a Ford SAT *Voyager* (G-ABHO) on a service between Heston and Berck. The route was extended on 29 June to include Dieppe (Pourville) at weekends and on 12 July, the same Ford aircraft was flown by T W Morton between Heston and Deauville on a daily basis until 3 September. The Dragon *Vagrant* was used to operate a Heston-Saarbrücken service from 22 December that continued on a daily basis from 27 December-22 January 1935.

An hourly ferry service was launched by a company called Southend-On-Sea Flying Services Ltd on 9 June in conjunction with the aircraft manufacturer, Short Brothers, between Southend and Rochester. Beyond 7 October the frequency was cut to four flights daily at a single fare of 8s 0d (40p); 12s 0d (60p) return. A Short Scion and a Fox Moth were used on the route.

A rather strange start-up, at least in terms of potential commercial viability, took place when Robert Boyd and T W J Nash began an experimental service on 13 June using a GAL Monospar (G-ACCP) between Barnstaple, Devon and Lundy Island. Apart from the carriage of day trippers and a few local residents in need of medical attention provisions and livestock were also flown between the mainland and the small island. Although the viability of this operation might have been in doubt, the service continued and became a regular feature that by September 1939 had made over 2,200 return flights. (See following chapters)

Northern Airways was another company that was linked with a bus operator; this time George Nicholson, a Newcastle owner that started flying on 1 July. The airline operated a Dragon (G-ACFG) flown by Ted Palmer on a cross-country route from Newcastle (Cramlington) to Carlisle and onward to the Isle of Man (Ronaldsway). There is a suggestion that the service was extended to Belfast during August. This ceased at the end of October having flown 11,000 miles, but it is believed to have carried only 182 passengers and the company became known as Northern and Scottish Airways on 21 November with services from Glasgow to Islay via Campbeltown that started on 1 December.

Other companies that were registered during 1934 were Guernsey Airways Ltd (24 November) and Channel Islands Airways Ltd (Registered in Jersey on 1 December) with a capital of £100,000 following the acquisition of Jersey Airways by Whitehall Securities. A few companies attempted to launch services with very little financial security; one was a company called Air Commerce Ltd that started with a capital of just £1,000.

In December Parliamentary approval was given for Imperial Airways to place an order for a new class of flying boat. The company had approached Short Brothers with a brief to produce a design for a long-range aeroplane that would be an improvement on the Kent. The proposed aircraft would have four engines, a stipulated range of 800 miles and would cruise at 150 mph carrying a payload of 24 passengers and 1½ tons of mail. These specifications were put to Shorts after Imperial Airways had assessed their routes and traffic requirements across their entire network in relation to ground and air temperatures, meteorology, terrain etc. The Air Ministry also required Shorts to produce a military version of the flying boat to a similar specification and at first it was anticipated that Imperial Airways would require only two of the aircraft and the RAF one military version. It has been suggested that Oswald Short and his designer had been inspired by watching the KLM Douglas DC2 aircraft performing in the MacRobertson Air Race. Short and his test pilot, Lankester Parker, were said to have been so impressed that they immediately began designing a monoplane instead of the expected bi-plane. This theory appears to be pure speculation and the design concept may have been born from the sudden realisation that British designs had fallen far behind in the race to develop efficient aircraft. Perhaps the DC2 was the wake-up call needed to make industry come to terms with the trends that were evolving from America and Germany, where monoplanes were becoming the norm. In any event, from the early expectation of an order for just two flying boats, Imperial Airways amended this requirement to an initial order of ten that subsequently grew to twenty-eight. Shorts was ecstatic; the company realised it was sitting on an order worth £1,750,000 (£62,500 per aircraft). The design that the company produced was known as the S23 and although this was later changed by Imperial Airways to become known as the *C Class*, the aircraft were more popularly known as the Empire Flying Boats. From this evolved the Ministry of Defence military variant, known as the R2/33 Sunderland that did such sterling work with RAF Coastal Command during the Second World War.

CHAPTER THIRTEEN

ALL THE WAY TO THE CAPE
BY AIR – AT LAST

1935

THE blaze of publicity that surrounded KLM after its success in the MacRobertson Air Race during the autumn of 1934 was slightly calmed domestically when Imperial Airways grabbed the headlines by carrying the newly married Duke and Duchess of Kent at the start of their honeymoon. On 5 January, the happy couple boarded the HP42W *Heracles* (G-AAXC) at Croydon for their flight to Paris. The 'Royals' continued to Munich before finally heading for the West Indies. Ten days later *Horatius* (G-AAXD) scored another Royal success by flying Infanta Beatrice of Spain, her husband and brother to Croydon. Politicians were also starting to use the airline more frequently and when Anthony Eden travelled by air to Paris and Amsterdam he was flown on the DH86 *Delphinus* (G-ACPL). Whenever royalty, politicians and popular actors travelled on the airline, it was always seen to be a favourable endorsement of the company and any opportunity to make the most of such publicity was seldom missed.

Further valuable news coverage occurred on New Year's Eve when a London store booked the Short L17 Scylla *Syrinx* (G-ACJK) for a Champagne reception and fashion show for the benefit of 20 press photographers while flying over London. The first day of the year heralded the duplication of the Calcutta-London service with the eastbound flights following suit on 5 January. Two Boulton Paul P71a aircraft, *Boadicea* (G-ACOX) and *Britomart* (G-ACOY), were delivered to Croydon during the month and were used for non-scheduled private hire charters and VIP flights.

The major operational issue during January was the departure of the survey flight to check the potential of the flying boat route across India. Brackley, as usual, was despatched with his suitcase packed for another long mission that departed on 27th from Croydon on the 12.30 hrs HP42 flight with Horsey commanding *Heracles* (G-AAXC). There were still no through services for passengers in Europe and Brackley again endured two uncomfortable days on what he referred to as the '*dreadful train*' between Paris and Brindisi. He continued aboard the Short S17 Kent *Scipio* (G-ABFA) to Athens that landed at night allowing him to take the DH Dragon of the Egyptian airline, Misr Air (later changed to Misrair), to Cairo. After resting a day, he was joined by the normal mix of dignitaries who made it their business to accompany a special flight. On this occasion it was Brig Gen Sir Frederick Williamson (Director of Postal Services), Lord Guinness (Parliamentary Secretary to the Air Ministry), and a junior MP who tagged along for the ride. The party was there to witness conditions first-hand.

No other country in the world was carrying air mail without surcharge and the flat rate proposed for the Empire Mail Scheme was a pioneering move in postal history that was still surrounded by an air of uncertainty. The Director of Postal Services wanted to determine whether the flat rate would create any problems along the route. The eastbound HP42E *Hannibal* (G-AAGX) was boarded to Palestine, and by the 3 February the party had reached Karachi where Brackley remained for a few days to inspect the harbour facilities while the parliamentary delegation continued its junket by visiting Jodhpur and Delhi.

The Imperial Airways flight from Karachi was overbooked and Brackley, not one to abuse his position by deposing a fare-paying passenger, sampled the competition by taking the KLM flight to Jodhpur where he rejoined the Imperial Airways service to Calcutta and renewed his fond acquaintance with the Armstrong Whitworth Atalanta *Astraea* (G-ABTL) that he had flown on his demonstration tour of Australia. On 9 February the official dignitaries rejoined the flight in Bangkok. By July *Astraea* was back in Australia assisting Qantas on the Empire route while it waited for its small fleet of DH86s to arrive, but it was finding it difficult to cope with the increasing payloads of mail the route was receiving.

Brackley, by necessity, spent much of his time away from home. While abroad he was usually required to meet influential businessmen, petroleum executives, politicians, aviation contemporaries and other dignitaries wherever he ventured, and this trip was certainly no exception. During his time with Imperial Airways there were few prominent personalities within the industry that Brackley did not know, and his journeys to distant places were eased by the socialising that formed an essential part of his job. It is easy to appreciate the demands these travels had on him. His wife Frida's book at times relates a moving story of her often homesick husband counting the days before being able to return home. The narrative suggests that Frida's letters to Brackley were sometimes the only thing that kept him going on occasions. The book mentions how a lack of exercise and the sticky heat on this survey had made Brackley depressed despite being amongst '…*as charming a set of business people as one could possibly wish to meet.*' The remarks Brackley wrote in a letter to Frida about the air mail service are especially poignant: '*What a blessing the airmail is to this part of the world. In just over a week I can get letters from you, and by surface means it takes over a month. I wonder what people did in the old days when they were separated from their loved ones? It seems hard to realise – and yet I must consider ourselves very lucky to be living in these times to get the benefit of the great progress speed has made in transport.*' When this particular letter was written, Brackley had been suffering from a severe fever, caused by malaria that incapacitated him for most of March. This had forced him to take refuge at the New Delhi home of his friend, the Director of Civil Aviation of India, Frederick Tymms and his wife, Millie. But Brackley, ill or not, returned to his duties far sooner than his health

Two photographs of Boulton & Paul P71A G-ACOY 'Britomart' that crashed on landing at Brussels in 1935 (CAS)

really allowed and a few days later, feeling awful, he was back in Karachi making a second inspection of the harbour and West Wharf Reclamation that would be the safe haven for the new flying boats.

The commercial rivalry between KLM and Imperial Airways had grown in intensity and there was some conflict and differences of opinion between the British, Australians and Dutch created by the refusal to allow KLM to operate to Australia from Batavia. The parties argued specifically because the Dutch and their Netherlands Indies Government in Batavia favoured dealing with the Australian Government and not the British. This was perhaps justified considering the intransigent attitude that the British Government frequently

adopted. Nevertheless, KLM had been granted permission to fly over the British-controlled territories of Egypt, Palestine, Iraq, the Persian Gulf, India, Burma and Malaya, but the Dutch stubbornly refused to reciprocate by allowing British flights over their territories in South East Asia. Imperial Airways had only requested the right to use a few landing grounds, wireless and meteorological services across the Dutch territories, but these facilities were denied in retaliation for KLM being prevented from flying to Australia. Typically British politicians neglected to negotiate a two-way deal and they imposed no restrictions of passage over KLM who freely used British facilities paid for by UK tax payers. There was also concern that by using the Douglas DC2 bought in 1934,

KLM was already operating at an advantage with faster, more efficient services than Imperial Airways could hope to provide. From 12 June 1935 the Dutch were operating a fleet of five of these aircraft on the Batavia route twice-weekly, cutting the journey time to six days. They clearly had their eyes set on expanding their Amsterdam–Batavia route to Australia, but their path was blocked by the rights Imperial Airways had secured with Qantas Empire Airlines. At least Imperial Airways could boast that it had been flying passengers on the 12,754 mile through route to Australia since 13 April and it was also planning to open a branch to Hong Kong via Penang and Saigon. The Empire Route had become an immediate success but a lack of seating capacity prevented any passengers from being carried over the full route when it first opened. This was because all seats had been booked in advance by passengers wishing to fly only short sectors. The first two passengers to complete the entire route between Croydon and Brisbane had to wait until 20 April; three days after the first westbound flight had departed. The journey took twelve and a half days and with a one-way fare costing £195, it is surprising that there was much demand. This may not sound much but in current terms this would equate to more than £9,700, far beyond the reach of most wage earners.

When Brackley met his friend Prince Purachatra, the brother of the King of Siam, during a break in the survey, the conversation provided more than a pre-destined warning of the dangers that would later befall the world. Over lunch at Raffles in Singapore, Purachatra said that he viewed the '…*Japanese menace in this part of the world as being alarming.*' Brackley had flown the Prince in France during the War and they had established a good and trusted relationship. The Prince had become one of the first people to fly in Siam. The King and his brother had been forced into exile after a bloodless coup in Siam that had handed power to the army who had established a close alliance with Japan. Maybe the Prince knew more than he was telling when he warned of impending developments in the Far East. Brackley had spent time in Japan where he had worked with the famous aviator, the Colonel the Master of Sempill, training Japanese flying boat pilots. Ironically, after the Japanese had attacked Pearl Harbor during the Second World War, Sempill was suspected of spying for the Japanese.

One of Brackley's duties while in Singapore was to test fly the DH86 (VH-USF) that had recently had modifications made to the tail and fin. Having done this, his next task involved inspecting the aerodrome at Batu Pahat on the Strait of Malacca (Malaya) where the Armstrong Whitworth Atalantas would land. Brackley spent several days moving about the Malayan peninsula inspecting landing facilities on the mainland at Taiping and Kuala Lumpur and on the island of Penang. This done, it was time to rejoin his aircraft at Alor Star for the return to Bangkok via Bandor and onwards to Rangoon. On 1 March he returned to Calcutta from Rangoon in a Fox Moth with intermediary stops at Bassein, Akyab and Chittagong. His Asian work completed, Brackley left for home on 24 March reaching Croydon a week later. Despite still suffering the affects of malaria for most of April, he was forced to maintain a relentless schedule for as long as his health would permit. He had been given a new malaria drug called Atabrin. This appeared to work and gave him the strength to continue with his duties that included twice going to Shorts to inspect mock-ups of the new flying boat. He discussed the flying boat project with the Croydon pilots and flew with Olley in his new DH Dragon Rapide. Towards the end of April he met with the Air Ministry to discuss pilot testing, blind flying and the Empire Scheme and was also involved with a court of inquiry.

Imperial Airways had still not overcome the problem of being desperately short of aircraft. Its resources were further stretched by the increases made on the Africa services. In March the first of a pair of Avro

MAP OF THE AIR ROUTE★

IMPERIAL AIRWAYS

EMBARKING ON "HANNIBAL." ENTEBBE. UGANDA

652, civil prototypes of the Anson, were delivered and for a brief time were used on charter operations before being withdrawn from service in 1936. The European division was cut to just two Heracles and two Scylla aircraft with the old Argosies being held in reserve. The remaining Heracles class were transferred to work the Middle East and to operate the Cairo-Kisumu and Cairo-Karachi sectors. The three Scipios covered the Mediterranean (with the old Calcuttas in reserve) while the Atalantas operated the final sector between Kisumu and the Cape. Operationally, it was a stressful period that required complex aircraft movement planning. Some relief came when the third DH86 was delivered during April. This was used on the twice-weekly London-Paris-Marseilles-Rome-Brindisi freight and passenger route that connected with the Mediterranean services. By then the Italians had agreed a ten-year arrangement that would allow Imperial Airways more freedom of their airspace. Letters and parcels still continued to be carried by train from Paris to Brindisi until a new mail agreement could be reached. A prior insurrection in Greece had caused additional operational problems when night-flying over the country was forbidden. During this uprising, Imperial Airways flights were diverted via Malta and North Africa until 16 March and the company's motor yacht, *Imperia*, was moved to Tobruk to support the flying boats. On Wednesday, 15 May, a major breakthrough occurred when the entire Croydon-Cape Town route could be made by air for the first time. It had taken 39 months to overcome the problems that had made it necessary to use rail across Europe. Northbound flights from the Cape commenced on 7 May.

Imperial Airways' European services had expanded very little during the company's preoccupation with operations on the Empire routes. On 1 April a new service using the DH86A *Diana* class began operating from Croydon via Brussels, Cologne, Halle/Leipzig, Prague and Vienna to Budapest. Capt J P Percy operated the first service but bad weather forced the flight to terminate at Cologne. By 6 October, Leipzig and Prague were replaced as intermediary destinations by Nuremberg. A new service was introduced using the Avro 652 *Avatar* (later changed to *Ava*) (G-ACRN) and thereafter by the DH86 Diana class that continued twice-weekly during the summer with stops at Paris, Marseilles and Rome to Brindisi. Passengers could enjoy the prospect of flying the entire 1,352 mile route in a single day. Imperial Airways received no subsidy on this service and it eventually ceased operating in January 1937. Passengers found the complicated rules that applied to the various sectors difficult to comprehend.

- Passengers/freight *could be carried* London-Paris; London-Rome; London-Brindisi; Paris-Rome; Paris-Brindisi; Marseilles-Rome and Marseilles-Brindisi
- Passengers could *not be carried* London-Marseilles or Paris-Marseilles.
- Traffic *could also be accepted* Rome-Brindisi *but only if it was continuing on an onward service* on the Africa or on the India route.

These difficult traffic regulations had been devised to provide protection for the national and domestic carriers of France and Italy that might otherwise have lost revenue to Imperial Airways. The complexity also meant there was still no respite for passengers travelling on the Empire Route to Australia who still had to travel by train between Paris and Brindisi.

On 1 April Swissair commenced operating a Zurich–Basle–Croydon service using the impressive Douglas DC2. The service operated until October when there was a short lull before being re-commenced on 16 December to carry passengers destined for the Alpine ski resorts. Tragedy struck the previous evening when the Air France Paris-London inaugural service operated by a Farman F306 crashed near Rouen in bad weather killing renowned pilot Robert Bajac.

Disciplinary matters and incidents

Before leaving on the second flying boat survey of the year, Brackley was summoned to a meeting called by Woods Humphery on 21 May to discuss pilot discipline. A seemingly minor issue had become exaggerated concerning the use of the main booking hall cafeteria at Croydon Airport. Many of Europe's leading pilots had attained celebrity status and picture postcards of them in flying gear were produced. They enjoyed flaunting their popularity by mixing with passengers and joining them for refreshments. The public seemed to enjoy their company, but Imperial Airways viewed this fraternisation as detrimental. The pilots were ordered to stop using the booking hall facilities and to take their refreshments in the Airport Hotel beyond the terminal building. As there was seldom sufficient time to do this between flights, the pilots were angered by this restriction and, as usual, were quick to react, and the ban on using the facility once again created friction with the management.

There was also growing concern over the amount of fuel that aircraft had been carrying. On some routes, such as on the lengthy Mirabella-Alexandria sector, there was a lack of refuelling facilities that made it necessary to carry higher fuel loads. On others sectors there had also been cases of pilots carrying too little fuel. One flight almost came to grief when it landed with only 12 minutes of petrol remaining in its tanks. Despite the inherent dangers involved, there was no formal legal directive to force airlines to ensure that each flight departed with sufficient fuel to reach its destination. Matters were left to the pilot's discretion and they frequently came in for justified criticism when their fuel consumption was excessive or for carrying too much payload in relation to the fuel carried. Although Imperial Airways stressed that pilots should avoid taking risks, this often went unheeded and flights had to land or turn back when pilots ran out of petrol. It took a fuel related accident to a Calcutta flying boat for the warning to hit home before the pilots started taking it upon themselves to start carrying extra fuel as a safety precaution.

Despite warnings, official or otherwise, incidents had started happening with greater regularity. 1934 had been fairly incident-free for Imperial Airways but suddenly a sequence of things started to happen. The HP42E *Hanno* (G-AAUD) suffered considerable damage when it burst a tyre while landing at Kampala causing it to tip on its nose. The Avro 652 *Avatar,* the first aircraft type to be employed by Imperial Airways with a retractable undercarriage, received substantial propeller damage when the pilot forgot to lower the landing gear before touchdown. On 10 October, Wilcockson, taxiing the Short *Syrinx* at Brussels was hit by a severe wind gust that violently swung the aircraft round causing injury to a passenger. However, these were all comparatively minor compared to what happened on the last night of the year. The Short S8 Calcutta *City of Khartoum* (G-AASJ) was approaching Alexandria on a routine landing when the aircraft suddenly dropped out of sight of the illuminated flight path. The aircraft nosed into the sea killing nine passengers and three of the crew. The captain, Vernon Wilson, was the only survivor and he was found swimming near the wreckage by the search vessel five hours later. All three engines on the aircraft had suddenly stopped and the chief inspector of accidents concluded that the aircraft had run out of fuel despite refuelling at Crete. The same pilot had previously taken-off from Alexandria for Athens in *Satyrus* on 4 March 1933 with insufficient fuel to reach his destination. On that occasion fortune had been on his side and a safe landing had been made on the sea.

On 22 October the DH86, *Draco* (G-ADCM) crashed at Zwettl, Austria. This was followed three days later with the loss of one of the two Boulton Paul P71A aircraft, *Britomart* (G-ACOY) that crashed on take-off at Brussels. The Short Kent flying boat, *Sylvanus* (G-ABFB) was the next casualty when it caught fire while being refuelled at Brindisi on 9 November with twelve fatalities and one seriously injured survivor. Evidence pointed to the fire being started deliberately by an Italian saboteur but the reason remains a mystery. This was followed by an accident involving the DH66 Hercules, *City of Jodhpur* (G-ABCP) that crashed into a swamp at Entebbe while operating a mail-only flight for West African Airways. Overall, 1935 had been a bad year as far as

Captain A.S. Wilcockson.

safety was concerned. Air France, SABENA, Deruluft and Deutsche Lufthansa all had their share of accidents, fortunately mostly minor but on 14 July the KLM Fokker XXII, (PH-AJQ) claimed the lives of two passengers and five crew members. The aircraft lost two engines while attempting to take off from Amsterdam's Schiphol airport causing it to plough into a dyke where it burst into flames on impact. There were 13 survivors but the accident had provided the ammunition the British press needed to promote the dangers of flying. The adverse publicity, for a time, caused a decline in passenger numbers, but in spite of this, Croydon was handling 3,500 passengers per week and Imperial Airways had carried around 250 a day on its European services alone.

Trippe flies Imperial Airways

Juan Trippe of Pan American Airways and his wife were among those that flew into Croydon on an Imperial Airways flight after the couple had spent time in Hong Kong. On 30 October they had flown 500 miles across open sea to Tourane in French Indo-China (Vietnam) in the DH86 *Dorado* before continuing via Penang and stopping to refuel in Saigon. Next day they boarded the Atalanta *Aurora* (G-ABTM) to Bangkok and on the third day to Calcutta. The Trippes were unimpressed when it took ten hours to fly between Calcutta and Delhi and by the fact that it took Imperial Airways two days to accomplish the distance between Baghdad and Karachi; a journey KLM were making in one day with its DC2. The Trippes were also unhappy with the lack of comfort provided in the basic accommodation at the overnight stop at the desert fort at Sharjah. Trippe was derogatory about having to sleep within a compound surrounded by barbed wire in a bedroom that was clean but had no plumbing. This was in stark contrast to the amenities already being provided by Pan Am at Wake Island, a mid-Pacific island outpost where passengers on his airline were accustomed to sleeping in comfortable bedrooms with private bathrooms. He complained about dirty bed linen and the cold food at Baghdad; and he was not impressed by the differences in the cruise speeds of his China Clipper (140 mph) and the Imperial Airways flying boats that trundled along at a sedate 90 mph. But, once in England Trippe appeared more relaxed during discussions with the Imperial Airways board and when he visited Rochester to see the Empire flying boats under construction. These were a full six tons lighter than the Martin flying boats that Trippe was having built, but the British aircraft with its high cabin headroom gave the impression of being roomier and the comfort levels were a vast improvement on some of the older aircraft in the Imperial Airways fleet. Betty Trippe thought Mrs Woods Humphery's flippant remark *'Does it seem very much larger than your Clipper?'* complacent and her husband was privately dismissive after Mayo had discussed his Composite project with the American. During their time in Europe the Trippes also travelled to Foynes with Woods Humphery to look at the proposed flying boat site, but they were more impressed by KLM's DC3 that took them to Amsterdam for talks with Plesman and the Dutch company board. Further discussions ensued in Berlin where they were entertained by the Lufthansa directors, but the Trippes expressed their alarm at the way Germany was preoccupied with military aircraft and by the preparations the Third Reich already appeared to be making for war. Afterwards the couple took the opportunity to fly to Rio de Janeiro on the great Zeppelin airship, *Hindenburg.*

Hong Kong

Imperial Airways (Far East) Ltd was registered as a wholly owned company to operate the Hong Kong branch of the Empire Mail service to and from Australia. On 16 September the DH86 *Dorado* (G-ACWD) departed from Croydon with Capt William Armstrong commanding a crew of three including a first officer. The purpose was to survey a route between the beautiful Malayan island of Penang, Saigon and Hong Kong. Tourane (now Da Nang, Vietnam) was initially selected as an intermediary aerodrome but after the crew's first landing they considered it too dangerous and opted instead to use Hue on their first return flight. Three surveys were flown before the crew waited at

DH86 Diana Class –
G-ADCM, 'Draco' in 1935.
This aircraft crashed at
Zwettl, Austria on
22 October 1935.
(CAS/John Stroud)

Penang for the arrival of the first link with the Empire Mail from London. This was delayed and after receiving warning of this from Calcutta, Armstrong was faced with the dilemma to either keep the expectant people of Hong Kong waiting for their arrival or to attempt to complete the entire sector in a day. There was great public excitement in Hong Kong over the air link and the local people had been following the crew's progress throughout the test series with a great deal of optimism. Armstrong felt unable to let them down. Delaying the mail on its maiden flight would, he believed, make a poor impression. The alternative was to attempt the long, potentially dangerous 1,852-mile flight in a day even though he realised this might create a precedent that he was not keen to establish. Armstrong weighed up the situation with his first officer and opted to make a fast single-day flight and hoped that the weather would be favourable. The previous night had been extremely stormy and by the time the crew went to bed the lightning was still intense. They arose at 04.30 hrs with the storm still raging but decided to make the journey out to Penang aerodrome at Bayan Lapas. The storm continued to murmur as they took off and the aircraft rapidly climbed to a normal cruising height of 15,000 feet with thunder and lightning surrounding the small aircraft. Fortunately the air ahead was smooth and the conditions became more favourable as the flight progressed. It was a fairly clear morning and they steered by compass, navigating by dead reckoning across the Gulf of Siam. As the dawn broke it heralded in a fine tropical day and the north-east monsoon, typical in the region for this time of year, never came. They followed the coastal route to Saigon and by fortune the weather held good for the entire flight and they reached Hong Kong without any delays.

The first flight had worked out well for the crew of *Dorado* but the next was made in entirely contrasting conditions. As they ran into heavy black clouds and torrential rain they began to appreciate how quickly the weather can change in the tropics. The intensity of the rain had caused Armstrong concern for the safety of the aircraft. Poor visibility had forced them to fly just above the sea, barely able to follow the coastline and see the tops of the breaking waves. With nowhere safe to land they had no choice but to continue. There was an imminent danger that the strength of the rain could rip the doped fabric from the wings and the pilots were concerned that the engines might become water-logged causing them to stall. Heavy spray was entering the cockpit through the nose fabric and around the windscreen frame and it was starting to fail. As strips of fabric flew off in the 140 mph headwind, the first officer had to lean precariously out of a side window and hold the

remaining structure in place for the best part of an hour to prevent the windscreen from failing. Had the windscreen fallen out the pilots would have found it extremely difficult to control the plane in the strong headwind. Fortunately the rain ceased and the crew were able to land for repairs at Tourane despite their low opinions of the aerodrome's safety. On a subsequent flight they again were at the mercy of the weather. The rain had been even more intense and the crew barely managed to find Penang in appalling visibility and with the fabric almost completely stripped from the wing leading edges.

On 24 September Imperial Airways duplicated the London to Singapore service with return flights doubled from 3 October. Armstrong and his crew had completed their survey and had established the basic infrastructure for future flights. This included meeting agents to discuss load and ground facilities, working on radio frequencies, learning what to expect from the temperamental weather and getting to know the geography of the terrain along the route. With these tasks done every minor detail had been considered so that a proposed timetable could be compiled. By then the crew had gained first hand knowledge about the violent tropical storms, typhoons and the monsoon that were a prominent features of South East Asia.

There were other times when the safety of the mission was compromised, not just by weather. During the flight from England to Penang, Armstrong's first officer had been flying the aircraft over India when a huge bird appeared straight ahead and on a direct collision course. Armstrong saw the danger, immediately cut his engines and dropped the nose of the DH86 as soon as he saw '...*what looked like quite the biggest bird I'd ever seen, wings outstretched, apparently oblivious to us. And we were headed directly for it.*' The first officer became transfixed and stared in horror as the bird sailed inches over the top of the plane before hitting the tail section. This caused severe damage to the tailplane bracings, but by dropping dangerously to within a few feet of the ground, control was maintained to bring the aircraft safely to land at Jhansi in Uttar Pradesh. It was a tribute to the strength of the DH86 that it could continue flying and be landed safely after major structural damage to the tail. The incident had delayed the flight while the crew waited the arrival of spares from Karachi and for repairs to be carried out. With the success of the Hong Kong route, Imperial Airways considered establishing a branch to North Borneo and the Philippines from Kai Tak but nothing ever materialised of this idea.

During the formative period when the Far Eastern operation was establishing,. other wholly owned Imperial Airways companies were

The photographs on these pages show Imperial Airways HP42E, G-AAUD, 'Hanno', landing at Gaza in 1935, and being refuelled for her onward flight.
(US Library of Congress)

The refuelling of the HP42E 'Hanno' gets underway at Gaza. Imperial Airways was a keen endorser of Shell petroleum products and the branding of Shell appeared in a lot of the company advertising. (US Library of Congress)

AEROSHELL
LUBRICATING OIL

The Aristocrat of Lubricants

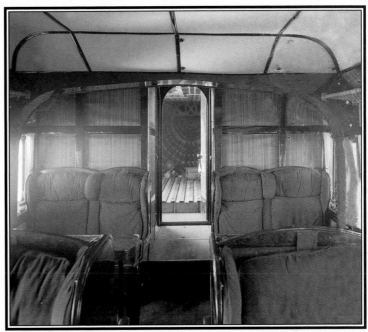

The almost Pullman railway car like interior of 'Hanno' photographed at Gaza. This is the rear of the cabin with a view into the rear fuselage. (US Library of Congress)

Left and above: The Imperial Airways stop-over site at Gaza, showing some of the buildings used for the comfort of passengers and Imperial staff, in this isolated post. (US Library of Congress)

Imperial Airways flight crew and
civilians pose with 'Hanno' at Gaza in
1935. The captain third from left with the
white gloves is believed to be
O. P. Jones. (US Library of Congress)

being registered. These were Imperial Airways (Nigeria and Gold Coast) Ltd; responsible for operating the Khartoum to West Africa service and Imperial Airways (Continental) Ltd that controlled the European services. The former was registered on 12 August 1935 in a joint operation with Elders Colonial Airways Ltd, a company that evolved from the British shipping company, Elder-Dempster Lines that was formed in 1932 after the African Steamship Company, British and African Steam Navigation Company and Elder Dempster and Company had merged. Based in Liverpool, Elder Dempster operated a large fleet of ships, but three, known as mail boats, sailed regular schedules between Nigeria and the Gold Coast with ports of call in Sierra Leone and Liberia.

For a company intent on expanding across many frontiers, nationalism could be a problem. As mentioned, Imperial Airways was subjected to considerable opposition over the Australia route from its critics who believed the service should be an all-Australian enterprise operated without external interference. Similar problems also had emerged in South Africa where there was a similar lobby by local organisations to share in the activities. When South African Airways (SAA) was formed this took away the need for Imperial Airways to fly beyond Johannesburg to Cape Town and led to Imperial Airways curtailing this part of the East Africa route. SAA took over the final Johannesburg-Kimberley-Cape Town sector on 1 April 1936 using Atalanta Class aircraft that it leased from Imperial Airways. The company had by then added a second service between Croydon-Johannesburg

'Hanno', at rest at Gaza.
(US Library of Congress)

(Germiston) that had started on 30 December 1934. These flights left London on Sundays and took eight days to complete the journey; the first northbound service departed from Johannesburg on 5 January 1935. Although schedules were not unduly affected, from March it became necessary to fly an additional 400 miles on the European sector when the Greek troubles (mentioned previously) caused the Brindisi–Cairo sector to be re-routed to Malta and the North African coast. On 1 July 1935 SAA had moved its base from Durban to Rand Field near Johannesburg and on 1 August it commenced flying Junkers Ju 52s on a weekly service between Johannesburg, Kimberley, Beaufort West and Cape Town.

An abundance of independents

The trend of the previous two years had continued and considerable progress was being made by the domestic airlines to establish regular services.

In Scotland Northern and Scottish Airways introduced a weekday service between Glasgow (Renfrew) and Campbeltown that extended to twice-weekly from 1 March. By 17 May Dragons had inaugurated a service between Renfrew and the Isle of Man (Hall Caine) that became daily from 1 June and twice-daily from 1 July. Whitehall Securities added the airline to its expanding portfolio on 23 May and increased the company's capital to £12,000. A further new service started on 5 December between Renfrew and the Isle of Skye (Glenbrittle) with Capt David Barclay making the opening flight in the Dragon

(G-ACFG). During the year the company also actively carried out extensive surveys of the Scottish Western Isles.

Aberdeen Airways began an Aberdeen–Wick–Thurso–Orkney service on 27 May and later added West Murkle and Clarendon to the route. This was operational until 8 November and by 16 December it re-opened the Thurso–Orkney sector. Highland Airways, which was also operating from Aberdeen moved their base to Seaton Aerodrome, Kintore in May and began carrying mail from Shetland on 1 June. This was taken by sea from Lerwick to Kirkwall before being flown south. Whitehall Securities also acquired United Airways a company that operated a number of routes in the north west of England between Liverpool-Blackpool-Isle of Man, Blackpool-Morecambe, Blackpool-Leeds (Yeadon) and Liverpool-Isle of Man with a mail contract.

This company was registered with £50,000 capital on 4 April 1935 by Whitehall Securities and Jersey Airways. By the end of April it was operating twice-daily between Heston and Blackpool (Stanley Park) and four times daily from Blackpool to the Isle of Man. This route was later extended to Carlisle. The Heston–Blackpool inauguration was flown by a formation of Jersey Airlines DH86 aircraft (G-ACYG and G-ACZN) with the United Airways DH89 (G-ADAE). Spartan Cruisers (G-ACDX and G-ACYL) opened the first day of the Isle of Man-Carlisle service. United later merged with Highland Airways although both companies continued to operate under their own names.

West of Scotland Air Services was a new company that was granted a five-year concession during July by the Stornoway Trust to fly

between Stornoway (Outer Hebrides) and Glasgow. A Fox Moth and a Short Scion (G-ADDP) were initially operated and a Short Scion Senior (G-AGNX) was later added to the fleet. An experimental Greenock-Isle of Arran service was also flown during August and September weekends.

From 4 March Provincial Airways began operating daily between Hull, Grimsby (on request) Nottingham, Leicester (Desford) and Southampton that connected with a Croydon–Plymouth service from July. The route was changed the same month to Hull–Croydon using DH Dragons (G-ACBW, G-ACDL and G-ACKD) and routes were introduced routes between Nottingham, Leicester, Le Touquet and Paris and Croydon-Le Touquet but the business was short-lived and ceased during September.

Crilly Airways also operated from aerodromes serving the Midlands and the north of England. This was formed by F Leo Crilly on 9 March with a capital of £12,000 and two days later flew Doncaster–Croydon with a DH Dragon named *Spirit of Doncaster*. By 9 April, twice-daily flights were added from Leicester to Bristol and Leicester-Norwich with Dragons. By 18 May a thrice-weekly service was added between Nottingham, Leicester and Northampton and during June/July a twice-daily Nottingham– Leicester– Skegness service was introduced to target holiday traffic bound for the popular east coast resort. Several other routes were added during 1935.
- Norwich-Ipswich-Southend-Ramsgate was flown on Sundays from 7 July until the end of September
- Leicester–Liverpool introduced 1 August
- Leicester–Norwich–Croydon introduced 1 October
- Leicester–Bristol introduced 1 October
- Leicester–Croydon introduced 1 October.

During the year the company operated two Dragons (G-ACDN and G-ACLE) and three Monospar ST35s (G-ADPK, G-ADPL and G-ADPM). Crilly also signed a mail contract with the Portuguese Government on 13 December to carry mail between Lisbon and London

Blackpool and West Coast Air Services was granted a Post Office contract to fly mail between the Isle of Man and Liverpool from 3 February. The first flight was operated by Capt J C Higgins in a Dragon (G-ACPY) to the Isle of Man and Capt O C Armstrong flying Dragon (G-ACGU) opening the service from Liverpool. Two further routes were added on 1 June; Isle of Man-Belfast and Isle of Man-Carlisle.

Lord Grimethorpe became chairman of a company registered with a capital of £20,000 on 4 March called North Eastern Airways that commenced operations between London (Heston), Leeds (Yeadon) and Newcastle (Cramlington) four days later with Airspeed Envoys. By 27 May the service had been extended to Edinburgh (Turnhouse) but the business got into trouble in July and all assets were transferred to a company called Alps Airline, also owned by Grimethorpe that intended to commence operating between London and Switzerland.

On the Channel Islands Jersey Airways (part of Whitehall Securities) began twice-weekly Jersey-Rennes flights that operated 8 January-29 March. On 7 March Capt B A Blythe inaugurated a Heston–Jersey–Heston service in a DH86 *The Giffard Bay* (G-ACYF). On the neighbouring island, Guernsey Airways began a Guernsey-Jersey service on 9 June using a Saunders Roe Windhover (G-AGJP) thrice-daily (except Wednesdays). Cobham Air Routes Limited also served the Channel Islands with twice-daily flights that began on 6 May between Croydon–Portsmouth–Bournemouth (Christchurch) and Guernsey (L'Eree). An Airspeed Courier was used on the Croydon-Bournemouth sector and a Westland Wessex on the remainder of the route. The Wessex (G-ADEN) was lost in the English Channel on 3 July causing the service to be suspended and the company was later acquired by Olley

Air Services. In its own right, Olley operated a Croydon–Brighton–Deauville service from 13 July until the end of September. Olley also acquired the £1,000 capital of a company called Isle of Man Air Services that registered on 21 January.

Commercial Air Hire Limited had the interesting idea of linking aerodromes in a ring around London, similar, in effect, to the present-day M25 orbital motorway which rings London, with a company called Inner Circle Airlines but although timetables were produced it is not known whether the service achieved any regularity. Four aircraft had been associated with the company; a Dragon (G-ACCR) and three Monospars (G-ADIK, G-ADJP, and G-ADLM). The Dragon and two of the Monospars crashed in 1936.

Following the experimental service started in 1934 by Boyd and Nash (see previous chapter), a company named Atlantic Coast Air Services was formed during April to provide one of the stranger domestic links. Using a Short Scion (G-ACUW), the firm flew from Barnstaple in north Devon to Lundy Island, the small outcrop famous for its puffin birds located in the Bristol Channel. The name of the company changed to Lundy and Atlantic Coast Airlines Limited on 26 April 1937 and it added a second Scion (G-AETT) and flew routes to Cardiff, Jersey and Plymouth to connect with flights to other parts of the country. The Scion (G-AETT) was eventually lost in a crash at Barnstaple but this was after the company had ceased trading in September 1938.

There were a few other notable movements on the domestic airways during 1935. One of these, Air Dispatch, an associate of Commercial Air Hire (as previously mentioned) operated an early morning freight service between Croydon and Paris using Dragons and an Avro 642 (G-ACFV). Passengers were later carried and from July-September, weekend flights had started between Croydon and Le Touquet.

GOING ABOARD IMPERIAL AIRWAYS LINER "SCYLLA"

"HANNIBAL" AT MALAKAL, ANGLO-EGYPTIAN SUDAN

Commercial Air Hire began a service during April that linked the two London airports at Heston and Croydon. In the same month, Wrightways re-opened an early morning newspaper delivery flight between Croydon and Paris (Le Bourget) that ran throughout the year. Norman Edgar (Western Airways) Limited operated weekend flights between Cardiff/Bristol, Le Touquet and Paris using Dragons and in December the company became known as Western Air Transport. A further company with its minds clearly set on international operations was registered as British Continental Airways Limited with a substantial capital of £25,000 on 15 April. By July the business was operating three times daily between Croydon, Ostend and Le Zoute that extended to Brussels at weekend until 28 September. During October a Croydon–Lille–Brussels service began and on 1 November a daily London-Antwerp-Amsterdam route was added.

Three further companies were registered during 1935; Cambrian Air Services on 25 April; British Scandinavian Airways Limited on 19 October and British American Air Services Limited on 6 April with a capital of £5,000.

In addition to the fledgling companies the more established domestic airlines were expanding. On 6 June, following the founder's untimely death, Hillman's Air Services continued to operate and began a service between Liverpool, Manchester and Hull. By 19 June a thrice-daily service was inaugurated between Stapleford (Essex)– Ostend–Brussels and Antwerp. This was amended from 1 October when Ostend was dropped. On 15 July a daily Stapleford–Ramsgate–Le Zoute service started with extra flights between Ramsgate-Le Zoute being made until the end of September. A strange incident occurred on 21 February when the Du Bois sisters, Jane (aged 20) and Elizabeth (23), daughters of Coert Du Bois, the American Consul in Naples, forced the cabin door of the Hillman's DH84 Dragon (G-ACEV) and jumped from the plane. John Kirton, the pilot, had been asked by the sisters to close the door separating the cockpit from the cabin when the girls complained of draughts as the aircraft flew through turbulence en-route to Paris. When he opened it later in the flight to

check his passengers were all right, they had gone. They had plunged to their deaths, hand-in-hand, from about 5000 ft above Abridge in Essex. The official hearing concluded a verdict of '... *suicide whilst the balance of their minds was disturbed.*' They were said to have been distressed at the deaths of two serving RAF officers, Flying Officer John A C Forbes and Flt Lt Henry L Beatty (half brother of Earl Beatty) who were killed when their Short Singapore had crashed near Messina, Sicily. The sisters had been dancing and were taken to dinner by the two airmen the night before the accident. Shortly before the suicides, while in charge of the same aircraft, a consignment of gold bullion had disappeared. Although he was not linked to either incident Kirton left the company's employ when the new board took over control following the death of Hillman.

"SCYLLA" LANDING AT LE BOURGET

Railway Air Services opened the *Manx Airway* between Manchester-Liverpool–Blackpool (Squires Gate) and the Isle of Man in an agreement signed with the Isle of Man Steam Packet Company Limited on 15 April. This operated:
- Three flights each way on weekdays
- On alternate Sundays flew Isle of Man–Manchester–Blackpool.

From 31 May daily services operated in both directions with:
- Three trips between Manchester–Blackpool–Isle of Man
- Two between Blackpool– Liverpool– Manchester–Isle of Man
- One between Liverpool–Blackpool–Isle of Man.

These services were timed to connect with other flights serving the South and West of England. During the same day the company made amendments to the LMS flights on the London–Glasgow route. These departed from:
- Renfrew at 08.45 hrs calling at Belfast, Liverpool, Manchester and Birmingham to arrive at Croydon at 13.05 hrs.
- Northbound services left London at 15.10 hrs to arrive at Renfrew by 19.30 hrs.

These flights connected at Manchester with the Isle of Man and Blackpool service and at Croydon with services to France, Denmark, Sweden, Holland, Spain and Switzerland. Much progress had been made to improve services and it was now possible to fly from Berlin, Copenhagen, Madrid and Zurich to Glasgow in a single day.

RAS took delivery of a pair of new DH89 Dragon Rapides on 18 May. These were registered G-ACPP *City of Bristol* and G-ACPR *City of Birmingham* and from 27 May they operated the twice-daily Liverpool-Birmingham-Bristol-Southampton-Portsmouth-Shoreham service that revised the former Birmingham-Cowes route. On the same day the Dragons *City of Cardiff* (G-ADDI) and *City of Plymouth* (G-ADDJ) re-established services on the Nottingham–Birmingham–Cardiff–Denbury (for Newton Abbot, Teignmouth & Torquay) –Plymouth route that had previously been operated from Liverpool. Both of these schedules formed part of the GWR West of England and the GWR/SR South of England services that were resumed during the summer. A Shoreham-Le Touquet excursion was added on 28 July with a DH89 Dragon Rapide at a fare of £3 single and £3 10s 0d (£3.50) return that included admission to the Casino and tea. This service was withdrawn on 1 September because of a lack of custom.

More route changes were made from 14 September. Nottingham–Plymouth and Shoreham–Liverpool were dropped from the schedules and winter timetables were introduced two days later. The Manx Airways flights were cut to two each way over the Manchester–Liverpool–Blackpool–Isle of Man sector. From the same date the London–Glasgow route was amended to London-Belfast with a connecting flight between Belfast-Glasgow. Manchester's Barton aerodrome had been considered unsuitable in winter and was dropped from the schedules.

However RAS amended its London-Glasgow service by making Birmingham a request stop and by adding Meir (for Stoke-On-Trent) as a second request stop, subject to 24 hours' notice. By 2 December the company had re-acquired a Post Office contract to carry mail between London, Belfast and Glasgow.

During the summer RAS participated in the London (Heston)-Cowes service operated by Spartan Air Lines. This was flown at varying frequencies depending on the date and the day of the week with as many as five flights daily each way on some occasions between Heston, Cowes, Bembridge and Lea (for Sandown and Shanklin). Spartan Cruiser II and III aircraft were operated on the services. RAS also ran an air ferry service on behalf of Spartan between Southampton, Cowes and Sandown using the Dragon (G-ACNI). This proved sufficiently popular to justify six each-way flights a day on weekdays, four on Sundays with two additional flights each-way every day during August.

Two further Dragons were added to the fleet during the spring. These were G-ADED and G-ADEE that were used on the Manx Airways service serving Liverpool, Blackpool, Manchester and the Isle of Man. Despite the Dragon's excellent safety record, these two particular aircraft were ill-fated. On 1 July Capt Robert Pierce was flying G-ADED with six passengers on the 11.50 hrs Ronaldsway (Isle of Man)-Blackpool-Liverpool-Manchester service when it crashed. It was reported that the air was still as the aircraft commenced its take-off run from Ronaldsway but it failed to gain height, ran out of runway and continued across a field before hitting a stone dyke. The pilot and two passengers were slightly injured; the remainder fortunately escaped before the Dragon caught fire and was destroyed. The sister aircraft, G-ADEE departed from Liverpool on 26 October in moderately bad weather. About 24 minutes after take off the aircraft had climbed to about 1,550 feet, too low to avoid hitting Snape Fell. The aircraft was far off track and about 19 miles from Blackpool when the accident happened killing the pilot and his only passenger. This Dragon was also destroyed by fire. In order to continue operating the service a Dragon G-ACHV from Airwork Ltd and another from GWR were called in as replacements.

RAS allowed passengers to carry 35 lbs of luggage. Anything beyond that was charged for at the appropriate freight rates for the distance being travelled. Heavy baggage and parcels could also be collected by the company for transportation by train and delivered to a passenger's destination to relieve them of the need to carry excessive loads on board an aircraft. RAS hade made every effort to establish an edge. Pressure on travel agents had given them a clear booking advantage over the many smaller operators that were scraping a living on the various UK routes. Passengers could buy RAS tickets at an increasing number of outlets that included the airline's own offices, main line railway stations, many travel agencies and the offices of Spartan Air Lines in Cowes (Isle of Wight). The smaller companies suffered badly as a result of the railway companies' greed and RAS had also promptly closed the accounts of any travel agencies that they found were selling tickets for other domestic airlines. This created a restrictive practice that was eventually challenged by the travel agencies and revoked in 1938 when the Amending Order of the 1936 Air Navigation Act made this activity illegal. But legislation came too late to help many of the smaller operators who had depended on travel agents for their bookings.

In July an important committee was set up under the chairmanship of Brig Gen Sir Henry Maybury GBE KCMG CB MICE '...*to consider and report upon measures which might be adopted by HM Government or by local authorities for assisting the promotion of civil aviation in the United Kingdom, and their probable cost. The Committee will take into account the requirements of the Post Office for air mails and the relation between aviation and other forms of transport.*' In typically long-winded fashion it took the Maybury Committee over a year to collate its findings and the report did not become available until 9 December 1936.

A development occurred on 30 September that would have a major affect on the future of British commercial aviation. A company became registered under the name of Allied British Airways that combined the interests of three existing airlines; United Airways, Hillman's Airways, and Spartan Air Lines, that were all under the control of Whitehall Securities. Two other companies, Highland Airways, and Northern and Scottish Airways were also absorbed into the conglomerate. On 29 October the name of the enterprise was changed to British Airways

The photographs on this page show the arrival of Imperial Airways G-ABFC, S17 Kent flying boat, 'Satyrus' on the Sea of Galilee in 1935. The Imperial Airways base was known as Tiberias.

The Captain of 'Satyrus' is seen here with Governor Keith-Roach and Imperial Airways officials.
(US Library of Congress)

Left: Passengers disembark with the Captain. The identities are unknown, apart from the little girl, who is Pamela Cross.
(US Library of Congress)

Refuelling gets underway for 'Satyrus' on the Sea of Galilee in 1935. (US Library of Congress)

A moment of reflection for passengers both civil and police on 'Satyrus' as she rides at her mooring on the Sea of Galilee. (US Library of Congress)

*Above left and above: As the setting sun heralds the end of another day on the Sea of Galilee, 'Satyrus' is readied for the following day.
(US Library of Congress)*

*The interior of the passenger cabin of 'Satyrus' at Galiliee in 1935. At the rear of the cabin is a map showing the 'Genoa to Alexandria Air Route', three instruments for the information of the passengers, two of which show air speed and time. To the right of the instruments is a builders plaque for 'Satyrus'.
(US Library of Congress)*

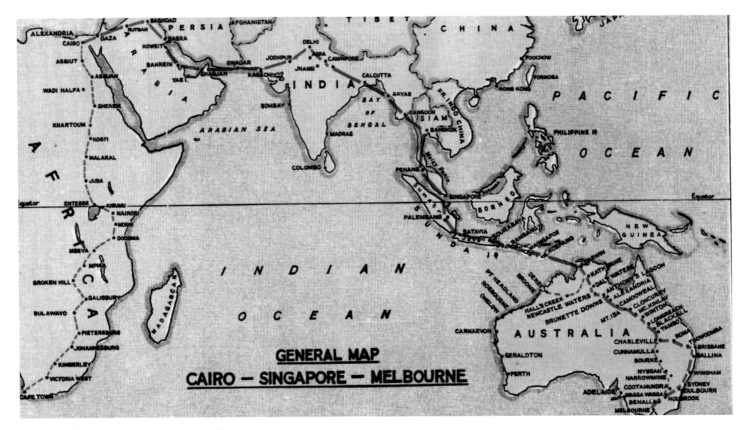

1935 Imperial Airways map showing the route via Gaza out to Australia.

Limited with a capital of £245,140. The new business began operating from Heston Airport on New Year's Day 1936, later moving to Gatwick the same year. Hillman's Airways, since the death of its founder, had been suffering a financial downturn. Gerald D'Erlanger had bought a large block of shares from the Hillman family and had also been guaranteed a further £15,000 to buy the company's other un-issued stocks. Spartan Airlines and United Airlines had been in favour of a merger with Hillman's that would secure their fate, and following discussions the formation of British Airways went ahead.

Alan Cobham was also involved as a consultant for the Irish Transatlantic Corporation that was registered in London during July 1935. Late in the year the company challenged Imperial Airways over its sole rights to operate on the proposed Atlantic route. The Air Ministry had approved the Irish involvement on the Atlantic but later retracted, seemingly, with no reason given. By then Juan Trippe's Pan American Airways had announced it was ready to operate to Europe via Bermuda and the Azores, but it was still waiting for permission to land on the Portuguese-controlled islands and it was yet to establish a base there. The US Postmaster, Gerald Farley, had asked Congress for funding to operate the service and Woods Humphery of Imperial Airways had been in discussion for some considerable time with Trippe and the US Government over a joint service. Woods Humphery was part of a delegation that included Sir Francis Shelmerdine (Director of Civil Aviation) and Post Office head, Sir Donald Banks, that joined an Irish contingent that visited Ottawa to discuss a route between Canada and the UK. This led to the proposal to form the Atlantic Company devised to prevent the Americans from participating. The intention was to make Montreal the terminal for North Atlantic flights that would continue to Vancouver with a branch to New York. The delegation travelled on to Washington where it attempted to establish reciprocal rights to fly to New York in exchange for granting Pan American Airways a route to England that had previously been unofficially sanctioned in a *gentleman's agreement* between Woods Humphery and Trippe. The Irish port of Shannon was put forward as the proposed eastern terminus. Canada wanted to be a member of the Empire Mail scheme and during the year

TEMPLE OF THE DAWN, BANGKOK

it was revealed the country had already signed a 55-year exclusive rights deal with Imperial Airways that had been kept secret from the Irish since its conception.

In Washington the delegation was met by members of the Inter-departmental Committee on International Civil Aviation recently set up by President Roosevelt. This was chaired by Assistant Secretary of State, R Walton Moore, an elderly gentleman with no experience of aviation. The politicians had taken control and despite Trippe's self-styled negotiations, even the forceful Pan Am chief had to concede that to deal with the British meant following the diplomatic route. He had already placed his application before the State Department in Washington to approach the British Government for Pan American's rights to fly between the USA and Great Britain and from the United States to Bermuda. But Moore was unable to condone the granting of rights to just one privately owned American company and he asked the British to open the route to any interested airline. They refused owing to the trust that had been established between Imperial Airways and Juan Trippe. The British would not allow a free for all, but diplomatically they could not name Pan American Airways either even though unofficially they favoured giving the rights to Trippe. Yet the British way meant that they had to be seen to be fair, so a press release was published inviting any other American airlines interested in flying the Atlantic to attend the meeting that had been set for the next day. None came forward leaving Pan American Airways the only contender. Although the US Government could not openly approve Trippe's company as the State's official representative, in the absence of competition they could hardly object either and this paved the way to progress with a transatlantic link. This arrangement raised hackles in some quarters after Trippe and Woods Humphery signed an agreement on 25 January 1936 that became known as the square deal. In what was tantamount to a cartel, this provided exclusive rights to the two companies that barred others from operating the route. Similarly Trippe and Woods Humphery had agreed that flights would only commence once both of their companies were ready and from the British point of view this was still a long way off.

The Short L17 Scylla was a development of the Short Kent flying boat - being essentially the wings and powerplants of the latter, married to a new fuselage with a fixed undercarriage. Two aircraft were built 'Scylla' right, (CAS/Edelsten) and Syrinx' below. (CAS) They both served with Imperial Airlines on its European routes until its merger with BOAC in 1939. A practical feature of the design was that the engine nacelles could take a variety of engines without modification. Both are seen here in 1935.

As prolonged negotiations were taking place, Ed Musick, the legendary Pan American Airways flying boat captain, climbed aboard the Martin M-130 *China Clipper* at Alameda, California for the epic flight to Manila. He departed on the afternoon of 22 November and the crew reached the Philippines during the afternoon of 29 November via Pearl Harbor (Hawaii), Midway Island, Wake Island and Guam. The Pacific had been breached and the Martin flying boat had crossed 8,210 miles of ocean in a flying time of 59 hrs and 48 mins, while the British were still struggling to build an aircraft capable of crossing the Atlantic.

In Europe Imperial Airways was carrying more passengers from Croydon than all of the foreign carriers put together. With a certain element of pride, Sir Eric Geddes stood up at the company AGM on 31 October and announced a net trading profit of £133,769. The profits were impressive even after taking into account that £192,960 book values had been placed on obsolescent equipment. Operationally it had generally been a progressive year for the airline and the board jubilantly recommended a dividend of 6% with a 1% bonus to be paid to shareholders. Geddes announced that the company planned to build a new London headquarters and passenger terminal to replace the existing facility that had become inadequate and overcrowded because of the growth of the airline. Geddes informed shareholders that further new aircraft had been ordered. These were the Armstrong-Whitworth Ensign four-engined land planes and the Short Empire flying boats.

The Imperial Airways board may have been comforted by the balance sheet but it could seldom ignore the periodic unease among its pilots, especially those that had joined the new Airways School at Croydon. The latest unrest was mainly over their rates of pay that they considered were inadequate. They were unhappy with the hourly rates; 10s 0d (50p) an hour on European routes; 15s 0d (75p) on overseas flying although the more senior pilots were paid extra. With the formation of British Airways many less experienced crew members had started to become disillusioned and were tempted to move. Some took

LAMBERT & BUTLER'S CIGARETTES

SINGAPORE HARBOUR

advantage by joining the Imperial Airways training course to gain their 2nd Class Navigation Licences and then promptly left to join the rival airline.

There was no escaping the fact that accidents were still causing the Imperial Airways management considerable concern. On 2 November a further incident occurred when the Atalanta *Astraea* overshot the runway while landing at Rangoon. The aircraft suffered damage to a wing tip and to the floor of the flight deck causing slight injuries to the pilot. Fortunately only two passengers were on board and both were unhurt. The aircraft was repaired locally and was put back into service. The very next day *Astraea's* sister ship, *Atalanta*, struck a tree while departing in the dark from Kisumu injuring the crew. Lord Balfour of Burleigh was one of the passengers aboard but he escaped unhurt. Elsewhere a far more tragic occurrence hit the headlines when the disappearance of the great Australian airman, Sir Charles Kingsford Smith, was reported. Smith had been attempting to break the England-Australia flight time in his American-built Lockheed Altair when he disappeared and was last seen crossing the Bay of Bengal, but was never heard from again and his body was never found.

A European timetable for Imperial Airways flights between the months of April-October 1935. (David Zekra)

IMPORTANT INFORMATION FOR PASSENGERS

The 24-HOUR CLOCK system is used in this timetable

(1) Terms and Conditions of Carriage. An extract from the conditions under which Imperial Airways undertakes to carry passengers and baggage will be found inside the cover of every air-ticket issued by the Company. The Company's *Conditions of Carriage* may be inspected at any office of Imperial Airways

(2) Alterations. This timetable, which gives an indication of average times of journey, cancels all previous issues, and is subject to alteration without notice

TICKET REGULATIONS

(3) Reservations. Seats should be booked in advance, and the principal travel agents can reserve a seat provided that accommodation be available. On the *Silver Wing* services between London and Paris, a passenger is able to reserve a particular numbered seat, subject to the seat being vacant and the loading rules of the Company being observed. The cost of any telegrams or trunk telephone calls in connexion with reservations will be charged to the passenger. Applications from intending passengers by telegram are only effected on the receipt of a telegraphic remittance, or the remittance by return of post. In no instance can accommodation be held in reply to a telegram or to a telephone message to the exclusion of other passengers who definitely wish to travel and are prepared to take up their tickets

Provisional reservations will be made only upon the payment of a deposit of 25 per cent. of the full fare. Such reservations automatically lapse unless the full fare is paid two clear days before departure. The 25 per cent. deposit will be transferred to any other service or will be refunded (less any cable or telegraphic expenses) if the passenger be unable to travel, or if accommodation be not available on the service on which a seat is desired

(4) Cancellations. In the event of a passenger wishing to cancel or to transfer a reservation and giving less than 24 hours' notice of this intention, the full fare may be forfeited or a transfer fee be charged

(5) Return Tickets. A return ticket does not give the holder any preferential claim to accommodation. Reservations for a return journey must be effected in the same way as for a single journey

(*a*) Refunds.—If no accommodation has been reserved, and should the passenger be unable to use the return half of a ticket, then the difference between the single and the return fares will be refunded

(*b*) A passenger who does not pay the return fare at the time of buying a ticket for the outward journey, cannot afterwards be put upon the same footing as the holder of a return ticket

(*c*) Return tickets are available for use on the return journey any day within the period of their validity

(6) Children. Children under three years of age and accompanied by an adult will be charged 10 per cent. (ten per cent.) of the fare. Those between three and seven years of age are carried at half the standard fare. The free baggage allowance of 15 kgs. is available for children over three years, but there is no free allowance for children if under that age

(7) Fares. The fare applicable to any journey is that which is published in the currency of the country of embarkation, after conversion, if necessary, to the currency of the country of purchase

TRANSPORT BETWEEN THE CITY AND THE AIR PORT

(8) Passenger Cars. Transport from the station of departure to the Air Port and *vice versa* is provided without extra charge

(9) Departure. Passengers must be at the Air Port, or at the departure station from which the car for the Air Port leaves, sufficiently in advance of the advertised time of departure for baggage and ticket formalities to be completed before that time. The departure of the passenger car from the station, or of the air-liner from the Air Port, cannot be delayed for passengers who arrive late. No guarantee can be given that passengers will be carried on a service if their arrival at the air port leaves insufficient time to complete loading formalities for a punctual departure of the service

BAGGAGE INFORMATION

(10) Baggage. Fifteen kilogrammes (33 lb.) of baggage are carried free of charge for each passenger when travelling on the services enumerated in this timetable. A concession is made for parties travelling together, whereby the allowance for the baggage may be 'bulked.' Excess baggage can accompany passengers (subject to the permissible load of the air-liner not being exceeded), but every kilogramme (2.2 lb.) in excess of this weight is charged for at the rates shown overleaf, and other *heavy baggage can be sent in advance at cheap rates.* Passengers' baggage must contain personal effects only. By Customs regulations all merchandise must be declared separately as freight, and entered on the aircraft manifest

(11) Registration of Baggage. Passengers' baggage is registered and labelled and a receipt is issued before departure. Passengers should guard against losing this receipt, or they may have difficulty in obtaining their baggage

(12) The Carriage of Livestock. Passengers are unable to carry with them, either as their personal baggage or in the saloon of the air-liner, any dog, cat, bird or any other animal, and all animals must be transported as freight

GENERAL INFORMATION

(13) Passports. Passengers are reminded that passports should be carried on the person. Imperial Airways or its agents will be pleased to obtain passports or visas on request provided that reasonable notice be given. *British, French and Belgian subjects do not require passports for week-end trips between London and Paris, Le Touquet, Belgian Coast, Ostend and Brussels*

(14) Meals. On the London-Paris services the air-liners are provided with a fully equipped restaurant, from which stewards serve breakfast, lunch, tea, dinner, or light refreshments as desired. There is also a bar supplying a full range of wines, spirits and other beverages

On other European services refreshment baskets can be provided if ordered at the time of booking

(15) Hotels. The names of personally inspected and recommended hotels in Great Britain and in all countries served by Imperial Airways are available at each of the Company's offices for the information of passengers. Imperial Airways will arrange hotel reservations if desired

SUMMARY OF THE SERVICES APPEARING IN THIS TIMETABLE

SUMMER 1935

DESTINATION	FREQUENCY OF SERVICE TO AND FROM LONDON	TIMES AND FULL DETAILS OF SERVICES ON PAGE
AMSTERDAM ...	Once daily, Sundays excepted	10 and 11
BASLE	Twice daily, Sundays excepted	6 and 7
BERLIN	Once daily, Sundays excepted	10 and 11
BRUSSELS ...	Three services each weekday, once on Sundays	8 and 9
BUDAPEST ...	Once daily, Sundays excepted	8 and 9
COLOGNE ...	Four services each weekday, once on Sundays	8 and 9
COPENHAGEN ...	Once daily, Sundays excepted	12
HALLE/LEIPZIG ...	Once daily, Sundays excepted	8 and 9
HAMBURG ...	Twice daily, Sundays excepted	10, 11 and 12
LE TOUQUET ...	Week-end services on Fridays and Saturdays, from London, returning on Mondays. Sunday day excursion	5
LILLE	Once daily, Sundays excepted	7
MALMÖ	Once daily, Sundays excepted	12
PARIS	Five services each weekday. Three services on Sunday	4
PRAGUE	Once daily, Sundays excepted	8 and 9
VIENNA	Once daily, Sundays excepted	8 and 9
ZÜRICH	Twice daily, Sundays excepted	6 and 7

GENERAL INFORMATION—*continued*

SEASON TRAVEL VOUCHERS (CARNETS DE BILLETS)

For the convenience of regular travellers Imperial Airways issues books of vouchers at reduced rates for travel on the services of the Company. Details on application to any office of Imperial Airways

BULK TRAVEL VOUCHERS

Imperial Airways offers bulk travel facilities at reduced rates to firms for use by *bona-fide* employees travelling by air on the firms' business. These vouchers are available for all routes of Imperial Airways in Europe. Details on application to any office of the Company

NO PASSPORT TICKETS

Special week-end no passport tickets, valid from Friday to Tuesday, are available for British, French, and Belgian subjects between London-Paris, London-Le Touquet and certain other places. See note 13 on inside of front cover

3

NORD AIR-EXPRESS
LONDON—BRUSSELS—HAMBURG—COPENHAGEN—MALMÖ (STOCKHOLM)

Operated in conjunction with Air France by the Belgian Air Lines (S.A.B.E.N.A.), for which Company Imperial Airways acts as the General Agent in Great Britain

1 APRIL—5 OCTOBER INCLUSIVE

WEEKDAYS ONLY

LONDON, Airway Terminus	dep.	07.15†
LONDON, Air Port	dep.	08.00†
BRUSSELS, Air Port	arr.	09.15
BRUSSELS, Air Port	dep.	09.30
HAMBURG, Air Port	arr.	11.30
HAMBURG, Air Port	dep.	11.45
COPENHAGEN, Air Port	arr.	12.50
COPENHAGEN, Air Port	dep.	13.00
MALMÖ, Air Port	arr.	13.10
MALMÖ, Central Railway Station	arr.	13.40

† One hour earlier from 1 April—13 April inclusive, owing to the introduction of Summer Time in Belgium

MALMÖ—STOCKHOLM

A train connexion to Stockholm is operated as follows :—

MALMÖ, Central Railway Station	dep.	14.22
STOCKHOLM	arr.	22.35

FARES

From LONDON to :	Single Fare	Return Fare (60-day)	**Return Fare (15-day)**	Rate per Kg. (2.2 lb.) for Excess Baggage
BRUSSELS ...	£4 0 0	£7 4 0	**£6 16 0**	0s. 9d.
HAMBURG ...	£8 15 0	£15 15 0	—	1s. 2d.
COPENHAGEN	£12 10 0	£22 10 0	—	1s. 7d.
MALMÖ ...	£13 0 0	£23 8 0	—	1s. 7d.

(STOCKHOLM) MALMÖ—COPENHAGEN—HAMBURG—BRUSSELS—LONDON

WEEKDAYS ONLY

MALMÖ, Central Railway Station	dep.	11.30
MALMÖ, Air Port	dep.	12.00
COPENHAGEN, Air Port	arr.	12.10
COPENHAGEN, Air Port	dep.	12.20
HAMBURG, Air Port	arr.	13.30
HAMBURG, Air Port	dep.	13.45
BRUSSELS, Air Port	arr.	15.45
BRUSSELS, Air Port	dep.	16.00
LONDON, Air Port	arr.	17.20†
LONDON, Airway Terminus	arr.	18.05†

† One hour earlier from 1 April—13 April inclusive, owing to the introduction of Summer Time in Belgium

STOCKHOLM—MALMÖ

A train connexion to Malmö is operated as follows :—

STOCKHOLM, Central Railway Station	dep.	22.35
MALMÖ, Central Railway Station	arr.	07.38

FARES

To LONDON from :	Single Fare	Return Fare (60-day)	**Return Fare (15-day)**	Rate per Kg. (2.2 lb.) for Excess Baggage
BRUSSELS ...	480 Belgian francs	864 Belgian francs	**816 Belgian francs**	4.80 Belgian francs
HAMBURG ...	120 R.M.	216 R.M.	—	1.20 R.M.
COPENHAGEN	240 D. Kr.	432.50 D. Kr.	—	1.25 D. Kr.
MALMÖ ...	225 S. Kr.	405 S. Kr.	—	1.00 S. Kr.

D. Kr.=Danish Kröne S. Kr.=Swedish Kröne

DEPARTURE AND ARRIVAL STATIONS

The scheduled number of minutes spent in transit between the stations and the Air Ports is given in brackets ( )

BRUSSELS—Bureau de S.A.B.E.N.A., 32-34 Boulevard Adolphe Max (45)
HAMBURG—Hapag—Reisebüro, Hauptbahnhof (40)
COPENHAGEN—D.D.L. Offices, Vesterport, Meldahlsgade 5 (50)

12

OTHER EUROPEAN SERVICES

Imperial Airways acts as General Agent in Great Britain for the German Airways (D.L.H.), the Belgian Air Lines (S.A.B.E.N.A.), the Swiss Air Line (SWISSAIR) and as agents for the Royal Dutch Air Lines (K.L.M.), the Swedish Air Transport Company (A.B.A.), Railway Air Services, and for all Air Transport Companies which are members of the International Air Traffic Association, and Imperial Airways will give information and book on their lines

Full details of all European services are given in *Bradshaw's International Air Guide*, which can be obtained from any newsagent. This Guide is issued every month at the price of one shilling

LONDON—OSTEND

A week-end service between London and Ostend is maintained by the Belgian Air Lines (S.A.B.E.N.A.), for which a separate timetable is published by the Company concerned

In addition to the offices shown on page 15, any air line operating company or the principal travel agents can supply information about the air services mentioned in this timetable

13

THE WEST AFRICA SERVICE OPENS, THE FIRST BRITISH AIRWAYS AND THE C-CLASS FLYING BOATS

1936

THE New Year celebrations began for some at Heston when British Airways' opened for business, but the nation's spirit was soon dampened by the announcement of the death of HM King George V at Sandringham on 20 January. It was a shock to the British public, more especially as the previous summer had been one of joyous activity when the King's Silver Jubilee was celebrated with all the pageantry the occasion could muster. The King was succeeded by Edward VIII, the former Prince of Wales, who was an extremely enthusiastic follower of civil aviation. However, Edward was never crowned, being forced to abdicate on 11 December because his love affair with the American divorcee, Wallace Simpson, was officially frowned upon. His painfully shy brother was left to take over the throne as King George VI.

During January Juan Trippe had signed an agreement with Woods Humphery (see previous chapter) that barred all competition from opposing it across the Atlantic between America and the UK. The French and Germans complained, sending delegations to lobby politicians in London. Eddie Rickenbacker, the former wartime ace who represented Eastern Airlines was also angered at its exclusion from the arrangement, and he flew to Croydon intent on gaining rights for his company. Pressures on both sides of the Atlantic led to politicians questioning the agreement and this in turn delayed the issue of permits. In America there was concern that the US Government had breached the Sherman Antitrust Act. The Germans petitioned the British for landing rights in Bermuda for their experimental Blohm und Voss Ha 139 catapult aircraft that they intended to launch from a depot ship in mid-Atlantic, but this was refused. The Americans gave their permission for the plane to land at Long Island Sound, and during the autumn of 1937, the Germans made seven return flights between Horta (Azores) and Long Island with their catapult aircraft. These were repeated with thirteen experimental flights in 1938 with a larger 'B' version of the aeroplane as a preliminary to regular services that commenced during the same year on the Bathurst-Natal/Recife sector of Lufthansa's South American service.

After the Air Estimates had been announced, the RAF received a small increase but the funding for civil aviation remained stagnant. There was still little official recognition of the role civil aviation was playing in the establishment of mail and passenger links with the Empire. The British Government was still providing far less financial support to commercial aviation than that being given to Air France, KLM and Lufthansa by their respective governments. It also suddenly dawned on a sleeping Government that the previously ignored warnings about Germany should be taken seriously. In April 1935 Britain joined France and Italy at the Stresa Conference to discuss what

should be done when it became evident that the Germany was re-arming, but Britain failed to adhere to the agreement that was reached.

Despite the inherent difficulties, the board of Imperial Airways, throughout its history, had retained a solid belief in its duty to link the far-flung reaches of the British Empire. As the chosen instrument of the Government it strived to open routes, wherever possible, to serve the substantial numbers of far-flung territories that still flew the British flag with pride. The colonies along the western side of Africa had been neglected while efforts had been concentrated on linking the towns of the East African states to reach Cape Town. By May 1935, with the South Africa route now open, an extension was being considered from Khartoum in line with the proposals made by Woods Humphery during the previous year. The new routing, using a locally based fleet of DH86 aircraft was planned to fly from the Sudanese capital to Lagos with stops at El Fasher, Fort Lamy, Maideguri, Kano and Kaduna. At Lagos it would connect with the newly formed airline Elder Colonial Airways that linked with the ships of its parent company, Elder Dempster Line, at Takoradi (see previous chapter). Gold was the major consideration and the precious metal was frequently carried on Imperial Airways aircraft for loading onto the ships.

LAMBERT & BUTLER'S CIGARETTES

G-ADHL

"CANOPUS"—NEW EMPIRE FLYING-BOAT

Capt O P Jones was appointed as operations manager, West Africa of Imperial Airways (Nigeria and Gold Coast) Ltd. Once in office, one of his initial tasks was to conduct exploratory flights as a matter of urgency over the proposed route. A DH86 Diana class aircraft, *Daedalus* (G-ADCN), was transferred from the European division and placed at his disposal. Jones departed from Croydon on 26 January. On the flight deck were K M Cass (first officer) and M Eddlington (flight engineer) while in the cabin were two Imperial Airways headquarters staff and a member of the Air Ministry. The imminent fear of disease forced the crew and passengers to take the precaution of having painful injections into their stomachs to vaccinate them against Yellow Fever that was extremely rife in West Africa. Once ready, *Daedalus* followed the regular route as far as Khartoum from where the crew faced the arduous task of checking every landing ground to Kano, investigate fuel supplies and meet with local dignitaries. Jones realised that the survey would be no holiday jaunt and the aircraft carried camping equipment, mosquito nets and a large supply of fresh water and food. Shell had previously despatched supplies of petrol by camel train to be available at landing grounds along the route in readiness for the aircraft's arrival. On 3 February, the crew reached El Obeid and then continued to El Fasher where they spent the night. There were no detailed maps and the aircrew had to use their experience and instinct to supplement the vague outline plans they possessed but these were little more than large

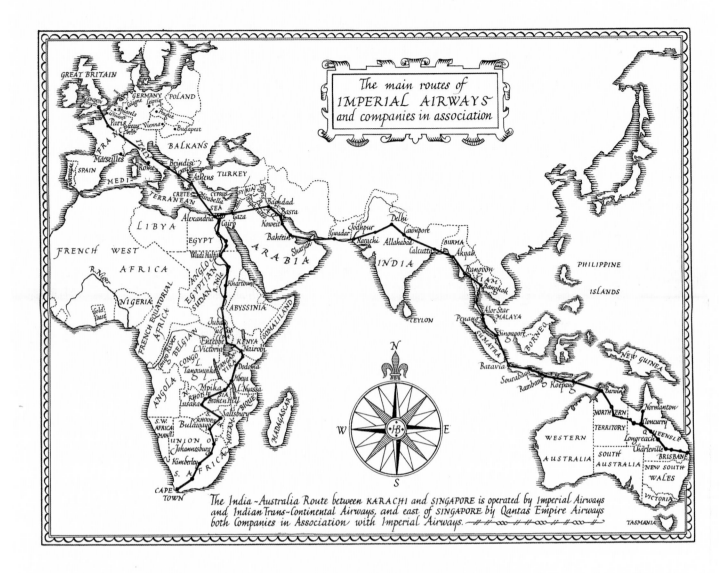

The main routes of IMPERIAL AIRWAYS and companies in association

The India–Australia Route between KARACHI and SINGAPORE is operated by Imperial Airways and Indian Trans-Continental Airways, and east of SINGAPORE by Qantas Empire Airways both Companies in Association with Imperial Airways. —#—#—∞—#—∞—#—∞—#—

blank sheets of paper with the occasional camel track or native village marked on them. The maps had been produced for a previous exploratory flight that the RAF had made ten years previously and none of the cartographic mistakes had ever been rectified. Geneina had been proposed as the first night stop once the route officially opened and this was their next port of call. The Sultan of Dar Masalite turned up to inspect the aircraft when it arrived and by the 5th the party had reached Abecher in French Equatorial Africa, spending the night at Fort Lamy. Although Imperial Airways had emphasised that Jones should avoid stopping overnight in French controlled territory, he was left with no option when the party arrived too late to continue to Maiduguri where it had planned to spend the second night. In good weather since leaving Khartoum, the DH86 had flown 1,700 miles to reach Kano in 15 hours.

The sun rays that penetrated the thin fabric cockpit roof of the aircraft had caused the crew to suffer a mild form of sunstroke. This was a minor inconvenience that was solved by strapping cork matting to the roof lining of the cockpit to insulate the crew from the penetrating rays. A little fever from sun stroke was considered a mild discomfort compared to what yellow fever or malaria had to offer and the crew had to be particularly vigilant to prevent any infestations from disease-carrying mosquitoes from entering the aircraft. To minimise the danger and to avoid the risk of transporting any infections back with them to East Africa, the interior of the aircraft was sprayed with DDT at every opportunity.

On the return from Kano the flight departed on 9 February making stops at Fort Lamy and Maiduguri, to arrive back in Khartoum two days later after short stops at Abecher, El Fasher and El Obeid and a night at

Geneina. The eastbound flight had spent just fourteen hours in the air. No time had been wasted and on the same day the first flight, on the proposed weekly mail service, left London to connect with the inaugural service from Khartoum on 13 February that would fly to Kano via El Obeid, El Fasher, Geneina, Abesher, Ati, Fort Lamy and Maiduguri. There were appropriate celebrations as the Shehu of Bornu provided a display of armour clad horseman and two bands played local music to welcome the flight's arrival at Maiduguru. The first scheduled return mail left Kano on 19 February to arrive in Khartoum next day. During the following weeks the service failed to operate as efficiently as planned. Imperial Airways services from London were, for one reason or another, often late causing havoc to the connecting West Africa services. On one occasion there was damage caused to a wing spar on the DH86 while operating the sixth service. This delayed it at Geneina until the old open-cockpit Avro X0 (G-AASP) arrived from Cairo to serve as substitute. Nicknamed 'The Last Gasp', because of its registration, this aircraft was considerably slower than the DH86. This necessitated Jones bringing in the DH86, *Delia* (G-ACWC), from London which only arrived in time to operate the eighth service. After this Jones was recalled to London and Capt R O Taylor took his place. The scheduled service included a night stop at Geneina where the crew initially had to rough it by sleeping in tents. The accommodation was slightly improved by the provision of straw huts, but after rain leaked through the roofs, these were later changed to waterproof mud huts. These were arranged in a compound that the crews named *Daedalus Camp* after the aircraft that had made the inaugural flight. In the weeks that followed the mail continued to grow and passengers also began travelling on the route.

The first British Airways begins operating

British Airways became operational on 1 January and services began with its Heston-Malmö (Sweden) service on 17 February that flew via Amsterdam, Hamburg and Copenhagen. The company, with an increased capital of £300,000, continued by taking over the routes it had inherited from the individual companies that had merged. After the nationalisation of the railway companies, British Airways had been operating the London-Isle of Wight service in conjunction with Railway Air Services and it also flew scheduled routes between the following destinations.

* London-Paris
* Liverpool–Belfast–Isle of Man
* Belfast-Glasgow
* Blackpool–Isle of Man
* Glasgow-Campbeltown–Islay (in conjunction with Northern & Scottish Airways)
* Glasgow–North & South Uist (in conjunction with Northern & Scottish Airways)
* Aberdeen and Inverness–Wick–Kirkwall–Lerwick (in conjunction with Northern & Scottish Airways)
* Isle of Man–Glasgow (in conjunction with Northern & Scottish Airways)
* Isle of Man–Carlisle
* London–Amsterdam–Hamburg–Copenhagen–Malmø–Stockholm

On 1 February Crilly Airways engaged in its first survey flight between London and Lisbon. The flight was made by G S Jones-Evans in a Fokker F XII (G-ADZJ) that reached the Portuguese capital next day after an overnight stop in Madrid. The granddaughter of the President of Portugal appropriately christened the aircraft *Lisboa* before it made the return flight to Croydon with stops at Madrid and Bordeaux. Because Spain was in a state of turmoil that developed into civil war following a well-planned military uprising on 17 July, subsequent flights were barred from flying in Spanish territory. The hostilities subsequently caused Crilly's proposed regular service to be cancelled. In May the company launched London 'theatre flights' from the Midlands and West of England to Croydon. Passengers were taken to the theatre of their choice and then, according to personal preferences, were flown back the same night or next day at an all-inclusive charge. The company also offered business houses and travel agents 1,000-mile travel vouchers for 10 guineas (£10.50) that could be used on all Crilly inland flights. During July the company began a Bristol-Bournemouth service but later in the year the business folded and it was absorbed, together with its fleet of six surplus KLM Fokker F XII tri-motors by British Airways. F Leo Crilly, a London businessman, had started the company in March 1935 but it soon got into financial difficulties after over-stretching its resources by buying the Fokkers. The company went into liquidation in September and Crilly, the founder, secured a contract with the Portuguese Government to carry mail between London and Lisbon.

On 7 February British Continental Airways (BCA) put out a challenge to British Airways by flying between London and Malmö twice-weekly, ten days before the comparative British Airways service. BCA inaugurated the route with the DH86 *St George* (G-ADMY) flown by Capt A P K Hattersley that, like British Airways, operated via Amsterdam, Hamburg and Copenhagen and returned to London next day.

British Continental was a private company fronted by the chairman of Lloyds of London, Sir Percy MacKinnon. The board was comprised of Sir Robert Burton Chadwick; The Hon A Morton Weir, F W Farey Jones (founder, managing director and chairman of F W Jones and Partners, the aviation insurers), John R Bryans, Graham McKinnon, Capt Henry Spry Leverton and Patrick Kilvington Hattersley (Chief Pilot). KLM was also listed as a minor shareholder and BCA cooperated with the Dutch airline on the Amsterdam-Doncaster-Liverpool service (see below). In July the company merged amicably with British Airways

and on 19 November Hattersley lost his life when his Fokker XII (G-AEOT) hit tree tops during a bad weather approach into Gatwick.

Brackley surveys the Empire Route

In March 1936 Herbert Brackley embarked on a survey that kept him abroad for a considerable period. This time he followed the proposed C-class Empire flying boat route in readiness for the new fleet of aircraft that were already in production at Rochester. The prospect of the new flying boats caused considerable excitement for those involved, not least Brackley who also had the task of ensuring that the new Shorts aircraft met everybody's expectations. During the previous autumn he had spent much of his time commuting to and from the Shorts works. On one occasion he was accompanied by Sir John Salmond who went to see the progress Shorts was making. In January Brackley had also conducted tests on a new Avro at Croydon. The second period of March was especially busy for him. His diary reveals that he attended an Air Ministry meeting on the 16th; an Imperial Airways board meeting next day; visited Rochester again with the chairman of the Parliamentary Committee on the 18th; held a Management Meeting on the 19th and spent the morning of 20th in his office prior to his departure the same day on the 12.30 hrs flight to Paris aboard *Scylla*.

After flying from Croydon, Brackley spent just 20 minutes in the French capital before boarding the next flight for Genoa. The punishing schedule of inspections, meetings and travel continued and even the

official survey party was not spared from enduring the train journey across Italy to Brindisi. The following day the party was airborne again between Brindisi and Athens and onward to Alexandria. The schedule was relentless and Brackley was frequently at work by 05.00 hrs inspecting sites. By 6 April he had visited Karachi, Delhi, Cawnpore, Allahabad, Calcutta and Akyab before moving on to Mergui and Rangoon. Extensive inspections of the landing areas at Karachi and Calcutta followed. In a letter to his wife, Frida, written while in the air between Victoria Point and Mergui on 11 April, Brackley described the conditions British settlers would have to tolerate in these places.

'I would hate to have to live in these parts… Mangrove swamp, dense jungle, rubber, coconuts, bananas and dirty natives. The aborigines we saw at Victoria Point have scales all over them. They live in grass huts without water and exist chiefly on fish… This route is not going to be easy to run, especially during the monsoon. The rain simply pours out of the sky.'

Brackley's party spent the best part of Easter in Rangoon before leaving at first light on 13 April. The return trip continued via Calcutta to Delhi and on to Jodhpur and Karachi before heading home with stops at Gwada, Bahrain, Baghdad, Habaniyeh, The Galilee and Dead Sea. However, any plans Brackley may have had about an early return to London were quickly dispelled by a telephone call from Burchall, Woods Humphery's assistant, who called with a renewed set of instructions. These counteracted Brackley's original brief by ordering him to continue following the Empire route to Sydney to report on the facilities being readied by the Australians. Brackley was not happy, but he was not really surprised by this sudden change of plans. He admitted to being homesick, but he was not one to disobey orders. With a stiff upper lip he ignored the inconveniences imposed by the gruelling task and concentrated his mind on whatever had to be done.

For the trip east arrangements had been made with the RAF to fly the party from Singapore in a Shorts *Singapore* flying boat. Hudson Fysh of Qantas had already flown from Darwin to meet the group that by then had grown to ten. Two Australian Government officials had joined Fysh at Darwin presumably to voice their Parliament's opposition to the use of flying boats on the service. The Australians were still not ready to accept the level of British involvement in the Empire Mail scheme and Brackley had anticipated some hostility from the politicians. Had the service been entirely organised by Australian nationals, their Government might have taken a more positive stance but the announcement of the Empire route had created considerable anti-British feeling.

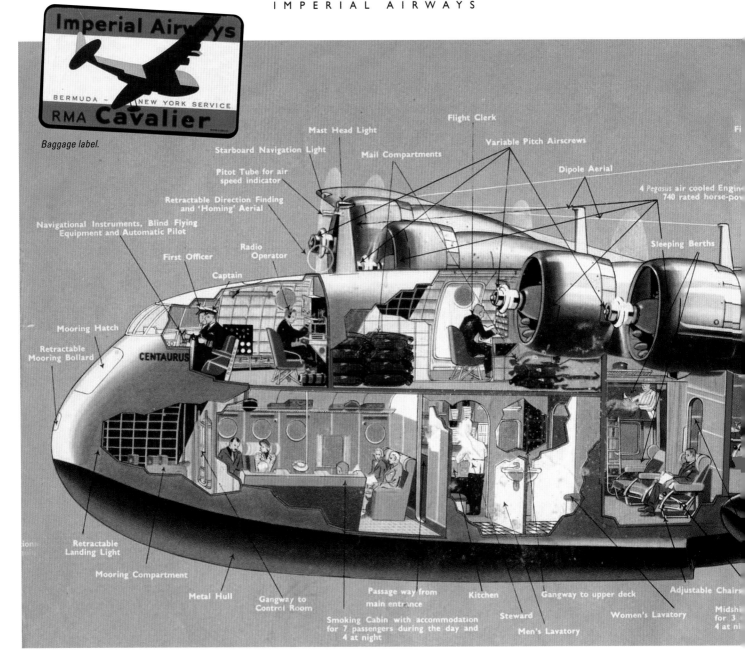

Baggage label.

Mast Head Light
Flight Clerk
Starboard Navigation Light
Mail Compartments
Variable Pitch Airscrews
Pitot Tube for air speed indicator
Dipole Aerial
Retractable Direction Finding and 'Homing' Aerial
4 Pegasus air cooled Engine 740 rated horse-po
Navigational Instruments, Blind Flying Equipment and Automatic Pilot
Sleeping Berths
First Officer
Radio Operator
Captain
Mooring Hatch
Retractable Mooring Bollard
CENTAURUS
Retractable Landing Light
Mooring Compartment
Metal Hull
Gangway to Control Room
Passage way from main entrance
Kitchen
Gangway to upper deck
Adjustable Chairs
Smoking Cabin with accommodation for 7 passengers during the day and 4 at night
Steward
Men's Lavatory
Women's Lavatory
Midsh for 3 4 at ni

The flight from Singapore was delayed by political red tape. The plan had been to fly to Australia via the Netherlands East Indies but the Governor of the Dutch Colony, angered by the refusal to award KLM the rights to Australia, claimed he had not been informed of the RAF flight and refused permission to enter Dutch controlled territory. Cables were despatched to London and after Air Ministry intervention access was finally granted to fly to Indonesia. The party eventually arrived in Brisbane on 22 May. The city proved to be one of the trickiest places on the entire route for Brackley to locate a suitable landing area for the flying boats. After checking various locations, a safe area of water was finally found, but Brackley had to file a report to London for approval before he and Fysh could present their report to the Director of Civil Aviation in Sydney for the Australian Government's approval. The party had planned to be in the city by 24 May to celebrate Empire Day; an auspicious time to have reached the eastern terminus of the Empire Route. The weather put paid to their optimism and the *Singapore* was forced to return to Brisbane after being beaten back by severe gales. They eventually reached Sydney the next afternoon but their time was taken up with an appearance at an Imperial Airways exhibition that was attended by many prominent Australians. Brackley was still unable to take any rest. His next task was to appear before the newsreel cameras to answer questions from an aggressive press that he referred to as '…*a positive menace.*' After this Brackley and Fysh took the night train to Melbourne for a busy round of conferences and meetings. By 13 June Brackley's return to London was finally underway via Darwin but he still had more landing sites to examine en-route. This

included inspections of some uninhabited islands and the Gulf of Carpentaria, an inlet of the Arafura Sea on the northern coast of Australia. The route from Darwin included Koepang, Bima and Sourabaya but the Dutch were still causing aggravation over landing rights. The return was further delayed waiting at Sourabaya to collect Air Commodore Smith who was flying on the regular Imperial Airways service to Singapore to meet Brackley. His flight had been held up in India and Burma by the monsoon. After leaving Sourabaya and flying via Singapore where he arrived on 18 June, Brackley parted company with the RAF flying boat and continued to Alexandria on the regular westbound Imperial Airways service. This flew via Penang, Alor Star, Bangkok, Rangoon, Calcutta, Allahabad, Cawnpore, Delhi, Jodhpur, Karachi, Gwardar, Sharjah, Bahrain, Basra, Baghdad, Rutbah, and Gaza to arrive at Alexandria six days later. Brackley arrived exhausted in London on 29 June. Without any respite, the next morning he had to be back at Airways House for a meeting with Woods Humphery.

As far as his flights went, there had been few problems, but a burst tailwheel tyre had delayed Brackley for 28 hours at Gaza awaiting a spare to arrive by train from Delhi. In modern times events of this nature would generally be taken with a pinch of salt, but in the 1930s having spare parts available at short notice far from home could create significant logistical problems that frequently could delay flights by many days.

Wherever Brackley went in the world his duties also required him to take responsibility for other matters. One such occurrence took place

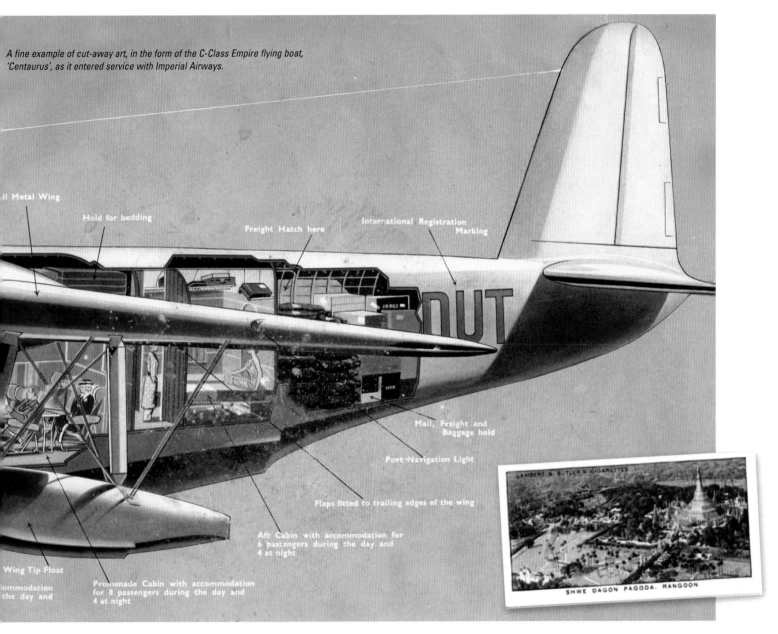

A fine example of cut-away art, in the form of the C-Class Empire flying boat, 'Centaurus', as it entered service with Imperial Airways.

All Metal Wing

Hold for bedding

Freight Hatch here

International Registration Marking

Mail, Freight and Baggage hold

Port Navigation Light

Flaps fitted to trailing edges of the wing

Aft Cabin with accommodation for 6 passengers during the day and 4 at night

Wing Tip Float

accommodation the day and

Promenade Cabin with accommodation for 8 passengers during the day and 4 at night

LAMBERT & BUTLER'S CIGARETTES

SHWE DAGON PAGODA, RANGOON

at Rangoon where he had to conduct an accident inquiry after the Short *Scion* floatplane that the aircraft manufacturers had sent to the Irrawaddy Flotilla Company to assist him had been completely wrecked in an accident.

During 1936 most of Imperial Airways fleet of DH86As were fully utilised on the European routes. While 12 of the type were being flown on the shorter routes, *Daedalus* (G-ADCN) had inaugurated the Khartoum-Kano service that was extended on 15 October to Lagos via Kaduna, Minna and Oshogbo.

On 14 March the first scheduled weekly Croydon to Hong Kong flight left London. More specifically this was the flight that would link with the Hong Kong feeder service at Penang also being operated by the Diana class DH86. The first departure left the Malayan island on 23 March and flew via Saigon and Tourane (Annam), where it stopped for the night. When the outbound flight landed at Saigon the famous veteran aviator, Charles Van den Born (1874-1958) was waiting to greet Capt Lock and his crew. Belgian-born Van de Born had settled in French Indo-China after he had been the first aviator to fly there.

Next day *Dorado* (G-ACWD) took-off at 06.00 hrs to cross shark-infested waters to arrive over Magazine Gap in Hong Kong at 11.30 hrs to be greeted by a squadron of aircraft from HMS *Hermes*. Large crowds had gathered for the arrival including the Governor of the Colony, Sir Andrew Caldecott. The waiting crowd expected to welcome only the aircraft's crew, but a veteran flyer by the name of Ong E Lim was sitting amidst sixteen bags of mail after flying his own aircraft to Penang to travel on the Hong Kong flight. Lim took the accolade as the first

official passenger ever to land at Kai Tak. The first return flight departed for Penang on 27 March. Once flights between Hong Kong and Penang became a regular weekly feature, the *South China Morning Post* monitored the services by publishing the names of passengers and details of the freight carried. With this branch open the Empire Mail service was progressing and by 6 May the London–Brisbane service was duplicated in association with Qantas. The duplicated westbound service to England was inaugurated on 16 May. However, the branch to Hong Kong did not meet everybody's approval and criticism came from a rather unexpected observer. During the reading of the Air Navigation Bill in Parliament, Lt Col J T C Moore-Brabazon, one of the very first British fliers, and only the second to be issued with a pilot's licence, uttered the derisory comment that the Empire route was *'Nothing to write home about.'* Mavis Tate, a member of the House, defended the service when she said that *'It is imperative for our interests in China and the Far East generally that we run a service from Singapore to Hong Kong and Shanghai.'* She added that British interests were under threat from Pan American Airways and Deutsche Lufthansa. KLM, by using faster, more efficient aircraft, had also cut 40 hours from the scheduled 144 hours it took Imperial Airways to reach Singapore from London.

The success of the Penang-Hong Kong connection was proving so successful that by 6 June a second DH86, *Delphinus*, (G-ACPL) had to be allocated. On 27 July Maj A Beckerleg of Marsman and Company became the first passenger to complete the entire Imperial Airways route between Hong Kong and London which, at that time, was quoted to be a distance of 15,000 miles. About 800 lbs of mail was carried

weekly between Penang and Hong Kong and during the first years of operation mail was given preference over passengers. On 5 November the China National Aviation Corporation, a company owned by Pan American Airways, forged another major external link with Hong Kong by commencing a service to Shanghai.

The expansion of British Airways

On 17 March there was an interesting incident; the very first case of its kind in Britain, when a passenger on the London to Paris flight aboard *Heracles* was fined at Croydon Police Court for smoking on board an airliner. On the same day British Airways began flying the first flat-rate air mail service between the UK and Scandinavia (Heston-Malmø) aboard their DH86 (G-ADEA) flown by Capt W F Anderson. The previous month the Air Ministry had handed a £20,000 subsidy to the airline and Royal Mail awarded a contract on the northbound routing between the UK and Sweden. Hillman's Airways had already been granted three mail contracts prior to the formation of British Airways and this had created some antagonism amongst the smaller companies who, with some justification, felt they were being denied their 'bite of the apple'. The Government, by announcing its support of British Airways, now had its second chosen instrument. In a quirky example of aviation trivia, it is believed that there had been no time to fully repaint the DH86 that operated the inaugural flight, and it is believed that it carried the names of British Airways as well as the previous owners, Hillman's Airways on the fuselage, although subsequent photographs of the aircraft appear to have been retouched to remove evidence of the Hillman's connection.

On 17 May British Airways transferred its operations to Gatwick Airport and by 27 July it had been awarded a contract to operate a mail service between Gatwick, Cologne and Hanover. This formed part of a joint operation with AB Aerotransport (Swedish Air Lines) which would fly the final Hanover-Stockholm sector. On the night of 15 September a second tragedy struck the airline when the former chief pilot of Hillman's Airways, Fraser Anderson, died in an accident during take-off at Gatwick in the DH86A (G-ADYF) en route with the night mail for Hanover.

Imperial Airways was boosted when the company was granted £204,000 from the Air Estimates to improve the ground facilities along the existing air routes '...*to speed up the services, and to organise modified routes that would be followed by the flying boats.*' The need to construct new bases for land planes and flying boats led to a further £75,000 being awarded in Government funding with an extra £20,000 paid towards experimental flights in preparation for opening a North Atlantic route. Subsidies for the year totalled £65,000 for the European Services; £105,000 for England-India and £18,300 for a New York-Bermuda service that was part-financed by The Government of Bermuda. There were also unfulfilled plans to provide a service to Greenland.

Northern and Scottish Airways was awarded a Post Office contract during February to operate between the Isle of Man and Liverpool that had previously been held by Blackpool and West Coast Air Services. On 21 January Northern and Scottish had extended its Glasgow-Skye routing to Askernish in South Uist and by 18 March it added South Uist to Sollas in North Uist. Enterprisingly it was also operating charter services at the same time from South and North Uist to Barra and Benbecula. On 30 June the company took delivery of nine additional aircraft from British Airways to meet its commitment to the airline on its English routes. These were the DH89s G-ADAG, G-ADAH, G-ADBU and G-ADDF; Spartan Cruiser IIs G-ACSM, G-ACVT and G-ACZM and Spartan Cruiser IIIs G-ACYK and G-ADEM. By 1 July the company had become a wholly-owned subsidiary of Whitehall Securities and British Airways, with Maj J R McCrindle, the British Airways managing director, appointed to the board of the Scottish company. During the same day, Northern and Scottish also took responsibility for the Irish Sea operations of British Airways. These were the mail contracts between Liverpool and the Isle of Man, Liverpool-Belfast-Glasgow, Belfast-Glasgow, Belfast-Isle of Man and Isle of Man-Carlisle. The company also began flying a circular route in opposite directions on alternate days that linked the Scottish Western Isles. The first of these was Renfrew-Skye-North Uist-South Uist-Renfrew with connecting flights from both Uists to Barra and Benbecula and from North Uist to Harris that were also met by a bus service to Lewis. The British Airways London-Sweden service with

Empire Airways Short C-Class, G-ADUV 'Cambria' was later transferred to BOAC.

Short S23 C-Class Empire flying boat, G-ADHL, *Canopus*, which entered service with Imperial Airways in 1936. The aircraft went to BOAC in April 1940 and was broken up at Hythe on 23 October 1946.

British Continental extended the routing from Malmø to Stockholm for the summer. At the same time British Continental Airways commenced a joint operation with KLM Royal Dutch Airlines to fly the previously mentioned Liverpool to Amsterdam via Doncaster service that ran until 30 October. The first of these services was operated by a KLM Fokker F XVIII that had been ferried specifically to Liverpool from Croydon the previous day.

Elsewhere in Scotland, Aberdeen Airways began flying between Aberdeen and Shetland as an extension of its Aberdeen-Stromness service. The first flight was operated by Capt Eric Starling on 2 June with the DH89 (G-ADDE). During the next day Highland Airways extended its thrice-weekly Inverness-Kirkwall service to Shetland (Sumburgh). This first flight was operated by Capt Fresson in the DH89 (G-ADAJ) and the service continued on weekdays from July until the end of October.

The Channel Islands airlines also added to their routes during the spring of 1936. Jersey Airlines opened a twice-weekly summer service between Jersey and Plymouth with Dragons and DH89s, but Plymouth was abandoned during 1937 in favour of Exeter. The small Channel Island

EL KADIMAIN MOSQUE, BAGHDAD

of Alderney was also linked with an on demand service as an extension of the airline's Jersey-Southampton route. Alderney was also added to the Guernsey-Jersey service operated by Guernsey Airways but this route was withdrawn after the Saunders-Roe Cloud amphibian *Cloud of Iona* (G-ABXW) crashed on 31 July killing all ten occupants.

On 22 May the Irish airline, Aer Lingus, was registered as a private company in Dublin with the full name of Aer Lingus Téoranta (Air Fleets Ltd) with £100,000. Five days later the company commenced services between Dublin (Baldonnel) and Bristol with a DH Dragon. This became known as Irish Sea Airways that was operated in conjunction with Blackpool and West Coast Air Services who had provided the funding for the first Aer Lingus aircraft. On 14 September a joint service began with a single each-way flight between Dublin and Liverpool on weekdays (withdrawn 24 October) and the Dublin-Bristol service was extended to Croydon with one weekday service in each direction flown by the DH86 *Eire* (EI-ABK).

British Airways was quickly earning a reputation for its professionalism. It invested plenty of money in its aircraft and equipped them with the latest navigational and weather aids. The fleet of DH86 express aircraft had APB three-axis auto pilots, Marconi directional finders, *Lorenz* blind-approach receivers, two-way radios, chemical de-icing, ice-proofed pitot heads and heated

carburettors. The latter anti-icing aids were considered essential to counteract the sub-zero temperatures encountered on the airline's Scandinavian operations. The cabins were also fireproofed and air conditioned to provide passengers with extra comfort and security while in the air.

On 27 July a DH86 was used to inaugurate the night mail service from London to Hanover and Cologne. After only a fortnight of successful operations this aircraft crashed at Altenkirchen near Cologne on 12 August and both crew members died in the resulting fire. The latest navigational aids had failed to assist the crew on this occasion when it was discovered that the aircraft was 30 miles off course and the accident was blamed on either a faulty radio-beam system or pilot error.

It had been another bad year for accidents. Two days before the British Airways crash, Imperial Airways had suffered another major loss when the pilot and two other crew members died at Croydon. They were testing the German developed Lorenz blind-landing system in the Vickers Velox (G-ABKY), an aircraft reserved mainly for freight and navigational aid testing. The incident occurred when the crew failed to gain sufficient height on take-off, struck houses on the edge of the airfield and the aircraft caught fire.

This was not an isolated incident and Imperial Airways experienced a sudden spate of accidents during the year. On 22 August the Short Kent flying boat, *Scipio* (G-ABFA), was about to land at Mirabella Bay in an abnormally rough sea. The aircraft was nose heavy due to the radio operator incorrectly setting the tailplane. Wilcockson, a highly experienced pilot, sensed a problem and opened up the throttles with the intension of making a renewed approach. However the extra thrust input worked against him and the aircraft pitched even deeper into a nose-down attitude causing it to crash into the sea. The Imperial Airways yacht *Imperia* anchored nearby headed for the crash scene. Two of the passengers aboard the flying boat were killed and the remaining nine were injured. The rough seas made rescue difficult and the *Imperia* crew was unable to bring them to land until next day. Another incident occurred when the HP42E *Horsa* (G-AAUC) was scheduled to make a night-landing at Bahrain, but considerably overshot the airport to end up 100 miles south of the intended destination. The captain had radioed to say that he was landing but contact was then lost and an RAF search party found the aircraft next day, but nobody was injured and the aircraft was undamaged in the incident. Bahrein at that time was unlit at night and pilots had to find their way by using direction finding wireless that they knew could be unreliable particularly during darkness.

Short C-Class under construction alongside some Kent's. G-ADHL, 'Canopus', the first type produced can be seen at far left with possibly G-ADHM, 'Caledonia' behind.

Imperial Airways was having no better fortune with its AW28 *Atalanta* class aircraft. On 10 February *Artemis* (G-ANTJ) was damaged at Pietersburg, South Africa after partially stalling on take-off and sinking on to ground beyond the airfield. The aircraft was repaired but another aircraft in the same class, *Athena* (G-ABTK) was written off having being gutted by fire at Delhi on 29 September after a bottle of oxygen exploded after it had mistakenly been used instead of air to start an engine.

With the numbers of passengers travelling through Croydon at an all-time high, the company introduced a fleet of silver and grey-painted luxury coaches to transport passengers in comfort from its headquarters at Airways House in Victoria to Croydon airport. During the mid-1930s the scheduled transit time between the London terminal and Croydon was just 45 minutes; today it would probably take closer to two hours!

From 24 March onwards all Imperial Airways flights bound for South Africa were cut to terminate at Johannesburg after South African Airways had taken over operations of the Johannesburg-Cape Town sector (see previous chapter).

The first 'C-Class' is launched

At the end of spring the first of the new Empire flying boats, the S23 *C-Class* was nearing completion at the Shorts plant at Rochester, Kent. G-ADHL *Canopus* left the line in June and following engine tests it was launched on the River Medway on 2 July. The test pilot, John Lankaster Parker, reported that the aircraft had been extremely responsive in taxying trials and on the first run he 'rotated' the big flying boat into the air and flew it for 14 minutes. On one occasion an engine failed on take-off but the aircraft responded perfectly well on the remaining three and was able to land safely after completing a few circuits. On 16 July, Parker took the aircraft to full speed at various altitudes and by 9 September it had completed load trials before being returned to the works to be fitted out. On 18-19 September the fully equipped version was demonstrated to Brackley. A week of demonstration flights followed and by 5 October it was the turn of dignitaries to experience a trip in the aircraft. Lord Swinton, the Air Minister and Sir Edward Ellington, Chief of the Air Staff and their entourages were the first to fly in the new flying boat. Next it was the turn of the Imperial Airways directors including Geddes and Sir John Reith, and on 6th Sir Samuel Hoare (First Lord) and the board of the Admiralty were taken up. On 20 September the aircraft was officially handed over to Imperial Airways with a certificate of airworthiness and two days later, Brackley flew it from Rochester to Rome stopping at Caudebec, Bordeaux and Marseilles on the way. At Lake Bracciano Capt F J Bailey took command for the proving flight to Alexandria. The return on 30 October was the first scheduled routing of the new C-Class. The journey made via Athens and Mirabella to Brindisi was completed in 7 hrs 20 mins. On 2 November the first scheduled southbound flight left Southampton. The Medway residents and members of their town council had been given the opportunity to officially celebrate the success of *Canopus,* already the world's fastest flying boat, on 25 September. But the airline's celebrations were marred by a further loss; this time the disappearance of the twin-engined Boulton Paul P71A *Boadicea* (G-ACOX) over the English Channel. The aircraft was never found despite extensive searches, but the body of the pilot was washed ashore a month later.

On 11 September the second of the first batch of 12 C-Class flying boats, G-ADHM *Caledonia*, was launched at Rochester. After some initial trials she was flown to Felixstowe for C of A tests, returning to the Medway on 1 October. *Caledonia* became the test bed for the planned North Atlantic service and was not fitted out as a passenger aircraft. During November she was flown to Hythe where long-range training and fuel consumption tests were conducted in preparation for the initial Atlantic survey that was due to start as soon as the winter ice flows had cleared from Botwood, Newfoundland. In December *Caledonia* was used to carry 5½ tons of Christmas mail bound for India and on 21st it departed on a proving flight to Alexandria. Imperial Airways was extremely impressed by the non-stop performance after it had flown the 1,700 mile Alexandria-Marseilles sector non-stop in just 11¼ hours. This was followed next day by a quick crossing of France from Marseilles to land at Southampton four-and-a-half hours later. Imperial Airways was about to enter an important new era in its history.

Full credit was attributed to Short Brothers for producing such an outstanding aircraft under difficult circumstances that at times seemed to be completely against the odds. The airline had entered a crucial phase and there was a vital and urgent need to re-equip the company to prevent it from losing too much ground to foreign opposition. KLM was already reaping the benefits of speed over long distances by operating the impressive DC2 on its overseas routes. The urgency to push the C-Class into service gave Shorts no time to produce a prototype. The aircraft evolved straight from the designs on the drawing board, only to be faced by production problems. Shorts had a large, skilled labour force, but by 1936 there was already a renewed German threat that forced the company to move all available men to

Short C-Class G-ADHM, 'Caledonia'.

the production of military aircraft for the RAF. This created a vast shortage of skilled workers forcing Shorts to employ unskilled labour to perform dedicated jobs. Such labour was put to work under the guidance of the few that could be spared from the skilled workforce. The experienced men trained and supervised the work as it was being done, but there was no opportunity to provide any pre-job training. In view of this, the management of Short Brothers was more than prepared to share in any failures, as well as successes, with their staff but things turned out successfully and everybody pulled their weight to produce an aircraft of exceptional quality. To increase the build speed, an efficient order of final assembly had to be devised to maximise the limited workshop space so that nine aircraft were in various stages of production all at the same time.

Political manoeuvring was seldom far away from the Imperial Airways boardroom. On 6 August 1936, *The Times* reported a certain intrigue had occurred linking Sir Eric Geddes, Woods Humphery and the Permanent Secretary to the Air Ministry, Sir Christopher Llewelyn Bullock KCB, CBE. The Civil Servant had reached the peak of his career but was dissatisfied and clamoured for ever greater recognition. Reports mentioned his desire to move into business and commerce and he attempted to coerce Geddes into supporting his efforts to gain a place at the helm of Imperial Airways. Rumours started to spread that Bullock was about to replace Geddes as chairman of the company and consequently this caused relationships between the men to sour. The previous year Bullock had recommended to Lord Londonderry that Geddes should be awarded an official honour for his work on the Empire Mail contracts. However Geddes received no such recognition and it appears this was because he had been able to see through the devious plan that was behind the gesture proposed by his sponsor. He found the unsolicited generosity of the Civil Servant distasteful, seeing it for what it was – a blatant attempt to gain support through favour. From the evidence, it must be said that Geddes was never in tandem with Bullock's indiscretions and he felt the civil servant had nothing to offer the airline. Nursing a feeling that he had been snubbed by Geddes, Bullock then tried to work on Woods Humphery. The two men dined together on 11 June and Bullock attempted to butter-up Woods Humphery by suggesting that he (Bullock) was about to replace Geddes as chairman. He suggested how he felt he and Woods Humphery could make an ideal partnership for the good of Imperial Airways, proposing himself as chairman and with Woods Humphery his deputy/managing director. In a subsequent committee of enquiry orchestrated by the Government, Bullock was deemed to have broken the very principles that regulated the conduct of civil servants that forbids them from soliciting public support in order to make personal gains, although they made no reference to outright corruption. The conclusion reached by the committee was that '…*in 1928 the principles were formulated regulating the conduct of Civil Servants in relations with the public, and these were commended by the Service generally as a true presentation of its traditions. They were enjoined by the Government and ordered by a Treasury circular dated 13 March 1928, to be incorporated with the rules of every department. We cannot escape the conclusion that Sir Christopher Bullock's conduct was completely at variance with the spirit of this code, which in our view clearly precludes a Civil Servant from interlacing public negotiations with the advancement of his personal private interests.*'

Bullock made a pitiful effort to defend himself by excusing his behaviour as a '… *passing phrase uttered in an unguarded moment*', but his superiors viewed his indiscretions otherwise and he was correctly dismissed by the Prime Minister from the post he had held since 20 January 1931. Bullock had been a prominent figure in aviation; he had served as an observer and as a pilot in the Great War and later rose through the ranks of the Civil Service, but his attempts to coerce the senior management of Imperial Airways were rightly seen as a total disgrace. Bullock was not always popular and it was said that he would only show respect to those he felt had earned it. The current Director General of the Post Office, Donald Banks, was appointed to replace him.

Short C-Class G-ADHM, 'Caledonia', passes low over the River Medway at Rochester.

Plans for the North Atlantic

On 30 July the British Government unveiled the plans that had been discussed during the previous year for the North Atlantic route. It was announced that a joint venture, with a director from each company, would operate the route. The three countries concerned in the plans were the United Kingdom, Ireland and Canada, and Imperial Airways was the nominated British airline. The split of the shareholding was to be 24½ per cent each to the Canadian and Irish interests; and 51 per cent to Imperial Airways. The proposed route would operate from the UK via Ireland and Newfoundland to Canada with Bermuda being considered as an intermediary destination during the winter months. Imperial Airways was charged with the task of conducting the experimental flights. Subsidy payments were agreed, with Canada providing 20 per cent up to a maximum of £75,000; 5 per cent from Ireland to a maximum of £12,000 and the remainder to be provided by the British Government. At the time no subsidy figure had been agreed for Newfoundland. The proposals never reached fruition and for whatever reason no joint company was ever formed to operate the route. However, on 22 August, a new company, Imperial Airways (Bermuda) Ltd was registered to manage a New York-Bermuda service.

As Imperial Airways was exercising its muscle on the wider-based international front, at home the smaller airlines were enjoying their own levels of success. Railway Air Services had continued to run a very enthusiastic service throughout the year. On 25 May it re-opened the South and West of England routes and operated Liverpool-Birmingham-Bristol-Southampton-Ryde-Shoreham with additional request stops at Meir for Stoke-on-Trent and Staverton for Gloucester. The Plymouth-Haldon-Cardiff-Weston-Super-Mare-Bristol route was also re-opened. On the same day, the company moved its Belfast operations from Aldergrove to Newtownards. By 5 July RAS had commenced a service between Cardiff and Shoreham via Weston-Super-Mare, Bristol, Southampton and Ryde that was timed to connect with the Jersey Airways Channel Isles service at Southampton. From 21 August to 12 September RAS added an hourly air ferry service across the Severn Estuary connecting Cardiff to Weston-Super-Mare. Norman Edgar (Western Airways) Ltd had also been operating fourteen flights a day on the same route from 31 May, but the frequency of their service was reduced in October and a Weston-Super-Mare to Birmingham route was introduced during July. RAS also experimented with a Glasgow-Perth service on 10 September with officials of the London Midland and Scottish Railways accompanying journalists aboard the DH 86. Finally, on 2 December RAS was re-awarded the London-Liverpool-Belfast-Glasgow mail contract. The RAS *Manx Airway* also opened services between Yeadon (for Leeds and Bradford) and Manchester, Yeadon-Manchester-Liverpool-Isle of Man from

The leading edge of the wing could be folded down to make a practical working platform on which to work on the four 920-hp (686-kW) Bristol Perseus radial piston engines on the Empire flying boats.

25 May, Yeadon-Manchester-Blackpool-Isle of Man and Isle of Man-Glasgow from 5 July, and Isle of Man-Belfast and Isle of Man-Carlisle (Kingstown) also during he summer.

A new airline, Channel Air Ferries Ltd, was registered on 8 May as a subsidiary of Olley Air Services Ltd and by 23 May it began operating daily between Brighton and Ryde (Isle of Wight) until the end of September with a Short Scion (G-ADDO).

The Maybury Committee that had commenced its work in July 1935 produced its long awaited report on 9 December. Principally the committee recommended the licensing of all internal airlines to ensure the most effective services to the public without uneconomical overlap. It further recommended that a single company be formed with the responsibility to operate a series of routes linking key population centres within the UK from a central junction airport. The committee felt this would provide the right conditions and opportunities for such a company to become self supporting. The report said the British Government should take responsibility for the provision, maintenance and operation of all radio facilities covering the UK and Northern Ireland as well as for the provision of a meteorological organisation and a comprehensive air traffic control service responsible for the safety and regulation of all air communications. Such suggestions were hardly mind-blowing and although the central hub junction system was given copious amounts of publicity, like so many Government sponsored schemes, it was never implemented and much of the work completed by the Maybury Committee became little more than a waste of time and public money. Certain of the Committee's findings were more positive and as a result of the report internal routes became licensed and a system of subsidies was introduced.

There were two major breakthroughs during the latter part of the year. In what might have been considered as a snub to British aircraft manufacturers, British Airways received Government approval to buy German-built aircraft (8 December) and later, American machines (24 December). In retrospect it had very little choice because there were no suitable British-built airliners available forcing the company to buy from abroad. At the time Airspeed Ltd had been approached by British Continental Airways to tender for a licence that would have allowed them to build 12 Douglas DC3 aircraft in the United Kingdom, but a cautious Airspeed board that lacked sufficient funding blocked the idea and the scheme never progressed. At least this move could be taken as a

sign that British enterprises were preparing to stretch the boundaries of aeronautical design beyond their normal comfort zones. For far too long the industry had been unwilling to consider building anything other than outmoded bi-planes. Home-based manufacturers really only had themselves to blame for their failure to meet the demands of the airlines to build large modern monoplanes of the kind commercial operators required for their continental routes. When the time came for British Airways to expand its fleet, it is a poor reflection that it had to look overseas to have its specifications met, and the company bought twin-engined, metal-skinned Lockheed Electras and the Ju 52 from Junkers.

While tests were progressing on *Caledonia* (G-ADHM), a brief interlude entered the life of Herbert Brackley when the air superintendent was summoned to a reception at London's Mansion House. During the evening of 12 October 1936, the Lord Mayor of London, supported by The Master, Wardens and Court of the Guild of Air Line Pilots and Navigators of the British Empire presented 'Brackles' with the Guild's Cumberbatch Trophy for Reliability. This was the first time that the award had been made and it was a fitting tribute that Brackley had been selected as the recipient. He had been one of the founder members of The Guild when it was formed to provide commercial pilots with the same status as sea mariners. The award was presented by the Grand Master of the Guild in the presence of Prince George, the Duke of Kent who had flown with Brackley on several occasions.

The programme for the ceremony justified why the award was made: *'But what is reliability? Clearly it is not merely a matter of keeping to regular time schedules. Does it lie only in the avoidance of accident, or does it lie also in the minimising of the worst results of an accident which circumstances may have rendered inevitable? Whatever definitions may be placed upon it, it is the quality of flying which, above all others, the Guild seeks to encourage. Many meetings of the Court of the Guild have been held and much thought devoted to deciding on the recipient of over fifty pilots, including airline, instructors and test pilots all of whom have over 5,000 hours flying to their credit, were carefully examined. It was only natural that choice should eventually narrow itself down to the 'skippers' of our oldest airline, Imperial Airways. Of the captains who joined that Company on its formation in 1924, eight are still with it today. Not one of them is less than 37 nor more than 44 years of age – not one has less than 8,000 hours commercial flying experience, whilst some have more than 12,000. At least one has fifteen years service without accident of any kind. Their names are as follows: O P Jones, L A Walters, W Rogers, A S Wilcockson, F Dismore, F J Bailey, H S Horsey, A B H Youell: lastly I should mention Squadron Leader Brackley, air superintendent of that great Company.'*

The commendation continued with a brief summary of Brackley's career and concluded by saying that the award would be held by him '*... both for his own record and also to hold for one year on behalf of the other eight. Their names will all be engraved upon the base of the trophy.*' With this brief interlude concluded, at the end of the month Brackley delivered *Canopus* (G-ADHL) to the Mediterranean and then flew home with Jimmy Youell one of the pilots cited in the Award. By the end of the year two further Empire flying boats had been delivered; *Cavalier* (G-ADUU) and *Castor* (G-ADUW), and the previously completed flying boat, *Caledonia* (G-ADHM) had been sent to the Hythe training base and *Centaurus* (G-ADUT) to Bordeaux.

Financially Imperial Airways was continuing to operate on a sound footing. Shareholders were given a double-bonus and a 6 per cent dividend when the company announced profits of £140,705 for the financial year 1935-36. Geddes announced the company's performance by commenting: '*For some time the directors have been quite inadequately remunerated, so I feel sure you will desire to pass a resolution increasing the fees from £6,500 to £12,000 a year.*' This was not a bad sum when viewed in comparison to 21st century values: today this would equate to approximately £240,370-£443,760.

CHAPTER FIFTEEN

NON-STOP FROM ALEXANDRIA, THE MAYO PROJECT AND THE DEATHS OF GEDDES AND SAMUEL INSTONE

1937

HAVING already put the first two of the new C-Class flying boats through their paces on proving flights and by employing *Caledonia* (G-ADHM) to carry the Christmas mail to Alexandria and back, Imperial Airways wasted no time putting the aircraft into service. *Castor* (G-ADUW), the third aircraft to be delivered, commenced operational flying from Marseilles to Alexandria via Rome (Lake Bracciano), Brindisi and Athens on 4 January 1937 with Captains Powell and Store at the controls. Eight days later the company operated the all-air trans-Mediterranean proving flight from Alexandria to Southampton, with a night stop at Brindisi, as part of the India service. On this auspicious occasion the aircraft was under the command of Capt L A Egglesfield in *Centaurus* (G-ADUT). On 16 January the first eastbound proving flight commenced between Southampton, Marseilles, Rome, Brindisi, Athens and Mirabella arriving in Alexandria next day. The first African service was next, departing from Southampton on 26 January with Capt Powell in command of *Cassiopeia* (G-ADUX). At last passengers bound for Egypt and beyond could relax aboard a comfortable aircraft instead of having to be transferred, like cattle, to the train for the journey across Europe.

During early January, Captains Wilcockson and Messenger visited Southampton and Hythe to become familiar with *Caledonia* under the guidance of Brackley. With the proving flights accomplished, the first regular service had been scheduled to leave Southampton for Alexandria on 6 February, using *Castor* flown by Capt H W C 'Jimmy' Alger. After conducting a smooth take-off, the engines were not running smoothly and Alger was forced to return with oiled-up plugs. It took much longer to change these than expected and the departure was seriously delayed. Rough water further prevented the cured aircraft from leaving next day but by the 8th the service got under way. However, this was delayed again by bad weather in the Rhône Valley that forced an unscheduled stop at Hourtin to refuel. In the early days there were few bowsers and Alger and his crew had to refuel the aircraft themselves by manhandling the petrol from heavy four-gallon cans; a slow operation that took three hours. By the time Marseilles was reached the aircraft was by then already two days behind schedule and the air mail subsidy looked in jeopardy. The terms of the mail contract reasonably demanded the consignments to arrive on time. Alger, conscientious and determined not to let the company down, broke company regulations by making a night landing at Alexandria. This was quite a dangerous manoeuvre but Alger calculated that the risk had to be taken to ensure that the company's mail contract remained intact.

The return flight was just as eventful. With the newly appointed Imperial Airways line manager, Charlie Cross, on board things started to go wrong after leaving

Marseilles when the crew was informed that Southampton Water was shrouded in fog and there would be no possibility of landing. There was only one alternative – to put down on the Saône at Mâcon. Cross ordered Bill Morgan, the flight clerk, to send the passengers on to England by train. The mail should have gone the same way, but Alger had other ideas that he kept from his line manager. Alger decided to press on regardless and after what he described as a *'hairy'* flight the crew managed to land at Southampton leaving Morgan just enough time to catch a train to Waterloo where he was reunited with Cross and the passengers.

By 18 February another breakthrough occurred when *Caledonia* flew an impressive 2,222 miles between Southampton and Alexandria non-stop in 13 hrs 5 mins. By the end of the month, eight S23 C-Class flying boats had been certificated. These were G-ADHL *Canopus,* G-ADHM *Caledonia,* G-ADUT *Centaurus,* G-ADUU *Cavalier,* G-ADUV *Cambria,* G-ADUW *Castor,* G-ADUX *Cassiopeia* and G-ADUY *Capella.* With more aircraft now at its disposal, Imperial Airways confidently increased its schedules to four flights weekly from the start of March. Production at Rochester was proceeding well and Shorts expected to deliver two new flying boats every month. At the time the HP42s were still faithfully plodding their way along the Cairo to Great Lakes sector of the South Africa route although they were expected to be withdrawn once the full compliment of flying boats were operational.

The positive aspects of aviation were still being overshadowed by the tragic. Fate played an unkindly hand again on 2 February when a

Short S23 C-Class Empire flying boat, G-ADVE 'Centurion', in flight. (CAS)

DH Dragonfly operated by London Express Newspapers crashed, killing the air correspondent of the *Daily Express*. The journalist had been flying the junction routes that had been defined in the 1935 Maybury Report to rationalise competition between the British internal airlines. The flight had departed from Liverpool (Speke) but all contact was soon lost. After an extensive search over a two-day period, the wreckage containing the bodies of those on board was found on a 1,500-foot hillside at Darnaw in Kirkcudbrightshire. Ironically, the dead journalist was making the flight to ratify the feasibility of the suggestions published in the report. It was poignant that one of the criticisms referred to by Maybury concerned the current state of equipment for flying in bad weather and the crash had merely emphasised the need for safety to be radically improved.

On 26 February the Air Registration board was formerly set up as a limited guarantee company without share capital to commence operating four specialist groups; 1) construction and maintenance; 2) insurance; 3) commercial operators and 4) piloting. The board comprised George Woods Humphery (Imperial Airways), L T H Grieg (Jersey Airways) and Eric Gander Dower (Aberdeen Airways). The organisation had been established as a result of the findings of the Gorell Report that was published in 1934 that had led to the Air Navigation Bill being passed as law in June 1936.

Trippe had telephoned Woods Humphery on 17 February informing him that the American dirigible concerns were partitioning the US Government for rights to cross the North Atlantic. By the 22nd the British Air Ministry had issued Pan American Airways with the rights to fly to the United Kingdom, Newfoundland and Bermuda. Similar rights were issued soon after permitting the airline to operate to Canada, Ireland and Portugal. The various permits, with the exception of the Portuguese, were handed to Trippe on 20 April at a ceremony held at the Washington office of the Secretary of Commerce. With the Atlantic route now looking more certain, work had commenced to establish a flying boat base at Foynes on the southern bank of the River Shannon estuary.

Hythe opens to flying boats

On 5 March Imperial Airways opened the Hythe flying boat base on Southampton Water. With the introduction of the C-Class flying boats on the long-haul Empire routes, the company's Croydon-based land operations were reduced to serve only Europe. On the previous day the final Imperial Airways landplane to operate the African Empire Route arrived at Croydon. The flying boats had already started to make a major impact and at Hythe the base became a centre of activity when, as the year progressed, flights arrived and departed with increasing regularity from Egypt, Africa, India, Australia and the Far East.

The spread of schedules kept the ground staff active throughout the week and many crew members were happy to work seven-day shifts without a break. Despite the criticism often levelled at the company, Imperial Airways was highly regarded as an employer and the spirit of the workforce was said to be extremely high.

In 1937 the amount allocated by the annual Air Estimates was beginning to look a little more realistic, although in terms of the total pot it was still a pittance. Civil aviation was allocated £2,315,000 from the £56.5m total. In his speech of 14 March, the Air Minister, Sir Philip Sassoon was buoyant about the immediate future of Imperial Airways. He announced that by the following year all first class mail bound for India, Australia and Africa would be carried on the company flying boat services with some additional landplane transportation to India. The flat rate would be 1½d for each ½ ounce carried. The Minister informed the Commons how aircraft would fly by day and by night in all

Passengers take lunch prior to boarding Short S23 C-Class Empire flying boat, G-ADVE 'Centurion', at Galilee during the mid-1930s. This aircraft capsized at Calcutta on 12 June 1939. (US Library of Congress)

Short S23 C-Class Empire flying-boat, G-ADVB 'Corsair' takes off from Galilee in the mid-1930s. 'Corsair' later served with BOAC. (US Library of Congress)

weathers over thoroughly organised routes that were equipped with modern navigational aids and radio that would ensure punctual and efficient operations. His remarks emphasised how the equipment to be used would safeguard against crashes.

As it turned out this proved to be an ill-timed statement in view of what happened the following day. Sassoon was not to know that Wolley Dod, the highly skilled former Imperial Airways pilot, was to die while conducting an experimental flight. Dod had been appointed European manager and was travelling in a DH86 that crashed in sleet and snow at Alsdorf between Croydon and Cologne. It was assumed that a build-up of ice on the aircraft wings had caused it to come down in the trees where it swiftly caught fire and Dod perished in the flames. On the 24 March a memorial service was held for the pilot, but fate played a wicked hand once more when *Capricornus* (G-ADVA) crashed at Mâcon, France. Ice was once more blamed as the likely culprit and it was also suspected of bringing down a number of American aircraft but little was known about the effects it caused on air frames. *Capricornus* had left Hythe for Australia, flown by Paterson and Weir carrying the first through air mail when the crew reported they were lost in a snow storm. Not long after, it ploughed into a mountain in the French Alps killing the pilots. A woman passenger on board survived the impact but died in a Mâcon hospital and the injured radio operator battled through the snow to reach a farmhouse two miles away to summon help. Brackley, was extremely concerned by the dangers caused by ice forming on aircraft wings and control surfaces and communicated the problem to Sir Robert Mond, his father-in-law, the chairman of ICI. Mond suggested that a type of Vaseline, later referred to as political paste, could be injected onto the upper surface of the wings to prevent ice from adhering to the metal or fabric. The DH86 was said to be an ideal victim for icing because of the '*struts and flying wires*' on the bi-plane, according to Capt Cripps, a pilot critical of the aircraft type. He complained that the DH86 was not even equipped with a heated pitot head and the gyro instrumentation operated by something known as the *venture system* was also prone to freeze.

In 1934 Imperial Airways had commissioned Armstrong Whitworth to build fourteen new AW27 Ensigns at a unit cost of £53,000 but two years on the new landplanes were still not ready. The manufacturers claimed that Imperial Airways had created the delays by making repeated demands for design changes, but the company blamed the aircraft manufacturer for prioritising the supply demands of the RAF which was increasingly concerned about the political activities developing in Germany.

There was also evidence that Imperial Airways was starting to come adrift in some areas of its operations; most specifically on the European routes. KLM, who had won the England–Australia air race with the impressive Douglas DC2, had already put fourteen of the type into service leaving Imperial Airways stranded as far as speed was concerned. The Dutch had also bought eleven of the later DC3s, and the type had successfully been introduced on the Amsterdam-Croydon route that KLM operated eight times daily before moving them to the Amsterdam–Batavia service. Douglas had taken little time to

demonstrate the merits of their all metal aircraft that were already regarded as world leaders. KLM was the first non-American company to order the aircraft and although it acquired these through Fokker, Douglas was quick to announce that it had plenty of aircraft to spare just waiting for operators to snap up. But, apart from the development of the flying boats, Imperial Airways and the British Government had shown a remarkable level of complacency by overly relying on aircraft that were showing distinct signs of old age. Aircraft such as the HP42 may have been comfortable, but in contrast to the sleek airliners that were evolving from America, the old bi-planes were lumbering dinosaurs operating in an age where passengers were expecting a faster and more efficient level of service. It is interesting that only one other European country ever bought a large British-built airliner during the inter-war years. The Belgian operator SABENA had bought the Handley Page W8f and 8b as well as a few Westland Wessex aircraft to add to a fleet that mainly consisted of Fokker F7b/3ms. Surprisingly, when the Belgians decided to re-equip, they remained loyal to Europe by buying Italian built Savoia-Marchetti S73 machines that worked their long distance routes between Europe and the Belgian Congo on the Brussels-Leopoldville service.

It was a further condemnation of British engineering when British Airways, now with the former AT&T pilot, Alan Campbell Orde as test pilot, chose to buy German aircraft when it next 'went shopping'. Instead of buying British it opted for the Junkers Ju 52/3m G-AERU *Juno* that it acquired from the Swedish Air Line (AB Aerotransport) to operate the London-Hanover mail service. The German tri-motors (favoured by Adolf Hitler) were highly efficient workhorses. Two further Junkers were added during the year: *André* (SE-AES) from AB Aerotransport in March (re-registered G-AERX *Jupiter*), and a brand new aircraft that arrived direct from the manufacturers during August that was registered G-AFAP and named *Jason*. These admirably complemented the fleet of ten Lockheed Electras that the airline had ordered in 1936 which had been introduced on the London-Paris route on 5 April. The Electras later operated the London-Malmö service from 17 April (until it was suspended on 4 October) and on the re-opened London-Stockholm route two days later that was flown impressively in 7 hrs 20 mins. The London-Lille service had also previously been suspended on 6 March. The airline was showing steady growth and on 7 February it moved its base for a second time, leaving Gatwick for Croydon. Imperial Airways meanwhile re-routed its London-Budapest service from 5 April to include Frankfurt-am-Main to connect with the

German Transatlantic Zeppelin operated by Deutsche Zeppelin-Reederei that flew to Rio de Janeiro and New York (Lakenhurst). As a result of this route change, Imperial Airways curtailed its services to Cologne and Leipzig. On the same day North Eastern Airways extended its Croydon-Perth (Scotland) services to Aberdeen, but operations were terminated in the autumn due to a lack of adequate radio facilities along the route.

Domestic activities

The carriage of mail was often favoured over passengers and the smaller companies keenly tendered for any available contracts. During February West Coast Air Services was re-awarded the Post Office contract to carry first class mail between the Isle of Man and Liverpool. This had previously been granted to the company in 1935 but was lost to Northern and Scottish Airways who had taken it during 1936 but failed to keep it.

The spring of 1937 brought a considerable flurry of activity from the small independent companies. The previously mentioned Atlantic Coast Air Services Ltd was re-registered on 26 April to become Lundy and Atlantic Coast Air Lines Ltd, a rather grandiose title for a company that operated a very limited number of services mainly between Barnstaple and the tiny Bristol Channel Island. On 10 May, Railway Air Services resumed the Manx Airway that connected the Isle of Man with Carlisle, Belfast and Glasgow. Four days later Aer Lingus re-opened their seasonal service that carried mail between Dublin and the Isle of Man in conjunction with Blackpool and West Coast Air Services. The Irish company operated the DH89 *Iolar II* (EI-ABP) on the inaugural service that was flown until 4 September when it was suspended for the winter.

On 13 May a Monospar ST4 (G-ACEW) owned by Highland Airways flown by Capt Eric Fresson with one passenger became the first aircraft to land on Fair Isle, one of the Shetland group of islands. A small operator calling itself Utility Airways, a subsidiary of the Merseyside Air Park Company, began flying four times daily across the Mersey from Hooton

An evocative photograph of the apron at Croydon Aerodrome during 1937 with the Air France Bloch, M3221, F-AOHD, Auvergne about to depart. (CAS)

to Liverpool (Speke) using a Monospar ST12 aircraft. This service was reduced from the end of June to a by-request operation suggesting it was not entirely viable. Although a further route, Hooton-Blackpool was added during July, it is doubtful whether the company made a profit and both services ceased on 1 October and were never re-opened. By 31 May all air operations for Blackpool were transferred from Squires Gate aerodrome to Stanley Park.

May had been an eventful month, for aviation and for the nation. Baldwin resigned, handing over the premiership to Neville Chamberlain. King George VI was crowned at Westminster and Lt Col A J Muirhead displaced Sir Philip Sassoon as Under Secretary of State for Air while Sir Francis Shelmerdine's title was 'upgraded' from Director to Director General of Civil Aviation. The Government was widely condemned when it appointed a non-aviation businessman, Sir Francis L'Estrange Joseph as its representative to the board of Imperial Airways to replace Sir Walter Nicholson. Operationally there was an air of excitement when the new, sleek, four-engined DH91 Albatross (G-AEVV) built to succeed the DH86 flew for the first time on 20 May. When test pilot Bob Waight flew the aircraft on her maiden flight, he applauded the Albatross as *promising* after making several passes in front of the proud de Havilland workforce. This was intended to be the long overdue extended-range aircraft, officially named the *Frobisher* (F Class) that was expected to operate the transatlantic route. Waight's life was tragically cut short when he was killed near Hatfield on 1 October while testing the TK4, an aircraft built by de Havilland to compete in the Kings Cup Air Race.

On 20 May British Airways introduced a two-class system on its services between London and Paris using different aircraft types. The first class service was operated by its Lockheed Electra in 1 hr 20 mins at a single fare of £4 10s 0d (£4.50). A weekend return was offered at £6 6s 0d (£6.30); a 15-day return for £7 10s 0d (£7.50) and a 60-day return for £8. The second class service took 20 minutes longer and was flown by a DH86 with fares ranging from £4 single to £7 2s 6d (£7.12½) for a 60-day return. Meanwhile, on 21 May Railway Air

Services took over the existing bookings on the Liverpool-Blackpool-Isle of Man-Belfast-Glasgow services previously operated by Northern and Scottish Airways, but the Scottish company re-opened its Glasgow-Isle of Man service on 1 June. North Eastern Airways opened experimental services a month later between Manchester, Doncaster and Hull and between Hull-Grimsby Ferry. These were extended during September to include Liverpool but the sector between Liverpool and Doncaster was subsequently cancelled in February 1938.

North Eastern Airways also featured in a further new service that was started by a company called Allied Airways (Gandar Dower) Ltd that commenced a five-times-weekly service between Newcastle (Woolsingham) and Stavanger, Norway using a DH86B *The Norseman* (G-AETM) flown by Capt Eric Starling. The service connected with North Eastern's services at Newcastle that linked Edinburgh, Perth and Glasgow with the North Eastern Railway's prestigious *Coronation Express* to London (Euston). The Stavanger flights also connected with Norwegian Air Lines Oslo service. Invariably many airline services had to be suspended due to adverse winter weather and the Oslo service closed from 20 September until the following April. A further short-lived service was also operated by North Eastern Airways briefly between London-Knocke/Le Zoute from 29 July to 16 September.

Jersey Airport was officially opened at St Peter on 10 March and by the end of the month Jersey Airways commenced flying Jersey-Brighton and Jersey-Exeter during the summer. This provided a connection with the RAS Bristol-Plymouth link that the Channel Islands company had operated during 1936. RAS later added Exeter as a request stop on the service from 1 June and the following day the airline began its first air mail service between Jersey-Southampton operated by the DH89 (G-ADBW) flown by Capt B Walker, with the return made by Capt W B Caldwell in the DH86 *The Giffard Bay* (G-ACYF). From 1 July, Channel Air Ferries began operating a Brighton-Bembridge (Isle of Wight)-Bournemouth route and opened a weekend Croydon–Deauville cross-Channel service two days later. During August and September the company also operated from Brighton to Deauville.

The Railway Air Services G-ACVZ
'Jupiter' that crashed while in the
service of Imperial Airways during
March 1937. (CAS)

On 9 August British Airways commenced a night mail service in co-operation with Deutsche Lufthansa between London and Berlin. This extended its existing London-Cologne-Hanover route that carried first class mail destined for Central and Eastern Europe. British Airways operated the Junkers Ju 52/3ms on the sector to Cologne that departed each week night and the Cologne-Berlin sector was flown on alternate nights by both airlines.

Three days later Scottish Airways was incorporated as a private company after Northern and Scottish Airways had joined forces with Highland Airways to serve the domestic requirements of British Airways, the London Midland and Scottish Railway and the ferry company David MacBrayne Ltd.

The world was stunned by the tragedy that occurred on 6 May when the Deutsche Zeppelin Reederei (DZR) airship *Hindenburg* burst into flames as she moored at Lakenhurst in New Jersey killing 35 people. Highly volatile hydrogen was the major contributor to the severity of the accident proving just how dangerous this form of transport could be. Juan Trippe and his wife would have breathed a deep sigh of relief that the tragedy had not occurred as they travelled incognito as Mr and Mrs Brown from Frankfurt to Brazil aboard the craft during their 1938 world tour.

The Bermuda service

The reality of a transatlantic operation was looking more positive. Woods Humphery had been in protracted negotiations with the Pan American Airways chief, Juan Trippe and simultaneous flights in each direction between Britain and the USA were planned. By the end of May, the operating company, Imperial Airways (Atlantic) Ltd had been registered and the nominal capital of Imperial Airways was increased from £1m to £5m. As a prelude to transatlantic operations, the two airlines had agreed to run a joint Bermuda-New York service. Imperial Airways had specifically ordered two modified C-Class flying boats; *Cavalier* (G-ADUU) and *Centaurus* (G-ADUT) to operate the service and these had been fitted with additional fuel tanks in each wing to increase their range to 1,078 nautical miles. Even with this extra capacity, the British flying boats did not have sufficient range to reach Bermuda from the UK and *Cavalier* had to be dismantled and transported aboard the SS *Loch Katrine* from London Docks for re-assembly on arrival. The components were packed in waterproof crates but those containing the wings were so large that they hung over the sides of the ship. During loading there was an anxious moment when the fuselage was almost lost when the crane lifting the crate collapsed.

Cavalier was test flown from Bermuda by Capt Armstrong with First Officer Richardson on 19 February with further proving flights operated by both airlines prior to the start of regular services. The first joint services departed mid-morning on 16 June when Capt Cumming commanded *Cavalier* with fourteen passengers aboard. The flight arrived late after Cumming treated his passengers to a sight-seeing diversion over Manhattan. The Pan American Sikorsky S-42 *Bermuda Clipper* (NC16735) carrying twenty-eight passengers departed in the opposite direction simultaneously. Bookings had been good and 405 passengers

had paid (£20 single: £36 return) in advance for the privilege of taking the six hour flight. *Cavalier* flew the return from New York on 19 June and each airline initially made a weekly return flight. Imperial Airways left from Grand Sound, Bermuda on Wednesdays and returned Saturdays; Pan Am departed from Port Washington, New York on Sundays, returning on Thursdays. By August the service was doubled and *Cavalier* operated services from Bermuda on Mondays and Fridays and returned next day. During the winter Baltimore replaced New York as the American terminal. *Cavalier* successfully maintained the service for eighteen months but ice was once more the cause when the aircraft was lost on 21 January 1939. The flying boat had taken off from Port Washington on its 290th flight commanded by Capt Alderson and was about two hours into the flight when icing caused the carburettors to fail that led to a loss of power in all four engines. The aircraft had been carrying eight passengers and a crew of five. Two passengers and the steward died in the accident.

As 1937 progressed Short Brothers continued to deliver the C-Class flying boats that were quickly absorbed into routine operations. On 15 May *Capella* (G-ADUY) was the first of the later batch of aircraft to operate south of Cairo when it flew to Kisumu on Lake Victoria. This was followed eight days later by Capt D C T Bennett completing the first dawn-to-dusk single-day Alexandria-Southampton flight. *Cassiopeia* (G-ADUX) carried 14 passengers and 1½ tons of mail on the 18-hour journey.

The first England-South Africa through flight opened when *Canopus* (G-ADHL) departed from Southampton on 2 June flown by Capt Attwood. The route operated via Marseilles, Rome, Brindisi, Athens, Alexandria, Cairo, Wadi Halfa, Khartoum, Malakal, Butiaba, Port Bell, Kisumu, Mombassa, Dar-es-Salaam, Lindi, Mozambique, Beira and Lourenço Marques to Durban. Optional stops were at Mâcon, Mirabella, Luxor, Kareima, Laropi, Quelimane and Inhambane. The inaugural flight northbound was made by *Courtier* (G-ADVC) on 6 June.

Two days earlier *Cambria* (G-ADUV) commanded by Capt Egglesfield completed a 20,000-mile survey of the flying boat routes. On 7 June Capt Travers commanded the final Imperial Airways landplane flight from Johannesburg (Rand airport) aboard the Armstrong Whitworth XV *Amalthea* (G-ABTG) carrying mail. Henceforth all Imperial Airways flights terminated at Durban and South African Airways took over the sector to Cape Town.

The HP42s had been providing loyal service and were still making a profit despite their slothfulness, but on 31 May one of their number, *Hengist*, (G-AAXE) was destroyed in a hangar fire at Karachi.

Sir Eric Geddes

On 22 June the aviation world learned of the death of Sir Eric Campbell Geddes, the chairman of Imperial Airways. He had been suffering from a lengthy illness and was also having to contend with his invalid wife, Alice, who outlived him by eight years. Geddes was born in Agra, India in September 1875 and was the second of five children born to a Scottish engineer and his wife. After attending various public

schools, Geddes went to America where he proved his versatility in a variety of jobs including typewriter salesman, labourer, lumberman and railway brakeman. In his formative years he had viewed himself as a failure, especially during his time at various public schools. His work on the railway systems of America may have forged his later career. He went first to India, to manage forest land before moving to the Powayan Steam Tramway, and then joined the Rohilkhand and Kumaon Railway where he served as traffic superintendent. Eventually he took a job in England on the North Eastern Railway (NER) under its traffic apprenticeship scheme, becoming goods manager three years later. By 1911 his prowess as a hard working and highly organised executive had been recognised and Geddes was appointed deputy general manager on a hefty salary of £5000 a year (over £365,000 today). With the outbreak of war he joined the 17th (Service) Battalion Northumberland Fusiliers, a company sponsored entirely by the NER comprised of their employees. Lloyd George later called upon his skills, appointing him deputy director of munitions responsible for the supply of weapons, field kitchens and vehicles for the war in France. This role gave Geddes temporary Civil Service status and he started to become involved in politics. By then he had been appointed head of the gun ammunition department which earned him a knighthood in 1916. He was also serving as the Director-General of Railways at the War Office and was given the rank of Major-General. His success at organising a light railway to move munitions to the front lines in France during wartime led to Geddes being appointed inspector-general of communications covering all theatres of war. Lloyd George and Haig had appreciated the way Geddes had developed an approach for '*civilianising*' the malfunctioning aspects of the War Office and in May 1917 he was appointed Controller of the Navy responsible for dockyard facilities and shipyards. He added the rank of Vice-Admiral to the officer status that had previously been bestowed on him by the army. Internal quarrelling developed within the navy's hierarchy and the Prime Minister replaced the existing First Lord of the Admiralty, Carson with Geddes. He then stepped into the political arena to become the Unionist MP for Cambridge University. His naval work continued and he visited Italy and Russia on troubleshooting missions and to the United States to review their naval war efforts. Geddes was never happy in his role of MP and viewed it as an '*insufferable idea.*' After the war he became involved with organising demobilisation and industrial rehabilitation and by 1919 he was fighting the railway's corner against nationalisation in favour of private ownership. From 1919-21 he became chairman of the Supply and Transport Committee (STC) where he co-ordinated the Labour government's strike breaking organisation. When he resigned his political role in February 1922 it came as a release and Geddes joined the board of the Dunlop Rubber Company, becoming chairman by December of that year. Two years later his involvement with Imperial Airways commenced when he was appointed part-time chairman, initially for one day a week but later extended. His work at Dunlop was highly inspirational as he moved the company beyond tyres to become a major producer of general rubber products. From 1925-28 the output from Fort Dunlop dramatically increased and the company became extremely successful. Geddes adopted imaginative business management practises that were probably far ahead of his times that included time and motion studies, technological innovation and *creative* accountancy. Many of his ideas were adapted from what he had seen on management trips to the United States where he picked up the latest business trends. At Imperial Airways he became a leading advocate of '*air mindedness*' and he became the key protagonist for developing the airline's Empire routes. He was not averse to confronting those that stood in his or the company's path, including any governments that refused to allow passage rights to the airline. Geddes once aptly said to Lord Hoare that his involvement with Imperial Airways had led to the '*...steady, conservative building-up of the company.*' His methods were not approved by everyone and Geddes was often regarded as brash, ruthless, impatient and a hard task master who could be very single-minded to get his own way. Although he was admired within the industry, many of his staff were fearful of his methods and viewed him as a martinet. After being cremated, Geddes' ashes were put aboard an Imperial Airways flying boat and scattered in the English Channel just off the Isle of Wight. He was replaced as chairman of Imperial Airways by Sir George Beharrel.

Despite the death of their chairman, the progressive work of Imperial Airways continued uninterrupted. Two days later, Capt H W C

Alger flew an Imperial Airways survey between Alexandria and Singapore using the Short Scipio flying boat *Satyrus* (G-ABFC). Then, on 29 June the Secretary of State for Air, Rt Hon Viscount Swinton and the Postmaster General, Rt Hon G C Tryon MP inaugurated the Empire Air Mail service in a special ceremony held aboard the MV *Medina* moored on Southampton Water. This was the first stage of the scheme envisaged by the late George Holt Thomas and the late Sir William Sefton Brancker seventeen years before. After the speeches, Capt F L Bailey, one of the earliest flying boat captains, took-off aboard *Centurion* (G-ADVE) carrying 3,500 pounds of un-surcharged mail. First class mail was carried between the participating nations at 1½d per ½ ounce for letters; 1d for postcards. As tends to happen on these auspicious occasions, the usual gremlins were at work to ensure that the occasion would not go without a hitch, and there was an embarrassing delay of about 25 minutes to the departure caused by a problem starting one of the flying boat engines. After the aircraft had got on her way, Beharrel spoke at a commemorative lunch at Southampton's South Western Hotel and during the meal Lord Swinton read a wireless report from the aircraft to say that it was already approaching Marseilles.

On 5-6 July the first commercial survey flights of the North Atlantic took place to herald another major breakthrough in the link between the UK and North America. Many believed that this important route should have been surveyed long before but progress had previously been delayed because no British aircraft was available capable of completing the Atlantic crossing. To conduct the survey Imperial Airways specifically converted the C-Class flying boat *Caledonia* for long range operations. This was flown westbound by Capt Wilcockson while the Pan American Airways Sikorsky S-42 *Clipper III* (NC16736) was simultaneously operated eastbound by Capt E H Gray. Wilcockson left Foynes on the River Shannon estuary at 1957 hrs for the long crossing to arrive at Botwood, Newfoundland at 1100 BST. The *Caledonia* had been specifically prepared to carry extra fuel and special radio equipment and to reduce weight the passenger cabin had not been fitted out. The flight schedule had been mutually agreed between the two companies and at the mid-point of the flight the two captains, one British, the other American, exchanged pleasantries by radio.

Juan Trippe had already invested more than $5.5m in expenses and new aircraft, much of it his own money, in his attempts to cross the Atlantic. Despite this he was concerned that another nation would beat his airline to the coveted prize. Unlike the British, French, Germans, Dutch and Italians that were under pressure to link their far flung colonies, America had no colonies and Trippe's priority was to expand his airline with the prime aim of making money. The ethos of this is made clear in Robert Daley's book *An American Saga – Juan Trippe and his Pan Am Empire* (Random House 1980) that compares the vastly contrasting profits of Imperial Airways and Pan Am in 1932. The British had made £52,894 that year (about $250,000) but the Americans, despite heavy expansion costs, made $698,526 in the same period. Britain, in the beginning, had very briefly led the way in the burgeoning airline industry, but as Dailey also pointed out, by 1932 France had 269 aircraft regularly employed in air transport; Germany 177, Pan Am already 121 and Britain just 32. Britain rapidly lagged behind and this was owed largely to the attitude of successive governments. The failure of Britain to develop commercial transport aircraft continued to be evident in 1937 when, despite the development of the C-Class, they were unable to match the power and range capabilities of the Sikorsky S-42 and Martin M-130 'leviathans' that Pan American had commissioned. These were already capable of flying vast distances carrying full loads; but the Shorts flying boats were incapable of reaching a range of 1,000 miles before running out of fuel. Imperial Airways had also been criticised, albeit they had been pushed by the Government, for ordering twenty eight flying boats costing £41,000 each before they had even been built, let alone flown. Trippe had been far more cautious, restricting his orders to a maximum of three at a time. There had also been a great deal of controversy surrounding the Atlantic negotiations. Trippe and Woods Humphery had been exchanging correspondence and telephone conversations since 1928 but while Trippe was able to negotiate as *his own man*, Woods Humphery had to follow the Government line and this ultimately resulted in interference that hampered progress. The British Government were no different to the French and Germans in this respect; all were merely protecting the subsidies that they were providing from the public purse.

This led to frustrations. At one point, high ranking British Civil Servants who knew little to nothing about commercial aviation, became engaged in meetings with the Americans without inviting Woods Humphery to attend. Most of these meetings were chaired by Sir Francis Shelmerdine (Director of Civil Aviation), or by Sir Thomas Banks, the head of the Post Office and it seems preposterous that Imperial Airways were not represented.

The first Atlantic crossing may not have been as efficient as Imperial Airways may have led people to believe. A former Pan Am captain, Sandford B Kauffman reveals in *A Manager's Memoir* (edited by George Hopkins; Texas Tech Press 1995) that Pan Am landed on schedule but the British flying boat had got lost. He claims they were close to the Newfoundland coast but even with radio direction finders, they were unaware of their location and had to wire for directions. This was picked up by a Canadian radio station who instructed the crew to turn north and once they had located Newfoundland they were able to find Botwood.

Kauffman also claims that the British flying boat was *'a disgrace.'* The Newfoundland Governor had apparently gone on board and found a dishevelled crew and the plane was dirty and greasy and not up to the high standards set by Pan American. Sandford also claimed that the governor was *'… discouraged when he considered the poor level of competence the British had put forth and I guess he sent back a pretty sharp report on the poor British chaps.'* He then offered some defence for the Imperial Airways crew: *'But, in fairness they had a problem with the airplane. It had just barely enough range to make the trip, and after that it was never used on the transatlantic scheduled service.'* This revelation might be a case of 'sour grapes' and I have been unable to unearth any evidence to support Sandford's story. Nevertheless, having completed the Atlantic crossing, *Caledonia* flew to Montreal on 8 July and New York next day before returning to the UK via Botwood on 12 July. There were enthusiastic celebrations on both sides of the Atlantic as the respective aircraft reached their destinations that were repeated when the pilots returned to their home ports on 15-16 July.

The tragedies that had marred 1937 unfortunately continued when word filtered through that on 2 July that the great female air ace, Amelia Earhart, was missing on an attempted 29,000 round-the-world trip with her navigator, Fred Noonan. The aviator was last heard from at 0845 hrs when she reported her position near the tiny mid-Pacific atoll of Howland Island but the aircraft had been running short of fuel as it headed across the great ocean. The twin-engine Lockheed Electra and its occupants was never seen again.

A key milestone was reached on 23 July when the hard working Handley Page HP42W (G-AAXC) *Heracles* completed a million miles in the air. The same aircraft had also made the airline's 40,000th Channel crossing on 2 May. During her time in the fleet the aircraft had safely carried approximately 80,000 passengers during 10,200 flying hours. The one millionth mile was announced as passengers tucked into lunch aboard the aircraft. Capt Dismore emerged from the cockpit at around 1415 hrs with a glass in his hand to make the historic announcement and the steward served a celebratory birthday cake.

The Mayo Composite Project

In July 1937 the lower component of the Short-Mayo Composite aircraft was flown for the first time for 20 minutes. A seaplane would later be attached to the top of a C-Class flying boat in a 'piggyback' (referred to by the company as 'pick-a-back') arrangement. The design was devised by Major Robert Mayo, the General Manager (Technical) of Imperial Airways as a way to overcome the problems of crossing the Atlantic from Ireland to Newfoundland. The Americans were ready with their flying boat programme, but Britain was still trying to develop a long-range passenger aircraft capable of flying the Atlantic with a sufficient payload of fuel to complete the journey.

In April 1932 Mayo had been granted approval on his first patent for an *'aircraft carrying other aircraft'*. The initial patent was considered too risky because the separation of the two aircraft depended on the use of the upper machine's elevators to launch it from the host with the inherent danger of the two aircraft colliding. Subsequently patents were approved that amended the separation method by using differential lift-coefficients of aerofoils on both aircraft that allowed the upper component to accept a greater share of the lift as speed increased. This was sufficient to overcome the spring detents that would bind the

Major Robert Mayo (centre), General Manager (Technical) of Imperial Airways and inventor of the Short-Mayo Composite, poses for a photograph on the slipway at Rochester during flight trials in 1938. With him is Major Stewart and Arthur Gouge.

aircraft together allowing the upper aircraft to pull clear safely. The system relied on the controls of the upper aircraft remaining locked until a safe height and sufficient speed had been attained to affect a separation. When the correct height/speed combination was reached, the flying controls of the seaplane became activated at the precise moment of separation allowing it to climb clear of the flying boat without experiencing any yawing. To further improve the safety aspect, another patent was passed that applied to a barometric control that acted as a failsafe to prevent the aircraft from separating if the altitude was too low. Until the controls on the seaplane became activated, the composite flew as a conventional single aeroplane with all flying manoeuvres being made by the pilot operating the lower, C-Class component.

Two other ideas had also been proposed in an attempt to find a solution to the problems associated by the distance involved in the Atlantic crossing. The first relied on a method used quite successfully by the Germans on their mail-carrying operations to South America that involved catapulting an aircraft from a water-based pontoon or mother ship. This method was dismissed as too risky after some pilots complained of back problems caused by the considerable G forces associated with being launched from a catapult. Sir Alan Cobham came up with his own proposal; in-flight refuelling. This would use a tanker aircraft based at Horta in the Azores to rendezvous with the C-Class flying boats that had departed from Lisbon to cross the Atlantic. The aircraft would link up over the Azores harbour where pipes extended from the tanker would be coupled to the flying boat allowing fuel to be transferred. This idea was initially dismissed although later adopted for a time on some flights between Ireland and Newfoundland.

Mayo's idea at the time seemed the most feasible, once the mechanics of separating the two component aircraft could be overcome; it relied only on a larger host aircraft taking off from water in the normal way to launch the smaller aircraft. The combined power from the eight engines of the two aircraft was used to provide the necessary lift to get the composite airborne. Once the correct altitude/speed combination had been attained, the pilots used a system of levers to separate the two aircraft. The smaller mail plane would fly to its destination, burning enough fuel in the process to make a normal safe landing and the host aircraft would return to base and be free to fly other duties. There was one inherent disadvantage to the concept. In order to make it viable a second host aircraft would also need to be permanently stationed at the other end of the route to provide the launch platform for the mail plane when it was due to return. Economically Cobham's in-flight refuelling system made far better sense.

The idea of a composite aircraft was not new. On 17 May 1916 Cmdr John Porte had previously conducted an experiment at Felixstowe using a Porte Baby flying boat that was carried on the central upper section of a Bristol Scout. The idea was to provide an aerial

Captain A.S. Wilcockson (centre) of Imperial Airways, flew the 'Maia' lower component of the Short-Mayo composite during fuel consumption tests and in-flight separation trials. Wilcockson is seen here on the occasion of the commencement of the England-India air route in March 1929.

The Short S.21 (G-ADHK) 'Maia' sits on the slipway with its four 920 hp Bristol Pegasus Xc radial engines idle.

The elegant Short S.20 (G-ADHJ) 'Mercury' seen on a rain-dampened slipway.

Hoisted by crane, the S20 'Mercury' is carefully brought towards the support struts located on top of the S.21's fuselage.

Commander Porte's composite – featuring the Porte Baby seaplane as the lower component and a Bristol Scout C as the upper component – waits on the slipway at the RNAS Felixtowe in May 1916. Thought to have been the largest aeroplane built in England at the time, the Baby boasted a span of 124 ft. and a loaded weight of 16, 500 lbs. It had a maximum speed of 78 mph and could climb to 9,000 ft in nine minutes.

twelve years later Norman MacMillan, the Fairey test pilot, patented a similar idea of *'aircraft being coupled in pairs or trains.'* This time the idea was conceived to provide an aerial launch platform for a type of gliding bomb. It seems the idea was never used but it was later adapted to launch gunnery practice targets in place of the self-propelled bombs.

Mayo, undeterred by any development problems pursued his composite until he patented the fully developed design jointly with Shorts in January 1936. Three months later Mayo was granted a patent to cover the added possibility of in-flight refuelling of the upper component. The Empire flying boat used as the composite host was specifically adapted for the purpose by Shorts and the upper plane was designed to be ultra-efficient. Initially the Empire boat had been conceived as a bi-plane that would have continued the British manufacturer's obsession for double-winged aircraft. However Oswald Short and his test pilot, Parker had been encouraged to radically change their thinking after they were said to have witnessed the sleek lines and performance of the Douglas DC2 perform in the MacRobertson air race. Fortunately the Empire design evolved as a cantilever monoplane. Had it been developed as a bi-plane the success of these flying boats as long-range transports could have been left in considerable doubt.

The contract for the Short-Mayo Composite between the manufacturer and Robert Mayo was signed in 1935 at an estimated total cost of £60,000 for both components after approval had been given by the Air Ministry and Imperial Airways. The development was known as specification 13/33 and the production costs were shared between Imperial Airways and the Air Ministry and given the serial number S20 for the upper component with S21 for the lower. The upper aircraft was

platform that would enable a smaller aircraft to be launched in mid-air to rapidly engage enemy Zeppelins. The Scout, flown by Flt Lt M J Day already had its engine ticking over when the host aircraft reached 1,000 feet. At this point Day opened the throttle allowing his aircraft to climb away from the Scout once the quick release toggle had been activated. He later described the experience as being *'like a dove rising from a roof'* but despite praising the experiment it was never repeated although

The Short-Mayo Composite moored on the River Medway.

The Short-Mayo Composite on the Medway with all engines running.

The Short-Mayo Composite in flight over the Kent countryside.

Captain Donald C.T. Bennett of Imperial Airways who flew the S.20 'Mercury' upper component. He found the delays to the completion of the Composite '... insufferable'. Bennett is seen here later in his career as an Air Vice Marshal of the RAF.

Caught on camera, S.20 'Mercury' lifts away from the S.21 'Maia'.

later registered as G-ADHJ *Mercury* and the lower, G-ADHK *Maia*. *Maia* was launched at Rochester on 27 July 1937 and flown by Parker for 20 minutes. The pylon structure that would cradle *Mercury* had not been fitted at that stage and the converted Empire flying boat was initially equipped with temporary four-bladed wooden propellers. These were later changed to three-bladed variable pitch airscrews before the aircraft was flown to 6,000 feet for level speed checks on 9 August. The pylon assembly was only added just prior to a check flight that was made in preparation for the press launch on 12 August.

The lower component was not vastly different to the other operational C-Class flying boats but certain modifications were required. A higher centre of gravity was created to account for the placement of the upper aircraft and the flying boat needed greater lateral stability on water. This was achieved by extending the beam of the planing bottom and by displacing and lowering the wing floats so that both would be awash simultaneously. The beam was also made slightly wider than on the conventional flying boats. The wing span remained the same but the overall wing area was increased by 250 sq ft and the tailplane surfaces were increased pro-rata. The hull, that could accommodate up to 18 passengers, was swept upwards at the stern to cause the tailplane to be raised, and the cabin had rectangular windows, otherwise the aircraft looked very similar to the other Empire boats.

The S20 *Mercury* was a clean twin-float mid-wing seaplane that was powered by four air-cooled Napier-Halford Rapier engines that were flared into the cantilever wing. The aircraft could carry 1,200 imperial gallons of fuel, enough to cruise in smooth air for up to 3,800 miles. The aircraft was constructed mainly of Alclad sheets although the control surfaces were fabric covered. The pilot and navigator sat in tandem fashion in the enclosed cabin forward of the wing and 1,000 pounds of mail could be carried in the aft hold. The S20 *Mercury* was launched and flown by Parker for fifteen minutes on 5 September and 40 minutes next day before being unveiled to the press three days later.

When in flight and the *Mercury* was trimmed, the C-Class pilot would see four lights illuminate on his control panel to provide the signal that would be passed to the pilot of the seaplane that his aircraft was ready for release. At this moment both pilots would activate their release levers simultaneously allowing *Mercury* to separate, climb vertically and accelerate clear of *Maia*. Separation could only be achieved once 3,000 lbs of tension had been attained on the aft linking hooks and 5,000 lbs on a third hook. Although neither pilot could see the other as they parted, as the upper aircraft climbed away the C-Class immediately dropped to prevent any chance of a collision. Although the test flights continued on the individual components during 1937, they were not flown as a composite until 1 January 1938. When the combined unit was ready, Parker carried out taxying trials at the

controls of *Maia* with Harold Piper aboard *Mercury*. During the first day of trials, the unit completed only an hour of taxying. Flight trials had been scheduled for 19 January 1938, although as gales lashed at the aircraft's moorings there was some concern for the aircraft but it survived unscathed. Bill Hambrook, in charge of the project, spent part of his time during the taxying trials closely observing the release gear by holding on to the pylon on the top of the flying boat. During one trial he remained in his precarious position as the aircraft reached near take-off speed and momentarily became airborne. On 20 January the combined unit was ready, and without Hambrook clinging to the structure, flew for 20 minutes. Because the load separators had not been correctly set, no attempt was made to part the two aircraft. The first in-flight separation scheduled for 5 February 1938 was also postponed due to bad weather, but next day conditions improved allowing the first separation to be successfully completed. The moment went unrecorded because it had been carried out on the spur of the moment and was seen only by a few people who were in the area at the time. The first official public separation had to wait until 23 February when it was filmed by British Movietone News cameras while the aircraft were at 700 feet. On that occasion Capt Wilcockson of Imperial Airways sat alongside Parker as co-pilot and observer.

New routes surveyed

During September 1937 the C-Class flying boat, *Ceres* (G-AETX), completed a survey flight between Alexandria and Karachi just prior to the regular service commencing on 3 October. The first sector of the scheduled service between Southampton and Alexandria was operated by *Clio* (G-AETY) with *Calypso* (G-AEUA) flying the final sector that arrived on 7 October. The route flew via Marseilles, Rome, Brindisi, Athens to Alexandria and then onward via Tiberias, Habbaniyeh, Basra, Bahrein, Dubai and Jiwani. The first flight to operate the entire westbound route was made by *Camilla* (G-AEUB) between 7-10 October. *Caledonia* (G-ADHM) also left Southampton for a survey flight to the Azores on 6 October to investigate the possibilities of a South Atlantic crossing via Lisbon.

On 15 October the Shorts Scipio flying boat *Satyrus* (G-ABFC) was next to survey a sector of the Empire Route when she departed from Alexandria for Singapore arriving two weeks later. The following month *Cordelia* (G-AEUD) conducted the first survey of the Karachi-Singapore sector where it arrived on 21 November. This was followed at daybreak on 3 December, after a two-hour delay, by *Centaurus* (G-ADUT) that left Southampton for the ultra-long survey to Australia and Auckland, New Zealand with Capt John W Burgess in command. Burgess, a New Zealander, was accompanied by a crew consisting of First Officer C F Elder; flight engineer Mr F Murray; two wireless

DH84 Dragon of Commercial Air Hire operated by Air Dispatch c1936-37. (CAS)

operators, H Dangerfield and A Low, and steward, H J Bingham. An overnight stop was made at Marseilles after the aircraft had diverted because there were no night-landing facilities available at Lake Bracciano, their intended destination. They continued via Singapore and Klabat Bay and took a break for a day at Batavia before continuing to Surabaya, Bima, Kupang and Darwin where the crew rested before reaching Brisbane on 21 December. When the flight arrived at Sydney on Christmas Eve, large crowds had turned out to witness the arrival of the first Empire flying boat to land in Australia. There had been little advanced warning and Imperial Airways had missed a wonderful opportunity to publicise the event. But, there was continuing displeasure from some who felt Imperial Airways had used the opportunity to deliberately upstage Qantas who were still awaiting the arrival of their own flying boats. The Qantas chief pilot, Lester Brain, was less concerned and had accompanied the crew from Darwin, but the Australians felt he should remain on board for the flight across the Tasman Sea. Burgess however refused him permission, allegedly claiming the flight was too heavy. *Centaurus* arrived at Auckland's Waitemata harbour on 27 December in brilliant sunshine after an

"HANNO" OVER THE DEAD SEA

uneventful 9 hrs 10 mins crossing from Sydney. Burgess was met by the New Zealand Premier, the Mayor of Auckland and by Edwin C Musick, the renowned Pan Am flying boat captain. The aviators ceremoniously shook hands in a show of friendship across a table suitably draped with the Union Jack. Musick's Sikorsky S42B, *Samoan Clipper*, was moored alongside *Centaurus* having completed a second Pan American Airways survey flight to New Zealand that had crossed the Pacific from Honolulu. Afterwards *Centaurus* toured New Zealand for a fortnight before returning to Sydney on 10 January 1938.

As the work of Imperial Airways progressed in Asia and Australasia, British Airways had been surveying a sector of the proposed South Atlantic route between Lisbon and Bathurst with officials from the Air Ministry.

During the autumn of 1937 RAS handed operations of the *Manx Service* to Isle of Man Air Services along with the five Dragon Rapides that had served the route. The new company was allocated £75,000 capital which RAS shared equally between Olley Air Services, the London, Midland and Scottish Railway and The Isle of Man Steam Packet Company Ltd. On 2 November the company was awarded a Post Office contract to carry mail between Liverpool, the Isle of Man and Belfast previously held by the Blackpool and West Coast Air Service. The latter had merged with Isle of Man Air Services on 27 September, but for operational purposes had retained its own identity until the name was shortened to West Coast Air Services.

On 15 September Channel Air Ferries commenced a service linking the Scilly Isles with Penzance to connect with the London-Penzance *Cornish Riviera* express operated by the Great Western Railway.

Accident at Phaleron Bay
On 1 October the flying boat *Courtier* (G-ADVC) was making an approach at Phaleron Bay in Greece in poor visibility en-route to Southampton from Alexandria. Capt Poole was flying the aircraft when he misjudged the height of his approach. Poole claimed to have been blinded by the sun reflecting from the surface of the sea and apparently thought he was on the water when he was still 50 feet above. He had become victim to a phenomenon known as 'glassy calm', a condition that makes it difficult to determine a visual separation between sky and water. The aircraft hit the water heavily, the hull split open and three passengers drowned. They were identified as Wing Commander W R Dyke Acland DFC AFC, Commander of 70 Squadron RAF Bomber Command in Iraq; an American theatrical agent, John Raymond Henderson and a Greek national, Alexandre Elefterakis. Capt Poole and four other passengers were slightly injured but the remaining crew members were unhurt.

The British government, for once, reacted quickly. On the day the accident occurred it announced that seat belts, fire extinguishers, blind-flying instruments and some de-icing equipment would become mandatory on all British transport aircraft. Ironically it had waited for

another fatal accident to occur before making it compulsory to carry safety equipment that had been standard on the commercial aircraft of most other countries for some time. Concern over the number and regularity of fatal accidents led to Parliamentary debates. Robert Perkins, the MP for Stroud (see below) raised issues on 17 November prompting the Under-Secretary of State for Air to announce that a committee of inquiry would be formed to investigate the workings of civil aviation. The committee began work on 2 December on what became the Cadman Report (named after the reporting committee chairman, Rt Hon Lord John Cadman GCMG, chairman of the Anglo-Iranian Oil Company). This document was to have widespread implications that would shape the airline industry of the future. From December 1937 to mid-February 1938 the committee held 30 meetings and interviewed 50 witnesses before preparing an 85-page report mainly concerning issues relating to Imperial Airways.

Sir Samuel Instone
On 9 November 1937 an unexpected tragedy befell the industry when the great shipping and aviation entrepreneur, Sir Samuel Instone, died in the London Clinic after what should have been recoverable surgery.

Instone was born in 1878, one of three brothers, the others being Theodore and Alfred. After being educated at Tunbridge Wells and Boulogne, Samuel started working in shipping at the age of fifteen. After marrying in 1910, he had started S Instone and Co Ltd in Cardiff, and mainly traded coal between Cardiff, London and Antwerp. He bought the former site of the Thames Iron Works at Bow Creek on the River Thames and established the Instone Wharf to allow easier transference of cargo from his ships directly on to the railways. The three brothers formed a private airline in 1919 to overcome delays caused to their ships when their bills of lading between ports had taken too long to arrive. The airline also carried staff between Cardiff, Hounslow and Paris and in 1920 the London-Paris service became a public service under the name of The Instone Air Line. In 1924 Instone was one of the original companies that merged to form Imperial Airways and Samuel remained on the board until his unexpected death.

S Instone & Co Ltd went public in 1921 with a nominal capital of £500,000 (£300,000 issued). Samuel became chairman of the Askern Coal and Iron Company Ltd and of the Bedwas Navigation Colliery Company where he came into conflict with the mining unions. After the failed general strike of 1926 his cost controls and modern methods of mining led to further disputes with the miners and some of his employees labelled him 'one of the bloodsucking rich.' Running disputes with the South Wales Miners' Federation continued until the year before his death causing his business to incur more than £1m in debts. Despite this, Samuel established a model housing estate in Yorkshire known as Instonville for his workers and contrary to the opinions of some of those he had been in conflict with, he had great sympathy for the miners, but this did not stop him winning an action for libel against the president of the Miners' Federation of Great Britain, Herbert Smith.

Despite being strong-minded, Instone was generally well liked. He was a Lieutenant of the City of London and a liveryman of the Worshipful Company of Loriners and knighted in 1921. He was a strong advocate of modern transport and in addition to his interests in shipping and aviation, he started one of the first waterbus services to operate on the Thames. He and his wife, Alice Maud Lieberman, had five daughters and they lived in central London. Instone was buried on 10 November at the Jewish Cemetery in Willesden, North West London.

The British Airline Pilots Association
There was renewed unrest within the ranks at Imperial Airways after several pilots had been dismissed. The newly formed British Airline Pilots Association (BALPA) that was acting in a role of quasi-trade union, met on 9 October to decide what action to take. It was fortunate for them they had the Unionist Member of Parliament, Robert Perkins (Stroud) to fight their corner. On 28 October he stood up in the Commons to proclaim his concerns over the way Imperial Airways had

been treating its pilots. One of the issues related to the company's refusal to accept BALPA's rights to collective bargaining. The case relating to the dismissal of Capt Wilson was raised. Wilson had allegedly been dismissed, without any reason given, two years after he had crashed *City of Khartoum* in the Mediterranean. The politician accused Imperial Airways of sacking him because he had dared to '… *open his mouth too wide when the inquiry took place.*' Concern was also shown over the firing of Captains Rogers and Lane Burslem who had both signed a letter in support of cancelling the winter services to Budapest over their concerns that the aircraft were not suitably equipped. Perkins continued '*This is victimisation. Imperial Airways has done everything to break the Association and refuses to recognise it or discuss with pilots at all. Another grievance is the question of wages: while director's fees have been increased, they have cut pilot's wages.*' He added that the majority of Imperial Airways pilots were dissatisfied with the equipment being provided because it was not good enough. This included the fact that blind-landing equipment had been fitted to only a few machines; few had de-icing facilities and: '*… very few, if any, with a spare wireless set.*' He ended his tirade: '*Finally machines on the London-Paris route are obsolete and certain others on European routes are definitely unsuitable for winter service. We have no alternative but to ask for an impartial inquiry into the whole position of pilots engaged by Imperial Airways, and in fact into the whole organisation.*'

Although *Albatross* (G-AEVV) had been successfully demonstrated during May, after lengthy manufacturing delays, Imperial Airways eventually placed an order for three DH91 Albatross airliners; G-AFDI *Frobisher*, G-AFDJ *Falcon* and G-AFDK *Fortuna* on the same day as the company AGM. It was revealed that profits had increased by £24,000 to £164,735. This announcement served to worsen the mood of the pilots and only succeeded in rubbing salt still deeper into their wounds when they also learnt that the directors had awarded themselves £5,000 in additional fees on top of the £12,000 previously allocated. Substantial increases totalling £42,126 had also been allocated by the company to increase the shareholder's dividends to 7% plus a further bonus of 2%. The pilots had good cause to be disgruntled considering that many were still expected to fly aircraft that were long out of date. There was also animosity in some public quarters from those that believed it was immoral to pay dividends to shareholders of any company that was receiving funding from the Treasury.

Robert Perkins was still not through with his condemnation. On 17 November he delivered a further assault in Parliament against the Air Ministry in what *The Times* described as '*a really thrilling debate.*' This time Perkins cast his concern over issues such as safety in the air, the stranglehold of the railways over internal air transport and the lack of blind-approach equipment. He criticised how two major financial corporations, Whitehall Securities and d'Erlanger, had control over the domestic airlines, suggesting that nationalisation might have been a better alternative. He argued that both Imperial Airways and British Airways were public utility companies that were heavily subsidised by the State. He went on to say: '*Both ran services to Paris and were faced with the Gilbertian situation of subsidising two lines to compete in cutting each other's throats on the same route. British Airways, the chosen instrument of the Government desired to buy more aeroplanes, but could not get them and had to buy both German and American machines.*' Perkins now on a roll turned his attention to the Government for: '… *encouraging the creation of municipal aerodromes and a number have been built at considerable cost to the ratepayers. They had however proved to be nothing more than white elephants, having involved losses varying from £2,800 to £20,000. There was complete stagnation in that matter; the Air Ministry sat back in their chairs with arms folded and did nothing to help those aerodromes. Nothing has been done or would be done in the near future for a creation of an adequate airport for London.*' The House cheered when he added: '*Whatever was spent on Croydon aerodrome he did not believe that it could ever be made a first class airport.*' Perkins attacked safety: '*They* (Imperial Airways) *were not even the safest line. So far this year the German Luft Hansa had flown more mileage and lost one passenger*[1] *compared with the eleven fatalities of Imperial Airways.*'

Perkins vehement attack was probably warranted and he could muster no better ally than Moore-Brabazon, who praised his colleague's courage. Moore-Brabazon remarked that previously any criticism against Imperial Airways had been seen as an attack on the Government and he appreciated that it was operating in difficult times and should not be seen as a '*wicked organisation*' and he hoped that an inquiry would take aviation away from party politics. This prompted Lt. Col Muirhead to respond by calling for a public inquiry to admit that '*all was not well*' but went on to say '… *the idea of a public inquiry might be attractive … but the need for it must be ascertained first. The field has recently been covered by the Gorell Committee in 1934 and the Maybury Committee in 1936.*' Muirhead followed up by confirming that the Secretary of State would discuss with the Government directors on the Imperial Airways board their system for dealing with staff grievances although he added the Government would not extend this to dictating to the company whether or not it should recognise a particular union.

The heated exchanges in Parliament led to the resignation of Air Vice Marshal Sir Tom Webb-Brown who had been Staff Manager at Imperial Airways for four years. R E Richardson replaced him and Brackley continued as Air Superintendent, although his efforts to liaise with the pilots was made more difficult after Perkins compared Croydon to a '*second rate Balkan State*' a statement that prompted one pilot to wear a bulging skirt and green hat in place of his company uniform.

The situation in Parliament remained heated. On 24 November the Under-Secretary had little option other than to announce the formation of a committee to investigate the allegations against Imperial Airways. The committee was headed by two Permanent Secretaries, Lord Cadman and W W Burkett, Assistant Director of the Air Ministry, who conducted witness interviews *in camera*. The airline produced a defence statement, but Woods Humphery and the board concluded that the Cadman Committee had really been formed more to investigate a merger between Imperial Airways and British Airways than to concern itself with the company's disputes with BALPA.

The attacks made by Perkins may have been quite timely and the remarks he made during November 1937 coincided with the cancellation of many flights from Croydon and several more from the Continent had to be turned back because they were unable to land. During murky weather on the night of 26 November events reached boiling point at Croydon when a Lufthansa Junkers Ju 52 carrying freight crashed into the KLM hangar and another parked Lufthansa Junkers before catching fire killing the three crew members.

It seemed to be a regular occurrence for a year-end to be marred by an Imperial Airways tragedy. 1937 was no different. On 5 December, Capt R P Mollard was in command of the Empire flying boat, *Cygnus* (G-ADUZ), that was returning to the UK from Australia and India when it crashed during a morning take-off at Brindisi. The likely cause of the accident was put down to Mollard incorrectly setting the flaps to a fully down position. This caused the flying boat to bounce several times on the water before 'nosing in' causing the bow to collapse. The aircraft subsequently sank and the steward, Frederick Lawrence Stoppani, and one passenger were drowned. Six passengers (among them Air Marshall Sir John Salmond, a Government director of Imperial Airways) were injured, one seriously and the five crew members were also hurt. Imperial Airways was later censored in the official inquiry for failing to have sufficient push-out windows and escape hatches which only added fuel to the fire from the critics who were increasingly considering the airline to be unsafe.

THE THADA, JODHPUR

LAMBERT & BUTLER'S CIGARETTES

---

[1] There had been several fatalities although these are all believed to have involved crew members: On 12 March 1937 a Lufthansa Heinkel He 111V2 (D-ALIX) crashed into a swamp near Bathurst, Gambia killing 4; on 25 May a Heinkel He70 (D-UXUV) crashed on take-off at Stuttgart killing 4; On 13 August a Boeing 247 (D-AKIN) crashed at Hanover with no fatalities and soon after Perkins' speech, a Junkers JU52/3M (D-AGAV) crashed into a hangar at Croydon killing 3 crew.

CHAPTER SIXTEEN

NEW MONOPLANES AND THE CADMAN REPORT
1938

THE fatal accident involving a flying boat that marred the end of 1937 was followed at the start of 1938 by news of another major tragedy although this time there was no British involvement. The incident involved the Pan American Airways flying boat *Samoan Clipper* (NC16734). The Sikorsky S.42B was being flown by the company's most eminent skipper, Edwin C Musick, who had greeted Capt Burgess of Imperial Airways when he arrived at Auckland in *Centaurus* at the end of 1937. The big American flying boat had left Honolulu to cross the Pacific on 9 January and had arrived in Samoa the following day where the crew rested for the night. The next morning, the Clipper took-off at 05.37 hrs from Pago Pago bound once more for New Zealand. The flight time was scheduled for 18 hours and the aircraft carried 2,300 gallons of fuel, enough to complete the long journey. An hour later Musick radioed that an oil leak in the number four engine had necessitated a return to Pago Pago. At 07.08 hrs the crew radioed again to say that the engine had been shut down and that fuel had been dumped to reduce weight in preparation for a three-engine landing. The crew called again to say that more fuel would be dumped and for safety radio silence would be maintained until after this had been completed. At 09.07 hrs a concerned radio operator, having heard nothing further from the Clipper decided to break silence, but failed to gain any response. Shortly after, a navy aircraft reported seeing an oil slick 12½ miles from Pago Pago along with some debris and it soon became obvious that there had been a major accident. A witness reported seeing the aircraft jettisoning fuel from both wings as it flew to the west of Pago Pago at around 08.35 hrs. The flying boat had appeared to descend abruptly and there was a flash followed by an explosion. The most probable cause of the accident had been that the fuel being jettisoned had ignited causing a massive explosion that destroyed the aircraft killing all seven of the crew.

The accident was a devastating blow to Pan American Airways who had flown more than 2,000 passengers over more than 1,300,000 miles in their flying boats without incident. Musick had been a superb flyer, a stickler for safety, and he was an acclaimed expert on flying boats. He was a friend of Lankester Parker who, with his assistant Harold Piper, conducted the first flight of the complete Mayo Composite on 20 January. The dreadful fate of Ed Musick and his crew nine days earlier must have been on the test pilot's mind as he climbed aboard the Mayo composite. Parker had kept himself busy; during the course of the day he had carried out the first in-flight refuelling test by flying the Imperial Airways C-class flying boat *Cambria* (G-ADUV) that linked with the Armstrong Whitworth AW 23 (K3585) above Southampton Water. The twin-engine former bomber, flown by Geoffrey Tyson, had been converted to an in-flight tanker and this was used to transfer up to 2,300 gallons of petrol to *Cambria*, the flying boat previously flown on the transatlantic experiments. With the initial flight completed this paved the way for a series of all-weather refuelling flights that were conducted under the direction of Sir Alan Cobham.

On 24 January, the long overdue prototype Armstrong Whitworth AW 27 *Ensign* (G-ADSR) finally made an appearance and was flown by C R Turner-Hughes and Eric Greenwood at Hamble. Brackley had motored down the day before, hoping to witness the first flight, but the aircraft was still not ready and he could only watch as it was towed across the road from the workshops to the apron. Brackley journeyed on to Southampton and Hythe where he inspected the flying boat facilities before returning to his office and missing the airliner's brief maiden flight the following day. Turner-Hughes and Greenwood conducted four ground run trials to gain a feel of the controls and to test the brakes before a brief 15-minute flight. There were some problems with the rudder control that required the combined strength of both pilots to move, otherwise the flight went well. Two days later the control had been adjusted allowing Turner-Hughes to fly the aircraft to Baginton (Coventry) where the manufacturer's tests were conducted.

During a flight on 8 March there was concern when all four engines stopped simultaneously. Turner-Hughes had fortune on his side because the failure occurred at sufficient altitude to permit him to glide the heavy aircraft to a safe dead-stick landing at RAF Bicester. After investigation the cause of the engine stoppage was linked to the incorrectly set fuel cocks; ironically the same thing that had occurred previously when *Atalanta* was being tested. Another obstacle the engineers had to overcome was a strange phenomenon that caused the elevator controls to lock while flying at high altitudes. After considerable brainstorming it was discovered that the fuselage of the *Ensign* shrank slightly when the aircraft operated in the low temperatures common at high altitude and this had caused the control wires to the rudder to become slack and to become trapped. This was soon cured and the aircraft went to Martlesham Heath for certification. After a take-off run of 350 yards, with an all-up-weight of 49,000 lbs

A Sikorsky S.42 flying boat of the type operated by Pan American.

Rudder

Fin

Fixed Aerial

Starbo

Tailplane

Lavatory for Coupé

International
Registration Marking

Coupé for 4 passengers

Coupé Entrance Door

Elevator

G-A

Metal Fuselage

Aft Cabin with accommodation
for 12 passengers

Ensign AIR LINER
FOR EUROPEAN SERVICES

the climb out was considered slow and it took a minute to reach 500 feet, not helped by the drag being caused by the undercarriage that took 1½ minutes to retract. Although the aircraft reached 200 mph in level flight, it could only remain at that level with two engines shut down and with the flaps and undercarriage fully retracted. In an attempt to improve the climbing ability, larger propellers were fitted but with little success. As a result the RAF pilots at Martlesham concluded that the aircraft was underpowered although they had been impressed by the controls and handling. There had also been occasions during certification when an engine had cut out, once on take-off, caused by oil clogging problems. The aircraft needed a whole string of minor modifications, but after taking three months for these to be carried out, at the end of June certification was granted. By the time *Ensign* was flown to Croydon during July for a short flight to Paris it was already two years behind the original delivery date. There were further delays when the aircraft had to be returned to Coventry for more modifications and *Ensign* did not go into service with Imperial Airways until October and then only on the London–Paris route.

On 27 January Brackley flew the second new aircraft; the DH91 *Albatross* (Frobisher Class), at Hatfield for an hour with Geoffrey de Havilland Jnr and Capt Butler. He reported that the sleek, four-engine airliner created by Arthur Hagg had '*Very impressive handling performance.*' The new airliner had the accolade of being the fastest commercial aircraft of the period, but it was built of wood during a time when other

designers were already using metal. The design was deceptive and the wooden construction's weakness was discovered when one of the test aircraft made a heavy landing and split in two. The same thing happened to a second aircraft after it had entered service with Imperial Airways. On a further occasion during testing at Hatfield, Geoffrey de Havilland experienced problems with the undercarriage operating system forcing him to make a belly-landing inflicting extensive damage to the propellers, engine nacelles and undersides of the wings. There was further concern for Imperial Airways when rumours spread that British Airways was also to receive the *Albatross* although this proved to be unfounded.

The Cadman Report

On 8 February the Cadman Committee presented a controversial report concerning all aspects of civil and commercial aviation. It suggested that the State subsidy to civil aviation must be doubled immediately from £1.5m to £3m. Surprisingly, for once, the Government complied and by the time the next Air Estimates were due, the money had been made available. Initially £2,925,500 was allocated from the total of £73,500,000 but this subsidy was later increased to the full £3m by 16 April.

The 85-page Cadman Report contained little that was not already known: '*There is not today a medium sized airliner of British construction comparable to the leading foreign types. Foreign manufacturers, American in particular, dominate the European market.*'

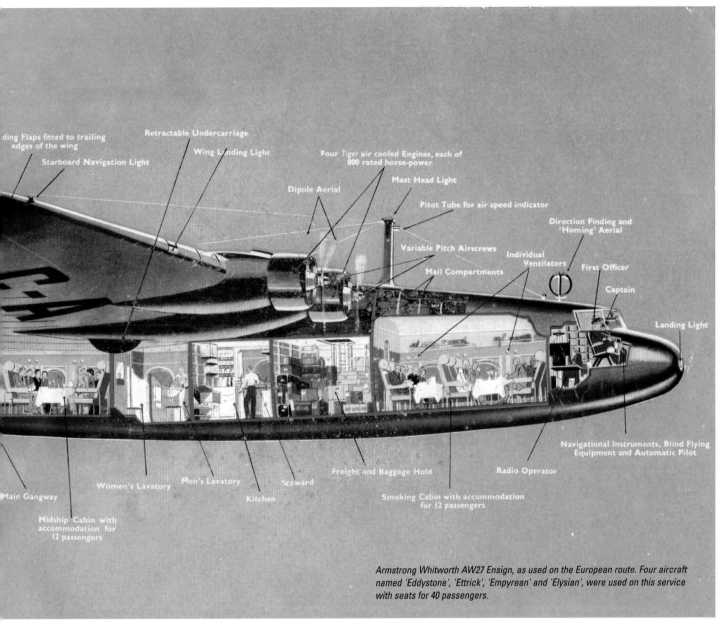

Armstrong Whitworth AW27 Ensign, as used on the European route. Four aircraft named 'Eddystone', 'Ettrick', 'Empyrean' and 'Elysian', were used on this service with seats for 40 passengers.

In a specific referral in the report, Imperial Airways and British Airways were targeted:' … *Management has been defective … intolerant of suggestion, unyielding in negotiation. Air services to the West Indies and across the Pacific are an uncontested monopoly of an American Company.'* The report recommended that the services operated between the United Kingdom and mainland Europe needed to be expanded and there was criticism for the way the Government had subsidised two companies that were competing with each other on the same overseas route. They suggested that British Airways should be responsible for developing the European services, leaving Imperial Airways to concentrate on the Empire routes.

The repercussions of the report were such that on 11 November the Government responded by announcing its intention to encourage a merger of the two chosen instruments to form a single State-financed corporation. This led to the eventual formation of the British Overseas Airways Corporation (BOAC) that became operational on 1 April 1940. By then much of Europe was at war and many of the objects of the new corporation had to be put on hold.

The Cadman Committee was particularly scathing about the way Imperial Airways was being run. This ultimately led to the resignation of George Woods Humphery as managing director. The report also mentioned the need for the company to accept collective representation and for improvements in the personal contact between employer and employees. However, Imperial Airways adamantly refused to accept any interference from BALPA. The Government began investigating a replacement chairman for the company, someone who would be full-

time, and initially offered the position to its prime candidate, Air Marshal Sir John Salmond, who was already a board member. Salmond declined the invitation and so too did the Government's second choice, Sir John Anderson. Instead the position was offered to the director-general of the British Broadcasting Corporation (BBC), Sir John Reith, who accepted. On 14 June, Sir Kingsley Wood announced in the Commons that Reith would replace Sir George Beharrel as chairman. At the same time Sir James Price, former deputy secretary of the Minister of Labour, was named as the new appointee to the board with the responsibility of taking care of Cadman's alleged wrongdoing by the airline's management. This proved to be the straw that broke the camel's back for Woods Humphery and although the board fought against his resignation his departure seemed inevitable. Burchall could offer only praise to his colleague: *'We have intense indignation at the campaign of calumny waged against the company and our chief for whom we have the respectful affection and loyalty. We know his immense drive, his vast ability and his everlasting energy. Under his guidance the finest commercial aviation service in the world has been produced.'*

Forty-eight-year-old Reith was not a popular appointment with everyone. He was regarded as a martinet by some and he had ruled with almost total autonomy during his long reign at the BBC where he had built his own kind of fiefdom. Arriving in 1927, he had established a public enterprise that was virtually free of any Government interference but had turned it into a highly regarded public service. Reith had worked with Woods Humphery previously when they both served their

A fine air-to-air publicity photograph of Armstrong Whitworth 27 Ensign, G-ADSR, 'Ensign' in 1938. (CAS)

Armstrong Whitworth 27 Ensign G-ADSY 'Empyrean', photographed in 1938. (CAS/Peter Clinton)

apprenticeships together. Reith was also best man at Woods Humphery's wedding and his father, the Rev J Reith, had officiated at the ceremony. But although they were friends, Reith concluded that the two men could never work together. Despite this, Wood Humphery must be applauded for remaining in his post long enough to initiate Reith into all aspects of his new role at Imperial Airways.

Woods Humphery's supporters believed he had been harshly targeted by the Cadman Committee who had levelled a great deal of criticism at him that was widely considered unjust. Imperial Airways responded to this attack by sending letters to its shareholders. The first of these, circulated on 10 March, included a copy of the Cadman Report. This was followed by a further communication distributed on 30 March that staunchly supported its managing director: '*Until the Cadman Report was published, neither your board nor Mr Woods Humphery had the least idea that Mr Woods Humphery had been charged with being 'intolerant of suggestion and unyielding in negotiation' and with 'taking a commercial view of his responsibilities that was too narrow'. The fact therefore is that Mr Woods Humphery has been condemned by the Committee without opportunity of saying a word in his defence*

on the matters in question. You will appreciate that these allegations are matters of vital importance to Mr Woods Humphery who has devoted himself so wholeheartedly to the interests of the company since its formation, first as general manager and later as managing director. The board desire to record their high appreciation of the part Mr Woods Humphery has played in the advancement of the company and of civil aviation generally.'

The company also refuted the allegations that obsolete aircraft were in use on the European routes. The letter to shareholders continued: '*... this was entirely beyond the company's control and expresses regret that, although evidence of the causes was laid before the Committee, no explanation was included in the report. There was no lack of foresight on the part of the board in this matter for 1934 an order was placed with an important British company for 12 large landplanes comparable in every way with the flying boats which are now so successfully operating the Empire routes. The first of these landplanes was due for delivery in September 1936, but in spite of the efforts made by the Air Ministry and your company not one of these has yet been delivered.*'

The company also publicly hit back at the report by claiming the Government had procrastinated in many matters. This included letters,

contracts and subsidies and that it had caused the Empire mail negotiations to drag on for four years and the proposals to use Langston Harbour[1] (Hampshire) as a base for the Empire flying boats for two years. The Captains Committee added its unanimous support of the company's management in a letter to Sir George Beharrell and added that in its opinion Woods Humphery had been singled out for unwarranted criticism.

On the issues discussed in the report that related to the worsening staff relationships at Imperial Airways, C G Grey penned his opinions in *The Aeroplane* and emphasised his view that the trouble had mainly been caused by the late Sir Eric Geddes: '*His principle, which may have brought him to his outstanding success in the material things of life, was to build up a system of almost inhuman mechanical efficiency. The one thing that is needed when you are dealing with such temperamental people as the pilots and the crews of the aeroplanes is the intimate personal touch. They need a dictator, but he must be ... a personal leader which Sir Eric Geddes was not. To the employees of Imperial Airways he was a machine to be feared rather than a human being to be loved and followed. Even many of those who admired him because of the kind of outward efficiency which he forced on to other people, could never bring themselves to regard him as a human being.*' Grey added that the Cadman Report was '... *the most sensible document that has yet been issued on civil aviation...* '

Grey also used his editorial sword in support of Woods Humphery: '*The best thing would be to make George Woods Humphery full time chairman and then find a couple of other full time directors. Quite definitely, his resignation would be the very worst thing that could happen to Imperial Airways and for British Civil Aviation. Besides being a good engineer, Woods Humphery was a competent pilot in the war and kept his licence until recently. Consequently he can talk to his pilots as one pilot to another and to his engineering staff as an engineer.*'

While furore surrounded the Cadman Report, the Secretary of State for Air, Lord Swinton, resigned during May and was replaced by Sir Kingsley Wood, a man with no experience of aviation. Harold Balfour, a director of British Airways, resigned his position to become Under Secretary of State for Air. Over the next six months the new broom Wood, and his staff, followed the proposals of Cadman by conducting negotiations with the airlines in an attempt to agree a

An Armstrong Whitworth Ensign being worked on at Croydon.
(CAS/Robert Pearson Brown)

favourable share price for the Treasury with the intention to nationalise the companies as a single entity. Imperial Airways settled on 32s 9d (approx £1.63); 2s 9d (13p); more than the share value on the Stock Exchange.

Aside from the upheaval within the company caused by the Cadman Report that had led to the well publicised resignation of Woods Humphery on 30 June, normal operations continued unhindered. On 6 February, following many months of delays, the first separation of the Short-Mayo composite took place over Rochester. There had been some communications problems between the two aircraft previously and the upper component had also experienced difficulties with the trim indicator. This had implied the correct speed and altitude settings had been attained when, in reality, this was not the case causing previous separations to be cancelled. On another occasion, the indicator system had been working correctly but the air had been too turbulent for a separation to take place. When the conditions had finally become favourable, *Mercury* was loaded to about 14,500 lb. At a height of around 700 feet and with the speed at 110 knots, the levers

---

[1.] Langston Harbour was considered as an alternative flying-boat base but subsequently dismissed

Armstrong Whitworth 27 Ensign, G-ADSR, 'Ensign'.

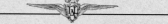

Cockpit view of a DH91 'Frobisher' Class Albatross in 1938. (Larry Williamson - CAS)

Interior of DH91 'Frobisher' in 1938.(CAS)

A superb air-to-air publicity photograph showing the sleek lines of the prototype E2 all-wood DH91 Frobisher Class Albatross. Originally built as a fast mail plane (two were built - 'Faraday' and 'Franklin'), five passenger versions were built for Imperial Airways carrying 22 passengers, and used on the routes from Croydon to Paris, Brussels and Zurich. These five were named 'Frobisher' , 'Falcon' , 'Fortuna', 'Fingal' and 'Fiona'. (CAS)

De Havilland DH91 Albatross
Frobisher class G-AFDI
'Frobisher' in front of the
control tower at Croydon in
1938. This aircraft was
destroyed on the ground during
a Luftwaffe air attack on
Whitchurch Airport on 20
December 1940. The DH 91s
held the possible distinction of
being the only aircraft in the
fleet to carry the famous
speedbird emblem on the
fuselage. All other uses were
restricted to sales literature.
(CAS)

De Havilland DH91 Frobisher
class – G-AFDL 'Fingal' being
serviced in 1938. This aircraft
was destroyed in a crash-
landing near Pucklechurch
in Gloucestershire on
6 October 1940.
(CAS/Peter Clinton)

were pulled to separate the two aircraft. Parker, who was flying *Maia,* claimed as the separation occurred, it had felt like his aircraft had released a heavy bomb. Piper meanwhile had to ensure that he had *Mercury* fully under control to prevent the upper component from climbing too abruptly. Apart from the safety precautions, the separation had gone extremely well. *Maia* returned to land on the Medway while Piper continued some high speed runs in *Mercury* before also landing on the river. A series of further tests followed and the weight of *Mercury* was gradually increased until it reached a maximum 21,000 lb but there was considerable public criticism caused by the need to dump fuel from the payload of *Mercury* when too much remained to make a safe landing.

On 17 February the Empire flying boat, *Coogee* (G-AEUG), left Southampton for the final survey flight to India and Singapore with Capt Alger in command. Six days later the Empire Air Mail service was extended to Egypt, Palestine, India, Burma, Ceylon and Malaya carrying the first un-surcharged air mail. *Centurion* (G-ADVE) later accompanied the Qantas C-Class *Coolangatta* (VH-ABB) commanded by Capt Allan for the aircraft's delivery flight to Australia. Both aircraft arrived at Karachi on 27 February before the Qantas crew continued to Australia via Singapore. From 10 April, Imperial Airways had cut the flying time to Karachi to just 3 days; the UK to Singapore to 5½ days and UK-Sydney to 9½ days. Capt J S Shepherd operated the first accelerated service for Imperial Airways in *Centaurus* (G-ADUT). Rapid progress had been made to cut journey times to distant parts of the British Empire. The C-Class flying boats had also shortened the UK-South Africa journey time from more than 6 to 4½ days with Kisumu reached in just 3 days.

Reith Arrives

By the start of summer things at Airways House were still suffering in the wake of the Cadman Report. Reith took up his appointment in June but he was not convinced he had done the right thing. There was still plenty of ill-feeling among the staff over the treatment of Woods Humphery and Reith was far from impressed by the conditions confronting him at Victoria. His biography *Into the Wind*, published in 1949, relates his feelings: '*I was brought to the door of an old furniture depository behind Victoria Station. It was Imperial Airways – a plate on the wall said so. Inside were some counters, luggage on the floor, a few people standing about – a booking office evidently. I enquired of a young man behind one of the counters where the Head Office was. He pointed to a dark and narrow staircase. "Up there" he said. The managing director's office "second floor" he thought. Having ascended thither I went along a passage, also dark and narrow, between wooden partitions, peering at the doors and wondering which to try first. Here it was – a bit of paper with "managing director" written upon it. From Broadcasting House to this!'*

Subsidies to the internal airlines

On 18 May the Secretary of State for Air announced that £100,000 of the £3m allocated in the Air Estimates to civil aviation would be used to assist the progress of the internal airlines. The subsidy was made on the proviso that the recipient companies should endeavour to operate on a paying basis during the five year period that the subsidy would operate. On 12 December the Government published a White Paper that named the companies that would be subsidised. The money was split between eleven operators; each was awarded an upward limit of £15,000 (approximately £706,000 today) that was paid on approved services at a rate of 6d (2½p) per capacity-ton-mile. This subsidy, due to commence on 1 January 1939, was set to reduce by ½d a year to 4d by the fifth year. The rules required the airlines to employ British aircraft, equipment and staff and a *'suitable proportion'* of staff had to be present or past members of either the Air Force Reserve or the Auxiliary Air Force. The following selected subsidised companies were given provisional licenses on the approved routes by the Air Transport Licensing Authority on 21 October (from 1 November it became an offence to operate an air service within the United Kingdom without a license):

- Allied Airways (Gander Dower) Limited: Aberdeen-Thurso; Thurso-Kirkwall; Thurso-Stromness
- British American Air Services Ltd: Heston to 30 destinations connected with race meetings
- Channel Air Ferries Ltd: Lands End-St Mary's (Scilly Isles)

- Isle of Man Air Services Ltd: Manchester-Isle of Man; Liverpool-Isle of Man; Liverpool-Manchester; Belfast-Isle of Man; Carlisle-Isle of Man
- Jersey Airways Ltd: Southampton-Jersey; Heston-Jersey
- Lundy and Atlantic Coast Air Lines Ltd: Barnstaple-Lundy
- Norman Edgar (Western Airways) Ltd: Weston-Super-Mare-Cardiff; Weston-Super-Mare-Swansea
- North Eastern Airways Ltd: Croydon-Perth; Croydon-Glasgow; Hull-Doncaster; Grimsby-Hull
- Portsmouth, Southsea and Isle of Wight Aviation Ltd: Portsmouth-Ryde; Bournemouth-Ryde; Portsmouth-Lea; Southampton-Ryde
- Railway Air Services Ltd; Croydon-Glasgow; Glasgow-Belfast
- Scottish Airways Ltd: Inverness-Shetland; Kirkwall-Longhope, Westray, North Ronaldsay, Sanday, Stronsay and Wick
- Western Isles Airways Ltd: Glasgow-Islay; Glasgow-North Uist

The domestic companies were now anxious to get their 'houses' in order to comply with the subsidy regulations. On 28 February Jersey Airways introduced an on demand stop at Portsmouth as part of their Jersey-London (Heston) service. This was set up as a direct result of the Southern Railway electrification between Waterloo and Portsmouth that had occurred the previous year. By 28 May Portsmouth had become a regular port of call with some services flown only between Jersey and Portsmouth during the summer. The airline embarked on a pooled service with Air France between Jersey and Dinard on 9 August that was operated by each company twice-weekly using the DH86s of Jersey Air Lines and Wibault Penhoet 282/283 three-engined monoplanes of the French company. This was in addition to the summer Air France Paris-Dinard-Jersey service that began a month earlier. Wrightways also began flying to France after starting a weekend, on demand, Croydon-Le Touquet service. North of the border, Scottish Airways inaugurated a new route between Renfrew-Perth-Inverness-Wick-Kirkwall and Lerwick (Sumburgh) that commenced on 26 April.

The European airlines were also increasing their services to the UK. The Italian company Avio Linee Italiane began flying to Croydon on 1 June as an extension to its Venice-Milan-Turin-Paris service using Fiat G 18V aircraft. This was the first time that an Italian airline had flown a regular service into Britain. On 25 June, Deutsche Lufthansa began operating its impressive Focke-Wulf Fw 200 *Condor* aircraft on an irregular basis from Berlin. The type was also chosen by the Danish company DDL Danish Air Lines when it made the inaugural flight to Croydon with *Dania* (OY-DAM) to begin a regular service from Copenhagen (via Hamburg) on 28 July.

As the domestic airlines began to establish routes, it was inevitable that casualties would occur among those weaker companies which were unable to comply with the licensing requirements and be forced out of business. The regulations that came into force during late autumn were preliminary to the full licence application hearings that began in December. On 20 June a company called the Straight Corporation (Southern Airways) started flying between Ipswich and Clacton and is believed to have operated a Short Scion (G-ADDV), but this was brief and ceased in September. On 26 July the same company attempted to operate between Ramsgate and Ilford (Essex), an odd choice of route that also only lasted until September. However, during October the company acquired control of the Norman Edgar (Western Airways) company and renamed it Western Airways Limited. On 27 July, Norman Edgar had extended their Weston-Super-Mare to Cardiff service to Swansea.

Railway Air Services began a local Shoreham-Ryde-Southampton service on 7 March using the DH Dragon (G-ADDI) that had been renamed, *Island Maid.* On 2 May a Liverpool-Glasgow service was introduced and on the same day the company transferred its Belfast operations from Newtownards to Sydenham's Harbour Airport, a new facility that Mrs Neville Chamberlain had opened on 26 March. RAS aircraft were used on the Bristol-Cardiff-Plymouth service from 8 August, but by 11 September the company ceased operating all West Country and South of England services. On 5 December a new company, Great Western and Southern Air Lines Ltd, was formed with a capital of £100,000 split between British and Foreign Aviation (50%), Great Western Railway (25%) and Southern Railway (25%). The

A Lockheed Electra L-10 of British Airways. (CAS)

company took over some of the services previously operated by RAS and bought its DH89s (G-ACPP and G-ACPR) together with the Dragon (G-ADDI). Great Western and Southern also took over the operations of Channel Air Ferries although services continued under the name of the original company until 24 March 1939. In June, a twice weekly international Croydon-Luxembourg service was added that was largely employed to carry the staff and gramophone records for Radio Luxembourg that had been founded in 1933. During the year, Channel Air Services also amended several of its routes. The Scilly-Penzance service was extended to Plymouth and the Brighton-Bembridge-Bournemouth service was amended to Croydon-Brighton-Bembridge-Bournemouth-Bristol-Cardiff. A summer on demand service was also operated between Heston-Croydon and Bembridge and between London, Brighton and Le Touquet.

During April, North Eastern Airways announced they would fly between Newcastle and Glasgow in connection with the Empire Exhibition held in the Scottish city. Flights were continued until October when the company replaced it with a Doncaster-Glasgow service via Edinburgh. By 3 October they had started southbound-only mail flights between Perth, Newcastle, Yeadon (Leeds and Bradford), Doncaster and London. Mail from Dundee was loaded at Perth and Edinburgh and at Newcastle, but the intricacies of the contract only permitted cargo to be offloaded at Newcastle and Croydon. The DH89 (G-AFEP) was operated from Perth and an Airspeed Envoy from Doncaster. During December the company informed RAS of its intention to re-organise its routes to bring them in line with the proposals formerly made in the Maybury Report. It also intended to form a new company that it called Co-ordinated Internal Air Lines Ltd and an application in this name was lodged with the Air Transport Licensing Authority to operate existing services with RAS, but this was later withdrawn and things continued as they were.

A new company called International Air Freight of Pall Mall was registered in January 1937 as a cargo-only airline and managed by a group of prominent businessmen, among them Daniel Metz (formerly UK manager of Citroen) as managing director, Capt W Lawrence Hope (formerly founder of Air Taxis), W I Stephenson (chairman of F W Woolworth), Sir Louis Sterling (managing director of HMV), Sir Percival Perry (chairman, Ford Motor Company) and Malcolm McAlpine (head of Sir Robert McAlpine). The company aimed to deliver goods direct to customers' doors combining the use of aircraft with a fleet of vans. It invested in a fleet of four American-built Curtiss

T-32 Condor biplanes (G-AEWD, G-AEWE, G-AEWF and G-AEZE) that had formerly been supplied to Eastern Air Transport. These were used by International Air Freight to carry cargo between Croydon and Amsterdam with a further route added between Croydon and Brussels. The company became the first regular non-passenger carrying airline to be awarded a GPO mail contract and it is believed that it also sub-contracted some of its freight work to British Airways. There is some confusion over when the company began, but conflicting reports suggest that Amsterdam was first flown on 27 March 1938 and Brussels on 3 May of the same year. There is speculation that the company had planned to develop and build its own aircraft but, despite the heavyweight board members, services were short-lived and it is believed that this ambitious company ceased operations by 20 September.

On 29 May British Airways had transferred most of its operations from Croydon and Gatwick to its next new base at Heston, although its night mail flights continued to operate from Croydon. In keeping with the findings of the Cadman Report, an agreement had been made with the Air Ministry on 24 March to manage and survey proposed routes between the United Kingdom and South America via West Africa. By 11 June the first ground survey had began on the Natal-Buenos Aires sector followed by the initial survey flights over the first sector of the proposed routes. These began on 7 October when two Lockheed 14s departed from Heston for Lisbon (Cintra) piloted by Capts V E Flowerday and E G L Robinson. One flight made the journey non-stop while the second made an intermediary landing at Bordeaux with Clive Pearson and the other Whitehall company directors on board. A further non-stop flight was made on 25 October and another between Lisbon and Seville occurred two days later. On 28 December Flowerday commanded the Lockheed 14 that left for Bathurst (Gambia) that reached Lisbon during the same day. It continued to Casablanca and Agadir on the second day and Dakar-Bathurst the next. Despite the good intentions, political problems hampered any progress and the Lockheed 14's limited range was also a concern particularly as the Spanish authorities had refused to provide landing rights because of the civil war, preventing the service from making a start.

Across the Atlantic

On 20-21 July the first heavier than air commercial crossing of the Atlantic was flown by Capt Donald C T Bennett (later known as 'Pathfinder Bennett' of the RAF) in the Short S20 floatplane *Mercury* (G-ADHJ). In the seat behind Bennett on this flight, sat radio officer

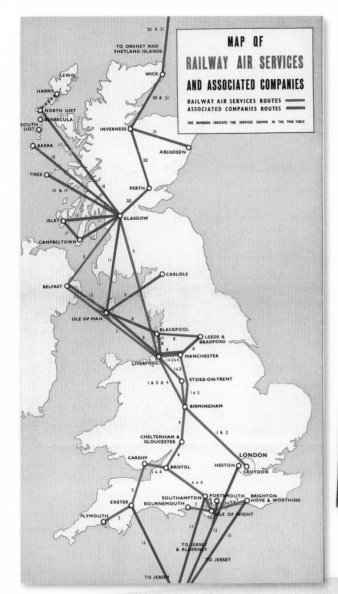

MAP OF
RAILWAY AIR SERVICES
AND ASSOCIATED COMPANIES

RAILWAY AIR SERVICES ROUTES ═══
ASSOCIATED COMPANIES ROUTES ═══

THE NUMBERS INDICATE THE SERVICES SHOWN IN THE TIME TABLE

A Railway Air Services route timetable and fares and freight rates tariff from 1938.

FARES AND FREIGHT RATES

FARES AND FREIGHT RATES—continued

NOTES:—

a—By Jersey Airways Ltd. between Southampton and Jersey.
b—By Portsmouth, Southsea and Isle of Wight Aviation Ltd. to and from Ryde.
c—By Isle of Man Air Services Ltd.
d—By Scottish Airways Ltd.
(d)—Excess baggage rate only.
*—Excess baggage only; must be rebooked at Southampton. Free allowance, 25 lbs.
**—Excess baggage only; must be rebooked at Ryde. Free allowance, 25 lbs.
†—Excess baggage rates see Jersey Airways publications.
††—Fares as for Glasgow/North Uist, plus 30/- in each direction—passengers are carried on charter basis to and from North Uist.

DAY EXCURSION tickets are issued as indicated below (service permitting) for return the same day.
A—Daily.   D—Tuesdays, Wednesdays, Thursdays and Sundays.

MID-WEEK FARES.
M—Mid-week fares, available outward on Tuesday, Wednesday or Thursday only, and for return on any Tuesday, Wednesday or Thursday within one month from date of outward journey. Passengers may return on any day within three months on payment of the difference between the mid-week return and the ordinary return fare.

HOLIDAY TICKETS.
H—Jersey Airways Ltd. issue, at the fares indicated, holiday tickets available outward on Wednesday, Thursday or Friday, for return any day up to and including Monday fortnight after date of outward journey excepting Saturdays in July and August.

CHILDREN under three years of age and not occupying a separate seat, carried free. Three years of age and under seven, and younger children occupying a seat, half fare. Seven years and under fourteen, two-thirds fare. Fourteen years of age and over, full fare.

FREIGHT.

Freight will be accepted (at Owner's Risk) at any Air Office of departure for conveyance to an Air Office of arrival at the rates per lb. shown. R.A.S. minimum charge per consignment is 1/6. Freight will also be accepted for delivery to consignee after air conveyance, and for transit, partly by air and partly by rail. Particulars on application.

Livestock (suitably crated) will be accepted at Air Freight rates plus 50 per cent. Minimum charge, 2/4. Details of the arrangements for the conveyance of livestock by Jersey Airways and Scottish Airways may be had on application to those Companies.

BAGGAGE.

Each passenger is allowed 25 lbs. of personal baggage free of charge. No free baggage is allowed to children travelling at reduced fares or travelling free. Baggage in excess of the free allowance—Air Freight rates. (Minimum charge not made.)

Through booked passengers to and from the Continent are allowed 15 kgs. (33 lbs.) baggage free.

IMPORTANT INFORMATION
FOR PASSENGERS

The 24-HOUR CLOCK system is used in this time-table

[Dense passenger information text including sections on:]

1. TERMS AND CONDITIONS OF CARRIAGE.
2. ALTERATIONS.
3. CONNEXIONS.
4. PASSPORTS.

TICKET REGULATIONS

5. FARES.
6. RETURN TICKETS.
7. CHILDREN.
8. RESERVATIONS.
9. CANCELLATION.
10. INTERCHANGEABILITY OF TICKETS.

BAGGAGE INFORMATION

11. BAGGAGE ALLOWANCE.
12. BAGGAGE.

INFORMATION (continued)

13. EXCESS BAGGAGE.
14. ADVANCE BAGGAGE.
15. LABELLING OF BAGGAGE.

SURFACE TRANSPORT

16. TRANSPORT BETWEEN AIR PORT AND TOWN.
17. DEPARTURE.

GENERAL INFORMATION

18. MEALS ON BOARD THE AIR LINER.
19. NIGHT STOPS.
20. INSURANCE.
21. CURRENCY COUPONS.
22. SMOKING.
23. QUARANTINE.
24. INOCULATION AND VACCINATION.
25. FIREARMS AND WIRELESS APPARATUS.
26. CAMERAS.
27. LIVESTOCK.
28. HOTELS.

SOME OF THE OFFICES AND AIRPORTS
OF IMPERIAL AIRWAYS

GREAT BRITAIN

LONDON: PASSENGER DEPARTURE STATION, Airway Terminus, Victoria Station, S.W.1.

WEST END BOOKING OFFICE, Airways House, Charles Street, Lower Regent Street, S.W.1.

SOUTHAMPTON: Imperial Airways, New Docks, Southampton.

FRANCE

PARIS: PASSENGER DEPARTURE STATION, Airway Terminus, Rue des Italiens.

MARSEILLES: Imperial Airways.

ITALY

BRINDISI; ROME; ATHENS (GREECE); ALEXANDRIA, JERUSALEM, TIBERIAS (PALESTINE); BASRA ('IRAQ).

INDIA

KARACHI; CALCUTTA.

BURMA

RANGOON.

SIAM

BANGKOK.

HONG KONG

HONG KONG.

MALAYA

SINGAPORE; BATAVIA, SOURABAYA (NETHERLANDS INDIES).

AUSTRALIA

SYDNEY: Qantas Empire Airways.

UNITED STATES OF AMERICA

IMPERIAL AIRWAYS GENERAL AGENTS IN U.S.A.

BERMUDA

IMPERIAL AIRWAYS

ENGLAND
EGYPT
'IRAQ
INDIA
HONG KONG
MALAYA
AUSTRALIA

SUMMER TIMETABLE
IN FORCE FROM 16 AUG. 1938 UNTIL FURTHER NOTICE
This timetable cancels all previous editions and is
subject to alterations without notice

An Imperial Airways Australia route timetable 1938. (David Zekra)

Passengers spend the night at:

Townsville, Queen's Hotel
Darwin, Resthouse
Sourabaya, Oranje Hotel
Penang, Eastern and Oriental Hotel
Rangoon, Strand Hotel
Gwalior, Grand Hotel
Dubai, Resthouse
Alexandria, Hotel Cecil
Brindisi, Hotel Internationale
Rome, Grand Hotel de Russie
Marseilles, Hotel de Noailles

AUSTRALIA — INDIA — ENGLAND SERVICES

AUSTRALIA (Sydney) — MALAYA — HONG KONG — SIAM — BURMA — INDIA — PERSIAN
GULF — 'IRAQ — PALESTINE — EGYPT — ENGLAND   •   WESTBOUND SERVICES

AUSTRALIA–INDIA–ENGLAND
By *Imperial flying-boat*

Miles from Sydney	Junctions and Termini are shown in CAPITALS	Local Standard Time	Days of Services
			Every
	SYDNEY *New South Wales* dep.	07 00	Tues., Thur., Sat.
482	Brisbane *Queensland* dep.	11 05	
756	Gladstone *Queensland* dep.	13 45	
1190	Townsville *Queensland* arr.	Aftn.	
1606	Townsville dep.	07 00	Wed., Fri., Sun.
2393	Karumba *Queensland* dep.	10 30	
	Darwin *N. Australia* arr.	Aftn.	
2926	Darwin dep.	06 30	Thur., Sat., Mon.
3710	Koepang *Netherlands Indies* dep.	09 15	
	Sourabaya *Netherlands Indies* arr.	Aftn.	
4172	Sourabaya dep.	06 00	Fri., Sun., Tues.
4735	Batavia *Netherlands Indies* dep.	09 35	
5126	Singapore *Malaya* dep.	15 00	
	Penang *Malaya* arr.	Even.	
5706	Penang dep.	06 30	Sat., Mon., Wed.
6077	BANGKOK *Siam* (B) dep.	11 25	
	Rangoon *Burma* arr.	Aftn.	
6398	Rangoon dep.	06 00	Sun., Tues., Thur.
6747	Akyab *Burma* dep.	08 55	
7204	Calcutta *India* dep.	11 40	
7450	Allahabad *India* dep.	15 10	
	Gwalior *India* arr.	Aftn.	
7720	Gwalior dep.	06 00	Mon., Wed., Fri.
8157	Raj Samand *India* dep.	08 55	
8897	Karachi *India* dep.	12 40	
	Dubai *Oman* arr.	Even.	
9197	Dubai dep.	06 00	Tues., Thur., Sat.
9542	Bahrein *off Arabia* dep.	08 40	
9855	Basra *'Iraq* dep.	10 40	
10344	Habbaniyeh *'Iraq* ‡ dep.	13 25	
10697	Tiberias *Palestine* dep.	16 15	
	ALEXANDRIA *Egypt* (A) arr.	Even.	
	Alexandria dep.	06 45	Wed., Fri., Sun.
11284	Athens *Greece* dep.	12 05	
11663	Brindisi *Italy* dep.	14 20	
11983	Rome *Italy* arr.	Even.	
	Rome dep.	07 00	Thur., Sat., Mon.
12364	Marseilles *France* dep.	10 15	
12988	SOUTHAMPTON *England* arr.	Aftn.	
	LONDON (*Waterloo*) arr.	Even.	

B Junction for Hong Kong (see timetable on the right)
‡ For Baghdad
★ For Jerusalem and Tel Aviv
A Junction for East, West and South Africa (see company's African timetable)

EGYPT–ENGLAND
By *Imperial flying-boat*

Miles from Alexandria	Junctions and Termini are shown in CAPITALS	Local Standard Time	Days of Services
			Every
	ALEXANDRIA *Egypt* dep.	04 45	Sun., Mon., Thur.
587	Athens *Greece* dep.	10 05	
966	Brindisi *Italy* dep.	12 20	
1286	Rome *Italy* dep.	15 25	
1667	Marseilles *France* dep.	15 25	
	Marseilles dep.	06 15	Mon., Tues., Fri.
2291	SOUTHAMPTON *England* arr.	Morn.	
	LONDON (*Waterloo*) arr.	Aftn.	

These services have come from Africa

INDIA–ENGLAND   By landplane from Calcutta–
Alexandria, thence by *Imperial flying-boat*

Miles from Calcutta	Junctions and Termini are shown in CAPITALS	Local Standard Time	Days of Services
			Every
	CALCUTTA *India* dep.	05 30	Wed., Sat.
475	Allahabad *India* dep.	10 20	
586	Cawnpore *India* dep.	11 40	
830	Delhi *India* dep.	15 05	
1133	Jodhpur *India* dep.	18 30	
1520	Karachi *India* arr.	Even.	
2257	Karachi dep.	04 00	Thur., Sun.
2581	Shariah *Oman* dep.	11 35	
2934	Bahrein *off Arabia* dep.	15 10	
3241	Basra *'Iraq* dep.	20 20	
3805	Baghdad *'Iraq* dep.	00 05	Fri., Mon.
4113	Lydda *Palestine* dep.	06 48	
	ALEXANDRIA *Egypt* (A) arr.	Morn.	
	Alexandria dep.	13 30	
4700	Athens *Greece* dep.	18 30	
5079	Brindisi *Italy* arr.	Even.	
	Brindisi dep.	06 00	Sat., Tues.
5399	Rome *Italy* dep.	09 05	
5780	Marseilles *France* dep.	13 20	
6404	SOUTHAMPTON *England* arr.	Aftn.	
	LONDON (*Waterloo*) arr.	Even.	

Passengers travel by rail between Southampton and London

Calls will also be made at Groote Eylandt, Birma, Klabat Bay, Koh Samui,
Iwasc, Mirabella and Macon if inducement offers and circumstances permit

BANGKOK—HONG KONG SERVICE
(See note B)   By *Diana* class landplanes

Miles	Junctions and Termini are shown in CAPITALS	Local Standard Time	Days of Services
Miles from Southampton	**EASTBOUND**		*Every*
7282	Southampton *England* dep.	05 15	Thur., Sat., Sun.
	Bangkok *Siam* arr.	Aftn.	Mon., Wed., Thu.
Miles from Sydney	**WESTBOUND**		*Every*
5706	Sydney *New South Wales* dep.	07 00	Tues., Thur., Sat.
	Bangkok *Siam* arr.	Morn.	Sat., Mon., Wed.
Miles from Bangkok	**EASTBOUND**		*Every*
283	BANGKOK *Siam* dep.	05 30	Tues., Fri.
606	Udorn *Siam* dep.	08 30	
896	Hanoi *French-Indo China* dep.	11 50	
1178	Fort Bayard *French-Indo China* dep.	14 40	
	HONG KONG *China* arr.	Even.	
Miles from Hong Kong	**WESTBOUND**		*Every*
282	HONG KONG *China* dep.	06 00	Tues., Fri.
605	Fort Bayard *French-Indo China* dep.	07 40	
895	Hanoi *French-Indo China* dep.	10 30	
1178	Udorn *Siam* dep.	14 00	
	BANGKOK *Siam* arr.	Aftn.	
1178	Bangkok *Siam* dep.	11 30	Wed., Sat., Mon.
8460	Southampton *England* arr.	Aftn.	Mon., Thur., Sat.
	EASTBOUND		
1178	Bangkok *Siam* dep.	05 30	Thur., Fri., Tue.
6884	Sydney *New South Wales* arr.	Aftn.	Mon., Tue., Thur.

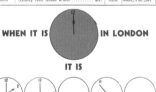

WHEN IT IS [clock] **IN LONDON**

IT IS

at Athens, Alexandria and Tiberias

at Baghdad and Basra

at Karachi, Jodhpur, Raj Samand, Delhi, Gwalior, and Allahabad

at Calcutta

at Akyab and Rangoon

at Bangkok, Udorn, Hanoi, and Ft. Bayard

at Penang and Singapore

at Hong Kong

at Darwin

at Karumba, Townsville, Gladstone, Brisbane and Sydney

The Shorts S23 C-Class
Empire flying boat, VH-ABC
'Coogee', that was
previously registered
G-EAUG, circa 1938.

A J Coster. *Mercury* flew 2,930 miles to Montreal in 20 hrs 20 mins after being launched from the Short S21 flying boat *Maia* (G-ADHK) near Foynes. The seaplane carried newspapers and mail and the aircraft continued to Port Washington, New York before returning via Botwood, the Azores and Lisbon on 25-27 July in a flight time of 25 hrs 35 mins. The aircraft had flown against 25 mph headwinds but had consumed less fuel than anticipated (54 gallons per hour) and maintained an average speed of 160 mph. Six days before starting the Atlantic crossing, *Mercury* had been launched from *Maia* over Southampton to be flown by Bennett on a 2,000-mile round trip to Foynes. He went on to create a long distance record for seaplanes by flying *Mercury* from Dundee to the Orange River in South Africa in 42 hrs 5 mins between 6-8 October. *Maia* had taken-off from the River Tay to launch *Mercury* on her 6,045 mile journey. The return flight was made via Cape Town, Durban, Beira, Kisumu, Khartoum, Alexandria and Marseilles.

The day after *Mercury's* eastbound Atlantic crossing (28 July), the Empire Air Mail programme was extended to include Australia, New Zealand, Tasmania, Fiji, Papua, Norfolk Island, Lord Howe Island, Nauru, the Mandated Territory of Western Samoa and the territories of the Western Pacific that were under the jurisdiction of the Region's High Commissioner. The inaugural mail was carried aboard the C-class flying boat *Calypso* (G-AEUA) following a ceremony at Southampton aboard the MV *Medina*. During the same day, Qantas Empire Airways commenced westbound Empire Mail services along the entire Sydney-Southampton route although Australian-registered aircraft and crew only operated as far as Singapore. By 2 September mail was carried from Hong Kong to Bangkok to connect with the Australia-England flight officially connecting the Crown Colony to the Empire Mail Service. By the summer of 1938 there were eight services a week between the UK and Egypt; three to Central Africa; two to South Africa; five to India and three to Australia.

Although the Imperial Airways dream to link the Empire was now a reality, the political situation was becoming extremely tense in Europe and another war was looming. On 15 September, Prime Minister Neville Chamberlain flew to Munich from Heston in a British Airways Electra (G-AEPR) to discuss the German-Czech political situation. He returned on the new Lockheed 14 (G-AFGN) without any agreement being made and went back to Germany a week later, again without reaching a settlement. After a third visit on 29 September at Hitler's invitation, Chamberlain attended talks with the German Chancellor, Italian dictator Mussolini, and Daladier, the French Premier. He returned jubilantly waving a piece of paper, signed by Hitler and declared at Downing Street that he had achieved '*Peace with honour* ...

I believe it is peace in our time.' The four leaders had agreed to allow the Germans to annex the Sudetenland region of Czechoslovakia and Chamberlain believed that they had resolved their differences through consultation to preserve peace. But he had, of course, been hoodwinked. In reality the document he had put so much faith in was worthless and it was not long before the country was placed on a confirmed war footing.

Prior to Chamberlain's visits to Germany, British Airways made a non-stop flight to Stockholm in 4¼ hrs using the Lockheed Electra 14 (G-AFGN) that had been delivered to Heston on 3 September, and returned in 6 hrs 10 mins.

Undeterred by the worsening diplomatic situation, autumn brought an increase in traffic to Imperial Airways. The heavy volume of Christmas mail led to a report in *The Times* on 28 October that declared: '*The Christmas mails have closed the doors of the Empire flying boats to those that want to fly along their routes in the early part of December. No more passenger bookings can be accepted...*' Business was brisk and flights between India and Australia had to be doubled with a third service added between Singapore and Sydney. In Africa the situation was much the same and flights on the Johannesburg-Salisbury sector were increased to six flights. The East African services between Khartoum-Lagos, Lagos-Accra and Bathurst-Freetown also began operating. By December the success of the Empire Air Mail route to Australia had reached manic proportions. Imperial Airways and Qantas jointly flew well over a million miles including 282,000 on special Christmas mail flights. Every available aircraft was pressed into mail service on the Australian and African routes. The normal C-Class flying boat operations were joined by the Ensigns, Frobishers, Atalantas, HP42/45s, DH86s and the reliable Avro Ten (G-AASP). *Mercury* also played a key role after launching from *Maia* to make a non-stop overnight flight to Alexandria with a ton of mail and 1,000 gallons of petrol. The increased demand also required the company to charter aircraft from Swissair, Olley Air Service and Wrightways and the RAF also contributed. During the six weeks prior to Christmas an estimated 197 tons of mail was flown to the Empire destinations. Loads amounting to 20 flying boats were carried to Australia and New Zealand (65 tons) and 46 tons to India.

On 24 October Imperial Airways had taken delivery of three of the 12 Armstrong Whitworth AW 27 aircraft that had been ordered. *Ensign* (G-ADSR) had been delivered to Croydon on 5 October although it had briefly made an appearance in July. On 20 October, Jones and Horsey commanded relay flights carrying invited British and French travel agents and journalists who were given luncheon or tea while in flight over London or Paris. Four days later regular services commenced

Bangkok — Hong Kong — Bangkok

Wed.	Fri.	05.30	dep.	Bangkok	arr.	Even	Mon. Fri.
»	»	08.30	dep.	Udorn	dep.	14.00	» »
»	»	11.50	dep.	Hanoi	dep.	10.50	» »
»	»	14.40	dep.	FortBayard	dep.	07.45	» »
»	»	Even	arr.	Hong Kong	dep.	06.00	» »

Connecting with East Bound Flying Boat Service
ex Alexandria, on Mondays and Fridays.
Operated by Land Plane

Alexandria — Basra — Alexandria

Tuesday	04.00	dep.	Alexandria	arr.	Even	Friday
»	08.35	dep.	Lydda	dep.	15.50	»
»	14.25	dep.	Rutbah	dep.	11.30	»
»	17.35	dep.	Baghdad	dep.	08.00	»
»	Even	arr.	Basra	dep.	04.00	»

Operated by Land Plane

FULL
INFORMATION
MAY BE HAD
FROM

IMPERIAL AIRWAYS

ALEXANDRIA
AIRWAYS HOUSE
Rue des Fatimites
Telephone 23086
Telegr. "AIRWAYS"

CAIRO
Rod El-Farag
Telephone 55167
Telegr. "AIRWAYS"

JERUSALEM
King David Hotel
Telephone .. 2353
Telegr. "AIRWAYS"

TIBERIAS
Tiberias Hotel
Telephone 22
Telegr. "AIRWAYS"

BAGHDAD
West Air Port
Telephone ... 277
Telegr. "AIRWAYS"

LOCAL AGENT

IMPERIAL AIRWAYS
And Associated Companies

ENGLAND
EGYPT
INDIA
MALAYA
HONG KONG
AUSTRALIA

TIMETABLE
in force from
10th APRIL 1938

UNTIL FURTHER NOTICE
SUBJECT TO ALTERATION WITHOUT NOTICE

1938 Imperial
Airways time-table.
(David Zekra)

ENGLAND — INDIA — AUSTRALIA

Southampton .	dep.	05.15	Sun.	Wed.	Thu.	Fri.
Marseilles	dep.	10.32	»	»	»	»
Rome	dep.	13.35	»	»	»	»
Brindisi	dep.	16.20	»	»	»	»
Athens	arr.	Even	»	»	»	»
Athens	dep.	06.00	Mon.	Thu.	Fri.	Sat.
Alexandria ...	dep.	11.40	»	»	»	»
Tiberias	dep.	14.50	»	»	»	»
Habbaniyeh (Baghdad)	dep.	19.40	»	»	»	»
Basra	arr.	21.45	»	»	»	»
Basra	dep.	05.30	Tue.	Fri.	Sat.	Sun.
Bahrein	dep.	08.35	»	»	»	»
Sharjah	dep.	11.35	»	»	»	»
Gwadar	dep.	16.45	»	»	»	»
Karachi	arr.	18.45	»	»	»	»
			*	†	*	†
			Wed.	Sat.	Sun.	Mon.
Karachi	dep.		05.00	04.00	05.00	04.00
Jodhpur	dep.		08.35	07.45	08.35	07.45
Delhi	dep.		11.00	10.55	11.00	10.55
Cawnpore	dep.		—	13.05	—	13.05
Allahabad	dep.		13.15	14.30	13.15	14.30
Calcutta	arr.		16.40	18.35	16.40	18.35
Calcutta	dep.	05.30	Thu.		Mon.	
Akyab	dep.	09.10	»		»	
Rangoon.....	dep.	12.05	»		»	
Bangkok.....	arr.	15.10	»		»	
Bangkok.....	dep.	05.30	Fri.		Tue.	
Penang	dep.	11.05	»		»	
Singapore ...	arr.	Aftn	»		»	

Mon.	Fri.	Aftn	dep.	Singapore
		Even	arr.	Penang
Tue.	Sat.	06.30	dep.	Penang
»	»	11.30	dep.	Bangkok
»	»	Aftn	arr.	Rangoon
Wed.	Sun.	06.00	dep.	Rangoon
»	»	09.00	dep.	Akyab
»	»	10.40	arr.	Calcutta
»	»	11.40	dep.	**Calcutta**
»	»	15.10	dep.	Allahabad
»	»	Even	arr.	Delhi
Thu.	Mon.	06.00	dep.	Delhi
»	»	08.35	dep.	Jodhpur
»	»	11.40	arr.	Karachi
»	»	12.40	dep.	Karachi
»	»	15.20	dep.	Gwadar
»	»	Even	arr.	Sharjah
Fri.	Tue.	06.00	dep.	Sharjah
»	»	08.05	dep.	Bahrein
»	»	10.10	arr.	Basra
»	»	10.40	dep.	Basra
»	»	13.25	dep.	Habbaniyeh (Baghdad)
»	»	16.15	dep.	Tiberias
»	»	Even	arr.	Alexandria
Sat.	Wed.	06.45	dep.	Alexandria
»	»	12.05	dep.	Athens
»	»	13.50	dep.	Brindisi
»	»	14.20	dep.	Brindisi
»	»	Even	arr.	Rome
Sun.	Thu.	07.00	dep.	Rome
»	»	10.15	dep.	Marseilles
»	»	15.15	arr.	Southampton

Services ex Singapore on Mondays & Fridays
Call at Raj Samand and Gwalior instead
of Jodhpur, Delhi & Cawnpore.
Operated by "C" Class Flying Boat.

CALCUTTA SERVICES ONLY

Calcutta	dep.	05.30	Tue.	Fri.	Land Plane Service Only
Allahabad	dep.	10.20	»	»	
Delhi	arr.	14.05	»	»	
Delhi	dep.	15.05	»	»	
Jodhpur	dep.	18.30	»	»	
Karachi	arr.	Even	»	»	
Karachi	dep.	07.00	Wed.	Sat.	
Gwadar	dep.	10.00	»	»	
Sharjah	arr.	11.25	»	»	
Sharjah	dep.	12.25	»	»	
Bahrein	dep.	15.00	»	»	
Basra	arr.	Even	»	»	
Basra	dep.	04.00	Thu.	Sun.	
Habbaniyeh (Baghdad)	dep.	06.45	»	»	
Tiberias	dep.	09.35	»	»	
Alexandria	arr.	12.05	»	»	
Alexandria	dep.	13.00	»	»	
Athens	dep.	18.30	»	»	
Brindisi	arr.	Even	»	»	
Brindisi	dep.	06.00	Fri.	Mon.	
Rome	arr.	08.35	»	»	
Rome	dep.	09.05	»	»	
Marseilles	dep.	12.20	»	»	
Southampton	arr.	Even	»	»	

† Saturday & Monday service from Karachi-Calcutta
Via Jodhpur, Delhi, Cawnpore, Allahabad,
operated by Landplane.

* Services ex Karachi on Wednesdays & Sundays,
call at Raj Samand and Gwalior instead of
Jodhpur, Delhi and Cawnpore.
Operated by "C" class Flying Boat.

ALL TIMES IN LOCAL STANDARD TIME

Particulars of Extra Landplane Service from Alexandria to Basra overleaf.

between the cities. It was a further grim reminder of the dark days to come when *The Times* reporter aboard a Paris flight wrote that passengers were offered copies of *Mein Kampf* on the streets of the French capital. Passenger impressions of *Ensign* were extremely favourable and they praised being able to use the smoking lounge and having the space to walk about the cabin. It is a pity that Imperial Airways could not share their enthusiasm. Three of the class pressed into service to assist with the Empire mail to Australia during December failed to arrive. The recently delivered aircraft had all developed major mechanical problems. *Egeria* (G-ADSS) required an engine change and failed to get beyond Athens; *Elsinore* (G-ADST) suffered the same fate at Karachi and *Euterpe* (G-ADSU) never got beyond India owing to an unspecified fault. *Elsinor's* return was also marred by a faulty landing gear that had to be lowered by hand and could not be retracted until it had received workshop attention. In consequence the pilots were forced to fly 2,500 miles with the wheels down.

At least Imperial Airways could put more faith in its other new aircraft, the DH91 Albatross, known as the F Class *Frobisher* (G-AFDI) that had taken part in acceptance tests on 17 October and flew to Paris from Croydon in 53mins on 25 November. The *Frobisher* was the first airliner to carry the recognisable *Speedbird* logo that was designed for Imperial Airways in 1932 by graphic artist, Theyre Lee-Elliott, a designer who had also designed posters for London Transport.

Incidents continued to haunt the airline at the tail end of the year. Capt E H Attwood and crew members, A N Spottiswood (first officer), F G Ubee (flight officer) and B B Rees (wireless officer), died on 27 November when *Calpurnia* (G-AETW) crashed on Lake Habbaniyeh (Iraq) 15 miles from the marine station. The flying boat, en route to Australia had been making a night landing during a sandstorm. Ironically, the Inspector of Accidents at the Air Ministry, Capt Wilkins, was on his way to the accident aboard a Lufthansa Berlin-Kabul flight when that too crashed near Vienna but Wilkins was only slightly injured. Then, on 3 December, another aircraft was destroyed when the DH86 *Daedalus* (G-ADCN) caught fire at Bangkok while the engines were being started. Fortunately nobody was on the aircraft and there were no casualties.

Night scene at Croydon, as DH91, 'Fortuna' waits for her next departure.

A study in sleekness: DH91 'Frobisher' shows off her lines against two EW 27s Ensigns at Croydon, 'Egeria' and 'Elsinore'. These two Ensigns served on the Empire routes.

G-ADUT, 'Centaurus', C-Class flying boat of Imperial Airways gathers speed for take-off. 'Centaurus' surveyed the Far East route to Australia and New Zealand and subsquently was transferred to the Royal Australian Air Force (RAAF) in 1939 (carrying the military serial A18-10).

G-AFDM De Havilland DH91 Albatross Frobisher Class 'Fiona' with glove hanger under construction in 1939. This aircraft was scrapped in September 1943. (CAS/Miss Tuckwell)

CHAPTER SEVENTEEN

SCHEDULED TRANSATLANTIC OPERATIONS BEGIN, BOAC AND THE OUTBREAK OF WAR

1939-1940

O N 10 July 1939 the debate for the second reading of the British Overseas Airways Bill took place in the House of Commons and the Minister for Air, Sir Kingsley Wood defended the Government's nationalisation of the airlines by saying: *'Another important aspect of the financial side of the matter was referred to by the Cadman Committee, who expressed the opinion that the subsidies granted to air transport companies should not be used for raising dividends to undue levels. They also added that it was desirable to take steps to ensure that the large additional capital needed for development would be raised on terms which would not prove unduly expensive to the Exchequer ... I do not hesitate to say that this can without doubt be best secured by the issue of stock with a Treasury guarantee. In fact neither of the two operating companies could raise the capital that is needed for replacement and new equipment except on onerous terms. If present arrangements continue, the taxpayers might well have to pay increasing sums to provide interest on capital.'*

The writing was on the wall for Imperial Airways as an individual entity but until BOAC took over the reins there was no reason why normal business should not resume. It was becoming a regular occurrence for the management of the airline to have the onerous task of having to deal with a catastrophe at the start of every New Year. The year 1939 was no exception. Capt Griffith Powell, the regional manager of the Imperial Airways Bermuda-New York service had the initial responsibility of dealing with the latest tragedy. On 21 January the C-Class *Cavalier* had ditched en route between New York and Bermuda (see Chapter 15) after a suspected ice build-up had caused two engines to fail and the remaining pair to be deprived of power. Capt Alderson had been in command and although he did his utmost to save his aircraft without sufficient power, he had no option but to ditch. The water was rougher than it appeared and the aircraft hull broke in two and sank 15 minutes later. Reports later claimed there were insufficient lifebelts for the survivors and those that were wearing them had not put them on correctly. Fortunately some of the cushion-style life preservers floated up from the wreckage and survivors were able to cling to these. A rescue had been swiftly implemented, but darkness fell and it took more than ten hours to locate the survivors, who had huddled together in a tight group. But one passenger, J Gordon Noakes, had received a serious head wound when the aircraft hit the sea and he succumbed to his injury, slipped from the group and was lost. At 23.35 hrs New York time the survivors were spotted by the crew of the *Esso Baytown*. Bobby Spence, the steward had become delirious and started thrashing about in the water. He was pulled back to the group by the others but died soon after. A second passenger, Donald Miller, also died before the rescue ship could arrive. In March, Miller's widow brought a law suit against Imperial Airways (Bermuda) Ltd and Imperial Airways, alleging her husband's death was *'...due to wilful neglect and misconduct on the part of the company and its representatives aboard Cavalier.'* Mrs Katherine Miller, who had also been on the flight, claimed $201,109 (£33,700) in damages and during Sir John Reith's visit to New York where he was visiting the World's Fair during August, her

lawyer served a subpoena requiring the Imperial Airways chairman to attend court to be questioned.

Although the remaining survivors suffered from shock and exposure, it was nevertheless miraculous that so many survived. The water had not been as cold as it might have been and the Gulf streams had kept the survivors from freezing to death. The cause of the accident was attributed to icing on the butterfly valves of the throttles and carburettors of the Perseus engines. This had been causing considerable consternation for some time and there was a call that the problem should be cured before the replacement flying boat, the later S30 Cabot Class launched in December 1938, *Champion* (G-AFCT) was sent to Bermuda.

In January the DH91 Albatross Frobisher Class were briefly grounded after a freak incident at Croydon. One of the aircraft had been taxying and making a turn, when mud on the apron caused the aircraft to slip so that a wheel came into contact with the edge of the tarmac causing the undercarriage to collapse. When no design or mechanical fault was discovered the fleet was put back into service and the following Saturday *Falcon* (G-AFDJ) flew the evening service to Paris in 76 minutes in spite of appalling weather. The same aircraft was setting a trend for speed and efficiency. On 8 January it was flown by Capt E R B White to Marseilles from Croydon in three hours, and two days later, it set a new Croydon-Brussels record in 48 minutes with Capt J T Percy in command. The sister aircraft, *Fortuna* (G-AFDK), flown by Capt Jimmy Youell became the first F-Class to operate between Croydon and Zurich on 13 January, but the route was closed at the end of the month until 16 April when an intermediary stop was added at Basle.

Collaboration between BA and IA

As a formative build-up to a British Airways/Imperial Airways merger, there were a number of personnel changes made during the early part of the year as well as route modifications that affected both companies. Brackley was devastated when it was announced that A C Campbell-Orde would be moving from British Airways to take up the newly created post of Operations Manager at Imperial Airways. This effectively made Brackley's role as Air Superintendent redundant although the company required him to concentrate on *'... special duties for which his experience fits him well. In future he will undertake, among other duties, the survey and development of new routes.'* Brackley's diary entry for 20 March recorded: *'Told of Campbell Orde's appointment as operations manager. Dejected.'* The company issued a bulletin: *'By virtue of the creation of the Office of Operations Manager, the consequent appointment of Mr Campbell Orde, and the transfer to him of the operational duties formerly attended by the Air Superintendent (personnel matters having already been transferred to the Flying Establishment officer), the office and title of Air Superintendent now ceases to exist. On return from a Survey on which he is proceeding, the former Air Superintendent, Major H G Brackley, will be attached to the Department of the Operations Manager.'* It appears Brackley was unsettled by this

Probably photographed in 1939, the German Lufthansa Junkers Ju 52, D-ASIS. (CAS)

appointment and a poignant section in Frida's book based on her husband's diaries at the outbreak of war sums things up:

'Brackles entered the war after years of immense strain and overwork organising the Empire Air Routes: the year preceding the war added disillusionment through the political set-up and trend of events which took place behind the scenes over the amalgamation of Imperial Airways and British Airways into BOAC. The placing and treatment of personnel of Imperial Airways to satisfy certain vested interests and produce a public scapegoat was disgraceful; whatever their personal deficiencies had been, the devotion of the men to the work had been unquestionable.'

Brackley had been specially screened for BOAC but he used his connections to become a reservist in RAF Coastal Command[1].

On 15 April Imperial Airways withdrew from the Croydon-Brussels-Cologne-Frankfurt route and during the same day, British Airways also flew its last Croydon-Paris service. Thereafter the two airlines jointly operated eight return flights daily using Imperial Airways DH91 Frobisher Class aircraft until they signed an agreement with Air France on 25 July to share resources. The new services commenced next day and operated eight return flights during weekdays with five on Sundays. On 17 April British Airways re-opened its Heston-Brussels service using Lockheed Electras that operated twice-daily on weekdays. It also opened a once-daily Heston-Frankfurt-Budapest service using Lockheed 14s and extended the Heston-Hamburg-Copenhagen-Malmö service on weekdays to Stockholm with Electras, but Malmö was later dropped. This became known as the *Viking Royal Mail Service*. After the declaration of War this route was amended to Perth-Stavanger-Oslo-Stockholm. In the prelude to hostilities, British Airways also began a weekday Heston-Berlin-Warsaw service the same day using Lockheed 14s. It seems strange that during the immediate prelude to war, Deutsche Lufthansa was able to fly into England on a joint Oslo-Gothenburg-Copenhagen-Hamburg-Croydon service introduced during April with DDL Danish Air Lines using the impressive Focke-Wulf Fw 200 *Condor* on a daily basis.

As responsibility for the European routes was gradually being transferred to British Airways, Imperial Airways was actively forging ahead with the Empire routes. On 16 April the time taken to reach South Africa was cut to 4½ days and to 5½ days to Hong Kong. On 4 April an experimental flight was operated jointly with Elders Colonial Airways between Lagos and Takoradi (Gold Coast) to connect with the Imperial Airways services at Khartoum. The first service left Khartoum for London for London on 30 April.

On 19 May Imperial Airways placed a display advertisement in *The Times* proudly listing their Empire destinations as –

* Egypt in 28 hours — 6 Services a week
* East Africa in 3 days — 3 Services a week
* West Africa in 4½ days — 1 Service a week
* South Africa in 5 days — 2 Services a week
* Malaya in 5½ days — 3 Services a week
* Hong Kong in 6 days — 2 Services a week
* India in 3 days — 5 Services a week
* Australia (Sydney) in 10 days — 3 Services a week

Following the appointment of Campbell Orde, Brackley was despatched on a confidential survey of the projected *reserve route* across the Sahara and Belgian Congo that was being considered as an alternative because of the threat of war in the Mediterranean. He left on 10 May and travelled via Marseilles, Algiers and El Golea before crossing the Sahara from Gao (French Equatorial Africa) in an Air Afrique Potez Type 66. Brackley recorded in his diary that the senior pilot allowed him to fly in '*… a delightfully comfortable and airy cabin with superb chairs. Better than ours.*'

On 14 March another C-Class flying boat was added to the incident statistics that thus far had claimed eight hull losses. *Corsair* (G-ADVB) ran out of fuel in the Belgian Congo and was badly damaged when it landed on the shallow waters of the River Dangu. It hit a rock and had sunk in mud although nobody had been injured. E J 'John' Alcock was the captain of the stricken craft. During the flight from Lake Victoria to Juba he had left the flight deck in the care of his first officer while he took a break. Unbeknown to the crew the direction finding equipment that had replaced a faulty set the previous day had been wrongly poled and the *Corsair* had been flown 200 miles off course. Believing the aircraft to be salvageable, Imperial Airways sent a team to retrieve it and in the process a small village had to be constructed that became appropriately named *Corsairville*. The heat, humidity and insects provided the most appalling working conditions. When repairs had been completed Kelly Rogers attempted to make a take-off but the shallow river was also too narrow and the aircraft hit a rock, again damaging the hull. Repairs had to be started again but by January 1940 *Corsair* was successfully re-launched and was on her way home.

On 1 May there was a further fatal accident involving a flying boat *Challenger* (G-ABVD) was attempting to land at Mozambique Harbour but the aircraft approach had been off-course causing it to run into

[1]. Herbert Brackley later became Senior Staff Officer with RAF Transport Command and was promoted to Air Commodore in 1943. After the war he became assistant to the BOAC Chairman, Lord Knollys, before being appointed Chief Executive of the British South American Airways Corporation (BSAA) following the sudden departure of the former Imperial Airways pilot, Air Vice-Marshal Don Bennett. Brackley drowned while swimming at Rio de Janeiro on 15 November 1948 and was buried at Blakeney, Norfolk.

shallow water and the keel struck the bottom. The flight clerk, George Knight, was killed in the impact, wireless officer Tom Webb was drowned, and the four remaining crew members and one passenger were injured.

There was further criticism of Imperial Airways during the debate that followed the Air Estimates. This was quite academic considering that the days of the company were limited, but the Air Ministry announced orders for three Short G-Class Golden Hind Class flying boats.

1st Day air mail cover from the Pan Am Montreal-Foynes route, 1939. (author)

Marseilles as the penultimate to the survey from Baltimore to Foynes on the North Atlantic winter route. *The Times* reported that the Imperial Airways flying boat, *Coonemara*, was dwarfed by the *Yankee Clipper* when they ceremonially flew alongside each another over the Solent.

Pan American could wait no longer for the British. On 20 May the Boeing 314 *Yankee Clipper*, returned to Europe under the command of Capt A E La Porte on the first commercial crossing between Port Washington and

The Easter holiday had brought exceptionally fine weather and there was a clamber for seats as passengers took the opportunity to cross the Channel. More than 1,000 flew from Croydon; 530 aboard Imperial Airways Paris flights, 165 on British Airways and 365 on Air France. Forty flights left for Paris, thirty for Le Touquet and extra services had to be added to other European destinations to cope with demand. Many passengers probably realised this would be a final opportunity to travel to the Continent prior to war. On one flight *Heracles* experienced a massive 'bump' while returning to Croydon from Paris and Capt Jones was forced up from his seat causing his head to go through the roof lining. Other crew members were also injured but the passengers, by then, had been instructed to wear their recently introduced seat belts and they were unhurt.

On 5 June the new company headquarters opened at Buckingham Palace Road next to Victoria Station. This was an impressive stone building with a central clock tower between two wide, outstretched wings and was named Airways House (as was the former HQ). The building was stylishly designed by A Lakeman to provide a spacious, modern and comfortable point-of-departure and passengers could board special trains from a private railway platform (Victoria Station platform 17) that adjoined the rear of the building. These reached Southampton in 90 minutes to connect with the flying boat departures and passengers flying on the European landplanes from Croydon boarded coaches from a covered bay at the front of the building.

During the week following the official opening, Sir Kingsley Wood presented the Commons with the results of the Government negotiations to buy Imperial Airways and British Airways. Although Parliamentary approval still had to be given, the Government had sanctioned the purchase of Imperial Airways at 32s 9d (£1.76) for a £1 ordinary share and an estimated 15s 9d (76p) for each British Airways £1 share. This would pay £2,659,086 to Imperial Airways and £311,000 to British Airways. *The Times* of 13 May reported: '*The boards of the two companies were recommending those offers to the shareholders for acceptance.*' At the time Imperial Airways shares were listed at 29s 0d on the Stock Exchange; British Airways shares were unquoted. By the end of May the shareholders of both companies had formerly agreed to the sales and on 12 June, the British Overseas Airways Corporation Bill was introduced to the Commons, given a second reading on 10 July, a third on 26 July and gained Royal Assent on 4 August. BOAC was due to take over operations from 1 April 1940 but by the time this could be implemented, Britain was already at war with Germany.

Opening the Atlantic for business

In May two Handley Page Harrow tankers, owned by Alan Cobham's company, Flight Refuelling Ltd, capable of carrying up to 900 gallons of petrol, were shipped to Hattie's Camp (later known as Gander), a large aerodrome close to the Newfoundland coast. A third tanker was despatched to Rineanna (Shannon) to perform air-to-air refuelling on the westbound flying boat. One of the later S30 C-Class boats, *Cabot* (G-AFCU), was refuelled over the Atlantic and similar practice runs were made over the Solent in preparation for the start of regular trans-Atlantic operations. In all, 15 successful refuelling operations were carried out although there was a danger that fuel could ignite after it was found to leak into the bilges of the flying boats. A proving flight commanded by Capt Harold Gray had been made on 4 April by Pan American Airways to Southampton via Horta, Lisbon, Biscarosse and

Marseilles via Horta and Lisbon. The flight continued to Southampton, arriving on 23 May and returned to New York next day. The same aircraft, once more commanded by Capt Gray, later opened the North Atlantic mail service that reached Southampton on 28 June carrying dignitaries including Juan Trippe and 1,734 lbs of mail. The first passenger services were started by Pan Am on 22 June, but the new British S26 G-Class flying boat, *Golden Hind* (G-AFCI), was only launched five days before. This was the first of three larger Shorts flying boats designated for the Atlantic services. Although these were destined for Imperial Airways, they were delivered too late to go into service and the airline's inaugural mail services, due to have started on 1 June had to be postponed. The British contribution to the Atlantic air mail service had to wait and did not get underway until 5 August. Capt Long joined Kelly Rogers, now back from his exploits with *Corsair* in the Belgian Congo, operated the first British scheduled Atlantic service using the S30 C-Class *Caribou* (G-AFCV). After leaving Southampton, the flying boat was refuelled by the Harrow above Foynes and continued to Botwood, Montreal and New York. *Maia* carrying an assortment of dignitaries escorted *Caribou* over Ireland. *Caribou* reached Botwood in 16 hrs 32 mins but the aircraft had been delayed by the adverse Newfoundland weather. After being refuelled from the second Harrow tanker based in Newfoundland, the flight continued to Montreal and Port Washington (Long Island) arriving 36½ hours after leaving Foynes. The return flight left on 9 August and three days later Capt Donald Bennett left Southampton on the second service with *Cabot* (G-AFCU). By 30 September the aircraft had completed the 16th North Atlantic crossing and a week earlier (23-24 September) *Cabot* had set a new record by flying between Foynes and Botwood in 13 hours.

The three G-Class flying boats should have been delivered at monthly intervals. They were nearly twice as large as the C-Class, with an overall length of 103 ft (15 ft longer than the C-Class) and a wing span 20 ft longer. The aircraft had a loaded weight of over 70,000 lbs and was powered by four Bristol Hercules engines, each driving three-bladed constant-speed propellers and capable of producing 1,380 lbs of power at take-off. Compared to the C-Class, the new flying boat had a range of about 3,000 miles and could cruise at 180 mph. The aircraft was put through a month of flotation tests and engine runs and was flown for the first time by Parker on 21 July and then for 72 minutes four days later. Two further test flights followed before the aircraft was handed to Imperial Airways to make proving flights. But the G-Class was another example of how late deliveries of new aircraft had marred the efficiency of Imperial Airlines. The Armstrong Whitworth *Ensigns* that had been intended to work the India route were still not ready and on 3 July the S30 C-Class, *Clyde* (G-AFCX), was the first of the type to be pressed into service on the Southampton-Karachi service.

Mishaps had also been continuing to occur with familiar regularity. On 12 June *Centurion* (G-ADVE) operating from Sydney to Southampton carrying four passengers nosed-in while landing on the Hooghly River at Calcutta. One passenger suffered a broken leg but fortunately nobody else was injured. The company managed to salvage two of the engines from the partially submerged aircraft, but the hull snapped into two while it was being lifted. The fire that engulfed the S30 *Coonemara* (G-AFCW) flying boat was far more serious and claimed the life of one man. The aircraft was being refuelled half a mile offshore at Hythe when fire broke out in the engine room of the petrol barge carrying 20,000 gallons of fuel. There had been an explosion and

Evocative cover for an Imperial Airways brochure which contained information on the company's Ensign airliner and C-Class flying boat.

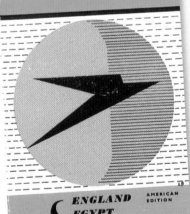

Above and opposite page: Imperial Airways, England/Australia timetable, April 1939. (David Zekra)

the fire quickly swept to the aircraft and completely destroyed her. The two further hull losses had cost the company more than £150,000.

Similarly, British Airways was experiencing catastrophes. On 11 August a carburettor caught fire on a Lockheed 14 on the London–Zurich service and a quick emergency landing had to be made into a field. The crew and passengers escaped unhurt but the aircraft caught fire and was completely burnt out. Four days later all four passengers and the radio operator were drowned when the Electra (G-AESY) had to be ditched in the Störstroem Straits near Copenhagen on the Stockholm service, although the pilot survived.

The approaching war was causing contingency plans to be put in

AUSTRALIA—INDIA—EGYPT—ENGLAND SERVICES

AUSTRALIA (Sydney)—MALAYA—HONG KONG—SIAM—BURMA—INDIA—PERSIAN GULF
'IRAQ—PALESTINE—EGYPT—ENGLAND • WESTBOUND SERVICES

Passengers spend the night at:

- TOWNSVILLE Queen's Hotel
- DARWIN Rest House
- SOURABAYA Oranje Hotel
- PENANG Eastern and Oriental Hotel
- CALCUTTA Great Eastern Hotel
- KARACHI Carlton Hotel
- BASRA Shatt al Arab Hotel (Margil Airport Hotel)
- ALEXANDRIA Hotel Cecil
- MARSEILLES Hotel Splendide

AUSTRALIA—INDIA—EGYPT—ENGLAND

By *Imperial* flying-boats
Beginning Saturday 8 April 1939

Miles from Sydney	PORTS OF CALL Junctions and Termini are shown in CAPITALS (*See Notes at right of page*)	Local Standard Time	Greenwich Mean Time	Days of Services (Every)
	SYDNEY *New South Wales* ... dep.	07 00	21 00	Tues. Thur. Sat.
482	Brisbane *Queensland* ... dep.	11 05	01 05	
756	Gladstone *Queensland* ... dep.	13 45	03 45	
1190	Townsville *Queensland* ... arr.	16 50	06 50	
	Townsville ... dep.	07 00	21 00	Wed. Fri. Sun.
1606	Karumba *Queensland* ... dep.	10 30	00 30	
2393	Darwin *Northern Australia* ... arr.	16 10	06 40	
	Darwin ... dep.	06 30	21 00	Thur. Sat. Mon.
2926	Koepang *Netherlands Indies* ... dep.	09 15	01 15	
3710	Sourabaya *Netherlands Indies* ... arr.	15 00	07 30	
	Sourabaya ... dep.	06 00	22 30	Fri. Sun. Tues.
4129	Batavia *Netherlands Indies* ... dep.	09 35	02 05	
4692	Singapore *Malaya* ... dep.	15 00	07 40	
5083	Penang *Malaya* ... arr.	17 40	10 20	
	Penang ... dep.	05 30	22 10	Sat. Mon. Wed.
5663	BANGKOK *Siam* (B) ... dep.	09 30	02 30	
6034	Rangoon *Burma* ... dep.	12 25	05 55	
6355	Akyab *Burma* ... dep.	15 15	08 45	
6704	Calcutta *India* ... arr.	17 10	11 17	
	Calcutta ... dep.	06 00	00 07	Sun. Tues. Thur.
7161	Allahabad *India* ... dep.	09 20	03 50	
7407	Gwalior *India* ... dep.	11 45	06 15	
7677	Raj Samand *India* ... dep.	14 25	08 55	
8114	Karachi *India* ... arr.	17 40	12 10	
	Karachi ... dep.	07 00	01 30	Mon. Wed. Fri.
8854	Dabai *Oman* ... dep.	11 45	07 55	
9154	Bahrein *off Arabia* ... dep.	14 00	10 40	
9499	Basra *'Iraq* ... arr.	16 30	13 30	
	BASRA ... dep.	07 00	04 00	Tues. Thur. Sat.
9812	Habbaniyeh *'Iraq*‡ ... dep.	10 00	07 00	
10301	Tiberias *Palestine** ... dep.	13 10	11 10	
10654	ALEXANDRIA *Egypt* (A) ... arr.	15 55	13 55	
	Alexandria ... dep.	04 45	02 45	Wed. Fri. Sun.
11241	Athens *Greece* ... dep.	09 45	07 45	
11620	Brindisi *Italy* ... dep.	12 10	11 10	
11940	Rome *Italy* ... dep.	15 10	14 10	
12321	Marseilles *France* ... arr.	18 00	17 00	
	Marseilles ... dep.	08 00	07 00	Thur. Sat. Mon.
12945	SOUTHAMPTON *England* ... arr.	12 40	11 40	
	LONDON (Waterloo) ... arr.	Aftn.	Aftn.	

EGYPT—ENGLAND (Additional Services)

By *Imperial* flying-boats
Beginning Sunday 16 April 1939

Miles from Alexandria	PORTS OF CALL (*See Notes at right of page*)	Local Standard Time	Greenwich Mean Time	Days of Services (Every)
	ALEXANDRIA *Egypt* ... dep.	04 45	02 45	Sun.★ Mon. Thur.
587	Athens *Greece* ... dep.	09 45	07 45	
966	Brindisi *Italy* ... dep.	12 10	11 10	
1286	Rome *Italy* ... dep.	15 10	14 10	
1667	Marseilles *France* ... arr.	18 00	17 00	
	Marseilles ... dep.	08 00	07 00	Mon.★ Tues. Fri.
2291	SOUTHAMPTON *England* ... arr.	12 40	11 40	
	LONDON (Waterloo) ... arr.	Aftn.	Aftn.	

These services have come from Africa

INDIA—EGYPT—ENGLAND

By landplanes from Calcutta to Alexandria, thence by *Imperial* flying-boat to England
Beginning Saturday 15 April 1939

Miles from Calcutta	PORTS OF CALL Junctions and Termini are shown in CAPITALS (*See Notes at right of page*)	Local Standard Time	Greenwich Mean Time	Days of Services (Every)
	CALCUTTA *India* ... dep.	05 30	23 37	Wed. Sat.
475	Allahabad *India* ... dep.	10 20	04 50	
586	Cawnpore *India* ... dep.	11 40	06 10	
830	Delhi *India* ... dep.	15 05	09 35	
1133	Jodhpur *India* ... dep.	18 30	13 00	
1520	Karachi *India* ... arr.	22 00	16 30	
	Karachi ... dep.	04 00	22 30	Thur. Sun.
2260	Sharjah *Oman* ... dep.	11 35	07 45	
2584	Bahrein *off Arabia* ... dep.	15 10	11 50	
2937	Basra *'Iraq* ... arr.	18 30	15 30	
	Basra ... dep.	04 00	01 00	Fri. Mon.
3244	Baghdad *'Iraq* ... dep.	07 45	04 45	
3807	Lydda *Palestine** ... dep.	14 00	12 00	
4115	ALEXANDRIA *Egypt* (A) ... arr.	17 45	15 45	
	Alexandria ... dep.	04 45	02 45	Sat. Tues.
4702	Athens *Greece* ... dep.	09 45	07 45	
5081	Brindisi *Italy* ... dep.	12 10	11 10	
5401	Rome *Italy* ... dep.	15 10	14 10	
5782	Marseilles *France* ... arr.	18 00	17 00	
	Marseilles ... dep.	08 00	07 00	Sun. Wed.
6406	SOUTHAMPTON *England* ... arr.	12 40	11 40	
	LONDON (Waterloo) ... arr.	Aftn.	Aftn.	

BANGKOK—HONG KONG SERVICE

By *Diana* class landplanes

Miles	PORTS OF CALL	Local Standard Time	Greenwich Mean Time	Days of Services (Every)
Miles from Southampton	EASTBOUND			
	Southampton *England* ... dep.	05 00	04 00	Wed. Sat.
7282	Bangkok *Siam* ... arr.	15 30	08 30	Sun. Wed.
Miles from Sydney	WESTBOUND			
	Sydney *New South Wales* ... dep.	07 00	21 00	Tues. Sat.
5663	Bangkok *Siam* ... arr.	09 05	02 05	Sat. Wed.
Miles from Bangkok	EASTBOUND *Commencing Monday 24 April 1939 from BANGKOK*			
	BANGKOK *Siam* ... dep.	05 30	22 30	Mon. Thur.
283	Udorn *Siam* ... dep.	08 20	01 20	
606	Hanoi *French Indo-China* ... dep.	11 25	04 25	
896	Fort Bayard *China* ... dep.	14 15	07 15	
1178	HONG KONG ... arr.	17 35	09 35	
Miles from Hong Kong	WESTBOUND *Commencing Tuesday 11 April 1939 from HONG KONG*			
	HONG KONG ... dep.	06 00	22 00	Tues. Fri.
282	Fort Bayard *China* ... dep.	07 40	00 40	
572	Hanoi *French Indo-China* ... dep.	10 30	03 30	
895	Udorn *Siam* ... dep.	13 35	06 35	
1178	BANGKOK *Siam* ... arr.	16 05	09 05	
1178	Bangkok *Siam* ... dep.	09 30	02 30	Wed. Sat.
8460	Southampton *England* ... arr.	12 40	11 40	Mon. Thur.
	EASTBOUND			
1178	Bangkok *Siam* ... dep.	05 30	22 30	Thur. Mon.
6841	Sydney *New South Wales* ... arr.	16 15	06 15	Mon. Fri.

NOTES

★ The service on Sundays between Alexandria and Marseilles and on Mondays between Marseilles and Southampton will operate 30 minutes earlier throughout
By train between Southampton and London
* For Jerusalem and Tel Aviv
‡ For Baghdad
(A) Junction for East, West and South Africa (see Company's Africa timetable)
(B) Junction for Hong Kong (see timetable above)
Calls will also be made at Groote Eylandt, Bima, Klabat Bay, Koh Samui, Jiwani, Mirabella and Macon if inducement offers and circumstances permit
In the event of any such calls being made then the times of arrival at or departure from subsequent stations will be later than those shown above

ENGLAND—INDIA—AUSTRALIA SERVICES

ENGLAND—EGYPT—PALESTINE—'IRAQ—PERSIAN GULF—INDIA—BURMA—SIAM
HONG KONG—MALAYA—AUSTRALIA (Sydney) • EASTBOUND SERVICES

Passengers spend the night at:

- SOUTHAMPTON South Western Hotel
- ATHENS Hotel Grande Bretagne
- BAGHDAD Maude Hotel
- BASRA Shatt al Arab Hotel (Margil Airport Hotel)
- SHARJAH Rest House
- KARACHI Carlton Hotel
- JODHPUR State Hotel
- CALCUTTA Great Eastern Hotel
- BANGKOK Oriental Hotel
- SINGAPORE Raffles Hotel
- SOURABAYA Oranje Hotel
- DARWIN Rest House
- TOWNSVILLE Queen's Hotel

ENGLAND—EGYPT—INDIA—AUSTRALIA

By *Imperial* flying-boat
Beginning Saturday 15 April 1939

Miles from Southampton	PORTS OF CALL Junctions and Termini are shown in CAPITALS (*See Notes at foot*)	Local Standard Time	Greenwich Mean Time	Days of Services (Every)
	LONDON (Waterloo) ... dep.	19 30	18 30	Tues. Fri. Sat.
	Southampton *England* ... arr.	21 28	20 28	
	SOUTHAMPTON ... dep.	05 00	04 00	Wed. Sat. Sun.
624	Marseilles *France* ... dep.	10 10	09 10	
1005	Rome *Italy* ... dep.	13 15	12 15	
1325	Brindisi *Italy* ... dep	16 00	15 00	
1704	Athens *Greece* ... arr.	19 50	17 50	
	Athens ... dep.	04 30	02 30	Thur. Sun. Mon.
2291	ALEXANDRIA *Egypt* (A) ... dep.	09 30	07 30	
2644	Tiberias *Palestine** ... dep.	12 30	10 30	
3133	Habbaniyeh *'Iraq* ‡ ... dep.	17 10	14 10	
3446	Basra *'Iraq* ... arr.	19 20	16 20	
	Basra ... dep.	05 00	02 00	Fri. Mon. Tues.
3791	Bahrein *off Arabia* ... dep.	08 05	04 45	
4091	Dabai *Oman* ... dep.	11 15	07 25	
4831	Karachi *India* ... arr.	18 50	13 20	
	Karachi ... dep.	05 00	23 30	Sat. Tues. Wed.
5268	Raj Samand *India* ... dep.	08 25	02 55	
5538	Gwalior *India* ... dep.	10 50	05 20	
5784	Allahabad *India* ... dep.	13 05	07 35	
6241	Calcutta *India* ... arr.	16 50	10 57	
	Calcutta ... dep.	05 30	23 37	Sun. Wed. Thur.
6590	Akyab *Burma* ... dep.	09 15	02 45	
6911	Rangoon *Burma* ... dep.	12 15	05 45	
7282	BANGKOK *Siam* (B) ... arr.	15 30	08 30	
	Bangkok ... dep.	05 30	22 30	Mon. Thur. Fri.
7862	Penang *Malaya* ... dep.	10 25	03 05	
8253	Singapore *Malaya* ... arr.	13 15	05 55	
	Singapore ... dep.	08 00	00 40	Tues. Fri. Sat.
8816	Batavia *Netherlands Indies* ... dep.	13 10	05 40	
9235	Sourabaya *Netherlands Indies* ... arr.	16 05	08 35	
	Sourabaya ... dep.	05 30	22 00	Wed. Sat. Sun.
10019	Koepang *Netherlands Indies* ... dep.	12 50	04 50	
10552	Darwin *Northern Australia* ... arr.	18 10	08 40	
	Darwin ... dep.	06 00	20 30	Thur. Sun. Mon.
11339	Karumba *Queensland* ... dep.	13 25	03 25	
11755	Townsville *Queensland* ... arr.	16 20	06 20	
	Townsville ... dep.	06 30	20 30	Fri. Mon. Tues.
12189	Gladstone *Queensland* ... dep.	10 15	00 15	
12463	Brisbane *Queensland* ... dep.	12 55	02 55	
12945	SYDNEY *New South Wales* ... arr.	16 15	06 15	

ENGLAND—EGYPT (Additional Services)

By *Imperial* flying-boat
Beginning Tuesday 18 April 1939

Miles from Southampton	PORTS OF CALL (*See Notes at foot*)	Local Standard Time	Greenwich Mean Time	Days of Services (Every)
	LONDON (Waterloo) ... dep.	19 30	18 30	Tues. Thur. Fri.
	Southampton *England* ... arr.	21 28	20 28	
	SOUTHAMPTON ... dep.	05 30	04 30	Wed. Fri.★ Sat.
624	Marseilles *France* ... dep.	10 40	09 40	
1005	Rome *Italy* ... dep.	13 45	12 45	
1325	Brindisi *Italy* ... dep.	16 30	15 30	
1704	Athens *Greece* ... arr.	20 20	18 20	
	Athens ... dep.	05 00	03 00	Thur. Sat. Sun.
2291	ALEXANDRIA *Egypt* ... arr.	09 00	07 00	

These services go on to East, West and South Africa

ENGLAND—EGYPT—INDIA

By *Imperial* flying-boat to Alexandria, thence by landplane to Calcutta
Beginning Sunday 16 April 1939

Miles from Southampton	PORTS OF CALL Junctions and Termini are shown in CAPITALS (*See Notes at foot*)	Local Standard Time	Greenwich Mean Time	Days of Services (Every)
	LONDON (Waterloo) ... dep.	19 30	18 30	Sun.† Wed.
	Southampton *England* ... arr.	21 28	20 28	
	SOUTHAMPTON ... dep.	05 00	04 00	Mon. Thur.
624	Marseilles *France* ... dep.	10 10	09 10	
1005	Rome *Italy* ... dep.	13 15	12 15	
1325	Brindisi *Italy* ... dep.	16 00	15 00	
1704	Athens *Greece* ... arr.	19 50	17 50	
	Athens ... dep.	04 30	02 30	Tues. Fri.
2291	ALEXANDRIA *Egypt* (A) ... dep.	11 30	09 30	
2599	Lydda *Palestine** ... dep.	15 55	13 55	
3162	Baghdad *'Iraq* ... arr.	23 45	20 45	
	Baghdad ... dep.	07 00	04 00	Wed. Sat.
3469	Basra *'Iraq* ... dep.	10 35	07 35	
3822	Bahrein *off Arabia* ... dep.	15 10	11 50	
4146	Sharjah *Oman* ... arr.	18 55	15 05	
	Sharjah ... dep.	04 20	00 30	Thur. Sun.
4886	Karachi *India* ... dep.	15 30	10 00	
5273	Jodhpur *India* ... arr.	18 45	13 15	
	Jodhpur ... dep.	05 00	23 30	Fri. Mon.
5576	Delhi *India* ... dep.	08 10	02 40	
5820	Cawnpore *India* ... dep.	10 20	04 50	
5931	Allahabad *India* ... dep.	11 45	06 15	
6406	CALCUTTA *India* ... arr.	15 50	09 57	

By train between London and Southampton
* For Jerusalem and Tel Aviv ‡ For Baghdad
(A) Junction for East, West and South Africa (see Company's Africa timetable)
(B) Junction for Hong Kong (see timetable overleaf)
Calls will also be made at Macon, Mirabella, Jiwani, Koh Samui, Klabat Bay, Bima and Groote Eylandt if inducement offers and circumstances permit
In the event of any such calls being made then the times of arrival at or departure from subsequent stations will be later than those shown above
★ The service on Friday between Southampton and Athens will operate 30 minutes earlier throughout
† The departure time of the train from Waterloo on **Sunday** will be 18.30 L.S.T., arriving Southampton 20.18 L.S.T.

SOUTHAMPTON
MARSEILLES
ROME
BRINDISI
ATHENS
MIRABELLA
FOR SERVICES TO AFRICA SEE COMPANY'S AFRICA TIME TABLE
ALEXANDRIA
LYDDA
TIBERIAS
HABBANIYEH
BAGHDAD
BASRA
BAHREIN
DABAI
(SHARJAH)
JIWANI
KARACHI
JODHPUR
RAJ SAMAND
DELHI
GWALIOR
CAWNPORE
ALLAHABAD
CALCUTTA
AKYAB
RANGOON
BANGKOK
UDORN
FORT BAYARD
HANOI
HONG KONG
KOH SAMUI
PENANG
SINGAPORE
Flying-boat routes are shown in orange
Landplane routes are shown in black
SYDNEY
IMPERIAL AIRWAYS
Between Singapore and Sydney by QANTAS EMPIRE AIRWAYS *
IMPERIAL AIRWAYS AND INDIAN TRANS-CONTINENTAL AIRWAYS *
* Companies in Association with Imperial Airways

place to re-route airline services likely to be caught in a war zone. The Australian Government, in collaboration with the British, looked at alternatives that would keep their links open. A return survey across 9,022 miles of the Indian Ocean was flown by Capt P G Taylor in a Consolidated PB2Y flying boat *Guba* (NC777) that left Port Hedland on 4 June and arrived back in Sydney after pioneering the 'reserve route' from Australia to Africa that routed via Batavia, Cocos, Chagos and the Seychelles to reach Mombasa on 21 June.

By the end of August Imperial Airways had received 12 of the modified Ensigns but they were still proving troublesome. The constant speed propellers were problematic and oil was overheating. Despite high expectations, the company was forced to revise its plans to operate these

in the Middle East because they were considered no longer suitable. Instead the airliner subsequently went to work on the less demanding European routes.

A suspension of passenger services

During August all of the British civil airports, particularly Croydon, had reported extremely heavy traffic, but Imperial Airways made the announcement that all passenger bookings on the Empire routes had been suspended. The company claimed this was due to the increasing daily mail demands and the need for aircraft to carry extra fuel. But it was also caused by the company still being short of suitable aircraft, a situation not helped by the unexpected flying boat losses and the failure to order enough some years before. The mail loads during the first six months of 1938 had reached 1,400,000 lbs but this had increased to 2,116,000 lbs during the first half of 1939. *The Times* of 9 August was scathing: '*The poorest advertisement for the corporation which is about to take over the two principal British air operating companies is the announcement that from today Imperial Airways will cease to book passengers for its Empire routes.*' The report blamed the Air Ministry and '*... those who controlled the companies ... This is a situation for which the mistakes or misfortunes of the past may largely be blamed. It is a condition which the new corporation must not allow to recur. The corporation is not yet in existence; but the machine it will administer has been built up and that machine has begun to prepare for the day when the present fleet of aircraft will have to be replaced...*'

In view of the situation, by November the company had announced that a second weekly land plane service had been introduced between London and Calcutta with extra flights between Karachi and Calcutta to cope with passenger demands. A special land plane service had also been added to Alexandria via Marseilles, Tunis and Malta to provide transportation for passengers denied seats on the flying boats.

On 24 August, Parliament was called to enact on the Emergency Powers (Defence) Bill and all military reservists were called up. Hitler had threatened Poland and Chamberlain had warned him that Britain was unprepared to stand by and would intervene if Germany invaded. The warning went unheeded and on 1 September German infantry and Panzers entered Poland. British armed forces were mobilised and a dawn to dusk blackout was ordered throughout the country in anticipation of air raids. From midnight, under the Air Navigation (Restriction in Time of War) Order 1939, civilian flights could no longer operate over the eastern half of England and Imperial Airways, British Airways and the Civil Aviation Department of the Ministry of Defence were transferred from Croydon and Heston to Whitchurch near Bristol. Flying boat operations were transferred from Hythe to Poole in the neighbouring county. By 3 September Chamberlain had confirmed that Britain was at war with Germany. As a result all European services were suspended until further notice. On the day war was declared, some of the Imperial Airways and British Airways fleets, and the aircraft of Railway Air Services, were flown to Exeter to operate National Air Communications flights on behalf of the Government under the terms of the subsidy agreements the airlines had signed.

By 22 September, at the request of the Air Officer Commanding, Egypt, a UK landplane route was re-established from Shoreham (Sussex) via Bordeaux, Marseilles, Tunis, Malta and Sollum to Alexandria that extended to India. The first flight, commanded by Capt A C P Johnson, was operated by the DH91 *Fortuna* (G-AFDK) and the service continued until Italy entered the War in 1940.

Since the internal route subsidies had come into effect on 1 January, the Air Transport Licensing Authority was kept busy during 1939 considering applications. The Authority had approved 32 route applications from 11 airlines and by the end of the August these had increased to 47 licences and 14 operators that were awarded for a variety of periods that ran from one to seven years. In addition to the 12 companies that had been granted provisional licences (see previous Chapter), Great Western and Southern Airlines Ltd, Guernsey Airlines and Olley Air Services Ltd (London to race meetings) were approved. Channel Air Ferries that had previously applied during 1938 had been taken over by Western and Southern Airlines and Norman Edgar (Western Airways) Ltd had dropped the founder's name to become Western Airways.

The first new services of the year began on 3 April between Brighton-Ryde and Ryde-Bournemouth, and were flown by Great Western and Southern Air Lines Limited. The new company had been incorporated on 5 December 1938 when the Great Western and Southern Railways had reached an agreement with British and Foreign Aviation Ltd. GWR and SR each held a 25 per cent shareholding and British and Foreign the remaining 50 per cent. The company was based at Brighton, Hove and Worthing Airport (better known as Shoreham) and operated the following services:

- From 3 April: Brighton-Ryde and Ryde-Bournemouth.
- From 1 May: Liverpool-Manchester-Birmingham-Bristol-
- Southampton-Ryde-Brighton.
- From 5 May: Bristol-Exeter (on request)-Plymouth-Lands End-Scilly. The Lands End-Scilly sector flew six-times daily on weekdays; five times on Sundays.
- From 8 May: Cardiff-Bristol-Bournemouth-Ryde-Brighton.
- From 16 May: Croydon-Luxembourg (flown twice-weekly mainly on behalf of Radio Publicity Ltd for the carriage of gramophone records).
- From 26 May: Heston-Croydon-Ryde, four-times weekly.
- From 26 May: Croydon-Deauville.
- From 26 May: Croydon-Le Touquet.
- From 26 May Croydon-Brighton-Le Touquet.

Great Western and Southern Airlines provided the same interchangeable services that enabled passengers to use their tickets on rail and air transport that had previously been offered by RAS, and they also offered circular tours using rail, air and sea. On 22 May Railway Air Services was still operating a daily London-Liverpool-Belfast-Glasgow mail service with a change of aircraft in Belfast. A four times daily service was also added between Liverpool-Manchester and London with request stops at Birmingham (Elmdon from 1 May) and Stoke-on-Trent, but Stoke was dropped during the summer. Connections between Liverpool and Manchester were operated by Isle of Man Air Services. The RAS summer schedules were hampered by cancellations caused by RAF exercises. The services had been allocated Line numbers, (for example: the London-Liverpool-Manchester-Glasgow service was Line No: 652) and services were timed to connect at Croydon with the arrivals and departures of other flights.

Western Airways began a daily Swansea-Barnstaple-Newquay-Penzance service on 8 May and Weston-Super-Mare-Bristol-Birmingham-Manchester thrice-weekly from 17 June. Guernsey Airport at L'Erée had been officially opened by the Secretary of State for Air on 5 May and Jersey and Guernsey Airlines commenced new services from Guernsey to Alderney, Jersey, Southampton and London. On 27 May, the companies inaugurated Guernsey-Exeter and Guernsey-Brighton services. After the outbreak of War, the company resumed limited services between Jersey-Shoreham and Guernsey-Shoreham from 24 October using DH86s. By 1940 Shoreham became unserviceable and between 8-11 February and 18 February-2 March 1940 RAF Tangmere was used. Guernsey Airways commenced a Southampton-Guernsey mail service on 8 May using a DH86 *The Belcroute Bay* (G-ACZP) flown by Capt B Walker with the first return mail flown on 22 May. On the same day mail flights were started between Jersey and Guernsey (first return mail flown on 10 July). Jersey Airlines had taken delivery of a stylish-looking prototype de Havilland 95 Flamingo (G-AFUE) on 3 July that was kept busy during the summer carrying 1,373 fare-paying passengers over 25,915 miles in under two months. During the same month the company founder, W L Thurgood, sold his interests to Whitehall Securities and the Great Western Railway and Southern Railway.

North of the border, Scottish Airways commenced a Kirkwall (Orkney)-Glasgow-Kirkwall circular service on 15 May and by 31 July added an Inverness-Wick-Kirkwall-North Ronaldsway air mail service three times a week using a Dragon (G-ACIT) flown by Capt Fresson. The start of the War was causing the airline few disruptions and on 11 September, the Renfrew-Campbeltown-Islay service was re-opened that had been previously suspended. Next day an inter-island route from Inverness to Wick, Kirkwall and Orkney using the DH89 (G-ADAJ) began. This was extended on a charter basis to Shetland on 1 November and the company gained a regular mail contract that operated between Glasgow and Campbeltown.

Wartime services

By the autumn the war was beginning to disrupt many civil operations due mainly to the uncertainty of the situation and the German advance through Europe. On 11 October, a joint Heston-Paris service was operated by Imperial Airways with Air France using British Ensigns and French Dewoitine D338s. Aer Lingus re-opened its Dublin-Liverpool service and Isle of Man Air Services re-opened its Isle of Man-Liverpool and Belfast routes that had been suspended. DDL Danish Air Lines briefly resumed Copenhagen-Amsterdam-Shoreham services on 13 November but when its Focke-Wulf Fw 200 *Dania* (OY-DAM) arrived on the regular service on 8 April 1940 it was seized by the British authorities and not permitted to return. The aircraft name was changed to *Wolf*, re-registered G-AGAY and passed to BOAC. The aircraft was never repatriated due to being damaged beyond repair by the RAF (as DX177) in an accident at White Waltham in July 1941.

The two Danish Focke-Wulf Fw 200 Condors, W.Nr. 2993, OY-DEM 'Jutlandia' in the background with W.Nr. 2894, OY-DAM 'Dania' in the foreground. At the time of the photograph, OY-DAM had not yet had its name applied.

Tragically, the Imperial Airways HP42E *Hannibal* (G-AAGX), that had served the airline so well during the pre-war period, was lost on 1 March 1940 over the Gulf of Oman between Jiwani and Sharjah on the Karachi-Alexandria route. Some wreckage, but not the aircraft cabin, was spotted three days later strewn along a beach at Ras al Kuh and identified as being from the HP42, but the cause of the accident remains a mystery that has given rise to a certain amount of speculation. The crew consisted of Capt Townsend; first officer C J Walsh; radio officer A H H Tidbury and steward, C A Steventon.

During the early part of 1940 German advances were interrupting international services between Britain and Western Europe. Following the invasions of Denmark and Norway, the British Airways Perth-Oslo-Stockholm service was suspended on 9 April. This had been operated by Junkers Ju 52/3ms and Lockheed 14 aircraft. The Junkers *Jason* (G-AFAP) never returned from Oslo after it was captured by the Germans. On 4-5 May, the former Imperial Airways S30 C-Class flying boats *Cabot* and *Caribou,* assigned to No 119 Squadron, RAF, as V3137 and V3138, were destroyed by German bombing while participating in a mission to the Allied base at Harstad in northern Norway. By 10 May, Belgium and the Netherlands had fallen, forcing all SABENA and KLM flights to Shoreham to cease. Five days earlier the Associated Airlines Joint Committee (AAJC) was formed by an agreement between the Secretary of State for Air and Air Commerce Ltd, Great Western and Southern Air Lines, Isle of Man Air Services, Olley Air Services, Railway Air Services, Scottish Airways and West Coast Air Services. Allied Airways had a separate agreement with the Secretary of State and Jersey Airways and Guernsey Airways were beyond the jurisdiction of the Committee and not party to the agreement.

Although RAS had re-opened its Liverpool-Belfast-Glasgow route and Scottish Airways its Glasgow (Renfrew)-Tiree-Barra-Benbecula-North Uist service, with an extension to Stornoway, by 17 May the Air Ministry ordered the cancellation of all services. The aircraft belonging to the member companies of the AAJC were ordered to various RAF stations, but this was cancelled the same day allowing normal services to resume on 20 May. However, this was short-lived and two days later these aircraft were required to assist in the evacuation of the British Expeditionary Force from Dunkirk. The aircraft remained at the disposal of the Government until 2 June when they were returned to airline services once it was considered too dangerous for unarmed aircraft to participate in the evacuations. Services were suspended once more on 15 June at which point the aircraft were flown to Exeter and were again required to assist evacuation duties from France. On 18 June four aircraft (DH86s G-AEFH & G-AEWR & DH89s G-AEBW and G-AEPF) that had flown to Bordeaux had to be abandoned.

The Scottish Airways Glasgow-Campbeltown-Islay, Glasgow-Hebrides and Inverness-Kirkwall routes that had also been suspended,

were resumed between 24-29 June and on 7 November, the Inverness-Kirkwall-Shetland service was re-opened along with the RAS Liverpool-Belfast-Glasgow service on 27 June.

On 1 April the British Overseas Airways Corporation (BOAC) was formerly launched and took over the assets of Imperial Airways and British Airways to form the new chosen instrument. Services commenced with the first BOAC Empire service to Durban that departed on 3 April. Prior to this, Clive Pearson had replaced Lord Reith on 6 March as chairman of Imperial Airways in readiness to for the start of the new corporation. BOAC was soon embroiled in wartime operations on 22-23 May that began with the *Ensigns* flying food to Merville to supply troops that had been surrounded. During this operation *Elysian* (G-ADSZ) was destroyed on the ground by a German air attack. On 1 June, the AW27 *Ettrick* (G-ADSX) had to be abandoned at Le Bourget following a German air raid. Three days later, regular DH91 Frobisher flights had began operating from Heston to Lisbon twice-weekly, initially landing at Bordeaux until the city was captured. KLM also began operating under charter to BOAC between the UK and Lisbon to connect with the Pan American Airways Lisbon-New York *Clipper* service. By 13 June all flights to Paris were suspended for the remainder of the war.

Once Italy entered the war, overseas flights became severely restricted and although some African destinations were maintained using land planes, the French banned British flights from crossing the Sahara from 28 June. For a while a few services were maintained between the UK and Khartoum via Bordeaux, Lézignan, Oran, Gao and Fort Lamy. The Mediterranean routes were by then curtailed and the Horseshoe Route was introduced that linked Durban to Australia via Cairo on 18 June. C-Class flying boats operated this service on a weekly basis from 19 June. Singapore-Sydney continued to be flown by Qantas; Sydney-Auckland by Tasman Empire Airways Ltd (TEAL) who received three Empire flying boats, *Aotearoa, Awarua* and *Australia,* with an increased range of 2,000 miles. Other destinations linked by the route were Lourenço Marques, Beira, Dar-es-Salaam, Mombasa, Kisumu, Khartoum, Cairo, Habbaniyeh (for Baghdad), Basra, Karachi, Calcutta, Rangoon, Bangkok and Penang.

All Channel Islands services were suspended from 15 June and by 1 July the islands were under German occupation. Jersey Airways and Guernsey Airways had transferred their termini to Heston but shortly after moved to Exeter. From 19-21 June, the unarmed DH86s of the companies had successfully evacuated 319 people from the islands.

Between 3 August-23 September BOAC made four round-trips using the C-Class *Clare* (G-AFCZ) to carry mail and officials between Poole-Botwood-Montreal and New York. *Clyde* (G-AFCX) made a

further round trip between 4-11 October and the same aircraft was used by Capt Loraine to survey a route between Poole and West Africa between 6-9 August that connected Lisbon-Bathurst-Freetown and Lagos. Flights at ten-day intervals operated from 19 October carrying Government personnel, freight and mail using *Clyde* and *Clare*. Capt Loraine continued on to Leopoldville where talks were held aboard the moored flying boat to bring French Equatorial Africa on to the Allied side. Between August and December the former British Airways Lockheed 14s, Electras and Junkers Ju 52/3ms, now owned by BOAC, resumed the Takoradi-Khartoum service that had been suspended during June. By the end of the year they were making seven flights a fortnight and the route had been extended to Cairo. The C-Class flying boats, *Cassiopeia* (G-ADUX), *Corinthian* (G-AEUF) and *Cooee* (G-AFBL) were also used to operate services between Poole and Lagos. Capt Bailey continued on the latter to Leopoldville and afterwards the three aircraft operated the Horseshoe Route from Lake Victoria. During October SABENA also opened a weekly Takoradi-Lagos-Douala-Libenge-Stanleyville-Juba-Khartoum-Cairo service by arrangement with BOAC. In the Far East, difficulties obtaining rights to cross French Indo China forced BOAC to suspend services to Hong Kong on 15 October and by Christmas 1941 the Colony has been invaded by the Japanese.

At the end of the 1938-39 Imperial Airways fiscal year, figures showed a substantial increase in traffic. The company's aircraft had completed 8,958,400 miles in the previous 12 months (compared to 6,224,000 to April 1938 and 853,042 during its first year). In spite of the inherent problems, the company had achieved considerable growth See table below..

Passenger figures however have been queried in a study published by Gordon Pirie in The *Journal of Transport History* (March 2004) titled *Passenger Traffic in the 1930s on British Imperial Air Routes*. This suggests the airline may have distorted these figures by failing to make a clear definition between paying customers and staff. Pirie's argument appears quite well founded because load factors that have been published in various sources do tend to show an amazing lack of consistency. At the time of writing the report is available on the internet and makes an interesting read.[1]

According to Pirie: '*The standard passenger traffic data used in both popular and academic writing about British Empire civil aviation are taken from a narrow and limited set of figures. Without other numerical information, statistical records produced by Imperial Airways for operational and accounting*

reasons, and released by the airline for public consumption, have their use Yet these figures are not easy to comprehend, and they are difficult to rework into meaningful categories. Annualised data, and figures aggregated across the two European and the two empire trunk routes, obscure monthly and geographical variations in passenger traffic. The data also fails to distinguish between paying and non-paying passengers, and between seat bookings and actual travel.'

Imperial Airways achieved much during the 16 years of the airline's existence and it managed to grow exponentially despite having to overcome much adversity, not least from apathetic British Governments that refused to provide the adequate subsidies necessary to survey and open the Empire routes to India, Africa, and Australasia. Financially this left the company exposed, especially in Europe where foreign competition was generously state funded. In later years this had an even more profound affect. By this time the company's main European competitors were already operating all-steel monoplanes while Imperial Airways remained for too long trapped in a time warp and was expected to struggle on with an outdated collection of biplanes. Even by the time the S23 C-Class flying boats had been introduced, they were already technically inferior to and unable to compete on range and payload with Pan American's *Clippers*. Imperial Airways was widely criticised, usually with good reason, for the safety and unreliability of its aircraft. Accusations of serious mismanagement, similarly well-founded, were aimed at the board of directors, especially over the manner in which it conducted staff relations. The company had been criticised for expecting non-flying staff to be sent abroad at short notice with no consideration being given to their families. There were ongoing disputes with many of the pilots who, it seems, did not always have the backing of Brackley. Had the merger with British Airways to form BOAC, not been forced upon it, there is no way of knowing how long Imperial Airways could have survived without the need for major expenditure to upgrade its fleet. With an increasing likelihood of intense competition from abroad, the company's days may well have been numbered. Britain could have been a world leader in civil aviation from the start, but successive governments procrastinated allowing the industry to become second rate. As it transpired, the formation of BOAC was probably a good move by the Government but the new company was unable to make a major impact owing to the interruption of war. Nevertheless the initial period of commercial airline operations had been as interesting as it was challenging and we owe so much to the staunch efforts of the early pioneers who left behind a legacy that shaped the future of a global airline system.

Traffic statistics on Imperial Airways and Associated Companies, with annual profit and loss and government subsidy payments to Imperial Airways 1924-25 to 1938-39

Fiscal Year	Route Mileage	Aircraft Miles Flown	Passengers Carried	Total Ton Miles	Profit or Loss	Government subsidy
1924	1520	699,900	10,321	350,700	£-15,217	
1925	1368	805,300	11,027	383,800	£-20,415	£137,000
1926	1368	733,000	16,621	493,500	£11,461	£137,000
1927	2355	719,000	19,005	539,600	£72,567	£152,600
1928	2215	911,300	27,303	798,800	£78,861	£235,100
1929	5305	1,166,000	28,484	994,300	£60,139	£230,600
1930	5570	1,104,900	24,027	921,700	£27,140	£364,650
1931	7760	1,276,900	23,817	1,060,800	£10,186	£340,325
1932	11,263	1,733,700	45,844	2,013,800	£52,894	£467,513
1933	13,709	1,926,000	54,768	2,624,100	£78,572	£545,008
1934	13,471	2,315,100	54,875	3,152,400	£133,769 a	£543,694
1935	15,529	4,079,400	66,324	4,772,200	£140,705 b	£561,556
1936	19,351	4,789,000	60,374	4,868,600	£164,735 c	£426,595
1937	22,432	5,700,800	64,629	7,548,500	£92,267 d	£381,767
1938	24,904	8,958,400	51,287	14,200,000		£619,625★
1939						£1,233,614

Sources and notes: Government Subsidies from Command Papers 5685, 85: The other figures have been taken from Robin Higham's book *British Imperial Air Routes 1918-1939* (G T Foulis 1960) and are attributed to *Imperial Airways 1924-1940* and *The Journal of Transport History* (1 November 1954) and the annual reports of Imperial Airways. The profit and loss figures includes the following: a) Plus £31,593 not attributable to 1934 fiscal year; b) Plus £12,229 not attributable to 1935 fiscal year; c) Plus £7,487 not attributable to 1936 fiscal year and d) plus £1,205 not attributable to 1937 fiscal year. The traffic figures have been taken from the Air Ministry *Civil Aviation Statistical and Technical Review* (1938).

★Includes Empire Mail Service.

1. http://findarticles.com/p/articles/mi_qa3884/is_200403/ai_n9394507/

SOME ASPECTS OF   IMPERIAL AIRWAYS

In this and succeeding issues of the *Gazette* we are showing a number of photographs in an attempt to give some idea of the multifarious aspects of the organization behind the successful operation of Imperial Airways routes

THE COMMANDERS

To the public the Commanders are the embodiment of Empire air transport. Upon their shoulders lies the responsibility not only of flying and of navigating the company's airliners but of helping to maintain its prestige along nearly 30,000 miles of routes

They are members of a profession which demands a high degree of skill in pilotage, in navigation, in engineering, in a knowledge of meteorology and the technique of wireless operation

THE FIRST OFFICERS

The responsibility of flying regular services day in and day out to the 'uttermost ends of the earth' is a heavy one and a task for only the skilled and the experienced

Commanders begin their service as First Officers, in which rank they gain experience, but before they are appointed even Probationary First Officers they must have won knowledge either as pilots in the King's Service or in commercial life, and they receive additional training in the company's own school. Like the Commanders, First Officers are skilled pilots, navigators, wireless operators and engineers, for they share duty with the Commanders

THE RADIO OFFICERS

The story of the progress of air transport is largely one of the progress of radio communication. To the uninitiated, an airline may appear to be a number of aircraft moving apparently at random, whereas, in reality, they are in the grip of a vast and growing organization and controlled upon the ground and in the air. The essential element of this control is wireless; wireless to convey information from the ground; wireless to let airliner speak to airliner; wireless to give information about weather; wireless as an aid to navigation. This control needs skilled and experienced men and all airliners on the Empire routes carry radio officers

THE FLIGHT CLERKS

The airliners operating the Empire services carry 'ship's papers,' the compilation and the care of which require skilled attention, for any infraction of national regulations may cause delay in the transit of the mail, passengers and cargo

A Flight Clerk is entrusted with their care and with the stowing and the unloading of the mail and baggage; he also shares with the Flight Steward the task of seeing that the comfort of the passengers is observed

His is but one of the many new professions which have been born with the coming of air transport

THE FLIGHT STEWARDS

Air transport, while bringing the advantage of speed, must also offer a standard of comfort comparable with that of its competitors. To travel by air is to be comfortable. Cabins are quiet, large and lofty, warmed and ventilated, meals are served as they should be—but these are the mechanical aspects, lifeless if there is not the human spirit of service and understanding behind them. It is the Flight Steward who gives this—a man experienced in the art of pleasing and of giving attention

GROUND SERVICE

However perfect the airliners in design and in construction, and however skilled their officers and crews, yet if this mechanical state be not maintained at a pitch of perfection, then it will not be possible to operate the services efficiently

The State long ago decreed that no British airliner shall ever leave the ground or the water unless its condition be mechanically sound. Ground engineers, riggers, fitters, metal-workers, electricians, inspectors, carpenters, cleaners, craftsmen of every branch of aeronautical engineering—upon the work and the skill of each one of these rests largely the reputation of the Empire air routes

A period feature from Imperial Airways Gazette showing aspects of the running of the airline.

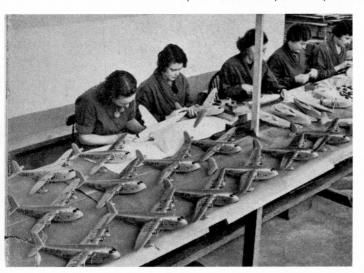

One aspect of promoting Imperial Airways in the eyes of the public was the creation of a series of models of the fleet – in this case the C-Class flying boats intended for use in travel agencies. They were made by International Model Aircraft Ltd, makers of the well-known Frog and Penguin aircraft models. The models proved very popular as window displays, so much so, that they became available in toy shops across the country, either ready-made or as a kit, comprising 33 parts moulded in plastic. Much virtue was made of the then fairly new injection moulded nature of the components for models of this size, as against Bakelite, a more brittle material.

APPENDIX 1 **BRITISH AIRLINES AND THEIR AIRCRAFT**

This list includes only the aircraft known, or thought to have been delivered, or in service during the period covered by this book

A full list of civil aviation registration for the period can be found on the internet at: www.goldenyears.ukf.net/home.htm

Note: The second column represents the manufacturer's serial number in the majority of cases, the third column the fleet name of the aircraft where applicable and the last column brief notes that are known about the aircraft.

AIRCRAFT TRANSPORT & TRAVEL LIMITED (AT&T) (1919-1920)

AIRCO de Havilland 4 (Introduced 1919)
G-EAEX	K142		}
G-EANL	F2671		} Registrations cancelled 4/1920
G-EANK	F2670		}

AIRCO de Havilland 4A (Introduced 1919)
G-EAHF	F2699		Crashed Caterham 11/12/1919
G-EAHG	F2694		Forced landing English Channel 20/10/1919
G-EAJC	F2702		Scrapped November 1920
G-EAJD	F2704		Scrapped November 1920

AIRCO de Havilland 6 (Introduced 1919)
G-EAAB		formerly K100 Sold to Marconi - Crashed Croydon November 1921

AIRCO de Havilland 9 & 9B (Introduced 1919)
G-EAAA	C6054		Crashed Portsdown Hill 1/5/1919
G-EAAC	K100 & H9277		Converted to DH9J
G-EAGX		Ancuba	Sold abroad August 1920
G-EAGY			Sold abroad January 1921
G-EALJ			
G-EAMX			Sold abroad April 1920
G-EAOZ	5889		To KLM July 1921 (H-NABF)
G-EAPL			To KLM July 1921 (H-NABE)
G-EAPO			Written off September 1920
G-EAPU			Written off November 1920
G-EAQA			Crashed January 1921
G-EAQL			Sold to Belgium July 1921
G-EAQN			Crashed Le Bourget 9/11/1920
G-EAQP			Sold to S F Cotton

AIRCO de Havilland 9A (Introduced 1919)
G-EAOF	E750	
G-EAOG	E752	
G-EAOH	F753	
G-EAOI	E754	
G-EAOJ	E756	
G-EAOK	E757	

This group of aircraft was Napier-Lion powered and was used for the carriage of mail to the Army of the Occupation and operated between Hawkinge and Cologne that was started by the RAF and taken over by AT&T. DH9s and 9As were used from November 1919

AIRCO de Havilland 16 (Introduced 1919)
G-EACT	K130		Crashed March 1920
G-EALM			to de Havilland
G-EALU		Arras	To de Havilland
G-EAPM		Agincourt	To de Havilland
G-EAPT			To de Havilland
G-EAQS			
G-EARU			
G-EASW			

AIRCO de Havilland 18 & 18A (Introduced 1920)
G-EARJ		Crashed Wallington 16/8/1920
G-EARO		To RAE Farnborough 1924
G-EAUF		To Instone, written off 13/5/21

HANDLEY PAGE TRANSPORT LIMITED (1919-1924)

Handley Page 0/400 (Introduced 1919)
The HP number was allocated after military use

G-EAAE	D8350	HP16	Vulture	Scrapped August 1920
G-EAAF	F5414	HP13		to USA May 1920 rebuilt as 0/7
G-EAAG	F5418	HP18	Penguin	Crashed April 1920
G-EAAW	F5417	HP14		Withdrawn April 1920

G-EAKE	J2252		Crashed Sweden June 1920
G-EAKF	J2249	HP19	Scrapped October 1920
G-EAKG	J2250	HP20	Scrapped August 1920
G-EALY	J2247	HP24	Scrapped October 1920
G-EALX	J2251	HP21	Scrapped April 1921
G-EAMA	J2248	HP25	Crashed Cricklewood 12/1920

Handley Page 0/11 (Introduced 1920)
G-EASL	C9699	HP30	Crashed April 1920
G-EASM	C9731	HP31	Withdrawn April 1921
G-EASN	D4611	HP32	Withdrawn April 1921
G-EASO	D5444	HP33	Withdrawn April 1921
G-EASZ	F310	HP36	To India April 1921

Handley Page 0/10 (Introduced 1920)
G-EASY	D4614	HP35	To India April 1921
G-EATG	D4618	HP37	Withdrawn April 1921
G-EATH	D4631	HP38	To IA – Broken up June 1925
G-EATJ	F307	HP39	Withdrawn April 1921
G-EATK	J2262	HP40	Scrapped August 1922
G-EATL	F312	HP41	Withdrawn April 1921
G-EATM	D4609	HP42	Wrecked Berck 30/12/21
G-EATN	J2261	HP43	Crashed Senlis, France 14/1/22

De Havilland 4A (Introduced 1920)
G-EAVL	H5905		Crashed April 1921
G-EAWH	F5764		Withdrawn 1922

Handley Page W8 (Introduced 1921)
G-EAPJ	W8-1/HP15	City of Newcastle	Later renamed: Duchess of York

Handley Page W8b (Introduced 1922)
G-EBBG	W8-2	Bombay	Later renamed: Princess Mary To IA
G-EBBH	W8-3	Melbourne	Later renamed: Prince George To IA
G-EBBI	W8-4	Prince Henry	To IA

De Havilland 18B (Introduced 1922 – On loan from Air Ministry)
G-EAWX	6	Returned June 1922

Bristol Type 62 Ten-Seater (Introduced 1922 – On loan from Air Ministry)
G-EAWY	6124	Returned June 1922

S INSTONE & COMPANY LIMITED and THE INSTONE AIR LINE LIMITED (1919-1924)

De Havilland 4A (Introduced 1919)
G-EAMU	H5939	City of Cardiff	Rebuilt as DH4A & renamed
		City of York	To IA

Bristol 47 Tourer (Introduced 1920)
G-EART	5876	Withdrawn Feb 1921

Vickers FB28 – Vimy Commercial (Introduced 1920)
G-EASI	41	City of London	To IA: After retirement believed to have been used as a summer house in Croydon

BAT FK26 (Introduced 1920)
G-EAPK		City of Newcastle	Crashed 31/7/22

Westland Limousine (Introduced 1920)
G-EAJL	WAC2	
G-EARE	WAC4	Scrapped 19/6/23
G-EARF	WAC5	Scrapped 1923
G-EAWF	WAC9	Scrapped April 1923

De Havilland 18 (Introduced 1921)
G-EARO	2 & E53	City of Cardiff	On loan to RAE 1924
G-EAUF	3 & E54	City of Paris	Crashed 13/5/21
G-EAWO	4		To Daimler Airways: mid-air collision Poix
G-EAWW	5		
G-EAWX	6		To Handley Page; dismantled 18/11/23

De Havilland 34 (Introduced 1922)
G-EBBR	28	City of Glasgow	To IA
G-EBBT	30	City of New York	To IA
G-EBBV	32	City of Washington	To IA
G-EBBW	30	City of Chicago	To IA

Vickers Type 61 Vulcan (Introduced 1922)

G-EBBL	1	*City of Antwerp*	To IA
G-EBDH	2		
Returned to Vickers June 1923			
G-EBEA	3	*City of Brussels*	Returned to Vickers June 1923

Bristol 75 Ten-seater (Introduced 1924)

G-EBEV	6145	*City of Bristol*	To IA

AIR POST OF BANKS LIMITED (1920)

Westland Limousine (Both aircraft loaned by Westland Aircraft Works)

G-EAFO	WAC1	Demolished by Fairey 3/9/25
G-EAJL	WAC2	Sold to Newfoundland 8/22

THE DAIMLER AIRWAY (1922-1924)

De Havilland DH18A (Introduced 1922)

G-EAWO	4	Mid-air crash between Poix & Beauvais 7/4/22

De Havilland DH34 (Introduced 1922)

G-EBBQ	27	*City of Glasgow*	To IA
G-EBBS	29		Crashed Ivinghoe Beacon 4/9/23
G-EBBU	31		Crashed Berck 3/11/22
G-EBBX	35		To IA 31/3/24; crashed Purley 24/12/24
G-EBBY	36		To IA 31/3/24; scrapped
G-EBCX	35		To IA 31/3/24; Crashed Croydon 23/9/24

THE BRITISH MARINE AIR NAVIGATION COMPANY LIMITED (1923-1924)

Supermarine Sea Eagle (Introduced 1923)

G-EBFX	1163	*Sea Eagle*	Damaged Alderney 13/10/23 not repaired
G-EBGR	1164	*Sarnia*	To IA
G-EBGS	1165		To IA; sunk Guernsey 10/1/22 Then burnt Heston 13/2/54

IMPERIAL AIRWAYS LIMITED (1924-1940)

Handley Page 0/10 (1924)

G-EATH	D4631	From HP Transport but never used

De Havilland DH34 (1924)

G-EBBR		From Instone - Crashed Ostend 27/5/24
G-EBBT		From Instone - Dismantled March 1926
G-EBBV		From Instone - Dismantled March 1926
G-EBBW		From Instone - Dismantled March 1926
G-EBBX		From Daimler Airways - Dismantled December 1924
G-EBBY		From Daimler Airways - Crashed Purley 24/12/24
G-EBCX		From Daimler Airways - Dismantled December 1924

Handley Page W8b (HP18) (1924)

G-EBBG	W8-2	*Princes Mary*	From HP Transport; crashed Abbeville
G-EBBH	W8-3	*Prince George*	From HP Transport
G-EBBI	W8-4	*Prince Henry*	From HP Transport

Vickers FB28 Vimy Commercial (1924)

G-EASI	41	*City of London*	From Instone

Supermarine Sea Eagle (1924)

G-EBGR	1164	*Sarnia*	From British Marine Air Navigation
G-EBGS	1165		From British Marine Air Navigation Rammed & sunk St Peter Port Guernsey 10.127

Vickers 4 Vulcan (1924)

G-EBFC	8	Withdrawn December 1924 – Dismantled 1927
G-EBLB	9	Crashed & Burned Purley 13/7/28
G-EBEK		Aircraft owned by Air Ministry & used for 1925 Empire Exhibition Display at Wembley

De Havilland DH50 (1924)

G-EBFO	74	Converted to DH50J. This aircraft was used on survey work: India to Burma, (1924-25). Cape Town (1925-26)

As twin-float seaplane:

		Australia (1926) To West Australian Airways January 1929 as VH-UMC
G-EBFP	75	To Iraq Petroleum October 1932 Scrapped 23/10/28
G-EBKZ	133	Crashed Plymouth 23/10/28

Handley Page W8f Hamilton (HP26) (1924)

G-EBIX	W8-7	*City of Washington*	Crashed Neufchatel 30/10/30

Bristol 75A (1924)

G-EBEV	6145	Used for cargo evaluation

Avro 563 Andover (1925)

G-EBKW	5097	On loan from Air Council for tests

Handley Page W9 Hampstead (HP27) (1926)

G-EBLE	W9-1	*City of New York*	To New Guinea January 1929 as VH-ULK

Handley Page W10 (HP30) (1926)

G-EBMM	W10-1	*City of Melbourne*	To National Aviation Day Displays Nov 1933
G-EBMR	W10-2	*City of Pretoria*	To National Aviation Day Displays Nov 1933
G-EBMS	W10-3	*City of London*	Crashed in English Channel 21/10/26
G-EBMT	W10-4	*City of Ottawa*	Crashed English Channel 17/6/29

Armstrong Whitworth Argosy MK1 (1926)

G-EBLF	AW154	*City of Glasgow*	Withdrawn Sept 1934
G-EBLO	AW155	*City of Birmingham*	Crashed at Aswan 16/6/31
G-EBOZ	AW156	*City of Wellington*	Renamed *City of Arundel* Written off Oct 1934

De Havilland DH66 Hercules (1926)

G-EBMW	236	*City of Cairo*	Crashed at Timor April 1931
G-EBMX	237	*City of Delhi*	To South African Air Force Nov 1934
G-EBMY	238	*City of Baghdad*	Withdrawn 1933
G-EBMZ	239	*City of Jerusalem*	Destroyed by fire at Jask
G-EBNA	240	*City of Teheran*	Damaged beyond repair Gaza
G-AAJH	393	*City of Basra*	To South African Air Force April 1934
G-AARY	703	*City of Karachi*	Withdrawn Dec 1935
G-ABCP	347	*City of Jodhpur*	To West Australian Airways – Crashed Uganda 23/11/35
G-ABMT	344	*City of Cape Town*	To West Australian Airways – then to South African Air Force July 1934

De Havilland DH54 Highclere (1926)

G-EBKI	151	On loan from Air Ministry 7/11/26 – Destroyed when snow caused hangar roof to collapse at Croydon 1/2/27

Vickers 170 Vanguard (1926)

G-EBCP	1	On loan from Air Ministry for Tests – Crashed Shepperton 16/5/29

Supermarine Swan (1927)

G-EBJY	1173	On loan from Air Ministry – Scrapped 1927

Short S8 Calcutta

G-EBVG	S712	*City of Alexandria*	Capsized Crete 28/12/36
G-EBVH	S713	*City of Athens*	Renamed City of Stonehaven Dismantled 1937
G-AADN	S748	*City of Rome*	Forced down at Spezia 26/10/29
G-AASJ	S752	*City of Khartoum*	Crashed Alexandria 31/12/35
G-AATZ	S754	*City of Salonica*	Renamed *City of Swanage*. Scrapped 1939

Supermarine Southampton (1929)

G-AASH	1235	On loan from Air Ministry

Armstrong Whitworth Argosy MKII (1929)

G-AACH	AW362	*City of Edinburgh*	Crashed & burned Croydon 22/4/26
G-AACI	AW363	*City of Liverpool*	Crashed nr Dixmude 28/3/33
G-AACJ	AW364	*City of Manchester*	To United Airways July 1935
G-AAEJ	AW400	*City of Coventry*	Dismantled 1935

Westland IV (1929)

G-AAGW	1867	Later converted to Wessex

De Havilland DH61 Giant Moth (1930)

G-AAEV	335		Ex-Cobham's *Young Britain* – crashed Broken Hill 19/1/30

Handley Page HP42 Hannibal Class (1931)

G-AAGX	42/1	*Hannibal*	Lost Sharjah-Jask 1/3/40
G-AAUC	42/4	*Horsa*	
G-AAUD	42/3	*Hanno*	Later Converted to Heracles Class - Wrecked in gale Bristol 19/3/40
G-AAUE	42/2	*Hadrian*	To BOAC

Handley Page HP45 Heracles Class (1931)

G-AAXC	42/5	*Heracles*	Wrecked in gale Bristol 19/3/40
G-AAXD	42/6	*Horatius*	Wrecked in forced landing – Tiverton 7/11/39
G-AAXE	42/7	*Hengist*	Later converted to Hannibal Class. Burnt out in fire at Karachi 31/5/37
G-AAXF	42/8	*Helena*	Later converted to Hannibal Class

Short S17 Kent Scipio Class (1931)

G-ABFA	S758	*Scipio*	Sank Mirabella 22/8/36
G-ABFB	S759	*Sylvanus*	Burnt out in arson attack Brindisi 9/11/35
G-ABFC	S760	*Satyrus*	Scrapped Hythe June 1938

Westland Wessex (1931)

G-ABEG	1901		Damaged beyond repair Northern Rhodesia1936
G-ACHI	2151		

Avro Ten (Type 618) (1931)

G-AASP	384	*Achilles*	Charter– to BOAC 1939 destroyed 1940
G-ABLU	528	*Apollo*	Crashed Ruysselede, Belgium 30/12/38

Armstrong Whitworth XV Atalanta (1932)

G-ABPI	AW740	*Atalanta*	Transferred to Indian Trans Continental Airways as VT-AEF *Arethusa*
G-ABTG	AW785	*Amalthea*	Crashed Kisumu 27/7/38
G-ABTH	AW741	*Andromeda*	Retired June 1939
G-ABTI	AW742	*Atalanta*	To BOAC 1940
G-ABTJ	AW743	*Artemis*	To BOAC 1940
G-ABTK	AW744	*Athena*	Destroyed by fire at Delhi 29/9/36
G-ABTL	AW784	*Astraea*	To BOAC 1940
G-ABTM	AW786	*Aurora*	Transferred to Indian Trans Continental Airways as VT-AEG

Desoutter I B (1933)

G-ABMW	D28	*Air Taxi No 6*	Used until 1935

Short L17 Scylla (1934)

G-ACJJ	S768	*Scylla*	To RAF March 1940 crashed Drem, Scotland 14/4/40
G-ACJK	S769	*Syrinx*	To RAF March 1940. Broken up 1940

De Havilland DH86 Diana Class (1934)

G-ACPL	2300	*Delphinus*	To BOAC; undercarriage collapsed
G-ACWC	2304	*Delia*	To BOAC; crashed Nigeria 17/6/41
G-ACWD	2305	*Dorado*	To BOAC; damaged beyond repair 17/3/43
G-ADCM	2317	*Draco*	Crashed Zwettl, Austria 22/10/35
G-ADUE	2333	*Dardanus*	To BOAC; collapsed landing gear
G-ADUF	2334	*Dido*	To BOAC; withdrawn 3/5/52
G-ADUG	2335	*Danae*	To BOAC; Broken for parts
G-ADUH	2336	*Dryad*	Sold 1936 Ireland 1951
G-ADCN	2319	*Daedalus*	Burnt out Bangkok 1938
G-ADEF	2328	*Dione*	To BOAC; Collapsed Lydda 1941
G-ADUI	2337	*Denebola*	To BOAC
G-AEAP	2349	*Demeter*	To BOAC; Burnt out Sicily 1943

Boulton Paul P71A Boadicea Class (1935)

G-ACOX	P71A/1	*Boadicea*	Lost English Channel 25/9/36
G-ACOY	P71A/2	*Britomart*	Crash-landing Brussels 25/10/35

Avro 652 (1936)

G-ACRM	698	*Avalon*	To Air Service Training July 1938
G-ACRN	699	*Avatar*	Later renamed Ava: to Air ServiceTraining July 1938

Vickers 212 Vellox (1936)

G-ABKY	1		Used for cargo

Vickers 252 Viastra X (1936)

G-ACCC	1		Used for radio and icing tests

Shorts S8/8 Rangoon (1936)

G-AEIM	S757		Used for training

Shorts S23 C Class flying boat (1936)

G-ADHL	S795	*Canopus*	To BOAC Apr 1940 - Broken up 1946
G-ADHM	S804	*Caledonia*	1937 made 1st Atlantic crossing – to BOAC Apr 1940 – broken up 23/3/47
G-ADUT	S811	*Centaurus*	Surveyed Far East to New Zealand – to Australia Sept 39, destroyed at Broome 3/8/42
G-ADUU	S812	*Cavalier*	New York-Bermuda service, crashed 21 January 1939
G-ADUV	S813	*Cambria*	Used with G-ADHL on trans-Atlantic survey 1937 – to BOAC – broken up Jan 1947
G-ADUW	S814	*Castor*	Made 1st regular Alexandria flight 6/2/37 To BOAC – broken up 4/2/47
G-ADUX	S815	*Cassiopeia*	To BOAC – crashed Sabang 22/12/41
G-ADUY	S816	*Capella*	Damaged beyond repair Batavia 12/3/39
G-ADUZ	S817	*Cygnus*	Crashed Brindisi 5 December 1937
G-ADVA	S818	*Capricornus*	Crashed nr Macon 24 March 1937
G-ADVB	S819	*Corsair*	To BOAC – broken up 20/1/47
G-ADVC	S820	*Courtier*	Crashed nr Athens 1 October 1937
G-ADVD	S821	*Challenger*	Crashed at Mozambique 1 May 1939
G-ADVE	S822	*Centurion*	Crashed at Calcutta 12 June 1939
G-AETV	S838	*Coriolanus*	Later passed to Qantas as VH-ABG – to BOAC, broken up Sydney 1947
G-AETW	S839	*Calpurnia*	Crashed Lake Habbaniya 27/11/1938
G-AETX	S840	*Ceres*	To BOAC, destroyed by fire Durban 1/12/42
G-AETY	S841	*Clio*	To BOAC; impressed as AX659, crashed at Loch Indal 22/8/41
G-AETZ	S842	*Ciree*	To BOAC – shot down 28/2/42
G-AEUA	S843	*Calypso*	To BOAC – Impressed as A18-11 (RAAF) Crashed Daru Papua New Guinea 8 August 1942
G-AEUB	S844	*Camilia*	Passed to Qantas as VH-ADU, to BOAC, crashed Port Meresby 22/8/43
G-AEUC	S845	*Corinna*	To BOAC, destroyed at Broome in air raid 3/3/42
G-AEUD	S846	*Cordelia*	To BOAC, impressed as AD660, then back to BOAC, broken up6/3/47
G-AEUE	S847	*Cameronian*	To BOAC, broken up January 1947
G-AEUF	S848	*Corinthian*	To BOAC, crashed Darwin 22/3/1942
G-AEUG	S849	*Coogee*	Used under British Registration for part of 1938 - but was Qantas VH-ABC, crashed Townsville
G-AEUH	S850	*Corio*	Used under British Registration for part of 1938 – but was Qantas VH-ABD, then Australian Govt. Sept 39 shot down nr Koepang 10/1/42
G-AEUA	S851	*Coorong*	Used under British Registration for part of 1938 – but was Qantas VH-ABE, shot down Timor 30/1/42
G-AFBJ	S876	*Carpentaria*	Used under British Registration for part of 1938 – but was Qantas VH-ABA, broken up Hythe 19/1/47
G-AFBK	S877	*Coolangatta*	Used under British Registration for part of 1938 – but was Qantas VH-ABB, crashed Sydney 11 October 1944
G-AFBL	S878	*Cooee*	Used under British Registration for part of 1938 – but was Qantas VH-ABF, broken up Hythe 2/2/47

Short-Mayo Composite Aircraft (1938-1940)

G-ADHJ	S20/S796	*Mercury*	Upper component, scrapped 1941
G-ADHK	S21/2797	*Maia*	Lower component, Destroyed by German action, Poole 1942

Short S30 C class Empire flying boat (1938-1940)

G-AFCT	S879	*Champion*	To BOAC, broken up 19/1/47
G-AFCU	S880	*Cabot*	To BOAC, to RAF Sept 39, destroyed in air raid at Bodo 5/5/40
G-AFCV	S881	*Caribou*	Used for in-flight refuelling experiments, to RAF, destroyed in air raid at Bodo 5/5/40
G-AFCW	S882	*Connemara*	Destroyed by fire at Hythe 19/6/39
G-AFCX	S883	*Clyde*	To BOAC, wrecked in gale, Lisbon14/2/41

G-AFCZ	S885	*Clare*	To BOAC, then TEAL as ZK-AMB, then back to BOAC. Destroyed by in-flight fire nr Bathurst, West Africa 14/9/42
G-AFKZ	S1003	*Cathy*	To BOAC, broken up 9/3/47
G-AFCY	S884	*Captain Cook*	May have been used by Imperial Airways prior to going to Tasman Empire Airways (TEAL) as ZK-AMA Aurora during March 1940. later named Aotearoa. Broken up, Auckland 1953
G-AFDA	S886	*Cumberland*	To TEAL as ZK-AMC, broken up Auckland 1947

Shorts S33 flying-boat

G-AFPZ	S1025	*Clifton*	To BOAC, re-registered VH-ACD, crashed at Sydney 18/11/44
G-AFRA	S1026	*Cleopatra*	To BOAC, broken up 4/11/46
G-AFRB	S1027		Never completed, hull scrapped 1943

Armstrong Whitworth 27 Ensign (1938-1940)

G-ADSR	AW1156	*Ensign*	To BOAC and used by military Dismantled, Cairo Jan 1945
G-ADSS	AW1157	*Egeria*	Allocated to Indian Trans-Continental Airways as VT-VAJE but not delivered Wartime service, broken up 13/4/47
G-ADST	AW1158	*Elsinore*	To BOAC, broken up Hamble 28/3/47
G-ADSU	AW1159	*Euterpe*	Allocated to Indian Trans-Continental Airways as VT-AJR but not delivered, Dismantled Cairo 1946
G-ADSV	AW1160	*Explorer*	To BOAC, broken up Hamble 23/3/47
G-ADSW	AW1161	*Eddystone*	To BOAC, broken up Hamble 21/4/47
G-ADSX	AW1162	*Ettrick*	After German raid on Paris abandoned and later used by Germans
G-ADSY	AW1163	*Empyrean*	To BOAC, broken up Hamble 21/4/47
G-ADSZ	AW1164	*Elysian*	To BOAC, Destroyed by German action at Merville, France 23/5/40
G-ADTA	AW1165	*Euryalus*	Allocated to Indian Trans-Continental Airways as VT-AJG but not delivered: Damaged on supply mission to France Scrapped for spares 1941
G-ADTB	AW1166	*Echo*	To BOAC, broken up Hamble 20/3/47
G-ADTC	AW1167	*Endymion*	Allocated to Indian Trans-Continental Airways as VT-AJH but not delivered: To BOAC, burned out in air raid at Whitchurch 24/11/40
G-AFZU	AW1821	*Everest*	Delivered direct to BOAC, broken up at Hamble15/4/47
G-AFZV	AW1822	*Enterprise*	Force-landed during military use in West Africa, salvaged by French and registered F-AFZV, later F-BAHD and then used by Germans

De Havilland DH91 Albatross Frobisher Class (1938-1940)

G-AFDV	6802	*Frobisher*	To BOAC – destroyed Whitchurch in air raid 20/12/40
G-AFDJ	6803	*Falcon*	To BOAC, scrapped Sept 1943
G-AFDK	6804	*Fortuna*	To BOAC, crashed nr Shannon 6/7/43
G-AFDL	6805	*Fingid*	To BOAC, crashed Pucklechurch, nr Bristol 6/10/40
G-AFDM	6806	*Fiona*	To BOAC scrapped Sept 1943
G-AEVV	6800	*Faraday*	Ordered by Air Ministry for RAF, crashed Reykjavik 11/8/41
		Franklin	Ordered by Air Ministry for RAF, crashed Reykjavik 7/4/42

Saunders-Roe A19 Cloud (1940)

| G-ABHG | 19/2 | | For crew training. Damaged beyond repair June 1941 |

Short S26 G Class flying-boat

G-AFCI	871	*Golden Hind*	To RAF as X8275 1940; Destroyed by gale on River Swale 3/1954
G-AFCJ	872	*Golden Fleece*	To RAF as X8274 1940; destroyed 20/6/41
G-AFCK	873	*Golden Horn*	To RAF as X8273 1940; Crashed River Tagus, Lisbon 9/1/43

The G-Class was built for Imperial Airways but never went into service with the airline and were transferred from the Air Ministry to BOAC

The Fleets of the other Domestic Airlines

HILLMAN'S AIRWAYS LIMITED (1932-1935)

De Havilland DH60G Moth

| G-ABCW | 1552 | | Sold to India April 1933 as VT-AEC |

De Havilland DH60 GIII Moth

| G-ACGX | 5029 | | To Cinema Press 1936 |

De Havilland Puss Moth

G-ABSB	2213	*Sonny*	Withdrawn after accident at Clacton 7/5/33
G-ABSO	2217	*Babs*	Sold to Brian Lewis 1933
G-ABVX	2228	*Gifford*	To British Airways Oct 35 - Not used

De Havilland Fox Moth

G-ABVI	4004	*Chris*	To Essex Aero 1936
G-ABVK	4005	*Doreen*	To British Airways
G-ABWB	4007		Sold to Scottish Motor Traction 7/7/32 then to North Sea General 9/7/33, then to India
G-ABWF	4008		Sold to Scottish Motor Traction 31/1/33 Sold to India Oct 34. Crashed 1935

De Havilland DH84 Dragon

G-ACAN	6000	*Maylands*	Delivered by Amy Johnson – sold to Aberdeen Airways 16/8/34
G-ACAO	6001	*Goodmayes*	Sold Norman Edgar 15/10/35
G-ACAP	6002	*Romford*	To British Airways Dec 1935
G-ACBW	6009	*Gidea Park*	To Provincial Airways July 1934. Retired 1941
G-ACEU	6022	*Brentwood*	To British Airways 1935.
G-ACEV	6023	*Ilford*	Sisters committed suicide by jumping 21/2/35. To Airwork Dec 1935

De Havilland DH89 Dragon Rapide

G-ACPM	6251		Crashed Nr Folkestone 2/10/34
G-ACPN	6252		To British Airways Dec 1935 then Highland Airways Sept 1936
G-ACPO	6253		To British Airways
G-ADAG	6266		To British Airways then Northern & Scottish
G-ADAH	6278		To British Airways then Northern & Scottish
G-ADAJ	6276		To British Airways Jan 1936
G-ADAK	6281		To British Continental Airways, then British Airways 1/8/36
G-ADAL	6263		To British Airways 11/12/35, not used
G-ADDF	6284		Ordered by Aberdeen Airways but not delivered - to British Airways 27/8/35, then Northern & Scottish Airways 1936

De Havilland DH86A Express

G-ADEA	2323	*Drake*	To British Airways 11/12/35
G-ADEB	2324		To British Airways 11/12/35
G-ADEC	2325		To British Airways 11/12/35

PORTSMOUTH, SOUTHSEA AND ISLE OF WIGHT AVIATION (1932-35)

Westland Wessex

| G-ABVB | WA2156 | | Damaged beyond repair at Ryde 30/5/1936 |

De Havilland DH83 Fox Moth

| G-ACCA | 4041 | | To Australia as VH-UTY Feb 1936 |
| G-ACIG | 4072 | | To RAF March 1940 |

Airspeed AS5 Courier

G-ACLR	11		To RAF March 1940
G-ACLF	12		To RAF March 1940
G-ACNZ	20		To RAF March 1940
G-ACZL	25		Leased from Airspeed
G-ADAX	26		Leased from Airspeed
G-ADAY	27		Leased from Airspeed

De Havilland DH85 Leopard Moth

| G-ADBH | 7030 | | |

De Havilland DH84 Dragon

G-ACRF	6077	To Australia as VH-UXG Feb 1936

Airspeed AS6A Envoy

G-ADCA	36	To Spain August 1936

MIDLAND & SCOTTISH AIR FERRIES LIMITED (1933-34)

Airspeed AS4 Ferry

G-ACBT		Dismantled at Renfrew
G-ACFB		To Air Publicity Nov 1936

De Havilland DH83 Fox Moth

G-ACBZ	4040	To Australia as VH-UZD
G-ACCB	4042	To Giro Aviation – Ditched 25/9/56
G-ACCT	4047	To West of Scotland Air Services August 1935
G-ACCU	4048	To Australia as VH-UZC

De Havilland DH84 Dragon

G-ACCZ	6015	To Crilly Airways May 1935
G-ACDL	6016	To Provincial Airways Sept 34
G-ACDN	6018	
G-ACJS	6042	To Northern & Scottish Airways Jan 35
G-ACNI	6071	

Avro 618 Ten

G-ACGF	527	Registration Cancelled Dec 46

Avro 642

G-ACFV	642	Marchioness	To Commercial Air Hire May 35 of Londonderry, then to Australia as VH-UXD Mandate Airways, New Guinea Destroyed by Japanese 1942

Avro Cadet

G-ACFX	647	To Perck Flying Club as VR-RAJ 1936
G-ACIH	657	To North of Ireland Aircraft Nov 38

NORMAN EDGAR/WESTERN AIRWAYS (1933-1938)

De Havilland DH84 Dragon

G-ACAO	6001	To RAF April 1940
G-ACJT	6043	Crashed 20/12/1939
G-ACMJ	6058	To RAF April 1940
G-ACMP	6063	Crashed 23/7/1935
G-ACPX	6075	To RAF April 1940

De Havilland DH89A Dragon Rapide

G-ACTU	6258	Crashed after modification as AW115
G-ADBV	6286	To RAF March 1940
G-ADDD	6283	To RAF January 1940
G-AFSO	6445	Destroyed in enemy action – France 31 May 1940

De Havilland DH86B Express

G-AETM	2353	To Finland as OH-SLA Dec 1939

De Havilland DH90 Dragonfly

G-AEDH	7510	To RAF May 1940

Percival Q6

G-AFIX	Q31	Owned by H F White but used by Western Airways – to RAF Apr 1940

ATLANTIC COAST AIR SERVICES

Short Scion S16/1

G-ACUW	S775	To RAF May 1940

General Aircraft Monospar ST4 MkII

G-ACCP	10	Withdrawn from service Aug 1939

SOUTHEND-ON-SEA FLYING SERVICE

Short Scion S16/1

G-ACUY	S777	To Short Brothers

Short Scion 2

G-ADDN	S785	To Aircraft & Allied Enterprises March 1940

JERSEY AIRWAYS & GUERNSEY AIRWAYS (1933-40)

De Havilland DH84 Dragon II (Introduced by Jersey Airlines 1933)

G-ACMC	6053	The St Brelade's Bay	Prototype MKII, to Airwork
G-ACMJ	6058	The St Aubin's Bay	To Airwork
G-ACMO	6062	The St Ouen's Bay	To Northern & Scottish 4 July 1935
G-ACMP	6063	The St Clement's Bay	Leased to Norman Edgar May 1935

Crashed nr Cardiff 22 July 1935

G-ACNG	6069	The Portelet Bay	To Spartan 27 June 1935
G-ACNH	6070	The Bouley Bay	To Northern & Scottish 4 July 1935
G-ACNI	6071	The Bonne Nuit Bay	To British Airways Feb 1936
G-ACNJ	6072	The Rozel Bay	To Allied Airways

De Havilland DH86A (Introduced by Jersey Airways 1935)

G-ACYF	2313	The Giffard Bay	To Wearne's Air Services
G-ACYG	2314	The Grouville Bay	Impressed as AX840
G-ACZN	2316	The St Catherine's Bay	Leased to Imperial Airways 8/11/35-22/1/36 crashed Jersey 4 Nov 1938
G-ACZO	2318	The Ouaine Bay	Damaged St Aubin's Beach, Jersey 17/8/35 – To Royal Navy
G-ACZP	2321	The Belcroute Bay	Leased to British Airways Dec 1936 Impressed as AX83
G-ACZR	2322	La Saline Bay	Leased to Imperial Airways 11/11/35-18/12/35

De Havilland DH86B (Introduced 1936)

G-ADVK	2339	To Guernsey Airways 22 April 1939
G-AENR	2352	Impressed as AX842

De Havilland DH89 Dragon Rapide (Introduced 1935)

G-ADBV	6286	The St Ouen's Bay II	From United Airways 28/5/35 – to Jay Dade May 1937
G-ADBW	6288		To Isle of Man Air Services Oct 1937

Saunders-Roe A21 Windhover (Introduced by Guernsey Airways 1935)

G-ABJP	A21/2	Windhover	Guernsey Airways for Alderney service

Saunders-Roe A19 Cloud (Introduced by Guernsey Airways 1936)

G-ABXW	A19/4	Cloud of Iona	Guernsey Airways for Alderney service Crashed 31 July 1936

De Havilland DH95 Flamingo (Introduced by Jersey Airways 1939)

G-AFUE	95001	To RAF Oct 1939
G-AFUF	95002	Delivered direct to Royal Navy

Avro 642

G-ACFV		On hire 1935

Short Scion Senior

G-AECU		On hire 1935

HIGHLAND AIRWAYS LIMITED (1933-37)

De Havilland DH60 Moth (Introduced 1931 for route surveys)

G-AAWO	1235	Ah-Wo	Leased from Miss Heloise Pauer, used only for survey flights. Bought 1934, sold 1948. Used in Highland commemorative ceremony 1/8/86

Monospar ST4 (Introduced 1933)

G-ACEW	11	Bought new. Crash-landed Kirkwall 3/7/33, sold 30/6/37 then damaged beyond repair Croydon 13/12/37

De Havilland DH84 Dragon (Introduced 1933)

G-ACCE	6010	Caithness	On hire from Brian Lewis, written off Kirkwall 29/8/34
G-ACET	6021	Kirkwall	From SMT
G-ACGK	6033	Loch Ness	From E C G England, crashed into sea nr Inverness 8 January 1935
G-ACIT	6039	Aberdeen	Bought new. To BEA April 1948
G-ADCT	6095	Orcadian	Bought new. Written-off after crash landing at Inverness Feb 1940

De Havilland DH89 Dragon Rapide (Introduced 1935)

G-ADAJ	6276	*Inverness*	Transferred from BA, but originally owned by Hillmans. To BEA then to French Colonies
G-AEWL	6095	*Zetland*	To BEA and then to French Ivory Coast

SCOTTISH AIRWAYS

De Havilland DH60G Moth

G-AAWO	1235	From Highland Airways

De Havilland DH84 Dragon

G-ACIT	6039	From Highland Airways
G-ACMO	6062	From Northern & Scottish Airways
G-ACNG	6069	From Northern & Scottish Airways
G-ACOR	6073	From Northern & Scottish Airways
G-ADCT	6095	From Highland Airways

Spartan Cruiser II

G-ACSM	10	From Northern & Scottish Airways
G-ACYL	12	From Northern & Scottish Airways
G-ACZM	14	From Northern & Scottish Airways

Spartan Cruiser III

G-ACYK	101	From Northern & Scottish Airways
G-ADEL	102	From Northern & Scottish Airways

De Havilland DH89 & 89A Dragon Rapide

G-ADAJ	6276	From Highland Airways
G-AEWL	6367	From Highland Airways
G-AFEV	6402	Delivered 7/3/38 – crashed Kirkwall 18 March 1940
G-AFFF	6386	From Railway Air Services – crashed Milngavie 27 September 1946
G-AFOI	6450	To BEA
G-AFRK	6441	From Isle of Man Air Services 12/5/1939

NORTHERN & SCOTTISH AIRWAYS LIMITED (1934-37)

De Havilland DH84 Dragon (Introduced 1934)

G-ACFG	6027	Sold abroad Feb 1937
G-ACJS	6042	Registration cancelled Nov 1936
G-ACMO	6062	To Australia as VH-ABK March 1937
G-ACNG	6069	To Scottish Airways – crashed Kirkwall 19 April 1940
G-ACNH	6070	Registration cancelled January 1937
G-ACOR	6073	To British Airways March 1937

De Havilland DH83 Fox Moth (Introduced 1935)

G-ACED	4064	To Australia as VH-UZL March 1937

Spartan Cruiser II (Introduced 1936)

G-ACSM	10	To Scottish Airways, then RAF 1940
G-ACVT	11	To Scottish Airways
G-ACYL	12	
Crashed Isle of Man 23/3/1936		
G-ACZM	14	To Scottish Airways – withdrawn Jan 1940

Spartan Cruiser III (Introduced 1936)

G-ACYK	101	Crash-landed at Largs 14/1/1938
G-ADEL	102	To Scottish Airways, then RAF 1940
G-ADEM	103	To Scottish Airways – crashed Blackpool 20/11/1936

De Havilland DH89 Dragon Rapide (Introduced 1936)

G-ADAG	6266	To Airwork Sept 1937
G-ADAH	6278	To Airwork Aug 1937
G-ADBU	6280	Damaged beyond repair Nov 1936
G-ADDF	6284	To Airwork Aug 1937

NORTH EASTERN AIRWAYS

Airspeed AS 6A Envoy Series 1

G-ADAZ	32	To Air Service Training, Hamble Nov 38
G-ADBA	33	To RAF Jan 1939
G-ADBB	34	To Spain Sept 1936
G-ADBZ	35	Leased to Air Dispatch – crashed near Croydon 22/1/1937

De Havilland DH84 Dragon

G-ACLE	6044	To Allied Airways Dec 1937

De Havilland DH89 Dragon Rapide

G-ADDE	6282	To RAF March 1940
G-ADWZ	6309	To RAF March 1940
G-AEMH	6336	To RAF March 1940
G-AEXO	6368	To RAF March 1940
G-AEXP	6369	To RAF March 1940
G-AFEO	6405	To RAF March 1940
G-AFEP	6406	To RAF March 1940

BLACKPOOL & WEST COAST AIR SERVICE (1933-1937)

De Havilland DH83 Fox Moth

G-ACFC	4053	*Progress*	To Olley Air Services Jan 1936
G-ACFF	4060	*Progress II*	To Great Western & Southern Airlines July 1939

De Havilland DH84 Dragon

G-ACGU	6034	Crashed on take-off at Heston 16/7/35
G-ACPY	6076	To Aer Lingus as EI-AB! May 1936; shot down Scilly Isles 3/6/41
G-ADCP	6092	To RAF April 1940
G-ADCR	6094	Crashed 25 June 1938

De Havilland DH86B Express

G-AENR	2352	To Royal Navy July 1940

SPARTAN AIR LINES

Spartan Cruiser I

G-ABTY	24M	To The Hon Mrs Victor Bruce Feb 1936

Spartan Cruiser II

G-ACBM	2		To British Airways March 1936
G-ACDW	3	*Faithful City*	To Misr Airwork as SU-ABL April 1934
G-ACDX	4		To British Airways April 1934
G-ACSM	10		To British Airways February 1936
G-ACVT	11		To British Airways February 1936
G-ACZM	14		To British Airways January 1936

Spartan Cruiser III

G-ACYK	101	To British Airways April 1936
G-ADEL	102	To British Airways October 1936
G-ADEM	103	To British Airways March 1936

De Havilland DH84 Dragon

G-ACNG	6069	To British Airways March 1936

INNER CIRCLE AIRLINES

De Havilland DH84 Dragon

G-ACCR	6011	Lost in English Channel 22/1/1936

General Aircraft Monospar

G-ADIK	27	Crashed May 1936
G-ADJP	28	To R K Dundas May 1936
G-ADLM	30	Crashed Croydon 16 May 1936

CRILLY AIRWAYS

De Havilland DH84 Dragon

G-ACDN	6018	To Commercial Air Hire May 1937
G-ACLE	6044	To North Eastern Airways Feb 1937

General Aircraft Monospar ST25 Jubilee

G-ADPK	55	To PSIOWA December 1936
G-ADPL	56	To PSIOWA December 1936
G-ADPM	57	To H S Ashworth Dec 1936

Fokker F XIII (all ex-KLM)

G-ADZH	5284	To British Airways ex-PH-AFV
G-ADZI	5285	To British Airways ex-PH-AFU Crashed 15 August 1936
G-ADZJ	5292	To British Airways ex-PH-AIE
G-ADZK	5301	To British Airways ex-PH-AII Destroyed 16/8/1936

SCOTTISH AIRWAYS LIMITED (1937-47)

De Havilland DH60G Moth
G-AAWO

De Havilland DH84 Dragon

G-ACIT	6039	Aberdeen	From Highland Airways
G-ACMO	6062		From Northern & Scottish Airways
G-ACNG	6069		From Northern & Scottish Airways
G-ACOR	6073		From Northern & Scottish Airways
G-ADCT	6095	Orcadia	From Highland Airways

Spartan Cruiser II

G-ACSM	10		From Northern & Scottish Airways
G-ACYL	12		From Northern & Scottish Airways
G-ACZM	14		From Northern & Scottish Airways

Spartan Cruiser III

G-ACYK	101		From Northern & Scottish Airways
G-ADEL	102		From Northern & Scottish Airways

De Havilland DH89 & 89A Dragon Rapide

G-ADAJ	6276	Inverness	From Highland Airways
G-AEWL	6367	Zetland	From Highland Airways
G-AGDH			
G-AGED			
G-AGLE	6784		
G-AGOJ	6850		
G-AFEY	6402		Crashed Kirkwall 18 March 1940
G-AFFF	6386		From RAS 26/5/39. Crashed Milngavie 27 September 1946
G-AFOI	6450		To BEA
G-AFRK	6441		From Isle of Man Air Services

RAILWAY AIR SERVICES LIMITED (1934-47)

De Havilland DH84 Dragon (Introduced 1934)

G-ACHV	6035		To De Havilland Air Taxis Dec 1938
G-ACNI	6071		Operated under Spartan Airways name Passed to British Airways Feb 1936
G-ACPX	6075		To Western Airways
G-ACPY	6076		To Channel Air Ferries
G-ACVD	6084	Star of Cheshire	To Brian Allen Aviation July 1935
G-ACXI	6087		Sold abroad December 1935
G-ADDI	6096	City of Cardiff	Later changed to Island Maid To Great Western & Southern Jan 1939
G-ADDJ	6097	City of Plymouth	To Australia as VH-UZZ March 1937
G-ADED	6098		Crashed Isle of Man 1 July 1935
G-ADEE	6099		Crashed at Fair Snape Fell 26 Oct 1935
G-ACNG	6069		May have been used by RAS

De Havilland DH86 (Introduced 1934)

G-ACVY	2302	Mercury	Scrapped 1948
G-ACVZ	2303	Jupiter	Crashed while with Imperial Airways 15 March 1937
G-ACZP	2321		To Skytravel 1948
G-AEFH	2350	Neptune	DH86A. Lost in evacuation from France 1940
G-AENR	2352		DH86B. Scrapped November 1948
G-AEWR	2354	Venus	DH86B. Lost in evacuation from France 1940

De Havilland DH89 & 89A Dragon Rapide (Introduced 1935)

G-ACPP	6254	City of Bristol	To Great Western & Southern March 1939
G-ACPR	6255	City of Birmingham	To Great Western & Southern 19/2/39
G-AEAJ	6320	Star of Lancashire	To Isle of Man Air Services Oct 1937
G-AEAK	6324	Star of Mona	To Isle of Man Air Services Oct 1937
G-AEAL	6325	Star of Yorkshire	To Isle of Man Air Services Oct 1937
G-AEAM	6326	Star of Ulster	To Isle of Man Air Services Oct 1937
G-AEBW	6327	Star of Renfrew	To Isle of Man Air Services Oct 1937
G-AEBX	6328	Star of Scotia	Crashed nr Belfast 3 July 1938
G-AFFF	6386	Juno	Later unnamed. To Scottish Airways – crashed at Milngavie 27 September 1946
G-AGLE	6784		
G-AGLP	6780		
G-AGLR	6781		
G-AGUU	6908		
G-AHGF	6903		
G-AHGG	6902		
G-AHGH	6934		
G-AHGI	6935		

G-AHKS	6812
G-AIHN	6498

PROVINCIAL AIRWAYS

De Havilland DH83 Fox Moth

G-ACCF	4046		To British Air Transport May 1936
G-ACEX	4056		To Pines Airways April 1936
G-ACEY	4057		To Crilly Airways April 1935

De Havilland DH84 Dragon

G-ACBW	6009	Neptune	To Air Dispatch Nov 1939
G-ACDL	6016		To Luxury Air Tours June 1936
G-ACKD	6052		To League of Nations Dec 1935

ABERDEEN AIRWAYS LIMITED and ALLIED AIRWAYS (GANDAR DOWER) LIMITED (1934-47)

Short Scion

G-ACUV	S774		Sold to Gandar Dower to replace DH86 G-ACRH that crashed

De Havilland DH84 Dragon

G-ACAN	6000	The Starling	Prototype Dragon for Hillman's. Crashed Dunheath, Caithness 21/5/41
G-ACLE	6044	Old Bill	Crashed South Ronaldsway 1939 – rebuilt and sold to Western Airways 1939
G-ACNJ	6072	Sir Rowland	To Jersey Airways – scrapped 1946
G-ACRH	6078	Aberdonian	Crashed on take-off at Aberdeen 13/7/34
G-ADFI	6100	The Silver Ghost	Crashed Thursoe 3/7/37

De Havilland DH86B Express

G-AETM	2353	The Norseman	To Western Airways April 1939 then to Finland as OH-SLA. Destroyed Malmo 2/5/40

De Havilland DH89 Dragon Rapide

G-ACZE	6284	The Don	Crashed Orkney 27/12/45. Restored and stored at Dyce until 1966
G-ACZF	6268	Carina	Crashed Orkney 27/12/45
G-ADAH	6278	Pioneer	Crashed Kirkwall 1940 but repaired then preserved at Royal Scottish Museum
G-ADDE	6282	The Aberdonian	To RAF 23/3/40 then sold for spares to Allied Airways
G-AGDM	6584	Eldorado	To BEA 15/1/47 then to France
G-AGHI	6455	The Shetlander	Withdrawn Croydon Sept 1950 G-AIDL
6968		The Wanderer	To BEA 1/2/47 then private owners

UNITED AIRWAYS LIMITED (1935)

Armstrong Whitworth Argosy II

G-AACJ	AW364		To British Airways January 1936

De Havilland DH60 Gipsy Moth

G-AAYY	1251		To Ceylon as VP-CAC Dec 1936

De Havilland DH60 GIII Moth
G-ACNS

De Havilland DH84 Dragon

G-ACMC	6053
G-ACMJ	6058
G-ACNI	6071

Spartan 3-seater II

G-ABTR	101		To British Airways May 1936

Spartan Cruiser II

G-ACDX	4		
G-ACSM	10		
G-ACYL	12		To British Airways December 1935
G-ACZM	14		

De Havilland DH89 Dragon Rapide

G-ADAE	6272		
G-ADBU	6280		To British Airways Jan 1936
G-ADBX	6289		To British Airways Jan 1936

ISLE OF MAN AIR SERVICES LIMITED (1937-47)

De Havilland DH89A Dragon Rapide

G-EAAJ	6320	RMA Castletown
G-AEAK	6324	
G-AEAL	6325	
G-AEAM	6326	
G-AEBW	6327	
G-AFEZ	6408	
G-AGLP	6780	
G-AGSJ	6888	
G-AGUP	6780	

GREAT WESTERN & SOUTHERN AIR LINES LIMITED (1938-47)

Short Scion Major

G-ADDO	S786	From Olley Air Services; to Allied Enterprises; impressed 1940

De Havilland DH83 Fox Moth

G-ACFC	4053	
G-ACFF	4060	

De Havilland DH84 Dragon II

G-ACPY	6076	
G-ADDI	6096	From RAS; sold America 11/1970

De Havilland DH89 & 89A Dragon Rapide

G-ACPP	6254	
G-ACPR	6255	
G-ACYM	6269	
G-AGEE	6622	
G-AGUV	6912	

BRITISH AIRWAYS LIMITED (1935-40)

Armstrong Whitworth Argosy II

G-AACJ	AW364	From United Airways – Cancelled Dec 1936

De Havilland DH60G Moth

G-AAYY		From United Airways – to Ceylon Dec 1936 AS VP-CAC

De Havilland DH60 GIII Moth

G-ACGX		From Hillman's Airways - to London Transport Flying Club Feb 1939

De Havilland DH60 GIII Moth Major

G-ACNS		From Air Hire – to South Africa March 1940

De Havilland DH80A Puss Moth

G-ABVX		From Hillman's Airways – Impressed as X5044 Nov 1939

De Havilland DH83 Fox Moth

G-ABVI	4004	From Hillman's Airways – Destroyed in bombing 6 February 1940
G-ABVK	4005	From Hillman's Airways – to Pines Airway February 1939

De Havilland DH84 Dragon

G-ACAP	6002	From Hillman's Airways– to Commercial Air Hire Feb 36 – Crashed Lyndhurst 26 March 1936
G-ACEU	6022	From Hillman's Airways – sold to Airwork 13/1/36 then to Spanish Civil War
G-ACEV	6023	From Hillman's Airways – sold to Airwork Dec 35 then to Spanish Civil War
G-ACMC	6053	From United Airways to Airwork 23/1/36 then to Australia as VH-UXX
G-ACMJ	6058	From United Airways to Airwork 25/1/36 then to Norman Edgar
G-ACNG	6069	From Spartan Air Lines, to Northern & Scottish 19/1/37, then back to BA 29/10/37 then to Scottish Airways 14/6/38
G-ACNI	6071	From United Airways. To Airwork 31/12/36 then to Irish Air Corps as DH18
G-ACOR	6073	From British Continental Airways, to Northern & Scottish March 1937, then to New Guinea as VH-AEA

De Havilland DH86A

G-ACZP	2321	Loaned from Jersey Airways – Impressed 21/7/40 as AX843 – Returned to RAS August 1940
G-ADEA	2323	From Hillman's Airways, to Wearnes, Malaya as VR-SBC June 1938
G-ADEB	2324	From Hillman's Airways – Crashed nr Cologne 12 August 1936
G-ADEC	2325	From Hillman's Airways to Pluna Uruguay as CX-AAH Sept 1938
G-ADMY	2327	From British Continental Airways, to Royal Navy Nov 1940
G-ADYC	2340	From British Continental Airways, to RAF Nov 1937
G-ADYD	2341	From British Continental Airways, to RAF Nov 1937
G-ADYE	2346	From British Continental Airways, to Pluna, Uruguay a CX-ABG
G-ADYF	2347	From British Continental Airways Crashed Gatwick 5 September 1936
G-ADYI	2345	To Wrightways March 1940, Impressed as AX795 RAF May 1940
G-ADYJ	2348	To 24 Squadron RAF October 1937

De Havilland DH89 Dragon Rapide

G-ACPN	6252	From Hillman's Airways, Not used by BA to Airwork then to Spanish Civil War and shot down 27/8/36
G-ACPO	6253	From Hillman's Airways, not used by BA to Airwork then Australia as VH-UBN 17/8/46
G-ADAE	6272	From United Airways, to Denmark as OY-DIN 28/5/38
G-ADAG	6266	From Hillman's Airways, to Northern & Scottish 19/8/36
G-ADAH	6278	From Hillman's Airways, to Northern & Scottish 19/8/36
G-ADAI	6287	From British Continental Airways, to Airwork 28/8/37
G-ADAJ	6276	From Hillman's Airways, to Highland 22/9/36, then to BEA, then France Crashed in Laos 2o August 1954
G-ADAK	6281	From British Continental Airways, not used by BA. Sold for Spanish Civil War
G-ADAL	6263	From Hillman's Airways, not used by BA, to Airwork then to Wrightways 4/6/36
G-ADBU	6280	From United Airways, to Northern & Scottish 11/6/36
G-ADBX	6289	From United Airways, crashed Isle of Man 3 March 1936
G-ADDF	6284	From Hillman's Airways, to Northern & Scottish 29/6/36, sold for Spanish Civil War
G-ADIM	6293	From British Continental Airways. To Airwork 29/8/37

Spartan Cruiser II

G-ACBM	2	From Spartan Air Lines, to Straight Corporation Nov 1937
G-ACDX	4	From United Airways, scrapped 9/10/35
G-ACSM	10	From United Airways, to Northern & Scottish Aug 1936
G-ACVT	11	From Spartan Air Lines, Crashed Isle of Man 23 March 1936
G-ACYL	12	From United Airways, to Scottish Airways June 1938
G-ACZM	14	From United Airways, to Scottish Airways June 1938

Spartan Cruiser III

G-ACYK	101	From Spartan Air Lines, to Northern & Scottish Aug 1936
G-ADEL	102	From Spartan Air Lines, to Northern & Scottish Jan 1937
G-ADEM	103	From Spartan Air Lines, to Northern & Scottish Aug 1936

Spartan 3-seater II

G-ABTR	101		From United Airways to F G Barnard September 1937

Fokker F XI1 (Introduced 1936)

G-ADZH	5284	ex PH-AFV	From Crilly Airways. sold to Spanish Nationalists Aug 1936
G-ADZI	5285	ex PH-AFU	From Crilly Airways, sold to Spanish Nationalists, crashed Biarritz 15/8/36
G-ADZJ	5292	ex PH-AIE	From Crilly Airways, sold to Spanish Nationalists & shot down Leon 16/12/36
G-ADZK	5301	ex PH-AII	From Crilly Airways, sold to Spanish Nationalists, crashed La Rochelle

16/8/36

G-AEOS	5291	ex PH-AID	From KLM, to RAF, scrapped by BOAC May 1940
G-AEOT	5300	ex PH-AIH	From KLM, crashed Gatwick 19/11/36

Fokker F VIII (Introduced 1937)

G-AEPT	5043	ex PH-AEF	From KLM, withdrawn 12/1/38
G-AEPU	5046	ex PH-AEI	From KLM, sold to Sweden as SE-AHA 25/5/39 then to Finland

Junkers Ju 52/3m (Introduced 1937)

G-AERU	5440	*Juno* ex SE-AER	From AB Aerotransport, passed to

G-AERX	5518	*Jupiter* ex SE-AES	BOAC 22/8/40 then SABENA for spares From AB Aerotransport, passed to BOAC 22/8/40 then SABENA as OO-CAP in 1941
G-AFAP	5881	*Jason*	Seized by Germans at Oslo 9/4/40

Lockheed L-10A Electra (Introduced 1937)

G-AEPN	5440		Impressed April 1940 as W9105
G-AEPO	5518		Impressed April 1940 as W9106
G-AEPP	5881		To BOAC
G-AEPR	1083		To BOAC
G-AESY	1102		Crashed Denmark 15 Aug 1939
G-AFCS	1025		To BOAC
G-AFEB	1122		Impressed April 1940 as W9104

Lockheed L-14 (Introduced 1938)

G-AFGN	1467		Burnt out after forced landing, France 11 August 1939
G-AFGO	1468		Crashed Somerset 22 November 1938
G-AFGP	1469		To BOAC
G-AFGR	1470		To BOAC
G-AFKD	1484		To BOAC
G-AFKE	1485		To BOAC
G-AFMO	1490		Crash-landed Heston 15 January 1940
G-AFMR	1491		To BOAC
G-AFYU	1444		Lost off Malta 21 December 1939

MAJOR ACCIDENTS & INCIDENTS INVOLVING BRITISH REGISTERED COMMERCIAL PASSENGER AIRCRAFT 1919-1940

This is not a fully comprehensive list although the majority of known accidents, fatalities and casualties are shown. The list has been compiled from a number of sources including 'The World Directory of Airliner Accidents' by Terry Denham (Patrick Stephens Ltd 1996) and the Aircraft Crashes Record Office at Grand-Lancy, Switzerland (www.baaa-acro.com). Wherever possible I have attempted to verify the accuracy when different sources have conflicted. This mainly occurs over casualty numbers, incident date and aircraft registration.

Date	Registration	Aircraft Type	Operator	Incident
1/5/1919	G-EAA (C6054)	De Havilland DH9	AT&T	Crashed Portsdown Hill, Hants
31/5/1919	G-EADF	Blackburn Kangaroo	Grahame White Aviation	Crashed on take-off Hendon
29/6/1919	G-EADE	Blackburn Kangaroo	Grahame White Aviation	DBR Hendon
15/8/1919	G-EALT	Armstrong Whitworth FK 8	London Provincial Aviation	Crashed Great Yarmouth
2/10/1919		De Havilland DH4	AT&T	Crashed Newcastle
29/10/1919	G-EAHG	De Havilland DH4A	AT&T	Forced-landing English Channel
8/12/1919	G-EAOW	Blackburn Kangaroo	Blackburn Aeroplane & Motor Co	Damaged on landing Suda, Crete
11/12/1919	G-EAHF	De Havilland DH4A	AT&T	Crashed Caterham, Surrey
23/2/1920	G-EANV	Handley Page HP07	SA Transport Co	Crashed Acacia Siding South Africa
25/2/1920	G-EANO	Handley Page HP12	HP Transport	Crashed Al Shereik, Sudan
25/3/1920	G-EACT	De Havilland DH16	AT&T	Crashed Nr Brighton, Sussex
10/6/1920	G-EARU	De Havilland DH16	AT&T	Crashed Swanley Junction, Kent
-/7/1920	G-EAGW	Avro 504K	North Sea Arial Navigation Co	Crashed Scarborough
16/8/1920	G-EARI	De Havilland DH18	AT&T	Crashed into garden Wallington, Surrey
16/8/1920	G-EALW	Armstrong Whitworth FK 8	By Air	Crashed Nr Bedford
-/8/1920	G-EAGX	De Havilland DH9B	AT&T	Crashed Unknown location
14/12/1920	G-EAMA	Handley Page HP12	Handley Page Transport	Crashed Cricklewood: 4 fatalities, 4 injured
-/1/1921	G-EAQA	De Havilland DH9	AT&T	Crashed location unknown
14/1/1922	G-EATN	Handley Page 0/10	Handley Page Transport	Crashed Senlis, France: 5 fatalities
13/8/1921	G-EAUF	De Havilland DH18	Instone	Crashed Location unknown
24/8/1921	2R2	R38 Airship	Royal Airship Work	Crashed River Humber: 44 fatalities; 5 injured
28/11/1921	G-EAZF	Avro 504	Avro	Crashed Croydon: 2 fatalities; 2 injured
7/4/1922	G-EAWO	De Havilland DH18A	Daimler Airway	Mid-air crash with Farman Goliath F-GEAD of Grand Express Aériens, Grandvilliers, France: 5 fatalities
13/4/1922	G-EBBZ	Vickers Viking	Vickers	Crashed Brooklands, Surrey
31/7/1922	G-EAPK	BAT FK26	Instone	Crashed Location unknown
3/11/1922	G-EBBU	De Havilland DH34	Daimler Airway	Crashed Berck, France
-/-/1922	G-EBOH	Vickers Vulcan	Instone	Crashed Oxted, Surrey
14/9/1923	G-EBBS	De Havilland DH34B	Daimler Airway	Crashed Nr Ivinghoe Beacon; 6 fatalities
22/11/1923	G-EAPJ	Handley Page W8	Handley Page Transport	Crashed Poix-de-Picardie, France
13/10/1922	G-EBFK	Supermarine Sea Eagle	British Marine Air Navigation Co	Damaged beyond repair Alderney, Channel Islands
27/5/1924	G-EBBR	De Havilland DH34	Imperial Airways	Crashed Ostend, Belgium: 0 fatalities
24/12/1924	G-EBBY	De Havilland DH34B	Imperial Airways	Crashed Purley, Surrey: 6 fatalities
5/5/1925	G-EAIT	Blackburn Kangaroo	North Sea Aerial Transport	Crashed Brough, Yorkshire
21/10/1926	G-EBMS	Handley Page W10	Imperial Airways	Ditched English Channel: 0 fatalities
10/1/1927	G-EBGS	Supermarine Sea Eagle	Imperial Airways	Struck by ship St Peter Port, Guernsey and Sank
1/2/1927	G-EBKI	De Havilland Highclere	Imperial Airways loaned from Air Council	Destroyed when hangar collapsed Croydon Airport
12/3/1927	G-EBPZ	Fairey III	North Sea Aerial Transport	Crashed Victoria, East Africa
15/2/1928	G-EBBG	Handley Page W8	Imperial Airways	Crashed Abbeville, France: 0 fatalities
13/7/1928	G-EBLB	Vickers 74 Vulcan	Imperial Airways	Crashed & burned Purley, Surrey: 4 fatalities
25/9/1928	G-EBOM	Blackburn Kangaroo	North Sea Aerial Transport	Crashed Brough, Yorkshire
23/10/1928	G-EBKZ	De Havilland DH50	Imperial Airways	Crashed on take off Plymouth: 0 fatalities
16/5/1929	G-EBCP	Vickers Vanguard	Imperial Airways on loan from Air Ministry	Crashed Shepperton, Middlesex: 2 fatalities
17/6/1929	G-EBMT	Handley Page W10	Imperial Airways	Engine failed: crashed English Channel: 4 fatalities
6/9/1929	G-EBMZ	De Havilland DH86 Hercules	Imperial Airways	Caught fire after crashing Jask, Iraq: 3 fatalities; 2 injured
11/9/1929	G-AALC	Fokker F III	British Air Lines	Crashed Croydon
26/10/1929	G-AADN	Short Calcutta	Imperial Airways	Force landed and sank under tow Spezia, Italy: 7 fatalities
19/1/1930	G-AAEV	De Havilland DH61 Giant Moth	Imperial Airways	Crashed Broken Hill, Rhodesia: 0 fatalities
14/2/1930	G-AAJH	De Havilland DH66 Hercules	Imperial Airways	Damaged beyond repair on landing Gaza, Palestine: 0 fatalities
21/7/1930	G-AAZK	Junkers F13	Walcot Airlines	Crashed Gravesend Kent; 6 fatalities
5/10/1930	G-FAAW	R101 Airship	Air Council	Crashed Beauvais, France: 48 fatalities; 5 injured
30/10/1930	G-EBIX	Handley Page W8g Hamilton	Imperial Airways	Crashed in fog Neufchatel, France
19/4/1931	G-EBMW	De Havilland DH66 Hercules	Imperial Airways	Crashed-landed after running out of fuel Kupang, Timor: 0 fatalities
16/6/1931	G-EBLO	Armstrong Whitworth Argosy I	Imperial Airways	Crashed Aswan, Egypt: 0 fatalities
7/1/1932	G-EBKF	Blackburn Dart	North Sea Aerial Transport	Crashed Digby, Derbyshire
29/1/1932	G-AAJH	De Havilland DH66	Imperial Airways	Crashed Salisbury, Rhodesia: 0 fatalities
28/3/1933	G-AACI	Armstrong Whitworth Argosy II	Imperial Airways	Crashed Nr Dixmude, Belgium: 15 fatalities
7/5/1933	G-ABSB	De Havilland DH80A Puss Moth	Hillman's Airways	Written off after accident Clacton, Essex
21/10/1933	G-ABYK	Boulton & Paul P64 mail plane	Boulton & Paul	Crashed on test flight, Mousehold, Norfolk:1 fatality
30/12/1933	G-ABLU	Avro Ten	Imperial Airways	Crashed into radio mast – off course Nr Ruysselade, Belgium: 10 fatalities
13/7/1934	G-ACRH	De Havilland Dragon 2	Aberdeen Airways	Crashed on take off Aberdeen
29/8/1934	G-ACCE	De Havilland Dragon 1	Highland Airways	Written off after bad take-off Kirkwall, Orkneys
24/9/1934	G-EBMM	Handley Page HP W10	National Aviation Day Displays	Crashed Aston Clinton, Bucks: 2 fatalities
29/9/1934	G-ACSY	Airspeed Courier	London, Scottish & Provincial Airways	Crashed Sevenoaks, Kent: 4 fatalities
2/10/1934	G-ACPM	De Havilland Dragon Rapide	Hillman's Airways	Crashed in bad weather Folkestone, Kent: 7 fatalities
17/10/1934	G-ACLS	Airspeed Courier	Air Taxis	Crashed Grenoble, France
8/1/1935	G-ACGK	De Havilland Dragon I	Highland Airways	Crashed into sea and written off, Inverness, Scotland: 3 injured
11/5/1935	G-ABTY	Spartan Cruiser I	Commercial Air Hire	Crashed English Channel: 2 injured
1/7/1935	G-ADED	De Havilland Dragon 2	Railway Air Services	Crashed on take-off Ronaldsway, Isle of Man
3/7/1935	G-ADEW	Westland Wessex	Cobham Air Routes	Crashed English Channel
16/7/1935	G-ACGU	De Havilland Dragon 1	Blackpool & West Coast Airways	Crashed on take-off Heston
22/7/1935	G-ACMP	De Havilland Dragon 2	Western Airways on lease from Jersey & Guernsey Airways	Crashed on mud flats Splott, Cardiff
9/10/1935	G-ACDX	Spartan Cruiser II	British Airways	Damaged in forced-landing Gosport, Hants
22/10/1935	G-ADCM	De Havilland DH86	Imperial Airways	Crashed Zwettl, Austria: 0 fatalities
25/10/1935	G-ACOY	Boulton & Paul P71A	Imperial Airways	Crashed on landing Brussels, Belgium: 0 fatalities

Date	Registration	Aircraft Type	Operator	Incident
26/10/1935	G-ADEE	De Havilland Dragon 2	Railway Air Services	Crashed Fair Snape Fell, Lancs
9/11/1935	G-ABFB	Short S17 Kent	Imperial Airways	Destroyed by fire Arson Brindisi, Italy: 12 fatalities; 1 injured
23/11/1935	G-ABCP	De Havilland DH66	Imperial Airways	Crashed in swamp Entebbe, Uganda: 0 fatalities Hercules
31/12/1935	G-AASJ	Short S8 Calcutta	Imperial Airways	Crashed after running out of fuel Alexandria, Egypt: 12 fatalities; 1 injured
22/1/1936	G-ACCR	De Havilland Dragon 1	Commercial Air Hire	Crashed English Channel
11/2/1936	G-ABTJ	Armstrong Whitworth AW8 Atalanta	Imperial Airways	Accident Pietersburg, South Africa 0 fatalities
23/2/1936	G-ACUT	Spartan Cruiser II	British Airways	Crashed Ronaldsway, Isle of Man
3/3/1936	G-ADBX	De Havilland DH89 Dragon Rapide	British Airways	Crashed Isle of Man
23/3/1936	G-ACYL	Spartan Cruiser II	Northern & Scottish Airways	Crashed Isle of Man
26/3/1936	G-ACAP	De Havilland Dragon 1	Commercial Air Hire	Crashed Lyndhurst, Hants
22/4/1936	G-AACH	Armstrong Whitworth Argosy II	Imperial Airways	Crashed and caught fire, Croydon: 0 fatalities
16/5/1936	G-ADGX	De Havilland DH89	British Airways	Crashed into hangar on landing, Ronaldsway, Isle of Man
16/5/1936	G-ADLH	GAL ST-4 Monospar	Commercial Air Hire	Crashed on take-off Croydon
30/5/1936	G-ABVB	Westland Wessex	Portsmouth, Southsea & Isle of Wight Airways	Damaged beyond repair Ryde, Isle of Wight
-/5/1936	G-ACVH	Airspeed Envoy	Airspeed	Forced landing Langstone Harbour, Hampshire
16/5/1936	G-ADIK	GAL ST-4 Monospar	Inner Circle Air Line	Crashed Croydon
27/6/1936	G-ADDT	Short Scion 2	Pobjoy Air Motors	Crashed Porthcawl, Glamorgan
31/7/1936	G-ABXW	Saro Cloud	Guernsey Airlines	Crashed off Jersey: 10 fatalities
10/8/1936	G-ABKY	Vickers Velox cargo aircraft	Imperial Airways	Crashed during night take-off, Croydon: 4 fatalities
12/8/1936	G-ADEB	De Havilland DH86	British Airways	Crashed Altenkirchen, Germany 2 fatalities
15/8/1936	G-ADZI	Fokker FXII	British Airways	Crash-landed Biarritz, France
16/8/1936	G-ADZK	Fokker FXII	British Airways	Damaged landing in fog, La Rochelle, France
22/8/1936	G-ABFA	Short S17 Kent	Imperial Airways	Sank on landing Mirabella, Crete: 2 fatalities
5/9/1936	G-ADYF	De Havilland DH86	British Airways	Crashed during night take off, Gatwick: 3 fatalities; 1 injured
25/9/1936	G-ACOX	Boulton & Paul P71A	Imperial Airways	Crashed English Channel: 2 fatalities
29/9/1936	G-ABTK	Armstrong Whitworth XV Atalanta	Imperial Airways	Destroyed in hangar fire, Delhi, India: 0 fatalities
7/10/1936	G-ABWI	Blackburn B2	North Sea Aerial & General Transport	Crashed Nr Selby, Yorkshire: 1 fatality
19/11/1936	G-AEOT	Fokker FXII	British Airways	Crashed Tilgate, Surrey: 2 fatalities; 2 injured
20/11/1936	G-ADEM	Spartan Cruiser II	Northern & Scottish Airways	Crashed Blackpool, Lancs
-/11/1936	G-ADBU	De Havilland DH89 Rapide	Northern & Scottish Airways	Damaged beyond repair, location unknown
28/12/1936	G-EBVG	Short Calcutta	Imperial Airways	Destroyed by storm Mirabella, Crete
-/-/1936	G-ABEG	Westland Wessex	Imperial Airways	Damaged beyond repair, Chirindu, Northern Rhodesia
22/1/1937	G-ADBZ	Airspeed Envoy I	Air Dispatch, leased from North Eastern Airways	Crashed Titsey Hill, Surrey: 2 fatalities
2/2/1937	G-AEHC	De Havilland DH90 Dragonfly	London Express Newspapers	Crashed Newton Stewart, Lancs
15/3/1937	G-ACVZ	De Havilland DH86	Railway Air Services on charter to Imperial Airways	Crashed Nr Elsdorf, Germany: 3 fatalities
24/3/1937	G-ADVA	Short S23	Imperial Airways	Crashed in snowstorm Nr Ouroux-en-Morvan, France: 5 fatalities
29/5/1937	G-ACSZ	Airspeed Courier	North Eastern Airways	Crashed Doncaster
31/5/1937	G-AAXE	Handley Page HP45	Imperial Airways	Destroyed in hangar fire, Karachi, India
3/7/1937	G-ADFI	De Havilland Dragon 2	Aberdeen Airways	Crashed Thurso, Caithness
1/10/1937	G-ADVC	Short S23	Imperial Airways	Crashed on landing Phaleron, Athens, Greece: 3 fatalities
5/12/1937	G-ADUZ	Short S23	Imperial Airways	Crashed on take-off Brindisi, Italy: 2 fatalities
13/12/1937	G-AEPP	Lockheed Electra 10A	British Airways	Crashed into petrol pump on landing, Croydon
14/1/1938	G-ACYK	Spartan Cruiser II	Northern & Scottish Airways	Crash-landed Largs, Ayrshire
25/4/1938	G-ACHX	De Havilland Dragon 1	Wrightways	Crashed Purley
25/6/1938	G-ADCR	De Havilland Dragon 2	Blackpool & West Coast Airways	Crashed, location unknown
3/7/1938	G-AEBX	De Havilland DH89 Rapide	Railway Air Services	Crashed Nr Belfast, Northern Island
27/7/1938	G-ABTG	Armstrong Whitworth XV Atalanta	Imperial Airways	Crashed Kisumu, Kenya: 4 fatalities
4/11/1938	G-ACZN	De Havilland DH86	Jersey Airways	Crashed Jersey: 14 fatalities
22/11/1938	G-AFGO	Lockheed 14 WF62 Super Electra	British Airways	Crashed Walton Bay, Somerset: 2 fatalities
27/11/1938	G-AETW	Short S23	Imperial Airways	Crashed in sandstorm, Lake Habbaniyah, Iraq: 4 fatalities
3/12/1938	G-ADCN	De Havilland DH86	Imperial Airways	Destroyed by fire, Bangkok, Siam
21/1/1939	G-ADUU	Short S23	Imperial Airways	Sank after ditching due to icing, between Atlantic Ocean between New York & Bermuda: 3 fatalities
12/3/1939	G-ADUY	Short S23	Imperial Airways	Destroyed, Batavia, Dutch E. Indies
18/3/1939	G-AFMO	Lockheed L14 Super	British Airways	Crashed Heston
1/5/1939	G-ADVD	Short S23	Imperial Airways	Crashed Mozambique Harbour: 2 fatalities
18/5/1939	G-AEAK	De Havilland DH89D	Isle of Man Air Services	Crashed Speke, Liverpool
1/6/1939	G-ABTH	Armstrong Whitworth AW28 Atalanta	Imperial Airways	Incident - Aircraft retired from service, Cairo, Egypt: 0 fatalities
12/6/1939	G-ADVE	Shorts S23	Imperial Airways	Capsized and sank while landing Calcutta, India: 0 fatalities
19/6/1939	G-AFCW	Shorts S30	Imperial Airways	Destroyed by fire after fuel bowser caught fire, Hythe, Dorset: 1 fatality on bowser
21/7/1939	G-AEXN	De Havilland DH90 Dragonfly	Mutual Finance	Crashed Buckinghamshire
11/8/1939	G-AFGN	Lockheed 14 WF62 Super Electra	British Airways	Destroyed by fire after forced landing, Luxeuil, France 12 casualties
15/8/1939	G-AESY	Lockheed 1A Electra	British Airways	Crashed in sea after fire off Denmark: 5 fatalities; 1 injured
7/11/1939	G-AAXD	Handley Page HP45	Imperial Airways	Wrecked in forced landing, Tiverton, Devon
20/111939	G-AFFM	Airspeed Oxford	British Airways	Crashed after striking balloon cable, Gosport, Hants: 2 fatalities
20/12/1939	G-ACJT	De Havilland Dragon 1	Western Airways	Crashed Weston-Super-Mare, Somerset
21/12/1939	G-AFYU	Lockheed 14-WF62 Super Electra	British Airways	Crashed off Valetta, Malta: 5 fatalities
10/1/1940	G-AEDY	GAL ST-25 Monospar	Utility Airways	Crashed Nr Hanworth
13/2/1940	G-AETT	Short Scion	Lundy & Atlantic Coast Airways	Crashed Barnstaple, Devon
13/2/1940	G-AEHJ	Heston Phoenix	British American Air Services	Crashed Mersey, Liverpool
14/2/1940	G-ADCT	De Havilland DH84	Scottish Airways	Crash landed & written off, Inverness
19/2/1940	G-ACPR	De Havilland DH89	Great Western & Southern Airways	Crashed Burford, Oxfordshire
2/3/1940	G-AAGX	Handley Page HP42	Imperial Airways	Crashed – cause unknown, Gulf of Oman between Jask & Sharjah: 8 fatalities
18/3/1940	G-AFEY	De Havilland DH89	Scottish Airways	Crashed Kirkwall, Orkneys
19/3/1940	G-AAXC	Handley Page HP45	Imperial Airways	Wrecked in gale, Bristol
19/4/1940	G-ACNG	De Havilland DH84	Scottish Airways	Crashed, Kirkwall, Orkneys
22/4/1940	G-AFKD	Lockheed 14 Electra	BOAC	Crashed, Loch Lomond, Scotland: 5 fatalities
24/7/1940	G-AFZZ	Lockheed 14 Electra	BOAC	Crashed, Bucharest, Romania

SOURCES AND BIBLIOGRAPHY

The Following Archives were used

Flight International Magazine On-Line – **www.flightglobal.com**
Imperial Airways Gazette
Oxford Dictionary of National Biography (on-line resource) – **www.oxforddnb.com**
The Minutes of Imperial Airways Board Meetings
The Times Newspapers On-Line – **http://archive.timesonline.co.uk**
The British Airways Archives at the BA Museum, London Heathrow Airport – **www.bamuseum.com**
The Croydon Airport Society Archives – *Croydon, Surrey* – **www.croydonairport.org.uk**

Books

Allen, Roy: *Pictorial History of KLM Royal Dutch Airlines,* Ian Allan 1978
Altschul, Selig & Bender, Marilyn: *The Chosen Instrument – The Rise & Fall of an American Entrepreneur,* Simon & Schuster, New York 1982
Andrew, C F & Morgan, E B: *Vickers Aircraft Since 1908,* Putnam 1995
Archbold, Rick: *Hindenburg – An Illustrated History,* Warner Communications 1994
Armstrong, William: *Pioneer Pilot,* Blandford Press 1952
Bamford, Jack: *Croissants at Croydon – The Memoirs of Jack Bamford,* London Borough of Sutton Libraries & Arts Service 1986
Banning, Gene: *Airlines of Pan American since 1927,* Paladwr Press 2001
Barnes, C H: *Handley Page Aircraft Since 1907,* Putnam 1987
Barnes, C H: *Shorts Aircraft Since 1900,* Putnam 1997
Brackley, Frida H: *Brackles – Memoirs of a Pioneer of Civil Aviation,* W & J Mackay & Co 1952
Brittain, Sir Harry: *By Air,* Hutchinson & Co, 1933
Cluett, Douglas: Learmonth, Bob & Nash, Joanna: *The First Croydon Airport,* Sutton Libraries & Arts Services 1977
Cluett, Douglas: Learmonth, Bob & Nash Joanna: *Croydon Airport 1928-1939 – The Great Days,* London Borough of Sutton Libraries & Arts Service 1980
Cobham, Sir Alan: *Australia and Back,* A & C Black 1926
Collier, Basil: *Heavenly Adventure – Sir Sefton Brancker & the Dawn of British Aviation,* Secker & Warburg 1959
Conrad III, Barnaby: *An Aviation Legend – Pan Am,* Woodford Press 1999
Corbett, David: *Politics & the Airlines,* George Allen & Unwin 1965
Coster, Graham: *Corsairville – The Lost Domain of the Flying Boat,* Viking, 2000
Daley, Robert: *An American Saga – Juan Trippe & His Pan Am Empire,* Random House, New York 1980
Davies, R E G: *Airline of Asia Since 1920,* Putnam 1997
Davies, R E G: *British Airlines – An Aircraft & Its Aircraft – Volume 1 1919-1939,* Paladwr Press 2005
Davies, R E G: *Fallacies & Fantasies of Air Transport History,* Airlife Publishing 1994
Davies, R E G: *History of the World's Airlines,* Oxford University Press 1967
Davies, R E G: *Lufthansa – An Airline and Its Aircraft,* Airlife Publishing 1991
Davies, R E G: *Rebels & Reformers of the Airways,* Airlife Publishing 1987
Denham, Terry *World Directory of Airline Crashes.* Patrick Stephens 1996
Dickson, Charles C: *Croydon Airport Remembered,* London Borough of Sutton Libraries & Arts Service 1985
Doyle, Neville: *From Sea Eagle to Flamingo: Channel Islands Airlines 1923-1939,* The Self Publishing Association 1984
Doyle, Neville: *The Triple Alliance – The Predecessors of the First British Airways,* Air-Britain Publications 2001
Ekins, H E: *Around the World in Eighteen Days & How to Do It,* Longmans, Green & Co 1936
Ellis, E & F H: *Atlantic Air Conquest,* William Kimber 1963
Ellis, Paul: *British Commercial Aircraft – Sixty Years in Pictures,* Jane's Publishing Co 1980
Finch, Robert: *The World's Airways,* University of London Press 1938
Frater, Alexander: *Beyond the Blue Horizon – On the Track of Imperial Airways,* William Heinemann 1986
Fysh, Sir Hudson: *Qantas Rising – Autobiography of the Flying Fysh,* Angus & Robertson 1966
Gandt, Robert L: *China Clipper – The Age of the Great Flying Boats,* Naval Institute Press 1991
Graham-White, Claude & Harper, Harry: *Our First Airways – Their Organisation, Equipment & Finance,* John Lane 1919
Grant, R G: *Flight – 100 Years of Aviation,* Dorling Kindersley 2002
Gunn, John: *The Defence of Distance – Qantas 1919-1939,* University of Queensland Press 1985
Guttery, Ben R: *The Encyclopaedia of African Airlines,* on-line at **http://books.google.co.uk**
Harper, Harry: *The Romance of the Modern Airway,* Sampson, Lowe, Marston & Co
Higham, Robin: *Britain's Imperial Air Route – The Story of Britain's Overseas Air Route 1918-1939,* G T Foulis 1961
Hill, W/Cdr Roderic: *The Baghdad Airmail,* Nonsuch 2005
Hoare, Sir Samuel: *India By Air,* Longmans, Green & Co 1927
Holt-Thomas, G: *Aerial Transport,* Hodder & Stoughton 1920
Hooks, Mike: *Croydon Airport – The Peaceful Years,* Tempus Publishing 2002
Hooper, Meredith: *Kangaroo Route,* Angus & Robertson 1985
Hudson, Kenneth: *Air Travel – A Social History,* Adams & Dart 1972
Ilsey, John William: *In Southern Skies – The Pictorial History of Early Aviation in Southern Africa 1816-1940,* Jonathan Ball Publishers, Johannesburg & Cape Town 2003
Instone, Alfred: *The Early Birds,* Western Mail & Echo 1938
Jackson, A J: *Avro Aircraft Since 1908,* Putnam 1990
Jackson, A J: *British Civil Aircraft – Vols: 1, 2 & 3 – 1919-1959,* Putnam 1959-1960
Jackson, A J: *De Havilland Aircraft Since 1919,* Putnam 1978
Jackson, A S: *Imperial Airways & The First British Airlines 1919-1940,* Terence Dalton 1995
James, Derek N: *Westland Aircraft Since 1915,* Putnam 1991
Jublonski, Edward: *Atlantic Fever,* Macmillan 1972
Lawford, Hayden K: *Pioneer Airline Pilot – The Life & Times of Capt E H Lawford AFC,* Hayen K Lawford 2006
Lissitzyn, Oliver James: *International Air Transport & National Policy,* Council of Foreign Relations, New York 1942
London, Peter: *British Flying Boats,* Sutton Publishing 2003
London, Peter: *Saunders & Saro Aircraft Since 1917,* Putnam 1988
MacMillan, Norman: *Sefton Brancker,* William Heinemann 1935
McIntosh, W/Cdr R H: *All-Weather Mac,* MacDonald 1963
Munson, Kenneth: *Airliners Between the Wars 1919-1939,* Blandford Press 1972
Munson, Kenneth: *Pictorial History of BOAC & Imperial Airways,* Ian Allan 1970
Orde-Hume, Arthur W J G: *British Commercial Aircraft – Their Evolution, Development & Perfection 1920-1940,* GMS Enterprises 2003
Penrose, Harald: *British Aviation – The Adventuring Years 1920-1929,* Putnam 1980
Penrose, Harald: *British Aviation – Widening Horizons 1930-1934,* HM Stationery Office 1979
Penrose, Harald: *British Aviation – Ominous Skies 1935-1939,* HM Stationery Office 1980
Penrose, Harald: *Wings Across the World – The Illustrated History of British Airways,* Cassell 1980

Pudney, John: *The Seven Skies – A Study of BOAC & Its Forerunners Since 1919*, Putnam 1959

Quinn, Tom: *Tales From the Golden Age of Air Travel*, Aurim Press 2003

Sanford, Kendall C: *Air Crash Mail of Imperial Airways & Predecessor Airlines*, The Stuart Rossiter Trust 2003

Sassoon, Philip: *The Third Route*, William Heinemann 1929

Sherwood, Tim: *Coming In To Land – A Short History of Hounslow, Hansworth & Heston Aerodromes*, Heritage Publications 1999

Sims, Phillip E: *Adventurous Empires – The Story of the Short Empire Flying-boats*, Airlife Publications 2000

Smith, Graham: *Taking to the Skies – The Story of British Aviation 1903-1939*, Countryside Books 2003

Stroud, John: *Annals of British & Commonwealth Air Transport 1919-1960*, Putnam 1962

Stroud, John: *European Transport Aircraft Since 1910*, Putnam 1966

Stroud, John: *Passenger Aircraft & Their Interiors, 1910-2006*, Scoval Publishing 2002

Stroud, John: *Railway Air Services*, Ian Allan 1987

Stroud, John: *The Imperial Airways Fleet*, Tempus 2005

Tapper, Oliver: *Armstrong Whitworth Aircraft Since 1913*, Putnam 1988

Templewood, Viscount: *Empire of the Air – The Advent of the Air Age 1922-1929*, Collins 1957

Thomas, Lowell: *European Skyways*, Windmill Press 1928

Trippe, Betty: *Pan Am's First Lady – The Diary of Betty Stettinius Trippe*, Paladwr Press 1996

Veale, S E: *Tomorrow's Airliners & Airports*, Pilot Press Ltd 1945

White, Gay Blair: *The World's First Airline – The St Petersburg-Tampa Airline*, Aero Medical Consultants, Florida 1984

Wilson, Stewart: *Airliners of the World*, Aerospace Publications, Australia 1999

Winchester, Jim (Edited by): *The Aviation Fact File: Biplanes, Triplanes & Seaplanes*, Amber Books 2004

Wingent, Peter: *Movement of Aircraft of Imperial Airways Africa Route 1931-1939*, Peter Wingent 1991

Wynn, Group Capt W E: *Civil Air Transport*, Hutchinsons Scientific & Technical Publications 1945

Also:

No Author listed: *Wings Over Hong Kong – A Tribute to Kai Tak*, Odyssey, Hong Kong 1998

On-Line Resources

http://airminded.org

http://aviation-safety.net

www.imperial-airways.com

www.planecrashinfo.com

www.timetableimages.com